HISTORY OF THE AMERICAN FRONTIER
1763-1893

Frederic L. Paxson

History of the American Frontier 1763 - 1893

Simon Publications

2001

PREFACE

WHEN I began my studies in the history of the West some twenty years ago, the State of Colorado, where I worked, still bore the imprint of the struggle of the preceding decade. The frontier was gone; and the frontiersmen there as elsewhere in the United States were adapting themselves to the life of a new century. Turner had already pointed out the significance of the frontier in our history, but the occasional historical pioneer who followed his lead must make his own tools, find his sources, and assemble his bibliographies.

This is all changed to-day. The *Mississippi Valley Historical Review* has become the organ of the Westerners, while the sound scholarship of Alvord and his host of associates has cleared the ground. The time is ripe for this synthesis, in which an attempt is made to show the proportions of the whole story. My successors will of course do better, but none will complete his task with a firmer conviction than I possess that the frontier with its continuous influence is the most American thing in all America. In future generations we may perhaps become an amalgam of the European races and lose the advantage of a fresh continent, but we shall still possess and be shaped by a unique heritage.

My debt to my indexer, Mr. David M. Matteson, is real, for he has at many places given me the advantage of his wide and accurate scholarship.

FREDERIC L. PAXSON

MADISON, *March*, 1924

CONTENTS

CHAPTER XXIV

MISSOURI: THE NEW SECTIONALISM

CHAPTER XXV

PUBLIC LAND REFORM

CHAPTER XXVI

FRONTIER FINANCE

CHAPTER XXVII

THE AMERICAN SYSTEM

CHAPTER XXVIII

JACKSONIAN DEMOCRACY

CHAPTER XXIX

THE EAST, AND THE WESTERN MARKETS

CHAPTER XXX

THE WESTERN INTERNAL IMPROVEMENTS

CHAPTER XXXI

THE PERMANENT INDIAN FRONTIER, 1825–1841

CHAPTER XXXII

THE MISSISSIPPI VALLEY BOOM

CHAPTER XXXIII

THE BORDER STATES: MICHIGAN AND ARKANSAS

CHAPTER XXXIV

THE INDEPENDENT STATE OF TEXAS

CHAPTER XXXV

1837: THE PROSTRATE WEST

CHAPTER XXXVI

THE TRAIL TO SANTA FÉ

CHAPTER XXXVII

THE SETTLEMENT OF OREGON

CHAPTER XXXVIII

THE "STATE" OF DESERET

CHAPTER XXXIX

THE WAR WITH MEXICO

CHAPTER XL

THE CONQUEST OF CALIFORNIA

CHAPTER XLI

FAR WEST AND POLITICS

CHAPTER XLVII

"PIKE'S PEAK OR BUST!"

CHAPTER XLVIII

THE FRONTIER OF THE MINERAL EMPIRE

CHAPTER XLIX

THE OVERLAND ROUTE

CHAPTER L

THE PUBLIC LANDS: WIDE OPEN

CHAPTER LI

THE PLAINS IN THE CIVIL WAR

CHAPTER LII

THE UNION PACIFIC RAILROAD

CHAPTER LIII

THE DISRUPTION OF THE TRIBES

CHAPTER LIV

THE PANIC OF 1873

CHAPTER LV

FRONTIER PANACEAS

CHAPTER LVI

THE COW COUNTRY

CHAPTER LVII

THE CLOSED FRONTIER

CHAPTER LVIII

THE ADMISSION OF THE "OMNIBUS" STATES

CHAPTER LIX

THE DISAPPEARANCE OF THE FRONTIER

LIST OF MAPS

HISTORY OF
THE AMERICAN FRONTIER
. .

CHAPTER I

THE AMERICAN FRONTIER OF 1763

THE frontier of the British Empire made its foothold at the river mouths on the Atlantic side of the North American continent at the beginning of the seventeenth century. For one hundred and fifty years thereafter its lodgment was precarious, as its scanty peoples struggled with the adversities of nature, the long communication line to the base at home, the hostility of the native races that were dispossessed, and the jealousy of the other European nations whose realm was thus invaded. France, with a growing power over the whole St. Lawrence Basin, and Spain, with an uncontested grip upon the Gulf of Mexico and its hinterland, lacked the imperial agents with which to expel the interloping British, but not the will. The second generation of British colonials saw the rivalry of the nations turn to war, and then for a century there was intermittent contest for the empire. King William's War and Queen Anne's, the struggle over the Austrian succession, and the Seven Years' War, were but phases of the effort to reach a state of equilibrium in Europe. For America these wars kept the border of the British Empire red with the blood of the regular troops, the Indians, and the settlers whose homes lay beneath the feet of the combatants to be devastated by them. At the end of the contest, in 1763, the isolated colonies were no longer bound only by their imperial bond and their British past. They had acquired a common experience. Their own effort had helped to break the enemy. And they had been transmuted in the fight with nature and the alien until they had become the units of a new race. The American frontier takes shape in the final years of the century of colonial wars, and upon the return of peace starts upon the conquest of the continent. Its British origins survive to mould its life, but its destiny and its spirit have become American.[1]

[1] The story of this struggle is best told in the writings of Francis Parkman, whose brilliant style and vivid historical imagination have made him first among American literary historians.

The European settlement of 1763 followed the greatest military effort that Britain has ever made in America. Fighting took place at every strategic point along the line of contact with New France, and considerable armies were for the first time maneuvered in the wilderness. At the Forks of the Ohio, where Pittsburgh was soon to arise, at Niagara, along the route leading from New York by way of Lake Champlain to Canada, and at Quebec itself, the expeditionary forces of Great Britain, aided by colonial levies, kept so effective a pressure upon the French that the latter empire broke. France surrendered her American colonies at the end of the war, leaving to England and Spain the control of North America. The Mississippi River was made the common boundary of the survivors. England, relieved of the French menace, turned to the enjoyment of her new domain, when there arose from the colonies the ominous question — Who won the war? and an affirmative American spirit took the place of the eliminated France.

The peoples of the British colonies, who were ceasing to be British in 1763, and were assuming the new aspect of American, were not above two million strong. In the absence of any census, it has been necessary to arrive at the population of the colonies by estimates based upon casual accounts, figures of immigration, and conjectures as to the birth rate. In 1760 there were perhaps 1,600,-000 persons within the thirteen colonies. Fifteen years later, on the eve of independence, there may have been 2,600,000. In another fifteen years, in 1790 when the first census under the Constitution was taken, there were 3,929,214. An overwhelming proportion of the population of 1763 was American born, and in parts of the colonies there were many families that could trace five generations of unmixed ancestry, leading back in nearly every instance to immigrants who came to America speaking the English language and familiar with the institutions of British life.

Among the little groups that clustered about the harbors of the seaboard there were only four towns that could with reason be described as cities. Boston, Philadelphia, New York, and Charleston were the points where such wealth as had been produced in America tended to concentrate, and where the colonial aristocracies had their root. But most of the colonists were farmers, living on or near their property. Virginia, as the largest, was the most populous colony, and after her followed Massachusetts, Pennsylvania, North Carolina, and New York. The most characteristic figure of these towns was the merchant, for commerce was the only industry besides agriculture that had been allowed to flourish by the policy of the mother country. Banking was rudimentary, transportation on land was unorganized, and manufacture was forbidden by the navigation laws. The colonial supplies that could not be made within the home by domestic manufacture came chiefly from the British exporters, were carried often in American-built ships, and were distributed by colonial merchants whose British connections kept them always in close grips with the hands across the seas. But the life outside the towns was simple and the needs were primitive. The deprivations due to the ban upon American industry were slightly appreciated by the farmer who lived almost entirely to himself, and whose accumulated earnings and savings were never enough for the immediate needs of agricultural expansion, let alone purchases or investment in other fields.

Although the British origin of most of the American population was patent, there were considerable areas in the colonies where alien accents and non-British blood were common. There had been foreign strains associated in the first settlements, and there had come waves of various European continental emigrants. The Dutch of old New Amsterdam remained to found a sturdy aristocracy for New York, and to dominate much of the agricultural development of the Hudson Valley up to Albany and the Lower Mohawk. The handful of Swedish families, settled along the Delaware, made a slighter impression. The stray Huguenot immigrants had planted here and there a group among the southern settlements, while individuals among them had been dispersed throughout the whole British area in America. Not until the first century of British occupation was over, however, had additional races come in large numbers. It is with the German and Scotch-Irish migrations of the first half of the eighteenth century that the social historian has his first serious problem in appraising the materials in the American melting pot.

The German flood came largely from the Palatinate after 1710. War, famine, and persecution were the forces which prepared the mind of the German peasant for emigration, while the open lands at the rear of most of the colonies provided abundant places for their lodgment. The great proprietors, like the family of Penn, saw profit in the quit-rents to be derived from numerous settlers on the family lands. Colonial politicians saw advantage in colonizing newcomers along the Indian border where their bodies might be a buffer between the French or Indian raiders and the

British settlers. In the twenty years after the Peace of Utrecht, in 1713, the frontier of New York received the Germans along the Mohawk, and took on the name of German Flats. They pushed southward, up the Schoharie, towards the headwaters of the Susquehanna, and made a connection with other groups that were working their way inland from Philadelphia. These latter followed the ridge between the Schuylkill and the Susquehanna. By 1729 Pennsylvania found it necessary to divide the huge original Chester County and to create Lancaster County out of its western end. The road from Philadelphia to Lancaster, ultimately to become the Lancaster Turnpike, was soon a crowded highway of migration, while from a river valley near its Susquehanna end came the name of the heavy, covered, Conestoga wagon, that was destined to be the vehicle of empire. Following the valleys southward to Carolina, and picking out the fertile limestone soil with sound farming judgment, the German settlers cleared a large part of the border as it stood at the middle of the eighteenth century.

Almost simultaneously with the Germans came the Scotch-Irish. The particular group that bears this name emigrated from Scotland to Ireland shortly after 1600. Their descendants who remain in Ulster are to-day as little assimilated by the native Irish as they were at the time of the first invasion. After a century of residence in the north of Ireland, many of them, singly and by congregations, sought out a better livelihood and more tolerant surroundings in the colonies. By shiploads they came, to Boston, New York, and Philadelphia. Like the Germans, they found the near-by farm lands already occupied, and pushed on to the great open stretches where land was cheap, and where provincial policy preferred to have the newcomers. "The settlement of five families from Ireland gives me more trouble than fifty of any other people," lamented James Logan, the agent of the Penns, in 1730. But the qualities of temper that made trouble for the proprietors made also for independence and courage in the frontiersman. Less than the Germans did they go as directed, or await the order of authority. Perseveringly they pushed their settlements ahead, title or no title. When political conditions of the provinces displeased them, they turned to politics to capture the provincial legislatures. They spoke the dogmatic language of the frontier in the colonial towns where property and place had dominated. And in their political activities they showed the result of long training in self-ruling churches, where the Presbyterian order created institutions of representative government.

Mingled with the Irishmen of Scotch antecedents came other but un-numbered settlers from the Catholic counties of the south of Ireland. Many of these came as indentured servants, and most of them left fewer literary sources for the study of their culture than did the Scotch-Irish. Less clannish than their compatriots they formed no distinct group that can be readily isolated from the larger body of colonists. Another century was to elapse before the Irish of Irish extraction became a notable current in American immigration.

A process of Americanization began as soon as the members of the alien races touched upon American soil. The change wrought thus upon the foreign language group made them obviously into a different race. Not less fundamentally, though less visibly, the English-speaking pioneers lost their identity with the England of the later Stuarts and the house of Hanover, and became American without immediate consciousness of their change. The course which development and life followed from the moment when the earliest settlements were planted, provides a basis for understanding the transmutation.

The first foothold on the Atlantic seaboard was gained at the convenient landing places, such as the peninsula of the James River, or Boston Bay, or Manhattan Island, or the highlands on the Delaware above the mouth of the Schuylkill. It would have been difficult to maintain a settlement at any point not accessible to ocean-going ships. Around such focal points there developed thirteen colonies; and in each colony much the same forces helped to direct the lines of growth. The early maps show how settlement, as it spread, kept within easy reach of navigable water, and how the colonial farmer preferred to go many miles upstream, rather than penetrate a few miles into the roadless country. Not until the eighteenth century did a colonial postal service become either a possibility or a fact, and until the nineteenth century was well advanced the land traveler met hardships at every turn.

Before 1763 the spread of occupation passed through two distinct phases, corresponding to the geographical contours of the continent.[2] The rivers were the natural lines of penetration, so

[2] Justin Winsor, *The Westward Movement* (1897), describes this from the angle of the cartographer and bibliographer. His greatest disciple, Edward Channing, in Volumes I–III of *History of the United States* (1905–12), not only retells the narrative of colonial life, but prints population maps that are a contribution to our knowledge of the course of settlement.

long as they were navigable. At the places where the Atlantic streams emerge from the piedmont and start across the more level coastal plain, the waterfalls or rapids constitute obstacles that in nearly every instance induced a change of tactics by the invading settlers. Above these points navigation was broken. At the falls the boat with its cargo of pioneers and their goods must in any event be lightened for the portage. Traders' posts developed naturally near these strategic spots, and around them there have in later days grown up industrial communities, making use of the generous water powers that the falls provide. Settlement in the vicinity of the falls was no longer governed by a narrow river route, but spread out in every direction where the land invited.

The falls line that can be shown on a map, connecting the lowest break to navigation in the several streams, follows the meeting line of the piedmont and the coastal plain, and separates two social areas as clearly as two geological. Below the falls line each colony kept to itself, and each river valley constituted a separate cell in which to generate British institutions in a new world. Above the falls line there was less marked separation, and a growing tendency for the outlying settlers of any group to form acquaintance and contacts as readily with their neighbors on either side as with their relatives downstream. By 1700 settlement had reached the falls line in most parts of the English colonies. In those southward from New York, where the rivers run most nearly at right angles with the Atlantic Shore, the settlers above the falls were already well on their way inland.

Above the falls line, and running roughly parallel to the seacoast, lay a barrier to expansion, in the form of the Appalachian system, with its multitude of parallel river valleys. Here, for one thousand miles, extending from northern Alabama to the watershed of the St. Lawrence, the advance into the interior of the continent was impeded, or deflected into such channels as nature had provided. Many of the eastern valleys of this system are cut across by the rivers emerging from the higher ranges, while the interior valleys themselves carry the headwaters of great rivers. The tributaries of the Potomac and the Susquehanna, the Shenandoah and the Juniata, and the tributaries of the Ohio and the Tennessee, interlock sources and share these parallel channels. The incoming settlers, as they passed the falls line and climbed the eastern ridges of the first tier of valleys, found in this valley system a destination in itself that met the frontier needs for advance from early in the eighteenth century until after the peace of Paris in 1763.

It was a characteristic of the Appalachian valleys that they stayed the course of westward advance, and distributed north and south the families that ascended above the falls into the piedmont and the mountains. Mingling together, for the first time on a generous scale, the settlers from New York and Pennsylvania, or from Virginia and Carolina, found themselves cheek-by-jowl with the new-come Germans and the aggressive Scotch-Irish. The provincial attribute of every group was checked somewhat by the hostile attitude of other groups. The common qualities and experiences inherent in a struggle for livelihood in the wilderness built up for them a universal background of immediate needs. The children of the first entrants soon began to intermarry, for family life began early on the frontier, and the economical unit was neither the spinster nor the laborer, but the married couple. The divergent and contradictory traits with which the colonials came into the melting pot of the interior valleys were speedily submerged in the common nationality. Here, with the mingling of the social streams, the American character seems to have been born. Before any of the mountain settlements was a generation old it had begun to react upon the classes in control of the colony and resident in the older regions. The clash between the older regions with their desire to control the provinces, and the frontier areas with special and often antagonistic needs, enlivens colonial politics from an early period. It was the perennial struggle between the landless and the well-established. It led to political maneuvers and gerrymanders for the control of colonial assemblies. It brought forth from the new frontiers an early formulation of the distinctive American demand for a right to self-determination.[3]

Before 1700 the spread of life in America was confined chiefly to the seacoast and the plains below the falls. Between 1700 and 1763, the valleys were occupied and occasional adventurers crossed the mountains for a glimpse of the western slopes beyond.[4] At the moment when the French and Indian War (1756–1763) became

[3] The name of Frederick Jackson Turner easily leads those of the historians of the frontier. All American historians have reshaped their views of the meaning of our history since the publication of his "Significance of the Frontier in American History," in the *Proceedings* (1893) of the State Historical Society of Wisconsin.

[4] Clarence W. Alvord and Lee Bidgood, *The First Explorations of the Trans-Allegheny Region by the Virginians, 1650–1674* (1912).

the closing struggle between England and France, the colonials of the frontier region were so numerous as to make a large part of the force relied upon by England for imperial extension.[5] In the deliberations at the Albany Congress of 1754, when the colonial officials met to plan for the common defense, a keener establishment than the British had erected might have seen a movement ominous for the continuance of the empire. It might have foreseen that the reorganization of the intercolonial post-office, that Benjamin Franklin had just been allowed to carry through, would be as likely to break down colonial isolation as to help the empire. It might have mistrusted the nose for news that was being developed in the rising list of colonial newspapers. The notable services of Franklin among the Pennsylvania farmers provided the expeditionary forces with supplies and transport. It was behind a provincial leader rather than a regular officer that they turned back the French at Lake George. Colonial self-consciousness and solidarity, with men who knew the actual frontier in the lead, were stimulated by the successes of this war; and when at its close England seized the moment as propitious to reorganize the empire, the provinces had been educated past the point at which this was possible.

The British readjustments after 1763 were based upon the facts that the French menace had been dispelled, that the burden of maintaining peace ought to be spread over all subjects of the empire, that the confusion of colonial boundaries ought to be removed, that the outlying Indian tribes ought to be pacified and satisfied, and that the area of settlement ought not to be allowed to grow in disproportion to the number of inhabitants.[6] To the colonial population of about two millions there were now added the French of Canada and the French and Spanish of Florida and Eastern Louisiana. It was as necessary to provide a government for these latter as to improve the organization of the older subjects. The fiscal provisions that Parliament enacted in the next few months aroused dissent and protest from the moment of their passage, stirring up a cry of "no taxation without representation," that could not be silenced within the empire. The provisions for local government produced an irritation as weighty, for they struck at the inherent traits and needs of border life.

[5] Eugene I. McCormac, *Colonial Opposition to Imperial Authority during the French and Indian War* (1911), was the first of the University of California *Publications in History*.

[6] Clarence W. Alvord, *The Mississippi Valley in British Politics* (1917), is not only a learned treatment of this theme, but reveals in its author an unusual sense for values; Clarence E. Carter, *Great Britain and the Illinois Country, 1763–1774* (1910).

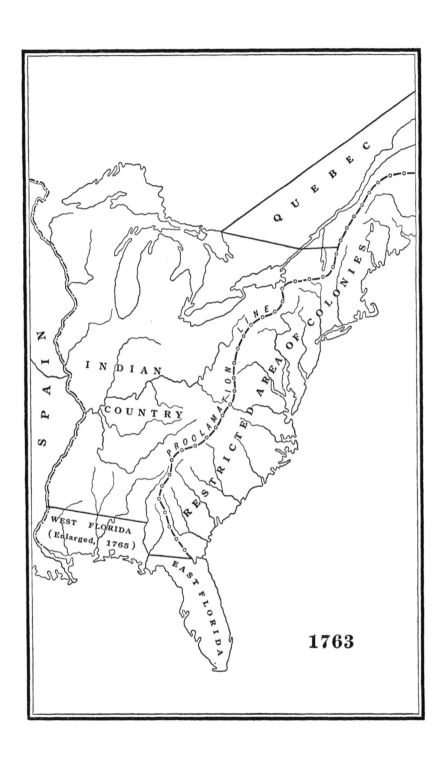

SPAIN

QUEBEC

INDIAN

COUNTRY

PROCLAMATION LINE

RESTRICTED AREA OF COLONIES

WEST FLORIDA
(Enlarged, 1765)

EAST FLORIDA

1763

By proclamation of George III, dated October 7, 1763, three British colonies were added to the original thirteen. Each was to be a crown colony, governed directly from England, and each included a fraction of the recently acquired population. Quebec, the northernmost, embraced the drainage basin of the St. Lawrence to Lake Nipissing and the region of the Hudson's Bay Company. Maine, New Hampshire, Vermont, and New York found in Quebec a northern neighbor and a newly defined boundary. Mountainous northern extremities had already constituted a practical northern limit for these colonies. Quebec both removed the danger of French attack and made the limit definite.

The Spanish Floridas, acquired from Spain in exchange for Havana which had been occupied by a British fleet during the war, were divided by the Chattahoochee and Apalachicola rivers into the provinces of East Florida and West Florida. The new northern boundary of East Florida was the St. Mary's River, and a line from its source to the junction of the Chattahoochee and the Flint rivers. It would have been easy to mark this line if it had been possible to agree on the tributary of the St. Mary's that was to be treated as a source. West Florida was for the time being bounded on the north by the line of the thirty-first parallel, north latitude; but this was in a few months pushed further north to the mouth of the Yazoo River.

Between the new dominions of Quebec and the Floridas, stretched the thirteen colonies, all along the seaboard; and west of them the mountain valleys whose occupation was just beginning, and the great tract of Eastern Louisiana, still possessed by its aboriginal owners and the handful of Frenchmen and half-breeds at Vincennes, Kaskaskia, and Detroit. Here and there, west of the Appalachians, and north of the Ohio, was a fur-trading stockade and a corn patch or two, but generally the Indian Country extended unbroken from Quebec to Florida, and from the watershed to the Mississippi and beyond. The original boundary claims of six of the thirteen colonies traversed this western area, for England had been generous in making the "sea to sea" grants of territory that she did not own, and in nearly every province speculative men were considering the possibility of getting new grants or founding new settlements west of the mountains. To all of these the Proclamation of 1763 brought disappointment, for by specific mandate "all the lands and territories lying to the westward of the sources of the rivers which fall into the sea from the west and northwest are reserved under the sovereignty, protection, and dominance of the king." Colonial officials were forbidden to grant additional lands west of this proclamation line. A new crown policy was provided, in place of the old one which had permitted easy extension of settlement and widespread speculation. Growth in the future was to be personally conducted, with all the safeguards of government control, and with the Indians pacified in advance. The hardy border settlers, who had lived thus far in a realm little affected by effective law, were now to await the arrival of law and order before advancing further. Adventurers who had already possessed themselves of claims to thousands of acres along the Upper Ohio were cut off from the enjoyment of their ventures. From the standpoint of the empire it meant the beginning of an orderly policy. For the mixed population that thronged the valleys of the Appalachians and was already conscious of common interests acquired as they won their lands, the proclamation line was a vexatious restriction. It was not to be respected or tolerated. Instead of constituting the final limit of promiscuous expansion of the frontier in America, the proclamation line is the starting-point for the winning of the West by a people already Americanized, and no longer either exclusively European or wholly provincial. East of the frontier of 1763 the American groups are best to be examined as European frontiers in America; west of the line is an American frontier to be studied in contrast with the East.

CHAPTER II

THE FORKS OF THE OHIO

The line of the most advanced settlements in 1763 reveals the western front not of a single column of frontier homeseekers, but of several. In the region south of Albany, New York, and north of Knoxville, Tennessee, the various forces were somewhat blended because of the unifying influence of the transverse mountain ranges. North and south of this region, the flanks of the frontier were checked in their advance by other causes.[1]

The northernmost end of the frontier, behind the outlying settlements of New England and New York, began at the St. Croix River, which was already established as the eastern boundary of Maine. This stream, whose name was carried on the maps of the New England coast, though not in use among the actual residents, received its designation at the time of De Monts, founder of an unsuccessful colony in 1604 on an island off its mouth. Diffused along the coastline, west of this point, but never penetrating far inland, the settlements of Maine were devoted to the industries of fishing and the production of naval stores. In a governmental way they were attached to Massachusetts, but that government had experienced little difficulty in preventing them from pushing to the interior. It had more than once offered special inducements, in the form of relief from taxation, to frontiersmen who would police the border. The province of Maine had few agricultural attractions that could compete with those of the Connecticut valley and its neighborhood.

The Connecticut River was the most eastern of the important routes of frontier advance. On both sides, across the colonies of Connecticut and Massachusetts, it spread a zone of clearings, and before 1763 its upper reaches were occupied by the overflowing population from the coast settlements. The conflicting territorial claims of Massachusetts and New York, as well as those of New Hampshire, kept the country of the upper Connecticut uncertain as to its land titles until well into the eighteenth century. The

---

[1] Ellen C. Semple, *American History in its Geographical Conditions* (1903), and A. P. Brigham, *Geographical Influences on American History* (1903), were pioneer works, and are still of great value in the study of physiographic sectionalism.

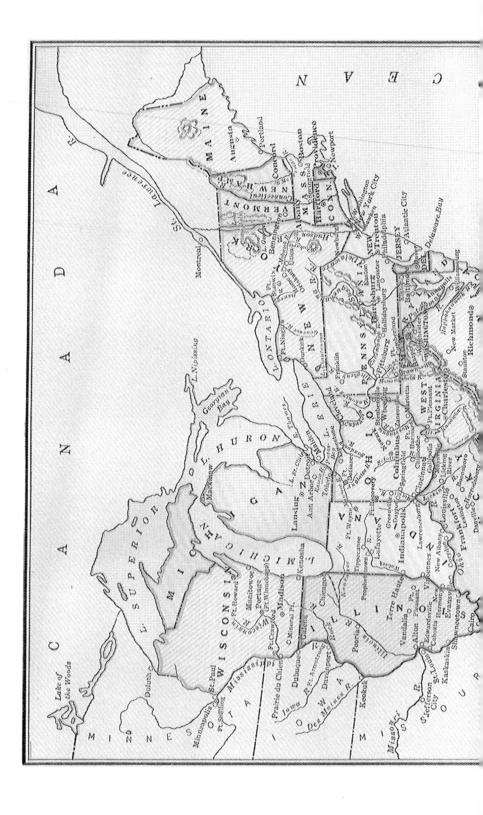

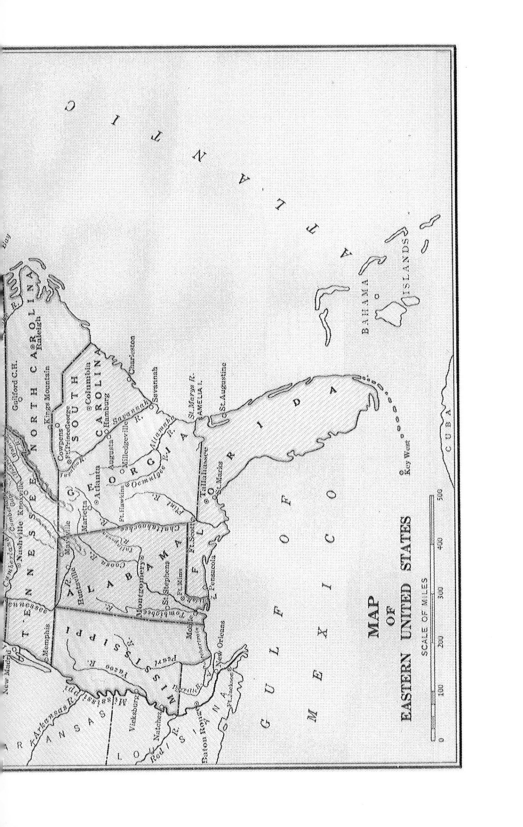

MAP
OF
EASTERN UNITED STATES

SCALE OF MILES

0   100   200   300   400   500

administration of New Hampshire was detached from that of Massachusetts when Governor Benning Wentworth was commissioned for the former province in 1741. In 1764 the claim to Vermont was decided by an Order in Council assigning to New York the country north of Massachusetts and west of the Connecticut. But the ownership of the farm lands involved continued for many years a matter of concern for all settlers.

The claim of New York to extend as far east as the Connecticut was based on ancient grants to the Duke of York, but it was probably allowed in the region north of Massachusetts for the sound military reason that between the Connecticut River and the western shores of Lake Champlain lay the southern end of the road from Canada. Repeatedly bands of French and Indians had descended upon the northern frontier along the route of the River Richelieu and Lake Champlain. In the war just closed when the boundaries were adjusted, there had been heavy fighting here. Massachusetts was in no position or disposition to defend this route. New York was better placed, and more responsive to influence from England. The allotment of the Green Mountains to New York must be regarded as one of the acts taken in the imperial readjustment that followed the Treaty of Paris.

The frontier settlements in the New Hampshire grants, as the country west of the Connecticut was sometimes called, stopped short of the southern tip of Lake Champlain. The hills east of the Hudson had few inhabitants, and that river was a channel of settlement only as far north as Albany. The Mohawk from its mouth to near its source at Fort Stanwix was narrowly lined with German settlements. But the resistance of Indian tribes rather than difficulties of geography prevented extension west or south of that river.

The great barricade at the northern end of the colonial frontier line was maintained by the Six Nations of Indians, or Iroquois. The Mohawk, Seneca, Cayuga, Oneida, Onondaga, and Tuscarora formed a loose confederacy, with a strong hostility towards European intruders. In a triangle of country, indicated by Niagara below Lake Erie, Oswego on Lake Ontario, and Easton on the upper Delaware River, their control of the situation discouraged either prospectors or settlers. Generally in alliance with the English, and backed up against a convenient line of communication in the Lakes and the St. Lawrence, they resisted encroachment until after 1763. Then, at Fort Stanwix, in 1768, they made a

general peace and settlement. There had been occasional crossings from the Schoharie to the Susquehanna earlier in the century,
but the full development of the upper Susquehanna in central
New York was reserved for the period after the French had gone.
From this northern frontier, and the country of the Six Nations,
the Appalachian valleys extend southward to the Cherokee upon
the southern flank.

The mountain buttress, in which rise the sources of the Savannah, Chattahoochee, Coosa, and Tennessee rivers, forms the
southern shoulder of the Appalachians and the northern limit of
the group of southern Indians. Five tribes, later to be generally
known as the "five civilized tribes," ranged the plains beyond the
mountains and west to the Mississippi. On the eastern front were
the Cherokee and the Creeks, with the Seminole projecting down
into the wilderness of Florida. Westward, and along the Mississippi below the bluffs on which Memphis now stands, were the
Chickasaw and the Choctaw. Of these the Cherokee had been
long in residence, and were much affected by contact with the
Gulf settlements of New Orleans, Mobile, and Pensacola. Many
traders had married Indian women and settled among them.
Half-breed children had grown to be leaders of the tribes. More
than the other Indians adjacent to the English colonies, the
Cherokee had begun to abandon their wild habits and to reside in
villages among their cultivated fields. Before they were finally
displaced, they built churches and schools, reduced their language
to a written form, and gave promise as to the possibility of civilizing the Indians. The natural routes from the English seaboard
settlements to the interior went around the southern tribes, rather
than through them. These thus escaped the disintegrating influences of contact with a farming frontier, and maintained their own
identity for two generations after the close of the French and
Indian War.

By the Treaty of Hard Labour, in 1768, the Cherokee agreed
to an eastern boundary line, adjacent to the British colonies, much
as the Iroquois agreed to one at Fort Stanwix in the same year.
There was a clear British policy to separate the colonized area
from the Indian Country by a neutral strip, bounded on the east
by the Proclamation Line, and on the west by a composite line
based on Indian treaty provisions. From the head of the Savannah
River, near Fort Prince George, to the head of the Mohawk near
Fort Stanwix, the Indian Country took shape behind the barrier

of the Appalachian system in the years after 1763. There was not much pressure from white population at either the northern or the southern end. But in the middle, where the main roads from the Atlantic came near to the chief valleys leading into the Mississippi, the Forks of the Ohio were already a main objective of the colonial thrust.

The southern boundary of Pennsylvania, which is not wrongly described as the Keystone State, runs through the region of the best approaches to the junction of the Allegheny and Monongahela rivers, where the Ohio takes its rise. Here is the gateway to the Mississippi Valley. By way of either the Potomac or the Susquehanna, in this latitude, the settler easily advanced from tidewater to the foothills of the mountains. Each of these rivers cuts across the easternmost of the mountain valleys. Near the point in the Susquehanna where the Juniata enters it, and the point on the Potomac where it receives the Shenandoah, the tributaries of the streams tend to run with the mountain folds instead of across them. From central New York to southwest Virginia they open up the Appalachians. And it was an added advantage to their region as a route of entry that land titles between the Potomac and the Susquehanna were in confusion. The courageous squatter might with impunity defy the claims of both the Penns and the Calverts who were lords proprietors of the soil.

The boundary controversy between William Penn and Lord Baltimore originated in the uncertainties of language in the charters of Maryland and Pennsylvania. The earlier grant, in 1632, cut away from Virginia for the benefit of Lord Baltimore, the wedge of land between the fortieth degree of north latitude and the south bank of the Potomac, as far west as the "first fountain" of that stream. Nearly fifty years thereafter, in 1681, a later king presented to William Penn a rough rectangle of territory, extending five degrees of longitude west from the Delaware River, and from the "beginning of the fortieth degree of Northerne Latitude" to the beginning of the "three and fortieth." The inaccuracy of contemporary maps, and the confusion of words in the grants, made it possible for the Penns to claim that the "beginning of the fortieth degree" was in fact the thirty-ninth parallel, and that Pennsylvania had received from the crown one full degree of land formerly allowed to Maryland. Lord Baltimore naturally contested this reading of the charters, asserting a right to the fortieth parallel. Philadelphia, however, had been founded by Penn on the

Delaware about midway between the parallels of contest; and the Quaker founder could not surrender his contention without losing his fair seat of government.[2]

The inevitable result of the contest of jurisdiction was a dual assertion of ownership to the strip between the fortieth and thirty-ninth parallels, and repeated conflicts in the effort to exercise control. The enterprising squatter, playing one claimant of quit-rents against the other, was often able to avoid both. Along the boundary line, and west of the Susquehanna to the source of the Potomac, the area began to fill up in the middle third of the eighteenth century. Beyond the Potomac, Virginia became Penn's opponent in place of Maryland, for the ancient Virginia charter of 1609 could be construed as founding a claim to country well north of Pittsburgh and the Ohio Forks.

The adjustment of the Pennsylvania-Maryland boundary was not reached until the French and Indian War was in progress. In 1760 the proprietors compromised on a line to be surveyed fifteen miles south of the latitude of Philadelphia; and in the next eight years the imported surveyors, Mason and Dixon, ran the boundary that has thenceforth borne their name. The controversy between Virginia and Pennsylvania was unimportant in 1768 when the line was finished, since few settlers had reached the southwest corner of Pennsylvania. In the next few years, however, there was what closely resembled a little civil war on this border. Pennsylvania reinforced its claim by creating in 1773 the county of Westmoreland, west of the Youghiogheny and north of the projection of the Mason and Dixon line. But Virginia had already claimed that this was a part of its own Augusta County. Lord Dunmore, the Virginia governor, sent his agents to Pittsburgh to give reality to his claim, but the outbreak of the Revolution drove him from his post. In 1779 Pennsylvania and Virginia at last accomplished what their royal and proprietary governors had failed upon, and compromised upon the angle that now forms the southwestern boundary of the former State.

The approach of the settled frontier to this disputed area began with the creation of Lancaster County, Pennsylvania, in 1729. English, Scotch-Irish, and German farmers were by this time prospecting beyond the Susquehanna, and the Germans were beginning to dig in along that river, in communities that have not even

[2] Winfred T. Root, *The Relations of Pennsylvania with the British Government, 1696–1765* (1912).

yet been dissolved or broken up. As "Pennsylvania Dutch" some of them retained their identity and language, and made a striking exception to the general rule that along the frontier the marks of race were speedily blended in the common American type. Harper's Ferry and Harris's Ferry, below the mouths of the Shenandoah and Juniata respectively, were in use by this time. And Robert Harper, who opened the former in 1734, is claimed by the German-American historians as German, and by the Scotch-Irish as Scotch-Irish. He may indeed have been both without violating any of the probabilities of the frontier.[3]

While most of the incomers were content to buy land rights and settle in the valleys, there moved among them men of older establishment in the country who engaged in larger schemes of land speculation. In Virginia there was a boundary uncertainty similar to that along the Pennsylvania line. The grant to Lord Culpeper of the "northern neck" which was the peninsula lying between the Potomac and the Rappahannock rivers, detached this tract from the ownership and management of the Old Dominion. The northern limit of the tract depended upon agreement as to the sources of the two rivers concerned. In 1745 Lord Fairfax, into whose hands the northern neck had descended by inheritance, made his surveys and built the Fairfax Stone at what he declared to be the head of the Potomac. Beyond this point the way was clear for new speculations, and the young George Washington, his friend and employee, was already infected with the common virus of land desire.

By royal charter of 1748, a group of Virginia and British men of affairs were incorporated as the Ohio Land Company, and were given a grant of 200,000 acres of land west of the Allegheny Mountains. Lawrence Washington, elder brother of George, was one of their number; and Christopher Gist, who was known along the Virginia border as surveyor and prospector, was sent out as their advance representative. As far as the mouth of Will's Creek, on the Potomac near its northernmost bend, the river and the settled trails were convenient guides to Gist's party. He built a stockade at Will's Creek that was named Fort Cumberland, in honor of the British duke whose exploits in the recent war had thrilled the souls of loyal subjects. Fort Cumberland was erected in 1750, and in

[3] C. A. Hanna, *The Wilderness Trail* (1911), and *The Scotch-Irish, or the Scot in North Britain, North Ireland, and North America* (1902), trace the advance of the frontier towards the Ohio, with much learning and no more controversy than is general in racial histories.

the few years ensuing the Virginia speculators pushed out from it towards the Forks of the Ohio where their enterprise inspired counteraction by the French.

The breathing stages in the century of French wars were reached in the treaties of Ryswick (1697), Utrecht (1713), Aix-la-Chapelle (1748), and Paris (1763). After Utrecht there was a cession of Acadia to the British, although France soon regretted and tried to retrieve the loss. After Aix-la-Chapelle the *status quo ante bellum* was promised to be restored, and the great French fortress at Louisburg that the New England troops had seized was given back. But the approach of the Ohio Land Company towards the Ohio River, where the French had hitherto held uncontested sway, brought forth positive assertions of French ownership from Canada. An expedition was sent southwest from Montreal under one Céloron de Bienville in 1749. Leaving the St. Lawrence route at Niagara, Céloron cut across New York to the Allegheny River, and buried near its head, on July 29, 1749, a lead plate claiming the country for his master the king of France. As he traveled down the Allegheny River and the Ohio, Céloron continued to plant his plates and raise the arms of France. He descended the Ohio to a point below the mouth of the Miami, the future site of Cincinnati and beyond the region of immediate danger from the English, and then returned to Canada. The relative effectiveness of buried tablets and cabins set in frontier clearings as a means of determining ownership was now to be worked out.

A French fort, Duquesne by name, in the angle between the Allegheny and Monongahela rivers, was erected to challenge the power of the Virginia speculators to realize upon their Ohio Land Company grant. The youthful mission of Washington[4] to demand the surrender and abandonment of this post is the prelude to his public life, and marks an opening gesture of the French and Indian War that broke over the border somewhat before its European counterpart, the Seven Years' War, became a reality. In 1754 the colonial delegates gathered at Albany to discuss plans for common defense and imperial union. The following year the decisive contest broke out.

In the struggle in America in this final war for control, the nature of the effort of each of the contestants indicates its resources as an imperial power. The French, whose policy had been to leave the Indians alone and to exploit their trade, operated with de-

---

[4] Archer B. Hulbert, *Washington and the West* (1905).

tached expeditions, supplemented by bands of savages. The British, on the other hand, made the regular troops only the nucleus of the effort, and attached to them large bodies of volunteers and militia, and found it possible to derive supplies and transport from the settled counties that were fast approaching the scene of actual hostilities. When a French force retired from the field, it left an empty country. When a British force retired, it marched back through a zone of farmsteads, that had been growing while the column advanced. Many of the militia that formed the army kept their eyes open in the new country, picked out advantageous sites, and hurried home to hurry back with their families, and extend the frontier zone, French or no French.

Washington failed in 1754 to induce the French to abandon Fort Duquesne, and was himself taken prisoner at Fort Necessity. When this news reached the seaboard and crossed to England, a great expedition was prepared to move against the fort in 1755. An army under Braddock was dispatched to the Chesapeake, and disembarked at Alexandria, Virginia. Thence they moved up the Potomac to Fort Cumberland, and beyond that point into the wilderness. In a general way Braddock's march followed the trail that Christopher Gist blazed for the Ohio Company, but Braddock cut away the underbrush and removed some of the standing timber so that the army wagons and artillery could move westward with his force. In June, 1755, Braddock was advancing with some twenty-two hundred men from Fort Cumberland to the Forks of the Ohio. If he had known how to use the knowledge of Indian fighting that George Washington and the colonial troops possessed, he might have avoided disaster. As it was, he was surprised and destroyed on July 9, on a field upon the right bank of the Monongahela somewhat below the mouth of the Youghiogheny, and about seven miles above Fort Duquesne. The militia convoyed back to safety what there remained of his defeated troops.

There was Indian war along the whole French border after the failure of Braddock, for fear of retaliation, the one thing that held the apprehensive Indian in check, was now dispelled. And it was three years before the next British force was ready to bring peace to the settlers of the border and disaster to the French. William Johnson had meanwhile commanded at the victory at Lake George (1755), but had been forced back to Fort Edward on the Hudson. In 1758 England prepared the largest forces that had been sent to America, intending to move simultaneously against Louisburg and on to Quebec, against the forts around Lake George, against the French at Niagara, and against Fort Duquesne. The last expedition was put in charge of Brigadier John Forbes, who completed his organization at Philadelphia, and moved west along the roads of Pennsylvania to a mobilizing point across the Susquehanna.

The first military decision of Forbes was whether to follow the trail that Braddock had blazed in 1755, which involved a short detour to the south, or to cut his own way through Pennsylvania to his destination. His Virginia aids urged the advantage of their route, but he determined to cut a second road to the Ohio. With the commander generally sick and at the rear, his army of over seven thousand men crossed the Susquehanna at Harris's Ferry, passed through Carlisle and the site of Bedford, and was by November, 1758, approaching the place of Braddock's defeat. The army of Forbes escaped the efforts of the French to ambush or destroy them, and left in their rear another route for the farmers who were behind them. The French at Fort Duquesne did not wait for the inevitable. As Forbes approached they destroyed their supplies, burned their buildings, and departed for Canada, abandoning the valley of the Ohio to the British. The other campaigns, that drove them from Niagara and reduced Quebec, followed in the next few months. In 1760 the military conquest of Canada was complete.

The poetic license of Dr. Holmes has perpetuated the memory of that year, 1755, when "Braddock's army was done so brown," and the American historian has generally interpreted this defeat as evidence of the ineffectiveness of British regulars in the wilderness. They were indeed ineffective. But they were also there; and maintained by their artillery and trains. More correctly than by Dr. Holmes, the event has recently been explained by Archer Butler Hulbert,[5] who calls it Braddock's victory; for it was the ability of the British to make a road across the country from the Potomac to the Ohio, and to make a second three years later, that really won the Ohio country. In the contest of the two civilizations, the French were outweighed by the numbers and habits of the British. And in the rear of the British armies of frontier defense there poured an unbroken stream of homeseekers, with

---

[5] The sixteen small, thin, and valuable volumes of this writer, comprised in his *Historic Highways* (1903), cover the historical geography of most of the migrations east of the Mississippi. He is also responsible for *The Ohio River. A Course of Empire* (1906), and *The Niagara River* (1908).

Scotch-Irish leaders at the front, to hold the lands. The survey of Mason and Dixon's line (1760–1768) followed the military victories of the war. The struggle for the farms of southwest Pennsylvania began at once. And the colonials who believed that they had won the war felt deep indignation and sense of keen injustice when the immediate result of their victory was the proclamation of 1763, and the prohibition to extend their settlements beyond the headwaters of the streams flowing into the Atlantic. They had reached the Youghiogheny and the Monongahela. Pittsburgh was already named at the Forks of the Ohio, and they could not retreat.

CHAPTER III

THE SHENANDOAH COUNTRY AND THE TENNESSEE

THE full intention of the British Government (if indeed it had a real intention), when it proscribed the occupation of the West beyond the sources of the rivers flowing into the Atlantic, is not yet known. There was at least a new feeling of imperial responsibility, and a hope to make the colonies more fruitful. In 1768, for the first time, one of His Majesty's principal secretaries of state was made Secretary of State for the Colonies, and the share of the Board of Trade in colonial government was somewhat lessened. It was the opinion of Washington, whose hopes may have shaped his judgment, that the proclamation was only "a temporary expedient to quiet the minds of the Indians," and one sure to be abandoned "when those Indians consent to our occupying the lands." In the treaties of Fort Stanwix and Hard Labour, the Royal Government accepted cessions of land from the tribes in the country beyond the line, and neither then nor later did it refuse to listen to colonial overtures for the erection of additional provincial establishments in the West.

The history of these projected colonies, the creation of any one of which might have changed the course of American development, throws light upon the lust for lands with which many Americans were inspired.[1] The possibility of their creation for barrier purposes was discussed by Benjamin Franklin and Thomas Pownall, both of whom were members of the Albany Congress of 1754. In the following year, Samuel Hazard of Philadelphia aspired to form a colony abreast of Pennsylvania, Virginia, and Carolina, and running from one hundred miles west of Pennsylvania to the Mississippi, and even beyond it. "Charlotiana," to embrace the triangle between the Wabash, the Mississippi, and the Upper Lakes, was discussed at about the same time. The proclamation did not stop the hopeful speculation, and two schemes known by the names of Illinois and Vandalia were under consideration until the Revolu-

[1] F. J. Turner, "Western State Making in the Revolutionary Era," in *American Historical Review*, vol. I; G. H. Alden, "New Governments west of the Alleghanies before 1780," in University of Wisconsin *Bulletin* (Historical Series, vol. II), and "The State of Franklin," in *American Historical Review*, vol. VIII.

tion checked their course. These had the support in England of Dr. Franklin who was there as colonial agent, and in the colonies of William Johnson, now Sir William and superintendent of Indian affairs because of his military services.[2] From 1767 to 1772 the various branches of the British Government were pondering whether a petition supported by colonial magnates of such eminence ought to be rejected, and in August of the latter year the Board of Trade was directed to go ahead with the details. The proposed boundaries for Vandalia fix its location southwest of Pennsylvania, with the Ohio at its north, an irregular mountain line between the Fairfax Stone and Cumberland Gap on its south, and the Kentucky River on its west. The transaction went so far that the governor of Virginia was warned not to grant lands in trespass upon the proposed colony, a warning that could not have been needed had the Proclamation of 1763 been vigorously in effect. Independence came before the new charter was issued, leaving Virginia still able to claim the full extent of her own charter boundaries.

While the speculators were thinking in terms of huge provincial grants, the frontier farmers continued steadily at their task of clearing farms. From southwest Pennsylvania they advanced up the Shenandoah and its parallel neighbors into the valley country beyond the Blue Ridge. For half a century after the initial settlements at Harris's Ferry and Harper's Ferry the overflow from Virginia and Pennsylvania, strongly reinforced by immigrant home-seekers, sought out new locations behind the counties of the low-land region. About ninety miles southwest of Harper's Ferry, another gap through the Blue Ridge let in a secondary stream of men who had crossed Virginia along the line of the James River. The organization of Frederick County, with Winchester as its seat, occurred in 1743. Staunton, the seat of Augusta, held its first court in 1745. And in 1749 Virginia and North Carolina found it profitable to extend their common boundary westward until it reached the Laurel Fork of the Holston.

The Cumberland Mountains form to-day a part of the boundary of Kentucky and Virginia. On either slope their streams drain not into the Potomac basin, but the other way, into the Mississippi. On the west, the Cumberland River here starts its way across Ken-

---

[2] The State historian of New York, Dr. James Sullivan, has recently edited three fine volumes of *The Papers of Sir William Johnson* (1921), which are particularly rich for the years 1745 to 1774.

tucky to its entrance into the lower Ohio. East of the Cumberland Mountains are the upper tributaries of the Tennessee River, of which the Clinch and Holston are the most imposing. Between the tributaries of the Potomac, flowing northward, and those of the Tennessee and Cumberland flowing southward there is no pronounced watershed to obstruct the course of frontier advance. Easily the pioneers passed along the parallel valley trails, with minor trails entering from east of the Blue Ridge, and with corresponding ways opening west, where the New River cuts across to a junction with the Great Kanawha, or where the Cumberland Mountains are broken by Cumberland Gap (which is where the southern boundary of Virginia crosses them). As a military measure the Virginia troops crossed the low watershed in 1756, and descended the Holston to a point some twenty-five miles below the present site of Knoxville, where they built Fort Loudoun. For the same reasons Fort Prince George on the Savannah, near its head, was constructed in the same year. The settlements were well in the rear of these outposts when they were planted, and Fort Loudoun could not be held with the troops available. But with the return of peace, the military trails became the roads of entry for the people.[3]

Virginians dominated in this expansion of settlement, as was natural because of their situation, but it is impossible to overlook the North Carolinians who joined the march after it came abreast of their own colony. The great difference between the relation of North Carolina to the mountain colonies, and that of Virginia, is that the settlements of North Carolina had not ascended the eastern slopes of the mountains. In Virginia by 1760 the seaboard plantations merged gradually into those of the up-country, and these in turn were continuous up to the Blue Ridge. In North Carolina there was a broad expanse of unoccupied land between the main colony and the tributaries of the Tennessee River.

The development of county government in Virginia and North Carolina kept uneven pace with the need for it among the border settlements. Heretofore there had often been a lapse of several years after the legal creation of a county before its first officers qualified. Now there were frequently many settlers and a need to

[3] This is the theme of Theodore Roosevelt, *The Winning of the West* (1889–96), romantically written, with emphasis upon the heroic virtues. Archibald Henderson, *Conquest of the Old Southwest* (1920), traverses much of the same ground, helped by the mass of monographic literature that has appeared since Roosevelt wrote, and inspired by family enthusiasm and a real literary zest.

register land titles and probate estates before the colonial legislatures became aware of the fact. Wherever it happened that a group of settlers outran the operation of established law there was a tendency for them to frame some kind of legal institutions for themselves. They were never embarrassed by isolation, though sometimes exasperated by apparent neglect. The Pilgrim group on the *Mayflower* in 1620 set a precedent that their successors followed in unnumbered cases. Along the southern borders of the Virginia-Carolina valleys there were four clearly defined experiments of this sort in the fifteen years after the treaties of Fort Stanwix and Hard Labour. In their earlier phases they seem to represent a protest against colonial or imperial attempts to restrict their spread; later they are merged in the aftermath of the American Revolution.

The Watauga settlement was made about 1769, and gave rise to an early exhibition of the frontier aptitude for self-government.

It began in the normal expansion from what is now the southwest corner of Virginia into what has become the northeast corner of Tennessee. The Watauga River is an eastern tributary of the Holston, making a junction with the latter a little south of the Virginia line. In the absence of surveys, the settlers picked the choice locations for themselves before they learned that they were encroaching upon the lands of North Carolina. They claimed their title under the Virginia cabin right, by which one cabin and an acre of corn gave foundation for a claim to four hundred acres. In 1771 and 1772 the settlement grew in size because of the entry of a rebellious group of North Carolina colonists who had been on the losing side at the battle of the Alamance.

The factions in North Carolina politics that produced this insurrection, with its culminating conflict on May 16, 1771, show a social cleavage. Similar classes prevailed in nearly every other colony, and tended sharply to divide the people according to their property interests.[4] The first made counties in a colony gained representation in the assembly, and used their votes to prevent the extension of representation after the growth of the community made additional counties inevitable. There was everywhere

[4] John S. Bassett, "The Regulators of North Carolina," in American Historical Association, *Annual Report*, 1894; C. H. Lincoln, *The Revolutionary Movement in Pennsylvania* (1901); William A. Schaper, "Sectionalism and Representation in South Carolina," in American Historical Association, *Annual Report*, 1900; Charles H. Ambler, *Sectionalism in Virginia from 1776 to 1861* (1910); are among the most useful studies of this social sectionalism.

irregular and discriminating representation; but rarely was it as pronounced as in North Carolina where the original counties clung to their five assemblymen, allowing the new counties only two. The resentment against this injustice was increased by questions of land ownership. The strip of territory along the Virginia line belonged to Earl Granville who was loath to grant land titles, but preferred a quit-rent. The taxes levied by the province, when added to the claims of Granville, made a burden heavier than the frontiersmen were willing to carry. The injustice was aggravated by a loose method of accounting, and a wasteful fee system that made it possible for the sheriffs to abuse their position to their private profit. The remoteness of the courts, and the cost of attending them, gave additional grievance. The result was mob violence — a real peasants' revolt — in which the regulators tried to improve their situation by force. In retaliation the provincial government took punitive measures against the frontiersmen that culminated in the pitched and disastrous battle of the Alamance. The "regulation" was ended in blood and the leaders of the regulators were hanged. Many of their followers left North Carolina in indignation, and shifted to the Watauga district, only to find that here too they were under the jurisdiction of the native colony.

The participants in the movement into new lands were generally unimportant men, whose very names can be determined only after a more careful search of title deeds and recorded wills than any historian has yet made. Often only partly literate, or worse, they left few formal records of their life, and their monument in tilled fields tells nothing of their personality except as it reveals their stubborn industry. In the Watauga, however, two men stand forth whose names personify the movement in which they led. James Robertson, whose origin appears to have been Scotch, was under thirty years of age when he took the lead in the group. Born in Virginia, in Brunswick County in 1742, he drifted south into North Carolina when Raleigh was still unfounded, and Wake County, in which it now exists, was an active frontier. The rough-and-tumble of border existence here is suggested by the fact that within two years of its creation the court of Wake County had to do justice twice in the case of ears bitten off in personal encounters. Here too was a center of the violence of the regulators, although Robertson left the community before the battle of the Alamance. In the Watauga region he was a natural leader, with a fame little dimmed by that of his great associate, John Sevier.

The Huguenot ancestry of John Sevier may have contributed to the making of his character, but more is due to the frontier of the Shenandoah Valley, where he was born in 1745.[5] His biographer describes him as the son of a Virginian, who was a "considerable planter." He was better educated than most of the men he worked with, but resembled them in early marriage and speculative zeal. At seventeen he took him a wife, and laid out and named the township of Newmarket, Virginia. He knew the Indians, and how to trade with them as well as fight them, before he moved to join the colony of Robertson on the Watauga in 1772. Year after year this settlement remained isolated and in danger. Under its leaders it blocked the trail of the Cherokee against the settlements of both Carolina and Virginia, and "stood, from first to last, the immovable rear-guard of the Revolution." In 1772, tradition has it, the Watauga group formed a written "association" in which they agreed to stand together, as indeed they must; and in which they provided for the minimum institutions of government which neither Virginia could nor North Carolina would establish. The text of this agreement is not known, but the evidence as to its existence seems to be conclusive. Certainly the bond of existence and agreement was alive, whether on paper or not.

Out of the Watauga settlement there germinated similar groups of pioneers who risked the wilderness in their determination to live their own life and to advantage themselves as best they could. In 1775 Judge Richard Henderson found here recruits for one of the most spectacular of border enterprises. In 1779 James Robertson led an emigration hence to the Cumberland. In 1784 under John Sevier there was formed the short-lived but significant State of Franklin.

The Transylvania speculation of Richard Henderson is connected both with the movement for new colonies after the Treaty of Fort Stanwix, and with the advancing occupation of the Virginia-Tennessee valleys. The permanency of the adjustment made by the Proclamation of 1763 had already been brought into doubt many times before the settlement at Watauga was planted, to overrun the line. In 1768 the British acquired the claim of the Six Nations to an indefinite tract south of the Ohio River, which appeared to be a step preliminary to a new opening of lands. In 1774 the province of Quebec was swung south from the trail to Lake Nipissing to the line of the Ohio and Mississippi rivers. The east-

[5] J. R. Gilmore, *John Sevier as a Commonwealth Builder* (1887).

ern colonies felt that this was both a new colonial venture and a threat at their peace and safety. In the same year Lord Dunmore, the Virginia royal governor, concluded a warfare on the Ohio River below Pittsburgh, that brought the area of West Virginia under his control.

Lord Dunmore's War was a result of continued encroachment of white settlement in spite of the treaties with the southern Indians.[6] A trail had been cut across from the Monongahela through the bustling southwest corner of Pennsylvania, to the Ohio River, which was reached at the mouth of Wheeling Creek. The island in the Ohio River here made a convenient place for a settlement and a post, and the brothers Zane, whose initiative brought about the establishment, were followed by others whose cabins crept down the left bank of the Ohio. The Indians were irritated by this crowding process, and, maddened by the whiskey that they could get from the settlements, made attacks upon isolated homes. At this moment Lord Dunmore was making a vigorous assertion of Virginia title to Pennsylvania lands, and had an agent named Connolley in actual possession of Pittsburgh. He took the aggressive against the Shawnee tribe in the country below Wheeling, and defeated Cornstalk with his Shawnee braves on a field known as Point Pleasant, at the mouth of the Great Kanawha. The unquestioned jurisdiction of his province was by this campaign extended over most of West Virginia. Among the men who fought for him at Point Pleasant were many who left their homes on the Watauga or the New, or in the Shenandoah Valley. Isaac Shelby was there, and William Cocke, as well as Daniel Boone who was on the verge of a much greater venture in the valley of the Kentucky River.

Throughout its relations with the various Indian tribes the British Government sought to maintain the general principle of law that title to Indian land could be acquired only by public authority. The desire to speculate in such land repeatedly induced colonial subjects to negotiate directly with the Indians, who were easily influenced by their friends, and who responded readily to the offer of presents, food, and drink. But the royal governors

[6] The Draper Manuscripts of the State Historical Society of Wisconsin contain the most important single collection of sources for this time and place. From them came the papers that Reuben Gold Thwaites and Louise Phelps Kellogg edited as *Documentary History of Lord Dunmore's War, 1774* (1905), *The Revolution on the Upper Ohio, 1775–1777* (1908), *Frontier Defense on the Upper Ohio* (1912); and that Dr. Kellogg edited alone, *Frontier Advance on the Upper Ohio* (1916), and *Frontier Retreat on the Upper Ohio* (1917).

discouraged and disavowed such agreements, while in the proprietaries such land was a legitimate monopoly of the proprietor himself. This was the subsequent view of the United States Government, that "deeds obtained by private persons from the Indians without any antecedent authority, or subsequent confirmation, from the Government, could not vest in the grantees mentioned in such deeds a title to the lands therein described." The few exceptions to this law were not enough to warrant a hope, but created only a speculative chance that such transactions might be legitimated. Such a chance Judge Richard Henderson took when he negotiated a treaty with the Indians of the Kentucky country in March, 1775.

James Robertson, of Watauga, and Daniel Boone, were among the border leaders associated with Henderson in the attempt to found a great land company to operate west of Virginia. They negotiated a private treaty at Sycamore Shoals, that is reported to have been clearly and honestly explained to the Indians who signed it. The land described, to which Henderson sought title, was the area between the southern watershed of the Cumberland River (separating it from the Tennessee), and the Ohio River. To-day it represents all of Kentucky and much of middle Tennessee. According to his own notion, Henderson was within his rights in going through the forms of the purchase, although Virginia disavowed it at once. The dissolving authority of England could not be invoked against him. The Transylvania Company was organized to exploit the lands, and Daniel Boone, most famous of all the scouts, was hired to mark a road from the settlements into the Kentucky Valley and the Blue Grass region.

Boone had already hunted over the land transferred at Sycamore Shoals, and knew that the easiest road ran down the east side of the Cumberland Mountain, turning sharply northwest at its tip to go through Cumberland Gap. He blazed the Wilderness Trail along this path immediately after the treaty, and in April, 1775, was building himself a cabin at Boonesborough, by a salt lick on the south side of the Kentucky River. From Watauga to the new settlements appearing at Harrodsburg and Lexington, his trail was soon beaten by the feet of hundreds of immediate followers; while the name of Lexington commemorates the doings in New England at the moment when Henderson joined Boone at the stockade on the Kentucky River. James Harrod was already in Kentucky, with a station of his own, when Boone arrived to serve notice that this land had been bought by Judge Henderson from the Cherokee. As early as May 23, 1775, the Transylvania settlers held a local convention to make preliminary laws for themselves, in spite of the denial by Virginia of their right to exist. But when Henderson and the Transylvania Company sought to fix a price for their land many of the settlers shifted their allegiance to Virginia. The Continental Congress, now in session, knew better than to offend Virginia by recognizing Transylvania as a separate state; and before the end of 1776 Virginia caught up with the development of its frontier, creating Kentucky County with the same dimensions that Kentucky has to-day.

The Transylvania Company was not able to maintain its claim to the legality of the Treaty of Sycamore Shoals against the authority of Virginia and the indifference of Congress. Henderson was eventually compensated for his loss of the tract by grants in the Cumberland Valley, made by both Virginia and North Carolina, and retained his colonizing zest in spite of his misfortune. In 1780 he and James Robertson were at it again, this time in western North Carolina, where they founded Nashborough, or Nashville, in the bend of the Cumberland River.

This settlement in middle Tennessee was not the result of single family pioneering, but was another of the group movements in which a large land speculation was united to the desire for independence and autonomy. On May 13, 1780, the Cumberland agreement was signed by two hundred and fifty settlers, and included a basis of government as well as a contract with what remained of the Transylvania Company. With this venture Robertson separated himself from the colony at Watauga, which he had helped to found ten years before, and which had begun to throw its feelers along the other tributaries of the Tennessee — the Clinch and the Holston. Richard Henderson headed the list of signers of the Cumberland agreement, and drafted the document. Colonel John Donelson of Virginia was with the first detachment. The uncertainty whether Nashville was in Virginia or North Carolina was eventually settled after Robertson represented Cumberland in the North Carolina Assembly and that body created Davidson County for the government of the new group in 1783.

The American Revolution was running its uneven course between the founding of the Watauga settlement and that of Nashville. The names of the heroes of the eastern conflict found their way to places on the western map. Washington, Sullivan, and Greene counties, North Carolina, were spread over the mountain regions. But the spirit of equal representation that inspired the States in their demands upon Great Britain was stifled when it came to the recognition of their own new offshoots. In North Carolina twenty-eight of the thirty-five counties were still east of Raleigh when that State revised its constitution in 1835. And since the legislature was based upon county representation, the people in the large and few counties of the West were systematically outvoted by the more compact groups of the East. The fact that property and safety went with eastern compactness, and that on the border was debt and Indian danger, kept a sharp cleavage alive in North Carolina politics, as it did under similar conditions in the States further north and south. Virginia, Georgia, Pennsylvania, New York, and Massachusetts had much the same sectionalism, with the same causes and consequences.

The settlers on the Watauga and the Holston came there largely from Virginia, but held the State of North Carolina responsible for what they lacked in facilities of government. When Congress in 1780 made an appeal to the States to surrender to it all the unused western lands, they looked to that body for recognition of their existence. When North Carolina ceded its western claim in 1784, and Congress made no motion to accept or govern, the citizens of the Tennessee Valley followed the dictate of their history and character, and organized for themselves not a mere association but the State of Franklin.

John Sevier was the inspiration of the State of Franklin. Now at the crest of his life, his success and courage made him natural leader of his community. The Indians feared and respected him in equal degree. His tactics of defending a frontier by carrying an aggressive war against the Indian villages, commended itself to his admirers and gave him weight with the savages. In August, 1784, he presided over a convention of delegates from Washington, Sullivan, and Greene counties in the ceded part of North Carolina; and he became head of a provisional government which was a year later made as regular as the citizens of Franklin could make it. Congress ignored the overtures of Franklin for admission, as it ignored those of Transylvania. To its fears of alienating the parent States was now added the decrepitude that grew as the Confederation decayed. A reaction from the zeal for independence in Franklin came when the tax-gatherers went round, and after 1786 North Carolina was successful in reasserting its control. Sevier was outlawed as a traitor first, then pardoned and honored as the hero that he had become. The autonomous spirit of the frontier, and its disposition to penetrate the Indian Country, had however spread something of American institutions over the Shenandoah country and through the southwest gateway of the valleys into central Kentucky, and middle and eastern Tennessee. The movement began as England sought to check it in 1763. In another twenty years it was become the conscious agent of a new sort of imperial expansion. The American Revolution gave it legitimacy, and it gave to America its meaning.

CHAPTER IV

THE REAR OF THE REVOLUTION

THE contrast between the old England and the new Englands that developed in America before 1763 was obscured by the fact that one language in general served the needs of both nations. On neither side of the Atlantic was there clear realization of the creation of a new nationality. So long as England refrained from ruling her English-speaking subjects the recognition of the difference was deferred. When she tried to reorganize and systematize the empire after the Seven Years' War she stumbled upon obstacles that startled and grieved the leaders of opinion on both sides; but even then America knew its separate nationality long before England could bring herself to see it. Of all the frontier struggles that the American historian has to deal with, the first and greatest is this one, in which the overseas frontier of Britain carried to its logical completion the development of local self-governing institutions, and then defended its independence through seven years of war. In this revolution the frontier bore its full part. In the ensuing war that secured independence, most of the heavy fighting was along the seaboard, but the lesser engagements of the interior border reveal the personality and resources of the frontiersmen, and count heavily in the further pressure against the unoccupied West.[1]

The half-century after the creation of the Ohio Land Company in 1748 is one of continuous growth along the border, in spite of French wars, British policy, and revolution. It divides easily into three periods with tolerably clear limits. The first decade, ending with the capture of the site of Pittsburgh by the army of Forbes, is marked chiefly by the approach of the settled area to the valleys of the Appalachians and the outlets on the west. The second stage is one of conquest and covers the early years of the Revolution, until George Rogers Clark found himself in possession of

[1] Channing's theory of the Revolution is laid down in his vol. III. Since the publication of Sydney George Fisher, *True History of the American Revolution* (1902), many of the younger historians have felt it necessary to give their interpretation of these events, among the more notable being Claude H. Van Tyne, *The Causes of the War of Independence* (1922), James T. Adams, *Revolutionary New England, 1691–1776* (1923), and Arthur M. Schlesinger, *The Colonial Merchants and the American Revolution* (1918).

Vincennes and the Illinois country in 1778–1779. The valleys were occupied in these years, the wilderness was subdued both single-handed and by group effort, and before the later date was reached, conquest had given place to peaceful occupation in many parts. The period of occupation comes third in the series, but overlaps that of conquest. It may be said to begin about 1770 when the Watauga pioneers made their lodgment. There was no let-up in occupation thereafter. Before the end of the century the persistent attempts to make new states west of the mountains reached success. The governments that blocked them were displaced, and the new republic took to itself as equals both Kentucky and Tennessee. The Revolution on the border played a part in both of the later periods.

The history of the old French wars repeated itself when England undertook to bring her rebellious colonists to terms and to undo the Revolution. On the seaboard, of course, every port lay open to any fleet that might invest it. But along the border the routes that the French had known were all that the English could find or use. The Lake Champlain route regained its importance immediately on the outbreak of hostilities. At either end of Lake Ontario an entry was sought to central New York. The Allegheny River continued to run an easy approach from Lake Erie to Pittsburgh. And the Indians found themselves courted once more, by emissaries from either side, with promises that neither side was able to fulfill. The English military posts in Florida proved to be unimportant, because of the vast distances against the current of the Gulf rivers before any colonial habitations could be reached. When the British wished to strike against the southern border, the penetration was made at Charleston, and an inland march through South Carolina led them to the back country.

The struggle for Quebec, which might have been the fourteenth colony had Benedict Arnold been successful, has been described in picturesque detail by Justin H. Smith.[2] It served only to reveal to Americans the fact that the French *habitants* of Canada were not the stuff for either martyrs or revolutionists, and that the cry of liberty and free government raised an echo only where generations of English past had educated the subject to an appreciation of them. The counterstroke of England from the St. Lawrence to the Hudson by the way of Lake Champlain gave the basis for the strategy of 1777, in which it was hoped to cut the New England

[2] *Our Struggle for the Fourteenth Colony — Canada and the American Revolution* (1907)

States away from the Middle Colonies. Three columns were designated to (1) ascend the Hudson to Albany, (2) descend the Mohawk from Fort Stanwix to its mouth, and (3) join these two by the direct route from Montreal. The concerted movement was broken down. At Oriskany, near the site of Fort Stanwix, the invading force of General St. Leger was checked on August 6, 1777, by a patriot army under Nicholas Herkimer, a descendant of one of those immigrants whose name had clung to German Flats. The hope of uniting the Six Nations and inspiring the morale of the Tory population of central New York, evaporated with this rebuff. On August 16 the Hessians of General Burgoyne were routed at Bennington "at the foot of the Green Mountains" by a militia force from New England, while his major army was entangled in the wilderness between Lake George and the Hudson. Sir William Howe, meanwhile, instead of ascending the Hudson to coöperate with Burgoyne, set sail for the Chesapeake, and was at Elkton when he ought to have been at Albany. The victory he gained when he occupied the rebel capital at Philadelphia in September was a costly compensation for the disastrous defeat of Burgoyne at Saratoga, or for the surrender of the northern army to the Americans on October 17, 1777.

In the early years of the Revolution, the border between the Mohawk and the Tennessee was without formal protection, bustling though it was with new families. The refusal of the crown to authorize these to extend themselves, or to organize new colonies, was a grievance that kept them sore. The soreness turned to anger when Quebec was enlarged on the eve of the Revolution. To Quebec and Montreal, which were hitherto centers of Canadian influence, Detroit was now added as the western post in the enlarged province. Recent historians have proved that the Quebec Act of 1774,[3] that worked this change, was not intended as a stroke against the English-speaking colonies, or as a punishment. But the colonials could see in this change that spread the French law and the established Catholic church of Quebec over the Ohio Valley, nothing but a deliberate attempt to set up an enemy in their rear. West and south of Detroit were little French communities that justified the enlargement of Quebec. At the outlet of the Upper Lakes stood the trading post at Mackinaw. On the Wabash was Vincennes. The east bank of the Mississippi was occupied at Cahokia and Kaskaskia, a little below St. Louis. Neither

[3] Victor Coffin, *The Province of Quebec and the Early American Revolution* (1896).

the ousting of France in 1763 nor the extension of Quebec in 1774, made much difference to the placid hunters and traders of these villages. Never used to share in government, and expecting little from their rulers, they took one flag or another without excitement or regret.[4]

The British officers at Detroit saw a chance to distress the American border as soon as hostilities commenced. By turning loose the Indians against the scattered settlements, it might be possible to force the diversion of a considerable amount of military strength from the main campaigns in order to protect the outposts; and the outlying settlements might be prevented by their own danger from carrying aid to the new national cause. Sir Henry Hamilton, at Detroit, was under the orders of Sir Guy Carleton who commanded at Quebec, and both suggested plans and executed them. The Indians of the Ohio Valley were warned that American victory meant for them an extension of white settlement north of the Ohio River. The tales they were hearing of the treaty of Richard Henderson at Sycamore Shoals was earnest of this, for the Transylvania Company brought the aggressive farmers into the fair land of central Kentucky. Another step and they would pass the Ohio River itself. The Virginia claim to all the West made that State the chief agent in the struggle against Detroit, as it sought to prevent both private intrigue with the Indians and the machinations of the enemy.

A proclamation addressed by Hamilton to the Indians in June, 1777, started two movements towards the defense of the Pennsylvania and Virginia borders. Congress sent a general named McIntosh to Pittsburgh in the following spring, and one of the young leaders of the frontier went himself to the seat of the Virginia government at Williamsburg, to seek assistance in carrying the war into the enemy's country. George Rogers Clark, who performed this mission, was twenty-five years of age in 1777, and was already proficient in the arts of the new settlement. He had an interest in speculation, knew how to run a surveyor's line, and was

[4] *The Centennial History of Illinois*, a monument worthy of frequent imitation, has for its first volume Clarence W. Alvord, *The Illinois Country* (1920). Professor Alvord and Professor James A. James have edited for the *Collections* of the Illinois State Historical Library many papers on George Rogers Clark and his predecessors. R. G. Thwaites, *How George Rogers Clark Won the Northwest, and other Essays in Western History* (1903), is somewhat out of date, but is by a master of popular narrative. F. J. Turner, "George Rogers Clark and the Kaskaskia Campaign," in *American Historical Review*, vol. VIII, is critical and detailed.

able to shift for himself in open country. At Williamsburg he found Patrick Henry installed as governor and engaged in making the most of the insurrection he had pressed against England.

Virginia was big with ideas, but had an empty treasury, and a reluctant tax-paying populace. The proposal of Clark to raise a force of troops and descend the Ohio River against the French towns called for both money and men; the latter to be found in the new communities, the former hard to find at all. Keeping the project secret from all save an informal group of political leaders, Governor Henry sanctioned the measure, gave Clark his commission, and authorized him to raise seven companies of fifty men each, and to meet his expenses with Virginia scrip. With this warrant, dated January 2, 1778, Clark hurried back to the Monongahela country to enlist his followers. Of formal military training or discipline they had none. There was almost no military appearance in their band. If they had a flag, it is almost impossible to say what one; — although at Oriskany an amateurish stars and stripes was improvised from rough materials found in the patriot camp. But there were men ready to enlist in such a campaign, though not the three hundred and fifty that Clark's commission contemplated.

The potential military strength of any American border settlement needs to be understood in order that the capacity of the frontier for war may be realized. In nearly every case the unit working on the frontier was a young married couple. Bachelors could not operate to best advantage with both farm and cabin to be developed. And spinsters, wherever they appeared, were in slight danger of remaining such for long, because of the crying masculine need for helpmates. As soon, therefore, as a new community took shape it had women as well as men, and children who arrived even more rapidly than did the terrible diseases of undoctored childhood which carried them to the little graveyards. For many years there were few unmarried men in any community, and as soon as boys grew to manhood they were likely to marry and proceed on their own account to found new homes in the forest. Recruits for an army could hardly be found, though every man carried a deadly gun, and knew how to use it to advantage, to economize on precious powder and ball, and to take cover from the Indian behind any tree or hillock. For a few weeks men might get away from home. But the wife and little ones played upon the frontiersman's imagination as soon as his term of service lengthened enough for him to become proficient in any of the specialized duties of the soldier. Desertions soon became numerous. What had to be done needed to be done quickly while the enthusiasm lasted, and needed to involve no special organization or training. A commander of troops who could find any basis for holding his men together after the first three months, and for using them in organized strategic efforts, deserves to rank high on the score of both human quality and military skill.

George Rogers Clark learned all these things before the expedition to the Illinois country was accomplished. By May he got together his first band at Redstone on the Allegheny, and started down the Ohio with them in flatboats. The incorrigible propensity of the settlements to keep on spreading even in time of war led a group of families to trail him to the Falls of the Ohio where they made a landing and a settlement. Louisville assumed, appropriately enough, the name of the French king whose alliance with the United States was consummated almost as Clark came to the falls. Thereafter it found a certain reason for existence and growth in the necessity of nearly every boat that descended the Ohio either to have its goods portaged around the rapids, or to be steered through them by a professional pilot.[5] A "pincers movement" upon the blue grass region of Kentucky begins at this moment; one arm of the forceps reaching it through Cumberland Gap, the other touching it at the Falls of the Ohio.

From the site of Louisville Clark advanced by boat to the mouth of the Cumberland River, where he landed to make the rest of his journey overland. The French alliance doubtless made it easier than it otherwise would have been for the French of Kaskaskia to accept his control when he took their town on July 4, 1778. Hamilton at Detroit, meanwhile, was hearing fragments of report upon the success of Clark, and was preparing to meet and check him. After holding a council with the Indians in June, he marched in the autumn through their villages, and descended the Wabash to Vincennes, where he arrived in December. The road he followed was better known to the tribes than any other in the interior of America. For centuries the Canadian Indians and those of the South had visited, and fought, each other up and down the Wabash route. No other tributary of the Mississippi gives a better approach to the Great Lakes than does this stream, or reaches them at a better point. From Toledo Bay, at the northern end of the route, Lake Erie provides a natural way to all parts of Ontario.

[5] Robert M. McElroy, *Kentucky in the Nation's History* (1909).

Ascending the Maumee River from Toledo Bay to its source, there is an easy portage to the navigable head of the Wabash. The Indian canoeist, followed in turn by the French missionary, explorer, and trapper, used this route from the beginning. Along both the Maumee and Wabash were many of the permanent homes of the tribes living between the Lakes and the Ohio. Visitors and courtship were linked together. Here on the Wabash were Indians of mixed tribal origin, connecting those of the North with those of the South. In one of the tepees, perhaps, as Hamilton floated down the stream, was a papoose who was destined in the next generation to try to unite the western tribes on the basis of blood and the control of the Wabash. This was Tecumseh; but before his day the destiny of the Old Northwest was to be worked out.

Clark wintered at Kaskaskia, while Hamilton wintered at Vincennes, the difference being that the one thought himself secure while the other sensed a task not yet done. In the dead of winter Clark led his men out of quarters for a march across country to the Wabash. The journey, through the marshes of southern Illinois, was one of those exploits that sensible men know cannot be accomplished; and Hamilton gave no thought to possible attack. His surprise and enforced surrender came unexpectedly in February, 1779. Thereafter England made no show of force in the lower Ohio country, although there was another expedition in a vain attempt to seize Pittsburgh. The frontiersmen whose power to fight as individuals helped to break the New York campaign of 1777 at Bennington and Oriskany, proved capable of an aggressive measure when under proper leadership. The historian who has tried to identify and describe Clark's services of supply concludes that the campaign was waged on hopes and promises, some of which were long in realization. The frontier soldier at his best could accomplish things impossible for an army with its traditional impedimenta.

Further south than the Ohio, the frontier bore its share of the brunt of the Revolution when in 1780 Cornwallis proposed to envelop Carolina and Virginia, after making a landing at Charleston in May. The British were in complete possession of South Carolina within a few weeks after the surrender of that city, and what American forces there were operated only as irregulars and guerrillas in the hills of the back country. In August the army that Washington sent to the relief of the State was destroyed at Camden in what John Fiske has characterized as "the most disastrous defeat ever inflicted upon an American army, and ignominious withal, since it was incurred through a series of the grossest blunders." [6]

From Charleston to Camden was about halfway to the back country of North Carolina where the embattled farmers fought the courts and the provincial troops at the Alamance in 1771. The advance of Cornwallis's troops to the interior, in the autumn of 1780, called the frontier rifles from their cabins to help check the invader. It was the kind of attack that border men could well engage in. They came from South Carolina and Virginia, as well as from the Tennessee. John Sevier was there, and Isaac Shelby; but it is hard to tell who was captain, or who devised their tactics. In October, 1780, they found a detachment of the British penned on top of King's Mountain, in North Carolina, near its southern line; entrenched, the commander said, in a "place from which all the rebels outside of hell cannot drive us." One by one they picked the British off, and rushed the rest from their position. Each little group fought by itself with a minimum of direction, but in each the average man was trained in the arts that Indian fighting had taught him. King's Mountain turned the southern invasion towards its ultimate defeat. The Quaker blacksmith general, Greene, took command of the American forces in this last winter of the war, and worried the British. He beat them at the Cowpens, and held them at Guilford Courthouse. In the fall of 1781 Cornwallis was maneuvered into that peninsula of the James River, where British dominion began in 1607; and here it was substantially ended when he surrendered in October, 1781.

The revolution that had taken place in America between the landing at Jamestown and the surrender there, owed much to the constant influence upon standards and ideas exerted by people who were living a life dominated in its form by the log cabin. It was a frontier influence that changed the British, and merged them with their co-workers into the American. In actual grievances the men of the border had less cause for complaint than either the commercial people of the seaboard whose routes and markets were being brought under regulation by the navigation laws, or the southern planters whose heavy debts to their English factors kept them always depressed. The limitation upon the right of the border to

---

[6] John Fiske, *The American Revolution* (1891), is based on lectures that were deservedly popular, and that have not yet been excelled in interest for the general reader. The illustrated edition of 1897 is all that can be desired in the way of maps and illustrations.

take the land it wanted was the chief grievance in the realm of real things. Less tangible was the spirit of independence that throve there, and the resentment against any form of control of the individual.

The independence for which the war was waged was a condition precedent to the negotiation of peace after the surrender of Cornwallis. There was no doubt as to the status that must be accorded the thirteen colonies and their actually settled areas. On three sides, however, there was room for discussion and compromise. Quebec had resisted the overtures made by the Continental Congress, and had avoided either conversion or conquest. It remained in hands that valued it for the fur trade of the country behind. Florida, at the other end of the seaboard strip, had remained uninterested in the thought of independence, and had not been in danger of conquest. England was free to dispose of it at pleasure. The country west of the Appalachians was an area of controversy, with enough evidence of occupation or conquest to warrant an American claim, yet with a bearing upon the western half of Louisiana, and Canada, that inspired the British negotiators with a desire to retain it. The American commissioners, Franklin, Jay, and Adams, soon found that the zeal of the French ally had cooled off with victory; and that France, glad enough to cripple England, had no enthusiasm for erecting an America both independent and powerful. The other ally, Spain, watched with jealousy the progress of a negotiation that might extend the borders of the United States until they joined her own at the Mississippi River. It was proposed to the peace commissioners, on behalf of France and Spain, that in settling the boundaries England should retain all of Canada, and that Canada should include the whole of Quebec as enlarged in 1774. Spain was suggested to receive back Florida, which she had lost in 1763. The Indians were to retain the area between the Appalachians and the Mississippi, and were to be divided by an arbitrary line east of which they should be under American control, and west of which they should owe devotion to Spain.

The frontier, and the events along it during the Revolution, seem to have had no direct effect upon the negotiations at Versailles, that resulted in the preliminary articles of peace in 1782. With both allies willing to restrict American limits for reasons of their own, the Americans were driven back to their own courage and sagacity in framing the agreement. Their instructions, which showed the skillful hand of the French agents in Philadelphia, were inadequate and had to be disregarded. Even the commissioners, with all the knowledge they could acquire, could not learn enough of the terrain to make a final boundary. In the outcome it was not the conquest of Clark that gained the Ohio Valley for the United States, but the hope of England to develop a cleavage between the former colonies and France, and to reëstablish a basis for intimate and friendly trade. By the terms of the Treaty of Versailles, concluded on September 3, 1783, the thirteen States were recognized as extending to the Mississippi, over the stretch of Indian country between Lake Superior and the Lake of the Woods on the north, and the thirty-first parallel on the south. Spain received back her provinces of Florida, but there was a secret article in the Anglo-American treaty relating to the northern boundary of West Florida that was provocative of trouble for her and the United States.

CHAPTER V

THE LAND PROBLEM

THE Treaty of Versailles left in American hands the future of American life, but there was little in the past of the former provinces to warrant a belief that these hands could grapple with the problems of independence, or steer a course at once leading to a useful goal and acceptable to all. So uncertain was their unity, that England made the treaty not with the United States, but with the thirteen States, which were carefully enumerated. The colonial history of their governments was drenched with separatism, which the navigation laws and the various English councils dealing with colonial affairs had carefully cherished. Wise observers in England believed that the American edifice would soon collapse, and wise Americans feared it. After five years of freedom, Washington was constrained to tell the weightiest assembly that has ever gathered in America — the Constitutional Convention in Philadelphia — that "it is too probable that no plan that we propose will be adopted." The worst years of the critical period were those that preceded the ratification of the Federal Constitution made in Philadelphia, but for more than half of the next century it was easy to find respectable leaders who thought that separation from the Union was a probable and proper course.[1] The strongest of the slender bonds that held the States together until common interests grew sufficiently close to dominate the local, are to be found in the opportunities created and the duties entailed by the huge areas of open land, extending along the rear of every State, and filling the unoccupied expanse between the ill-fated Proclamation Line and the Mississippi River. Easy access to the land was indispensable to frontier communities, and common interests here engendered common purpose.

The American frontier was a line, a region, or a process, according to the context in which the word is used. As a *process*, its most significant meaning is found. A universal common task was impressing its standardizing influence upon all the people who came within its reach. Everywhere on the frontier civilization was

---

[1] The extreme independence of the States and their reluctance to admit Federal control are shown in C. H. Van Tyne, *The American Revolution* (1906).

being manufactured out of raw material and personnel. Few persons came to the frontier except to make homes for themselves, and to stake their hardihood and fortune against the chances of isolation and hardship. Most of them had little to hope for in their older homes, and made the emigration to advance their chances and their children's. For the interval between two generations, in any frontier region, the typical life was that of the frontier farmer clearing his fields and building his cabins. The immediate family need came first, then came the group — the school and the church, local government and statehood — and the crafts of industrial supply followed the more primitive ones of agriculture. After the lapse of twenty or twenty-five years these needs had ordinarily been met in any typical frontier region, and the first-born children of the early households had grown to maturity and gone off in couples to a newer frontier to repeat their parents' experience. In the multiple repetition of this, at every crossroads in America, through nearly three centuries, each generation has in turn been able to challenge the social values of the common heritage, and to modify its institutions to fit the shifting need. History has here more nearly repeated itself than in the other experiences of the past. This was a social laboratory for the mixed races that thronged the continent. The frontier process and its consequences give the special meaning to American life.

The frontier as a *region* was that area of the United States in which the frontier process was going on at any moment. In the early seventeenth century it was along the lower courses of the Atlantic rivers. In the early eighteenth century it was along the piedmont. At the date of the Proclamation Line, it filled up many of the parallel valleys of the Appalachians; and until the end of the story it was an irregular strip extending across the whole width of the United States, and advancing relentlessly towards the setting sun. Not until 1790 is it possible to speak with precision of the frontier *line*. In the absence of census reports and data on the exact location of frontier homes, the historian must write in somewhat general terms. In 1790, however, the first census under the Constitution enumerated enough of the population for it to be possible to shade a map showing the average densities, county for county. After this date, at each ten-year period, the maps of the census reports reveal the unoccupied West, and show the regions in which the social average is under two, or six, or eighteen, or forty-five, or ninety persons per square mile. The lines that can be drawn delimiting the zone of from two to six to the square mile are frontier lines, that help the historian to fix his attention upon the frontier of any date.

The American frontiersman had to erect, in the course of a lifetime, all of the institutions of private or public life that he desired. At the start, he was forced to sift them over, and decide which duty first. Invariably the earliest of his problems was that of land, since his first need was to find a place that he might call his own, and build his home. The conditions under which, from decade to decade, the frontier farmers acquired their land titles, shaped the course of their immediate growth, and left habits of thought or antipathies that have moulded public opinion and given direction to national government. No disturbance has ever succeeded in diverting their attention from the land. In the French wars and the Revolution the common soldiers were ever thinking of new homes to be acquired, and their officers were debating the chances of profitable speculations in western titles. In all of the States there was yet, in 1783, an abundance of land waiting to be developed; but nowhere was this so in the forefront of public interest as along the border, from Albany to Knoxville, in a zone perhaps seven hundred and fifty miles long by one hundred miles wide, where the average density of population as late as 1790 ranged between two and six to the square mile. The landless man and the landless State were in the spell of such opportunity; their common bond operated to hold the tottering Union upright while it was learning how to walk.

The United States started with persons whose European background of experience left them convinced of the importance of the ownership of land, and whose energy and character planted them in a continent of vast wastes, with nothing between them and landed estates but the shadowy title of the Indian occupant, and the real barrier of crown control. Such as it was, the Indian title covered the whole of North America. The Indian tribes knew nothing of the title in fee simple that the English colonists valued, and had hardly any glimmering of private ownership or leasehold. Rarely did any tribe have undisputed possession of the hunting fields it used. Indian titles were plastered over the land, and in any tract there were likely to be several tribes to be placated before it could be claimed that the crown had acquired title to it. But the crown in general established its right to be the sole buyer of the tribal lands, and the sole vendor to the colonists. Whether it disposed of the land directly to the settler, as in the crown colonies, or indirectly through the proprietor, as in the proprietary colonies, it stood ever between the Indian and the colonist.

In the administration of the lands acquired from the Indians but unoccupied by whites, the crown and the proprietaries differed in general policy. For the crown it was sufficient to take only a fee from the purchaser, sixpence an acre, more or less, to ensure the regularity of the deed. The proprietor, on the other hand, had ambitions to build up forever a landed family estate, and sought to make the land a source of perpetual revenue. His desire was either to sell for a substantial price, or to grant the land subject to a small annual quit-rent in perpetuity.[2] To the settler, with his passion for land of his own, this proprietary demand was a source of continuous grievance. The clash of desires enlivened the politics of every province, and carried over into the free States, after independence.

Whether in the crown or the proprietary colony, the right of the squatter was generally one that could be protected. There were no preliminary surveys, and no descriptions of the land until some desirous settler wrote down the metes and bounds of his tract and opened negotiation for a deed. As between two claimants to a tract, the occupier or squatter had precedence. That any one should be excluded from unoccupied land merely because of the demand of the crown, the proprietor, the large owner, or even the State, ran against frontier opinion. A more congenial idea was the notion that such land was by nature free until some squatter should improve it, and then it belonged to him.

The shock of independence severed the connection of the crown, and that of most of the proprietors, from the ownership of the unoccupied lands. There were confiscations of Tory property or estates that added even occupied land to the tracts to which the several independent States laid claim after 1776. Every State became something of a landed proprietor by revolutionary right, and from the mere possession of land took on something of the proprietors' point of view. Instead of the instant determination to dispose freely of this land, as the frontier would have wished, the thought arose that here was a visible asset. The lands were State property, and might be administered to produce revenue to

[2] Beverly W. Bond, *The Quit-Rent System in the American Colonies* (1919), is standard on this.

maintain the State. The colonial idea that had been strongest in the proprietaries spread over all the States, and carried the social clash of the colonial period over into the Union.

A second clash, rooted in the confiscated lands, and serving to disturb the spirit of unity, followed independence, as the States realized that some had great holdings or claims, and some small. The landless States resented the lack of a land endowment, and were jealous of the acreage of the former sea-to-sea colonies. In New Hampshire, Rhode Island, New Jersey, Delaware, and Maryland,[3] the established boundaries of the States were narrow and more nearly filled than in New York or Pennsylvania where the admitted limits were still far beyond the line of population; or in Massachusetts, Connecticut, Virginia, North Carolina, South Carolina, or Georgia, where the sea-to-sea limits of the old charters founded hopes of tracts of land beyond the Alleghanies.

In every State, and in the Continental Congress, the two controversies based upon the future of the lands provided an enduring basis for political division. In Pennsylvania the agrarian leaders from the Susquehanna and Juniata valleys fought the Philadelphia aristocrats, and the comfortable farmers of Bucks and Delaware at every turn. In Massachusetts, before the end of the seventeen-eighties, the farmers of the Connecticut Valley challenged the General Court and defied the law of the State. The piedmont farmers of Virginia and Carolina realized instinctively the difference beween their interests and those of the farmers of the coast. And in addition to the wrangle visible in the delegation of nearly every State, the smaller States bluntly refused to go ahead with Union until their safety was assured, and their aspirations recognized.

The first Continental Congress was a revolutionary body, pure and simple, deriving its right to exist from the sanction of common consent and force. From the earliest meeting in 1774 until nearly the surrender of Cornwallis in 1781, it remained a voluntary body, without formal authorization or a deliberate constitution. The States wanted independence, but were jealous of their complete freedom of action. The Congress proposed the adoption of Articles of Confederation, but saw the weary years roll round with-

[3] The Johns Hopkins University *Studies*, edited by Herbert B. Adams, opened a new era in American historical writing; his own monograph in vol. III, "Maryland's Influence upon the Land Cessions to the United States," was among the earliest critical studies of the Confederacy.

out the unanimous concurrence that was necessary to turn the revolutionary basis into one of law.

The Articles of Confederation were weak and inadequate at best. They provided only a meeting place for debate and recommendation, without power to enforce a decision or to protect the majority will. No State was bound to coöperate. No executive was maintained. All revenue was based on quotas paid through good will. No important acts could be taken without a two-thirds vote of States. But inferior as the Articles were, they hung in suspense from the moment of their submission to the States in 1777, until the end of 1780. The States were both dilatory, which was overcome by time, and suspicious, which was overcome by compromise. The menace of unsettled boundaries was everywhere. New York was vexed by the aspirations of Vermont to independence. Connecticut and Pennsylvania had bitter litigation over conflicting claims. The northern boundary of New Jersey was too important to be left to chance. South Carolina and Georgia were at odds over the location of the source of the Savannah River, upon which their boundaries depended. Maryland became the spokesman of the smaller States, and a proper spokesman since she had suffered curtailment and compression at the hands of wealthy and influential neighbors.

The background of the Maryland unwillingness to bind herself in advance of a satisfactory land settlement begins with the original charter of 1632 granting to the Calverts the tract of Virginia lying between the south bank of the Potomac River and the fortieth parallel of north latitude. The crown had at this date taken back the original company charter of Virginia, and had thus acquired the right to readjust the limits of that province.

The Maryland provincials had constant friction with their well-established neighbors, the Virginia planters. The peculiarity of the charter that made the boundary not the usual channel of the river, but the southern bank, was an outrage in Virginia eyes, for no Virginian could wet his feet in Potomac water without committing a trespass upon Maryland. But the western end of Maryland was described as a line drawn north from the source of the Potomac River, and Virginia set about finding as easterly a source as topography and interpretation would allow. Lord Fairfax, the proprietary owner of the Northern Neck of Virginia, which was bounded by the Rappahannock and the Potomac, planted a stone in 1745 at what he claimed on his own survey to be the "first fountain of the Pattowmack." It was not so far west as Maryland thought the source ought to be; nor yet so far east as Virginia once insisted when she advanced the claim that the real Potomac begins at Harper's Ferry where the Shenandoah enters. Maryland felt defrauded, but was as impotent to better herself on the west as she was on the north where the impressive colony of William Penn bore down upon her.

The Penn contention to a southern boundary at the thirty-ninth parallel, because the charter of 1681 read from the "beginning of the fortieth degree," threatened to deprive Maryland of a sixty mile strip along her greatest length. The tardy settlement of this contest, and the survey of Mason and Dixon's line, stilled the dispute but cost Maryland much of the debated strip. She had long before lost the three counties on the Delaware, below Philadelphia, that became the State of Delaware.

Basing her opposition on her fear of the western lands in hostile hands, and the claim that having been won by the common effort they ought to be used for common purposes, Maryland did not ratify the Articles of Confederation until Congress had taken up her cause and the larger States had yielded. In 1780 Congress, with the Articles still ineffective, and with only a revolutionary basis of authority, invited the States claiming western lands to cede them to the United States for common use. It pledged a fair distribution, and application of the proceeds to the common purpose, and the ultimate creation of new States as the ceded lands filled up.

New York led the larger States in accepting the condition of union, perhaps because the validity of her title was slighter than that of the others. Connecticut followed, with a partial surrender that Congress could not at first accept. Virginia agreed to give up the lands north of the Ohio River, and upon this evidence of good will and common spirit, Maryland avowed herself satisfied. Every State but Maryland had ratified the Articles before the end of 1780. On March 1, 1781, by the direction of the legislature of Maryland, her delegates in Congress signed the Articles, which became effective at once. A Union was established, but, more important perhaps, the Union had a definite task for which its authority was adequate. The Articles of Confederation did not create a sufficient Union to govern the United States; but the Congress as trustee had a property problem that kept it from vanishing into nothingness.

CHAPTER VI
CREATION OF THE PUBLIC DOMAIN

IN the dark autumn of 1780, with Carolina and Virginia overrun by British troops, and with the gleam of hope that came from the inspiring news of King's Mountain not yet visible, Congress made its desperate effort to procure at least an act of government. On September 6 it urged the States with western lands to cede them to the Union; and on October 10 it repeated the urging, promising that they should "be disposed of for the common benefit of the United States." It pledged its faith that as the lands were occupied they should be divided into new commonwealths, with admission to the Union as a natural goal. With Vermont maintaining an independent though not recognized government, with the settlers along the Watauga now eight years old in their aspirations, and with James Robertson and his Cumberland pioneers in the act of formulating their Nashboro agreement, it was evident that the number of the States would not long remain thirteen. The world has few earlier glimpses than this of a growing federal commonwealth, with increasing members, and with no desire for permanent dependents. The fate of the Articles hinged upon the response to this appeal; and with it perhaps the fate of the Union itself, and the world's most promising experiment in federalism. The suggestion of an appeal had been made by New York for the sake of harmony. Connecticut welcomed it as "an Event most desirable and important to the Liberty and Independence of the rising Empire."

The legal basis of the claims, whose surrender was asked by the nervous little States, was in the series of charters issued by the English crown to various companies, proprietors, or colonies. The list begins with the first Virginia charter of 1606. The last colony charter was that of Georgia in 1732. After this time there were numerous proclamations and orders of the king in council that affected the boundaries, but the period was one of detailed adjustment rather than of new creation. The English law permitted the king to treat the overseas lands as dependencies of himself, and Parliament had not meddled with colonial limits. In general the crown reserved to itself the right to alter boundaries that it had fixed. The latest grant was the effective one. The proprietaries were a partial exception to this, for the crown regarded the gift of land to a lord proprietor as a closed transaction, not subject to modification more than the property rights of any other subject. The Proclamation of 1763 did not change the ultimate legal right of any of the various claimants to colonial lands. It merely deferred their enjoyment; and in the absence of any new colonial creations after 1763, except Quebec, which was based on act of Parliament in 1774, the independent States retained whatever claims they had. None of the States treated the Quebec Act as legally changing their status, and the United States did not advance the claim that it might well have pushed, that the country north of the Ohio River having been cut off by English law had become national property, with succession to the Union rather than to the original claimant States. The Quebec Act was regarded by the United States as an act of war and not of law.

The New York proposal for a general cession was embodied in a tender, dated February 19, 1780, "to facilitate the Completion of the Articles of Confederation and Perpetual Union among the United States of America." When Charles II granted the New Netherlands to the Duke of York, the charters of 1664 and 1674 conveyed a tract of land between the Delaware and Connecticut rivers and dominated by the settlements already planted along the Hudson. In spite of the assertion of the charters that the Connecticut River was to be the eastern limit, it was never practicable for New York to establish it. Both Massachusetts and Connecticut were already in possession, with groups of settlers in the valley that could be neither dispossessed nor displaced. It was convenient to compromise. In 1731 a definite agreement was reached with Connecticut, and in 1783 with Massachusetts, by which irregular lines some twenty miles east of the Hudson were established in provincial law. They had been reached *de facto* many years earlier, when the contesting jurisdictions there took a state of practical equilibrium.[1]

But north of Massachusetts, New York pressed the claim to extend to the Connecticut, with a logic that increased in weight after England separated and delimited New Hampshire. It took an

[1] Henry Gannett, *Boundaries of the United States and of the Several States and Territories* (3d ed., 1904), was printed as *Bulletin*, No. 226, of the United States Geological Survey. It is the most convenient summary of boundary matters, and contains valuable maps which are generally accurate.

order in council in 1764 to settle the dispute so far as Massachusetts was concerned. But the local population was a different matter and rejected the jurisdiction of New York, aspiring to statehood as Vermont.

West of the Delaware, New York had no charter claim, but no subsequent colony received a grant of the lands between the Delaware and Lake Ontario. The Treaty of Fort Stanwix procured, in 1768, an Indian cession of title south of an irregular line, and New York, when independent, laid claim to what the crown had thus acquired, as well as to whatever the Six Nations might own, wherever situated. In assuming to be the successor of the crown as to the Six Nations, New York took over an indefinite assumption that ran as far as the Ohio River and Kentucky, for the Six Nations were mighty warriors with a place in the sun that spread far into the continent.

Massachusetts, senior to New York in creation, accepted the hard fact that New York cut across her on the west, but kept alive a claim to land beyond the Delaware and comprehended in her sea-to-sea grant of 1629. It was not certain how good this claim was, for the second Massachusetts charter, issued in 1691 after the New York grants, described her domain as "parte of New England in America," and did not mention a sea-to-sea extension. Weak as the Massachusetts claim was, that of New York was no stronger. The two States had not come to an agreement as to their property west of the Delaware when New York offered to cede to Congress whatever she might have of title west of Lake Ontario and the Niagara River. Congress accepted a quit-claim from New York in 1781. Five years later New York and Massachusetts divided the title to the land between the Niagara and the Delaware, and vested the political sovereignty of all of it in New York.

All that Congress could accept from New York was a quit-claim, since the territory covered by it was claimed with just as much show of right by Virginia, Connecticut, and Massachusetts. The Virginia claim was based on the mystifying description in the second charter of the province, issued by James I in 1609. The seaboard limits conveyed were entirely clear, extending from Old Point Comfort two hundred miles in either direction along the coast. But at this point the inspired draftsman who drew up the charter made a rhetorical flourish incapable of application. He wrote: "up into the Land, throughout from Sea to Sea, West, and Northwest."

No court and no cartographer could ever have drawn a boundary line running at once west and northwest. It became a common Virginia interpretation, though without sanction, that one of the lines should be drawn west, and the other northwest. Virginia naturally enough preferred that it should be the southern boundary to run west, and the northern, starting not far from the present site of Atlantic City, to run northwest. In the course of years the location of the southern charter boundary became academic, for the crown issued a Carolina grant that drew a new and immovable line. To the north, Maryland and Pennsylvania removed tracts that had fallen within the limits of the Virginia claim. But in 1781 Virginia was still unmoved in her contention that of right her northwest line, beyond the area of Pennsylvania, ran through the Great Lakes and included the whole of the Old Northwest.

Not only had the Old Dominion the broadest of pretensions, but she had made the most lavish use of them. The speculations of the Virginia gentry touched the Ohio River before the middle of the eighteenth century, and each of the colonial wars was followed by the issuance of a shoal of warrants to officers and men, entitling them to bounties from the open lands. The heaviest settlement of the Appalachian valleys, outside Pennsylvania, was on Virginia soil and under her titles. The Great Kanawha and Cumberland rivers tempted her citizens to further fields within her jurisdiction. And the victories of George Rogers Clark were under her commission, while his conquests were organized by her legislature as Illinois County. When Maryland called upon Virginia to deliver the western lands to Congress, the latter could truthfully say that she no longer controlled most of them. The best estimates of the acreage granted in sales or bounties to 1781 (for her bookkeeping was far from precise and surveys were often poetic in their inaccuracy), indicated that already more than the area of West Virginia and Kentucky would be required, and that there was a substantial amount to be taken from the country north of the Ohio. It was impossible to cancel the grants already made or the warrants outstanding. The Virginia offer of January 2, 1781, was of a cession to Congress of what there remained north of the Ohio, reserving for warrants that could not be satisfied in Kentucky as much of the country between the Scioto and the Great Miami rivers as might be needed.

There was much dickering between Congress and Virginia before they were able to agree upon the phraseology of a deed, and execute it May 1, 1784. In this, as in other cases, Virginia desired to receive in exchange for what she surrendered a guarantee of title to what she retained. In particular she desired to be protected in her claim to all of Kentucky. Congress could accept only what the States had to give and was in no position to admit that they really owned it or to stabilize the title to anything else. Eventually they compromised, as the cessions proceeded far enough to indicate that all would yield and that there would be no movement to dispossess any. There had been pioneer settlements in Kentucky for many years before the northwest country was thus transferred to Congress, and the completion of the transaction marks a beginning of a Kentucky movement for the creation of an independent State within the limits of the old Kentucky County.

The Massachusetts western lands followed those of New York and Virginia into the public domain. As a part of the negotiations over the New York cession that State and Massachusetts determined to let Congress have whatever there was west of the Niagara River. In November, 1784, Massachusetts transferred her claim to the strip across Michigan and Wisconsin, extending to the Mississippi River. In the next two years, and after threats of referring the matter to a land court to be organized by Congress under the Articles, the New York compromise was reached. The western limit beyond which both New York and Massachusetts gave up their claims, was defined as a line that should run due south from the western tip of Lake Ontario, or twenty miles west of the Niagara River, according as the surveys should determine which of the lines was westernmost. When this was run a few years later, the line of the Niagara was found to be too far east to meet the requirement; the line of the tip of Ontario fell a little east of the western boundary of Pennsylvania, and cut off a little triangle of Congress lands above the northwest corner of that State. This later became the Pennsylvania "triangle."

The completion of the Connecticut cession was delayed until 1786. The original charter of 1662 described a tract bounded on the north by Massachusetts and on the south by the South Sea; and only a moderation unusual among colonies kept Connecticut from claiming under it a title to the whole southern end of the continent. The erection of New York established a practical western limit to Connecticut, and it was expedient to compromise upon a convenient *de facto* line somewhat east of the Hudson. But, like Massachusetts, Connecticut admitted only what she must and kept alive her claim to the western extension of her strip beyond the Delaware. When William Penn received his grant in 1681, extending from the Delaware five degrees of longitude to the west, and in latitude from the beginning of the fortieth to the beginning of the forty-third degrees, Connecticut refused to be reconciled. Even when fixed on the north at the forty-second parallel (for Penn's interpretation of his south line was used against him at the north), Pennsylvania stretched like a barrier across the whole width of Connecticut. In spite of this, the Connecticut general court disposed of lands in the Pennsylvania tract and tried to defend the titles by force. A civil war threatened, when Congress intervened as judge to stop it. In 1782 a special court upheld the superiority of the Pennsylvania claim. West of Pennsylvania the Connecticut pretension remained, and like Virginia she wished to retain part of the area to satisfy grants to her revolutionary soldiers and sufferers from pillage and destruction by British troops. As finally accepted by Congress, the cession commenced one hundred and twenty miles west of the Pennsylvania line. The Connecticut Reserve east of that point was retained in both title and jurisdiction for the present.

It was the creation of the province of Carolina in 1663, with a modified boundary in 1665, that gave to Virginia a limit on the south that could not be contested. South of thirty-six degrees, thirty minutes of north latitude, Carolina stretched down the Atlantic shore to a point so far in Florida that no one ever seriously believed that the English crown could bestow it. There was never a fixed settlement with Spain upon the limits between Florida and Carolina; but in 1732 England reduced the province by establishing Georgia between the Savannah and Altamaha rivers, and their sources projected westward from sea to sea. If England owned anything south of the Altamaha, which is highly doubtful, Carolina might have retained some sort of title to it. At any rate South Carolina long nourished such a claim. The division of the two Carolinas in 1729, along the thirty-fifth parallel, continued by an arbitrary line down to the coast, did not alter the gross claims of the two provinces.

After 1732, South Carolina disputed with Georgia the location of their common boundary, west of the "most northern part," or head, of the Savannah. Like the Potomac, and the Connecticut, and the St. Croix, each of whose headwaters was the origin of boundary litigation, the Savannah originates in a group of streams converging from every angle near the head. Georgia sought to defend the most northern head that could be found. South Carolina argued that the name Savannah was not locally used to describe the stream above the point where the Tugaloo from the north meets the Keowee, from the west, and that at this junction the western parallel must start. The strip that South Carolina ceded to Congress on March 8, 1787, existed only if her title against Georgia was valid. On April 28, in the same year, in a treaty between the two States made at Beaufort, South Carolina yielded to the Georgia interpretation and accepted the Tugaloo as the Savannah, and its source as the starting-point. Geographers have differed as to whether this left any strip north of this point and south of the North Carolina line of thirty-five degrees that would warrant South Carolina to be included among the States having western lands to cede.

North Carolina had ceded, repented of it, and recalled the cession before South Carolina acted.[2] Her western claim was as nearly uncontested as that of Virginia to Kentucky. No other colony had ever encroached upon it. There were difficulties in marking, due to faulty surveys made by the amateur engineers who tried to run the lines, but there was no dispute in principle. The Watauga and Cumberland settlements, both within the North Carolina zone, showed the accessibility of the country to the pioneers crowding over the western rims of the Appalachian Valleys. The suggestion by Congress that the State quotas for common expenses ought to be based upon land areas, induced a willingness to cede this unoccupied land to Congress. But the cession of 1784 was not accepted promptly, and when the mountaineers rose up to create their State of Franklin, North Carolina reëstablished her authority in the West and held it for five years more. On December 22, 1789, after the new Federal Constitution was in force, the cession was renewed; and in the following spring Congress provided it with a government. But by this time there was no area left unclaimed that could be included in the public domain. The cession was one of sovereignty rather than of land title. In neither Kentucky nor Tennessee were there ever any public lands belonging to the United States.

After South Carolina, only Georgia remained with anything to

[2] J. C. Welling, "States' Rights Conflict over the Public Lands," in American Historical Association, *Papers*, 1889; St. George L. Sioussat, "North Carolina Land Cession in its Federal Aspects," in Mississippi Valley Historical Association, *Proceedings*, 1908–1909.

cede to Congress. The moderate clearness of her original charter limits had been lost after the Proclamation of 1763 when it suited the convenience of England to enlarge the jurisdiction of the newest colony. In that proclamation, in the adjustment of the boundary of East and West Florida, there was left unclaimed a tract lying between the St. Mary's River, the northern limit of East Florida, and the Altamaha, the southern limit of Georgia. This, the English Board of Trade recommended, should be annexed to Georgia, and it was done.

Since the same document that extended Georgia to the St. Mary's forbade the issuance of any grant of lands beyond the Proclamation Line, it seems doubtful if Georgia could acquire by it any title to lands west of the Atlantic rivers. But Georgia construed the extension as extending to the Florida line throughout and following the thirty-first parallel even to the Mississippi. When England expanded West Florida to the parallel of the Yazoo River, Georgia was thereby restricted; but when the United States in the Treaty of Versailles received the thirty-first parallel as its boundary, Georgia asserted that its territory had been returned to it, and claimed this Yazoo strip. South Carolina, too, claimed this strip, and the United States itself; while Spain, because of the secret article relating to the strip (it was to have remained English had England decided to keep Florida for herself at Paris) believed that the true boundary of West Florida as ceded to her in the treaty, was at the Yazoo line.

Not until April 24, 1802, was Georgia willing to surrender to the United States either this Yazoo strip, to which her title was so flimsy, or the extension between the heads of the Savannah and Altamaha, to which her claim was good. She had meanwhile speculated in part of the area, and her legislature had yielded to temptation and furnished one of the most glaring cases of public corruption that the United States has known.[3] The Yazoo lands became a public scandal, and eventually the Supreme Court of the United States, in Fletcher vs. Peck, handed down one of the most momentous of its decisions in a case arising from these speculations. The responsibility for corrupt officials was placed squarely upon the constituency that elected them, and the State was held bound by the acts of whomsoever it entrusted with responsibility. But, in the end, Congress was induced to compensate the

[3] Charles H. Haskins, "The Yazoo Land Companies," in American Historical Association, *Papers*, 1891.

citizens who were defrauded by the corruption of the Yazoo speculators.

Between 1780 and 1802 the public domain was in process of creation. From the earliest cession, Congress became involved in a trust that no other authority could share. As the area of cession grew, the power to make or mar an empire was lodged in the United States. Before the series of surrenders was completed by the Georgia act population had begun to flow over the public domain in a broad wave, and two new States had been organized in the West. The Articles of Confederation had by this time revealed all their weaknesses and had been overturned by a revolution so negligent that the old Congress was never adjourned, but simply died from lack of delegates and quorum. The new Constitution arose from the experiences of the critical period. The function of the Articles was to hold the thirteen States convergent until their majority was ready for Union. The common property in the public domain prevented the abandonment of the Articles before the people had learned the lesson of the "more perfect union."

CHAPTER VII
THE NATIONAL LAND SYSTEM

BEFORE the final deeds were executed transferring to Congress the land cessions of New York and Virginia, movements had begun for the developing of the public domain, and it was necessary for Congress to adopt some policy for its management and distribution.[1] The two basic ideas upon land policy from which it was free to make a selection were those of New England and the South. There was little tendency to improvise a doctrinaire theory, for most of the men concerned were hard-headed owners of the land themselves. But there had been two sharply defined systems in force, each with its merits and defects.

In the southern colonies the planter had operated as an individual, prospecting for himself, selecting his tracts for purchase, defining the meanderings of his boundaries with as much accuracy as he could, and then procuring title from the province and record of his deeds at the county court. The method harmonized with the strong individuality of the frontier farmer and his uneasiness under restraint. But it produced conflicts of claims and interminable litigation over titles, much of which was not susceptible of precise adjudication. When the United States Government, in recent years, purchased large tracts of mountain land for the Appalachian Forest Reserve and insisted upon clear titles from the beginning, it found frequent discrepancies in the descriptions of property in the original deeds. Overlaps were common; and often it happened when the boundaries were plotted that little tracts of no-man's-land appeared between two defined lines that had been supposed to be identical. In the rapid settlement of Kentucky and Tennessee, where the southern system prevailed, the frontier lawyer sharpened his wits and filled his purse for years from the proceeds of boundary suits.

New England, with a stronger community sense and a different

---

[1] Payson J. Treat, *National Land System, 1785–1820* (1910), is excellent so far as it goes, but there is still great need for a general historian of the public lands. Thomas Donaldson, *The Public Domain, Its History* (1884), has all the defects of government documents, but the historian cannot get along without it. Its tables may be supplemented by those in the *Report* of President Roosevelt's Public Lands Commission (58th Congress, 3d Session, Senate Document 189, Serial 4766).

type of farming, never became addicted to the loose system of the South, but adhered to the town or township method. The land was granted in large lots to town groups and subdivided and recorded within the town. There was less straggling of the frontier as a result and greater certainty as to property rights. The boundaries of the towns could be defined in advance of the grant, leading to a system of prior survey before settlement that avoided many of the vexations from which the southern planter suffered.

In Congress there were men experienced in both systems and advocates of each. As soon as the policy towards the ceded lands came under discussion, there was clash of views and in the outcome a compromise that contained more of the northern practice than of the southern. The soldiers of the Continental Army, still under arms in 1783, were among the earliest applicants for western rights and started with their petitions the chain of events that ripened in 1787 into the Ordinance for the Government of the Lands Northwest of the Ohio River.

The troops at Newburgh on the Hudson, in 1783, knew that they would be happy some day but were filled with immediate discontent as they thought of the return to private life. In May the officers formed the hereditary Society of the Cincinnati, that they and their sons might properly remember and commemorate the hardships and glories of the Revolution. In June, the men, under the lead of Rufus Putnam and with the approval of their officers, demanded that Congress make provision for their needs out of the western domain. Washington received their memorial and forwarded it with his endorsement to Congress. What they wanted was a soldiers' State, west of the Ohio, with land payments to supplement the scanty pay and depreciated money that they were offered. Washington approved this scheme, though he had for himself a larger project. In 1784 he traveled through Western Virginia, almost to the Ohio, looking over the prospects for the development of a Potomac Company that was to speculate in lands towards the Ohio and build a canal along the Potomac that should direct the trade of the new settlements forever to the East. He was afraid that unless directed firmly the straggling West would get beyond control and so he gave his moral sanction to Jay's proposal to agree with Spain that the Mississippi River should be closed to navigation for a term of years. Out of the Virginia and Maryland conferences that his Potomac Company engendered grew the trade convention and finally the Constitutional Convention in Philadelphia, in 1787. But before this date Congress had laid down the general principles of a land policy.

With the cessions of New York and Virginia completed, Congress signed a treaty with the New York Indians at Fort Stanwix, October 22, 1784. With the approval of Red Jacket and Cornplanter, the elder statesmen of the Seneca, who knew the futility of Indian resistance, the Six Nations confirmed the old Treaty of Fort Stanwix (1768) and added a cession of their whole claim to any part of Pennsylvania. They pretended as well to cede the country north of the Ohio River, to which their title was founded on shadowy conquests which the resident tribes in Ohio would not recognize. On January 21, 1785, Fort McIntosh on the Ohio River thirty miles below Pittsburgh was the scene of another treaty in which Wyandot, Delaware, Chippewa, and Ottawa braves agreed to a southern boundary in the vicinity of the watershed between Lake Erie and the Ohio River and west of the Cuyahoga. A handful of Congress troops moved down the Ohio River at once and planted at the mouth of the Muskingum a station that took the name Fort Harmar. The treaties had little effect upon the minds of the occupying Indians who did not recognize their cessions for another decade, but they constitute the beginning of the acquisition by the United States Government of Indian titles which remained, as ever, a condition precedent to private development.

Thomas Jefferson of Virginia, who was chairman of a committee of Congress that brought in a scheme for the partition of the ceded lands in March, 1784, knew the disadvantages of an uncertain land policy. In his forty-first year now, he was already a distinguished statesman. He had seen service in Congress and in the Virginia House of Burgesses. He had followed Patrick Henry as governor of Virginia in 1779 and was shortly to go abroad on that trip of European residence that brought him into intimate touch with the philosophers of the new era in France. As governor of Virginia he had both adjusted the contested boundary with Pennsylvania and directed the transfer of the Virginia lands to Congress. He knew about soldiers' bounties, and squatter rights, and the impatience of frontier opinion when the activities of their governments did not suit them. No mind in America was more fertile in drafting schemes for the common benefit, many of which worked well in practice.

The report of 1784 and the Ordinance of April 23 that was based

upon it have slipped attention through the greater interest that
the later Ordinance of 1787 has aroused. It contained, however,
the basis of a colonial policy elaborated out of the pledges that
Congress had already given as to the custody and future of the
western lands. The perpetual guarantees that Jefferson desired

Jefferson's Proposal of 1784

to have form a bill of rights for the new colonies contemplated
that they (1) should forever remain a part of the United States,
(2) be subject to the Congress and the Articles of Confederation,
(3) pay their share of the revolutionary debts, (4) maintain governments republican in form, and (5) be free from slavery after
1800. The last of these guarantees was stricken out before the
ordinance passed.

As to statehood, Jefferson proposed loose and inadequate terms of admission and a whimsical scheme for the partition of the Northwest. New States were to be admitted from the Northwest when they had a population equal to that of the smallest State already in the Union and when Congress by two-thirds vote (nine States) approved; and they were to come in on terms of equality. The scheme was weak because it provided no machinery for organizing the States and no preliminary government before the population became adequate for statehood; both of which points were remedied before the first new State was admitted to the Union. The partition arrangement paid no attention to waterways or to drift of population but called for ten States, eventually, with artificial boundaries along the parallels of latitude, and with names which show how erratic a sensible man like Jefferson could sometimes be: Sylvania, Michigania, Assenisippia, Illinoia, Polypotamia, Cherronesus, Metropotamia, Saratoga, Pelisipia, and Washington. Congress omitted the boundary scheme from the final ordinance.

The Ordinance of 1784 indicates a quickening of Congress's interest in the task ahead, but the creation of new settlements along the Ohio was not yet practical politics until the treaties had been arranged with the Indians. A second report from the committee on the western lands, in the spring of 1784, brought in matters upon the survey and subdivision of the public domain to which Jefferson had given much attention before sailing as minister to France. It became the Ordinance of May 20, 1785.

"The principle of rectangular surveys was established in our national land system," by the Ordinance of 1785, says Professor Ford, who has made the most careful study of the colonial precedents of the public domain. The rectangular system was by no means new in concept, but no colony had possessed the means to administer a large scheme of preliminary surveys before the lands in question came upon the market. The novelty of the method as here applied lay in the determination to make careful surveys of townships six miles square, and of the thirty-six internal sections in each, before disposing of the public lands.[2]

The small beginnings of the public land survey took place in 1785–1786 under Captain Thomas Hutchins, geographer of the United States, who was assisted by a board of surveyors, upon which each State was entitled to place a member of its own choice.

[2] Amelia C. Ford, *Colonial Precedents of our National Land System as it existed in 1800* (1910).

Massachusetts nominated General Rufus Putnam for its surveyor, but subsequently substituted Benjamin Tupper, to whom with Putnam, the United States is much indebted for the immediate outcome of its plan. It was proposed, first, to establish a principal meridian, along which to lay the parallel ranges of townships. The intersection of the Ohio River with a western projection of the southern boundary of Pennsylvania was made the starting-point; and between the meridian of this point and the western boundary of Pennsylvania the seven ranges of townships, for which there was room, were marked in the next few months. The Indians, who had not realized that the surrender of their lands would be followed by the entry of survey gangs, obstructed the running of the lines, but were held away by United States troops; while the enterprising squatters who had sneaked in their cabins on the right bank of the Ohio were dispossessed by the same force. By the survey law, one seventh of the land as surveyed was reserved to be distributed among the men of the Continental Army who held land warrants. The balance was to go to the States by lot according to their quotas of taxes. Alternate sections were to be disposed of as a whole; the others were to be broken up and sold in tracts as small as single sections. The town of Wheeling, in Virginia, on the upper Ohio River, now acquired a rival in Steubenville, farther up on the western bank. The soldiers and the surveyors made this the gateway to the Seven Ranges of Ohio.

There was still no provision for the erection of government among the buyers of the Congress lands or the settlers in the Virginia Military Reserve, and while the survey of the Seven Ranges was under way the need for this became imperative. Putnam and Tupper were prime movers in advancing this necessity, for to an innate desire to speculate in unoccupied lands the experience of Tupper in the Ohio country added a local knowledge of the resources of this region. Putnam and his friends had for three years been cherishing the idea of a western soldiers' State, and when Tupper visited him at his home in Rutland early in 1786, the plan ripened into action.

On the first of March they called a caucus of their military friends at the Bunch of Grapes tavern in Boston to discuss the formation of a land company to be financed with the worthless continental currency that Congress had forced upon them while in the service.[3] The group had much in common, as Professor

[3] John Bach McMaster discussed these matters in vol. I of his monumental *History of the*

Hulbert has shown. Besides their military recollections, many were brothers of the Society of the Cincinnati, and a large number of them were members of that famous Masonic Lodge that had been formed at Washington's headquarters and had followed with the commander-in-chief all the wanderings and vicissitudes of the Revolution. At this meeting it was decided to form a company of one thousand shares, of one thousand dollars each, payable in continental money, and to ask Congress to be allowed to buy a tract of land with the capital thus raised. The money was worthless in ordinary use, but it had been issued by Congress accompanied by a public promise to pay, and Congress could not well refuse to receive it back. Since under the Ordinance of 1785 no provision existed for the sale of more than one township, it would be necessary to have a new law passed; and since no scheme of government was ready, one would have to be provided. Putnam, Parsons of Connecticut, and the Rev. Manasseh Cutler became the first agents of the Ohio Associates, as they called themselves, to present their demand to Congress after a second meeting for organization held in 1787.[4]

The Continental Congress, when Samuel Parsons presented his memorial to it on May 9, 1787, had ceased to be an imposing body. Its appeals to the States for amendments that would enable it to carry on the public business had been ignored. The indifference of the States made it uncertain whether even a quorum of members could be maintained. A Constitutional Convention, to meet in Philadelphia in May, was about to drive it into oblivion. Only the business of the public lands kept it alive but not too active. No immediate attention was given to the memorial of the Ohio Associates, but on the following day James Monroe brought in a report on the government of the Northwest that would have received consideration had there been a quorum to debate it. From

People of the United States from the Revolution to the Civil War, which appeared in 1883. No other general writer has given as much space or as careful attention to the details of western local history as he has done in his eight great volumes. Five years after his first volume the ground was again traversed by John Fiske, *The Critical Period of American History* (1888).

[4] The chance that placed Archer B. Hulbert in a professorship at Marietta College for several years, gave him access to valuable manuscripts. He improved the opportunity in *The Records of the Original Proceedings of the Ohio Company* (1917), "Andrew Craigie and the Scioto Associates," in the *Proceedings* of the American Antiquarian Society, N.S., vol. xxiii, and "The Methods and Operations of the Scioto Group of Speculators," in *Mississippi Valley Historical Review*, vol. i. See also W. P. and J. P. Cutler, *Life, Journals, and Correspondence of Rev. Manasseh Cutler, LL.D.* (1888), and C. S. Hall, *Life and Letters of Samuel Holden Parsons* (1905).

May 12 to July 5 it was impracticable to get a quorum competent to transact business, and Congress could only adjourn from day to day, while Parsons preached his doctrine to the members out of hours. When business resumed, Cutler had arrived and had taken charge of the negotiation, and events moved forward to a quick conclusion, whose details are never likely to be known. On July 13 the Northwest Ordinance was passed; two weeks later the special act for a sale to the Ohio Associates became a law, and on October 27 the final contract was signed and sealed.

Alone among the acts of the old Congress this Ordinance of 1787 stands out as a great constructive measure. That its genesis may be found in Jefferson's Ordinance of 1784 is entirely clear, but the elaborations upon his idea and the practical improvements are so sweeping as to show the touch of other hands and interests. The report of Monroe that was handed to Congress in the spring of 1787 shows that he was not conscious of the project of the Ohio Associates. When after the lapse of quorum the matter was taken up again, the influence of Cutler, unmeasured but manifest, was at work. A new committee with a different personnel was charged with the task, and the names upon it are those of friends upon whom Parsons and Cutler had been exerting their powers of persuasion. On July 9 the report went back to this new committee; on the 11th a new report was made; on the 13th it was adopted.

It seems improbable that the authorship of the resulting law can be established or that there can be a precise measuring of the forces behind it. The long-realized need for a workable law was there. The dazzling influence of a request to purchase a million dollars' worth of land — even a million continental dollars' worth — cannot be ignored. It would certainly have received considerate attention at any time, for Congress was still full of the hope that the lands might produce a revenue that it could spend. With such a demand before it, Congress might well have been moved to insert in the basic law such guarantees as the buyers wanted. A third influence, and a sinister one, seems to have been exerted by the cupidity of certain public characters who wanted to share in whatever profits the speculation might produce, and who saw no impropriety in their indulging in it while authorizing it.

The eighteenth century was not one in which public men drew as sharp a line between public trust and private gain as now. In its last decade an absolute majority of the Georgia legislature was bought over by the Yazoo speculators and bribed to betray their trust. The only active fields of investment were lands and public bonds, and nearly every man of prominence who had money took chances on the rise and fall of these. So common was this business that one of our recent historians has convinced himself that a corrupt or selfish interest was the chief factor giving stability to the Government of the United States after the adoption of the Constitution and that the real motive in the honorable assumption by the United States of the debt of the revolution was the desire of speculators to enrich themselves.[5] Whatever the interpretation may be, the line of private conduct of public men ran through a shady twilight zone in 1787. The Ohio Associates were not able to get the votes for their act of government or their contract until they agreed to buy enough land to let in with them the Congress members who were jealous of their profits. With this assurance given, as Cutler tells us that it was, their course became smooth.

The Ordinance of 1787 included a partition scheme, a plan of government, and a bill of rights. The first provided for the ultimate division of the Northwest into three or five States, as need might dictate. If three, the separating boundaries were to be the Wabash River and the meridian of Vincennes, and a meridian to be drawn through the mouth of the Great Miami River, corresponding with the present boundaries between Indiana and her neighbors. If five States should be admitted, then a line drawn east and west through the southern tip of Lake Michigan should cut off the two peninsulas that were eventually to become Michigan and Wisconsin. This was made an eternal and solemn compact among the States so far as Congress could compass it.

So far as government was concerned the act provided for three progressive stages, the last of which should bring the State into the United States as a full participating member. England, too, at this same time and in the century ensuing was working upon an empire, and used three stages of similar import — with one marked exception that to-day distinguishes the British Empire from the American, since the fulfillment of statehood for British colonies has tended to leave them outside the Empire claiming independent rights, whereas the American State has become progressively amalgamated with the nation in whose government it has an organic share.

[5] Charles A. Beard, *Economic Interpretation of the Constitution* (1913), and *Economic Origins of Jeffersonian Democracy* (1915).

In the first stage, a territorial government was to be erected by Congress with governor, secretary, and judges, competent to make the laws and administer them without consulting the wish of any settler. It was an autocratic establishment, to be justified only by its temporary character and the infancy of the social group. In the second stage, to be reached when there should be five thousand adult males in the territory, an elected legislature was provided for, giving to the citizens that control over law-making and the purse that British peoples have so consistently demanded. When the total population reached sixty thousand, the Ordinance provided that it should be competent to hold a constitutional convention, frame its own basic law, and enter the Union. No new State had been added to the thirteen as yet, and the future of the Union was shrouded in the secrecy of the Philadelphia Convention when Congress sketched the future American colonial policy as firmly as though it thought it was legislating with full authority and assurance.

The bill of rights that was incorporated in the document shows resemblance to the similar pronunciamentos that appear in the Declaration of Independence and that are attached to many of the earliest State constitutions. The Ohio Associates doubtless wished to make the new world as attractive as possible to their prospective customers. Some of the guarantees were separated in the text of the Ordinance as "articles of compact," forever "unalterable, unless by common consent." Others are scattered through the miscellaneous provisions. First of the unalterable rights was freedom of religion: "No person, demeaning himself in a peaceable and orderly manner, shall ever be molested on account of his mode of worship or religious sentiments, in the said territories." After this came the promise of uninterrupted right to the writ of *habeas corpus*, to jury trial, to compensation for property seized, and to freedom from *ex post fac o* laws. "Religion, morality, and knowledge being necessary to good government and the happiness of mankind, schools and the means of education shall forever be encouraged," ran a sentence pregnant with meaning for the new communities. The abolition of slavery which Jefferson had sought in vain to incorporate in the Ordinance of 1784 was now pledged. Equal distribution of property among brothers and sisters, heirs to the estate of intestates, was guaranteed, reflecting a reform that Jefferson again had fought for in Virginia and that was a protest against the Old World law of primogeniture. The tottering Congress provided, moreover, that the "said territory, and the States which may be formed therein, shall forever remain a part of this confederacy of the United States," and insisted that they should be responsible for their share of the common debt, and refrain from questioning the full right of Congress to dispose of the title of the soil within their limits.

The Ordinance of 1787 became a law by the unanimous vote of the eight States present in Congress on July 13, 1787. One individual member voted no, but the delegations were a unit otherwise. Its significance as the basis of the American colonial policy gives importance to the fact that no word in the Articles of Confederation seems to confer upon Congress the explicit power either to accept or dispose of a public estate; and that the method of its passage was irregular, since a mere majority of the thirteen States had no power to do any business under the Articles. On all ordinary matters two-thirds, or nine, were required; on amendments unanimity of the whole thirteen. This was the only great work that the Congress transacted under the Articles, and it was of dubious constitutionality. The Constitutional Convention at Philadelphia was moreover well upon its work of disregarding the Articles, framing a peaceful revolution, and ratifying a new Constitution by less than a unanimous vote.

The requisite agreements had all been made by Cutler and Parsons before the Ordinance was passed. The "wrecking crew" that insisted on being let in with them, William Duer, Andrew Craigie, and the rest of the Scioto Associates, had been satisfied. On July 27 the ordinance of sale was passed authorizing the transfer of nearly seven million acres to the men who wanted them. The price agreed upon for all was the same — one dollar an acre, payable in continental money with a discount of one-third on account of the swampy or otherwise useless lands that might be scattered through the tract. It was arranged that 1,781,760 acres should go to the Ohio Associates, to be paid for with $500,000 in cash and the balance on survey. The Scioto group took option on 4,901,480 acres, payable in six installments and divided the option into thirty shares which they allotted among themselves.

The close interlocking of interests in the transaction is revealed by the fact that Winthrop Sargent, secretary of Congress, was also secretary of the Ohio Associates and acted with Cutler in completing the purchase. Two of the new judges elected to go to the Northwest Territory were Parsons and Varnum, both of whom were directors of the Associates. And General Arthur St. Clair, president of Congress, and a former western agent of the Penns at Pittsburgh, was not only a stockholder of the Associates but was chosen by his colleagues to be the first governor of the first territory of the United States. Under Governor St. Clair, life and meaning were given to the political principles laid down in the Northwest Ordinance.

CHAPTER VIII
THE OLD NORTHWEST

THE active mind and the careful erudition of the late B. A. Hinsdale have anticipated much of the work of the historian who proposes to follow up the Ordinance of 1787, and to trace the extension of settlement into the Old Northwest.[1] Between 1787 when the Ohio Associates' contract was closed, and 1795 when "Mad" Anthony Wayne induced the Indians of the Wabash to sign a quittance to the lands along the Ohio River, a new colony was planted in the West. The conditions of frontier life that were already well established between the Ohio River and the Tennessee were extended across the former river to its Indian shore. And the mother country that had in 1783 agreed to the Great Lakes as a boundary between Canada and the United States, was persuaded to keep the promise and withdraw her posts to her own dominions. On the southwest frontier, in the same years, Spain accepted the inevitable fact of American independence and complied in words, at least, with the description of boundary incorporated in the Treaty of Versailles. Kentucky became a State, and Tennessee followed in 1796. The century was to end with what was new frontier in 1763 transformed into happy and prosperous farmlands; and with the pioneers of the earlier date now the grandparents of pioneers who were thrusting their cabins towards Detroit, Mobile, and St. Louis.

The site for the purchase of the Ohio Associates was fixed by elimination at a point on the Ohio River below the western limit of the Seven Ranges. Further upstream, there were no tracts large enough. Further down, the reserved lands of Virginia barred any sales between the Scioto and the Great Miami. Thither General Rufus Putnam was sent in the spring of 1788, as superintendent of the new settlement; and opposite Fort Harmar, which the army had placed in 1786 at the mouth of the Muskingum River, he determined to plant the first new town. He traveled

[1] B. A. Hinsdale, *The Old Northwest. The Beginnings of our Colonial System* (1888); F. L. Paxson, "The Gateways of the Old Northwest," in Michigan Pioneer and Historical Society, *Collections*, vol. xxxviii. R. G. Thwaites, "The Boundaries of Wisconsin," in *Wisconsin Historical Collections*, vol. xi, contains a complete series of sketch maps showing the progress of political subdivision of the Northwest.

west by the familiar road from Philadelphia, and on reaching the Youghiogheny paused to have his carpenters cut timber and build boats for the river portion of the trip. It was a sentimental touch that gave to the boat that carried his group of pilgrims through the Ohio gateway to the Old Northwest, the sacred name of *Mayflower*.

On May 7, 1788, the first advance guard of the Ohio Associates arrived at the Muskingum, and started to build the town of Marietta. In the ensuing summer more adventurers joined them, and the farm cabins began to emerge among the clearings in the country behind. Governor St. Clair arrived in July to take up the thankless task of administering the Ordinance, creating counties, pacifying the Indians, and explaining to the settlers the reasons why it was dangerous to build their homes in the remote interior.[2] In the following spring he moved his headquarters further down the river to the mouth of the Miami, where he built an army post, Fort Washington. He found a small community already on the ground as the result of the speculation of one John Cleves Symmes.

The purchase of Symmes from Congress took place in the spring of 1788, and was on terms similar to those granted the Ohio Associates. For the sum of one dollar per acre, reduced by one third on account of probable bad lands, he contracted to buy an inverted wedge of land touching the Ohio between the mouths of the Great and Little Miamis, and expanding north into the Indian country. Neither of the boundary streams that determined his location was as well known as the southern tributary of the Ohio, the Licking, that has its mouth opposite the Symmes grant. Accordingly when it came to providing a name for the new venture, the fancy of the speculators was allowed full play. *L* for the Licking; *os* for its mouth; *anti* for the opposite shore; and *ville* for a termination; produced the name Losantiville, under which Symmes sent his first settlers west. Governor St. Clair did not like the name, and one of the virtues of his autocratic power was his ability to change it. The word of his preference was Cincinnati, a tribute to the society of which he was a member, and a suitable name for a region in which the activities of the officers of the Continental Army had such great influence.

[2] Dwight L. McCarty, *The Territorial Governors of the Old Northwest. A Study in Territorial Administration* (1910), is one of the few attempts to analyze American colonial policy; compare Max Farrand, *Legislation of Congress for the Government of the Organized Territories of the United States* (1896), and David W. Parker, *Calendar of Papers in Washington Archives relating to the Territories of the United States* (1911).

The population under the guidance of St. Clair grew slowly. In Kentucky across the river, where the Indian danger had been passed, the numbers grew from 73,000 in 1790 to 221,000 in 1800. The Northwest Territory had reached a maximum of only 51,000 by the later date. There was slow expansion in the vicinity of Marietta and Cincinnati, and a sifting of settlers into the Seven Ranges. The Virginia and Connecticut Reserves showed small growth until well after 1790.

The Virginia surveyors came into the valley of the Scioto River in 1790–1791 and ran lines that were gradually occupied by residents of Kentucky holding Virginia warrants. It was more a speculation than a migration of soldiers claiming their own bounties. The warrants were bought and sold freely, and the promoters of the Scioto towns invited associates, with the offer of an in-lot, an out-lot, and one hundred acres as the standard allotment. Between Wheeling and Limestone, on the Ohio River, the latter being opposite Maysville in Kentucky, an old Indian trail was developed as a road that paralleled the river. In 1796 Congress employed Ebenezer and Jonathan Zane of Wheeling to mark the route, so that the prospector might follow it with reasonable safety. The trail, generally known as Zane's Trace, crossed the Scioto at an Indian village of Chillicothe, by the mouth of Paint Creek. On either side of it, as well as along the river itself, the Virginia warrant holders made their settlements. They took the name Chillicothe for their principal town, and before the decade ended St. Clair had reason to appreciate the solidarity of the Virginia frontier point of view as contrasted with that of his New England subjects. Two methods of land occupation clashed, and two political opinions. Even to-day, the student of Ohio politics needs to bear in mind the southern origin of many of the people of central Ohio.

Moses Cleaveland, in the employ of the Connecticut Land Company, led a band of settlers to the Western Reserve of Connecticut in the summer of 1796.[3] Part of the strip that Connecticut insisted on retaining when she made her cession was given as the Fire Lands, to the sufferers from British raids along the towns of Long Island Sound. The rest was passed over to a land company with so generous a grant that the company was disposed to claim

[3] The *Tracts* of the Western Reserve Historical Society, and the *Fire Lands Pioneer* of the Fire Lands Historical Society contain many volumes of documents and literary papers relating to the Connecticut Reserve.

a right of government as well as the ownership of the land. In surveying the tract a five-mile township was used instead of the six-mile area of Congress, and Moses Cleaveland selected a site at the mouth of the Cuyahoga River, on Lake Erie, as the place for their first main town. Until Connecticut surrendered to Congress the jurisdictional right over the Reserve in 1800, the settlers at Cleveland got along with few institutions of established government. Then they became a part of the Eastern Division of the Northwest Territory.

Another early group that left its mark upon the virgin soil of the Old Northwest was made up of French emigrants who were persuaded to seek a Garden of Eden in Ohio by the siren voice of Joel Barlow, an early American minor poet. Barlow was sent to France by the trustees for the Scioto Associates to dispose of lands that they had the right to buy from Congress. They had nothing but an option, which they never exercised; but in some manner that has never been fully explained, Barlow sold a tract of three million acres to a French Scioto Company that proceeded to retail farms to peasants and artisans who were willing to emigrate. In the spring of 1790 some six hundred of these arrived at Alexandria, Virginia, to the dismay of William Duer who was as nearly the moral head of the Scioto Associates in America, as they had. There were neither agents to meet them nor lands awaiting them. In great haste, as the prospect of hundreds of clamorous and deceived purchasers bore upon him, Duer arranged to buy a portion of the Ohio Associates' lands for them. The Ohio group owed him money, for their own finances had nearly broken down, and he had carried them through their Marietta purchase. They now sold him for this debt, 196,544 acres on the Ohio River opposite the mouth of the Great Kanawha in the seventeenth range; and thither they fetched the Frenchmen, to found Gallipolis in October, 1790. Rufus Putnam was engaged to build their huts, but no human could be found to fulfill the promises of Barlow's prospectus or to provide profitable occupation for the skilled craftsmen who were among the emigrants. Colonel Duer failed in 1792 before the titles at Gallipolis had been straightened out, the settlement withered away, and Congress for many sessions listened to the tale of disappointed hopes and fraud. Ultimately the sufferers were compensated in part, but Gallipolis remains a scar upon the surface of the Northwest.

In every settlement west of the Ohio River there was an encroachment upon the Indian lands, whose title was not fully quieted until 1795.[4] When the Six Nations agreed to the second Treaty of Fort Stanwix, they yielded only a claim that the tribes living west of Pennsylvania did not admit. When the Lake Erie Indians confirmed the cession at Fort McIntosh, they surrendered what they did not occupy. Early in 1789 St. Clair called the tribes into council with him at Fort Harmar where these grants were reaffirmed, and the local tribes were brought unwillingly into the negotiation. Most of the Indian villages of importance were situated along the Wabash and Maumee rivers, but certain of the tribes hunted freely over and were closely identified with the Ohio shore. These were the Miami, Shawnee, Kickapoo, Potawatami, Wea, and Delawares. After the long succession of conferences at Fort Harmar, for the tribes began to gather in September, 1788, and the treaty was not signed until January 9, 1789, all of the tribes concerned had been brought into association with the United States. But there were at least three reasons why the surrender of the right bank of the Ohio was not yet assured.

In the first place the tribes had only a hazy notion of what a cession meant. To them, air, wild game, running water, and the land were common property, over which no absolute or exclusive title was recognized. It was possible for tribesmen to attend a council and not realize from the interpretations of the commissioner's speeches that they heard, that they were doing more than grant to the newcomers the same free usage that they enjoyed themselves. Without private property in land, they were unable to grasp the full significance of land to the whites until after they had seen the growth of farms and cabins.

In the second place, the clan organization that prevailed over the tribes was less than national in character, and produced no government comparable to that of the whites, with power through recognized officers to bind all the citizens of the State. The Indian generally recognized the binding force of his personal promise. When he made his own mark at the foot of the treaty and received and enjoyed the gifts and entertainment that preceded it, he felt himself bound by it. But the Indian who did not sign felt himself free to repudiate the whole transaction and to assert his continuing

[4] Charles C. Royce has prepared a definitive series of maps of Indian land cessions which is printed in Bureau of American Ethnology, *Annual Report*, vol. xviii, 1896–1897, under the title "Indian Land Cessions in the United States." With this, and the texts of the treaties in Charles J. Kappler, *Indian Affairs. Laws and Treaties* (1913), the student is in a position to check up on all details relating to cessions and migrations.

privilege to enjoy what had formerly belonged to his tribe. When there was dissatisfaction with a treaty, the non-signatory braves were its natural leaders.

In the third place, all of the Indians of the Northwest were aware that the new United States had been unsuccessful in securing the possession of the full territory granted by England in 1783. The posts along the Great Lakes, from Niagara to Green Bay, were still in possession of English garrisons, and the factors of the British fur companies still did business as in the past. Every year the Indian hunters brought their furs to Detroit or other posts, and here exchanged them for guns, ammunition, scalping knives and hatchets, frying pans, needles, and blankets; and it is too much to expect of human nature that some of the agents did not remind them that the continued extension of the American settlements would destroy their game and force them to seek new homes. The papers of the British Board of Trade contain many references to the desire of the fur traders that the south side of the Great Lakes be never surrendered to the United States. And when England was in these years urged to fulfill the treaty, her reply was that the retention of the posts was in retaliation for the American failure to allow her subjects to collect their pre-revolutionary debts.

In spite of the treaties, the Ohio Indians remained along the Ohio, and brought danger to every outlying cabin. In 1790 General Harmar was sent to the Maumee villages with the first of a long series of military expeditions whose purpose was to make such a demonstration as would overawe resistance, and quiet the border. But the commander could not control his own regulars and militiamen, was surprised in the autumn when on the Maumee near its source, and was driven back to Fort Washington in disorder. The following winter was one of terror in the Northwest, and the ensuing spring saw St. Clair himself in the field by order of President George Washington.[5] There was no successful preparation for St. Clair's maneuver, in either personnel or material. His plan was fundamentally sound, contemplating the erection of a chain of forts from Fort Washington to the Maumee, from which garrisons would be able to police the border. He built Fort Hamil-

[5] William H. Smith, *The St. Clair Papers* (1882); Charles J. Stillé, *Major-General Anthony Wayne and the Pennsylvania Line in the Continental Army* (1893), devotes its concluding chapters to Wayne's western exploit. There are many local papers in the *Publications* (originally the *Quarterly*) of the Ohio Archæological and Historical Society, and the *Quarterly Publications* of the Historical and Philosophical Society of Ohio.

ton and Fort Jefferson before winter set in, but was himself surprised while on a branch of the Wabash near the present western boundary of Ohio. Under the leadership of Little Turtle, whom the Shawnee Brave, Tecumseh, was serving as a scout, he was worried back to his seat of government.

Anthony Wayne was Washington's personal choice as commander to retrieve the situation and build up a sort of prestige for the United States among the tribes of the Northwest. Against the judgment of his advisers, for Wayne was mistrusted as rattle-brained by many of his associates, the President commissioned him to raise an army. This Wayne did near Pittsburgh, in the summer of 1792; but instead of hurrying his untrained force to the Maumee, he held them in camp and under discipline until in the spring of 1793 he was ready to take them down the Ohio to Fort Washington. Even here he was in no hurry, despite the nervousness of the border settlers. He marched north along St. Clair's cordon of forts to a point some six miles beyond Fort Jefferson, where he erected Fort Greenville and wintered in 1793–1794.

The Indian curiosity grew as Wayne led his legion into their midst. Under the discipline of Harmar and St. Clair they had been allowed to visit the camp of the army even while the war was on, and had been able to stroll among the tents and pilfer under the very eyes of the troops. With Wayne there was a sentinel that challenged the Indian at the limit of the camp, and either turned him back or escorted him under guard to the tent of the commander, where there was a parade of troops under arms. There was no straggling of men and no free pilfering. Instead of seeking a fight in 1793, Wayne was content to march a detachment to the site of St. Clair's defeat and build and garrison there a new post that bore the significant name of Fort Recovery. In the summer of 1794 Wayne took to the open.

A certain Major Campbell, of the English establishment, commanded at Detroit, and watched the approach of Wayne with as much curiosity as did the Indians. He warned the American officer that a further penetration might bring him into trouble; to which Wayne replied not only with stern words, but with an advance to the Maumee, where the Auglaize enters, and with the construction there of Fort Defiance. In August he moved on down the Maumee, towards the head of Toledo Bay where was a British station, but before he arrived there the Indians blocked his track. Some forty miles below Fort Defiance, where a tornado had left a natural breastwork of trees and brush, Little Turtle marshaled his braves. There may have been some English and Canadians fighting with him; Wayne at least thought so. It was as unusual, and as little in accord with the ordinary tactics of Indian warriors, for them to lie quietly behind cover and await attack as it would have been for them to enter into a pitched battle with an entrenched enemy. On August 20, 1794, they were totally defeated, their picked warriors were slain, and the demoralized survivors were brought to the frame of mind that both Harmar and St. Clair had previously sought to establish. With the campaign over, Wayne marched without hindrance to the source of the Maumee, and there erected Fort Wayne.

The Treaty of Greenville was concluded by the conqueror on August 3, 1795. Little Turtle, of the Miami, who had now had his fill of warfare with the whites, became an influence towards conciliation and peace; and the numerous tribes whose homes between the Wabash and the Ohio were threatened by the American influx, accepted the unavoidable recognition of American title. The boundary line that was here established started on the Ohio shore opposite the mouth of the Kentucky River; thence it ran east of north to Fort Recovery, at which point it turned sharply to the east, running through central Ohio to the head of the Cuyahoga, and down this stream to Lake Erie. Fort Wayne, a little beyond the boundary, became a military post, but it was not greatly needed, for while the generation that fought the Battle of Fallen Timbers dominated, the Old Northwest enjoyed a lasting peace.

CHAPTER IX

THE WESTERN BOUNDARIES

WITH "dry decency and cold civility," the English Government allowed John Adams, minister from the United States, to reside in London for the four years after the signing of the Treaty of Versailles. But when he gave up as hopeless the task of negotiating a satisfactory treaty of commerce with that country and took his departure in 1788, he had nothing to show for his efforts; and in the audience of departure King George III bluntly informed him that when the United States fulfilled its part of the treaty, he would execute his. In vain Adams endeavored to procure the evacuation of the western posts. In formal arguments, he was ever confronted with counterclaims regarding the British debts, for the States had disregarded the recommendations of the treaty that British subjects be allowed to recover their pre-war debts, and that the laws discriminating against the Tories be made less onerous. If Adams could have gone behind the claims of unpaid bills and an unfulfilled treaty, he would have found in the papers of the British offices a multitude of protests from British merchants and subjects residing in Canada, directed against the transfer of the region of the Great Lakes to the United States at any time. The British commandant at Niagara, in 1789, acted in this spirit and refused to let Americans even view the falls, alleging that "too many people have seen the falls already." The British debts, however, were a real grievance, and a better pretext. So long as the United States showed no sign of being able to safeguard itself or to protect its border population, there was small chance that the English side of the treaty would be carried out.

The campaign of Wayne played a part in solving the diplomatic tangles of the United States which was nearly as important as the part played in settling tangles of the border. Twice in the autumn of 1794, and each time in a frontier cause, the new republic showed a spirit to defend itself. The large army of militia that was marched to western Pennsylvania to put down the Whiskey Insurrection, indicated a determination to enforce the power of Congress to "lay and collect" taxes. Wayne's well-disciplined advance created in every month after 1793 a stronger disposition to respect the

military capacity of the United States. His erection of Fort Defiance, in the first week of August, 1794, was a gesture whose
meaning the British officers at Detroit could not mistake. The
crushing victory at Fallen Timbers broke at once the Indian power
of independent resistance, and the British disposition to give them
aid and encouragement. John Jay, whom Washington sent to
London in the summer of 1794 to make a peace that could be maintained, found in the affairs along the northern border almost the
only topic upon which he could make headway.

The outbreak of the French Revolution, and the general European war that came with it, brought to a crisis the question of
securing an understanding with Great Britain. The popular disposition in the United States was to support a war against England
regardless of American condition to maintain it. The alliance with
France, concluded in 1778, called for American aid in case France
should be attacked by her enemies, and the French Republic
interpreted the war as such an attack. It would have been easiest
for Washington to place himself at the head of this feeling of
popular sympathy, and plunge the country into warfare on the
side of France. Nowhere would such a decision have been more
popular than throughout the new settlements, where men responded readily to the ideas of liberty and democracy. But it
might well have been suicide, for there was neither army nor navy;
the militia was without organization; and in the spring of 1793
when Citizen Genêt arrived in Philadelphia bearing the suggestion
that America aid her ally, it had not been established that America could either enforce her own domestic laws or suppress a few
thousand resentful savages on her border. Not yet in possession
of her own conceded limits, the United States was hardly in a
position to bid defiance to Great Britain.

A wave of sympathy with France poured over the United
States. The course of Genêt to the seat of government from
Charleston, where he landed, was like a triumphal progress; with
civic banquets, denunciation of Britain, and flattery of France.
The democratic clubs of France became the model for political
clubs in the United States; and to these flocked the younger men,
east or west, who were outside the governing class and were disposed to believe that the friends of Washington contemplated, if
not a monarchy and another King George, at least a centralized
government in which State and popular liberty would disappear.

Genêt proceeded to outfit privateers in American ports, to prey upon British commerce, and to commission roving characters in the western settlements to organize raids upon the Spanish territory. The Secretary of State, Jefferson, was a pronounced Francophile, even though he yielded to the pressure of the Cabinet and wrote a famous proclamation of neutrality which was issued April 22, 1793. By order of Washington Genêt was soon disavowed as minister from France on account of his transgressions of neutrality; but he stayed in the United States and found a refuge with a family of Washington's opponents, where he married a daughter and bred a line of sturdy American descendants.

The one sure thing before Washington was the need for peace; and England itself was making this almost impossible by a rough and autocratic administration of maritime law as it affected the rights of neutrals. The mission of Jay was to prevent a war and to give a sign to the uneasy people that Washington was not sitting without action in the crisis. Jay found the British reluctant to make any commercial treaty with the United States. Before the Revolution, the colonies as parts of the British dominion had enjoyed a large measure of the trade in supplies with other British colonies, as well as with England direct. Outsiders were excluded by the commercial system from any part in this trade; but it missed the attention of the Americans that success in the Revolution would place them outside the protected circle, and deprive them of free access to the markets, especially those in the West Indies upon which they had long depended for sugar, molasses, and coined money. As an independent nation the United States asked England to admit it to the favors that only British colonies ordinarily enjoyed, and was vexed when England declined to grant the request. Jay could get no commercial privileges that Congress regarded as worth having, and when his treaty of November 19, 1794, was under consideration, the French party regarded it as humiliating and empty.

The treaty, however, accomplished the basic thing; it pledged "a firm, inviolable and universal peace, and a true and sincere friendship," between the two countries that were tottering on the verge of war. And in its second article the British sovereign promised to "withdraw all his troops and garrisons from the posts and places within the boundary lines assigned by the treaty of peace to the United States." This was to be accomplished by June 1, 1796, and in consideration for it (or for any treaty at all) the United States accepted the responsibility for and agreed to pay such debts to British subjects as could be shown to have been destroyed by legal impediments put in the road of their collection by the States.[1]

The British evacuation of the northwest posts took place as agreed. In the summer of 1796 Wayne's army pushed the military frontier of the United States from the Maumee line of Fort Defiance and Fort Wayne to Detroit, when they took over that post from the retiring British. It is Hinsdale's belief that England's "retention of the posts, so calamitous in results to the growing Western settlements, was largely due to a lingering hope that the young republic would prove a failure, and to a determination to share in the expected spoil. The fact is, neither England nor Spain regarded the Treaty of Paris [1783] as finally settling the destiny of the country west of the mountains." The first critical period in American history was ended when the States held together long enough to frame the Constitution and enter upon a "more perfect Union"; the second when the new government managed to enforce its laws against resistance, to keep the peace on its borders, and to procure the fulfillment of its rights to territory. The difficulty that was resolved along the frontier of the Great Lakes in 1795 and 1796 was paralleled by a similar controversy, and similar success upon the frontier of the Gulf of Mexico.

"The Mississippi," wrote an American Secretary of State, "is ... the Hudson, the Delaware, the Potomac, and all the navigable rivers of the Atlantic States, formed into one stream." In a century in which roads were non-existent, and wheeled vehicles an object of curiosity, the river constituted a highway that shaped the course of colonization and life. On the seaboard the dominance of the rivers determined the type of colonial life. Once the settler passed beyond the Appalachian watershed, the natural highways carried him readily towards the West; but instead of breaking up any possible community of interest into as many river valleys as there were, the western streams picked up the component parts of a newer solidarity, and as they merged into the Ohio and Mississippi, built up a powerful and dominant idea. France before 1763, and Spain thereafter, thought of the Mississippi system as a natural means of bringing to New Orleans the profits of the Indian trade of the interior of the continent. The American settlements in the Ohio Valley produced a contestant for those profits, and a

[1] Andrew C. McLaughlin, "The Western Posts and the British Debts," in American Historical Association, *Report* (1894).

rival to dispute with the owners of New Orleans the control of the traffic.[2]

At the date of the peace negotiations in Paris, 1781–1783, there were western settlements progressing under the grants of Virginia and North Carolina, and many of the more remote counties in Pennsylvania were upon the tributaries of the Upper Ohio. Beyond these colonies was the Indian tract, that France and Spain would willingly have kept Indian forever. Beyond this were the outposts of the fur traders. The English posts on the Great Lakes were matched by French and Spanish posts at St. Louis and along the Gulf Shore from New Orleans to Pensacola. St. Louis was a new dependency of New Orleans upon which the trading houses placed special reliance for the management of the fur trade of the Missouri Valley.

No serious attempt was made at Paris to carry the boundary of the United States across the Mississippi, or to contest the control of the town at the mouth of the Missouri, on its western bank. Pierre Laclede, of a famous New Orleans firm of fur traders, was responsible for the selection of the site, and Chouteau, his employe, for the planting of the post. In the winter of 1763–1764, they made their establishment, in time for many of the French residents in the Illinois country to cross the Mississippi upon receiving news of the cession of the east bank to England. Most of the French on the Wabash, or elsewhere in the Illinois country, were indifferent to the change made by the Treaty of Paris. Those who disliked it swelled the population of St. Louis, which was after all a better site for such a post than any that had been chosen east of the Mississippi. For the rest of the century, as the abundant manuscripts in the Missouri Historical Society show, there was continuous trade upon the Mississippi. Yearly the supplies of the traders were worked up against the current, in long keel-boats, and as often the bales of fresh furs collected by the Indian hunters were floated downstream to seek a European market from New Orleans. The traffic involved no trespass upon the territory of the United States, but the claim of the Spanish to own the Mississippi River on whose bosom it was carried was a constant exasperation. The grievance was made more burdensome because of the strategic

[2] Frederic A. Ogg, *The Opening of the Mississippi* (1904); James A. Robertson, *Louisiana under the Rule of Spain, France, and the United States* (1911); F. J. Turner, "Origin of Genet's Projected Attack," in American Historical Association, *Report*, 1896; Archibald Henderson, "Isaac Shelby and the Genet Mission," in *Mississippi Valley Historical Review*, vol. VI.

position of Spain along the Gulf of Mexico, and her refusal to recognize the boundary of the United States established here by the Treaty of Versailles.

A secret article in the preliminaries of peace between England and the United States, signed in 1782, furnished the pretext upon which Spain based her retention of part of the southwest corner of the United States. The open articles placed the boundary at the thirty-first parallel, but it was secretly understood that if Great Britain should retain West Florida after the conclusion of her peace with Spain, the boundary should be "a line drawn from the mouth of the river Yassous [Yazoo]," which is about one hundred miles further north. Spain felt somewhat defrauded by this quiet bargain at her expense, and having possession of the country in question, did without the law. Her post at Pensacola was within her unquestioned limits; likewise was the one at New Orleans; but above Mobile and above New Orleans, at Natchez, and elsewhere she held on to military posts within the defined boundaries of the United States. Holding both banks of the Mississippi at its mouth, she was in a position to render worthless the agreement between England and the United States that the navigation of the river "from its source to the ocean" should be free and open to the subjects and citizens of both. It was this control, and the resulting power to lay an embargo upon all western commerce, that irritated the western Americans more than the constant trafficking between the Spanish posts and the southwestern Indians. Continuously from 1783 to 1795 there were attempts to reach an agreement upon the status of the Mississippi and the Southwest.

In the earlier period of the negotiation, while Jay was in charge of the foreign relations under the old Congress, it was supposed that it might be safe to close the Mississippi to American trade. Spain showed a disposition to allow the United States a treaty of commerce, opening some of her colonial ports to the United States, in return for this price. Both Jay and Washington believed that it would be another generation before the actual needs of the western settlements would include the river. But Congress failed to approve the proposals, and the negotiation lapsed; not, however, until a rumor of it leaked out and penetrated to the Kentucky towns, where Brigadier General James Wilkinson was already exciting the western mind with a vision of profitable foreign trade.[3]

---

[3] The dubious career of James Wilkinson has aroused much controversy, and the doubtful esteem in which he was held by his contemporaries was responsible for his publication of *Memoirs of my own Times* (1816), an interesting but unreliable autobiography.

The Spanish administrators at New Orleans feared that the ready westerners might descend the river and take by force that which the policy of Spain would not concede. They insured against this catastrophe by allowing favored traders from upstream to violate the law. It was no novelty for infractions of the law to be sources of revenue for Spanish colonial officials. They also built up a pension list of important Americans in the Kentucky and Tennessee country, paying them private sums of money to secure friendship and the avoidance of overt acts against Spain. Many frontiersmen saw no sin in letting Spain pay them to obey the law.

The free initiative of the border, that worried Miro at New Orleans, worried Washington as well after he became President. The bond of Union was still slight, and among the settlements that had been refused admission and equality by the old Congress, there was restiveness that countenanced talk of separation and queries as to whether the Union was worth while. Vermont had maintained a State since 1777, without recognition. In Kentucky and Tennessee statehood had been demanded and denied. Nowhere was Washington's proclamation of neutrality defied with more zeal than in the new settlements where France was already intriguing to get filibusters to march against Spain. Simultaneously with the mission of Jay to England, and in much the same spirit, Washington made a final effort to get from Spain some action that would allay the passions of the West.

The details of the negotiation of the Treaty of San Lorenzo el Real, signed October 27, 1795, by Thomas Pinckney and Godoy, the Prince of the Peace, were vexatious and dilatory. Procrastination and evasion were used to fight off either compliance with Pinckney's demands, or rupture of the negotiation. Not until the American minister had given up the task and demanded his passports could he procure action. And then it appears to have been due, not to the strength of his case, but to a change in Spanish policy. The gossip that had reached Spain about the Jay treaty sounded as though the treaty was to be rejected by the Senate, and a war with England entered upon. Spain, too, was about to declare war on England. The desirability of an ally whose good will might prevent a British march from Canada across the Northwest against St. Louis and New Orleans, was obvious. Accordingly three days after Pinckney broke off the discussion, he signed a treaty in which Spain agreed to the boundary of the thirty-first parallel, promised to remove any garrisons stationed north of it, pledged the free navigation of the whole Mississippi River, and granted for three years a privilege to the up-river exporters to deposit their wares at New Orleans, and thence export them.

The situation in Europe changed almost the moment the treaty was signed, and Spain lost her interest in placating the clamorous elements in the United States. When American commissioners were sent to Natchez to run the boundary line they found delay until 1798. In this year the line was staked out, and with its establishment the United States came into full possession of its territorial limits, and passed out of the second critical period of its existence.

CHAPTER X

THE FIRST NEW STATES

GEORGE WASHINGTON laid down the office of President of the United States in 1797 with the new government a going institution. He had secured possession of the whole American territory, sketched a policy of international relationship, proved that it was possible to enforce the laws as well as to make them, and breathed into the dry bones of constitutional provision the spark of life. He had as well carried out the novel policy of imperial development sketched in the Ordinance of 1787, and signed the bills admitting to full brotherhood in the Union the three new States of Vermont, Kentucky, and Tennessee. No one of these was a public land State, for in none did the United States own the title to any of the soil. Only one, the last, had even been a territory in the sense of the Ordinance. But their admission was an earnest of the adherence of the Republic to the principle of free self-government. What the old Congress promised in the Ordinance and described as an eternal compact among the States, the new Congress reënacted August 7, 1791, when it adopted the Ordinance as a statute under the Constitution.

Vermont is associated with the western frontier only by a conscious effort of imagination, but its course of development, like the later course of Maine, ran true to the typical process of the border. It was a frontier of the Revolutionary period, and possessed a *de facto* independence as old as that of the thirteen States that were inside the Confederation. The long refusal of Congress, or rather inability, to admit Vermont helps to explain many strains of thought that pervaded the rest of the frontier and filled the hearts of Washington and Jefferson with a fear that the Union might not be maintained. From 1777 until 1791 Vermont maintained a republican form of government under a constitution, and asked without response for admittance.

The reasons for both the birth of Vermont and the reluctance to admit it as a State are to be found in the conflict of jurisdiction among Massachusetts, New Hampshire, and New York. The northern boundary of the Massachusetts settlement, fixed at the Merrimac River, was subject to a dispute in which that province claimed to run the line from the source of the river, and New Hampshire contended for a line of demarcation leaving the Merrimac at Pawtucket Falls, where is its most southern bend. There was involved the southern half of both New Hampshire and Vermont. While the matter was still in controversy both colonies granted lands to settlers in the area of contest. Their dispute was settled by the crown in 1741, when New Hampshire was given the whole region north of the present boundary of Massachusetts.

The award to New Hampshire left undetermined the old claim of New York to extend to the Connecticut River in the country north of Massachusetts, and New York took the aggressive as claimant against New Hampshire now that Massachusetts was eliminated. The governor of New Hampshire encouraged the settlement of the area beyond the Connecticut, and sold freely rectangular townships six miles square, for the purpose of strengthening his title to the land by actual occupation. The New Hampshire grants thus became a community whose peaceful existence depended upon a victory of New Hampshire over New York. In 1764 this hope faded, for the king recognized the title of New York as extending to the Connecticut River. The victor province invited the occupants of the soil, who had bought their titles from the illegal claimant, New Hampshire, to buy them again from it. It was hard enough to make frontier farmers buy their land once; to make them do it twice was beyond the possible. The New Hampshire Grants denied the claim of New York, set up an independence that New York was not able to break down before the Revolution began, and made a constitution under the name of Vermont when the other States made theirs. Whether Vermont was a State or not, the "Green Mountain Boys" played a useful part on the northern frontier during the Revolution.

The appeal of Vermont for admission came before Congress not far from the time when the settlements of the Blue Grass region of Kentucky were being planted by Judge Henderson's Transylvania Company, and were asking similar treatment. The Vermont constitution of 1777 copied a Pennsylvania provision for a council of censors and periodic revision. Neither New York nor Virginia was yet ready for partition, however, and the life of Congress was too precarious to make it wise to run the risk of alienating either or both of these great constituents. In 1786 a second constitution was made; but still the requisite nine States could not be got to vote for admission. In 1790, New York at last gave consent to the alteration of its boundaries, and released the land between Lake Champlain and the Connecticut. Congress thereupon, by act of February 18, 1791, declared that after the following March 4, Vermont should be a member of the United States. It had a few days earlier given a like permission to Kentucky.

The Kentucky settlements sprang to life along the middle border on the eve of the Revolution. Lord Dunmore's War, with its decisive victory in 1774 stimulated the advance out of Pennsylvania and Virginia into the West and gave new zest to speculation in land titles and colonial projects. In the following year Henderson made his attempt to buy lands directly from the Indian owners, and was sharply rebuffed by Virginia. At the time of the Henderson settlement there were already a few Virginians on the ground with prior claims as squatters. James Harrod brought in a group by way of the Ohio River and the Falls, and settled in the Kentucky Valley in 1774. Harrodsburg was the center of Virginia influence over the Blue Grass country before Daniel Boone established Boonesboro for Henderson's associates in 1775. The Boonesboro Convention that appealed to Congress for independent statehood was matched by a Harrodsburg Convention that memorialized Virginia for an extension of government by that State. Congress was inactive, but Virginia, at the end of 1776, organized a Kentucky County covering the whole area that she was already disposed to consider as a future State. Clark gave peace to the new county in the following years, and protected with his expedition the planting of Louisville at the Falls of the Ohio.

The new western settlements that were made in the ten years after the surrender of Lord Cornwallis were mostly directed to Kentucky County, with the Ohio River on its northern side, and the Cumberland near its southern. The great gateways at the Ohio Forks and Cumberland Gap let the settlers through. The hostility of the Indian tribes on the right bank of the Ohio retarded settlement there and repelled the pioneer invader. The opposition of the Cherokee, and the violent altercation between North Carolina and the followers of John Sevier concerning the State of Franklin, discouraged much emigration to the country south of the Cumberland. The friendly limestone soil of the Blue Grass invited occupation, and the parent State, Virginia, held out hopes of freedom and opportunity.

Here came James Wilkinson in 1784, with experience earned in the Revolution and with an eager mind roving over all the possibilities of the future for the Ohio Valley. Permanent attachment to Virginia was only one of the solutions; admission as a State was second; an inland confederacy linked together by the Mississippi River was a third; and there may have been another that contemplated an alliance with some foreign power that might secure both personal prestige and a market for the surplus produce of the farms.

Kentucky assumed self-consciousness at the moment when Congress was debating the question of a Spanish treaty and an agreement to close the Mississippi for a term of years. The garbled report of this that reached the West strengthened the suspicion that Congress might neither admit the West nor treat it fairly. The long-denied claims of Vermont provided ammunition for the advocate of a more local self-determination. The illicit profits of the river trade, that the compliant Spanish administrators allowed to Wilkinson and many of his friends, kept them interested in their immediate gains. The statehood movement ripened, but ripened slowly even after Virginia in 1786 stated the terms upon which she was ready to recognize Kentucky independence.

Three times more, before the decade ended, Virginia repeated her tender of freedom to her colony. Each time something occurred to keep Kentucky from taking effective action under it. In 1789 the Federal Constitution added a new safeguard to the State whose section aspired to separate autonomy. Under the Articles of Confederation, admission was authorized by vote of nine States, with no further requirement. Under the Constitution admission was based upon simple act of Congress, with the proviso that no State should be forced to contribute of its land to any new State without its consent. Even Congress added its authorization and fixed a date at which Kentucky should become a State before the tenth of the Kentucky conventions in her statehood series met at Danville and framed a constitution.

There were plenty of guides for the craftsmen of the new State.[1] Both Delaware and New Hampshire had just completed revisions of their revolutionary constitutions, and in Pennsylvania an uprising of the newer counties had dominated in a constitutional con-

[1] Archibald Henderson, "Creative Forces in American Expansion," in *American Historical Review*, vol. xiv. Francis Newton Thorpe, *A Constitutional History of the American People, 1776–1850* (1898), fully appreciates the meaning of the American process of constitution making; the texts of the various constitutions are most easily available in his *Federal and State Constitutions, Colonial Charters and other Organic Laws of the States, Territories, and Colonies now or heretofore forming the United States of America* (1909).

vention of elected delegates. The Virginia constitution of 1776 was still foremost in western minds as representing an advanced view of democratic right. The men who counted for most in the Kentucky convention were Virginia born; and in the constitution they made, may be seen the flowering of the Virginia spirit in a frontier soil. It was different from the Virginia bloom, as that of Virginia differed from that of Old England. It founded its electorate on manhood suffrage. George Nicholas, who probably drafted the document, showed his belief in direct representation by resigning his seat when he changed his mind upon a basic point, and by returning to his constituents for a fresh election. Most of the Kentucky delegates, when in the Virginia convention, had voted against the ratification of the Constitution of the United States; now that they had in sight a full participation in that Union, the spirit of national pride began to grip them. Before the date June 1, 1792, had arrived, at which Kentucky was to become a State, the constitution was in force, the State government had been installed, and senators and representatives were ready to take up their work at Philadelphia in the national Congress. They had perhaps one hundred thousand constituents with homes in or near the Blue Grass.

Tennessee became the sixteenth State in 1796, after a vexatious period of youth and adolescence. Its earliest settlements went back to the Watauga district, and the exodus from North Carolina after the Battle of the Alamance. The parallel tributaries that flow southwest and make up the Tennessee River drain a series of fertile valleys that attracted a small but consistent immigration in spite of the adverse claims of the Cherokee Indians and the attitude of North Carolina. So many of the newcomers came from the Virginia valleys, bringing with them a preconceived distrust of North Carolina that the heroes of the winning of this West had a special aversion to the state of dependence that the parent State maintained. In 1784 North Carolina ceded the western country to Congress, withdrawing the cession before the year expired. In 1789, after silencing the aspirations of the State of Franklin, the cession was repeated on terms that Congress could accept.

There were no public lands to be transferred to Congress, but the temporary jurisdiction over the people made necessary an act for their government. North Carolina specified in the cession that the guarantees spread over the Northwest by the Ordinance of 1787 should be allowed to her dependents. Congress, therefore, on May 26, 1790, created the territory south of the Ohio River for the benefit of Tennessee, and installed a government, sister to that which St. Clair was directing from his new seat at Cincinnati. In addition to Tennessee, the territory embraced the alleged strip ceded by South Carolina, and, in theory, the tract south of the Yazoo line. But since Spain was still in possession of the last, it gave small concern to Governor William Blount, whom Washington commissioned as first executive of the territory. There were not over 25,000 settlers in the new government when it was established; six years later when admitted to the Union it was alleged that the population of 77,262 was acquired only by counting in transients who were obliged to pass through eastern Tennessee on their way to Cumberland Gap and Kentucky.

The three districts that nature had created for the State of Tennessee made their impression upon the mind of the prospective commonwealth from its beginning. Eastern Tennessee is a region of parallel valleys, with high elevation, and with economic and agricultural resources different from those of the more level country on either side. Small farmers of the frontier type built it up; and in backwaters where there was no easy approach to any market, some of their descendants still remain and live the life of the eighteenth century in the twentieth. "Our contemporary ancestors," as they have been called, make it possible to visualize the life that was characteristic of the whole frontier in its earliest phase, with the exception of the aggressive spirit that speedily changed the face and prospect of the more favored regions. From the stagnant recesses of the mountains where economic development came slowly if at all, the pushing members of each succeeding generation have worked themselves out; leaving behind the dull ones and the unfortunates, whose retarded colonies are sprinkled among the valleys south of Pennsylvania.

Knoxville, founded on the Tennessee River in 1789, was at once the seat of eastern Tennessee and the capital of the territory. Here in 1794 the earliest legislature met, the population having grown enough to authorize it. And two years later, after the territorial census had been taken, here the convention met to frame a constitution and demand that Congress recognize Tennessee as a State.

Middle and western Tennessee, the other two districts, represent somewhat different geographic influences, that were followed by economic and social deviation. The middle region lies west of the mountains and is dominated by the Cumberland River. In an agricultural way, it partakes of the character that the Blue Grass region of Kentucky possesses. It was settled first by James Robertson's colony at Nashville, and expanded as a region of plantations. Slaves were profitable here, as they were not in eastern Tennessee, and the resulting system of slave agriculture bred a different social atmosphere. In western Tennessee, the tract actually west of the Tennessee River and east of the Mississippi, the Chickasaw Indians remained in possession through the first two decades of the nineteenth century. Ultimately the cotton crop came to control the interests of western Tennessee, and Memphis, with its strategic position on the high bluffs of the Mississippi (the first good high ground above Vicksburg), became a gateway for the extension of an economic imperialism over the country still further west. But in the end of the seventeenth century, when the territory south of the Ohio was transforming itself into the State of Tennessee, middle Tennessee was the remote frontier; west Tennessee was Indian country, and eastern Tennessee was the center of political activity.

On the frontier of the Tennessee River, Blount had to deal with Indian danger and alien intrigue, somewhat as St. Clair was forced to meet them on the Ohio in the same years. But no engagement with the Cherokee stands out with the strategic significance of the Battle of Fallen Timbers, and no treaty had the far-reaching effects of that at Greenville. Sevier and Robertson, leaders in the earliest stirrings of society, remained the prominent leaders through the Indian dangers and the political discussions. An element that was lacking in the Northwest Territory appeared in Tennessee in the chance for dubious speculation in Spanish profits. In Tennessee, more than elsewhere, the bond of interest in the United States was slight, and the temptation to make something out of the international situation was strong. We do not know quite the extent or the manner in which Blount and Sevier, and others of their associates, like Wilkinson in Kentucky, took profits out of Spain. Some of the leaders were kept on the pay roll at New Orleans; others, like Clark and Blount, were ready to accept pay from France for a filibustering attack on Spain. After Tennessee became a State and Blount a senator, enough evidence appeared to warrant his impeachment. There was no conviction, since the Senate had already expelled him, and doubted, moreover, whether a senator was liable to impeachment.

In the case of Kentucky, Congress declared that it might become a State on a given date in the future, and Kentucky proceeded to make a constitution, without outside oversight. In Tennessee there was no such recognition until a delegation appeared at Philadelphia, reporting that a constitution had been made and that congressmen were ready to take their seats. Thereupon there was debate upon the propriety of the formation of a State with no more authority than the general provisions of the Ordinance of 1787, and there were members of Congress who would gladly have disciplined the new commonwealth for its presumption. But since most of these were of the party that had lost its grip upon the West, and even upon Congress, they were unable to delay action. On June 1, 1796, by an act effective at once, Tennessee was declared a member of the Union. Sevier, who had been the territorial delegate in Congress, was governor, Blount was one of the first senators, and a Nashville lawyer, Andrew Jackson by name, became the earliest representative.

Times were changing, when Tennessee entered as the sixteenth State. Part of the West was no longer sheer frontier. In central Kentucky there were signs of stability and wealth, as there were in western Virginia and western Pennsylvania. Local leaders had begun to grow on local roots, and frontier points of view had gained coherent spokesmen. The ubiquitous printer had made his way across the mountains, with his irrepressible news sheets. The *Pittsburgh Gazette* (July 29, 1786) was the first west of the mountains. This was followed by John Bradford's *Kentucke Gazette* (August 11, 1787), and by William Maxwell's *Centinel of the North-Western Territory*, that made its appearance at Cincinnati November 11, 1793. The historian turns to the early issues of these newspapers in vain, when he hopes for details upon the settlement of the communities that maintained them. Only by accident does local news creep in. But in the large discussions of national policy, and in news of the foreign events upon which national policy was based, they provide a sure guide to both the political theories of the new frontier and the party practice.

CHAPTER XI

POLITICAL THEORIES OF THE FRONTIER

THE American frontier was not founded upon any antecedent theory of imperial or domestic growth, but emerged with a form largely dictated by the status of its land, the life that the early settlers could not avoid living upon that land, and the inheritance of ideas that the residents possessed. It was a common law process, similar to that which had in England built up the body of legal doctrine and political practice. The foreign experience that shaped American public growth before 1800 was so completely English that frontier society and institutions are plainly the result of old habits modified by new environment.

As frontier thought became weighty enough to be heard across the mountains, in the councils of the United States, it was both possible and necessary to analyze it and to identify those elements that were indigenous, and those that were inherited from either the colonial or the European past. The most important of those that were native and unavoidable grew out of the fact of isolation and distance, which bred self-confidence, equality, and distrust of the absentee.

Isolation is a condition precedent to the development of any frontier. Professor Turner has pointed out the differences between the various frontiers of the missionary, the hunter, the soldier, the stockman, and the farmer. Their common quality lies in the fact that a few men were making the first occupation of a vast waste, and when the farmer came along behind the roamers who had already traversed his region, and perhaps advertised it, he built his cabin in a loneliness that was lightened rarely by other human presence, Indian or white. For years the cabins remained far from each other, separated by wastes of forest. Among themselves, or with their former homes, there could be few connections. The frontier family could not escape the sense of loneliness and self-dependence that lessened the binding force of prior ties, and stressed the value of immediate experience. The recollections that they had of home were most often those of youth, that had never been fully admitted into the confidences of its elders, nor allowed to share and learn the responsible burdens of public life. A background of general impressions, not checked up with precise information, existed everywhere among them. And as the period of separation lengthened, the memories blurred. There developed both sentimental reminiscence and a full consciousness of separation.

The life of the average frontier settler provides the details that make up the picture of the whole; the experience of those that were successful built up the mental attitude. There were many failures, who never finished a farm, who lived always in squalor, and turned shiftless as lack of success became a habit. These made a vivid impression on the eye of the outside visitor who described the West; but the traits that frontiersmen valued in their leaders were those of their luckier or wiser neighbors. Self-confidence was the first of these.

Old age and middle life have always been restive under the aggressive nerve of youth. Ignorance and self-confidence seem to them to be bred together, while their own conservatism appears only the natural product of experience. Here along the frontier was a whole community of youth, thrown upon its own resources to make success or failure. The consequence of success was more self-confidence. The failures moved on, moved back, or died. The self-made man became the normal leader. Deprived of the restraining voice of age, and led by the intensified initiative of youth, the West became a seat of impatient independence.

The self-confidence of western thought operated against a background of equality. It was an equality of fact rather than of theory. It has been quite possible, as democratic ideals have developed, for a man to accept their principle but dislike their practice. Civilization is founded upon the subordination of individual aspiration and accomplishment to the common good, but not many men have loved the giving up that this entails. Along the frontier, men came to accept the idea of equality with greater ease than usual, because as they looked around them, they saw men equal.

In few communities have wealth, station in life, education, or refined taste brought less immediate profit to their possessor than on the frontier. It was as hard for the rich as for the poor to build the cabin, clear the cornfield, extract the first unwilling crop, and raise the children through the perils of childhood. There were few things that money could buy, in the form of either goods or service; and small leisure for the enjoyment of intellectual or social pleasure. There was grinding labor for all who made life go. The occupations at any stage of its development were identical for every family on a new frontier. The necessity to live the common life made them resentful of the pretensions of persons who tried to live it differently. In their minds the distinctions of the older States that were based on property or station lost much of their significance. Economic and social equality were hard facts that they could not evade.

To this self-confidence, and the insistence that none were better than themselves, the frontier life added a distrust of the absentee whether in the field of government or business. This absenteeism was close to the roots of the Revolution, as it has since been in the uneasiness of Ireland, of Egypt, of India, and of the Philippines. The American grievance was less that government was bad, than that it was remote and beyond control. Aspirations to self-government were intensified by this condition of dependence upon an absentee. When his claim was not the right to rule but the right to a share in the produce of labor, the distrust was as strong, however valid might be the law or the contract on which the claim was based. The Penns and the Calverts, great proprietors as they were, never succeeded in organizing their revenues on a permanent basis. It is hard enough to admit the claims of the creditor who lives neighbor to the debtor, and understands the situation of the latter, even though he does not share it. But when the creditor is remote, and has no interest in the debtor except the profits that he makes, the door through which misunderstanding may enter is wide open. The absentee landlord, or mortgage owner, or shareholder, can never expect to have his debtor see eye to eye with him along the line of obligation and profit. This absenteeism becomes a large factor in explaining the eager frontier demand for autonomy in government, and for laws that would help the debtor as against his creditor.

Self-confidence, equality, and the demand for autonomy, were unavoidable conditions that the frontier bred. They were expressed in a language of words and institutions that were quite as unavoidable an inheritance from the colonial past. In each of the thirteen colonies there had been similar drift from the ideas of England, and the years had built up in each a government that men took for granted in the era of independence.

Always there was a written charter of government. In England the lack of a written constitution has perplexed many who have been conscious of the dominance of such documents in America. But the American colony was in every case founded upon a charter and a body of instructions to royal officials in which the powers and limits of government were defined in words. Even the most revolutionary of Americans have begun their revolution by writing not manifestoes but new constitutions.

Next to the constitution, there was ever the right and duty of some authority to review the acts of government and square them with the basic law. In colonial days this had been the function of British courts of appeal, and of the king in council. Colonial legislatures had been accustomed to royal disallowance of their laws, and colonial courts knew that no doctrine was safe until it had run the gauntlet of the English judges. The frontier was not certain whether this power to disallow should be exercised by court, or governor, or by the people in their sovereign capacity; but it could not avoid the existence of the fact.

In every colony there had existed a governor, not because there was a king in England and in imitation of him, but because of the great rule of human affairs that some man must direct a work if it is to be done. It was a necessary result of independence that the selection of this official, whatever name he might bear, should be a public duty, and that his title to rule should be derived from the voters of his State.

No colony had even tried to live without an assembly, in which some measure of direct representation had a part. Invariably it was bicameral, one house owing its existence to the people and their votes, the other an outgrowth of the group of councillors that every governor gathered around him. The two principles that made a difference in basis between the houses were lost when both came to be elected, but the balance that two houses gave to government, and the power to check and revise, kept both of them alive.

The final authority in the colony, as in England, was an electorate, whose breadth and inclusive character are measures of the status of democracy at any time. The continuous struggle in colonial government was between the absentee principle that the governor represented, tending to follow the policy of king and parliament, and the self-governing principle that came up through the people to their elected representatives, who grasped the common purse, and sought to frame the law. It was long before Americans could convince themselves that it was possible for an executive to represent the people, and that governors elected could be free from the inclination to represent an alien power.

With these experiences, that were similar and common to all the colonies, the American people entered upon a course of self-education in politics when they broke their bond of dependence upon England. Twice before 1800, they tried as a whole to frame a common government. It was no advantage that an institution was English when they selected the parts of their scheme, for they had had enough of king and parliament. But it was much that an arrangement had worked well in their colonial life, and that they understood it. These things, and few others, contributed to the Articles of Confederation and the Federal Constitution, and to the twenty-five State constitutions made before their first quarter century of freedom was over.

Constitution making in the United States affords a measure of popular ideas of government such as no other community possesses. It was no accident that upon independence the States immediately proceeded to re-write the basic law. Congress early advised such procedure, and before 1780 eleven of the States had taken the advice. Rhode Island and Connecticut, whose colonial charters were substantially constitutions of free government, found it unnecessary to make more than verbal changes to signalize the fact of separation. The other States, either in their legislatures or in conventions specially assembled, wrote new documents. Their first instinctive feeling was that such constituent tasks could be accomplished by the legislature, as in England the constitution is whatever parliament amends it to be. But before the American revolutionary process was complete, this view had given place to the other idea that for a basic law there must be a special and solemn assemblage of popular sovereignty, and that in a convention this can best take place.

Before the end of the century four American States had made three constitutions each (New Hampshire, Vermont, South Carolina, and Georgia); three had two each (Pennsylvania, Delaware, and Kentucky); seven had a single constitution (Massachusetts, New York, New Jersey, Maryland, Virginia, North Carolina, and Tennessee); while two States were yet content with the ancient charters (Connecticut and Rhode Island). Every few months since 1800 one State or another has voluntarily passed through this process, and by its acts given evidence of its political faith. The men who have been used in the conventions have ranked high, above ordinary considerations of self-interest and party politics, so that the evidence has been deliberate and solemn. No im· portant movement in politics has been deprived of its chance at a hearing, or of a result upon the basic law. In all, as in the first twenty-five, can be seen the constant pressure of frontier environment lessening unreasonable restrictions, and expanding the share of the people in the direct management of their government.

The typical American State of 1780, as the first crop of constitutions was completed, retained the governor, the legislature, and the courts, much as they existed in colonial times, as well as declarations or bills of rights that as yet tended to repeat the phrases of the Declaration of Independence. Only five of the thirteen States elected the governor directly by popular vote; democracy had not yet gone so far. Nine States denied him the right of veto.

The legislature retained the conventional two houses and possessed powers that were enlarged in proportion as those of the governor were curtailed. In only five of the States was the voter freed from property qualifications; while in all the legislator must possess property. In most States the legislature took over the appointment of judges from the executive, but in eight it was still the opinion that judges should hold office during good behavior.

The three frontier States, Vermont, Kentucky, and Tennessee, made six constitutions in the last decade of the eighteenth century. If all the American constitutions were liberal, these were ultra. Manhood suffrage, based upon a residence of one year in the State, and an age of twenty-one, was adopted in all; except that Kentucky, in its second constitution, added the significant word white. Their legislators must in every case meet additional tests; of superior age, of longer residence, of freehold property, of American citizenship, or, as in Vermont, of a belief in God and the Scriptures, and membership in a Protestant church. Their governors, too, were protected by requirements of property, age, residence, religion, and citizenship. The West had not broken entirely from the ideals of the older order, but the advance to manhood suffrage was a distinctive sign of progress.

It is evident as one reads these constitutions that a belief in natural rights found ready lodgment in the minds of residents along the frontier. Thomas Jefferson, in the Declaration of Independence, and George Mason, in the Virginia Bill of Rights, wrote phrases that have been repeated in nearly every constitution that has since been made. As the crown, and religion, and property lost favor as the foundations of government, nature came to be the obvious parent of democracy. As jealousy of the crown, or the executive, or the courts spread, a belief in balanced powers came to pervade these documents. It became more important to preserve liberty than to get work done; more desirable to check a possible usurpation than to promote efficiency. The Federal Constitution was ratified while this period of State Constitution making was under way, and it contained no bill of rights. But so great were the apprehensions that this lack aroused that a tacit pledge was given that the new government should at once amend the Constitution to correct this defect. And ten amendments were written into it by the States. In the fight over ratification, the frontier borders of the thirteen States were suspicious that a game was being played against them. Their delegates in the State conventions voted against ratification, fearing a conspiracy to build up a centralized and autocratic power. The normal frontier trend against authority and absenteeism, and towards personal liberty, remained after the Constitution became effective, and provided the materials out of which to build up parties and to struggle for national control. Political theory gives us one side of the frontier State, but only one. The other must be sought in party practice.

CHAPTER XII
JEFFERSONIAN DEMOCRACY

NEITHER the theory nor the practice of politics is alone enough basis upon which to construct a picture of a state. The two must be taken together, and the outcome is so completely the result of their interplay that it is not safe to allow the contemplation of either factor to blind the observer to the other. The American frontier of 1800 was in political, spiritual, and economic revolt. A great religious awakening was either a cause or a consequence of the fact that men were deeply stirred. The expression of their political opinion swept from power a party that had come to believe itself indispensable to the nation. It swept to office Thomas Jefferson, as President of the United States; and the form of its expression was so nearly that of its leader that it has come to be known as Jeffersonian democracy. Once before, in the Revolution, such a wave of resentment broke down the British tie. There were later waves to come, with Andrew Jackson and Abraham Lincoln at their crest. Behind them all lies the mixture of political theory and party practice that distinguishes the American frontier areas from the rest of the nation. In each case the men broken by one wave had been among the leaders of the last, and the clearest voice of new guidance came out of the freshest frontier group.[1]

The growth of American parties began with the inauguration of George Washington as President and followed the course suggested by his experiences and those of his associates in the Revolution. His attitude towards the new government entrusted unanimously to his hands was founded on his experience. He, more than any other American, knew the costs of the Revolution, and the difficulties that had threatened to defeat it. State interest, private selfishness, inadequate control, indifference, and poverty, had made his task as commander in chief almost impossible. His per-

---

[1] Robert T. Hill, *The Public Domain and Democracy* was published in the Columbia University *Studies*, 1910, and endeavors to show something of this process. Andrew C. McLaughlin, "Social Compact and Constitutional Construction," in *American Historical Review*, vol. v, and "Democracy and the Constitution," in American Antiquarian Society, *Proceedings*, N.S., vol. xxii, are thoroughly reliable critiques; A. D. Morse, "Causes and Consequences of the Party Revolution of 1800," in American Historical Association, *Report*, 1894.

manent greatness is based on the character that helped him to fight every obstacle without losing sight of the end that his countrymen ought, at least, to be aiming at. He had learned that there could be no sure result under a divided command, nor any result without self-sacrifice. Unless a real government could be put together among the States there was no ground for hoping that independence might endure. Some of his wisest friends were open hopers for a monarchy, and were frankly disappointed when a government of enumerated powers under the Constitution was all they could attain. The men he trusted most were men who had shared with him the difficulties of the past, and who appreciated with him the need of a government that could maintain itself above either State or private opposition.

In addition to the special experiences of Washington that gave direction to the Federalist Administration of which he became the head, there were other influences that ever affect the man in office. What we call the "administrative point of view" is chiefly the understanding of men who are required to get things done; and who see the ways and means because they are in office. Whoever the leader, of whatever party, with whatever previous avowal of political belief, the public office and the open responsibility turn him towards the fulfillment of his task. He cannot escape learning something of public business when he assumes public responsibility, and the common complaint that men in office turn indifferent to their old ideals means chiefly that men in office have to serve the office.

What his public duty forced upon him as an administrator, Washington would gladly have undertaken from conviction and experience. Under his direction the dry bones of constitutional powers were covered with the flesh of statute and administration. His fellow citizens in the older communities did not like any too well the emergence of a real, central, national authority; and on the border, where any remote government was an affront, it was easy to believe that the liberties of the people were in danger. What reflections of this sort did not rise spontaneously were readily suggested by the facile pen of Thomas Jefferson, whom Washington had made chief of his cabinet and Secretary of State.

In every eastern State in 1789, there was clash of social and political interests. The organization of the States had not kept pace with the spread of population within their own limits. The districts from which legislators came had not been re-defined as

sparse counties grew in population. The lack of representation
among the newer counties created a State situation not unlike that
of the colonies against England, when they denounced taxation
without representation. And the desire of the older sections to
perpetuate the distinctions of property and religion tended to dis-
franchise their children who emigrated to the West. In States
where the frontiersmen were German or Scotch-Irish there was
racial as well as social or economic reason for the conflict. Students
who accept in full the doctrines of economic determinism have
suggested that after all the forces that adopted the Constitution,
and opposed it, were only those of the propertied and the property-
less. This is an inadequate explanation, and leaves out of account
the great forces of inheritance and ideals; but it is true that most
Americans who owned land or slaves or held the securities iss.ted
by the revolutionary States, were also believers in a government of
real powers. Whereas the younger communities, with less experience and fewer of the stabilizing bonds of fortune, contained many
who thought it possible to continue to exist in a freedom approaching a state of nature. The radical western counties of the eastern States waged a long struggle for equality or domination,
recording their victories as they won them in successive constitutions and legislative policies.

Along the frontier, whether in the older States or throughout
the new, there were social materials ready to be used in making a
party to oppose any administration, and specially the Federalists,
with their belief in firm government. Thomas Jefferson seized the
leadership in organizing them, and held for four years a strategic
position at the seat of Federal Government; for Washington had in
his simplicity thought that all good men might be brought to agree
in administration, regardless of their attitude towards life, or their
personal ambitions. The first Washington cabinet was a coalition
of points of view, if not of factions. To Jefferson nearly every
measure that Hamilton devised and Washington sponsored, was
full of danger to the liberty of the people; and what was not inher-
ently threatening was dubious at least, if Hamilton endorsed it.
Personality, political ambition, and theory of government made it
improper that these two men should ever have sat in the same
government. Jefferson had no sense of loyalty to his chief that
kept him from using his official position to provide jobs for useful
party workers and to give form to his urgings that Washington and
his friends were a menace to the country.

Not until 1793 did Jefferson leave the cabinet, and he was working all the while to nullify its endeavor. His own view of democracy was derived from philosophical reflection, much of it French in origin and similar to those musings on equality that the later nobles of the Old Régime in France had indulged in under Louis XV. He was himself a Virginia landowner, and near-aristocrat, and all his life he loved the comforts and generous existence of the southern planter. But his theories of liberty brought him into close alignment with the hundreds of thousands of frontiersmen to whom equality was an observed condition of life and who were somewhat fearful lest others should be allowed to rise above it. His political sagacity made of them a party machine on which he mounted to leadership. The episodes of policy upon which Washington was forced to take a stand were grasped by him, to point out that real democracy would have chosen the other side.

The political issues upon which the Jeffersonian Democracy, or the Democratic-Republicans, were founded, were primarily the assumption of the revolutionary debts, foreign, continental, and State; the whiskey insurrection of 1791–1794; the policy of neutrality of 1793; and the repressive measures written by the Federalists into the Alien and Sedition Laws of 1798. For each of these Jefferson and his friends had an explanation that impugned the honest motives of the Federalists and that went so far in the extremer forms as to suggest that there was on foot a serious attempt to make of Washington a king and to overthrow the experiment of Federal Government. The first of these issues was certainly Hamilton's; the second probably was; the third was Washington's; and the last represented the idea of the Federalists in their later phases of carrying through by force what they could not gain by favor.

The assumption of the revolutionary debts was advocated by Hamilton as finance minister, in his desire to establish national credit on a secure foundation. With them at large and unpaid as to principal or interest, new loans were impracticable, and the repute of the United States must be uncertain. Their assumption played a double rôle in his mind. It was at once honest and expedient. It would bring into existence a large number of responsible citizens who, holding the new securities of the country, would have a strong interest in its solidity. To the West, that held few of the old or new loans and was in chronic debt, the measure looked like a stock-jobbing enterprise; for the revolutionary securities that were to be funded were depreciated in value, and rose sharply to the profit of their holders, as soon as assumption was announced as a national policy. Many were in the hands of speculators, and some were owned by members of the Congress. It was not clear that some public officers had not used their prior knowledge of resumption to enrich themselves by speculating in the debt. The frontier leaders pointed to this as evidence that the new government was the tool of property.

In the whiskey insurrection the United States showed its new ability to collect as well as to lay a tax. The excise law of 1791 contemplated revenues to be derived from direct taxation, and it was in Hamilton's mind to establish at once whatever powers the Federal Government possessed. The law included a tax upon the manufacture of whiskey, which has ever been regarded as peculiarly fit for taxation; but in the western regions, and specially the new southwestern counties of Pennsylvania (where they had recently opposed the Federal Constitution and aided in overturning the eastern aristocracy in their own convention) the whiskey tax looked like a direct blow for their destruction.

The frontier farmer, after a year or two, always had enough to eat, and had a surplus of food that might mean solvency if it could be marketed. But there were few local markets and the bulky raw products could not stand a long haul and heavy freight charges. Corn was a staple. It could be turned into hogs and driven to market furnishing its own transport, and nearly every traveler to the West reported the meeting of persistent droves of swine, bound eastward. The corn could also be distilled into whiskey and with reduced bulk and concentrated value be available for a real export trade. Every farmer had his still. The whiskey excise struck him not as a manufacturer but as a farmer, whereas the eastern farmer bought his whiskey instead of making it, and dodged the inquisitorial tax. When the treasury agents came among the western counties, it was only thirty years after the arrival of the British stamp agents whose rough treatment in the seaboard colonies had been a preliminary of the Revolution. The western farmers discouraged their neighbors from taking treasury appointments, threw rocks at the collectors, shot at their lighted windows after dark, and occasionally burned their barns and haystacks. Through 1792 and 1793 the collection of the whiskey excise was made so difficult in western Pennsylvania that the Federal Government sensed a general conspiracy to prevent it. Extensive riots around

Pittsburgh in the spring of 1794 led Washington to vigorous acts to keep the Government from being flouted. By proclamation, August 7, 1794, he ordered the illegal obstructors to disperse; and then he collected from the neighboring eastern States a militia body of 13,000 men whom he mobilized at Carlisle, and marched to Pittsburgh. Here they overawed the population and there was no resistance. The alleged leaders of the rioting were arrested and taken east for trial in federal courts. To Andrew Gallatin, a Swiss immigrant who had taken up his home on the Youghiogheny, in Fayette County, this seemed like a tyrannous usurpation, and government by force.[2] Jefferson disliked it. It was further fuel to the fires of partisanship that were already burning fiercely. And the radical democrat saw in it proof that the monarchical party would found itself on military force.

The French War of 1793 gave rise to Anti-Federalist sentiments that were at the boiling point during the exciting days of the suppression of the whiskey insurrection, and that suspected a corrupt alliance with England, as well as monarchy. There was an instinctive feeling of sympathy for the attempt of France to establish a free government in place of the old monarchy, and the philosophic leaders of the French Revolution were the same men who had, a decade earlier, welcomed the American experiment. When France declared that now was the time for the alliance of 1778 to operate, and Genêt arrived to receive the coöperation of America, democratic feeling ran high everywhere, and on the border was hardly mixed with any other reflections. To Washington the French War was one of propaganda rather than of defense; and a neutral course was the only one that his country could afford. Washington could compel Jefferson to administer his policy of neutrality, but he could not prevent the Democrats, who were already denouncing him, from raising liberty poles, donning the red cap of revolution, and drinking copious toasts of sympathy to France. Western leaders, like George Rogers Clark, offered their services to Genêt without reserve, and so affected the mind of that young French minister that he ventured to intimate to Washington that he could safely appeal from the Government of the United States to the people. Genêt's course was short; but when Washington rebuked him and hurried John Jay to patch up

[2] Henry Adams, *Life of Albert Gallatin* (1879), was accompanied by three volumes of *Writings of Albert Gallatin* (1879); for Adams this was a preliminary to his *History of the United States, 1801–1817* (1889–1890). It provided a permanent monument for Gallatin.

a treaty with England, the pro-French and the anti-British and the Democrats fought the treaty with bitter earnestness. The treaty was ratified by the Senate, but party lines were drawn in the country that Washington had hoped to see develop free from faction.

After 1793 Jefferson was out of the cabinet. He devoted himself to the organization of a chain of Democratic clubs, aimed at the winning of elections and the wresting of the country from the Federalists. Everywhere the younger local politicians were with him, and in Congress a growing number of his followers made a nucleus for attacking Federalist policies. The aftermath of the Genêt episode placed them on the defensive for a time, for the three ministers whom President John Adams sent to France, Marshall, Gerry, and Pinckney, found the members of the Directory to be bribe hunters rather than the priests of liberty that the Democrats pictured them to be. When the ministers' dispatches were printed as the X Y Z correspondence, the country had a revulsion of Federalist feeling, and the Congress chosen during 1796 and 1797 was Federalist in both houses.

The Federalists, in their return to complete power, had neither self-restraint nor wisdom. In the choice of presidential electors in 1796, after Washington had declined to allow himself to be elected for a third term, they picked John Adams as the candidate whom they desired their electors to support. The Democrats centered on Thomas Jefferson without dispute, but could not elect him. The wave of Jeffersonian Democracy was rising, but so long as the monolithic character of Washington remained in public life, it could not hope to win. Some Democrats talked as though he aimed at kingship. Even Jefferson hinted at the danger of monarchy, but he was too intelligent an observer to believe the truth of the inference he spread. The repute of Washington was fixed. His steadiness and courage and his slow honesty were beyond serious question. His prestige carried the Federalists into another presidential term, with Adams in office. But from his residence at Mount Vernon, where he died in 1799, he could not give them breadth of vision. When the X Y Z dispatches were spread and they gained their respite in office, they passed laws to punish their political critics and opponents. When they provided for the possible deportation of aliens, they had in mind men like Gallatin and Philip Freneau, whom Jefferson had patronized; and they enacted the naturalization law in the same resentful spirit. In the Sedition

Law of 1798 they struck at the virulent opposition editors whose manners and fluency had kept the Federalists restive for the last five years. Political vituperation was a finished art in the eighteenth century, and the Jeffersonian Democrats heaped ridicule and insult upon the conservatives, attacking their morals, their intelligence, and their patriotism. The laws they passed were obviously in contravention of the Constitution or its amendments, which had aimed at securing freedom of speech and of the press; but the rage of Federalists was blinding upon them. In the summer of 1798 Jefferson was again at his desk pointing out to his friends how unconstitutional the repressive laws were and raising the question whether such laws could not be nullified by the refusal of the States to let them be enforced.

Most leaders of thought in the United States would perhaps have agreed with Jefferson that the Federal Government was yet an experiment and that a break-up was within the realm of possibility. He was not anxious to break the Union down when he suggested State action similar to nullification to his friends; he was only a politician taking advantage of the indiscretion of an Administration. But he was playing with high explosives in suggesting a remedy for unconstitutional law outside the courts or Congress. In the autumn of 1798 his aids, keeping his prompting secret, brought up in Virginia and Kentucky two sets of memorable resolutions dealing with the relative powers of State and Federal Governments. These were supported as party manifestoes by men who had no thought of more than party action; and in finished form they were transmitted to the several States inviting their coöperation in ridding the United States of the obnoxious laws.[3] Rebuffed by such States as chose to discuss the matter at all, Kentucky returned in 1799 to the argument and expressed a belief in nullification by the States as a possible remedy against usurpation. That men could still say this in 1799 gives special emphasis to the importance of the two Administrations of George Washington in carrying the Constitution from an atmosphere of frank experiment to one of stable expectation and in erecting a Government whose law could be "the supreme law of the land." For Jefferson, the Federalist mistakes and the Virginia and Kentucky manifestoes were the last steps in the organization of a victorious party.

[3] E. D. Warfield, *Kentucky Resolutions of 1798* (1887); Frank M. Anderson, "Contemporary Opinion on the Virginia and Kentucky Resolutions," in *American Historical Review*, vol. v.

In 1800 Thomas Jefferson received seventy-three electoral votes for President, against sixty-five for John Adams, and was inducted into the office after the House of Representatives had disposed of a dispute within the Democratic party over which Democrat, himself or Burr, was really chosen. The claim of Aaron Burr, decided against him, and giving evidence of a tough and unresponsive political conscience, became within a few years the motive force for an episode that reveals the West as it was in 1806. For the present it was enough that in 1800 the new party of the West, inspired by its equalitarian environment and skillfully led by a statesman of political genius, had gained enough momentum to break down in their old age the party of the men who had been leaders in the American Revolution. The perennial suspicion of youth for age was reinforced by liberal ideas against conservatism, and by the uniformity of a frontier section against the more diversified older part.

CHAPTER XIII

THE FRONTIER OF 1800

THIRTY-SEVEN years after the British Government placed a limit to western expansion at the watershed of the Appalachians, the people of the colonies had grown in number from perhaps 1,600,000 to 5,300,000, and in the region then closed to their entry nearly a million settlers had taken up their homes and built a new civilization. In 1800 this border area produced the party of Jefferson that took possession of the Federal Government. Even Americans were not prepared in their minds for the sudden shift of political power. The English bewilderment and dismay at the loss of the American colonies was fully paralleled by eastern discouragement at the victory of the Republicans. All along the seaboard, persons of position were irritated at the control by a new democracy. The resentment was keenest east of the Hudson, and here the unwillingness to endure it was most nearly uniform. There were Democratic-Republicans everywhere, for everywhere there were young voters, men without property, and farmers struggling under the burden of their debt. But the sectional distribution of interests and the uniformity of the West behind the leadership of Jefferson are so manifest that the year 1800 becomes the dividing point between two chapters of political history. The background of popular movements for the next two decades is to be found along the frontier revealed by the census of 1800. Not only its political theory and party practice, but its numerical strength, social and religious habits, and changing relation to the eternal problem of its land, are needed to show it as it was.[1]

In the ten years after the first census of 1790, the population of the United States increased about thirty-five per cent, from 3,900,000 to 5,300,000.[2] The increase would have been great

[1] Henry Adams, *History of the United States*, vol. I, opens with a brilliant and permanent picture of American society in 1801. His interpretations, as might be expected of a great-grandson of John Adams, do not always give Thomas Jefferson the benefit of the doubt. Historians are still struggling against the northern tide-water point of view which Richard Hildreth established in *The History of the United States of America* (1849–1856), in counterblast to the writings of George Bancroft. Adams was of the Hildreth tradition, and Channing in our day keeps it alive, all with great learning and complete sincerity.

[2] W. S. Rossiter, *A Century of Population Growth from the First Census of the United States to the Twelfth, 1790–1900* (1909), is a useful publication of the Bureau of the Census, with many maps and diagrams, but without the invaluable shaded population maps.

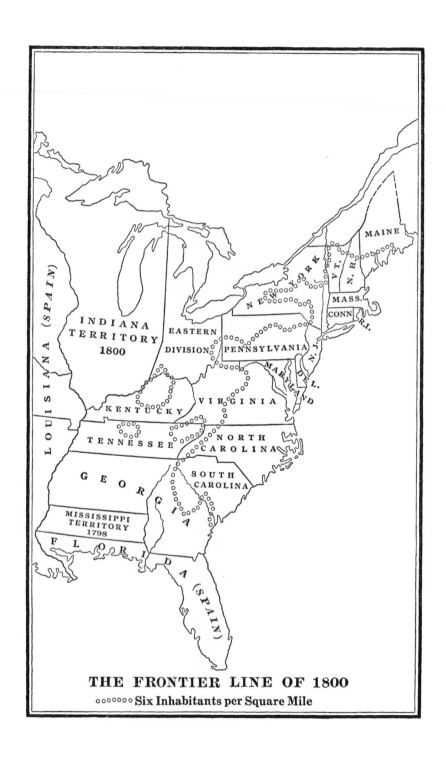

THE FRONTIER LINE OF 1800

○○○○○○○ Six Inhabitants per Square Mile

enough to disarrange relationships under any condition; it was the more notable because it came almost exclusively from excess of births over deaths. There was so little immigration that it may be ignored. The Americans of 1800 were American born of American parents, and had ceased to be conscious of even cultural association with outside sources, while the idea of a hyphenated nationality was not yet conceived. The non-English strains, except the Scotch-Irish, were disappearing as the prevalence of migratory habits, and the English language widened; or else were restricted and walled-off by the foreign language that they spoke. The German groups in Pennsylvania, and in parts of the mountain valleys, preferred to live a life apart. As individual members of their race acquired influence they appeared in history as Americans, with little beyond the German family name to distinguish them from their fellow citizens.

The frontier line of over six inhabitants to the square mile, in 1800, runs winding but unbroken from Lake Champlain to the Atlantic Ocean, a little south of the mouth of the Savannah River. Three marked protuberances westward from the general line of the watershed are in middle New York, where the Mohawk region was flourishing, in the upper Ohio Valley where a great colony covered the borders of Pennsylvania, Virginia, and the Northwest Territory, and in the upland country of Georgia, where travelers along the Falls Line trails crossed the Savannah at Augusta and were pushing into the future cotton country. West of the solid line were three great detached island tracts, indicated respectively by the Blue Grass of Kentucky, the valleys of East Tennessee, and the Cumberland district of Middle Tennessee. The other isolated settlements of even trifling density were small and unimportant, but in scattered clearings there were beginnings of civilized life over all the vast wedge of land that projects itself west from the mountains, between southern Indiana and northern Alabama, to the junction of the Ohio and the Mississippi. A rural economy prevailed over all the West even more markedly than elsewhere in the Union. Lexington boasted 1797 inhabitants, and Frankfort 628; Nashville reported 355, and Cincinnati 500; while Pittsburgh with but 1565 had not yet realized its future place at the head of the Ohio commercial area.

The social life of the frontier was as generally shaped by the factor of separation as was the political, and the more so on this transmontane border which the mountains cut off from their social base. The rough and winding paths through the mountain gaps forced the average migrant to abandon hope of quick return. The separation that induced self-reliance in government forced the pioneer to make his own furniture, build his own houses out of local materials, and get along with what his environment could supply him. The trails leading to the East were worse rather than better in 1800, for they had been heavily traveled without improvement. Where there were deep streams, private speculators conducted private ferries at extortionate rates. Elsewhere the rows of more or less parallel ruts that passed for roads forbade any traveler but the rider on horseback to make much progress. Wheeled vehicles for pleasure were hardly known, and the heavy farm wagons were moved only with disproportionate waste of strength. The leveling influence of frontier economy kept the well-to-do and the poor alike well fed but rough, in a world of simplicity.

Here and there, in the older parts of Kentucky and Tennessee, there was a house of stone or brick. Residences of sawed lumber were so rare as to attract attention. At Steubenville in 1807 a traveler counted one hundred and sixty houses — including a "gaol of hewn stone," a courthouse of squared logs, and a brick Presbyterian church. The typical home was the cabin built of logs, and limited by the shape of the material to small rooms, low ceilings, and single stories. In the cabin attic, reached by a ladder of saplings and restricted by the slope of a leaky roof, were pallets, and rough beds of log frame with rope or rawhide bottoms. The location of the home was generally determined by some natural spring, and the water that was carried for domestic use was heated in a swinging pot over an open fire, in a great fireplace. There were few artisans in the migration to the West, and the furniture proved it. What the axe, maul, and wedge could not produce was lacking from the ordinary home. Nails were too rare for common use, and wooden pegs did service for them. Mortar and plaster were beyond the domestic architect, but mud could and did stop the chinks between the logs.

By 1800 the external aspect of the landscape was changing, with the extension of cleared fields, and the gradual rebuilding of cabins over the older areas. But inside the cabins the family life still embraced the whole range of domestic manufactures. The frontier graveyards show how hard the early life was on the women of the family. The patriarch laid to rest in his family tract, beside two, three, or four wives who had preceded him, is much more common than the hardy woman who outlived her husbands. The housewife came to her new home young and raw, and found for neighbors other girls as inexperienced. She bore the children; and buried a staggering number of them, for medicine and sanitation, inadequate everywhere, were out of reach for the cabin on the border. She fed her men and raised her children, cooked their food and laid it by for winter. She was at once butcher, packer, and baker. The family clothes showed her craftsmanship, with skins playing a large part, and homespun or knitting revealing a luxury established. When one adds to the grinding and unavoidable labor, the anguish that came from sickness and danger, the frontier woman who survived becomes an heroic character, and the children who felt her touch become the proper material from which to choose the heroes of a nation.

The loneliness of frontier life made a craving for companionship that gives peculiar character to its religion, politics, and play. Nearly every traveler, whose journey took him to the region, noticed this trait and described the group activities that lightened it. The frontier social life may be said to have its beginning at the log-raising that attended the construction of the cabin. The single axman could cut his trees, and notch them, but he lacked appliances or strength to lay the logs in place. When the timbers were ready the neighbors of the countryside would ride in on horseback, from thirty or forty miles away. With wives on pillion and infants in arms they came; for where one went it was easiest for all to go. They made a picnic of the occasion, and the able-bodied men in a few hours, too few to spoil the play, piled up the logs and laid the roof. The frontier welcomed the legitimate excuse for such a gathering. Weddings became boisterous and rude, with home-stilled whiskey in an open tub, a drinking gourd at its side. Funerals lost something of their solemnity when relatives and friends so manifestly welcomed the opportunity to get together. The occasions came infrequently, but when they came there were stores of pent-up loneliness to be relieved. In politics and in religion, there was a formative condition in this fact that every gathering was a neighborhood festivity and that teaching and argument must be phrased in the language of excitement to meet the need of loneliness.

The habit of church-going, that was established in the middle and northern colonies, found little chance to indulge itself upon the border. There was neither church nor parson; nor funds to maintain them until after some years of successful farming. The occasional preacher found a flock awaiting him, regardless of creed; and willing to listen if he could speak its language. The generality of the congregation, got together for sporadic meetings, made narrow doctrinal sermons less available than humanitarian exhortations fitted to the Ten Commandments.

Since the dominant racial strains that filled the valleys west of the Susquehanna and that poured thence into Kentucky and Tennessee were Scotch-Irish, it was natural that the Presbyterian church had more adherents than any other on the border in the eighteenth century. This faith made a strong entry into America early in the century. As early as 1717 there was a synod at Philadelphia, and thereafter the church had a continuous organic existence. In 1802, David Rice and thirty-seven ministers founded a synod in Kentucky and claimed as their domain all the country west of the mountains. There can be little doubt that this Presbyterian predisposition had much to do with the border aptitude for self-government and federation. Within the Presbyterian churches self-government took root early and became ineradicable. The federal position of the synod made the members of the church ready to look on central government as the creature of the people rather than their master. A large proportion of the leaders of the Jeffersonian Democracy were pious members of Presbyterian congregations.

Behind the Presbyterians, but in the making, were the Methodist and Baptist churches. The last were well suited to frontier habits, but were less important in 1800 than those of the Methodist Episcopal faith, whose bishop, Francis Asbury, had led them without rival since his ordination in 1784. The evangelical zeal of the Methodists fitted them well for work upon the frontier, but they had first to overcome the long start that Presbyterians had acquired. Every year, however, helped them. The older Presbyterian congregations were firm in their desire for a learned clergy and possessed a religion with a tough intellectual content. In the United States there were few colleges that could fit men for the Presbyterian pulpit, and of the ministers who immigrated from England and Scotland, not many were allowed to go as far west as the border. The college at Princeton owed its foundation to the desire for more trained men of this faith. But when the church procured the men, it found that the frontier type of mind, craving companionship and warmth rather than close-reasoned theology, did not furnish the best field for their activity.

The Methodists and Baptists laid less stress on a learned clergy, and more on the power of exhortation. The rough and ready circuit rider was a natural democrat, with a message for every sinner.[3] Occasionally as he preached the burden of sin and the need for salvation, some preacher set the frontier ablaze with the fire of religious enthusiasm and started revivals that spread far from the scene of immediate origin. Among the meetings in the Kentucky settlements, as early as 1798, preaching is reported to have had unusual effects. Public conversion and confession of experiences became common. The meetings were marked by excesses of emotion, by jumpings and barkings of the conscious sinners, who often fell upon the floors exhausted in stupor, after their exaltation. The forms that mass religion may take in an untaught community, hungry for contacts, may be observed here. In August, 1801, at a camp meeting held at Cain Ridge in Kentucky, there were six continuous days of sustained religious enthusiasm, and contemporary accounts relate that as many as twenty thousand persons were in attendance. The revival of 1801 spread from this beginning until in a few months the whole border was stirred up over the deadly consequence of sin quite as completely as it had just been over the evil tendencies of the Federalist party. The religious revival and democratic partisanship seem to be different aspects of the same capacity of the frontier. They operated at the expense of intellectual religion and constructive statesmanship; but for nearly fifty years the religion, politics, and trade of the Mississippi Valley continue to show their impress.

Under these influences, and with educational opportunity limited, the Presbyterian church lost in relative standing after 1800. Not only the Methodist and Baptist congregations grew in number and strength, but within the Presbyterians there were democratic stirrings, to make the church more responsive to the frontier. Unable to change the whole, these movements became schismatic. The Cumberland Presbyterians were off on an independent course by 1810; the Christian Church followed a little later. The frontier continued for several decades to provide fol-

[3] Lorenzo Dow was among the most noted of these, *History of Cosmopolite: or, the Writings of Rev. Lorenzo Dow: Containing his Experience and Travels, in Europe and America, up to near his fiftieth Year. Also his Polemic Writings, to which is added the 'Journey of Life,'* by Peggy Dow. *Revised and corrected with Notes* (5th ed., 1857). Catharine C. Cleveland, *The Great Revival in the West, 1797–1805* (1916), ranks high among our histories of religion.

lowers for any teacher who proclaimed a new Gospel or interpreted an old one in a language comprehensible to its spirit. The old ties were broken, the eternal needs of the human soul continued to prevail, but the common experiences of religion needed to be restated in terms of frontier life.

The year 1800 witnessed many changes in American relationships, in the course of which the newer communities gained points of vantage for influencing the nation. Their spiritual upheaval brought religious organization into closer harmony with their habits of life; their political power brought their chosen leader into the chief office of the United States; their demands in a Congress that was listening with interest to their call procured a revision of the basic law that governed their access to the land.

Whatever social, religious, or political aspect they assumed, the early stages of their growth were dominated by the underlying structure of institutions arising from the land and its acquisition.

The ordinances passed in 1785 and 1787 sketched the outlines of the land system and the colonial system, so far as the States of the public domain are concerned. Before the century ended their administration had progressed far enough to reveal the character of the structure of which they were a part. In a colonial way, the Northwest Territory was running a bumpy course, amid Indian controversy and party faction. The Territory south of the Ohio lasted only until 1796, when it became the State of Tennessee. Then it passed into abeyance, for the detached strip which the United States claimed, south of the Georgia lands, was in actual possession of the Spanish outposts. Not until 1798 did these authorities, reluctantly and after every excuse for delay had been tried, surrender to the United States the country between the thirty-first parallel and the Yazoo line. The Territory of Mississippi was created in the same year to take over all American soil southwest of Georgia, and to receive a few years later the lands beyond the Chattahoochee when Georgia was at last ready to give them up.

Only a beginning of the administration of the land system by Congress had taken place before 1800. The rule of survey was permanently established, and every year men were in the field marking the corners of townships, and running the range and base lines. But the weight of the emigration went to lands in private hands.[4]   Kentucky and Tennessee and the Ohio end of Virginia,

---

[4] Catharine Van Cortlandt Mathews, *Andrew Ellicott, his Life and Letters* (1908), deals with the career of one of the most successful surveyors.

that has become the State of West Virginia, and the western end of Pennsylvania, contained so much available farm land that the exploitation of the Northwest languished. Even here the private lands were on the market earliest, outside the limited area of the Seven Ranges, that came on the market shortly after 1785. The Ohio Associates had land for sale, and Symmes in the hinterland of Cincinnati, and the Connecticut Land Company in its Western Reserve, and in the Scioto Valley every settler had Virginia scrip to sell. There was little pressure upon Congress to increase the area of its surveys as yet, and few buyers offered themselves after the first purchases.

Under the system of private sale of large tracts by Congress, there were only three transactions before the laws received their first revision in 1796. The Ohio Associates, Symmes, and the State of Pennsylvania were the three original purchasers of wholesale tracts. The first of these procured a right to buy five million acres, but was able to finance the purchase of only 822,900 acres. It is a matter of satisfaction that the Scioto Associates, whose greed held up for a time the legitimate proposal of Putnam and his colleagues, were a failure from the start and never bought an acre of the 4,900,000 included under their option. When they finally bought land to take care of the deluded French immigrants, they bought not under their option from Congress, but of the Ohio Associates. The contract of John Cleves Symmes, concluded at the same time, was only partially fulfilled. According to Donaldson, whose *Public Domain* is the standard quarry from which to extract figures relating to the lands, Symmes finally closed his deal after taking 248,540 acres. The State of Pennsylvania took nearly as much, 202,187 acres, when it bought a remnant of New York lands in order to procure a frontage for itself on Lake Erie.

The Pennsylvania "triangle" as it appears on the modern map was the result of the land cessions and compromises. When New York and Massachusetts resolved their dispute, they both abandoned to Congress the territory south of Lake Erie and west of the meridian drawn from the tip of Lake Ontario. As the surveys revealed it, for the fact was hardly suspected when the grant was made, this line cut the Pennsylvania boundary about forty miles east of the northwest corner of that State. The purchase was concluded in 1792, under an act authorizing it, passed four years before.

In the summer of 1790, at the request of the House of Representatives, Hamilton made a report upon the status of the public lands and their disposition. He discussed the two views of the domain that were already visible; the desire to sell in large tracts as a means of raising revenue, and the need of the local inhabitant, or future immigrant, to be able to buy what he could cultivate. Hamilton proposed that both purposes should be served, that a General Land Office be erected at the seat of Government, with local offices in the vicinity of the lands themselves, and that purchases be allowed ranging from one hundred acres to an individual farmer, to a township of one hundred square miles to the wholesale buyer. The inactivity of the system under the law of 1785 is revealed by the fact that Hamilton makes no mention of the six-mile township then established. It was over twenty years before Congress created the General Land Office he advised, and it paid no attention to his recommendation that the size of the unit be changed. In 1796 it passed a general law for the survey and sale of Ohio lands, adhering to the rule that Indian cession and survey must precede occupation, but admitting the plan of local administration of the sales. The smallest unit that could be bought was one section of six hundred and forty acres. Under this law 121,540 acres were sold by 1800, making at that time the total sale of lands for the benefit of the United States, 1,484,047 acres.

The considerable occupation of parts of the public domain begins after the Treaty of Greenville, and the quieting of the Indian threat against the households of the Northwest Territory. Thus far in the history of the public domain no one had made a source of revenue out of it. The fair hopes that Congress expressed in 1780 had failed so far as using the trust fund to reduce the Revolutionary debt was concerned. The large buyer had not been successful; the small buyer had no chance, for the unit of six hundred and forty acres was beyond his means. The terms of sale, laid down in 1796, allowed a credit of one year on half the purchase price of two dollars an acre. It was a rare local resident who had six hundred and forty dollars ready when he took up his land and could procure another six hundred and forty dollars to complete the transaction within a year. He was fortunate if after a year he had food for his family and stock and had escaped the perils of disease and accident.

There was no voice in Congress from the public land area to express the defects of the law of 1796 until after 1799. The southern territory had lapsed; the Northwest was in the first territorial stage with a governor and judges, but no self-government. In 1799 St. Clair found his population so large that an elected assembly was necessary. One of the first acts of this body was to select the delegate to Congress that the Constitution allows, and William Henry Harrison was the choice.

William Henry Harrison is a fair specimen of the Virginia strain that made that State the mother of western commonwealths. He was born in 1773, on a tide-water plantation on the lower James River in Virginia; and was son of a father who sat in the first Continental Congress and signed the Declaration of Independence. At the age of nineteen he was in the army of the United States, and at twenty-one he served under Wayne at Fallen Timbers. In 1798 he received a minor post in the employ of the Northwest Territory, and the following year the first territorial assembly elected him to Congress. He knew both the country opened by Wayne's victory and the point of view of the Virginia and Kentucky frontiersmen. In Congress he became the first spokesman from the public domain. He demanded a law for the farmer and secured its passage.

The land law espoused by Harrison was signed May 10, 1800, and, says McMaster, "did far more for the good of his country than his great victory over the Prophet at Tippecanoe, or his defeat of Tecumseh at the battle of the Thames." For the next forty years the personality of Harrison was an embodiment of the western spirit. For twenty of them every farmer who took up a residence on the public lands came beneath his influence. It was provided in the new law that the lands should be sold locally, in tracts of half-sections, or three hundred and twenty acres. At Cincinnati, Chillicothe, Marietta, and Steubenville, land offices were to be opened with registers in charge. For the term of three weeks the tracts were to be offered at auction to the highest bidder; after this time they were to be sold at private sale at two dollars an acre, on a credit extending to four years or more. The terms of the law required that the purchaser should pay the survey fee (six dollars per section) and deposit ten cents an acre when he filed his claim. The balance of the purchase price was spread in installments over four years; one quarter within forty days, a second fourth within two years, and the balance at the end of the third and fourth years after the contract. There were discounts for cash, and interest on the unpaid balances, but the substantial fact remains that under the Harrison Law, the United States became the partner of every settler who wished to try his luck upon the public domain, required him to put up only fifty cents an acre in advance and took its chance with him as to the success or failure of the enterprise. In four years, if successful, the settler expected to earn his farm out of its produce. Whether it was a good system for the country, or a vicious inducement to speculation and evasion of obligations, remained to be seen as the law directed the flow of settlers into Ohio, Indiana, Illinois, Alabama, Mississippi, Louisiana, and Missouri. It opens a fresh chapter in settlement, coincident with the other new chapters of 1800.

CHAPTER XIV

OHIO: THE CLASH OF PRINCIPLES

While the legislature of Kentucky, under the master hand of Jefferson, was avowing that the United States "are not united on the principle of unlimited submission to their general government," and was bringing to a focus the personal antipathies and sectional points of view that had arisen under the Federalist régime, the great and undenied principle that it asserted was receiving a concrete embodiment north of the Ohio, in the Northwest Territory. Here, for ten years, General Arthur St. Clair had governed as viceroy of Congress. That he was called governor instead of viceroy failed to hide the fact of autocratic control. In the scheme of things embraced in the Ordinance of 1787 there was no place for popular influence in territorial government during the first phase of the latter; and St. Clair belonged to the age and school that tended to distrust the popular influence in any form. By law and by temperament he represented the distasteful idea of "unlimited submission"; but his reign came to an end when the growth of numbers among his subjects entitled them in 1798 to elect members for a general assembly. In the meetings of this body in 1799 there was revealed the distance that the frontier had traveled since the Revolution. In Kentucky the constitution of 1792 was already outworn and replaced by a more generous basic law in this same year.

Even if there had not been a growth of national parties, there would still have developed many grounds for controversy in the Northwest Territory under St. Clair. The various little groups that planted themselves along the Ohio wanted to push into the interior faster than the Indians receded. The outlying districts were ever in danger of destruction and massacre, and the government never had at its disposal a force capable of policing the border. The wars of the early nineties were only aggravations of the situation until Wayne secured a victory. And it was but natural that the people should hold St. Clair responsible for the inconveniences they suffered.[1]

[1] Emilius O. Randall and Daniel J. Ryan, *History of Ohio* (1912), enlarges upon and replaces Rufus King, *Ohio: First Fruits of the Ordinance of 1787* (1888).

There was the constant factor of life under control, a situation annoying to Americans wherever they have found it. For over a decade they were thus suppressed, and in every section of the territory there was discontent. The criticism gained leadership and focus from the settlements in the Scioto Valley, where there were the special unities that came from a common Kentucky-Virginia origin and the Virginia land warrants with which they bought their land. Chillicothe was the very center of this, and a forceful personality showed itself in one Dr. Edward Tiffin, their leader. As Jeffersonian democracy gained within the States, the Jeffersonians here became ambitious for a new State dominated by his doctrines, and waited impatiently the time when it could be cut away from the Northwest. The first meeting of the legislature in 1799 started the movement that hereafter gained in speed and weight until it was successful.

The procedure of getting self-government under way was defined by the Ordinance. In December, 1798, representatives were chosen for the legislature, at the rate of one for each five hundred free male inhabitants in the population. These convened on call of St. Clair at Cincinnati, in February, 1799, to complete the work by nominating the members of council. They elected ten "residents of the district," each possessed of a "freehold in five hundred acres of land"; and from this list, the President of the United States caused the selection of five, to constitute the council of the territory. In September, 1799, the whole legislature met at Cincinnati, already indignant at the fact that St. Clair had of his own will determined their place of meeting. That he had presumed to provide a seal for the territory without consulting the will of the people added fuel to the flames. The session was one of denunciation and dispute. When it was over, St. Clair made the breach between himself and the Jeffersonians complete by vetoing every important statute that the territorial legislature had enacted.

With the beginning of self-government, came also the first step in federal relations. The territory was entitled to a delegate to sit in Washington. St. Clair desired the post for himself, but was beaten by Harrison, who proceeded to Philadelphia to sit in the last session held by Congress in that capital. Before the session ended and Congress packed up to move the seat of Government to Washington in the summer of 1800, two significant laws had been enacted upon Harrison's leadership. One, on May 10, laid the foundation for twenty years of land administration; the other, on May 7, divided the Northwest Territory and created the Territory of Indiana from its western half. Early in 1801, Harrison was back in Indiana, as its first governor, while his former fellow citizens were at work at statehood.

The division of the Northwest Territory was a concrete issue upon which the factions could express their views. Underneath the discussion lay the motive of Federalists, who feared that the new State would be Jeffersonian, and therefore urged such a division as would long defer its admission. St. Clair advocated the Scioto River as the western boundary of the projected State, and his friends advanced arguments against unwieldly extent for any State. The solemn agreement in the Ordinance of 1787 that the line of division should be the mouth of the Great Miami, weighed little with the men who saw in statehood a means of advancing or retarding party power. It had as little weight with Jeffersonians, who wished as soon as possible to get the requisite sixty thousand population in order to qualify for admission. They wanted generous boundaries, to get it the more quickly. The line of the Great Miami was a little too far east for them, because the drift of settlement had carried the population somewhat below Cincinnati, on the Ohio. The Miami region lay in a semi circle, with Cincinnati as its center; if the boundary started at the Miami mouth, it would not only cut off the people living further west, but would deprive the new State of needed numbers. They had the votes to prevent any reduction of the State. The eastern boundary of Indiana, as sketched in the division act of May 7, 1800, was a line starting on the Ohio opposite the mouth of the Kentucky River (and leaving the whole Miami settlement to its east). The boundary ran thence somewhat east of north to the post that Wayne had built in 1793, and named Fort Recovery; thence it ran north to the Canadian line.

The Eastern Division of the Northwest Territory was started towards statehood by this partition. It was not yet called Ohio, and it still embraced the settlements around Detroit, later to become Michigan. But St. Clair's dominance was over, even though he was allowed to linger in his post as governor for more than a year after Jefferson became President of the United States. Congress was listening to the radical population, and this element was drawing the lines of successful partisanship. To the special humiliation of St. Clair, the seat of government for the Eastern Division was shifted from Cincinnati, where his friends were most numerous, to Chillicothe, where he was a lonely and discarded figure.

In the two years after the division, the drift of settlement removed the necessity to worry over aggregate population. All the river towns became ports of arrival and centers of distribution for the interior. Nearly every town dreamed dreams of future greatness as a western metropolis, on the common border of East and West, with the surrounding country lying in economic dependence upon it. Wheeling, next to Pittsburgh, became the gateway, though neither of these towns lay in the Northwest Territory. From Wheeling, Ebenezer Zane had marked his southwest trace after 1796; and along Zane's Trace arose the first group of interior landlocked settlements. The land already on sale under the old grants of Congress became inadequate, and entries poured in upon the new land offices, opened under Harrison's law of 1800. It was an incentive that Congress under this law became a three-fourths partner in every venture. When in 1802 Congress took the next step, and authorized the Eastern Division to become a State, it was safe and convenient to draw in the western boundary, from the temporary line of the Kentucky River to the one originally designated in 1787: the meridian of the mouth of the Great Miami.

In no new State ahead of Ohio had it been possible for Congress to imagine that it was the real parent, with a controlling hand upon the acts of the people. Vermont, Kentucky, and Tennessee had made constitutions at their own convenience, and Congress had only had to name the day at which the fact of participation in the Union should begin. But in Ohio it was different, with the parentage of Congress completely established, and with a national administration desirous of shaping the result. On April 30, 1802, the people of the Eastern Division were authorized, or "enabled" by law to hold a convention, frame a constitution, and become a State. For more than a century thereafter Congress made a general practice of passing enabling acts when in its judgment a territory was ripe for statehood, and these laws became convenient places for the expression of opinion as to the character of government that the new State should assume. Once in the Union, the State was a free agent as to its internal organization, so long as it refrained from violating the Federal Constitution or laws of Congress, and maintained a republican form of government. But it could not get into the Union without the consent of Congress and the power to withhold this consent gave leverage to Congress in its demands upon the new States. A few of the later States made constitutions without enabling acts, but Congress always held such conduct against them.

Under the Enabling Act, the convention sat at Chillicothe in the month of November, 1802. Its meeting rang the knell of St. Clair's power. The convention was in the hands of his party enemies and proceeded to its work without any recognition of his existence. He resented this, demanded a hearing before the body, and indulged himself in a partisan attack upon the Enabling Act and the President of the United States. Upon receipt of a copy of the speech, Jefferson dismissed him from office, not as a Federalist but as a disloyal subordinate, and St. Clair lost the satisfaction of carrying to fulfillment the colonial venture over which he had presided from the start. The Virginia democracy finished what New England soldiers began.

The constitution of Ohio reflected in its articles not only the common experience of the men of the frontier, but the special hatred of autocratic power that had been created in the Northwest during the territorial period. Its outstanding spirit is that of distrust of executive government. There was as yet no recognition of the view that Andrew Jackson was later to acclimate in the West, that the executive could be strengthened if only he could be depended upon. Perhaps the greatest single difference between the democracy of Jefferson and that of Jackson was to turn on this; Jefferson revolted at government itself, while Jackson revolted at government by those whom he believed to be unfaithful and aristocratic. In 1802 the dislike of St. Clair was still too powerful for democrats to admit that any governor could be trusted. Accordingly the convention sheared away his power. The Ohio governor was given no veto, and no appointing power. He was merely an executive subordinate to the legislature, with a salary that the constitution limited, for the present, to a maximum of one thousand dollars a year.

The courts of the new State included justices of the peace, courts of common pleas, a supreme court, and such other courts as the legislature might desire to create. The supreme justices, like the governor, give a measure to the distance that the Ohio frontier had traveled from colonial precedents. They were to be appointed not by the executive for life, which was and remains the practice of English law, but by joint ballot of the two houses of the legislature, to "hold their office for the term of seven years, if so

long they behave well." Like other civil officers they were re-
movable by impeachment and conviction.

In the legislature, the supreme power of the democratic people
found its expression. The apportionment was based on the white
male population over twenty-one, which of itself gave an advantage to the newer regions where young men predominated, and
women and children were less numerous than in the older settlements. The franchise was granted to the same group, if only they
"have paid, or are charged with, a State or county tax." Those of
them who were of military age and so subject to duty, constituted
the militia of the State; and their officers, including the grade
of brigadier-general, were elected by the men whom they commanded. The statement of the "general, great, and essential
principles of liberty and free government," that takes up nearly a
third of the length of the constitution, begins with the harmonious
note that "all men are born equally free and independent."

In less than a month the convention at Chillicothe reduced to
writing a statement of basic principles and rules of government
that lasted until 1851 without revision. When the draft was
finished, the men who made it proclaimed it the constitution, to be
effective when the laws of the territory should cease. They not
only felt free to perform the final act of ratification themselves,
but they begged the assent of Congress to a boundary more generous than the Enabling Act authorized, and in violation of the
Ordinance of 1787.

The boundaries of Ohio, as fixed in the Enabling Act, were those
of the Ordinance, with a western line drawn through the mouth of
the Great Miami, and a northern line through the southern tip of
Lake Michigan. In the Ohio convention objection was made to
this because of the topographic uncertainty as to the location of
the south shore of Lake Erie. Men who had hunted in the north
suggested that the northern line of the Enabling Act might easily
run south of Lake Erie, and so separate Ohio from a lake frontage.
It was accordingly provided that if the Enabling Act line should
strike Lake Erie east of the Maumee River, or should miss it entirely, the northern boundary should, "with the assent of the Congress" be a line drawn from the southern tip of Lake Michigan to
the "most northerly cape" of the bay at the mouth of the Maumee
where Toledo now stands.

Congress failed to give the desired assent for a matter of thirty-
five years, but it recognized Ohio as a State in the Union by act of

February 19, 1803, in which it paid no attention to the suggested boundary change. The new State maintained that silence gave assent and eventually carried its point, after a vigorous controversy with its northern neighbor, Michigan, that struggled against the nibbling process at its southeast corner.

First of the public domain States and first to be nursed by Congress through all the stages of development, Ohio received from the United States the first of the land endowments that have since characterized the American colonial policy. The Ordinance of 1787 contained generous words for the encouragement of education. In the Enabling Act, section sixteen of every township of the public lands was granted "to the inhabitants of such township, for the use of schools." It was, in addition, provided that certain salt springs should be given to the State, and that five per cent of net proceeds of the sale of lands in Ohio should "be applied to the laying out and making public roads" in Ohio, and thence to the "navigable waters emptying into the Atlantic." In return for these grants the State agreed to leave tax-free for five years every parcel of land sold within its limits by the United States.

The new State government took hold in Ohio in March, 1803, with Edward Tiffin as the first governor. Among the earliest acts of its legislature was one incorporating the Miami Exporting Company, which became the first Ohio bank, and was expected to provide a paper money and advance the trade of the people with New Orleans and the outside world. At the moment of the act there was still uncertainty whether this outlet down the great river was to remain in hostile hands or to become American. It had just become known beyond doubt that Napoleon Bonaparte had acquired it, and that the local authorities had abolished the American right of deposit in New Orleans. Jefferson had just sent James Monroe as special envoy to France to try to buy a part of Louisiana, and he knew as well as did the men of the West that if the free use of the Mississippi should cease the Union would fall apart. That the first public land State should not be the last, depended in great measure upon his success in procuring an enlargement of the United States.

CHAPTER XV
THE PURCHASE OF LOUISIANA

THE leader of a rising opposition party nearly always finds a dilemma before him when the turn of the tide places him in the position of power and responsibility. In opposition it is safe to attack whatever the administration may do, and there is no means of testing the soundness of the criticism. In office, affairs look different. The theorist must test his capacity for the practical. Thomas Jefferson had no more than taken his oath of office in 1801 than there arose to haunt him his beloved France in the guise of a barrier to American unity and peace, and his own teachings upon the meaning of the Constitution as an inspiration to frontier self-determination.

The background of this new crisis was one of rosy hope for peace and growth. The new land act, and the final stages in the development of Ohio, were promises of sympathetic rule of the frontier regions. The surplus crops of the West were finding their way to a market. From the farm where they were grown, which was often on a stream navigable to light craft in early spring, the cargoes of wheat and corn, meal and flour, pork, bacon, and whiskey, found their way to the broad waters of the Ohio and Mississippi. In flatboats and barges, manned by local talent at the sweeps, they were floated south. In the long trip, drifting by day, and tied to some convenient shore at night, the farmer boatmen had time to gossip over the trade in which they ventured. The Mississippi dominated not their whole lives but their balance of profit. Before 1795, when Pinckney signed his Spanish treaty, the cruise to Natchez or New Orleans had been full of risk. The temper of Spanish officers was mercurial. It was always possible that they would enforce the law, which meant confiscation of cargo, and perhaps imprisonment. Whether they would succumb to bribery, and permit the speculator to share his profits with them, was uncertain until it was too late to give up the voyage. But after 1795 the right of deposit at New Orleans made the trade safe, and tempted its increase. The privilege was for three years, but at its expiration in 1798 the authorities took no step to reëstablish the former order; and the wars in Europe made a strong market that welcomed at

New Orleans the up-river crops. Natchez had meanwhile become the chief named place in Mississippi Territory, and the southwest corner of American power.

There was peace with France when Jefferson took office. The vexatious war of 1798 was over. The breach occasioned by the rapacity of the Directorate was healed by the overture of Napoleon, who invited John Adams to send him new commissioners. In a convention signed September 30, 1800, peace was established and indemnity was promised to those who had suffered at French hands. No foreign situation was more repugnant to Jefferson than hostility with France, save possibly an alliance with England which such hostility might engender. But he had been in office only a few months when the rumor leaked out, and would not down, that on the day after the convention with the United States was signed Napoleon had signed another with Spain that made it useless. To formal inquiry as to the existence of this other treaty, Napoleon blandly lied. But it was true that at San Ildefonso, on October 1, Spain had retroceded to France the Province of Louisiana that she had received from Louis XV in 1763. Napoleon had pledged himself here, never to alienate Louisiana to another power, and was forming visions of a rebuilt colonial empire with which to rival England.

The repeated denials of official France that such a transfer was contemplated were matched by specific news that it had taken place. In October, 1802, the Spanish agents at New Orleans confirmed the rumor by closing the Mississippi, under secret orders from the Spanish king. The privilege that Spain had tolerated since 1798, when the right of deposit expired, came to an end at the moment when Spain ceased to be a Mississippi Valley power. The bad news rushed up the trail from Natchez, and reaching Washington apprised the President that either the West would act, or he; and that his action must be prompt or not at all.

He knew his West. The independence that made it ready for lawless ventures, and that had shown itself in a willingness to intrigue either with Spain or against her, had been part of his arsenal to be used against the Federalists. The slack bond that held it to the Union, with the Appalachian barrier to keep it remote and the Mississippi to turn its eyes southwest, had made the western leaders receptive when in 1798 he preached a doctrine of limited government and suggested a right to nullify. He knew the real importance of the Mississippi and the passionate regard in

which the West held it. And he knew as well that New Orleans lay
unprotected at the mercy of a frontier expedition. Such attack
was likely to produce either the calamity of a war with France, or
a dissolution of the Union, or both.

On the other hand, Jefferson both hated war and believed, in
the bottom of his heart, that he lacked the power to avoid it.
"Peace is our passion," he wrote; and meant it. In his mind war
could be avoided simply by refraining from it. That it could or
would be forced upon a nation, or that there were other conditions
worse than war, he doubted. His instinct led him, in the open, to
play for time, and to decry the talk of war. In private, the crisis
forced him to realize that French control of the Mississippi meant
war with France and alliance with England, or else explosion.

Yet when he came to consider that a purchase of a part of Louisiana from France, so that the United States might be at least co-
owner of the river mouth, was the only probable means of averting
war, he hesitated, for he believed that the United States had no
constitutional right to make the purchase. No one more than he
had fulminated against abuse of power. His Attorney-General,
Levi Lincoln, confirmed him in the belief that it would be unconstitutional; and Jefferson with his own hand drew up an amendment to the Constitution to make it right. But his friends advised
him to act at once, and the real westerners among them, although
they had endorsed his Kentucky resolutions without objections,
saw no reason why the United States lacked power to expand. To
his eternal credit the statesman in him rose above the politician
and the doctrinaire. In the words of Henry Adams he "ordered
his ministers at Paris to buy this territory, although he thought
the Constitution gave him no power to do so; he was willing to increase the national debt for this purpose, even though a national
debt was a 'mortal canker'; and he ordered his minister, in case
Bonaparte should close the Mississippi, to make a permanent
alliance with England, or in his own words to 'marry ourselves to
the British fleet and nation,' as the price of New Orleans and
Florida."

In January, 1803, Congress was asked to provide a special fund,
and James Monroe was nominated as minister to France. The
fund was for the purchase; the minister was to assure the impatient
West that the Government was not asleep. The resident minister
in Paris, Robert R. Livingston, who might as well have been instructed to make the overture, was advised of Monroe's approach,

and noted in a sudden change of Bonaparte's policy that it might be possible to have the act accomplished before Monroe arrived.

No historian has gone further than Henry Adams in describing the play of forces around Napoleon that led him to coöperate with the desire of Thomas Jefferson.[1] It was not a fear of losing the province that moved him; nor the purchase price; nor the danger of making an enemy of America. His hope of founding an American empire had collapsed, and he possessed a rare self-restraint that stopped him from sending good money after bad. Already he had taken a step in the direction of New Orleans by sending an army to the island of San Domingo to occupy it and make of it a naval base. But in San Domingo the native revolt led by Toussaint L'Ouverture, and the yellow fever, swallowed up his force. He was unwilling to pay the price of conquest, and revived his hopes with a new project in the invasion of England. With the English war renewed, he knew he could not hold Louisiana against the English navy; hence he welcomed a chance to salvage something, and pass the province over to the United States. Before Monroe arrived in Paris, Livingston was in the thick of the discussion of price and terms, at Napoleon's own suggestion. On April 30, 1803, the two envoys dated the treaty by which they bought for the United States not merely the island on which New Orleans is situated, but the whole province.

The terms of the Louisiana Purchase were staggering to Monroe and Livingston, whose instructions contemplated nothing so extensive. The purchase price was sixty million francs, or, at the rate of exchange agreed to in the treaty, $11,250,000. In addition to this the United States agreed to pay the claims of American citizens against France for war depredations prior to the convention of September 30, 1800, an amount estimated at $3,750,000. The inhabitants of the ceded territory were to be incorporated in the United States, under the Constitution, "as soon as possible." And the ships of France and Spain were to be given special privileges in Louisiana ports for a term of twelve years, after which the ships of France were to be placed upon the footing of the most favored nation. In return for this price, the United States received the province of Louisiana "as fully and in the same man-

[1] Adams, McMaster, and Channing have traced this transaction in great detail; its diplomatic correspondence is accessible in the *American State Papers, Foreign Relations*, and more conveniently in a compilation made at the time of the World's Fair in St. Louis, *State Papers and Correspondence bearing upon the Purchase of the Territory of Louisiana* (57th Congress, 2d Session, House Document 431).

ner," as France received it from Spain in the Treaty of San Ilde-fonso, namely "with the same extent that it now has in the hands of Spain, and that it had when France possessed it; and such as it should be after the Treaties subsequently entered into between Spain and other States." No boundaries were mentioned, and none were intended. If a controversy over them should arise be-tween the United States and Spain, that was none of Napoleon's business, and may have been his desire, since the happiness of the United States was not included among his ambitions. Such as it was, Monroe and Livingston bought the province, and sent the treaty home for Jefferson to worry through the Senate.

With the ratification of the Louisiana Purchase the frontier had little special concern. It wanted the territory and felt none of the constitutional qualms that had distressed Jefferson. The Federal-ists of New England were thrown into the opposition and the minority, and now experienced fears of executive usurpation and constitutional violation that they would have scoffed at when in office. They fought in vain the ratification of the treaty, and the appropriation of the funds to pay for Louisiana. Over their ob-jections the transaction was consummated, and Congress passed as well the necessary laws to authorize an American government at New Orleans in place of that of Spain and France.

The actual transfer of Louisiana from Spain to France had not taken place, and France never took the trouble to set up a colonial establishment. Late in the fall of 1803, France took a formal pos-session of Louisiana at New Orleans, and delivered it at once, December 20, 1803, to the agents of the United States, James Wilkinson and William C. C. Claiborne. The upper portion of the province was transferred in the spring of 1804 to Meriwether Lewis, whose presence at St. Louis was in connection with a scheme of Jefferson's for the investigation of Louisiana.

Within a few days of the nomination of James Monroe as minis-ter to France, Jefferson sent a secret message to Congress asking authority for a venture whose meaning and propriety were then and still remain uncertain. He asked an appropriation to pay the cost of a reconnoissance of the Missouri Valley. Since this was French territory and he had no idea of its purchase as yet, the enterprise looks like an encroachment upon the rights of a country with which the United States was at peace. He planned to make the investigation with a detachment of the United States army, under military discipline. If his motive was not science alone, but possible preparation for a war of seizure, there was a special reason for his desire to keep the matter secret. Before the money was ready and the men were found, the consummation of the purchase removed all question of the reasonableness of the exploration; but it cannot yet be stated with certainty the part which it played in American policy at the moment of its proposal.

It is quite possible that Jefferson's motive may have been entirely scientific. His was an active mind and he found time to explore the whole field of scientific attainment as well as the intricacies of politics. His friends found him alert to new ideas, and those who had business with him more than once complained that they could not detach him from his speculations — or hold him to the exclusive consideration of one of these. In his work with the American Philosophical Society of Philadelphia, he found exercise for this side of his activities. As early as the Revolution he recorded a hope that it might be possible to send an expedition up the Mississippi and the Missouri and lift their topography and resources from the limbo of conjecture to a state of fact. As President, he could control resources that made this possible. Congress found the money in 1803; Jefferson found a leader for the party in a young friend, Meriwether Lewis; and Lewis selected as his second in command the brother of the conqueror of the Illinois country, William Clark.

The expedition of Lewis and Clark was organized in the summer of 1803, under instructions from the President dated June 20. It was to ascend the Missouri to its source, cross the continental divide, and descend the Columbia River to its mouth. It was to search for a route across the continent, and while doing this was to observe and record the lay of the land, the races of Indians that resided there, and the animal and vegetable resources. Trappers had long hunted over much of the region in question, and the Jesuit fathers had carried the influence of France to many of the tribes, but there was no description of Louisiana that could be relied upon for accurate information. Every member of the party was ordered to keep a record of the trip, was provided with notebooks and a water-proof cover for his papers, and was directed to keep his journal by him at all times. If there had been as much care taken to procure men trained to know the meaning of what they saw, as there was to procure a record and keep it safe, the expedition might have added much to the store of facts. But the men enrolled were sturdy products of the frontier, whose literary habits were untrained. They were able to live in the remote wilderness, but none of them was a scientist in thought or disposition. There was not even a professional physician among them, and no formal preparation was made for dealing with the miscellaneous Indian tribes who might block their way. The party was heavily armed and stocked with trading goods; but when Lewis wanted to converse with the Indians, he was forced to rely upon his mulatto body servant, who by chance spoke French. This servant translated the message to Charbonneau, one of the French guides, who could render it into the dialect he used in talking to his Indian wife, Sacajawea. She in turn translated it again into whatever tongue was necessary as the party met tribe after tribe along their way. She was a squaw of western origin who had been handed east among the tribes as a prisoner of war, and had taken on linguistic training as she came. With three translations between himself and the Indian chiefs, Lewis could not hope for intimate or accurate converse.

The enlisted men of the expedition were picked up where they could be found, according to their fitness for a prolonged trip. They mobilized at Pittsburgh and followed the river route past the new State of Ohio, and the older Kentucky, until they reached the Illinois shore, opposite St. Louis. Here they stayed for the winter of 1803–1804, because the Spanish officers at St. Louis would not honor their passports and were not instructed to give up the province. In March, Lewis was made the agent to receive the transfer, and on May 14, 1804, he led his band of thirty-two across the Mississippi and up the Missouri. They advanced in three small boats, ten miles or less a day, rowing, poling, towing, and pulling on ropes that they fastened to the shore. Their hunting parties marched with them, along the banks, shooting fresh meat and observing the country. When Lewis went ashore, Clark stayed with the boats. They found the Indians numerous, and generally friendly. Often hungry and always bored with their unlimited diet of meat, the Indians were greedy for sugar, molasses, coffee, and whiskey. They were willing petty thieves, but as yet they had little reason to be hostile to the whites; and the diseases occasioned by contact between the races were not yet serious.

After six months of laborious ascent, the expedition reached the village of the Mandan Sioux, where the Northern Pacific Railroad now crosses the Missouri; and here it went into winter quarters for 1804–1805. In the five months spent among the Mandan, the nature of the fur trade was forced upon their attention. The only resource the Indian had with which to enrich his life was fur. The traders who bought his pelts, paid low prices for them in blankets, ammunition, guns, and household tools, and maintained headquarters without regard to nationality. Lewis found English traders on the Upper Missouri, and saw the profits of the traffic passing to the Hudson's Bay Company or its rivals at Montreal.

The summer of 1805 carried the expedition from the Missouri to the Pacific. When they crossed the divide they left anything that could be called Louisiana behind them and entered a region where the scanty claims of foreign powers were divided among Russia, Spain, England, and the United States. They spent the next winter in a fort which they built at the mouth of the Columbia River, and in September, 1806, were back again at St. Louis.

The results of the Lewis and Clark expedition were not commensurate with the effort or the success that attended it. In a geographic way it greatly enlarged our knowledge of America. It made new and original contacts with many tribes of Indians. It provided descriptions, had any one cared to read them, of the Missouri and Columbia valleys. But it was many years before a fair compilation of the journals was prepared, and the century was nearly gone before the first critical edition appeared. Patrick Gass, one of the soldier-diarists, published his journal at Pittsburgh in 1807, in a small edition. Nicholas Biddle of Philadelphia began to edit them in 1811, but the war with England was a distraction, and his work did not appear until 1814.[2] Before the party arrived back at St. Louis the world had so changed that, whatever the original idea of Jefferson may have been, it was no longer a vital thing. If he feared the necessity to seize Louisiana, and was preparing a military survey, the ease with which the transfer had been accomplished destroyed it. No power contested the purchase, though Spain showed an irritation at being defrauded by Napoleon. If he hoped to make great scientific discoveries, the journals must have disappointed him for they contained nothing startling. By 1807 there was danger of war with

[2] Elliott Coues, *History of the Expedition under the Command of Lewis and Clark* (1893), was the first critical edition. It is still useful, although for matters of definitive erudition it is supplanted by Reuben G. Thwaites, *Original Journals of the Lewis and Clark Expedition, 1804–1806* (1904–1905). There is a convenient summary in R. G. Thwaites, *Brief History of Rocky Mountain Exploration with especial Reference to the Expedition of Lewis and Clark* (1904). Thwaites prepared himself for this work by editing *Jesuit Relations and allied Documents, 1610–1791* (73 vols., 1896–1901).

England. After that date the United States was being drawn step by step into the meshes of European politics, and Jefferson had little leisure to play the man of science. Not until after 1815 was the time ripe for a profitable interest in the trans-Mississippi; and then the legend was already in formation to which the remarks of Lewis and Clark gave credence: — that, after all, the country beyond the Missouri River was not fit for white habitation or use.

In 1806, the last year in which Lewis and Clark were in the field, another fragment was added to the scanty knowledge of the contents of the purchase by a lieutenant in the regular army, Zebulon Montgomery Pike. With a detachment of twenty-one men, in a good-sized keel boat, he was sent by General Wilkinson to ascertain the source of the Mississippi River.

At the time of the peace negotiations at Paris in 1782–1783 the best maps that were available indicated that the source of the Mississippi was well north of its real position. Counting on this, the boundary there described ran the line from the Lake of the Woods "on a due west course to the river Mississippi." It was impossible ever to mark this line, since no part of the Mississippi is as far north as the northwest angle of the Lake of the Woods. The defect in description of boundary was attempted to be cured by a convention signed in London by the American minister, Rufus King, in May, 1803, in which a direct line connected the source of the Mississippi and the Lake of the Woods. This treaty was never ratified, and there remained an uncertainty as to the Canadian boundary for another fifteen years.

Wilkinson sent Pike to ascertain the source at a time when the snow and ice of winter made it quite impossible to determine which of the swampy lakes of central Minnesota it really was.[3] Ascending the Mississippi, Pike found above St. Louis almost no signs of white habitation. In the lead country, from which in later years the northwest frontier was to draw the material for its bullets and shot, he saw and described the primitive workings of Julian Dubuque, who had been operating on the west bank of the river for some years. On the east bank, at the mouth of the Wisconsin, he found the ancient trading post of Prairie du Chien. Above this point the Indian country was unbroken. The Sioux awaited him at the mouth of the Minnesota River, and here he treated with

[3] Elliott Coues, *The Expeditions of Zebulon Montgomery Pike to the Headwaters of the Mississippi River, through Louisiana Territory, and in New Spain, during the years 1805-6-7* (1895).

them and took possession of the land as American soil. It was not a needless act, for the agents of the Montreal fur traders were here, as they were on the upper Missouri, and he found the English flag flying over their lodges. Not until 1819 was a permanent American post established here. In January, 1806, Pike determined upon Leech Lake as the source of the river, in which he was in error, and started back to St. Louis to report. By the date of his arrival there in April, the Mississippi Valley was astir with rumors of war and speculation, Wilkinson was treading a difficult course between treason and patriotism, and the fate of Louisiana was in the balance. The purchase of Louisiana had been completed, but while Jefferson was taking the measure of its physical contents, Aaron Burr was sounding its intellectual and moral depths, and tempting the ambitious leaders of the West with visions that perhaps were cloudy even to himself.

CHAPTER XVI
PROBLEMS OF THE SOUTHWEST BORDER

NAPOLEON BONAPARTE refused to go on record as to the boundaries of Louisiana, but we know to-day that it was his intention, had he completed his colonial experiment, to seize the Gulf of Mexico shore between the Mississippi and the Rio Grande, and claim it all.[1] When the province that he discarded into Jefferson's hands became the southwest border of the United States, its western limits were uncertain. And Spain, who had watched with apprehension the advance of both England and France, viewed with renewed alarm the presence at New Orleans of an American frontier force. The settlements in Texas had been planted in the eighteenth century to be a buffer for New Spain, the Internal Provinces had been organized, and Upper California had been colonized with the same intent. The Spanish officers who from New Orleans had watched the leaders of opinion in Kentucky and Tennessee with nervous fear since 1785, now took their station along the trail that ran from the head of the Sabine River to San Antonio, and determined to maintain an outpost here. In Louisiana, James Wilkinson was an unfit leader of the American army, for no one had illicit relations more than he with these Spanish officials. He was an unstable foundation for the cornerstone of empire.

After the delivery of New Orleans to Wilkinson and Claiborne in December, 1803, the latter became temporary governor, exercising in the name of the President full military power, and all the functions possessed by all the Spanish officials whom he displaced. Congress authorized such autocratic rule until it should have time to give further consideration to the government of the province. There were in Louisiana perhaps eight thousand whites in the vicinity of New Orleans, and fifty thousand south of the Red River. In Upper Louisiana, between New Madrid and St. Louis, there may have been six thousand more. Most of these were French or Spanish, though there was among them a new admixture

[1] The best treatments of these boundary matters are Isaac J. Cox, *The West Florida Controversy, 1798–1813* (1918), and Thomas M. Marshall, *A History of the Western Boundary of the Louisiana Purchase, 1819–1841* (1914).

of Americans, tempted across the Mississippi by easy naturalization and generous land grants. The people spoke French, lived
under the civil rather than the common law, and were in general
devout followers of the communion of the Catholic Church. They
contained little of the element that made American westerners
clamor for self-government before they were ripe for it. Instead,
the creoles of Louisiana, with the numerous half-breed mixtures,
accepted what government came to them with tranquil indifference. Their normal indolent politeness did not conceal their contempt for the American representatives of a rough and ready
civilization, but they made no resistance to their sale as chattels
by France to the United States.

In March, 1804, Congress divided the province of Louisiana by
the line of the thirty-third parallel running west from the Mississippi. South of this line, the Territory of Orleans was left in Claiborne's hands, as a territory of the lowest grade. North of the
line, the District of Louisiana was attached for purposes of government to Indiana Territory, where William Henry Harrison had
been in command since 1801. This latter combination was unsuccessful, and popular neither at Vincennes nor at St. Louis. In
1805, accordingly, Indiana was cut down. Michigan Territory
was launched, with seat of government at Detroit, under William
Hull; and Louisiana District was allowed to be a Territory, with
its government at St. Louis. Both Indiana and Orleans at this
time were raised to the second territorial status, and allowed a
legislature.

The exploration of the tract that thus became the two territories
of Orleans and Louisiana went on apace. Between 1804 and 1806
the northern and western limits were visited, without discovering
anything that called for or received immediate attention. But at
the south and west each year revealed increasing difficulty and
uncertainty. Pike, on his return from the Upper Mississippi was
transferred at once to this scene, and played there a part whose
meaning is as uncertain to the historian as it may have been to
him.

Under orders from Wilkinson, he left St. Louis July 15, 1806, to
escort a group of Indians to their homes in the Osage and Pawnee
villages, and then to proceed to the headwaters of the Arkansas
and Red rivers. The internal topography was as cloudy at the
border of New Spain as it was at that of Oregon. There would
have been good reason for an investigation of the region for the

simple purpose of ascertaining the facts, but the connection of Wilkinson with it makes such explanation of motive hard to accept. Somewhere to the southwest lay the frontier of Spain. It was fairly clear that on the Gulf Shore there would be established an equilibrium not far from the Sabine River; but inland neither Spain nor the United States knew what the limits ought to be. Pike was ordered to disguise his military identity, which would not have been necessary had his purpose been simply to explore the Territory of Louisiana; and he was given careful instructions and an untruthful story to be used in case he should fall in with troops of Spain. Like a good soldier he accepted his orders without question, and he does not seem to have suspected that anything but a proper military purpose was behind his mission. When he returned to the United States in 1807, and found that he was connected in the public mind with the plot of Aaron Burr, his indignation was so pronounced as to appear genuine.

Leaving the St. Louis border with his Indian charges, Pike visited their villages, and then struck off across what is now the eastern end of Kansas for the great northern bend of the Arkansas River. He followed the river to the Rocky Mountains, where it emerges through the front range at the Royal Gorge, where Pueblo now stands. From an examination of such maps as he could have seen, there was reason to believe that south of the Arkansas was the basin of the Red River. Certainly in their lower reaches these rivers lay parallel. The Sangre de Cristo range that Pike now crossed may have appeared to him to be the northern ridge of the Red River basin; but when he struck the stream beyond the range, which was the Rio Grande in San Luis Park, he built himself a fortified post on it. If he thought it to be the Red River, there was no occasion for a fort. If he knew it was the Rio Grande, he must have been conscious of a trespass, for his fort was on a western branch of the main stream. But he also knew that on the border, people were talking of a probable war with Spain. His commander, Wilkinson, had proceeded during the summer first to Natchez and then to the head of Red River navigation at Natchitoches, where he went through the motions of making a truce with the Spanish leaders who were in the vicinity of Nacogdoches. Between them they held the international boundary near the point where it was fixed by treaty in 1819. But while they were doing this downstream, Pike was building his fort upon the Rio Grande, and claiming that he thought himself upon the Red.

In February, 1807, Pike was visited at his camp by a courteous Spanish officer, with a detachment of soldiers and militia, and was invited to accompany him to his commander at Chihuahua. The force was so great that compliance could not be avoided. The Spanish relieved Pike of all his notes and papers, which were forwarded through military channels to headquarters at Mexico City (though no one seems ever to have read them).[2] The Americans were escorted as guests down the road that ascends the upper Rio Grande. They passed through Sante Fé, where New Spain had a civilization as ancient as that of New England. They continued to El Paso, where the river leaves the mountain trough that has become New Mexico; and thence they crossed the desert of Chihuahua. Spain had no use for Pike, though it desired to check his reconnoissance; and the impeding war failed to come about. From Chihuahua, therefore, Pike was escorted to the eastern road that led, and still leads, from Durango to Laredo, and thence across the Rio Grande to San Antonio. In the summer of 1807 he was passed along the whole length of the Texas road to Nacogdoches, and was delivered across the neutral ground to Wilkinson at Natchitoches.

By the time of Pike's arrival at the American border post, whatever may have been the original intention of Wilkinson in dispatching him had changed to patriotism and peace. Aaron Burr had been arrested, and the word treason had been noisily shouted at his followers. Pike found himself misjudged and minus the notes which might have made a valuable book upon his trip. However, his reputation was not permanently destroyed and he died a brigadier-general under fire at York in 1813. He had meantime brought out in 1810 a volume whose chief contribution lies in establishing the topographical data respecting the sources of the Arkansas and the Red and in describing the remote civilization of New Mexico. The picturesque life that Pike was taken through upon his enforced pilgrimage was new to him and interesting to his fellows. The scarcity of merchandise in New Mexico suggested a profitable field for border trade. But the time was not yet ripe for this. Santa Fé was a thousand miles away from St. Louis across the southern plains, whose inhospitality impressed Pike, as the northern plains had similarly impressed Lewis and Clark.

[2] These very papers were finally discovered by Herbert E. Bolton on one of his many visits to the Mexican archives. He found them covered by the dust of generations, and printed them so that all might see how valuable Pike was as an observer, in "Papers of Z. M. Pike," in *American Historical Review*, vol. XIII.

The mystery connected with the aims of Aaron Burr, and the devious course of James Wilkinson respecting them, is involved with the genuine tenseness of Spanish-American relations, and the old habit of the Mississippi Valley lightly to undertake ventures inconsistent with Federal law and duty. The arrest of Burr in January, 1807, brought his enterprise to an end, and was followed by peace and reaction in the West. He serves as a convenient scale upon which to measure frontier potentialities.

Aaron Burr was still in middle life and a national figure, when his career was suddenly terminated in 1804. He rose to power and repute through his skill in walking the shady paths of New York politics. Here as an organizer of Jeffersonian principles he became a democratic leader whose practical grip upon the vote gave him as much influence as Jefferson possessed with his power over the minds of men. He could not attain this position without brushing more than once against the sterner side of Alexander Hamilton, who as Federalist leader of the State and confidant of Washington, held a national position superior to his own. There have been times when the rival bosses of New York politics have at heart been friends, and in collusion against the public, but between Hamilton and Burr there was deep distrust and a genuine contempt.

The prominence of Burr led to his downfall. In 1800 by agreement among the Jeffersonian leaders, he became Jefferson's mate upon the party ticket. Under the Constitution the electors would ballot for two names, and the one receiving the largest number of votes would become President. But when the Democratic-Republicans determined upon their candidates it was clear to all that Jefferson was the party choice for President. The victory of 1800 was sweeping. Jefferson and Burr received more votes than their Federalist opponents, but the party organization was so effective that every Jeffersonian elector voted for both Jefferson and Burr, with the result that there was a tie that could be settled only by an election in the House of Representatives. This defect in the Constitution was corrected by the Twelfth Amendment; but in 1800 the contest produced a stubborn fight whose sole foundation was the lack of principle of Burr. He knew that morally no one had voted for him for President and that the course of honor was to procure the immediate election of Jefferson by the House. He nevertheless allowed his friends, and he had many, to try to secure the coveted post for him. The House was divided, with the

Federalist minority holding the balance of power, and with the personal enemy of Burr, Alexander Hamilton, holding the confidence of the Federalists. In the end, and through the efforts of Hamilton, Jefferson was seated; and to Hamilton is attributed the profound remark that though Jefferson had bad principles, Burr had none. Burr became Vice President, with his party turned against him because of his treachery, and with the personal antipathy to Hamilton deep and implacable.

On July 11, 1804, Burr killed Hamilton in a duel fought near the heights at Weehawken where there was a long-established habit of settling such New York disputes. These contests were frequent enough in American life in the eighteenth century, and the accident of killing an opponent was one that might easily happen to any gentleman. It was inconvenient, but not incurable. But Aaron Burr was already notorious, and Hamilton was a great national figure. Instead of easy forgiveness, Burr found indictment for murder in both New York and New Jersey. After his disaster, dueling rapidly gave way before adverse public opinion, and he became a victim of a suddenly shifted standard of manners and ethics. He returned to Washington where as Vice President he was secure from actual molestation, but as his term of office reached completion, March 4, 1805, he was a man without a party or a home. He became a man without a country.

In prospecting for a field in which to spend his later years (Burr was just forty-nine when he left office), his attention turned toward the West, which was natural because of two reasons. Federalism and Alexander Hamilton were so unpopular there that the killing of Hamilton was no affront; and personal encounters lasted much longer on the frontier than in the East. McMaster records that a traveling showman passed through Tennessee "exhibiting a wax figure of Burr as he appeared when he slew the leviathan of Federalism." There was here abundant opportunity for a man of resource and charm, and the affairs of Spain were so upset that almost anything might be made to happen.

Within a few days of the death of Hamilton it was suggested to Anthony Merry, the British minister in Washington, that measures for the rupture of the Union were under way. And in the ensuing months, Merry was led to believe that for a relatively small investment, £110,000 and the loan of a small fleet at New Orleans, England might procure this. A picture of a Mississippi Valley federation dazzled his eyes, and his dispatches to the

British Foreign Office show how fully he desired authority to encourage Burr. The British Government was not to be caught in such behavior. There was no allusion in its instructions to Merry that the Burr dispatches had even been received. And in the summer of 1806 Merry was mystified and chagrined to learn that he was to be allowed to come home on account of an ill health of which he was unaware.

The Spanish minister in Washington, the Marquis of Casa Yrujo, heard a different story. He thought he learned through an emissary supposed to be from Burr that the long-expected attack upon New Spain was about to take place; and that for a consideration Burr would prevent the expedition from succeeding: — would sell it out, in short. Yrujo heard wild talk of kidnaping Jefferson as part of the performance.

It is hardly to be believed that Merry and Yrujo could have been right, and Burr honest either with them or the United States. But the uncertainties that follow from a perusal of the correspondence of the English and Spanish governments are made worse by the tales that appear to have been told by Burr or his friends to the leaders of the West. In the summer of 1805 Burr, now a private citizen, made a trip to New Orleans by the river route. Ostensibly he was looking for a place to settle down, practice law, and start a western political career. He was received everywhere, and everywhere his personal magnetism overcame what doubts there were as to the legality or patriotism of his intentions. He found one western man of fortune who placed money at his disposal, Harmon Blennerhassett who lived in semi-feudal state on an island near Marietta in the Upper Ohio. Blennerhassett was dazzled by the idea of a career of conquest and a kingdom for Burr that should include the spoils of Spain, Louisiana, and Mexico. And he saw himself ambassador at a European court.

What Burr said to the western politicians like Andrew Jackson and Henry Clay, William Henry Harrison, and James Wilkinson can only be surmised. They may have thought it only a filibustering expedition at the expense of Spain, or a speculation in land titles on the Red River. They were not likely to have been interested in making a new king or emperor or in splitting the United States, now that the purchase of Louisiana had insured a western outlet to the sea. The evidence that exists is not enough to prove what Burr's intention was; but it is sufficient to establish the fact that to every hearer he told the story that he thought would interest. It has been common to speak of the Burr conspiracy and call it treason. Adams and McMaster, in their great histories, have leaned this way. McCaleb, who has made the most exhaustive study of the plot, holds that whatever was in Burr's concealed intent, it was not treason in the West.[3] The looseness of the federal bond there had endangered the Union since the beginning, and it is doubtful whether many Americans had as yet taught themselves to believe that the Union must last forever. The natural lawlessness of the border regions and the old habit of intrigue for advantage at New Orleans made the West ripe for illicit ventures. But as soon as the leaders of opinion heard that Jefferson called it treason they backed out.

After his trip of 1805, Burr returned by sea to New York and organized an expedition. He sent agents, some of whom talked too much, to arrange for building flatboats on the Ohio and to enlist adventurers to follow him down the Mississippi. The West in 1806 was filled with gossip about him, but if he was only proceeding against Spain there was no local feeling to block him. In the autumn he joined his parties, and in Kentucky was taken into court to explain himself. Henry Clay was his counsel, and convinced not only himself but the court that Burr had no evil intent. At Nashville it had to be explained again to Andrew Jackson; and Jackson, satisfied, continued to recruit for Burr. By December the party was again afloat, while Jefferson, now aroused by both his dislike of Burr and the rumors of military expeditions against Spain, issued a proclamation directing the conspirators to disband. The proclamation followed Burr down the Mississippi. In January, 1807, Burr abandoned his men and took to flight. James Wilkinson, who had been in his confidence and had appeared to be a part of the conspiracy, turned loyal. As commander of the army in the West, Wilkinson established a *modus vivendi* with Spain in November, 1806. He returned to New Orleans, warned Jefferson of danger, proclaimed martial law, and wrecked the effort. What he had promised Burr to do is not known; but what he did was to take the pose of savior of his country. The Spanish

---

[3] Walter F. McCaleb, before he turned banker, wrote the most discriminating of the Burr books, *The Aaron Burr Conspiracy* (1903); he did not give the vividness to Burr that is found in James Parton, *Life and Times of Aaron Burr* (1858), but there is more of Burr in his delineation than in Parton's. Until recently the British Foreign Office kept the ill-advised dispatches of Anthony Merry wrapped in red tape, and sealed with a great patch of red wax, lest the truth be allowed to bring pain to the people whom Burr once professed to serve.

minister, Yrujo, commenting on the affair after the arrest of Burr, accused Wilkinson of treasonable desire, but loyalty to the Spanish Government that so long had pensioned him. Wilkinson would now, he prophesied, make application for special compensation for extraordinary service; "he has sacrificed Burr in order to obtain . . . advantages."

The Burr conspiracy collapsed, and neither the United States nor Spain suffered from it. But the ease with which Burr obtained western aid for what was at best a shady venture, gives emphasis to the importance of the purchase of Louisiana as a means of holding the Union together. The separatist western spirit was dying, but by no means dead. The flame of national zeal, that in the next decade was to make a war with England unavoidable, was unlighted in 1803 and only beginning to burn in 1806.

With Burr arrested and on trial before John Marshall on charge of treason, the Mississippi Valley forgot this episode, and continued on its normal growth. The border territories, Mississippi, Orleans, Louisiana, Indiana, and Michigan, were increased by the creation of Illinois in 1809; and Louisiana, with some self-government after 1805, took the final steps towards the statehood guaranteed by the treaty of 1803.

The State of Louisiana was added to the Union April 30, 1812. From 1805 to 1811 Governor Claiborne and his subjects were in almost continuous open breach, there being few points at which the creole and the frontiersman could act in unison. The precedent established in the case of Ohio was followed by Congress, which passed an enabling act early in 1811, under which a convention met at New Orleans on November 4. The constitution of Louisiana was frankly based upon the second Kentucky constitution, framed in 1799. Although the French law that had prevailed in the former province was continued as the legal basis for the new State, the influences that were most vocal and effective were not French. The newly arrived immigrants from the southwest seized control of the new establishment. The convention met on the day upon which, at Washington, the new Congress convened to force war upon an unwilling President. Louisiana was an outpost in that war, and among the earliest measures preliminary to war was an enlargement of its territory to the northeast in the direction of Spanish Florida.

At the time of the Louisiana Purchase the United States raised the question whether the province included West Florida, but received no satisfaction from France.[4] The Gulf Shore was so important to the development of the Southwest, whose rivers crossed the Spanish strip, that the United States was bound to search for a theory that would include West Florida in Louisiana. The fact was that in 1762–1763, when France ceded Louisiana to Spain and England, the eastern boundary of the province extended to the region of the Perdido River, which now forms part of the eastern boundary of Alabama. England received from Spain in 1763 both Spanish Florida and the strip that Spain had just received from France. This became West Florida and was an administrative unit under England until 1783 and under Spain thereafter. The language of the treaty of 1803 referred to Louisiana as it was in 1800 in the hands of Spain, and as it had been in 1762 in the hands of France. By insisting upon the old French boundary, the United States made the point that West Florida ought to be included. By emphasizing the Louisiana that existed in 1800, Spain argued that West Florida was a thing apart.

The western end of West Florida reached the Mississippi between the thirty-first parallel and the River Iberville. Here American adventurers squatted before 1810, declared their independence of Spain, and invited annexation by the United States. Madison issued a proclamation in October, 1810, declaring that by purchase the United States extended as far east as the Perdido and directed Governor Claiborne to seize the territory as far as the Pearl River. On April 14, 1812, Congress added this tract to Louisiana; while that State entered the Union on April 30. A few days later, the rest of the strip, from the Pearl to the Perdido, was added to Mississippi Territory, thus bringing Mobile within American claim. General Wilkinson gave the claim reality a little later by occupying Mobile by force. The region that England might use as a military base against the United States was thereby somewhat reduced.

[4] Herbert B. Fuller, *The Purchase of Florida. Its History and Diplomacy* (1906).

CHAPTER XVII

THE BONDS OF UNITY

THE year in which Louisiana framed its constitution, 1811, was filled with significant events for the western future. There began at once a struggle between two forces, one disintegrating and one national, the one tending to develop Mississippi Valley entity at the expense of the United States, the other leading to a closer unity between the sections. As evidence of the latter, the first contracts for the construction of a great highway between the Ohio and tidewater were let in this year. As evidence of the former, the first steamboat floated on western waters, with a promise for New Orleans of a trade that could flow upstream against the current. In this year, also, the inevitable rivalry between the frontier and the native Americans whom it dispossessed revived in new hostilities, and Tecumseh was broken on the Wabash. At the same time the western "war hawks" descended upon the national government, organized the Twelfth Congress, made Henry Clay Speaker of the House and brought on the second war with England. The earthquake that shook much of New Madrid into the Mississippi, and the comet that set the heavens on fire, are only minor phenomena in a year of great events.

The promptness with which Jefferson acted to buy Louisiana is evidence of the fragile nature of the link that held the sections together before 1803; and the near-success of Burr shows the uneasiness that could still be counted on in 1806. With all the travel that poured from the region above the Falls Line into the great valleys, and out of these into the West, the routes remained in 1800 little easier to traverse than they had been a generation earlier. The old traces had become clear trails. Farms had appeared on either side, and branch paths led into innumerable communities a little off the main road west. Timber had been cut out and ruthlessly destroyed, for to the pioneer natural resources were as much an obstacle as an advantage. Oak and black walnut logs were felled for rude bridges or to corduroy a piece of quagmire. But there were no stone roads and few improvements. The toll ferries and bridges that enterprising men built for their own profit were as much exasperation as help to the migrant. And except the migrants, not many used the roads. There were too few wagons, and the ruts were too severe for hauling much of the crop from its place of production to any market. Unless a river provided a natural highway the farming region generally was forced to remain backwoods. No common demand of the pioneer region appeared more promptly than one for roads; and there is none that more completely baffled the country of magnificent distance, scant population, and low taxable values.

The European world, in the last quarter of the eighteenth century, was awakening to the values of easy transportation. Since the decay of the Roman Empire, few great roads had been made even in the countries of highest civilization, and life had been immobile for all but merchants and magnates. The accumulating wealth that came with the beginnings of the industrial revolution of the eighteenth century brought the costs of roads within the realm of practical politics, while the experiments of such engineers as Telford and McAdam yielded methods of wide and easy application. The movement for hard roads reached the United States before the eighteenth century was over. In its last decade Pennsylvania allowed a private company to build and operate a toll turnpike along the highway that led from Philadelphia to Lancaster and the Susquehanna. The Lancaster Pike was a marvel for the traveler, with its hard stone surface; and was an inspiration to other communities to imitate it.[1]

In the Enabling Act passed for Ohio in 1802, a fund was set aside out of the receipts from public land sales for building roads, and in the following spring part of this was dedicated to a tidewater road. The decade was over before the fund was large enough to be of use, or a decision could be reached as to the precise place to locate the road. But the start was made. By 1805 it was decided to build where every one who knew the West knew it must be built, along the general line of Braddock's route. From Fort Cumberland in Maryland, to which point it was possible to navigate the Potomac, and to which point as well the local roads of Maryland were passable, the new road was to go to the Ohio River at some spot between Wheeling and Steubenville. In this general region it would be as easy to build one place as another, but the

[1] R. G. Thwaites, *Early Western Travels, 1748–1846* (1904–1907), embraces thirty volumes of reprints of rare works of travel, and two volumes of comprehensive index. Together they constitute a gazetteer of the interior of America and are more usable than the originals from which they have been assembled.

local demands that every village of western Pennsylvania must be reached were so peremptory that it was still some years before the political deadlocks could be broken.

Jefferson was authorized in 1806 to appoint a board of three commissioners to lay out the Cumberland Road, and the States of Pennsylvania, Maryland, and Virginia were asked to assent to construction by the Federal Government within their limits. Except with their permission Congress could not own nor manage the land on which to build it.[2] The State of Pennsylvania withheld its consent until assured of a route acceptable to itself, and Albert Gallatin of Uniontown, the Secretary of the Treasury, had great influence upon the final choice. . The route as finally selected started at Fort Cumberland and followed thence a line somewhat less than direct through Uniontown to Brownsville on the Monongahela, to Washington, and finally to Wheeling. The combined influence of Kentucky and Virginia for Wheeling as a terminus broke down the claims advanced by Ohio for Steubenville. The fact that Wheeling was already the head of Zane's Trace across Ohio reinforced its claim. The road, as prescribed by law, was to be cut four rods wide, with a raised wagon way, with ditches and culverts, and permanent bridges where it crossed the streams. Hills were to be cut and grades smoothed, and the surface was to be of stone whose thickness and size were commanded by the statute. It was 1811 before the final route was at last approved, and by this time there was talk of continuing the project across the Ohio and through the Northwest States.

In the spring of 1811 the first contracts for building the road were let, mostly to farmer contractors who lived along the line. It was as heavy a piece of construction as had yet been undertaken in the United States, and many of the stone culverts and bridges are still serviceable in their second century of use. Before such actual construction had been completed, the War of 1812 broke out, and the work was put over until it ended. But after 1814, section after section was finished by the builders and turned over to the Government. It immediately came into heavy use — so heavy that before the western sections were opened in 1818, the eastern were worn out. The great wagons that carried freight

[2] Jeremiah S. Young, *A Political and Constitutional Study of the Cumberland Road* (1902), is more informing than most doctors' theses; there is a wealth of picturesque detail in Thomas B. Seabright, *The Old Pike. A History of the National Road, with Incidents, Accidents, and Anecdotes thereon* (1894), and there is a volume in Hulbert's series.

and farmers in endless procession cut deep ruts through the stone surface, and Congress made no provision to patch the holes or keep the road in use.

Some of the inhibitions that affected wise and practical men a century ago are unintelligible to-day. There was no opposition of consequence against the undertaking of the Cumberland Road as a national work. But when it came to keeping the road in repair either by government toll gates that should levy the cost upon the user, or through direct appropriations of Federal funds raised by taxation, a host of constitutional objections came to life. Pictures were drawn for the benefit of Congress of the sad condition of the States if such encroachment should be allowed. The sovereignty and independence of the States would be disturbed, and Congress would become a centralized autocracy. It was unthinkable that the United States should operate a continuing business within a State without destroying it. In 1819 John Marshall laid down the doctrine of implied powers that eventually put these qualms to rest; but until after 1824 it was impossible to get Congress either to maintain what it had begun or to start another public improvement.

The Cumberland Road was a symbol of Federal power, and a bond of union. It drew attention to something that the Nation was doing, rather than the States, and in a practical way it shortened the time and lowered the cost of communication between the sections. The mails that hurried along the road carried letters from Washington to Wheeling in the unheard-of time of thirty hours; and to Indianapolis in sixty-five hours and a half. The whole political population of Washington that came from western constituencies, gathered at Cincinnati or Louisville, ascended the Ohio to Wheeling, and there took stage to Baltimore or Washington. The homeseeker drove his own farm team and rode in his own covered Pennsylvania wagon. The average traveler for trade or politics found accommodations in the stage and in the inns that dotted the route. The professional freighters kept a constant cloud of dust above their slow-moving trains bound west. And the gentleman of means, in his own chariot or coach with his own servants on the box, passed between the sections at whatever rate he pleased. As late as 1837, when Andrew Jackson terminated his presidency in Washington and went back to the Hermitage in Tennessee to spend his declining years, he traveled thus.

The demand of the West for an extension of the Cumberland

Road belongs to the story of the fight over internal improvements that protrudes from national politics from 1816 to 1830. After 1824 the barriers were down. The following year, ground was broken for construction west of Wheeling, and for a project that was designated to thread upon a National Road all capitals of the western States. It was to connect Columbus, Indianapolis, and Vandalia (which was then the capital of Illinois), and then it was to cross the Mississippi at or near St. Louis, and proceed to the capital of Missouri. An occasional enthusiast grew romantic about extending it to the western boundary of the United States, or even to the Pacific. Once the idea of internal improvements at Federal cost was fixed there was no lack of local projects, and the Union took on for the western regions that needed aid, a shape and character that allayed forever the danger of disunion there.

Simultaneously with the Federal effort to bind the Union into an unbreakable unit, there came the change in water traffic that tended to emphasize the importance of New Orleans, and the sectional aspect of the West. Nicholas J. Roosevelt of New York sailed from Pittsburgh in the autumn of 1811 in his steamboat *Orleans* (or *New Orleans*) and heralded for the up-river towns the dawn of a new era. Heretofore the civilization of the transmontane settlements had been nearly indigenous, relying upon local produce, and a minimum of manufactured goods from the outside world. The wealth that was beginning to accumulate in the older settlements had no outlet except in purchase of land and stock. There was a public wanting to buy, and able; but the merchandise that could be hauled over the rough trails from Philadelphia or Baltimore, or be poled up the Mississippi in keel boats, was always less than what was needed, and ever more costly than was reasonable. The inland exasperation at the high freight rates of common carriers that to-day gives so much of the spirit to western politics, showed itself in 1811 in futile protests against the prohibitions laid by nature, and in eager welcome for roads and steamboats.

The use of steam was the prime influence in the industrial revolution. Early in the eighteenth century the attention of inventors was centered upon the construction of stationary steam engines that could be used to work pumps and lift loads. Soon they began to hitch them to textile machinery and the factory era was brought about. At an early date they experimented in the desire to make them travel on land or sea; and there are quaint steam

carriages of that century whose designers would be quite at home
in the age of gas internal combustion engines. The problems set by
the marine engine and the locomotive were so different that the
former was of necessity solved first. On land there could be no
smooth roadbed upon which the locomotive could function without shaking itself to pieces. Indeed until the use of the pneumatic
tire the land engine was substantially confined to tracks. But in a
boat, on quiet waters, the engine could and did run smoothly at an
early date. There was a steamboat on the Delaware in 1787 for
the amusement of the framers of the Federal Constitution. Its
inventor, John Fitch, lamented in his memoir: "I know of nothing
so perplexing and vexatious to a man of feelings as a turbulent
Wife and Steamboat building. I experienced the former, and quit
in season, and had I been in my right senses, I should undoubtedly
have treated the latter in the same manner." Dunbar, in his
monumental *History of Travel in America* (1915), tells the whole
story of Fitch, and gives cuts from which the evolution of the
steamboat can be clearly seen. Fitch was two decades too soon.
Not until 1807 did such a boat achieve success. This time it was
Robert Fulton with his *Clermont*.

The patent rights of Fulton, reinforced by monopoly charters
from New York and Louisiana, were for sale for use in various
regions. Under such rights, Roosevelt was the agent of the eastern
speculators who designed to exploit Ohio and Mississippi River
trade. In the summer of 1809 Roosevelt made the trip from Pittsburgh to New Orleans in a comfortable flatboat, with wife and
servants. He bore letters of introduction to be used at all the
more important river towns and appears to have been received as
a sort of amiable lunatic; whose design, magnificent and useful,
was impossible of fulfillment. Practical men who knew the river
current, knew no boat could hope to ascend against it. But Roosevelt stuck to his project, and gave guarantee of sincerity by making contracts for cutting and stacking along the banks the cord-
wood that his boat would need when it was built. He returned to
New York by sea, was back at Pittsburgh in 1810, and in the following year had his steamboat ready in a Pittsburgh yard.

The Roosevelt steamboat was about one hundred and sixteen
feet long, with a beam of twenty feet. Its carrying capacity was
rated at one hundred tons, and it cost about thirty thousand
dollars. It was propelled by a stern paddle wheel, but it carried
masts, and counted on using the wind whenever possible. For

many years steam was only an auxiliary propellant. The *New Orleans* challenged the doubters as it descended the rivers in the fall of 1811, and demonstrated to the satisfaction of the most captious that it could be driven upstream. Once in the lower Mississippi, it became a Natchez packet, until in 1814 it was destroyed.

An era of river traffic was brought to an end by the advent of the steamboat. It was, however, many years before the new craft were eitbcr numerous or safe, and there were survivals of the old that lingered through the century. The convenient cheapness of the raft or scow for one-way navigation made it impossible ever to displace these entirely; and Mark Twain eventually portrayed their spirit and displayed their limitations in *Life on the Mississippi* and *Huckleberry Finn*.

The old period that ended in the generation from 1811 to 1837 was dominated by the flow of current to New Orleans. Before the white man came, the Indians used the rivers, with their bark canoes, and sometimes built these large enough to carry numerous warriors for long distances. There was always visiting and fighting up and down the route from Toledo Bay to the lower Mississippi and the Mobile district. Occasionally the Indians found a convenient log, and hollowed it out, and roughly shaped its ends, so as to make a sort of war galley. But with few tools, it was impossible for the art of boat building to advance far before the European explorer and missionary arrived. Down to the time of the military campaigns on the Ohio, 1790–1794, there was little more river traffic than the canoe could carry; and almost none that went upstream. The erection of military posts, and the management of armies forced the development of a built-up boat that could be propelled against the current. The keel boat, forty or fifty feet long, and ten or twelve in width met this need. Polemen or oarsmen provided the motive power, but their needs for space and food took so much of the cargo room, that trade by keel boats was never large.[3]

When the settlers came, the bosom of the river was dotted with miscellaneous craft constructed out of rough planks, with designs and names that varied with their builders' whims. The records of the day are filled with mention of bateaux, barges, arks, scows, and flatboats. The pirogue was generally a boat hollowed, Indian

[3] Thwaites was not content to limit his studies to the library, and made an historical canoe trip along the Ohio shore, that is described in *On the Storied Ohio* (1903).

fashion, out of a single log; but the other boats grade off from what were only rafts surrounded by the gunwale, to long, slender, keel boats that responded to a rudder, and could be used for fairly rapid travel. The emigrant family, when it struck navigable water, built some sort of flatboat, nearly square, and without shaped contours. Part of the boat was likely to be roofed over, for shelter. There were sweeps at stern and sides, not for propulsion but for steering purposes. In such an ark, or scow, or flat, the family drifted to its destination; and there knocked the boat apart, to use the planks in building a house.

The exporting farmer, who had the accumulation of a prosperous season to dispose of, built such a craft, and took it down river in the late winter. For the farmer boy, a trip to New Orleans with a cargo of flour, meal, and whiskey meant a chance to see the world; and the homeward trip up the Natchez trace had all the thrills of exploration in the wilderness. At New Orleans the rough backwoodsman saw a civilization surrounded with articles of European manufacture. There was not much that he could take back home except the mental picture of luxuries and conveniences. He was likely to resume his normal life a convert to local manufactures, to road improvement, and to a national policy that would encourage these. The volume of river traffic, under these conditions, was so large as to affect the mental attitude of most of the West. An observer at Louisville, in the winter before Roosevelt took his steamboat down, counted one hundred and ninety-seven flats and fourteen keel boats that passed the Falls of the Ohio in two months. A traveler upsteam from Natchez to Louisville in 1816, met two thousand flats in a voyage of twenty-five days. When the traveler tied up at night at a convenient bluff, where he could get firewood and fresh water, he was likely to find numerous associates on similar errand clustered around him. Bradbury found thirteen arks moored at New Madrid, one day in 1811.

The traffic was nearly all one way. There were indeed importers who brought keel boat cargoes of store goods from New Orleans to the Louisville and Cincinnati markets, and it was reported that in 1800 this freight was cheaper than the wagon freights from Philadelphia, and could be procured for five or six dollars a ton. The competition between the Atlantic ports and New Orleans was indecisive for half a century after the building of the Cumberland Road and the advent of the steamboat. Not until the Civil War, and the closure of the Mississippi was the final answer given, whether the West was to be tributary to the East or to the South. In the end, the artificial routes across the mountains won the victory, and bound the interior of the continent in closest economic ties to the East. But the West extracted its price for this connection, by retaining complete freedom of political action for itself; and by throwing its vote first East and then South, it has been able to determine the political complexion of the nation.

The steamboat era begins about 1811, and advances slowly for a generation. The hopes of the first builders that the boats could be used effectively upstream were not realized at once. Not until 1817 did the first steamer from New Orleans, the *Etna*, reach Louisville. The *Western Engineer* that carried Long's exploring party in 1819, was one of the earliest of boats to try to ascend the Missouri; but by 1832 one of the fur companies sent its supply steamer up that river to the mouth of the Yellowstone River, where Fort Union was erected. The Mississippi was ascended to the site of St. Paul in 1823. Before the panic of 1837 there were nearly three hundred steamboats at work on the interior rivers; and ten years later there were nearly twelve hundred. From the panic of 1837 to the outbreak of the Civil War, the steamboat traffic was at its height. The older conveyances continued to be used for limited objectives; but the West that bordered on the Ohio and Mississippi had long since passed out of its condition of primitive frontier.

CHAPTER XVIII
THE WABASH FRONTIER: TECUMSEH, 1811

For fifteen years after Wayne's battle at Fallen Timbers the western frontier of the United States was generally at peace with its Indian neighbors. There was no protracted war on either northern or southern border, and in the middle region where the Ohio and Tennessee provide natural highways, the frontier farmers thrust a great wedge of settlement to the west, with its apex near the western end of Kentucky. The census of 1810, third under the Constitution, recorded more than seven and a quarter million inhabitants in the United States. Of these more than one in four lived in such communities as Kentucky and Tennessee, or in similar conditions in the older States. The log-cabin population of the absolute margin was a small fraction of the whole; but even the three fourths of the people in the older communities had not grown out of the recollection of primitive conditions. It was on the absolute margin that the contacts were made with the Indian tribes, and that the failure of the Federal Government to evolve an Indian policy became most clearly apparent.

The basic conditions of their life made it impossible for Indians and whites to live near neighbors. What had been true from the first colonial settlements until the Revolution remained quite as true, and more important, when the migrations to the West increased in volume after the Revolution. The heavier the white demand for land, the more clear was it that a race living by the chase could not withstand it. The Indian population was sparse; the thin white margin was based upon an immovable and aggressive civilization. If for no other reason than that the white farmers killed off and drove away the game, their appearance spelled disaster for Indian hopes.

But the other reasons were as compelling. The lust for land titles brought into the Indians' range of vision a new element which they could not understand. The more honorable and steady the farmer, the more determined he was to possess the attractive sites and exclude forever the trespasser. The tribal right of use, which was all the Indian had, was never clear or exclusive. And every misstep made by single brave, or tribe, was followed inevitably by demands for compensation in the form of cessions of land; and these by enforced migrations that kept the Indians in a life of endless change. Even if they had shown aptness in taking up the better customs of the whites, the shiftlessness that follows lack of private property and continual change of residence would have kept them demoralized.

The best virtues of the whites led to Indian undoing, by destroying their livelihood and occupying their land. The vices of the whites were as outstanding as their virtues, and even more disastrous. In whiskey the frontier farmer or trader had a cheap commodity for which the savage would pay a high price. The furs that had taken months to collect would be traded for a song — in whiskey. And after the Indian was drunk he would barter anything, or make his mark on any paper or treaty, and thus from the white standpoint dispossess himself of everything else he had. Whiskey was the most important of the evil influences that led to demoralization. The lust of white men, easily gratified by access to the Indian women, broke down whatever tendency to personal morality the Indians possessed, and sexual diseases spread quickly and inevitably through the tribes within a few years after each one was brought into contact with the border.

The first travelers invariably pictured an Indian civilization with an attractive dignity associated with it. After a few years squalor, degradation and disease destroyed most of this. There was never any law, or deliberate policy that the Indians must sell their lands, but it happened year after year, as the two civilizations touched, that for one reason or another it was possible to induce the tribes concerned to surrender their lands and move away. There was ever a public and sincere profession that the Indian had a right to live his life, and that he must not be destroyed, yet the habits of the races made residence together impossible, and the type of government that the American people desired tolerated no agencies powerful enough to administer a problem of such difficulty.

The Indian relations in the Northwest after the battle of Fallen Timbers and the Treaty of Greenville were generally quiet. The British garrisons surrendered the American posts along the Lakes and withdrew to Canada. Detroit ceased to be their center for the control of the fur trade, and in its place Fort Malden was developed. Amherstburg, at the extreme western tip of Ontario, now marks the site of Malden. The spot was nearly as accessible as Detroit, and the Indians crowded its environs during the trading season. From Malden to Pensacola there was a frequented trail beaten by the tribes as they came and went from the Spanish posts on the Gulf to the British on the Lakes. The density of Indian population along this route was greater than elsewhere in eastern America. The villages that they regarded as home were here, and their tribal burying grounds. Wild game was still their chief means of subsistence, but around many of these villages the braves had advanced enough in civilization to compel the squaws to clear and work an occasional cornfield or potato patch. As the frontier of settlement approached this line after 1810, the question rose to ominous prominence whether history would again repeat itself, and the tribes recede; or whether they might not make a stand here and resist eviction.

Governor William Henry Harrison presided at Vincennes on the Wabash for many years after the foundation of Indiana Territory in 1800.[1] Here he saw the procession of Indians pass up and down the river, carrying furs to trade at Malden, and guns and scalping knives as they returned. The scalping knife has a malevolent meaning in western literature. It was, however, a necessary part of a hunter's outfit, for it was only a skinning knife, and was necessary every time game was killed. Even the most bloodthirsty brave used it only occasionally to remove the hair from his enemy's head; but the war-time purpose gave it its repute. The Indiana settler, watching the procession, and observing the intimacy between the Indians and the British traders, found it hard to avoid the suspicion that every anti-American movement of the tribes was inspired at Malden, and that England was the inveterate enemy of the United States.

Governor Harrison witnessed this, and saw as well the fact that unless he should take the lead his territory could not grow. There was almost no land in Indiana in 1800 to which the Indian title had been quieted. At the eastern margin was a long wedge-shaped tract, known later as the gore. Its apex was at Fort Recovery; it widened towards the south until along the Ohio it extended from the mouth of the Great Miami to that of the

[1] Homer J. Webster, "William Henry Harrison's Administration of Indiana Territory," is in the Indiana Historical Society *Publications*, vol. IV; more recently there have appeared in *Indiana Historical Collections* the opening volumes of *Governors Messages and Letters*, of which the first two are Logan Esarey, *Messages and Letters of William Henry Harrison* (1922–1923). Esarey's work contains the best guide to Indiana history.

Kentucky River. In 1800 it was left in the Eastern Division, but when Ohio was enabled it was transferred to Indiana. Settlers could buy land here. They could buy it also at the Clark Grant, opposite Louisville; or perhaps from some of the French residents along the Wabash, whose rights to the soil they occupied were safeguarded in the various treaties of cession. There were also a few military reserves belonging to the United States, and specified in the Treaty of Greenville. But on the whole, Indiana was for the Indians and of them, when Harrison took hold.[2]

Steadily after 1800, Harrison pressed upon the Indians for further land sales, covering tracts west of the Greenville line. The miscellaneous tribes of the Wabash Valley used the land much in common. Delaware, Piankishaw, Wea, Miami, Eel River, Potawatami, and Kickapoo, they had all experienced white pressure before, and had sunk in their scale of civilization after a generation or more of white contact. In 1804 and 1805 Harrison procured a cession of a tract of their land along the right bank of the Ohio, about thirty miles in width, and this little opened the demand for more. In 1809 the governor held a conference with the tribes at Fort Wayne at which the United States bought three million acres, extended its holdings in southern Indiana, and broadened the "gore" by the addition of a twelve-mile strip on its western side. This final treaty brought the area of settlement within striking distance of the Indian country along the Wabash, and raised the practical issue of what the Indians would do next. Indiana meanwhile had been reduced in dimension by two partitions. The Detroit region was cut away in 1805, by a line drawn east from the southern tip of Lake Michigan, and organized as Michigan Territory. Illinois Territory was created in 1809, the dividing line ascending the Wabash River to a point north of Vincennes, and then due north along the meridian of Vincennes. Both of these lines were defined originally in the Ordinance of 1787. The one that established a northern boundary for Indiana was only temporary.

The treaties of Fort Wayne were denounced by the Indians who had not signed them; and in the attack appears a note that

[2] James A. Woodburn, in the centennial year of Indiana's admission, 1916, reprinted one of the finest classics of frontier description, *The New Purchase, or, Seven and a Half Years in the Far West*, originally produced in 1843 by Baynard Rush Hall, under the pseudonym of Robert Carlton, Esq. The New Purchase was in central Indiana, the time was in the decade after Tippecanoe. There is no better historical narrative of the Wabash country than Elbert J. Benton, *The Wabash Trade Route in the Development of the Old Northwest* (1903).

only occasionally was heard. The political capacity of the tribes and their leaders was generally weak, and what may be called statesmanship rarely shows itself above the level of their savage culture. The discontent of 1809 took the form of protecting the towns along the Wabash from further encroachment, and of repudiating the treaties by which cessions were made at Fort Wayne. Two brothers of the Shawnee tribe, Tecumseh and the Prophet, assumed the leadership of their race in opposing aggression and extinction.

The limitations of tribal authority were apparent when it came to land cessions. There was no government among the Indians such as white men maintained and tolerated. The chiefs were not real rulers; they pretended to rule, and sometimes were able to secure obedience, but their power was based upon an actual assent that often was withheld. Their signatures did not bind the tribe in a way that the tribe accepted. Non-signers considered themselves unbound, and individual warriors were always raising personal revolts. Tecumseh and the Prophet were not chiefs, but were agitators whose authority outran the chiefs. They were sons of a mixed marriage between a Creek woman and a Shawnee warrior, and had grown to manhood since the settlement of the Ohio country began. The military statesmanship of Tecumseh was supported by the mystical claims of the Prophet, who alleged that he had been dead and brought again to life. The vision of Tecumseh was founded upon the certain destruction of his people in case white encroachment should not cease.

Tecumseh repudiated the treaties of Fort Wayne on the ground that all the land belonged to all the Indians, and that not even the whole membership of a single tribe could alienate the property of the race. There was no foundation for this claim in law or history, but since the United States conceded that Indian tribes owned the soil it could not deny them the right to own it as they pleased. The theory was advanced in order to make it impossible for any tribe, or group of braves, to yield to white solicitation at the end of the orgies that preceded treaty making, and dispossess themselves. If the theory of Tecumseh should succeed, it would mean a permanent barrier of Indian residents across the northwest corner of Indiana, and would exclude the United States from further expansion. For two years Harrison and Tecumseh were rival statesmen, with antagonistic purposes, who avoided overt acts and watched each other for an opening. Tecumseh spent the months visiting the Wabash tribes, picturing the desolate future if they should have to go, and building up among them the will to resist as well as to follow his leadership. Harrison, meanwhile, watched for an outbreak that would justify retaliation, assuaged the irritation of the Indiana people at the effrontery of Tecumseh, and realized in full the crisis that Tecumseh threatened.

The political teaching of Tecumseh began before the treaty of 1809. In 1808 he located himself in a new village on the Wabash, below the mouth of Tippecanoe Creek and above the present site of Lafayette. As Prophet's Town this village grew to be the center of disaffection. He restrained his followers from attacks and murder, aware that he could not withstand an American army. He preached peaceful and passive resistance, that would attain its end and yet disarm the military branch of the American Government. Between Prophet's Town and Malden there was continuous intercourse that Harrison interpreted as positive English intrigue against American peace. The speeches of English traders and agents at Malden were incautious and often inflammatory. The gifts they made to American braves were at least indiscreet. The Indians acquired the belief that England would back them up in obstructing the advance of the American frontier.

The population of Indiana was so scanty in 1810 that the Indian hope to restrain it was not entirely visionary. The census recorded twenty-four thousand in Indiana, twelve thousand in Illinois, and forty-seven hundred in Michigan. There was no pressure of white farmers due to actual restriction of available lands. It was rather the generous idea of the frontier that wanted to be free in every direction, and the hope of speculators to operate over broad areas. The antagonistic racial ideas were dominant, and the national hopes of both Indians and whites were bound up with the future of the soil. Harrison, like St. Clair before him, had great difficulty in keeping the settlers within the ceded areas where there were lands for sale. They persisted in pushing into unceded regions, and in squatting where they had no right to be. When Indians protested against the theft of their land, the agitated squatter interpreted it as hostility; and when protests were followed by violence or murder, the border charged the Indians with war.

Harrison and Tecumseh were in correspondence for the two

years after the treaty of Fort Wayne. Occasionally the red statesman paid a visit of state to Vincennes, and more than once
Harrison fancied that open war was going to be thrust upon him.
He called upon the War Department for men and munitions,
and encouraged Ohio and Kentucky to be ready to assist him in
an emergency. Until the summer of 1811 actual war was avoided,
and the break was postponed so long as Tecumseh remained on
the Wabash to hold his followers in check.

In the spring of 1811, Tecumseh made a trip to visit the
southern Indians, and preach to them his doctrine of a general
strike against white demands. His absence revealed the shifting
sands upon which the aspiring Indian statesman had to rear his
structure. The braves, whom only he could hold back from hostility, were too much for the Prophet who tried to control them
in his absence. Reports of violence straggled in to Vincennes
in the summer, and throughout the border spread the conviction
that the Indians were at war. Harrison's conduct encourages
the belief that he was hoping for a cause for military demonstration against the Indians. He thought himself a military strate-
gist, and from his youth had studied the careers of military
heroes. He was not without hope to shine as Wayne shone in
the history of the Northwest, and to perpetuate his fame by
military glory. He was determined to find a means of breaking
down the resistance that Tecumseh's dangerous idea had built
up against the further acquisition of Indian lands.

Around Fort Knox, which was the military post at Vincennes,
Harrison collected a force in the summer of 1811. He accumulated about nine hundred men, mostly regular troops and Kentucky volunteers. Towards the end of September he began a
march up the Wabash, as a military demonstration, for the
intimidation of the Shawnee and their allies. In October he
paused at the site of Terre Haute to build Fort Harrison. Proceeding northward, and receiving frequent indications of the
Indian determination to hold their own, he came to Prophet's
Town early in November, and marched beyond it to the mouth
of Tippecanoe Creek. For several days he had been marching
through the unceded area, which might have been regarded as
an act of war; and each day as he advanced the number of Indians
seen upon his flanks and rear increased. They were sullen and
defiant, but did not fight. The officers of the American army
wanted Harrison to destroy the Indian village without waiting

for an attack; but the commander's caution made him wait, yet did not restrain him from taking, on the night of November 6, a camping site to which his Indian scouts had led him. He was one hundred and fifty miles away from his base at Fort Knox, in hostile territory, with insufficient supplies, and with troops that were restive under attempts at discipline.

The American camp was on a hog's-back south of the Tippecanoe Creek, as it enters into the Wabash. The American army did not entrench, for it lacked trenching tools. The men slept on their arms, through a rainy night. Sentries were placed, and one of these gave the warning about four o'clock on the morning of November 7, that the Indians were rushing the camp. From the moment of the onset until daybreak the outcome of the engagement was uncertain, but with daylight the American marksmen were able to drive the Indians back, and hold their ground. Through the next ten days Harrison worked his force back to Vincennes, and the further they marched the more they convinced themselves that they had won a great victory. As time passed on, the events of Tippecanoe ran the gauntlet of hostile controversy; but Harrison's supporters in the Northwest never wavered in their belief in his military genius.[3] He was the first personality of political consequence to emerge from the Northwest Territory, and throughout the remaining thirty years of his life the Hero of Tippecanoe was a personification of the frontier spirit. Had he not been as well the eager representative of the frontier desire to quiet Indian land titles, his vogue would never have been enough to make him President.

The Battle of Tippecanoe, doubtful victory as it was, did for the Wabash country what Fallen Timbers did for the Maumee. It broke the rising tide of Indian consciousness. Tecumseh never recovered his leadership; and after the War of 1812 was over, the United States extended its area of public lands to Lake Michigan without resistance. The generation that fought Harrison sent many braves across the Lakes to fight with England in the approaching war, but after 1815 they gave no further cause for American anxiety. For twenty years the tribes raised no problem that led to war. When their children came to manhood they listened to Black Hawk, and allowed themselves to be maneuvered into an appearance of war in 1832, but they never again interposed effective resistance to the advance of the Northwest border.

[3] Alfred Pirtle, *The Battle of Tippecanoe* (1900), in Filson Club *Publications*.

CHAPTER XIX
THE WESTERN WAR OF 1812

THREE days before William Henry Harrison escaped from destruction, and laid the foundation of his standing as a military hero, the Twelfth Congress assembled at Washington, chose Henry Clay of Kentucky as Speaker and organized its committees for immediate entry into war. The members of the new Congress, elected during 1810 and 1811, were chosen while American feeling against England was everywhere high. In the frontier States it carried all before it. The belief that England was behind Tecumseh and that his demonstration was in itself an act of war, was easily accepted in the West. The indignities that the United States had suffered at British hands on and off for eighteen years, aroused western resentment and stimulated another side of the western character from that which Aaron Burr had roused in 1806.

The frontier American has been capable of violent contrasts and has vibrated between individualism and localism at one extreme, and national idealism at the other. Foreign observers have been bewildered by quick American changes, and few Americans have been certain which, if either, tendency has represented the real American character. From 1783 until the collapse of the conspiracy of Burr, the forces that were in the lead throughout the West were indigenous, and grew out of the isolation of life and the importance of the individual. A low regard for Federal authority appeared. Angry legislatures scolded at acts of Congress and avowed belief in constitutional doctrines that could not have worked anywhere outside a state of anarchy. Leading citizens saw no wrong in intriguing with foreign nations. The danger of actual separation was present, and inspired Jefferson's prompt purchase of Louisiana when the closure of the Mississippi was threatened. The tendencies towards disunion were gradually lessened as the century advanced, but the West did not cease to look upon the affairs of the world from the viewpoint of the parish.

Directly opposite were the tendencies that induced a high regard for the ideal of a Nation as contrasted with the State.

Each of the thirteen original States had behind it a long history as colony, and a short period of real independence. Professor Van Tyne has shown beyond doubt how the States regarded themselves as sovereign during the Revolution, the most striking evidence being the fact that it was their several adoptions of independence rather than the declaration by Congress that gave weight to th:s momentous fact. Their actual independence, and their willingness to develop local aims at the expense of the National, caused Washington to age, and made his problem a general one of supreme politics and common sense, as well as one of military strategy. But this independence was confined to the original thirteen, or perhaps fourteen, if Vermont be included with them. No other State, except Texas, has had such experience. Instead, each new State as admitted to the Union has looked back to a period of growth under tutelage. One or two have broken off full-grown from a parent State, but most have begun as Indian country, occupied without controversy by Indian tribes. The quieting of Indian title, a necessary precedent to white occupation, has been a national duty. The settler has taken his deed directly from the Nation.

The Nation has stood behind and over the early stages of statehood development. By act of Congress the first government has been set up; by similar act a legislature has been allowed. In most cases an enabling act has been preliminary to the formation of a State constitution, and admission to the United States has been a privilege for which some States have waited long. The postal service has loomed big in western imagination, and has been a Federal function. In later years the Federal grant of land for schools and public institutions, and for railroad construction, has encouraged the local community to turn to Washington for aid. The Nation has ever been above the western State, and the free flowing imagination of the westerner has turned itself loose upon the Nation as an ideal. In personifying the United States, it was natural that the western traits should be those expected of the Nation. The sensitiveness of the westerner for personal honor and dignity was magnified as national honor. And in the two decades before the war Congress met in 1811, the United States had plenty of provocation to arouse the western sense of indignation and national resentment.

The grievances that justified the War of 1812 were mixed in character and long in accumulating. From the opening of the

European wars in 1793, England and France were in a struggle for survival. They fought on land and sea; and neutrals, met with on either element, suffered indignity and inconvenience. There was no real neutrality until Washington proclaimed it, and it was easier to proclaim than to make it respected. The Jay Treaty of 1794 gave respite that averted war with England at that time. The short naval war with France at the end of the century was terminated by a promise from Napoleon to show proper courtesy to the young republic. But when the wars were resumed, England and France tried to hurt each other by a policy of strangulation and trade curtailment. And the neutral carriers, who had taken over much of the commerce of the world, suffered. The British Orders in Council and the French retaliatory decrees were not inspired by special hostility to the United States. They indicated rather a determination on the part of both combatants not to risk injury by pausing to regard neutral convenience.

American grievances accumulated against both belligerents. Against England was the restraint of the colonial carrying trade, the maintenance of a virtual blockade of American ports, and the repeated seizure of seamen from American vessels on the allegation that they were of British origin. The United States admitted the right to search for contraband, to enforce actual blockades, and to determine the nationality and destination of the merchant ship. It denied a right to use the search for any other purpose, and regarded as insulting and degrading the British claim to enforce upon American ships the British doctrine of permanent allegiance. Against France the grievances were fewer in fact, and greater in outrage. Since French war vessels were unsafe at sea, there were few of them to search or injure American ships so long as these kept away from French ports. But in port in France, or wherever he could reach them, Napoleon caused the seizure and confiscation of American ships at will. France made no contention that her acts were lawful, as England did. She acted frankly in retaliation, and vented a weak maritime spite upon neutrals guileless enough to trust her. Great numbers of American vessels by putting themselves under British license, found the war trade profitable, and the States of New England that owned the ships were slow to resentment against the British acts. But elsewhere the searches and seizures roused the American spirit. Along the border they ranked with the supposed British intrigue among the Indians in preparing the American mind for war.

The escapades of Burr came at the moment when the West was ready to throw off the spirit of localism and to take on for a time the idea of a Nation. The attack of the British frigate *Leopard* upon the American *Chesapeake*, was perhaps the pivotal episode. This occurred in June, 1807, and the United States was wrung with impotent rage at the picture of the helpless seamen on the American warship as they stood up under the broadside fire of the British bully. The officer who fired a single gun in defense with a live coal carried in his fingers became a hero; but the fact remained that an American frigate had allowed its men to be taken from its deck without resistance. Jefferson reported that no event since the Declaration of Independence had so greatly aroused the people; but neither he nor they took it to heart as an evidence of inefficient administration and lack of power to enforce respect. The western desire for revenge grew steadily from this date, and Jefferson spent the rest of his days in office in the futile effort to procure respect by pacific means. Madison inherited his problem in 1809, without Jefferson's ingenuity in dodging the issue. Embargoes and non-intercourse of different types were tried. New England was making money, and was in favor of putting up with the affronts; the Middle States were divided; but the West and South were insistent for immediate war.

The young Democratic leaders of 1811 were required to win over President Madison to their program. Madison had a realization of both the extent of the grievance and the inadequacy of American means for war. His message to Congress in 1811 complained of unprovoked injustice on the part of both England and France, and invited Congress to put "the United States into an armor and an attitude demanded by the crisis." In March, 1812, he sent a special message, with papers showing a British intrigue in New England, and on June 1 he asked Congress to recognize the fact that England had created a state of war against the United States. It was alleged by northern critics of the President that he did this only under the threat that otherwise another man would be nominated for the presidency in 1812; but there is no evidence to prove the charge. He at least knew how little the country was ready, and coöperated in the passage of laws to increase the regular army, to utilize the militia, to assemble a body of volunteers, and to improve the organization and services among the land forces.

Madison had few trained officers or men to draw upon, and a War Department in which the Secretary was assisted by only a handful of clerks. The appointments of men to hold commissions went naturally to those who sympathized with the war, and Federalists complained of favoritism and sectionalism in making them. Winfield Scott, who had himself entered the service in the wave of enthusiasm following the *Chesapeake* affair, described his fellow officers as inefficient, lazy, uncouth, and often drunken.[1] For the high commands, in the absence of available men in the regular service, Madison dug out officers of experience in the Revolution, who had lived a quiet civil life for nearly thirty years. Governor William Hull, of Michigan Territory, became thus a brigadier general against his better judgment, and was sent to Ohio to create an army for operation in Ontario. Major-General Henry Dearborn, with qualifications similar to those of Hull, was sent to command in New York and New England, and cover the approaches at Niagara and Lake Champlain. Before the war was actually declared on June 18, 1812, movements had been made on paper for the capture of Canada and the defense of the southwest border.

The western demand for immediate war was associated with a belief that Canada could be easily overrun and added to the Union and an unwillingness to burden the people with taxes for paying the costs of the enterprise. There was no fear of immediate invasion along the seacoast, or from New Orleans. In the Northwest, where the rival fur traders had long contested for the business of the Indians, there was both a danger of border attacks and a chance for gains. The United States had already a show of force along the Upper Lakes. There were as many as one hundred and twenty men at Detroit, eighty-five at Fort Wayne, eighty-eight at Michilimackinac, fifty-three at Fort Dearborn, and similar numbers at half a dozen other posts. Along the Wabash and Maumee was a natural line of defense, which lay, indeed, one hundred miles or more beyond the outposts of the agricultural population, but which did not include any impossible salient in case there should be a British aggressive. The likeliness of this was disregarded, and Hull was expected to enter Canada at once.

[1] Winfield Scott, *Memoirs of Lieut.-Gen. Scott, LL.D., written by Himself* (1864).

Congress declared war while Hull's army was *en route* from Dayton, Ohio, to the Maumee River, making its way through a roadless and unsettled country. Arriving at Toledo Bay, and knowing nothing of the state of war, Hull took the chance of sending his baggage to Detroit by boat, in order to lighten his men and hurry up their march. The official runner bearing news of the declaration came too late; a companion, sent by business interests to protect their northwest trade, reached the British at Malden in time for them to pick up the sloop carrying Hull's baggage and papers as it passed their post.

This was the first calamity for the old, inexpert, and reluctant commander in the West. He reached Detroit and pushed on into Canada. He thought that Dearborn and the War Department were in coöperation, with counter measures at other parts of the Canadian frontier, to keep the English busy everywhere. But he had no knowledge of it, nor did the Department, nor even Dearborn.

The strength of Hull's army in Canada is variously reported to have been between one thousand and fifteen hundred effective men, while the British had against him nearly one thousand. They were concentrated at Malden, which place Hull approached in July. He convinced himself that he could not take it, as probably he could not, and retired in August across the river to Detroit. The arrival of Tecumseh with Indian allies for the British was the last item that went into his decision to withdraw.

Hull knew the difficulty of holding a salient at Detroit against British attack, but his men were unwilling to fall back to the Maumee, and he could not bring himself to lead them into action.[2] The British officer, General Isaac Brook, took advantage of every weakness, and knew as well that there was nothing to fear from Dearborn at Niagara. He crossed the Detroit River after Hull, and on August 16, 1812, received the surrender of the whole American force. By the same date the British and Indians had occupied all of the outlying American posts beyond the Wabash, murdering the garrison at Fort Dearborn the day before Hull's surrender.[3] The military frontier was now at the line

[2] M. Campbell, *Revolutionary Services and Civil Life of General William Hull; prepared from his Manuscripts by his Daughter. Together with the History of the Campaign of 1812, and Surrender of the Post of Detroit, by his Grandson, James Freeman Clarke* (1848); Ernest Cruikshank, "General Hull's Invasion of Canada in 1812," in Royal Society of Canada *Publications and Transactions*, 1707.

[3] There is no first-rate general history of the War of 1812, although Adams and McMaster

where sound strategy would have first established it, but only after humiliation and loss that ended Hull's honor and career.

The burden of frontier defense fell next upon the waiting shoulders of Governor Harrison, who received a commission as major general in the Kentucky militia in order to give him rank. It was politics as well as generalship that kept the Kentucky militia fighting on the Ohio line; but for the next year there was real doubt whether the line would hold. Winchester was beaten at the River Raisin in January, 1813, and the West gave up its hope of conquering Canada.

The construction of a small American flotilla on Lake Erie, and Perry's victory with it at Put-in-Bay in September, 1813, changed the military balance in Upper Canada, but did not give negotiable advantage to the United States. Harrison followed it by a second invasion of Canada, by way of Malden and broke the British forces at the Battle of the Thames on October 5; but at Niagara, and the eastern end of Lake Ontario, and on Lake Champlain, the military plans of Madison and his advisers miscarried, so that the final victories of Perry and Harrison did no more than bring safety to the Ohio and Indiana frontiers. The armies there were broken up in the autumn of 1813, and for them the war was over. The Indian hopes that Tecumseh had played upon were destroyed, and that brave himself lay dead on the battlefield of the Thames. Harrison who had meanwhile been made a major general in the regular army, found so little left for him to do that he resigned his commission in May, 1814, just in time for the Secretary of War to bestow it upon a new military hero of the southwest border, Andrew Jackson.

From the standpoint of the frontier, the Indian war of 1811, and the events of the War of 1812, were the means by which it became possible to push the area of American occupation from the line of the Wabash, to that of the Illinois River and Chicago. In similar fashion the events of the war made it possible to open the land southwest of the Tennessee and the Chattahoochee, and to establish direct connections between the farming frontier of Georgia and that of Louisiana. For two main reasons the Mississippi Territory that filled this gap after the Georgia cession of

have given it careful treatment incidental to their larger themes. Milo M. Quaife, *Chicago and the Old Northwest* (1913), is both interesting and learned. F. E. Stevens, "Illinois and the War of 1812–1814," in Illinois State Historical Library *Publications*, vol. ix, contains an abundance of local data. The various local historical societies have many papers upon special aspects of the frontier defense.

1802, was slow in its development. One was the normal direction of the roads running westward from Carolina and Georgia, which lay in general north of the Tennessee. The other was the resisting power of the Cherokee, and their neighbors, the Creeks and Seminole, the Chickasaw and Choctaw. These tribes were in possession of the southwest country when the War of 1812 broke out. Fort Hawkins on the Ocmulgee, in Georgia, was the jumping-off place, and there the Indian agent, Benjamin Hawkins, dispensed justice to both races, as he had done since his appointment by Washington in 1796.

The opening of Mississippi lands to settlement proceeded slowly. There were Choctaw cessions on the lower Mississippi, around Natchez, and along the thirty-first parallel that separated Mississippi from West Florida. A few white settlers leaked in at the bend of the Tennessee, where they squatted without right, and without much friction. There were more around Mobile and on the streams emptying into the bay of that name. St. Stephens was the center of American colonization of what is now southern Alabama, and by 1811 a new trace, the "three-chopped way," was blazed from Fort Hawkins through St. Stephens, and thence west to Natchez. At the outset of the war Wilkinson took possession of the strip of West Florida added to Mississippi, and bounded east and west by the Perdido and Pearl rivers.

The American collapse at Detroit in 1812 had an evil influence on the Indians of Mississippi, who were already uneasy with the teachings of Tecumseh. Among the Creeks the younger braves demanded war, and the nervous whites living near the Mobile River built themselves a stockade close by the junction of the Alabama and Tombigbee, which they called Fort Mims. Here they were attacked by Creek Indians on August 30, 1813, and in the resulting massacre nearly five hundred settlers lost their lives. The border filled with panic at once. The governor of the territory called upon Louisiana, Tennessee, Georgia, and the United States for help, and Tennessee provided it. Andrew Jackson, who had commanded an aimless march to Natchez in 1812, was placed in command of Tennessee militia, and in October, 1813, crossed the Tennessee River in search of hostile Indians and their main villages.[4] The troubles of a militia commander

[4] James Parton, *Life of Andrew Jackson* (1860), is a vivacious portrait that embodies the legendary traits of Jackson; it is still so interesting as to be dangerous, and must be checked at all points with the careful documentary treatment that prevails in John Spencer Bassett, *Life of Andrew Jackson* (1911). The writings of Jackson, which the General himself partly arranged for such use, are in process of publication under the editorship of Professor Bassett.

on the border were so inherent that few leaders ever rose above them. Jackson was greatest of those who did. There were no central supply agencies in the War Department, and each commander in the field was obliged to procure his own food, clothing, arms, and shelter; and then to persuade the Treasury to pay for them. Among the thirty-five hundred men whom Jackson led to the Alabama River were twelve-months men whose term of enlistment expired in December, 1813. There were also three-months men, due to be discharged in January, 1814, and after that some sixty-days men whose term expired in March. With such a system, typical enough of frontier forces, no training or discipline was either possible or profitable. The general could not build for the future; he was limited to such objectives as could be reached promptly, and to such maneuvers as could be undertaken by untrained marksmen.

In spite of difficulties in commissariat, pay, and personnel, Jackson reached the Horseshoe Bend of the Tallapoosa River in March, 1814, and found the "Redsticks" or hostile Creek warriors, sheltered behind breastworks in their camp. There were perhaps nine hundred braves who entered the fight on March 27, and perhaps a third that number who survived. The warrior band was destroyed, and the fugitives who escaped gave no further threat to the safety of the territory. Jackson continued his march down the Tallapoosa after the victory, as far as the Hickory Grounds below its junction with the Coosa River, which forms the head of the Alabama. He built Fort Jackson here, held it with a garrison, and sent his volunteers home for their discharge. He had met his problems of discipline, as his biographers, Parton and Bassett, show in great detail, by personal appeal and courage. He did not hesitate to violate the law or cut red tape when the safety of his army was at stake. He carried out the decisions of courts-martial with the death penalty, yet managed to hold the affection of his men upon whom he imposed his relentless will. He was the marked man of the West for the rest of his life.

The campaigns of 1814 opened Mississippi Territory as well as Indiana. In August, the Creeks were punished for their sins by a treaty which the victor dictated at Fort Jackson, in which they lost their lands between the Coosa River and the divide separating it from the Tombigbee. The braves who needed the punishment were dead or in flight; the quiet Creek warriors, many of whom had fought with Jackson, were the only ones who could be collected in the council. The injustice involved in punishing the good for the excesses of the bad was an ordinary part of the practice of handling the tribes.

The frontier enthusiasm for an easy conquest of Canada was disappointed. The high spirit with which the War of 1812 was undertaken was followed by discouragement at its failures. The administrative powers of the Government at Washington were so weak that the war must have blundered even if Congress had been willing to provide the means. But the war congressmen would not vote these. Gallatin had presided over the Treasury Department since his original appointment at the beginning of Jefferson's administration, and had become the leading financial statesman of his day. He gave up his office during the war in despair at the inability of his party associates to see the impossibility of getting victory without taxation. Peace commissioners, with Henry Clay as their western member, were sent abroad early in the war, in hope that England would yield something. They found instead a British desire to impose upon the United States an actual loss of territory. England talked of Tecumseh's warriors as allies and asked compensation for them in the form of an Indian state on the northwest frontier. It was victory for the American diplomats to avoid indemnity and partition. While they negotiated, a raiding force landed at the Chesapeake and burned Washington, in August, 1814, without meeting any effective resistance. The one thrill that might have contributed to some American advantage did not occur until two weeks after the commissioners had signed the peace of Ghent.

After the victory at Horseshoe Bend, Jackson received the major generalcy vacated by Harrison, and continued on the duty of covering the southwestern border. There was annoyance, and some danger, at Pensacola in the part of West Florida that the United States had not yet seized. The British naval forces took this town, in spite of its nominal Spanish and hence neutral character, and used it as a base to excite Indians against the Georgia and Mississippi settlements. Jackson invaded West Florida in 1814, and burned Pensacola; but he subsequently handed back the country to the protesting Spanish officials. After this he was sent to New Orleans, for the news was abroad that England had dispatched thither an army of veterans from the Peninsula to take the city.

Sir Edward Pakenham, brother-in-law of the Duke of Wellington, was given command of the raiding force that burned Washington, and of other troops made available by the ending of the war with France, and was directed to take New Orleans. His men landed in the autumn on the lakes below the city, and he joined them there at Christmas time. It is hard to believe that a professional force of veterans ought to have been broken by such an army as Jackson could assemble for the defense of New Orleans. Charles Francis Adams, who has given the engagement the most incisive criticism,[5] believes that the defeat was due to a proneness in British tactics to resort to "football" methods, and to the fact that Pakenham found that before his arrival his men had been placed in an untenable position between the Mississippi River and a huge marsh. Jackson, who was between the invader and New Orleans, and behind improvised trenches and breastworks of bales of cotton, outguessed him. Even thus, Adams concludes that Pakenham, having plenty of boats, ought to have thrown his force across the river, and flanked Jackson out of his defenses. But he did not; and on January 8, 1815, fifteen days after the Treaty of Ghent was signed, the British army was defeated, Pakenham was killed in action, and Jackson added to his trophies a new laurel as victor of New Orleans.

The western War of 1812 added no conquests to the United States, but it revealed both a capacity for high ideals and a weakness in administration. It also made two heroes, to both of whom time and good fortune gave the office of President of the United States.

[5] In *Studies Military and Diplomatic, 1775–1865* (1911).

CHAPTER XX
STABILIZING THE FRONTIER

THE military events of 1811–1815 were a failure, so far as they were an attempt to coerce Great Britain. None of the distinctive demands upon which the war was based were covered in the treaty at its end. England did not at any time exert her full strength to procure a victory, and the pressure of her merchants who preferred a good customer to a defeated enemy induced the British Government to sign a peace before it saw the effect of its expeditionary force under Lord Pakenham. The war was stopped, and the French war came to an end. Since many of the grievances of the United States were due to conditions rising out of the European war, these ceased with the passing of the war. But England made no acknowledgment of sin, paid no damages, and gave no pledges for the future.

The military events were a success in a domestic way, for they removed the last danger of an Indian obstruction to American expansion. The Mississippi River was now the objective of settlement. By 1815 there was no barrier in the road that reached it. The great Indian groups, whose physical union along the Wabash trail was a menace when they listened to a leader like Tecumseh, had lost their grip. Harrison and Jackson had finished any talk of their successful power of resistance. In the next half decade the people poured over the tracts where Tecumseh had hoped to see a permanent Indian civilization. The American Government, at the same time, stabilized the borders of the United States again, for it seemed as though destiny was fulfilled and national growth had reached its limit. Upon both the northern and the southern borders it was possible to extend the national boundaries to the natural limits of American occupation.

After the purchase of Louisiana in 1803 it was desirable to reduce to writing the boundaries of the United States, but this was impossible because of the preoccupation of England and France with greater things. With England, the northwest corner of the Lake of the Woods was still the furthest point upon which there was agreement. Beyond it, Canada and Louisiana met; but where, no man could say. The hunters sent out by the

Montreal Company and Hudson's Bay Company and the Americans at St. Louis, scrambled for the furs, and paid no more attention to national ownership than their fear of each other compelled. During the War of 1812, England became *de facto* possessor of most of the contested area, and even of much that lay inside the undisputed United States. Upon the outbreak of war, her agents, with Indian assistance, seized the American posts up to a line indicated by Toledo Bay, Fort Wayne, Peoria, and St. Louis. She occupied the trans-Mississippi, and on the Pacific took possession of the post at the mouth of the Columbia River that John Jacob Astor had caused to be erected.[1]

Astor was an active promoter of the American fur trade after he undertook to finance it in 1808. He proposed to trade out of St. Louis and to construct a chain of posts up the Missouri and down the Columbia. In 1810 he dispatched a ship to the mouth of the Columbia, to found Astoria as his western depot; and in 1811 he sent an overland expedition to pick the sites for the Missouri posts. Astoria was founded just in time to fall into British hands at the opening of the war, and the investments of Astor were tied up for the next three years. In 1816, with the war over and Congress in a mood to reconstruct and protect American interests, the western fur companies received friendly legislation. It was forbidden for foreign concerns to build and operate their stations on American soil. Wherever such posts were now found to be, Astor and his associates were in a position to buy them out at their own price. An American monopoly of the American fur trade was contemplated, and the importance of drawing a real boundary between Louisiana and Canada was increased. There was a new British settlement on the Red River of the North, at Pembina, that seriously encroached upon the Missouri River fur field.

After the war, England returned all conquests, and the United States reconstructed its defensive machinery to occupy them. The army reorganization was accomplished in 1815, with a reduction of the regular force and a discharge of the volunteers and militia who had been taken into Federal service since 1812. Small detachments of troops were sent to the old strategic centers

[1] When Thwaites died in 1913, the next piece of work waiting to be done by that indefatigable scholar was a history of the fur trade, for which the Draper manuscripts in his charge provided perhaps the richest single source. The standard book on the subject is Hiram M. Chittenden, *The American Fur Trade of the Far West* (1902), which is the work of an army officer who loved the historic background of his profession.

of Indian control. During 1816, Fort Howard was built at Green Bay, Fort Crawford at Prairie du Chien, and Fort Armstrong on Rock Island in the Mississippi, at the mouth of the Rock River. Fort Scott was built at the same time near the head of the Apalachicola to bring peace along the Florida frontier. There was every appearance of an intention to occupy the western frontier and to protect its settlements.

The negotiation of the line between Louisiana and Canada was taken up at London shortly after the War of 1812, with Albert Gallatin and Richard Rush as the American commissioners. There was no good reason why it should be one place rather than another. A strict logic might have called for the watershed between the Missouri and the Saskatchewan, but such a line would have been highly irregular. It was easier for the commissioners to make a compromise. There was already a starting-point at the Lake of the Woods. This was not so very far from the forty-ninth parallel of north latitude. An astronomical line was simple to describe and easy to locate, whereas that part of the existing Canadian boundary that depended on watersheds and river sources was a matter of endless controversy between England and the United States. It was accordingly agreed that from the Lake of the Woods the boundary should proceed in a direct line to the forty-ninth parallel, and thence westward.

The extension of this boundary raised a question over Oregon. Commissioners on both sides knew a little, but only a little, of the Pacific side of the continent. They knew that Russia held Alaska, and extended indefinitely southward; that Spain held Mexico and California and extended indefinitely northward; and that in the uncertain region of the Russian and Spanish claims, both England and the United States had some color of title.

The basis of the English and American claims to Oregon was equally good, or equally weak. The vessels of each nation had visited the country, an American master, Gray, having discovered the mouth of the Columbia River, and an English master, Vancouver, having visited Puget Sound. They had done something to found national claims. It was true also that citizens of each country had visited the region, overland. Mackenzie had crossed Canada to the coast, and Lewis and Clark had followed the line of the Missouri and Columbia thither. There were trading posts of both nations in the debatable land as well. The Hudson's Bay Company and Astor had both planted their establishments near the Columbia River, and the conquests of the former had been restored to their American owners after the War of 1812. To the commissioners of each country, such claims as these were too strong to be surrendered, but not important enough to wreck a negotiation over. The distances involved made frequent over-land communication improbable. Oregon was nearly as remote as China. The commissioners therefore agreed to disagree. They concluded a treaty in October, 1818, providing that the forty-ninth parallel should be the boundary to the summit of the Stony [Rocky] Mountains; and that the Oregon country beyond, whose title they contested with both Spain and Russia, should be held jointly without prejudice to the rights of either. There was to be joint occupation for ten years; and when this term expired, it was continued indefinitely, subject to annulment upon one year's notice by either nation. Oregon lay behind the horizon of practical politics, and even the Rocky Mountains were believed to be separated from the United States by a waste of uninhabitable desert.

While the northern boundary was being fixed at London, John Quincy Adams, now Secretary of State, fell heir to a discussion of the southern boundary. Spain was involved in this, and the Florida and Texas lines were balanced against each other in the treaty which he concluded at Washington, February 22, 1819. His negotiation was complicated by the claims of the United States to West Florida; the invasion of both the Floridas by Andrew Jackson; and the disintegration of the Spanish empire in America which Henry Clay was furthering by every means within his oratorical range.

The annoyances caused by Spanish weakness in Florida did not cease after Jackson burned Pensacola in 1814. The part of West Florida which the United States refrained from occupying (extending from the Perdido to the Apalachicola), and all of East Florida, possessed no government to speak of. Spain was unable to assert herself, and her provinces of South America were separating themselves one by one, and forming republican govern-ments of their own. The stockades on the Apalachicola con-tinued to be haunts for bad Indians, worse white men, and fugitive slaves. Their actual aggressions upon American settle-ments were less important than the fear that they might commit them. The State of Georgia complained that the United States garrison at Fort Scott was insufficient, and General Jackson

offered to invade Spanish Florida and destroy the centers of
danger on his own responsibility, if given a hint that such action
would be welcome to President James Monroe.

With the dispute between Monroe and Jackson as to whether
this hint was given, the western historian need have no concern.
Jackson believed he received it, was in any event ordered to the
junction of the Chattahoochee and Flint by the War Department,
and went the rest of the way himself. Early in 1818 he carried
out his offer, and went so far as to execute abruptly "two un-
principled villians," British subjects both, whom he found among
the Indians under suspicious circumstances. England was an-
nóyed by his summary procedure, and Spain was warned. The
negotiation of the Spanish boundary was now several years old,
due chiefly to the Spanish genius for delay. A fear of losing
Florida by force brought it to a conclusion in 1819.

The Spanish minister in Washington, de Onis, resumed his
relations with the American Government in 1815, after the
restoration of Ferdinand VII to the Spanish throne. There had
been a break in relations between the two countries after the
attempt of Napoleon to seat his brother, Joseph, there. The
United States had not recognized the government of Joseph as
being in accordance with the "consent of the governed," and had
withheld the recognition that American policy was already prone
to extend upon the slightest provocation. It seized part of West
Florida instead, and established temporary occupation over both
Pensacola, and Amelia Island on the east coast. It met the
demand of de Onis for the restoration of these by a suggestion
for the transfer of Florida, and an establishment of a Louisiana
boundary. Spain was not ready in 1815 to do either and played
for time. The negotiation was shifted back and forth between
Madrid and Washington, and dragged out as did the earlier one
that concerned the Yazoo strip.

Adams became Secretary of State when Monroe formed his
government in 1817, and Henry Clay, who had hoped to receive
the post, resumed his station as Speaker of the House of Representatives. The great task of Adams was to prevent Spain
from receiving European aid in an attempt to recover her lost
colonies. He was not averse to the independence of the colonies,
but was in no hurry to recognize them. Indeed he wanted to
defer this until he had brought about a settlement of the boundary
matters pending; and Spain was showing a disposition to seek

an American promise not to recognize their independence as a condition of the settlement of the boundary dispute.

Clay became the great congressional advocate of South American independence and recognition and thundered in their behalf for the next five years. His enthusiasm was a part of the normal American disposition to encourage self-government and republicanism. It was intensified by a willingness to embarrass Adams; and it did embarrass him.

The elements in the Spanish settlement were Florida, the southwest boundary, and the claims owing to American citizens for damage done by Spain during the wars in Europe. As for Florida, Spain had come to realize the precarious nature of her tenure and was disposed to sell out for the best price. By the second article of the treaty of 1819 "His Catholic Majesty" ceded to the United States "all the territories which belong to him, situated to the eastward of the Mississippi, known by the name of East and West Florida." The phrasing of the cession left undetermined the vexed fact whether he owned any or all of West Florida. However acquired, whether from France or Spain, the whole of Florida was now attached to the United States. It was speedily made a territory, bounded as at present by Georgia and Alabama and received as its territorial governor, Andrew Jackson, who had done so much to insure its transfer.

In consideration for the cession of Florida, Spain received an indirect payment in cash and a definite boundary for Texas. In article nine of the Treaty there was enumerated a long list of causes out of which had arisen claims by Americans against Spain, and by Spaniards against the United States. These were reciprocally renounced, except those of individual Spanish officers and inhabitants who might be able to prove that they had suffered injuries "by the late operations of the American Army in Florida." The United States agreed to reimburse these and to pay the lawful claims of Americans against Spain to the amount of five million dollars. It was agreed that the United States should set up a claims commission, and that Spain should furnish all evidence as required. To the extent that Spain was hereby relieved of the necessity of paying the American claimants, she was compensated for Florida in cash.

It is improbable that the clauses relating to the southwest boundary of the United States would have been agreed to if Adams and the Government of which he was a part had known all that his grandson, Henry Adams, knew when he wrote his *History of the United States during the Administrations of Thomas Jefferson and James Madison.* There was nothing in the treaty of cession by France, or the treaty of retrocession by Spain to France, or in the original treaty of cession by France to Spain, to indicate a certain boundary between Louisiana and the Spanish dominions. If Napoleon had been able to occupy Louisiana, he would doubtless have shown by his conduct what he believed himself to have received from Spain in 1800. But this never took place, and the historian has for his guidance only the secret instructions prepared for the prospective Captain General of Louisiana, which Napoleon approved November 26, 1802, before he decided to sell Louisiana to the United States. In this document Louisiana was described as "bounded on the west by the river called Rio Bravo [Rio Grande del Norte] from its mouth to about the thirtieth degree parallel." Beyond this point, even Napoleon was uncertain; but if the United States had been aware that he had included Texas in his Louisiana there could have been no willingness to give it up as compensation for Florida in 1819.

The American Secretary of State was reluctant to surrender Texas, unaware though he was of Napoleon's intention to occupy it. But the Government and the people still failed to see its importance in the territorial scheme of the United States. Florida was close-to, and imperative, if the Government was to have peace with the Southern States. Texas lay far to the West. Migration thither was not yet under way, and the line of the Sabine River, established in Wilkinson's *modus vivendi* with the Spanish military forces, still appeared to mark a point of easy equilibrium. What little was known of the country beyond the Mississippi River was discouraging. Along its immediate course lay many miles of inundated swamps. There was a narrow strip of habitable land, wide enough for a tier of new States, but beyond the lower Missouri and lower Arkansas were vast desert plains. Every traveler who had visited the buffalo range and the country of the wild Indians had reported adversely upon its suitability for white occupation. There was growing the myth of the American Desert that was to hold the United States contentedly within its boundaries for another generation. Deliberate expansion was never a part of American policy, and in 1819 it was easy to balance an immediate Florida against a remote Texas.

Before Adams and de Onis devised the boundary formula that

was finally inserted in their treaty, they discussed the possibility of reaching a compromise at nearly every stream emptying into the Gulf of Mexico between the Mississippi and the Rio Grande. De Onis demanded at first a line following the precise watershed of the Mississippi, which would have left much of present Louisiana in Texas. Both negotiators yielded reluctantly to persuasion and the inclusion of other desirable matters in the treaty, until at last the boundary was written upon a basis of the *de facto* military boundary, with deviation northward to keep the line away from the Spanish settlements on the upper Rio Grande in New Mexico. Beginning in the Gulf of Mexico, at the mouth of the Sabine River, the line followed the western bank of that stream to its intersection with the thirty-second parallel of north latitude; thence it ran due north to the Red River, and up the south bank to the one hundredth meridian of west longitude. Here it crossed the Red River and ran north along the meridian to the Arkansas River, thus making the desired detour around Santa Fé. It continued up the Arkansas to its source and north to the forty-second parallel of latitude and thence west to the Pacific. The two countries renounced forever their respective claims to lands lying beyond the boundary thus described.

The Spanish treaty was signed on February 22, 1819, some four months after the agreement with England upon a northern boundary for Louisiana. It was a frank compromise, concluded with difficulty amid a political din raised by Henry Clay, whose demand for immediate recognition of the Latin republics exasperated Spain and whose attack upon Adams for the surrender of Texas somewhat obscured the general nature of the settlement. It was, however, ratified in due time. For the moment it appeared as if the United States had reached its territorial growth. The military events of the early part of the decade had cleared the way for a wave of migration and settlement on either side of the Ohio, and along the Mississippi. Diplomacy had now stabilized the foreign boundaries, except the unimportant line along the Rockies between Louisiana and Oregon. No enemy, Indian or foreign, was able to stop the full development of so much of the area of the United States as was fit for settlement; and beyond this area, along its western edge, the arid uplands of the Rocky Mountains were believed to constitute both a barrier to too spacious expansion, and an insulator between the United States and its neighbors on the continent.

CHAPTER XXI

THE GREAT MIGRATION

THIS westward flow of population has been characteristic of American growth since the period of the earliest settlements. In an intermittent way it has been characteristic of British growth since the accession of King James I. It has been kept in motion by two forces, one of which is ever-present in society; the other has been peculiar to the British and American empires. The constant force is the necessity upon society to take care of the new adults, arriving each year at manhood, and requiring opportunity for livelihood. In a stagnant society these new arrivals find their niches arranged by the generation ahead of them and must take what they can get. Birth tends to determine station, and the rare individual who dies in a social position more elevated than his father held becomes a hero around whom legends accumulate as inevitably as those that make Dick Whittington a model for the nursery. If we could know for any society, at any age, the full story of the placement of each new generation, we should understand much of its history. In the United States youth rose to manhood as certainly as elsewhere, and boundless opportunity lay concealed beneath the stumps and sod of the frontier farms.

The peculiar force that directed the newer generation towards the West, as they sought their jobs, was the supply of unclaimed land that could be had in unlimited amounts. The American, who has ever thought of it as something to be bought when needed and scrapped when used-up, has difficulty in understanding the magnetic call of free land for those who have retained the European tradition of its scarcity. Throughout the time of American settlement, the lands of western Europe have been in private ownership. Values have not been fixed by productivity, but have been enhanced by the social prestige that has been associated with the freehold. In the United States the Government has been the primal owner but without a desire to maintain a "crown estate" or to retard its sale. To be able to acquire land at all was enough to turn the eyes of millions of Europeans towards the United States in the last century. To get it cheaply

was almost beyond belief. In the nineteenth century the immigrant came to settle on the western lands, following the Americans
who took it all for granted and who for several generations instinctively recalled the fact that farms were to be had in the
West, when they reached the age that calls for social independence
and self-support. The annual class of young people seeking work
is common to society; the call of the western lands is the peculiar
American note.

If there had been nothing more than these two forces, there
would have been a westward movement that would have played
a part in American history. There were, however, two types of
special stimuli that served to make the flow irregular and to
swell it at times to the proportions of flood. It was always true
that many of each new generation could be placed at home. Some
inherited wealth, and others married it. Many had positions waiting for them. Some were so timid that they accepted lowly occupations rather than risk the dangers of the unknown. The proportion
of each generation that was ready to follow the trails to the border
was subject to fluctuation; it could be increased by advertising
that drew attention to western opportunity or by hard times
that increased the difficulty of finding work. When it happened
that special notoriety for the West coincided with depression or
panic in the East the tide of migration reached its highest peaks.

In the middle of the eighteenth century came an early wave
that poured the Germans and the Scotch-Irish into the Great
Valley. Poverty, religion, and the devastation that followed war
were among the special causes; as was systematic advertising
of the attractions of the Pennsylvania and Virginia lands. The
movement never stopped, but it slowed down somewhat during
the years of the Revolution and prepared for a second crest to be
reached in the administrations of Washington and Adams. The
wars in the Northwest Territory, and the various intrigues in the
Southwest were among the western provocatives of this migration, for war and pestilence could advertise the West nearly as
effectively as peace and bumper crops. Hard times in the commercial towns of the Atlantic contributed the element of re-
pulsion. The Anglo-French war upset trade conditions, and by
interference and seizure both combatants created hard times for
Americans. Vermont, Kentucky, and Tennessee, with Ohio as
an aftermath, are the States of this second wave.

In the first five years of the new century the East was prosperous. The belligerents had to eat, yet they had cut down their own productivity by war. American foods and naval stores were in demand, as well as American-built ships to meet the naval shortage. Commerce and trade flourished in the artificial climate of foreign war, and the westward movement slumped.

About 1805 the rise begins again. The British merchants could no longer stand what they attacked as "The Frauds of the Neutral Flags," and brought effective pressure upon their Government to stop American profits incurred at their expense. England and France started upon their commercial war, with the "continental system" and by successive Orders in Council and Imperial Decrees struck at each other through the neutral United States. Jefferson retaliated in 1807 with his embargo. However effective this may have been in coercing Europe, it was a successful means of bringing an era of American prosperity to an abrupt end. Embargo was followed by non-intercourse in various shapes, and this by war; and at the wharves of New England and the Middle States the useless American merchant ships lay tied up until they rotted. Commerce went bankrupt with the ship-builders, the gay coast towns became dark and silent, and the younger generation remembered that after all there was the West as a resort. The depression that accompanied war increased the western drift. And after war followed peace with commercial horrors quite as great. Both commerce and manufacture had looked forward to peace as a means of reviving profits, but peace in Europe came at the same time and made it impossible for the artificial prosperity of the beginning of the century ever to recur. English ships could now carry British goods, and there was no place for Americans. English manufacturers dumped upon the American market their odds and ends accumulated during the prolonged contest with Napoleon; and sold them not through the American storekeeper but at special auctions and at bargain prices. The new American manufacturers that had built up business behind the protective bulwark of non-intercourse and war were a special object of enmity, and the British manufacturers suffered an immediate loss with complacency as they thought that by doing it they were driving to bankruptcy these American competitors. With trade, commerce, and manufacture hit again, the eastern depression outlasted the War of 1812, and was protracted through most of that decade, giving constant stimulus to the homeseeker in the West.

The prolonged unsettlement of the Eastern States was matched by spectacular advertisement of the Ohio Valley. Beginning with the purchase of Louisiana in 1803, there was hardly a moment for fifteen years in which the West was not attracting considerable attention from the whole nation. Published results of exploration began to be obtainable before the war was over. Pike's book on New Mexico was followed by the Biddle edition of journals relating to the Lewis and Clark expedition.

For nearly two years Aaron Burr was a focal point with reference both to the Mississippi Valley and the politics of Jefferson's Administration. His reconnoissance, his expedition, and his trial for treason brought into fierce publicity his own "damaged soul" (as Gamaliel Bradford puts it), as well as the resources that he sought to exploit. Interest in him was hardly gone, when the mutterings along the Wabash were heard, and the fame of William Henry Harrison began to rise. Indian wars were ever a means of official prospecting for desirable lands. The militiamen could not be restrained from observation, and the administration of the land law was for the purpose of advancing settlement. The normal course of the war brought western lands into further prominence, for Congress voted a land bounty for enlistments.

The land bonus of the War of 1812 was hoped to be an incentive to recruiting, but proved to be Dead Sea fruit for those who relied upon it. By act of December, 1811, a tract of one hundred and sixty acres from the public domain was promised, upon discharge, for every enlisted man and non-commissioned officer of the regular army. The unit was later increased to three hundred and twenty acres, and the eligibles were increased by the inclusion of certain of the volunteer troops. In all, nearly thirty thousand warrants for bounty lands were issued by the War Department, recorded on the books of the General Land Office in the Treasury Department, and allowed to be filled by lot from certain military tracts created in the West. The tract in Illinois, west of the Illinois River, was most important of these; but the settlers who moved into it were in few instances the veterans for whose recompense the warrants were issued. The bounty sounded important, but since the lands must be accepted in a predetermined tract, and by lot at that, it failed to accomplish its purpose. None the less it helped to announce the presence of open lands, and to increase the number of western-minded settlers. The wide notoriety of Roosevelt's steamboat, that was launched in 1811, worked to the same end.

Every campaign along the western border during the war with England prepared the way for a new rush of settlers after the war was closed. Hull and Harrison, in turn, led considerable armies beyond the line of the northwest farms into the Indian country between the Wabash and Detroit. The campaigns in New York, with Niagara, Sackett's Harbor, and Plattsburg in view, had the same result. Andrew Jackson led his southern troops first to Natchez, then through central Alabama to Mobile, and then to New Orleans, opening up as never before a knowledge of Mississippi Territory. Even the disasters of the war, like Detroit, Fort Mims, and the battle at the River Raisin broadened popular knowledge of the country; while such a victory as New Orleans meant its thousands of homeseekers headed thither.

The hard times that persisted in much of the East after 1807 were not fully relieved until after 1819. In all these years the West was continually before the public, with one spectacle after another to command the interest. The accelerated flow of population is clearly visible after 1811 and assumes huge proportions after 1815. It shows itself in the noise of the migration, in the heavy sales of western lands, and in the creation within six years of six new border States: Indiana (1816), Mississippi (1817), Illinois (1818), Alabama (1819), Maine (1820), and Missouri (1821).

The preceding wave of migration, that reached its crest about the date of the inauguration of Thomas Jefferson, was followed by the admission of Ohio, as a sort of aftermath. The great migration was preceded by Louisiana, and perhaps increased by it. Her two senators and single representative were added to the six senators and twenty-two representatives already in Congress, under the apportionment of 1811, who came from States lying wholly beyond the line of the Proclamation of 1763. New England was right in observing the shift in federal balance; but the worst was to come in the next years. Louisiana was a disconnected forerunner of the six border States that followed the War of 1812.

CHAPTER XXII

STATEHOOD ON THE OHIO: INDIANA AND ILLINOIS

THE career of William Henry Harrison, as governor of Indiana Territory, came to an end when he received a commission as major-general in the army of the United States and undertook the reorganization of the military defenses of the Northwest Border. Thomas Posey, who succeeded him, found a community less developed than Ohio had been when Arthur St. Clair retired, but one that had worked with instead of against its ruler. St. Clair had remained Federalist in spite of the temper of the frontier; Harrison was a Democrat at all times. Indiana, before 1810, was reduced to an approximation of its final shape, and separate governments in Michigan (1805), Missouri (1805), and Illinois (1809) administered parts of what was Harrison's domain.

The third census of the United States, taken in 1810, revealed the fact that the frontier of six settlers to the square mile still ran south of the line of the Indian cession at the Treaty of Greenville. There were indeed 230,760 inhabitants in Ohio, but most of them lived close to the Ohio River. Cleveland and the Connecticut Reserve were still unimportant, and into the Fire Lands tract at the west end of the reserve, settlers were beginning to enter in 1809. The Indians along the south shore of Lake Erie were dispossessed, and the Ohio legislature, creating Huron County in 1809 for the Fire Lands purchasers, was extending the initial stages of white government to its northern limits.

Below Cincinnati, the frontier line skirted the river in 1810. Most of Indiana lay beyond it. There were little localities of thicker settlement at Clark's Grant and Vincennes and on the Mississippi below St. Louis, but there had been little development beyond Cincinnati since the beginning of the century. At Detroit, Mackinaw, Green Bay, Prairie du Chien, and a few other spots were the communities of the fur traders, that the British took with ease in 1812 and restored in 1815. Real emigration was still running either to Ohio or south of it to Kentucky and Tennessee. The census enumerators found in Indiana 24,520 people; and in the outlying colonies fewer yet: Michigan 4762 and Illinois 12,282.

Throughout the decade just closing, Indiana had been handicapped by the presence of Indians, and Governor Harrison's greatest task was to find a means of persuading them to sell and move. There was no great difficulty in securing United States title to the lands along the Ohio River, for here few Indians maintained a permanent residence; the difficulty came in the center of Indiana and in the North. As early as 1805 successful treaties had been concluded with the Kaskaskia, the Piankeshaw, and the Sauk and Fox by which the whole right bank of the Ohio and the left bank of the Mississippi below Prairie du Chien, were conceded by these tribes to belong to the United States. The native tribes continued to live there, but if these treaties had any value they indicated cessation of Indian ownership. It was as Harrison moved inland that his troubles multiplied. His great conference at Fort Wayne in September, 1809, described by local historians as the most momentous since Greenville, was at once the first step to new occupation and the final stroke in welding an Indian opposition under Tecumseh. Richmond, Indiana, "Queen of all the Hoosier Plain," lay at the head of the old "gore," and became the "jumping-off place" at once for new occupants of the twelve-mile strip negotiated at Fort Wayne. The Quakers from North Carolina were already here, and their yearly meeting that was soon established, spread a new influence through the border groups. The central part of the territory, as reduced in 1809, was not ceded until 1818; the North remained Indian country for another decade. Simultaneously, in 1819, the Kickapoo ceded their claim south of Rock Island and opened central Illinois.

The advance guard of the great migration was showing itself at the time of the Treaty of Fort Wayne, and every year thereafter it pushed along the traces that the earliest pioneers had blazed. With the irresistible momentum of a glacier it chose the easiest routes and altered the aspect of the country as it passed. Before the fourth census was taken in 1820 the population north of the Ohio more than doubled, Ohio alone receiving more than that of the whole area in 1800. There were in Ohio in 1820, 581,295 settlers. Enough pushed beyond Ohio to lift Indiana out of the class of little border groups and to give it active self-consciousness with a population of 147,178. Illinois and Michigan grew with less freedom, the latter to 8765, the former to 55,162. In this increase of northwest population from 272,000 to 793,000 in a single decade is to be found the explanation of many of the social forces that have continued since 1820 to operate there.

The river towns received the incoming homeseekers. There was no local road of great importance. Zane's Trace across Ohio had no real parallel in Indiana, and the settlers stuck to the navigable streams with unfailing persistence. The valley of the White Water, in eastern Indiana, cutting across both the gore and the twelve-mile strip, was the earliest recipient of the new invasion. Somewhat below its mouth on the Ohio, Lawrenceburg was the furthest upstream of the Indiana towns and was a distributing center for settlers and trade after its founding about 1802. Regular river packets connected it with Cincinnati, which it was ambitious to outstrip; and past Lawrenceburg drifted the hordes of emigrants who sought homes less near to the settled parts of Ohio.

Jeffersonville and New Albany came next among the aspiring Indiana towns. The former of these lies just across the river from Louisville, at the Falls of the Ohio; the latter a few miles downstream. Both derived what importance they had from the speculations in land lying in the George Rogers Clark grant, and the residents of each hoped to capture some of the strategic importance held by Louisville. As the river traffic increased, with flats multiplying in number and the occasional steamboat snorting along after 1811, it was possible to capitalize the local value of the Falls, for here cargoes had to be repacked, pilots engaged, temporary lodgings secured, and supplies replenished. Behind New Albany and Jeffersonville, towards Salem and the east fork of the White River, another Indiana community was taking shape.

Corydon, in Harrison County, Indiana, became the seat of government of the territory during the War of 1812, although it was not on the Ohio River. Its situation on the Indian Creek, which empties not far below Louisville, was good enough however for it to be a fair rival of the immediate river towns, and politics gave to it an importance similar to theirs. Evansville, much further down the Ohio, and not far east of the mouth of the Wabash River, rose rapidly from its foundation in 1812 to county seat in 1814.

The Wabash, with its great eastern tributary, the White River, was a well-known highway before the era of American immigration into Indiana began. The French were here around Vincennes; and above Vincennes, past Fort Harrison at Terre Haute, past Prophetstown, and on towards Tippecanoe Creek, settlers were ready to force their way as soon as it was safe. During most of the second decade of the century the Indiana settlement was roughly U-shaped, following the course of the Ohio and the Wabash, with the extremities separated by unoccupied wilderness, through which ran the east fork of the White. To New Harmony, on the lower Wabash, there came about 1814 a religious colony of Rappists; and these were succeeded in the next decade by a community of Owenites, neither of them finding on the frontier the harmony or economic peace for which they were hopefully in search.

The catalogue of the river towns, through which settlement seeped into Indiana and Illinois territories, continues below the Wabash, and around the great peninsula that separates the Ohio from the Mississippi. There were fewer towns in Illinois, chiefly because Illinois was further away and because the homeseeker was likely to find satisfaction or lose his zest for penetration before he reached the mouth of the Wabash. St. Louis, on the Missouri side, was near to the northern limit of settlement before 1820. Alton, on the eastern bank between the mouths of the Illinois and Missouri, and Edwardsville, which lay a little inland, and a trifle further south, were the Illinois claimants for the greatness of St. Louis as New Albany and Jeffersonville were for that of Louisville. Shawneetown, on the Ohio just below the Wabash, had its ambitions; while Cahokia and Kaskaskia on the Mississippi were reminiscent of unimportant French beginnings.

The map of Indian cessions gives the other side of frontier extension after the War of 1812. It was only a matter of detail to get rid of the remaining tribes in the Northwest, but they were not removed until they came underfoot of the advancing population. In 1817, 1818, and 1819 there were considerable cessions along and north of what is now the direct route between Toledo and St. Louis. Until after 1817 the actual outlying settlements, beyond which there was no white life worth much attention, were in the Fire Lands, at Richmond and Terre Haute in Indiana and at Alton, Illinois. The Ohio River was parent of the communities as yet. No important land highway except Zane's Trace lay north of it. Not until 1818 was the Cumberland Road finished, to connect the Northwest with the East. From this date there rises a new spirit of demand for better roads, and at last penetration north of the frontier becomes more active. The National Road, west of Wheeling, begun in 1825, was to serve the newest settlements that had worked so far inland that the tributaries of the Ohio were shrunk too small to be of help. Each of the river towns at the entry thought of itself as a future metropolis of the West and built up arguments showing why it, rather than any neighbor, possessed the real assets for success. To-day, none of them between Cincinnati and St. Louis has achieved its ambition, and some of them have nearly disappeared.

From a population of 24,520 in 1810, Indiana grew to 147,178 in 1820 and was conscious at the close of the War of 1812 of having passed the mark of 60,000 set by the Northwest Ordinance. The statehood idea that had buzzed between 1800 and 1803 for Ohio, buzzed again in 1815 when a territorial census enumerated more than 63,000 Hoosiers in thirteen counties. Just why they were called Hoosiers and what unkind significance the term had when it appeared in print during the thirties, is not quite clear, but the name stuck and became a badge of pride. The population came predominantly from Kentucky or the South behind it. The local poet before long (1833) sang its praises:

> "Blest Indiana! in her soil,
> Men seek the sure rewards of toil. . . .
> Men who can legislate or plough,
> Wage politics, or milk a cow,
> So plastic are their various parts,
> That in the circle of the arts,
> With equal tact, the 'Hoosier' loons
> Hunt offices, or hunt raccoons."

The versatility of the frontiersman, and the political aptitude of the Hoosier, were apparent before 1815 in the maneuvering for county government and county seats. There are few themes in the recorded history of the early communities that yield more significant results than do these controversies, with reference to the extension of settlement. Herbert Quick, in *Vandemark's Folly* (1921), has told the tale in the truthful guise of fiction for a later frontier; but the story applies with equal truth to the process by which these unacquainted newcomers first shook down into a civic relationship.

Congress enabled Indiana to form a constitution by act of April 19, 1816, after receiving a petition to that effect from the legislature of the territory. In the enabling law a boundary problem, similar to that which had disturbed the Ohio convention and which remained unsettled until 1837, was settled to the satisfaction of the new State. The original boundaries, defined in the Ordinance of 1787 in case there should be three States in the Northwest, called for north and south lines fixed by the Great Miami, and Vincennes; and these were adopted without hesitation. If five States were to be formed, the divider should be drawn east and west through the southern tip of Lake Michigan. It was against this line that Ohio protested, asserting a claim to more territory and an assured frontage on Lake Erie, and defining a Northern boundary running directly from the tip of Lake Michigan to the north cape of the Maumee River. Indiana had a similar complaint, even more vexatious because the meeting point of its northern and western boundary lines left it intentionally with no room for a port on Lake Michigan. Congress recognized the grievance and established a new northern line to be drawn ten miles north of the original boundary. This allowed Indiana to have lake frontage wide enough for six ranges of townships, in which to-day a great industrial community has been developed. The fact that both the Ohio and the Indiana adjustment were at the expense of the future State of Michigan made no difference when Michigan was a territory with under ten thousand inhabitants.

The Indiana constitutional convention met at Corydon and sat for nineteen days in June, 1816.[1] No record of its debates was kept. Few of its members had received formal education, and none appears to have cared to keep an informing diary or to write instructive letters upon the discussions. The official journal is a barren skeleton of resolves and votes. The constitutions of the neighbor States were drawn upon, more perhaps because they expressed the prevalent ideas of government than because they were consciously copied. The members of the convention, unskilled though they were in formal letters, showed no diffidence about their task. In less than three weeks they met, appointed a dozen or more committees to bring in provisions for the several sections of the document, divided and sat in their various committees, reported back their results, brought the proposals into harmony in a committee on revision and adjourned after proclaiming the constitution to be the law of Indiana. Democratic

---

[1] Charles Kettleborough, *Constitution Making in Indiana* (1916), was prepared in connection with recent attempts made by that State to revise or amend its constitution of 1850, which is almost unamendable.

though they were, to a man, they saw no inconsistency in the promulgation of a constitution by a small group of framers. Congress admitted Indiana December 11, 1816.

Illinois was two years behind Indiana in time. Several years after admission the population was still under the required 60,000, but Congress that had fixed the figure could modify the test. There had been a legislature at Kaskaskia since 1812, and Ninian Edwards, the only territorial governor of Illinois, was a worthy peer of Harrison and St. Clair. He was born in Maryland, moved to Kentucky in the year of the Greenville Treaty, and was chief justice of Kentucky when named by President Madison as Governor of Illinois, at the age of thirty-four.

The Illinois Enabling Act passed Congress in April, 1818, as a routine procedure that had now become standardized. The most significant feature that it contained was again a boundary matter. Having given Indiana a little, Congress gave Illinois much. Instead of adhering to the Ordinance line, Illinois was offered the territory between Lake Michigan and the Mississippi River for some sixty miles north of the southern end of the lake, to 42° 30′ north latitude. What was cut off from Illinois Territory, with the remainder from Indiana, was added to Michigan Territory, which was thus extended to the Mississippi River.

When the convention met at Kaskaskia on August 3, 1818, to frame the Illinois constitution, it is doubtful whether there were forty thousand people in the prospective State, and they were sparsely spread over an unwieldy area. The farmer members, however, acted as promptly as though they represented an important community and framed and promulgated a democratic constitution in twenty-three days. Not for fifteen years did another free State frame an initial constitution, and never again was a western free constitution placed in force by promulgation. The effects of population shift and its liberalizing tendencies were bringing about another view of the meaning of democratic control.

The question of slavery made an appearance in Illinois as it had done in both Indiana and Ohio, in varying degrees, in spite of the prohibition of the Ordinance of 1787. Down to the date of the admission of Illinois it was hardly more than an incidental issue; a mild vexation that a slave-holding citizen of Kentucky or Virginia could not take his slave property with him into the public territory of the United States without running the risk of losing it. The Ordinance was explicit in its prohibition: "There shall be neither slavery nor involuntary servitude in the said territory, otherwise than in the punishment of ciimes, whereof the party shall have been duly convicted." It was regarded as a permanent provision, based upon a compromise made in the old Congress, but like most matters of American law, its enforcement was difficult in a community that failed to approve it, and it never escaped some violations. Occasional slaves were taken into the Northwest Territory, and later into the Territories of Indiana and Illinois. There was little sentiment for the use of slaves and little profit to be derived from their exploitation. But many of the colonists, especially those from slave-holding regions, inclined to resent the provision that forbade their bringing in slaves if they so desired. Few of the earliest settlers were well enough off to have many slaves, but there were occasional domestic servants, as much friend as property, who were brought north of the Ohio and kept there in what the law would have regarded as slavery, had it been enforced.

There was more of this sentiment in Indiana than in Ohio, for here the southern immigrant strain was more nearly dominant than in Ohio. Harrison knew there were slaves held in Vincennes and Kaskaskia and thought the fault was in the law rather than in the slavery. A convention held at Vincennes early in his career as governor begged Congress to suspend the slavery prohibition because it was driving settlers to Missouri at the expense of Indiana. The southern influence and origin became more powerful as it pushed further west. Illinois was more interested in slaves than Indiana. The division of Indiana in 1809 therefore cut off so many slavery supporters that in what remained Indiana it was not hard to prevent any considerable spread of slavery feeling. The Indiana constitution declared "that all men are born equally free and independent," and forbade slavery, in the very language of the Ordinance. It however recognized the southern parentage of most of its population in requiring that apportionments should be based on free white citizens as Ohio had done in 1803 and in excluding negroes from the militia.

Progressively, as the frontier moved down the Ohio Valley, the southern heritage became more complete, and the disinclination to exclude slavery became stronger. There were few settlers who desired to go to Illinois on any terms before 1820; and fewer still had slaves or could use them there with profit.

But the common sentiment was such that the apportionment and the vote in the constitution of 1818 were limited to whites; and the whole of Article VI was devoted to something less than a whole-hearted program that "Neither slavery nor involuntary servitude shall hereafter be introduced." The existing slaves and indentured servants were recognized, subject to the law that the children of negroes and mulattoes, the women at eighteen and the men at twenty-one, should become free. The first legislature of the new State adopted a black code that came near to reëstablishing slavery for the free negroes, and for several years there was an imposing movement to amend the constitution so as to admit slavery without question. The southern end of Illinois, the area of first settlement, became "Egypt" during this political struggle. In 1824, however, after a violent political campaign, a proposed slavery amendment was beaten by a vote of five to four. The slavery question was settled for Illinois; but it had become a larger issue, dividing the whole United States into divergent social groups.

CHAPTER XXIII

THE COTTON KINGDOM: MISSISSIPPI AND ALABAMA

IT is a matter of profound historical significance that the children of the South, educated in States in which slaves were chattels, could none the less free themselves from the institution of slavery during their first generation of residence north of the Ohio River. A heavy preponderance of the residents of the Old Northwest in 1820 came from Virginia or the country further south. Many to be sure had lived in the piedmont and mountain country where slaves were few, but the family names of tidewater, plantation Virginia were spread over the counties of the new States so freely as to prove the continuity of blood. Slavery was unpopular in the North, but more than that, it was unprofitable. An occasional domestic servant and a few field hands were found in the States of Ohio, Indiana, and Illinois, despite the Ordinance; but the movement to permit the general introduction of this type of labor was never able to command the support of more than a minority of the population. The Northwest was started free by the Ordinance of 1787; it remained free because of underlying economic conditions.

Slavery did not pay even in the southern States where it survived and flourished, but it was less unprofitable. If free labor had been available to do the work imposed upon the negroes, it would have been impossible for the system of slavery to stand up in competition with it. In only a few industries was the South able to work the slaves without absolute loss, and in these the method of work and the type of organization were dictated by the difficulties inherent in getting a safe profit out of ignorant and indifferent bondsmen. Never did southern capital produce as high a return as northern, never was it as abundant, never was its possessor as free to take advantage of opportunity. The southern planter owned his slaves, but in as true a sense they owned him and bound him to a narrow repetition of unprofitable operations. Except in the great fields devoted to cotton, tobacco, hemp, rice, and indigo, and in the domestic work around the planter's home, the South could not use slaves freely. In the typical process of clearing away the timber and making farms, that gave to pioneering its essential character, they were almost useless.

After nearly two centuries of existence in the English colonies, slavery was at the time of the framing of the Federal Constitution "in the course of ultimate extinction." There was hardly a person of importance in the South, where the slaves were most numerous, who did not believe the system was bad as well as unprofitable. The effects upon the negro as well as upon his owner were demoralizing and did not tend to perpetuate the type of character that the American frontier bred. It was possible to insert in the Constitution of 1787 a provision allowing the ultimate prohibition of importation of slaves and abolition of the slave trade. And when the date for this came round in 1808, it was possible to act upon it. Leading southerners still believed in emancipation and belonged to anti-slavery societies; and in the North where there was no problem of what to do with the freed negroes, slavery was rapidly disappearing. There was nothing that the slave could do that the white farmer could not do better; and there was no crop so profitable that it paid to exploit it at the cost that negro labor entailed. The children of these southern States, who knew slavery as it was before 1808, were able to live without it after they had gone through the experiences of frontier planting in the Northwest.

Cotton proved to be the crop whose profits made negro labor yield a net return. The economic historians have shown that the fiber of the cotton boll was only an interesting curiosity until near the end of the eighteenth century. It was possible to raise it in a large part of the South, and in a few spots, soil and climate were right for the production of fine qualities with long silky threads. But it was impracticable to prepare it for the wheel and loom because of the seeds entangled in the fiber. The problem of lowering the cost of cleaning it intrigued the attention of many planters, without result, until in 1793 the Yankee tutor, Eli Whitney, turned to it while residing with a southern patron. The cotton gin that Whitney made was so simple that he could never control the profits arising from his patent; and so effective that it brought about an economic revolution in the South and improved the comfort of mankind for all time.

Once it became possible to produce cotton at reasonable cost, its high adaptability for textile manufactures gave it a market. The textiles of the eighteenth century, whether wool, linen, or silk, were all expensive, and their cost limited most of the world to few garments, and these were worn indefinitely. The hand labor with needle and thread added to the expense. It may be doubted whether any inventions have done so much for human comfort as the gin which made cotton cheap, and the sewing machine which made clothing manufacture easy. But the benefits that Whitney offered to the world did not improve the condition of the negro barbarian in the heart of Africa whose body could be seized and turned by force to labor for another's benefit. The prohibition of the African slave trade had hardly become law before smugglers were ready to violate it, attracted by the rising price of prime field hands to work the southern cotton fields. By 1815, when the great migration was fully under way the southern stream of migrants had before them, and above all other ends, the hope of developing new cotton lands and making a crop for which there was an endless market. The trouble of the northern frontiersman in finding a market did not worry the South.

The plantation system that developed in the cotton fields had an economic organization determined not so much by slavery as by negro labor. The planter with a gang of negroes was forced to develop a system for their use, the controlling facts being that the workmen were fresh from barbarism where they were unaccustomed to labor, were illiterate and often unacquainted with the simplest words of English, and were in many instances of low grade intelligence. The illuminating research of Ulrich B. Phillips and Alfred H. Stone has made it possible to-day to see further into the real meaning of slavery than the abolitionists could, and to realize how inevitable the plantation was, once slavery and cotton were brought together.[1]

Because of the defects in the planters' labor supply, it was necessary to work the hands under close supervision. The brighter slaves found themselves in demand around the house or with the horses or in practicing the common crafts about the shop. But most of the slaves were useful only in the field; and hither they

[1] After years of preparation that began with his Justin Winsor prize essay, *Georgia and State Rights* (1902), and *A History of Transportation in the Eastern Cotton Belt* (1908), Ulrich Bonnell Phillips has at last produced his treatise on *American Negro Slavery* (1918). Probably none of our historians has more nearly mastered this theme. Alfred H. Stone, from the standpoint of a modern planter in the black belt, has done much to make it clear that the negro labor supply rather than the legal institution of slavery shaped the Old South; *Studies in the American Race Problem* (1908).

were sent with white overseers. Men and women worked together, and in common tasks they were happiest and most productive. It was the business of the overseer to simplify the routine of work. A gang of field hands, laboring side by side, each with his row of cotton to hoe or pick, singing crude chants to melodies that they had brought from Africa, did the best work of which they were capable. But the organization necessary for this division of labor tested the resources of the planter.

The economies of the plantation increased with its magnitude. An overseer was least expensive when his gang was as large as he could watch. The planters as they gossiped from year to year discussed their problems; whether, perhaps, it was better to let the married women return from field to cabin earlier than the rest to cook the food and wash the clothes, or to find a few intelligent laundresses and cooks and make them specialists. A planter who could afford to select and train a negro carpenter or blacksmith made larger returns per capita than one who had to hire or to use the slave at varying tasks. Simplicity, routine, and mental tranquillity were necessary to keep the slave productive. Kind words, a little sugar or molasses with his corn meal, tobacco as he wanted it, were parts of the regimen of every profitable plantation. The "slave driver" with whip, profanity and abuse, defeated his own ends, and led his employer to bankruptcy.[2]

But the consequence of owning a successful cotton plantation was slavery to the slaves. There was always the need to increase acreage and to enlarge the gangs to work it. This was the course of highest profit. The free capital accumulated by the planter was turned back into the business as he bought more improved land and more slaves. He could not well use uncleared land, like the pioneer, because his workmen could not clear it with economy. To send a single slave with his axe and grubber into the brush was to invite siesta rather than a clearing. Only the man who was working for himself was an effective clearer of the land. So the planter bought out the farms of his smaller neighbors and scoured the country for more slaves, if his own did not breed fast enough. His capital had no mobility. In good years when it paid to increase the crop both land and slaves rose to prohibitive prices. In bad years neither was marketable, yet

[2] J. D. B. DeBow edited from 1846 until the Civil War his *DeBow's Review*, in which southern economic problems had their day in court.

it would have been unsafe to sell the hands for they could not have been bought back as needed. The planter looked with a good deal of envy at the mill-owner of the North, who could stop buying cotton and lay off his hands when times were bad. The planter could not avoid turning the profits of good years into mere maintenance for bad.

Nearly everything he used the planter bought. He purchased meal and pork for the slaves instead of raising it with little cost. He bought his clothing and theirs and all the household equipment. And as he shipped most of his cotton directly from a near-by wharf to England, he tended to open an account with the factor who sold his cotton and bought supplies with the proceeds. Every year the planter had to have the supplies regardless of the price of cotton. His mortgages grew as surplus debts mounted against him. Before he died, in many cases, he was working for the factor and living in a semi-regal state, in the midst of a little court that was built on debt.

There was still another consequence of the plantation system that the slave States had to pay. The cotton planter stripped the fertility from his farms. He planted cotton, and only cotton, year after year. There was no rotation and no manure from live stock to be spread upon the fields. The best cotton soil was so fertile that for many years it continued to produce large crops in spite of this treatment, but the moment always came when the return began to diminish. Nothing in American agriculture is less attractive than the plantation going downhill. It meant poverty for the planter's children and dissipation of land and slaves. Foreclosures came in their inevitable course, and too often what had been flourishing cotton fields relapsed into the wilderness. The small, poor, white farmer who could and would live upon a few acres that had once been part of a plantation, had no surplus of either means or intelligence. The plantation era, with its soil destruction, passed over many an area, leaving it desolate until to-day.[3]

The sharp deviation between North and South became increasingly apparent after 1815, and in the end produced the conflict over secession. The frontier formed the cutting edge for both sections, as its children worked their way towards the

[3] In the first two volumes of John R. Commons, *Documentary History of American Industrial Society* (1910–1911), Professor Phillips has edited documents relating to the frontier and plantation.

unused lands. In the history of the country there are three clear phases, both North and South, but leading different directions.

In the earliest phase, the frontier is the frontier, wherever found. Here the typical occupation was that of the home builder; the man working out his salvation against the primitive enemies of timber, sod, and climate; the woman conducting the home and raising children. These were tasks for free men and women and for those who expected to grasp the rewards of success. Hired labor, or owned, was ineffective even where it could be obtained. Life was so relentless that the population was recruited, generation after generation, from youths who had little to start with but their own strength and hope. They owned neither slaves nor means. The conditions of equality that nature impressed upon their life lasted through the first phase, for twenty years or so in northern settlements, and for a somewhat shorter period in the southern.

In the second phase, differentiation began. In the northern border communities, by the time the first children married and moved on, the countryside was settled. The cabins and clearings had become farms and homes. The children withdrew to repeat the process, but did not prevent the home counties from doubling in population, or more, in ten-year terms. Newcomers were always taking up the sections of land that had remained unsold, in competition with such of the children as preferred to farm near home rather than emigrate. The older farmers and the more successful were out of debt, and some of them had money to lend at ten to twenty per cent a year. The county towns had grown, there was a local bank and a group of artisans, and a few of the older colonists had moved to town to live near the church and seminary, leaving the homestead to be farmed by a son or son-in-law.

In the plantation region the second phase witnessed the entry of the cotton planter. Ineffective as a pioneer, the planter allowed the free farmer to live through the first phase, as in the North, until he had cleared most of his acreage and brought it under plough. It took less than twenty years for this, and there developed a professional clearing group who made farms to sell. The second phase begins with the purchase of several adjacent clearings by the planter himself, or some middleman who proposed to re-sell to a planter. With the entry of the planter, the white families who had lived on the farms moved out, and there was a decline in white population not offset in numbers by the slaves brought in. The best of the farmhouses was taken over by the new owner, or he built himself a mansion. His overseer came next. The rest became cabins for the slaves, and if they were not conveniently situated they were abandoned, to be replaced by a cluster of negro cabins along a plantation street. Year after year, henceforth, the successful planter stripped his land with cotton crops. He enlarged his holdings when he could. His countryside maintained, not a host of simple, comfortable farmers but a few planter magnates, living in remote isolation and loneliness. The society of the plantation country was one of long distances and heavy journeys for recreation. And when the women of the planter's family had their way, they left the plantation for the winter and gathered with their equals in Charleston, Savannah, or Paris. Many of them became non-residents, and left the property to the exclusive control of hired overseers. More would have liked to do so. The period in which the North was becoming solvent and self-supporting was one in which much of the South was being robbed of its white population and despoiled of its fertility.

The third phase for the plantation region was one of decline. The shrewd planter saw it coming and knew that the normal consequence of the kind of farming slave labor forced upon him was soil exhaustion. If he died too soon, he left his heirs an impoverished estate, heavily in debt and lessening in productivity. If he were fortunate, he sold out just before the most profitable year was reached and found a northern buyer or a southern heir with means who could be captivated by the picture of a huge going plantation at the top of its performance. The history of the fortunes sunk in decadent plantations would make a long and illuminating story. It was rarely that the successful northern farmer emigrated again in middle life; but it was common to find the southerner of wealth, with gorgeous family and retinue of slaves, leaving the old homestead and migrating to a fresh plantation bought with part of the profits of the old. He left behind a collapsed community, with sparse population and little wealth, hardly able to bear its share of the weight of the State he abandoned.

The northern State, in the third phase, doubled again in population and more than doubled in wealth. The last remaining land found an owner. The county towns grew in size and wealth as they supplied the country with luxuries as well as necessities. The retired farmers moved to town with money to invest, and the last quarter of life found them sitting, conservative but solid, as directors of a bank, as merchants wholesale or retail, and as owners of budding manufactures that used the local water powers. There was wealth and diversification, and both were so outstanding that the casual traveler could not fail to note that the civilization brought about in fifty years made, out of similar elements, entirely different results north and south.

The deviation in type and interests that is clear enough to-day was not apparent before 1815, and in the twenties was producing discomforts whose causes were still obscure. The sections were conscious of their difference before they knew why they differed. Until the date of the Civil War the southern leaders tended to attribute the superior population and wealth of the North to sectional and protective legislation and to refuse to admit that their own inferior labor system and the immobile financial system on top of it had stopped their development. When cotton became king, the profits that part of the South enjoyed were an obstruction to clear thinking upon the slavery question.

The small amount of cotton that was raised in the United States in 1793 was grown in South Carolina and Georgia, chiefly in their lowlands along the coast; and these regions controlled three quarters of the crop until the War of 1812. The commercial supremacy of Charleston and Savannah in the South was unquestioned while this state of things lasted. With the shift of settlement beyond the Savannah to the waters of the Chattahoochee and the further streams of Coosa, Tombigbee, Pearl, and Yazoo, there came into existence a cotton belt tributary to the Gulf, and the southern Atlantic seaboard became nervous as to the future. Between 1811 and 1821, as the result of the southern drift of settlement, the cotton raised west of Georgia became nearly a third of the total crop. The eastern crop was greatly increasing in absolute amount, but was declining relatively to the whole. By 1831 a half of the crop was raised in the West; by 1834, two thirds. The crop that was worth about thirteen million dollars in 1810 was worth over seventy-five million dollars by 1834.

When the great migration took shape shortly before 1812, Mississippi Territory lay directly in the road of its southern advance. Erected in 1798, and enlarged after the Georgia cession of 1802, it included the whole of the present States of Alabama and Mississippi, north of the thirty-first parallel. The Spanish blockade along its southern side, due to the retention of Florida, was less important than it would have been if Mississippi had been growing rapidly, or if Florida had possessed an active and enterprising population. As soon as the territory began to grow, the United States acted upon the old claim to West Florida and appropriated the shore line west of the Perdido River, adding the strip to Mississippi. Mobile was occupied by Wilkinson in 1813, though Pensacola, taken a little later, was given back. There were under a hundred houses at either Mobile or Natchez when the war broke out, and the tide of migration had only just begun to flow.

The Natchez Trace cut across the western corner of Mississippi but was less used as an immigrant route than the Mississippi River. From Tennessee and Kentucky the migrants were most apt to take a flatboat downstream and make a landing near the mouth of the Yazoo River. Here begins a broad strip of deep black soil, with few equals in the world for cotton culture. The strip, with varying degrees of fertility extends east from the Yazoo bottom lands, across southern Mississippi and Alabama. The cessions procured by Jackson from the Creek Indians in 1814 opened a part of the strip to settlement. The Three Notch Road passed just south of the strip between Fort Hawkins and Natchez.

The Three Notch Road was a route of entry for settlers from Georgia and South Carolina. When the Northwest obtained legislation for the Cumberland Road to the Ohio, a southern demand was raised for a similar thoroughfare, and the Falls Line was the popular choice for its location. There could be no good road much further east, because of the great difficulty of crossing the numerous Atlantic rivers. Further west the rising piedmont made such a road a great engineering feat. But from falls to falls, the road would separate piedmont from coastal plain and would touch points at which natural water powers were being developed and where towns were springing to life. Richmond, Raleigh, Columbia, and Milledgeville, the capitals of their respective States, were all near this line, and it was reasonable to ask a Federal road that should reach the southern capitals and project itself to the southwest border at New Orleans.[4]

[4] The *Publications* of the Mississippi Historical Society, of which fourteen volumes were edited by Professor Franklin Lafayette Riley prior to the accession of Hon. Dunbar Rowland, the present editor, are prominent among southern historical collections in both bulk and importance.

Before the War of 1812, the southern line of settlement stopped short of the Ocmulgee River in Georgia, where Benjamin Hawkins had resided as southern Indian superintendent since 1796.[5] The reluctance of the Cherokee and Creek nations to make any cessions stood in the way of fulfilling the southern desire for a western road, and the Falls Line never became the site of a national thoroughfare. But west of Fort Hawkins a trail was blazed that crossed the Chattahoochee River at Fort Mitchell, reached the Alabama River at the Hickory Grove, where Montgomery was built, crossed the Tombigbee somewhat further south at St. Stephens, and thence ran close to the thirty-first parallel to Natchez. It was sometimes called the Federal Road, east of St. Stephens. West of this point it was more often the Three Notch Road, named from the surveyor's blaze. Nowhere was it more than an unimproved, though passable, trail, but along it came settlers that grew more numerous as the years advanced.

A third route to Mississippi Territory was directly from eastern Tennessee, with fertile lands in the bend of the Tennessee River, near Huntsville, as objective. The Natchez Trace crossed the Tennessee River not far from this region and was of local use. Jackson led his army of 1813 in this direction. By act of Congress, after the war was over, the men under his command marked a Federal road from the vicinity of Nashville, his home town, to Madisonville, Louisiana, on Lake Pontchartrain, a distance of over five hundred miles. Central Alabama was open to settlement by 1816, but until after 1830 there were large tracts in eastern Alabama and northern Mississippi that the Indians still held.

To these three districts of Mississippi Territory, at Yazoo, at Huntsville, and above Mobile, the tide of settlement turned in the years in which Indiana and Illinois were being lifted towards statehood. The population of Mississippi Territory in 1810 was 40,352 as against the joint population of Indiana and Illinois of 36,802. In the next ten years the two northern states reached a total of 202,340, while Mississippi and Alabama though less accessible grew to 203,349. In all the States the decade was one of crudest pioneer conditions, with few of the residents living in any but the earliest phase of social development. By 1830 the two northern States had risen to 500,476, while the southern

[5] His letters are in Georgia Historical Society, *Collections*, vol. IX.

lagged at 446,148; by 1850 the population of Indiana and Illinois was 1,839,886; of Alabama and Mississippi 1,378,149. The northern States were nearly thirty per cent ahead.

The division of Mississippi Territory took place in 1817 when Congress authorized the western side to form a constitution, and created the Territory of Alabama east of an arbitrary line running from the mouth of Bear Creek on the Tennessee River almost due south to the Gulf of Mexico. The Mississippi convention was held from July 7 to August 15, 1817, in Lorenzo Dow's old camp meeting house on the Natchez Trace at the first station above Natchez. The constitution was framed with the usual frontier ease, slavery was recognized as an existing institution without debate, and the document after its approval by the convention was given an endorsement novel among first constitutions. It was submitted to ratification by the voters of the State and set a precedent that thereafter was an additional measure of the extension of democracy.

The Territory of Alabama, created in 1817, grew much more rapidly than its parent, for more of its land was open to entry, and it lay nearer the main bodies of southern population. South as well as north, most of the settlers of a new district came from nearly adjacent communities. The great migration was nearing its crest as Alabama started its independent life, and the small farmers who cleared the land were rapidly pushed up into the hills or further west, as the planters with money to buy cleared land arrived in the lower valleys of the Alabama and Tombigbee. In 1819 Alabama was enabled to form a State, and the convention sat at Huntsville from July 5 to August 2. Like Mississippi, Alabama submitted its constitution to a popular referendum. It became a State December 14, 1819.

CHAPTER XXIV
MISSOURI: THE NEW SECTIONALISM

AFTER the admission of Alabama there were twenty-two States in the Union, eleven of which permitted and expected to permit slavery to exist. The hope or ideal that slavery would one day be discarded by the South itself had vanished. Instead there was developing a small and wealthy aristocracy that derived its importance from the exploitation of the cotton crop and the use of slaves. Like the bulk of the people of the South and West the plantation leaders called themselves Democrats, but they had little in common with the Democrats whom the frontier had bred until cotton became important, and who continued to be bred on the northern frontiers until the industrial aristocracy of the later nineteenth century arose. In the years of the great migration, after the entrance of Louisiana into the Union in 1812, attention was drawn to the equal balance of slave States and free, and the equilibrium in the United States Senate brought about thereby. This balance became a political condition to be maintained, and when the next new States appeared to ask the approval of Congress, the question was there raised as to the nature of the local institutions. The expanding frontier gave the background to the slavery controversy.

After the formation of Alabama, the region available for more new States was limited. There were the two detached corners of the United States, northeast and southeast. Maine and Florida were obviously destined for admission, one in the immediate future, the other more remotely. Between the western line of the last States (which ran from Toledo, Ohio, around the northern and western boundaries of Indiana, Illinois, Kentucky, Tennessee, Mississippi, and Louisiana) and the new international boundaries agreed to in 1818 and 1819, lay all the public domain that was left. Much of this was already conceded to be uninhabitable. North of Louisiana there was reason to suppose that additional States could be put in between the Mississippi and the eastern edge of the American Desert; certainly Arkansas, which was made a territory in 1819, and Missouri, above it. There were also two more to come from the Old Northwest, the last of the five,

Michigan and Wisconsin. If more than these four additional
States should be built along the border, it would be necessary
to force the Indians much further west than they were willing
to go, or to experiment with desert States. "The cultivated
frontier of the United States, with which the Indians are placed
in contact," said a writer in the *North American Review* in 1827,
"extends from Detroit to Nachitoches, a distance upon this line
of fifteen hundred miles."

So far as practical men could, or would, see in 1819 there were
thus six more States to be admitted before the Union should
reach its full dimensions. Maine, Michigan, and Wisconsin
would be in a latitude unfriendly to slavery. Florida and Arkansas would maintain slaves, without dispute. Missouri was
in doubt. For the sake of the balance in the Senate, now becoming precious, it must be made slave. But the experience of the
southern-born population in Indiana and Illinois, and its willingness to give up slavery, made it doubtful whether the southern
migrants into Missouri could be relied on to cherish the institutions of the land whence they came, or prevented from recognizing the northern fact that slave labor was not a source of profit
outside the plantation belt. The natural resources of Missouri
had something to do with the settlement of the question, and the
preferences of the population had some weight. The necessities
of a self-conscious section that feared to be overbalanced in the
Senate was the final deciding factor.

After a short period of dependence upon Indiana, a separate
territorial government was set up at St. Louis in 1805. It was
a government of the first stage, with all of its powers exercised
by governor and judges who were appointed by the President.
Its realm was huge, reaching from the Mississippi to the unknown
western limits of the province of Louisiana, whose name it bore.
Not until 1812 was it permitted to pass to the second stage, with
an elected assembly; and then it received the name of Missouri.
Few of its Indian inhabitants ever knew from contact with it
that such a government existed, and many of its white residents
were nearly as free from its control. St. Louis, its capital, was
center of the fur trade. The shifting traders only occasionally
returned to the center of the province, and for many years they
beheld few changes there. There was no considerable American settlement in Missouri Territory until the great migration.
Not until after 1815 did St. Louis emerge from the crude shell

of the frontier outpost and take on the semblance of a town. It did not call itself a city until after its incorporation as such in 1822; but by this later date the rise of steamboat traffic on the Ohio and Mississippi had changed the vision of its future. Between 1815 and 1822 a new State arose behind it.

In July, 1819, by an act passed the previous March, Missouri Territory was diminished to make room for Arkansas. There had been a secondary trading post near the mouth of the Arkansas River for a century or more. Arkansas Post was never as important as St. Louis, but there was enough traffic up and down the Arkansas to give it a precarious existence. There were few settlers in this valley when the new territory was created, but their distance from St. Louis and the chronic dislike of frontier residents for remote government, provided the excuse for slicing off a southern strip of Missouri. The parallel of 36° 30′ was made the dividing line, except for an irregular tract running south to 36°, between the Mississippi and the St. Francis River. This left in Missouri a group of river colonies around New Madrid that were midway between Arkansas Post and St. Louis, but were connected by straggling settlements with the northern capital. Arkansas Territory extended west between Missouri and Louisiana to the western boundary of the United States, which had been fixed a few weeks earlier in the same year at the one hundredth meridian. The Arkansas border, where it touched upon Texas, was the home of southern plains Indians who had never admitted white control, and who had ever been a difficult problem for Spain, on whose frontier they dwelt. Even before Arkansas was named, it had been determined to use part of this region for future homes for Indians from Alabama and Mississippi. Fort Smith, upon the upper Arkansas River, was erected to protect both the natives and the white colonists in the new territory and marked a point at which Arkansas was finally divided from the Indian country.

Fort Smith, which was erected in 1817 by Major Stephen H. Long and a detachment of the Seventh Infantry, U.S.A., was unable to obtain a population of five hundred before 1850. At the junction of the Poteau and the Arkansas, and some six hundred miles above Arkansas Post, it was a strategic spot, rather than a colony. It was the southern station of a chain of posts with which the War Department linked up the northern and southern frontiers of the United States after the end of the

War of 1812. The other forts in the series were Fort Howard and Fort Crawford in Wisconsin, Fort Snelling in Minnesota, Fort Armstrong on Rock Island in the Mississippi, and Fort Des Moines and Fort Leavenworth on the Iowa-Missouri border.

The planting of these forts began in 1816, and their location had significance as suggesting a permanent border between the farmers and the savages. Fort Howard, at Green Bay, was built in the summer of 1816, as was Fort Crawford at Prairie du Chien. Between them stretched the Fox and Wisconsin rivers and a famous thoroughfare that the French had used for a century and a half, and the Indians for unknown times. The easy portage for canoes, at the bend of the Wisconsin River, was slight impediment in the route. The northwest tribes, Sauk and Fox, Winnebago, Potawatami, Menominee, Chippewa, and Sioux, were all more or less in contact with the little garrisons that were maintained in these positions. Fort Armstrong, built at the same time, controlled the mouth of the Rock River and was in reach of the country identified with the Sauk and Fox.

West of the Mississippi, the garrisons came a little later. At the confluence of the St. Peter's and Mississippi, where Pike held his conference with the Sioux in 1805, was a strategic center that was occupied in 1819. This became Fort Snelling, and in another generation St. Paul and Minneapolis grew up around it. Colonel Henry Leavenworth, with troops from Detroit, began the structure, but Major Long had recommended the site, and Colonel Josiah Snelling finally completed it. Midway across Iowa, Fort Des Moines was established at a later date. In 1827 Fort Leavenworth, on the Missouri above its great bend, became the westernmost of the series.

A new law to regulate intercourse with the Indians was passed in 1816. The foreign traders who had hitherto captured much of the fur yield of Louisiana were excluded by this act, and licensed American citizens were given a monopoly of it. The American Fur Company benefited much by this legislation, and its subsidiaries that John Jacob Astor controlled speedily threw their agents into the remotest corners of the Louisiana Purchase. The British companies, operating out of London and Montreal, were brought into violent competition in the narrowed fields, and then were combined by act of Parliament in 1821. Their settlements on the Red River of the North, at Pembina, proved to be on the American side of the new international boundary of 1818, and they withdrew down the river to the mouth of the Assiniboin, founding there Fort Garry, later to ripen into Winnipeg.

In connection with the erection of frontier forts and a new law for Indian trade, the War Department contemplated another serious exploration of the western portions of Missouri Territory, and designated Major Long as the commander of the expedition.[1] It was hoped originally to make this exploration of such magnitude as to impress the power of the United States upon the minds of all the western savages and to clear up whatever geographical matters remained in doubt along the western boundary of the Louisiana Purchase. Funds were lacking for this, but with reduced dimensions the expedition was launched in 1819, when in the month of May, Stephen H. Long departed from Pittsburgh in his little steamboat, the *Western Engineer*.

The river steamboat had passed beyond the experimental stage by 1819, and the Pittsburgh shipwrights knew that to escape the bars and snags that gave variety to every river trip, the boat must be of light draught. The *Western Engineer* drew but nineteen inches, yet had its difficulties before it was far upon its journey. It left Pittsburgh on May 5 and started up the Missouri about the middle of June. By September it was near the mouth of the Platte River, in the vicinity of the Council Bluffs, where Long selected a site for his winter quarters, to be used during the first winter in the field. He left his men here during the winter of 1819–1820, returning to the States; but was back again in May, 1820, and ready to start west, up the shallow valley of the Platte on June 6. His orders directed him to ascertain the sources of the Platte, and then move south along the mountains to visit the headwaters of the Arkansas and the Red, to which Pike had been sent in 1806. He was to impress the Indians, and accumulate the scientific basis for an understanding of the country. He may have been successful so far as the red men were concerned, but his science, like his exploration, failed to reach its mark.

In the summer of 1820, Long made the easy circuit of the Platte, the foothills, and the Arkansas. He failed to find a source. He saw the great peak that now bears his name, and its southern sister, named for Pike, but did not penetrate behind them as would have been necessary to determine the origin of either river.

[1] This is well described in Cardinal Goodwin, "A Larger View of the Yellowstone Expedition, 1819–1820," in *Mississippi Valley Historical Review*, 1917.

He did not visit the source of the Red although one of his parties, on the homeward leg, made a detour to the Canadian Fork of the Red and descended into Fort Smith.

Long came back to St. Louis with conclusions whose substantial untruth was revealed in the century following: "In regard to this extensive section of country, I do not hesitate in giving the opinion, that it is almost wholly unfit for cultivation, and of course uninhabitable by a people depending on agriculture for their subsistence." Had he hesitated, he might have foreseen the expansion of the United States into Kansas, Nebraska, and Oklahoma. But he was convinced that he was right, and he had the support of Hugh M. Brackenridge, whose *Journal of a Voyage up the River Missouri* (1816), advised the reader that "compact settlements" might be expected along only the six hundred miles immediately above the mouth of that stream. "Above," said Brackenridge, "it becomes more dreary and desert till it reaches the Rocky Mountains, and can never have any other inhabitants than the few that may exist at certain stations along the river. ...It combines within its frightful and extensive territory the Steppes of Tartary, and the moving sands of the African deserts."

The vast region, Long wrote, "commencing near the sources of the Sabine, Trinity, Brazos, and Colorado [all in Texas], and extending northwardly to the forty-ninth degree of north latitude...is throughout of a similar character....This region, however, viewed as a frontier, may prove of infinite importance to the United States, inasmuch as it is calculated to serve as a barrier to prevent too great an expansion of our population westward." When his observations were printed, the *North American Review*, July, 1821, drew inferences that helped to shape public opinion for a generation. It called attention to the fact that the "acquired" territory of the United States between the Mississippi and the Rocky Mountains was "greater than that which belonged originally to the rest of the United States....It may be a question of political duty [it continued], whether our patriotism must expand with the extension of our territory, and require of us to look upon our French and Spanish brothers by purchase, to be as truly our fellow citizens, as the fathers who defended our soil, and the sons who have since tilled it. We...concur in the opinion...that there is great difficulty in sending out our patriotic affections beyond the Missouri and the Rocky Mountains. The natural tendency of an increasing empire to separation was counterbalanced in the new states we have formed, by their being peopled wholly from the older ones, and community of language, manners, interest, and ties, thereby preserved. This is not the case with part of Louisiana and Florida. . . . "

Long conceded that the eastern portion of the Missouri Territory was habitable and described so much of it as he observed along the river banks as he ascended. The census of 1810 had found 20,845 inhabitants in the territory; by 1820 the number had grown to 66,586 in the reduced Missouri, and 14,273 in Arkansas Territory. Most of the white inhabitants in both territories lived close to the great rivers. Behind St. Louis the settlements were pushing up the Missouri, and Long found the westernmost at Franklin, halfway between the mouth of the Kansas and that of the Missouri. About 1827 Franklin was washed away by the river, but in 1819 it was something over two years old and contained one hundred and twenty houses. There was here a weekly *Missouri Intelligencer and Boone's Lick Advertiser* that made its bow to the public on April 23, 1819, a few days before Long passed by. There were two brick houses among the one hundred and twenty, but the only building that had two stories was the jail. No church was mentioned, but there were four taverns and two billiard rooms.

Even before Long ascended the Missouri River, or made his discouraging report upon the future of the Far West, the people around St. Louis had begun to talk of statehood, as others were talking in the four other western territories that were admitted before 1820.[2] The fact that there were under sixty thousand inhabitants when the talk began was of no importance, since Congress had the power to determine the suitability of the territory to become a State. There was no good reason for failing to admit Missouri that would not have been equally good if urged against Indiana, Mississippi, Illinois, or Alabama; and there was no disposition to exclude the region.

There were memorials before Congress, praying for the admission of Missouri in 1817–1818, and they were reinforced in 1818–1819 by formal appeal from the assembly of the territory. The measure for the creation of Arkansas Territory that passed March 2, 1819, was accompanied by another enabling Missouri

[2] Floyd C. Shoemaker, *Missouri's Struggle for Statehood* (1916), is detailed, well-informed, and judicious. There is a good picture of "Missouri in 1820," by Jonas Viles, in *Missouri Historical Review*, 1920.

to form a constitution. But the latter was blocked on February 13, when a New York representative, Tallmadge by name, offered an amendment forbidding the further existence of slavery in Missouri. The superior growth of the free States had already given them more than half the total population in the United States, and accordingly a majority of the members of the House of Representatives. The Tallmadge amendment was accepted in the House; the Senate struck it out, and Missouri failed to be enabled at this session.

Between the adjournment of Congress in March, 1819, and its reassembling in December, the march of settlers into the Missouri Valley continued, and the determination of southern congressmen not to permit the exclusion of slavery from Missouri grew fixed. The Senate was evenly balanced. Missouri would turn it one way or another. And when Maine appeared on the program for 1819–1820 demanding admission as a free State, it was unthinkable for the South to surrender its hold on Missouri. Good observers were reporting that the Missouri settlers were bringing with them more slaves than had gone north of the Ohio River, and the temper of Missouri itself was in favor of slave labor.

The District of Maine was not one of the territories of the United States, and never had been one. It was instead a detached part of Massachusetts and partook of statehood already, having its share of representatives in the Massachusetts legislature and in the House of Representatives, under the Massachusetts apportionment laws. It had long indulged in talk of separate statehood and had grown much with the extension of settlement after the English war. Its constitutional convention met in October, 1819, and framed a document which the people promptly ratified. Massachusetts gave her consent to the separation, so that Congress had only to declare Maine to be a State. But the southern senators were now in earnest about Missouri, and Maine was accordingly paired with the former State, and threatened with exclusion unless Missouri came in slave.

The great debate in Congress in February, 1820, was the first formal display of the new sectionalism brought about by the renaissance of slavery. The virtues and defects of slavery as a system were brought in question, but more discussion was given to the power of Congress to place conditions upon the admission of a State, as Tallmadge desired to do, and to the rights of slave-holding citizens to a free and full use of the territory of the United States. Henry Clay, who was opposed to any restriction upon Missouri, gave his support to the compromise with which the deadlock between Senate and House was broken. Maine was admitted, by an act of March 3, 1820, effective March 15. Missouri was authorized to frame such a constitution as she desired, by act of March 6. And it was further provided, as a concession to the northern opinion that yielded regarding Missouri, that there should be no slavery in the remainder of the Louisiana Purchase, north of Arkansas Territory (or the latitude of 36° 30'). There is still some doubt as to who won by this compromise. It is certain, however, that slavery could not have been forced into any additional territory north or west of Missouri, and also that the slave-holder gained a right to enjoy slavery in all of the public domain in which it could be made to flourish.

Missouri remained outside the Union for seventeen months longer, not being admitted until August 10, 1821. The reason for the unusual delay is to be found in the procedure of the constitutional convention that began its sessions June 12, 1820. This body gloated too much over the southern victory and put into the constitution provisions excluding free negroes from Missouri, and restricting the power of the legislature to emancipate the slaves. The opponents of the compromise were so enraged at this that the act to admit Missouri under the new constitution could not pass the House of Representatives, and the debate over the status of slavery broke out anew in 1821. A committee of thirteen, presided over by Clay himself, failed to harmonize the conflict; a second grand committee of twenty-three brought forth a proviso that nothing in the Missouri constitution should ever be construed as denying to a citizen of any State any of the privileges and immunities to which he might be entitled under the Constitution of the United States; and that the Missouri legislature must assent to this. In this form the final phase of the Missouri Compromise became a law; and in accordance with its provisions Missouri came into the Union in August.

With the admission of Missouri the great migration came to an end so far as new States were concerned, and the heavy shift of population subsided for another ten years. The United States had gained six new States in the process and was now confronted with a period of getting used to its new dimensions. The economics of its growth and the politics of its reactions are uppermost until 1829.

CHAPTER XXV

PUBLIC LAND REFORM

THE creation of new States along the unsettled border is an excellent index to the shifts of population. The fact that six such commonwealths were added to the United States in the six years beginning with 1816, would of itself establish that period as one of marked migration. But even better than the States as an index are the figures that show the sales of public lands by the United States, for these figures measure not only the opening of new settlements, but the extent to which help had been found to finance the settlement.

In the first fifteen years of the public land system, that terminated with the passage of the Harrison Land Act in 1800, the total sales from the public domain were 1,484,047 acres. This total includes the operations under the three private sales to the Ohio Associates, Symmes, and the State of Pennsylvania, as well as under the law of 1796. The Harrison Act brought the land office to the buyer, opening at the start four local offices in the Eastern Division of the Northwest Territory. From year to year these offices were closed, shifted, or increased in number, in order to follow the business. Before the Harrison Act was revised in 1820, there were or had been in operation fourteen such offices in Ohio, four in Indiana, three in Illinois, and one in Michigan. Outside the Old Northwest, in the same period, there were three in Alabama, three in Mississippi, four in Louisiana, and two in Missouri.

The distribution of these offices indicates the regions where government sales were most numerous; the annual sales reveal the flow of occupation. But until after the beginning of the War of 1812 the volume of business showed no startling changes. Until this date the business of the land sales was managed in a bureau of the Treasury Department; on April 25, 1812, this was reorganized as a General Land Office, under Edward Tiffin of Ohio as Commissioner. After this date the business increased rapidly, the figures in millions of acres running as follows:

1813................ .14	1818................2.38
1814................ .82	1819...............5.11
1815................1.07	1820...............1.08
1816................1.47	1821............... .78
1817................1.92	

It is not to be supposed that the figures of sales of public land give a complete measure of the new settlement. Much of the land thus bought was held by speculators and was not cleared or farmed until these owners could find purchasers. There was still much land on the market from earlier grants, in which the emigrants could buy tracts. There were school lands for sale in most of the States. And in Kentucky and Tennessee, where there was no public domain, there was an abundance of private land for sale. No general study has yet been made to show how private land titles originated for any large tract along the frontier. The Wisconsin "Domesday Book," now under way, will show it for a single State; but for the present there is no better indication of the speed with which all lands were being used than the fairly accurate figures for the government-owned part of it. By 1820, according to Donaldson, the government had sold 19,399,158 acres; but nearly a third of this was beyond the power of the purchaser to pay for, and was eventually turned back into the public domain, to be sold again. The defects in the land law that Harrison had promoted as a reform were grievous and notorious before it had been in operation for ten years.

The minimum cost of making a farm under the Harrison Act cannot have been much different from that of making it on land purchased otherwise. This law provided for sale first at public auction, and then at private sale at two dollars an acre. The better lands were often bid up at the auctions to fancy prices, but Donaldson shows that the apparent sales of over nineteen million acres were for a total of only forty-seven million dollars. After the unpaid-for lands were surrendered, the United States received twenty-eight million dollars for thirteen million acres. The actual receipts averaged so nearly the minimum of two dollars an acre that it is clear that this price was not too low for unimproved land on the average frontier.

Under the Harrison Act the minimum amount sold to one buyer was half a section, or three hundred and twenty acres. In 1804 this was lessened to the familiar quarter section of one hundred and sixty acres, which was quite as much as the ordinary frontier farmer could operate, and more than he could expect to pay for. The government requirement for a quarter of the purchase price, or fifty cents an acre, to be paid within forty days of the purchase, meant that such a buyer needed eighty dollars in cash at the time he made his selection. The theory of the credit system, upon which the Harrison Act was based, was that payments after the first were to be earned from the produce of the land. The second quarter was not due until two years after the purchase; the other installments followed a year apart.

Most of the buyers of western lands were both poor and hopeful. Because they were poor, they found that the initial charge of eighty dollars was a large amount of money. Because they were hopeful, they were convinced that it would be easy to raise the later installments, and accordingly used all the ready money they could command in order to make the first payment on as large an acreage as they could get. This left many of them without cash, and the next two years saw few who were able to lay much aside. The number of defaulters at the second, third, and fourth payments increased progressively, and in the long run nearly a third of the lands contracted for were given up. By 1809 Congress began to pass relief acts extending the time of settlement for later installments; and in 1820 the twelfth such act was passed.

That the land system was vicious, was apparent by 1809, but the full extent of the injury it did has never been made clear. Its normal tendency was to create a region in which every citizen was in debt to the United States for a period of four years or more. The political consequence of such a situation, under a system of manhood suffrage, was an unavoidable tendency of public opinion to crystallize against the government. Every elector owed money, and voted to determine the policy of the government to which he owed it. No right of the government as a whole could stand out in his mind as clearly as did his own difficulties in making payments. Even if the whole frontier had been prosperous, there would have been an incentive to tinker with the law to reduce the payments and lighten the load. But the frontier was far from prosperous most of the time, and with every default on an installment, there was added to the electorate another voter in danger of having his farm taken away from him. The Harrison Act made it possible to reassert United States title to tracts that were not paid for, and the contractor was liable to lose his equity in the seizure. As the number of defaulters increased, the pressure increased upon congressmen to bring in acts to relieve their constituents. Even worse, as the number of defaulters increased because of inability to pay, it was further increased by unwillingness to pay. Nothing was actually done to dispossess the men who could not pay. The government threatened to exercise its right to seize the land, but did not do it. The successful farmer, who met his obligation and paid his debt when due, saw that the only difference between himself and his defaulting neighbor was that he had given up his hard earned money and his neighbor had not. He asked himself what use it was to pay, when nothing happened to the man who did not pay. In many cases, when his next installment came due, he let it pass unpaid. The larger the proportion of settlers that was in default, the less it was possible for the General Land Office to use successful pressure upon any of them. By 1812 the condition was one of general scandal, with no remedy except in a modification of the Harrison Act, and the total abolition of the credit system. The measurement of the injury done by the system to frontier standards of commercial honor would make an interesting study in group psychology.

A new view of the public lands was rising in the West between 1810 and 1820 as the people questioned the success of the old land policies. The leaders began to ask by what right the United States demanded any payment for its land. They challenged the basic idea upon which the public domain had been brought into existence. Congress had believed in 1780 that the western lands could be made a source of public revenue that would materially lessen the financial burdens left by the Revolution. The pressure from the smaller States for the cessions was based upon the belief that the lands were a source of wealth. But the experience since the United States took up their administration was that much money went into them and little came out. There was little net revenue, or none. When at first they were sold in competition with the lands still available in Pennsylvania and western Virginia they could not command either good market or strong price; and as these competitions lessened, the government found itself able to sell a considerable amount, at a nominal price of two dollars an acre, which it could not collect. Land legislation was a consistent source of business for Congress, and every western representative, as he took his seat, became a new obstruction in the way of making the public domain a source of profit. Towards 1820, the western congressmen began to lay stress upon the public services of the men who made new homes in the wilderness, and to demand that they be relieved from the financial burdens placed upon them. A new senator who took his seat from Missouri in 1821, Thomas Hart Benton, made free lands his objective; and after thirty years' service in the Senate, he lived to see his idea widely popular and brought to the verge of complete triumph.

So long as tidewater congressmen prevailed in Washington, there was no hope of victory for the notion that the United States ought to give free farms to the frontiersmen. The eastern desire for revenue was mingled with a genuine fear of the growth of the western States. There was a willingness to restrict the free settlement of the frontier that was more often effective than avowed. By 1820 Congress was convinced that the Harrison Act had broken down, but was not ready to give up the hope of revenue. The particular weakness of the law of 1800 had been the relatively large unit of sale, the system of credit, and the price. The unit was reduced in 1804, and now was reduced still further to half a quarter, or eighty acres. The principle of credit was now abolished; and by a new law passed April 24, 1820, sales were required to be made for cash. Upon the matter of price there was a compromise at $1.25 an acre. The farmers who were still in trouble, having defaulted upon installments and become liable to dispossession, were given the opportunity to make a compromise, and surrender to the United States the proportion of their lands that they could not pay for. They were thus enabled to start free once more.

The land law of 1820 was passed after the crest of the great migration had been reached. The year 1819, in which over five million acres of the public lands were sold, was also the year of general economic distress and panic. Not until 1834 was there another year in which the sales were nearly so great. For a decade after 1820 the frontier was assimilating the land it had acquired, and there was no strain that indicated special weakness in the new land act. In the thirties, when wholesale shift of population was resumed once more, the weakness appeared at a different spot; this time in the inability of the General Land Office to keep its surveys progressing as rapidly as the people demanded. The generation that established itself between 1800 and 1820 was grounded in the belief that a government price for land was one of the numerous financial extortions from which it had to suffer. It was generally convinced that the newer portions of the country were subject to financial exploitation by the older, and was more bitterly distressed by the financial bonds that bound it to fellow citizens than by those that were held by the lighter hand of government.

CHAPTER XXVI

FRONTIER FINANCE

THE need of the frontier citizen for credit was second in importance only to his need for land. First and most fundamental of his problems was ever that of acquiring a good title to the land he farmed. The contracts that had to be made in getting land left a mark upon the first generation, at least, in any frontier. The second need, to get the money to pay for the land, began to impress financial traits upon the community; and these in the next generation were sometimes more significant than even the land economics. Land was one of the occasions for cash and credit. But it was only one among a shoal of necessities that pressed down upon the young homeseeker and restricted his freedom of action until their demands were met.[1]

Any analysis of the financial requirements of the typical frontier family will reveal the fact that lack of financial opportunity was one of the compelling causes of migration; and that with migration determined upon, there were important financial necessities under at least three heads. The money for the cash payment upon the land was one of the three, and second in sequence in most cases. In point of time it was preceded by the fund to cover the costs of transportation; it was followed by a fund for maintenance until the new farm could become self-supporting.

The typical family on the agricultural frontier was young, poor, and ambitious. There were of course exceptions to the rule of poverty, but these were not enough to weaken its general binding force. Most young people, with either property or easy opportunity, were glad not to undertake the risks and hardships of the frontier life. Those who had neither were likely to make as short a migration as was consistent with finding cheap land and desirable living conditions. The exceptions, and numerous they were, to this rule, are to be found in colonies like that at Marietta or the Connecticut Reserve, or in the individual families who made the long trip from tidewater to the Ohio Valley. New England expanded into the West in some measure, but

---

[1] Murray S. Wildman, *Money Inflation in the United States. A Study in Social Pathology* (1905), is the clearest presentation of this theme.

when a census of origin was taken in any of the western regions it was commonly found that most of the dwellers in a new community originated in the immediately adjacent States, and sought their new homes with the minimum of travel.[2] Yet travel they must in any case. Every homeseeker needed means to get his wagon and team, to buy his simple outfit for operating the home and farm, and to maintain himself and family while on the journey. There is enough scattered evidence — it has never been assembled — to show that a large proportion of the travelers moved on borrowed money, and were unable even to start for their new homes until some obliging neighbor or relative took their notes and provided them with funds. In individual instances the amount was so considerable that many who desired to move were unable to raise the money for it; in the aggregate, the capital so invested became a heavy mortgage upon the future production of the new region.

After raising funds to cover the cost of migration and to make the initial payments upon the land, there still remained the necessity to support the family until crops could be extracted from the reluctant soil. The first harvest can rarely have done this, for the number of acres that could be cleared, planted, and cultivated in the first season was small. There are many estimates that show that the cost of getting a crop into the ground for the first time might be twice or thrice what the land itself would bring while unimproved. The average family lived in part upon the savings of some one else for a year or more. In many instances the newcomers made the first year partially supporting by working for wages for earlier arrivals who could use them on the farms. This naturally lessened, by the amount of the wages, the debt that otherwise must be incurred. But over the whole frontier, taking the average, the home maker continued to go into debt for a year or more after his arrival.

Under these three heads fall most of the debts that the frontiersman accumulated during the process of establishment. If there had been more capital available for loans, every region could have been developed more rapidly than it was. But the United States as a whole possessed little surplus capital for investment. The invasion of European capital had not yet begun on a large scale. There were few sums of eastern wealth that

---

[2] Lois Kimball Mathews [now Rosenberry], *The Expansion of New England* (1909), still needs to be paralleled by other studies as searching and convincing.

could be used for western development, no machinery for investing it if it had existed, and even less inclination to risk it there.
"I have found no evidence that any eastern capital was invested
in this way before 1815," said the late Professor Callender.
"The settler moved out into the wilderness with his own little
stock of household goods, farm implements, and cattle. No merchant with large credit in the East stood ready to advance
supplies of food and other necessities to him, while he devoted
his labor to the production of a crop to be sent to market, nor
was he assisted to clear his land and prepare it for cultivation
by loans of cash from individuals or mortgage companies."
Professor Callender minimized too much the family loans that
sent many an emigrant upon his way, and gives no recognition
to the fact that the average distance of the migrant was not many
miles — that his connections were not those of a westerner with
the East, but of a frontier farmer with a former frontier community, fifty miles or so behind him. But he is right in suggesting that there were few sources from which the pioneer could
borrow the funds necessary for the capitalization of his venture,
even on the most modest scale.

The development of social institutions provided a new financial
resource for the pioneer at the moment of the great migration,
and for two decades banks played a double rôle upon the frontier
stage. Cast as the hero in the first act, ready and able to save the
heroine from distress, the bank in the second act became the detected villain on the verge of strangling the confiding victim,
only to be foiled as the curtain fell by the protective efforts of a
new wave of fundamental democracy. Each of the parts played
by the banks was inevitable; together they form a contrast that
reveals much of the western spirit in its two phases of hopeful-
ness and despondency. And both prove beyond question the
high significance of financial institutions in the forming of a new
society.

Banks, in the modern sense, are largely the creation of the
half century that followed the American Revolution. Great
establishments, like the Bank of England, had long preceded this
period, but had revealed banking as a detached activity of the
state; not as an ordinary agent of commerce. The profits of the
banker, and his special interests, have received more attention
than the real contribution of banks as such to social finance.
It was not that they lent money. Money lenders are so ancient

that their origin is lost in antiquity, and they have continued to exist in every community with no perceptible change until to-day. They have been able to lend, however, only what they possessed, and the limits of their possible business has been the amount of savings that they have accumulated.

The banking idea added two conditions that together brought a fundamental change; these were currency and credit. As to currency, it was gradually learned that promissory notes, redeemable in coin on demand, were seized upon by every community as a convenient local currency. They were kept so busy that until the notes wore to rags they were not sent to the bank of issue for redemption. The world was currency-hungry during these early years of the industrial revolution and found the paper of solvent banks an excellent substitute for specie. The banks of issue soon learned of the long interval that would elapse between the issue of a promissory note and the date of its probable presentation for redemption. They learned that the coin held for redeeming the notes would not be needed, all or soon, and that they could extend credit to customers, not only to the amount of their coin capital, but to the amount of promissory notes that they could keep in circulation. The size of a prudent coin reserve, to be held on hand to redeem note issues, was a matter of estimate that ranged from one third to one fifth; but at whatever ratio it was fixed by the operators of the bank, there was a profitable margin of notes above the amount of capital that could be safely lent to borrowers. In the use of this margin, the banker made his profits, above those of the ordinary money lender, who could lend only what he had. For society, the discovery of this margin made the existing capital threefold, or fivefold as fluid as it would otherwise have been. The capital of a community with banks went several times further than the capital of the community without banks. Hence their spread.

Between 1791 and 1811 the United States possessed the Bank of the United States with a charter voted by Congress, and a small but growing number of local banks whose right to do business was based upon act of legislature in the various States. There were always a few informal banks that existed without legal sanction but because the men behind them deserved and held the confidence of the people to whom they lent their notes. There was no "free banking" in the sense that any group of men who complied with the provisions of the law could enter the business.

Instead each institution was supposed to derive its right to exist by a special act of the law-making body. There were only three of these in the United States before the inauguration of George Washington; at the end of his century there were only twenty-six. In 1811 when the charter of the Bank of the United States expired, there were only eighty-eight. The profitable nature of this business and the useful social character of their service had been found out by this time. The refusal of Congress to recharter its own creation opened a period of wholesale extension of private facilities that coincides with the great migration, and gives special form to its financial obligations and opinions.

It was natural that the American banks should appear earliest in the eastern towns where financial transactions were largest and where there were more men of means to appreciate the advantages of pooling their capital in such companies. But shortly after the beginning of the new century they made their appearance in the West. As in the East this function was sometimes acquired by indirection. Most famous of the early banking subtleties was that of the Manhattan Company, chartered in New York in 1799 for providing the lower end of Manhattan Island with drinking water and for other purposes. It construed its "other purposes" into a right to operate a bank of issue which has to-day become one of the great financial institutions of the United States. There appears to have been a Lexington (Kentucky) Insurance Company, of 1802, that quietly began to issue notes and to do a banking business. The Miami Exporting Company of Cincinnati was chartered by the Ohio legislature at its first session in 1803, to trade up and down the river with New Orleans; but it soon abandoned its first intention and became a bank. The profits to be gained by lending at interest the flexible credit that a bank of issue could control tempted numerous imitators to experiment with the new institutions, and to approach legislatures to solicit charters.

Between 1803 and 1811, banks appeared in one form or other in most of the frontier regions. There was a short-lived one chartered in Michigan Territory in 1806, only to be closed by refusal of Congress to approve the territorial act. It had meanwhile flooded the Detroit region with its notes. There was a Bank of Kentucky in 1806, and a Nashville Bank chartered the following year. This latter, until its suspension during the panic of 1819, was among the most famous of the western establishments.

But there was nothing in western banking until 1811 to indicate a "craze" or to suggest more than a reasonable adaptation of business to the tendencies of the times. In 1811 the charter of the Bank of the United States was refused continuance, it closed its doors, and the business it had done became a lure to tempt new ventures into the field.

There was more than the old business of the bank to attract new efforts. There disappeared with the bank a sort of control that had made every other bank in the United States somewhat more reliable than it would otherwise have been. Being the largest financial institution in the country it had occasion daily to do business with the notes of nearly all the eighty-eight other banks that were living independent lives. Each of these was under constant pressure from desirous borrowers to increase its issues beyond what it could safely redeem, and thus to lower its reserve below the danger line. Many of the weaker, or less experienced, or less honest did this; and took the chance of failure in case any holder of their notes should demand their instant redemption. The Bank of the United States was always a large holder of these notes, and was in a position at any moment, when it distrusted solvency, to test this by sending in for redemption of a large amount of its notes. The smaller institutions resented this, but could not well avoid it. Their representations, spread among their borrowers, that it was the restrictive policy of the Bank of the United States that kept them from being as accommodating as they desired, did much to stir up in Congress a dislike for the national bank and to prevent its recharter. With it gone, there was not only its business to be struggled for by new banks, but there was an assurance of lack of supervision and restraint that tempted speculators and crooks into the business. A boom struck the United States, under whose influence the banks of the United States multiplied to 307 by 1820. In this the West had more than its full share.

Most famous, perhaps, among the new banks created to replace the Bank of the United States was the Bank of Tennessee, opened in Knoxville, under the presidency of Hugh L. White, with Luke Lea as its cashier. Indicative of the lack of experience among its officers is the fact that upon its chartering, White was sent east to have its notes engraved, and to learn the "forms of financiering." He evidently learned them well, for it was continuously solvent until it wound up its affairs in 1827. As years

went on it had many competitors with varying degrees of intelligence and honor, but it never lost its grip on either. Ohio,
in 1816, noted the increase in private banking, and sought to
regulate and control it by passing a general act under which all
such institutions should pay tribute to the State. The State
became a partner in the ventures, and began to accumulate experience in the workings of State-owned business. Kentucky, in
1818, responded to the popular desire for easy credit and created
a chain of over forty banks with an aggregate capital above eight
millions. By law it authorized them to pay in their capital and
to redeem their notes, not in coin, but in the notes of either the
Second Bank of the United States or the earlier Bank of Kentucky.

Before 1819, when panic brought on a general reconsideration
of existing banking, there was a flood of paper money induced
by the demands of the West for credit.[3] The restraining influences
were abolished. The War of 1812 produced a condition in the
East that forced most of the banks south of New England to
suspend specie payments. It was the British raid on the Chesapeake in 1814, with the burning of the public buildings of Washington, that brought about actual suspension by those that were
fearful of either runs or seizure of coin by the enemy. When they
refused to redeem their notes in coin the notes remained in use,
for there was not much other money, but their value declined.
The western banks suspended, to keep what coin they had from
being drawn to the East. And with suspension general, there
was no possibility that an exigent note holder would bring down
the structure of speculation in a crash. "During this year [1814],"
wrote a western clergyman, "a money mania, like an epidemic,
seized the people. There were seven banking establishments in
Jefferson County [Ohio], one of which is said to have been kept
in a ladies' chest. But it did not stop here — merchants, tavern
keepers, butchers, and bakers became bankers."

The available banking capital of the West nearly doubled
between 1814 and 1818, and there is no way of determining with
precision the ratio of issues to capital, or the amount of the
ostensible capital that was real. In more than one case the subscribers to the stock of a new bank paid in a small fraction of the
price of the stock in coin, and received their certificates. They

---

[3] W. M. Gouge, *The Curse of Paper Money* (1833), is a quarry from which economic
historians still hew their facts. It was slightly supplemented by special studies made for the
Aldrich Monetary Commission.

then took the stock certificates to the bank, used them as collateral, to borrow back the coin and with the coin thus received paid the rest of the purchase price. The bank thus did business with a capital nominally of coin but really of notes of the stock subscribers, and was never in a condition to redeem any large portion of its notes.

The elements of strength for society in the new banking institutions lay in the provision of a convenient currency and the saving involved in making what capital there was several-fold more fluid. The dangers were in the inflation of currency that resulted, the inexperience and recklessness of the bankers, and the erroneous use to which nearly every bank devoted its capital. The inflation of currency was certain, with a resulting cheapening of the dollar, and a rise in prices. Economists are not agreed as to the amount of influence that quantity of money has upon its value; but most of them believe that a sudden increase in the volume of circulating medium is followed by a rise in prices. The sudden turning loose upon society of the extra credit made available by the banking circulation brought on such a period of inflation. To much of the United States, and to the West in particular, this rise in prices seemed one of the evidences of prosperity due to the banks, and stimulated the creation of more banks, to make more money.

The bankers of this period were mostly amateurs, who could not have had much knowledge of the institutions they were guiding because the institutions were so new. They learned their lessons as to amount of circulation that was safe, and as to kind of loan that was certain, at the expense of their customers; and when they made mistakes their customers paid. The business was dangerous enough in the hands of honest and careful men. But when banks were founded by speculators, or gamblers, or with deliberate intent to defraud, their notes were likely to gain wide currency before the error was detected, with resulting loss to every one who held them. The "saddlebag" bank appeared in many a community, when slick strangers came to town, opened an office, lent to patrons the clean, fresh money that had bulged their saddlebags on their arrival, disposed of the notes they took to local note-shavers, and disappeared by night with the loot. It was a common fraud to make notes that nearly resembled those of a well-known and solvent bank, and to pass them on confiding merchants fifty or a hundred miles away.

234 HISTORY OF THE AMERICAN FRONTIER

Counterfeiting was easy because most of the notes were poorly engraved, and could be imitated by any skillful and dishonest printer. These were the defects that might have been inherent in even a perfect system; but they were present in such proportions as to endanger the future of the whole principle of banking.

Worse than either the inflation or the defects due to the inexperience or dishonesty of bankers, was the type of loan that prevailed. Commercial bankers know to-day that all their obligations are demand obligations, payable on sight. So it was with the early bankers who lent to the borrower their notes redeemable on demand. It is now a commonplace that sight obligations may return suddenly for fulfillment, and that the harder the times, and the more uncertain the commercial situation, the quicker they come. The only safeguard against bankruptcy brought about by a sudden run is in an adequate reserve, and a set of assets that can be realized in a short time. Best of all the assets is commercial paper, running for short periods of thirty, sixty, or ninety days. A bank confining its business to loans of this type is continually turning over its capital and is ever in a position to watch the markets and trend of business and curtail or expand its loans according to the financial weather. Unless it has a large part of its assets in short-time paper, it is liable to be caught in a financial stringency with "frozen assets" on its hands, perhaps entirely good in the long run, but not negotiable in time to prevent a run from producing bankruptcy. The eastern banks were helped because their customers included the commercial institutions that needed short time loans. The western ones found among their customers a preponderance of farmers for whom a three-months note was worthless. The farmer who borrowed to cover the costs of transportation, land purchase, and maintenance, had no collateral to offer but his land title, and no means of repayment until he had completed his purchase from the government and earned the money from the land. He needed a long time mortgage, for three, five, or seven years. He was willing, or could be compelled, to agree to pay a high rate of interest; but he must have time. The result was a pressure upon the frontier banks to lend on mortgage and tie up their capital in slow-moving securities that offered no resource against sudden financial storm. The more prosperous the western bank appeared to be, in good and certain loans outstanding, the worse it really was because of the immense amounts of its notes that were subject to presentation for immediate redemption. So long as the war-time period of suspension lasted, the frontier banks financed the frontier farms, unknowing or careless of the danger they incurred. With the approach of peace, deflation, and specie payments, they saw the danger, and their customers felt it. The bank ceased to be the agent of easy prosperity, and soon assumed the popular appearance of a devouring monster.[4]

The financial crisis of 1819 marks the transition point between the two financial periods, but signs of anti-bank reaction appeared earlier than this. The chartering by Congress of a second Bank of the United States in 1816, and the efforts of this institution to bring about specie payments in 1817 started a new train of thought and action. There was no question at Washington but that the new bank was needed. After the disappearance of the first one, and the outbreak of war, even the Government of the United States had difficulty in maintaining solvency. There was no one bank on which it could rely. Its revenues were uncertain. Its credit was poor. The war loans were raised only in part, and even this only because of the heroic contributions of men of large private means, John Jacob Astor, Stephen Girard, and David Parish. When the war was over, Congress in its reconstruction session chartered a new bank, with the United States as a stockholder, and with power to run until 1836. It had the right also to open branches throughout the country, as opportunity offered, and to do the usual business of issue and discount.

This new bank, in its first two years, was nearly as reckless as the local banks with which it came into competition. It immediately opened sixteen branches, in addition to the main office in Philadelphia. Of these, five were east of Philadelphia and eleven were south and west. It never did a full share of business in New England. There were six distinctly southern branches, at Baltimore, Washington, Richmond, Norfolk, Charleston, and Savannah; and five western, at Pittsburgh, Chillicothe, Cincinnati, Lexington, and New Orleans. At all of these, loans were made and notes were issued. At one time the specie assets of the second bank were less than one ninth of its liabilities. In 1819, when the State banks suspended for a second time, the directors of the Bank of the United States became aware how greatly it

---

[4] It required another century for the United States to learn the difference between commercial and investment banking, and to devise the Federal Reserve Banks (1913), and the Federal Farm Loan Banks (1916) to serve the several needs.

had over-issued, and installed a new president with a stern command to curtail and save the institution. It did this at once, and by curtailing its issues increased the number of failures that the panic of 1819 had already made too large. It saved itself, but at the expense of forcing bankruptcy upon many of the smaller banks and weaker merchants, and thereby increasing the wave of resentment that was mounting up. The anti-bank movement became one against all banks, but specially against the Second Bank of the United States. The system of branches made it easy for local antipathies to merge in common attack upon the one symbol of monopolistic national banking.

Even before it curtailed in 1819, the Bank of the United States uncovered hostility to itself and its policies. It forced the local concerns to resume specie payments in 1817 by importing gold and maintaining them itself. Its refusal to do business with suspended banks created heavy pressure upon the latter to resume. As many of the local banks had yielded to the temptation to over-issue, they resumed with difficulty, or not at all. And as they made their own curtailments that were necessarily the price of resumption, they passed on to the disappointed customers as they refused them loans, the antipathy to the second bank.

The constitution of Indiana, framed in 1816, reveals an early phase of the suspicion of the Bank of the United States. It adopted two existing territorial banks, at Madison and Vincennes, as legal; and allowed the legislature to establish a State Bank, with one branch for every three counties in the State, but provided that other than these "There shall not be established or incorporated in this State, any bank or banking company, or monied institution for the purpose of issuing bills of credit, or bills payable to order or bearer." This would have prevented, had the prohibition possessed constitutional validity, the opening in Indiana of any branch of the Bank of the United States. The Illinois constitution, framed two years later, contained a similar prohibition of "banks or monied institutions" except those chartered by the State. The southern States, Alabama and Mississippi, and Missouri, that made constitutions during the great migration, provided for the creation of State banks, but omitted the prohibition against the existence of any others.

The coercive power of the Bank of the United States, that roused resentment against the first, roused it against the second. What Indiana and Illinois wrote into their constitutions, Ohio,

Kentucky, Tennessee, Maryland, North Carolina, and Georgia wrote into their statutes between 1816 and 1819. The common statutory way of excluding the branches of the Bank of the United States was to impose heavy taxes upon branches of "foreign" banks — $15,000 a year in Maryland, $50,000 in Ohio and Tennessee, and $60,000 in Kentucky. Before long the new bank was forced to decide how it should treat this attempt at prohibition. Its reluctance to submit brought the matter before the Supreme Court of the United States, and gave John Marshall the occasion to hand down the definitive decision in the cases of McCulloch *vs*. Maryland, and Osborn *vs*. United States Bank.

It was the need of the public domain for a policy of government that forced Congress in 1787 to take the first steps in asserting a national authority. From the frontier now, in the resistance against the power of this national authority to charter a national bank, came the stimulus to assert and define the nature of that power. It was not the East or the older sections that gave the most incentive to declare the meaning of the United States, but the frontier with its clear and uniform interests, and its institutions in formative stage. John Marshall seized the occasion arising in this controversy to assert the superiority of the Federal Government for all time. "Let the end [of Federal legislation] be legitimate," he wrote, "let it be within the scope of the constitution, and all means which are appropriate, which are plainly adapted to that end, which are not prohibited, but consist with the letter and the spirit of the constitution, are constitutional." Upon this argument rests the whole doctrine of implied powers, without which the United States Government would have been incompetent to meet the changing conditions brought about by the revolutions in life since 1787. To it may be attributed the steadiness with which the American Constitution has weathered the generations and watched with tranquillity the upheavals that have upset the rest of the world. The conclusion reached by Marshall was inherent in the Constitution, and would doubtless have been reached eventually by another, under a different provocation; but to the historian there is much significance in that the immediate provocation for the doctrine was the frontier experience with the new institutions of finance.[5]

[5] Charles Warren, *The Supreme Court in United States History* (1923), has done much to remove the Supreme Court from the level of partisanship, and to set it in a reliable matrix of historical facts. Albert J. Beveridge, *Life of John Marshall* (1919), is a distinguished monument to both author and subject.

Under the decision in the case of McCulloch *vs*. Maryland the States were denied the power to interfere in any way with the Bank of the United States, and it proceeded to extend its branches as it pleased. As the years elapsed after the depression of 1819, and as the debtors of that year became solvent again, the antipathies to the second bank dropped beneath the surface of opinion, until a casual observer might have believed that they had vanished. But the distrust for banks continued, and was shown in local struggles for relief in the years immediately following the panic.

Down to 1819 the western States generally encouraged the creation of local banks, and issued charters to them readily, under the belief that they made credit obtainable and were of general use. The result was a blanket of mortgage indebtedness over the region of new development, and a system of banks unable to meet financial stress. When hard times came, and the banks found it necessary to raise funds to meet their notes, they had only two options: — to require debtors as the debts came due to pay in cash; and to make new loans in smaller amounts than were needed by the borrowers. The result was general bankruptcy. The mortgagor was rarely able to raise the money to pay off the principal of his loan; often he could not even meet the high interest charges. When he became delinquent, the bank that owned the mortgage had to decide whether it was wise to foreclose and try to collect what was coming to it by legal process. If it failed to foreclose it drifted into trouble itself with worthless assets. If it foreclosed it made an enemy and terrified every debtor who feared similar treatment.

The uniformity of the burden of debt on the frontier made foreclosure there a more unpopular thing than it is in a mixed community where debtor and creditor rub elbows at every turn. At best it is an unlovely act to turn a debtor out of his property, and by forcing a sale compel him to risk and perhaps lose his equity. But in a mixed community there is a buyer at every sale, and the transaction speedily becomes *fait accompli*. On the frontier, however, with all the neighbors fearing similar treatment, foreclosure became not a regrettable necessity, but an act of malignity. The bank was blamed for an impossible interest rate, and for wanting its money. The buyer was criticized as a bloodless speculator, little better than a thief because he bought at forced and non-competitive sales, and acquired the former owner's equity for nothing. The bank that felt impelled to foreclose, needed to inquire whether it could find a purchaser brave enough to incur local hostility. Like-endangered neighbors often attended the foreclosure sales and by menace discouraged bidding. If no buyer could be found, the bank could not gain anything but odium by attempted foreclosure. The temper of the frontier made debt collection hard.

When the panic broke in 1819 there was the burden of heavy and uniform debt covering the new States and many regions of their elders. Often the farmer had no equity at all because in the enthusiasm of settlement he and the bank had marked his property far above its real value, and he owed on it more than its whole worth. Few frontier banks could adhere to the good rule of a fifty per cent mortgage on a conservative valuation. As money became scarce because of the curtailment, the western legislatures sought to ward off depression. Tennessee launched another Bank of Tennessee, and Kentucky incorporated the Bank of the Commonwealth. Each of these, in substance, lent the credit of the State to citizens.

The Kentucky attempt to fight panic with law deserved, and has received, much attention from historians. The Bank of the Commonwealth was intended to be a machine for note issue, and was relieved by law from the requirement to redeem its notes. Its loans were apportioned among the counties, and were meant to be granted to persons who could not borrow anywhere else. At the same time, in 1820 and 1821, Kentucky passed laws staying the legal action for collecting debts and placing obstacles in the road of foreclosure. The creditor who would not accept the notes of the Bank of the Commonwealth was required to postpone the forcible collection of his debt; foreclosed debtors were given a long period in which they could redeem their property; sales of land by execution were forbidden unless the property brought three quarters of an appraised value fixed by the neighbors — and these could be trusted to make the appraisals high enough. Public opinion fell away from the creditor who sought to protect his rights, as it had already fallen away from the United States when the General Land Office wanted to collect the installments due upon land purchases. The debtor community persuaded itself that it had been so badly treated that default was honorable. In Kentucky the legislature fairly represented the opinion of its constituents.

The Kentucky relief laws were forced to run the gauntlet of the courts, and in 1823 the highest court of the State declared them to be unconstitutional. The judges who handed down this decision were not greeted as courageous defenders of justice against passion, but were denounced as the friends of privilege. The State campaign of 1824 was fought over the issue of the decision, and the people won. The next legislature, finding it impossible to change the decision, repealed the judiciary act, and legislated the offending judges out of legal existence. It created a New Court, more accommodating to public opinion. But the Old Court refused to be abolished, kept up an extra-legal existence, and became the rallying point for the more conservative and the more far-sighted members of the State. As the years went on, the worst effects of the panic were outlived, and solvent farmers, with money coming to them, saw little good in preventing the collection of just debts. By 1826 the Old Court party carried the State, and its next legislature repealed the New Court law over the veto of the governor. Financial solvency had won in the long run, but its victory left permanent scars.

The West that was taking shape between 1819 and 1829 never entirely forgot its antipathy to banks, and its fear of financial institutions. It lost them for short periods, but the emotion was always potent in shaping western opinion, breeding a fear of privilege, and reinforcing the ideas of democracy that Jefferson had found so strong. Neither while the bank war was raging, nor after it subsided, can one understand the frontier States without taking this experience into full account.[6]

[6] William Graham Sumner, *Andrew Jackson as a Public Man* (1882), contains a pungent and faithful account of the relief system.

CHAPTER XXVII
THE AMERICAN SYSTEM

WHEN Congress assembled in the late autumn of 1815 to take up the various measures of reconstruction for the United States, there began a generation that was to be dominated by four great Americans, Andrew Jackson, John C. Calhoun, Daniel Webster, and Henry Clay. The age of the American Revolution was over, though John Adams and Thomas Jefferson lingered on in retirement for another decade. The period of tide-water ascendency was nearing its end — an end that had been foreshadowed when the western "war hawks" took possession of Congress in 1811 and forced a war upon James Madison. In the next thirty-five years, for Calhoun, Webster, and Clay were still on the stage in 1850, and the indomitable spirit of Andrew Jackson still inspired the majorities of the Mississippi Valley, the United States made its great strides towards nationality. And at nearly every step it took, the decision was made upon some point presented out of the experience or upon the insistence of the region commonly called the West. Part of this West was in the primitive stage of the new frontier, part had recently passed beyond it. The margin of occupation of the continent was relentlessly moving on, and the spirit that accompanied it remained a living force.

Clay and Calhoun came to the task of reconstruction as young and enthusiastic nationalists, as the word could be used in 1815. They had seen lessons in the experience of the United States in the war just closed, and sought to take advantage of them. Webster had not yet found his place, and was still the local politician, inspired chiefly by a vision of the interests of his section, that had opposed the war and fought the Democratic politicians who conducted it. Jackson was still in the regular army, a military hero after New Orleans, but not identified with any political theories.

In the legislation of 1815–1816, Clay as Speaker of the House of Representatives, and Calhoun, from the floor, joined in support of the new measures; a bank to straighten out the national finances, a protective tariff to provide revenue and safeguard the young manufactures to which the war had given birth, and the first step in a system of internal improvements that should make the United States more prosperous and more mobile in another struggle. Congress agreed with them in these measures, discussing each more from the standpoint of expediency and detail than from that of politics or theory. The bank and the tariff were enacted in 1816. The following winter a bill for internal improvements was sent to President Madison in the last weeks of his administration.

The bank act of 1816,[1] provided that the Bank of the United States should pay over to the National Treasury about half a million dollars a year, as the price of its franchise and as interest on the Government-owned stock. This bonus, as it was called, was not pledged to any special purpose; and the Bonus Bill was brought forward directing that it should be spent year after year upon internal improvements of national character. President Madison was himself convinced that the building of roads and other means for internal communication was necessary and had in his last two annual messages advised Congress to use what powers it possessed and to take steps to enlarge them by constitutional amendment. When, however, he received the Bonus Bill, he could not square it with his understanding of the Constitution, and returned it with his veto.

In the New England States, where internal improvements were disliked as another of the western schemes, and in the South, where a distrust of the exercise of Federal power was rapidly rising, the veto of the Bonus Bill was welcomed. Madison knew his Constitution. No member of the convention that framed it had been more methodical than he. His private notes enabled him to recall nearly every debate of consequence that took place during the summer of 1787 in Philadelphia. He now urged Congress to obtain by amendment the powers that he thought it lacked, but was constrained to veto the act in question because general internal improvements did not fall among the enumerated powers of the Constitution. Marshall had not yet thought out his decision in McCulloch *vs*. Maryland, and Madison's train of thought was similar to that of the elder statesmen of the outgoing generation.

The day after the veto of the Bonus Bill, James Madison left office, and James Monroe, next of the Virginia hierarchy, took his place. The new President agreed with the constitutional doctrines of his predecessor, and found that the veto forced him to a decision

---

[1] No historian has yet treated the tariff or internal improvements with adequate learning and dispassion; for the bank, however, all reasonable needs are met by Ralph C. H. Catterall, *Second Bank of the United States* (1903).

as to practical steps. The United States was, and had been since 1802, pledged to a road between the Potomac and the Ohio rivers. Since the close of the war this great turnpike had been built as rapidly as the contractors could work. It was now nearly finished and was drawing upon money in the Treasury as the bills came in. A strict adherence to the view of Madison's veto would compel an abandonment of the Cumberland Road and would prevent the undertaking of further ventures. In the various enabling acts passed for the new States, Congress was pledged to devote a part of the proceeds from land sales to road building; this now had to be reconsidered. If the policy was unconstitutional it must be stopped.

Monroe allowed the Cumberland Road, which was nearly done, to be completed; and it was opened throughout in 1818. But he applied the new policy to new improvements as they appeared, and discouraged the hope of the Middle States and the West that the United States would give them generous aid. The New England States, and the South, were so close to navigable waters that internal improvements never meant so much to them as to the West. It was the western demand that precipitated the debate over internal improvements and that stimulated a political movement to break down the obstruction of the President and his school.

The resistance of Monroe was required to show the western States how keenly they needed and desired the improvement of their roads. As their plans were blocked they came to realize that transportation was the price of their solvency and prosperity, and stood third at least among their basic problems. First was the satisfaction of their land hunger; next came the devices to which they resorted to raise what money they needed. But with only land and debts there was no hope ahead. Since all the western population expected to live by farming, there could be no local market for much of the agricultural produce that their farms yielded. Every farmer had, in a year or two after settlement, a rough abundance on his own table and in his own barns. But the only way he had to raise his interest and meet the installments on his principal was through the sale of his agricultural surplus. Grain, flour, whiskey, and pork he could produce in quantity, if he could only sell them. An early realization of this caused the western determination to control the navigation of the Mississippi River. As settlements pushed up into the country, away from the great rivers, the lack of roads was felt. There were no local means to build them. Reliance upon a general Federal Government was the only hope; and this was now chilled by the narrow vision of Madison and Monroe. From the moment of the veto of the Bonus Bill, the leaders of the West saw that their prosperity was tied up with the success of internal improvements. They did not have to be taught that these were needful; they had rather to learn how to make friends, and how to state their demands so as to procure results from Congress. Few leaders failed to try to break this barrier. The most successful at the task was Henry Clay, with his American System.

In order to procure congressional support for roads between the sections, two things were needful. One was to impress or convince the President, the other to get the votes in Congress. There were not enough votes in the West alone to bring success. By union with the Middle States the Bonus Bill majority was obtained; but this majority was too weak to pass the bill over the veto, and might not be counted on to continue in the face of persistent opposition from the President. If either the East or South could be persuaded that internal improvements were to its interest, the votes thus gained when added to those of the West, would make a safe majority. The most promising strategy was to approach the East, for this section had emerged from war conditions, ripe for local demands upon Congress and needing to make friends on its own account.

The situation uncovered during the debate over the Tariff of 1816 revealed the way in which the East could be approached. The new manufactures, chiefly in New England, were the creation of the war, and faced destruction after the return of peace. There was no serious difference of opinion in Congress that the existing industries ought to be protected enough to stay alive; the possibility of a general system of protective tariffs began to arouse eastern interest.

Until the beginning of the economic warfare in 1807, the United States was in an industrial way nearly as much a colony of England as the States had been before 1783. At the earlier date, except for the domestic manufactures that kept every rural housewife busy, the Americans either bought their finished products from European makers or did without them. The absence of available capital, and the immaturity of factory manufacture kept the United States backward and retarded the rise of a real industrial population. Eastern fortunes went into shipping or trade, not into manufacture. But with the embargo and the curtailment of the stream of goods from Europe, the prices of store goods rose, the supply lessened, and one by one, men were tempted to try to make in America for the American market. There were sets of plans of the new spinning and weaving machines that were smuggled to the United States before 1800. Samuel Slater began to operate the cotton factories of New England by 1790. But because of the high cost of American labor and its inexpertness there were few profits in the industry. At a normal competitive price the English mills could easily undersell those of the United States.

Between 1807 and 1815 the new American factories were launched, the cotton mills of Francis Cabot Lowell at Waltham being among the most important. Their rise gave a nervous shock to the European manufacturers who had hitherto had a safe monopoly of American trade; and before the news of the signing of the Treaty of Ghent reached America, there were British ships hovering off-shore with cargoes of British goods for the American market. The goods were sold at prices designed to drive the American competitors out of business and might have succeeded in the attempt had not Congress cheerfully responded to the manufacturers' plea for help by passing the Tariff of 1816.

With American manufactures once established and the principle of protection conceded, the debate was on. Matthew Carey, of Philadelphia, took the lead in popularizing the arguments for a protective tariff and attacking the free trade philosophy of Adam Smith. Hezekiah Niles, a Baltimore printer, who brought out the first issue of his *Weekly Register* in 1811, was an easy convert to the new thought, and used his columns to give it circulation. The individual manufacturers supported the debate from self-interest; and the communities into which they brought employment became interested in their success. It took ten years or more to bring New England to a general acceptance of the ideas of protection. The Middle States and West did not have to be converted, having no repugnance to the Federal Government to overcome and approving the ideas from the start. Before the agitation was far advanced the connection between the tariff and internal improvements was seen, and Henry Clay came to the front as its expounder.

The position of Henry Clay as Speaker after 1815 made his

support necessary for any promoter of a new legislative policy. The failure of Monroe to invite him to become Secretary of State in 1817, made him willing to lead in criticism of administration policies and in espousal of new ones that were likely to embarrass it. His position as the most important statesman that the West had produced kept him in touch with western needs and aspirations, and ambitious to be their champion. At nearly every session of Congress after 1816 he listened to new demands for protection; for higher rates on established industries, and additional rates for new ones. He came to see what the more theoretical advocates of protection were urging. By 1824, when the tariff revision of that year was under way, he had become the most important political leader of both internal improvements and tariff and was able to bring the two policies into a real unity of national significance.

The speech of Clay on March 30, 1824, urging the American System upon the country, has come to be a classic, and few protectionist orators since that date have added anything to it. He began with a gesture to secure the adhesion of the West. The West was prostrate, he said. He described the panic of 1819, the overproduction without a market, the dangers of foreclosure. He knew that the approaching campaign in his own State was to be fought upon the issue of the courts and their relation to debt collection. He pointed out the paradox of bankruptcy, existing and menacing, in a land of opportunity and plenty. He asked why the distress; and answered himself by asserting that "during almost the whole existence of this government, we have shaped our industry, our navigation, and our commerce, in reference to an extraordinary war in Europe, and to foreign markets, which no longer exist." Peace in Europe, he pointed out, was followed by a cessation of imports of food from the United States, for Europe in time of peace could and would feed herself. It was hopeless, he believed, to look to the European market for a remedy for American depression. Europe could not possibly consume the American surplus, for American population was doubling every twenty-five years, and production of food was ever increasing its excess over consumption. Europe would not take the American surplus, if it could, for every European country properly desired to develop its own agriculture and to exclude American competition in foods.

The only way that Clay could see to relieve the situation was to build up the American market. If this could be done, it would provide a steadier and more reliable market than Europe could afford, and would have the added advantage of making the United States independent of European fluctuations and upheavals. Clay might with propriety have referred at this point to Monroe's memorable message of the previous December, in which the President laid down for all time the doctrine of a set of American interests separate from those of the Old World. He was advocating an American economic system to parallel the political one of Monroe; and praised his system under the name American, in contrast with the non-American system that made American prosperity dependent upon world markets.

The virtue of a protective tariff was that it would at one stroke increase the degree of American independence in an economic sense, and improve the home market for food stuffs. Every new factory would by its output lessen the necessity to import foreign goods. It would moreover occupy in its shops men and women who would otherwise have been engaged upon the farms in raising food. They would continue to consume, making a market for the surplus, but they would cease to produce food, and so would reduce competition. The West could support a policy of voting protection to factories in the East, because thereby an eastern consuming population would be built up. It was even possible that some manufactures would cross the mountains, and take root in the towns of the Ohio Valley, thus bringing new home markets directly to the farms. The tariff system would reduce the proportion of agricultural workers, increase the demand for food, and perform the patriotic service of making the United States really independent.

In his other speeches, Clay elaborated the idea of internal improvements in connection with the tariff. By means of a proper system of these new highways, the farms and the markets would be brought together. Freights would be lessened, and by that amount would widen the radius within which the western farmer might hope to find a buyer. East and West were asked to support the new system, and Clay may well have had a vision of himself as building up the first constructive program of national development since that of Alexander Hamilton.

The difficulty that stood in the way of Clay's success as a legislative leader was the conscientious obstruction that Monroe offered to internal improvements. In the years immediately after 1817, Monroe saw no reason to change his conviction that the Bonus Bill veto represented a sound view of the Constitution. The Cumberland Road was completed and put to use. Over its course flowed that part of the great migration that moved from points east of the Susquehanna to the Ohio River. The eastern sections of the road were crowded with wagons before the western were done. Like any stone road, it began to deteriorate at once, and every season saw a larger number of holes and ruts that needed repairs, but got none. There was no provision in the law for keeping the road in good condition, and no precedent for the United States to manage and operate such a public work.

Five years after the veto of the Bonus Bill, Monroe, "with deep regret," vetoed "An act for the preservation and repair of the Cumberland Road." It was proposed in the bill to open toll gates, charge tolls of the users of the road, and devote the proceeds to maintaining the road in usable condition. This seemed to Monroe to imply "a power to adopt and execute a complete system of internal improvement"; a power which Clay believed to exist, and which was readily to be inferred from Marshall's recent decisions; but which Monroe denied. The President sent with his veto message an elaborate statement of his views upon constitutional powers and internal improvements, that may be regarded as the classic presentation of the views of the opposition. It was also one of the last presentations of the view, for in two years more Monroe found a way to reconcile his scruples with the attainment of the works. The complete leadership of Clay in presenting the proposals for internal improvements was reached during the tariff debate of 1824. It had been growing ever since 1817. The West had become a unit in accepting it; the eastern States were more approving every year. The pressure for new works, and the reasonableness of keeping up what had been done, did not miss the attention of the President.

A month after Clay's great argument for the Tariff of 1824, Monroe signed a bill authorizing the War Department to undertake a wholesale program of surveys of routes suitable for improvement. There was nothing in the Constitution that had not been there in 1817, but Monroe now convinced himself that the power to maintain an army and to establish military and post roads warranted the undertaking. His effective resistance to the western demand came to an end. On the last day of his presidency he signed a bill for surveying and marking a western road from the borders of Missouri to the Mexican frontier, in the direction of Santa Fé.

As the years rolled on, from 1815 to 1824, and Clay became the western exponent of the American System, no one could miss the political values in a western leader, with a western program, gaining the adherence of the eastern States. Clay, of course, wanted to be President, and his friends worked for him between 1820 and 1824. It was not worth while for any one to oppose Monroe in 1820, for there was no clarified issue, and no other leader with a standing more than local. The so-called era of good feeling was not one of unanimity, but one of unripened interests and unseasoned leaders. After 1820, however, the field was open to all aspirants, and every section produced at least one candidate. John Quincy Adams, from New England, had the advantage of the long tradition by which a Secretary of State acceded to the presidency, as well as his descent from a former President. William H. Crawford of Georgia was the southern candidate, with a strong following in Congress. Clay was, of course, brought forward as chief exponent of the American System — the only candidate who stood for a definite policy of government. And Andrew Jackson, of Tennessee, was produced as well, to represent a different phase of the opinion of the West.

Clay had succeeded in carrying with him on the tariff the middle tier of States — Missouri, Illinois, Kentucky, Indiana, Ohio, Pennsylvania, New Jersey, as well as New York, Connecticut, Rhode Island, and Vermont. The believers in his American System had the votes to elect him President if they would. But when the election came in 1824, John Quincy Adams carried away from Clay, New York and all of the New England States, though not differing from Clay in principle. And Andrew Jackson, whose views on public affairs were matters of profound uncertainty, carried the popular vote of Pennsylvania, New Jersey, Indiana, and Illinois. There was no election. Clay ran fourth of the candidates, and hence could not have his name appear before the House of Representatives whose duty it now was to elect a President. He presided over it as Speaker, and watched the contest between the two men, Jackson and Adams, who had cut into his field, and Crawford, whose strength was in the South which had been cold to the American System from the start. He threw his influence to the one who openly accepted his principles, and Adams was elected. When Adams responded by choosing him as Secretary of State, it may well be said that the American System of the West had triumphed, although its greatest prophet held the lesser post. After the approval of the Road Survey Bill of 1824, the United States possessed an administration pledged to the doctrine of internal improvements, and all that this implied.

CHAPTER XXVIII
JACKSONIAN DEMOCRACY

THE victory of Clay's system, together with the defeat of Clay, calls for careful examination.[1] The election maps show that in many States citizens who approved Clay's principles and who held the admiration of Clay that was general throughout the West, nevertheless were carried away by personal enthusiasm for another. They voted for Jackson, who received more votes than any other candidate. Yet Jackson in 1824 was only a military hero, and did not make clear his attitude upon the real issues in government until after his inauguration in 1829. The best general explanation of the paradox is that Clay represented the West truly, but Jackson more vitally; that the truths for which Clay stood were less compelling than those that were exemplified by his rival; that the intellectual and constructive program articulated in the American System was at a disadvantage as a procurer of votes compared with Andrew Jackson's personification of frontier democracy.

In the dark years that followed the boom period of the great migration, between 1819 and 1825, the West, like the whole United States, was crying for a leader who could sense its needs and translate them into phrases that every voter could understand. There was an economic situation that called for correction, if it was possible by conscious thought to correct the economic environment. There was the burden of debt that lay heavily upon the shoulders of the typical border citizen, and by its sheer weight perverted his judgments. There was the need of a market for the farmer's surplus. There were, too, the rough plenty of a generous land, and the universal chagrin that the opportunity so clearly visible was yet so elusive. Clay saw these elements, and constructed his system to meet as many of them as possible; and found few among his western countrymen who contradicted his diagnosis. Yet he failed to receive the full rewards, because there were additional common qualities of the West, capable of being

---

[1] The best analysis of sectionalism in the third decade of the last century is Frederick J. Turner, *Rise of the New West* (1906); his *Frontier in American History* (1920) is a useful collection of his various essays upon different aspects of this general theme.

stimulated into powerful political incentives and producing reactions that reached the heart as well as the brain. Clay's program
was of the intellect, but the West was more keenly conscious of its
heart.

In analyzing the psychology of the West, it must never be lost
sight of that the persistent fight with nature made of the pioneer
an individual with sharply developed peculiarities. It is a nice
question whether the equalitarian or the individualizing forces
were the weightier. The one condition that the pioneer could not
get away from was the oppressive similarity of his life with that of
his neighbors. He had a tendency to suffer from whatever affected
them; and when by chance he escaped the epidemics of thought or
condition that swept the West, his instinct of imitation made him
often assume the condition that he lacked. He resented the equality, but shrank from standing out as different. He was keenly resentful of anything that seemed like coercion, but saw nothing inconsistent in being intolerant of the habits or opinions of others.
The uniformity of frontier life did not make for toleration.

His intense individuation made him likely to admire those who
seemed to have the traits that he admired in himself. The dueling
code survived longest in the parts of the United States in which
frontier roughness lasted longest. In part this may have been due
to a real need for self help and to the fact that the man who was
quickest on the trigger finished the fight. But it was equally due
to the intense sensitiveness bred by loneliness and equality. He
could not bear the thought that another might look down upon
him. He could see the extra loneliness that peculiarities brought
to certain individuals and was quick to resent any slur or fancied
slight. The frontier rather admired Burr for his duel with Hamilton. It never thought less of Jackson because he carried in his
body for a quarter of a century a bullet he had stopped in an altercation with the Bentons in 1813. Popularity was easily built
up upon hero worship, and the best hero was he who had no traits
that the frontier could not understand.

The equalitarian conditions thus bred a dislike of superiority;
and the individuation produced a high regard for those in whom
it was most pronounced. There was also in the western character,
and quite as firmly grounded in experience as either of these, an
expansive trait that the word idealism only roughly describes.

The successful pioneer lived a life of progress. He began with
untouched nature, and each year saw a larger area of cleared lands.

a better group of buildings, a more selected herd of stock, and greater freedom due to increase in financial resources. The young and poor bore their lot the better because of the firm conviction that they were some day to be established and rich. There was no class of permanent farm laborers, and almost no certain domestic help. There were no barriers of caste to prevent a man from rising in the esteem of his community; and in spite of the language of democratic equality, influence was largely based upon attainment. The habit of believing in personal progress and growth had a parallel in the certitude of social progress and development. The first scattered farmers of a region knew that they were to become leaders in local and county government; that improvements would surely come; that statehood was inevitable. The mature men were entitled to believe that the senatorial toga might descend upon them; and they brought up their boys in the belief that any of them might be President. The American worship of the self-made man has been founded in this general knowledge that most Americans in the beginning were self-made. The frontier citizens saw the forest and prairie melting before the attack of the advancing farms. They saw the Indians recede towards further western homes. They heard that the United States was moving its empire west. Only the conviction that the country beyond the Missouri was worthless kept them, at the beginning of the nineteenth century, from visualizing the United States as a continental power. But they took for granted the idea that progress and expansion would come as needed. And none of them shied at a new idea merely because it had not yet come to pass. The life of change and growth they lived made them natural expansionists and idealists. And when they came together on their local feast days, the Fourth of July, or Washington's Birthday, or the anniversary of New Orleans, their orators let their fancy play around that future greatness of themselves which all conceded. The stabler communities, with less mobility for the individual, kept their fancies closer to the ground.

The West was impregnated with the potentialities of equality, individuation, and idealism in 1819, and was ready to follow a leader that it loved. The old men, of the revolutionary generation, had lost its confidence, and no new leader was in the year of the panic ready to assert a compelling leadership. The parties of the beginning of the century had lost their fire, and the cooling ashes had failed to bring to life a real or mythical phœnix.

caucus candidate. Adams was the choice of the New England leaders, strong because he had escaped the danger of taint of Federalism. Clay was backed by the middle group. Jackson was the hero of the West. It was entirely possible to support Jackson, yet believe in Clay; it was more thrilling than to stand for Clay. The Jackson men attacked the caucus because it could not be controlled, and developed a theory palatable to Democrats that it was a non-popular institution and hence unworthy. When Jackson appeared to have a plurality of the popular votes, though not a majority of the electoral college, his friends asserted that this plurality was a mandate upon the House of Representatives to elect him, as the leading of the three candidates. When the House passed over his claim to elect John Quincy Adams, Jackson became a martyr, and John Randolph thundered his denunciation of the "infamous coalition" of "Puritan and blackleg." During the whole of the Adams administration, while Adams and Clay were using all their powers to put the American System into effect, the Jackson men were fighting them for partisan advantage; and in 1828 Jackson was triumphantly elected. The West and South could vote as a unit upon frontier virtues and Jackson's popularity, whereas they were divided when it came to endorsing Clay's program. The Democratic party of which Jackson became the head had a new birth, freshly invigorated by contact with the fundamentals of the West, and managed by a group of political leaders new upon the national stage. The defeated elements of Jefferson's old party speedily ceased to be Democrats at all, and received a new name of National Republicans; and once more there was an opposition at Washington.

CHAPTER XXIX

THE EAST, AND THE WESTERN MARKETS

JOHN QUINCY ADAMS, Henry Clay, and the American System came into their own in 1825, and for four years gave expression to a new set of ideas that was working a transformation in the character of the United States Government. John Marshall, through his creative decisions in the Supreme Court, gave a new legal philosophy that percolated through the courts to the bar, and thence to the politicians and the people. By 1830 the fact that such a change was under way was clear enough for Webster to assume his nationalist rôle in his reply to Hayne; and for the forces that feared such transformation of the Government to take refuge in State rights and to find in the restrictive philosophy of John C. Calhoun an expression of their desires. The cleavage in opinion was sectional largely because cotton and slave labor built up a section that could not avoid serving its major interests. But between 1825 and the reply to Hayne in 1830 the southern opposition was not strong enough to block the rapid development of the United States along the lines pointed out by Marshall and Henry Clay.

From the passage of the Road Survey Act of 1824, Congress was ready to assist internal improvements in various ways. The topographical engineers of the army were at the disposal of the promoters of new highways, for there were as yet no civil engineers in civil life. The military engineer was an indispensable unit in the work. The list of works begun and carried through by Congress steadily increased, although not one attained the magnitude of the Cumberland Road. Its western extension, known as the National Road, was undertaken in 1825. Numerous schemes of river and harbor improvements were adopted. In many cases in which Congress could not be induced to take the full responsibility for a project, it was still possible to procure a generous Federal subscription in the form of purchase of stock, so that the Government became a partner in corporate enterprise, as it had earlier been a partner with every farmer who bought his land on installments. But the Government aid came too late to meet the full demands that were expressed during the years of the great migration; and it was never as generous as enthusiasts hoped for. Even before the obstruction from the White House had ceased, State efforts and private capital started upon the task of supplying the more imperative needs of commerce between the sections.

The first great efforts to bring together the eastern and western markets, after the inception of the Cumberland Road, were of eastern origin, and were based upon two main hopes. One of these was the normal desire to capture the markets created in the Ohio Valley by the great migration, and is to be regarded as a far-sighted reaching out for business. The other was the fear of a new competitor in New Orleans and the determination to keep the western settlements in trade relations with the East.

The development of the western trade of seaboard towns began with the extension of population into the Appalachian valleys. The first migrants were followed, at an interval, by the processions of covered wagons owned by the merchants of Baltimore and Philadelphia, carrying stocks of store goods to be sold or peddled on the frontier. As soon as the Forbes Road was passable, it was used by this traffic. Never was the business large enough to satisfy the merchants, and never was the supply of store goods large enough to please the westerners. The further the routes projected themselves into the interior, the higher went the freight charges; and by the time Pittsburgh arose at the head of the Ohio, the distance had become so long that few goods could stand the cost of shipment. The Cumberland Road was designed to carry this business, and, by improving the route, to lower the cost. To Philadelphia and Baltimore the Cumberland Road came as a natural and desirable improvement of what these regions already possessed. The other towns of the seaboard were less certain and were inclined to see in the road a special advantage which they coveted for themselves. New York and Charleston, particularly, had their attention directed to the western trade, and to the fact that Philadelphia and Baltimore had greater advantages than they possessed.

The desires of New York and Charleston grew in intensity with the progress of the great migration and were stimulated by the fear of what the steamboats might do. Roosevelt's boat on the Ohio was an object lesson, and a precursor of an inland trade whose natural outlet would not be any city on the Atlantic. Just so soon as the up-river boats could be relied upon, there was nothing to prevent New Orleans from becoming the great distributing center of the interior. The Appalachians presented a natural limit to the trading areas of the seaboard; there was no limit east of the Rockies, to the commercial empire of New Orleans. Between the desire for western trade and the fear that New Orleans would appropriate it, the East stirred itself to offer competition; and when Congress could not be induced to respond at once, the East used its own resources.

The State of New York was conscious from an early period of the natural highway that lay subject to its disposal between the upper reaches of the Mohawk River, the south shore of Lake Ontario, and the eastern end of Lake Erie. Because of French proximity and Indian occupation this highway was never frequented during the colonial period, and the safer routes from the Delaware and the Susquehanna to the "pleasant lands behind" monopolized the traffic. But with the end of the Revolution, the surrender of the forts by England, and the stabilizing of the Six Nations, there was no longer a reason for checking the flow of New York and New England at old Fort Stanwix. Before the year 1800 the ancient settlements of the Dutch Flats on the Mohawk had been extended for the whole length of the river, and the settlers had begun to use the Mohawk and the Hudson as their route of communication for whatever trade they had. The obstruction in the Mohawk at Little Falls, some seventy miles above its mouth, was a serious inconvenience to the settlers who lived around Utica and Rome, above that point. The Massachusetts land controversy was adjusted, the Holland Land Company had bought its tract near Lake Erie, the Connecticut Land Company was prospecting around Cleveland. There was growing promise of business in the country beyond the Mohawk.

The Western Inland Lock Navigation Company was ready for business in the winter of 1796, having been formed to meet the demand for river improvement on the Mohawk. It built a series of five locks around the rapids at Little Falls, and by thus overcoming the forty-two foot drop in the Mohawk here, made the whole river navigable for small boats as far inland as Fort Stanwix, or Rome. It also called attention to the fact, that dreamers had often noted, that there was no real obstruction in the way of extending the locks and canal from the head of the Mohawk to the Oswego, or the Genesee, or even to the Niagara River at some point above the falls. With a water route from New York City to Lake Erie before his mind, the pamphleteer or letter writer waxed poetic upon the future of New York. In this instance his wildest dreams could not approach reality. As the impending construc-

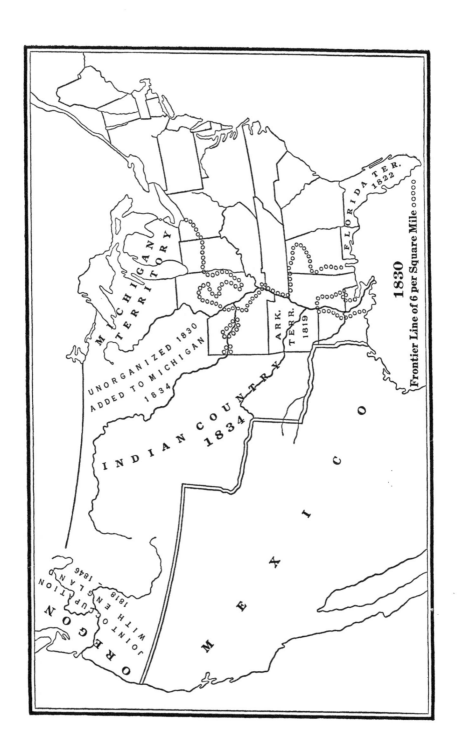

1830

Frontier Line of 6 per Square Mile ○○○○○

FLORIDA TER. 1822

MICHIGAN TERRITORY

UNORGANIZED 1830 ADDED TO MICHIGAN 1834

ARK. TERR. 1819

INDIAN COUNTRY 1834

MEXICO

OREGON

JOINT OCCUPATION WITH ENGLAND 1818 — 1846

tion of the Cumberland Road called the attention of New York to what Pennsylvania was to have, the project of an Erie Canal passed from the realm of prophecy to that of practical politics.

As early as 1810, at a time when Albert Gallatin was suggesting a chain of coast-line waterways at the expense of the United States, New York procured a survey of the route along which an Erie Canal must pass. DeWitt Clinton, son of a famous political family, was one of the first commissioners, and remained throughout the leading prophet of the canal. Federal aid was asked but was not obtained; and with the War of 1812 on hand, no one expected it. By 1816 New York had given up its hope of Federal aid and had crystallized its determination to have a canal. In Europe the advocates of canals were getting the better of the advocates of turnpikes, in the argument over trade extension. A new era of internal communication was dawning. In 1817, Clinton, who was now governor of the State, elected upon the canal issue, broke ground for the Erie Canal at a point near Fort Stanwix.

While the Erie Canal was under debate, there was a development of the idea respecting the significance of canals. First they were projected as river improvements, like the Little Falls canal. It was then thought that the loaded barges could be towed in the rivers, using canals merely as a means of getting around the falls and rapids. A little experience, however, brought forth the inadequacy of most streams for canal use. Unless a river, like the Hudson, was great enough for independent navigation, it was not satisfactory for transportation in both directions. The current was variable, the water's edge shifted after every shower. The towpath was in danger of being elevated beyond reach, or else submerged beneath the stream. There developed the advantage of a ditch, substantially level, with water fed in through sluice gates as needed, and run off when excessive. The capital outlay was heavy, but once built the canal could be owned like any other property, and all users could be made to pay for their share of it. The Erie Canal was at last projected from the Hudson to Lake Erie, its three main divisions being from Albany to Rome; Rome to the Seneca River; Seneca to Lake Erie. The size of the locks determined the capacity of the waterway, being ninety feet by twelve. The cross section revealed a stream four feet deep, forty feet wide at the surface, and twenty-eight on the bottom. The boats that could be floated and passed through the locks were estimated as carrying about one hundred tons.

It was a long distance in time and experience between the ground breaking and the completion of the Erie Canal. There was no American precedent for such a work, and no earlier need to accumulate so large a capital for a single enterprise. The credit of the State of New York did it; and Governor Clinton had continuously to hold the desire of the State up to the task it had undertaken. The panic of 1819 intervened, when sensible men knew that the money could not be raised; but Clinton kept his courage. Every year the population of the West was growing; and every year the steamboats built up for New Orleans a better organization of the river trade. But by 1824 the Erie Canal was nearly done, and in October, 1825, Clinton took part in the national celebration that signalized success.

On October 26, 1825, the canal boat *Seneca Chief*, with Clinton and his party as passengers, and with lesser participants following in other craft, started its triumphal procession from Buffalo to New York. There was no Buffalo before the canal, and no settlement along its route west of Rome. By the date of completion, homes dotted the canal zone throughout its length, and at Buffalo a lake port was developing a new group of western connections. For the first time the Upper Lakes were in real contact with the world. The *Seneca Chief* carried the news to the ocean. A salvo of artillery fire, relayed in advance, announced the coming of the procession. A keg of the waters of Lake Erie was carried in symbolic fashion to be emptied into the Atlantic. At every station along the canal banquets were eaten and toasts were drunk. At Albany, where the canal ended, the boats were taken in tow by a steamer; and on November 4, the ninth day of the trip, New York was reached.

The effect of the Erie Canal upon the development of both the city at its mouth and the country behind it was beyond any expectation. Before 1830 there developed an up-state frontier New York that would have become another State had it been further away, and whose significance was obscured because it lay inside a State already existing. But no New York politician has been unaware of it.[1] Before 1840 the south shore of Lake Erie was colonized with towns and communities all of which saw the world through New York eyes. Before 1850 both Michigan and Wisconsin had been added to the United States, largely as results of the

[1] Charles McCarthy, *The Antimasonic Party; A Study in Political Antimasonry, 1827–1840* (1902).

population shift that the canal occasioned; and the Old Northwest had become conscious of the fact that it contained two regions, the newer being a Yankee tract that fought the Democrats of the Ohio Valley at every turn. By 1860 the region tributary to New York was a sufficient unit to bind the East to the West, and to maintain the Union. New York City, meanwhile, had outgrown its fears and jealousies of Philadelphia and Baltimore, and had come into the full enjoyment of its imposing harbor and its trade control of the easiest route into the American continent. The desires of New York merchants for their share of the western markets started many things whose limits they could not foresee.

Before the completion of the Erie Canal in 1825, the people of Pennsylvania and Maryland were shaken in the complacency with which they had hitherto regarded their control of western trade. The Cumberland Road was worn out before it was finished, and Congress could not pass a law for its repair. New Orleans was rising in importance all the time, and New York, with upstart hopes, was threatening to upset the balance. With such a background, the activities of the merchant population of Philadelphia and Baltimore must be regarded after 1821.[2]

Pennsylvania had the same motives that New York possessed to improve upon the Cumberland Road. It had in addition a fear of the competition of New York. It had lost its faith in turnpikes by 1825, and in this year its legislature authorized the survey of the routes across the mountains between Philadelphia and Pittsburgh in the hope of finding a route for a canal, or for a tunnel through which a road might run. The next year the State started in upon the building of a composite engineering work, having found a group of engineer advisers whose consciences let them assert that it could compete with the Erie Canal. But whether it could compete or not, political necessity forced the government of Pennsylvania not to sit by idly while New York gathered in the western trade.

The Pennsylvania System, as it was called, for no single word could adequately describe it, was ready for use throughout in 1834. From Philadelphia to Pittsburgh, its total length was nearly four hundred miles. From Philadelphia to Columbia on the Susquehanna River, tracks were laid down for a tramway, over which it

<hr />

[2] M. Reizenstein, "Economic History of the Baltimore and Ohio Railroad," in Johns Hopkins University *Studies*, vol. xv; Wm. B. Wilson, *History of the Pennsylvania Railroad Company* (1899); and of course Hulbert, in his *Historic Highways*.

was proposed to haul wagons for any one who would equip his vehicles with wheels that would fit the tracks. At Columbia, a canal along the Susquehanna River continued the line to the mouth of the Juniata, the goods and passengers having been transshipped to canal boats. The canal followed the Juniata as far into the mountains as it could, coming to an end at Hollidaysburg. Even the hopeful Pennsylvania engineers were never able to procure water for the canal on top of the Alleghany Mountains. From Hollidaysburg, over the ridge and down to Johnstown on the Conemaugh River, there was a tramway running over a series of inclined planes and levels and through a long tunnel at the crest. Horse power was used to haul the wagons on the levels. Stationary engines and cables let the cars up and down the slopes, and between the terminals of this inclined railway there was overcome a combined ascent and descent of twenty-five hundred feet. From Johnstown another canal completed the route to Pittsburgh, by way of the Allegheny River.

There was no questioning the scenic beauties of the Pennsylvania System of improvements. For the decade of the thirties, the traveler in America felt that his opportunities were not fulfilled unless he had made the journey by the canal boat packets from Philadelphia to Pittsburgh. Eventually freight was hauled in sectional cars that could be taken off their trucks and put into water as boats so as to avoid the necessity for handling the goods. Steam locomotives were in use on the tramway end of the line before 1834. But the cost of operation was such that Pennsylvania could never earn interest on its investment, and in 1857 the State was glad to sell the system to the Pennsylvania Railroad Company, which scrapped it. The whole work is, however, of interest as showing the intensity of the Pennsylvania desire to retain and enlarge its share in the traffic of the western markets. The example of Pennsylvania was an immediate stimulant to the people further south who feared that this enterprise might cut them out of their share of western profits.

Maryland and Virginia, whose peculiar relationship to the Potomac River was one of the causes occasioning the creation of the Federal Constitution, were equally concerned in the commerce to which the Potomac Valley led. Washington's connection with the Potomac Company of 1784 was founded in the belief that a canal might be cut through from the Chesapeake to the Ohio. With the building of the Cumberland Road, the agitation of the canal promoters was stilled for the time; but with the undertaking of the New York and Pennsylvania works it came to life again. As discussed in the twenties, the project took the form of a canal from the rapids in the Potomac, above Georgetown, to the Ohio River. Between Georgetown and Fort Cumberland the canal could follow the familiar valley route that had been well known since the colonial days when Alexandria, Virginia, was port of entry for freight and immigrants. As the discussion advanced, the interest of Baltimore merchants in the scheme cooled off, because only by an artificial route could the canal be made to touch Baltimore or to add anything to the trading advantages of that town.

A separate Baltimore improvement plan was developed after Virginia had determined to proceed alone with its canal, and during 1827 charters were granted by both Maryland and Pennsylvania for the Baltimore and Ohio Railroad Company. "Little known as railroads are in America," said the *North American Review*, . . . "the scheme is certainly a bold one, of constructing a road of this sort, not less than two hundred and fifty miles in length, and surmounting an elevation of three thousand feet." The engineers of the army were relied upon for the preliminary surveys, and a surviving signer of the Declaration of Independence, Charles Carroll, of Carrollton, broke ground for the enterprise on July 4, 1828, after what *Niles' Register* described as "The most splendid civic procession, perhaps, ever exhibited in America." The charters of the road required it to be done by 1843, but before the line had even reached Fort Cumberland, the panic of 1837 intervened. Not until after 1850 was the work done. The competition for the western trade thus led Maryland to risk the venture with the newest of the devices in communication.

South of the line of the Baltimore and Ohio Railroad, the Chesapeake and Ohio Canal and the South Carolina Railroad were additional testimony to the lure of western business. The former of these was begun by President John Quincy Adams on the same day that ground was broken for the Baltimore and Ohio. It, also, was blocked by the panic; and unlike the railroad never recovered from the check. It was finished to Fort Cumberland, and stopped there.[3]

The South Carolina Railroad originated in Charleston's jealousy of the towns along the Gulf. As the cotton region spread over the

[3] Corra Bacon-Foster, *Early Chapters in the Development of the Patomac Route to the West* (1912).

lowlands of Carolina and Georgia, Charleston developed and consolidated its commercial leadership of the South. It was not as
immediately suspicious of New Orleans as were the cities further
north along the coast. But it watched the extension of cotton
acreage into the uplands of Georgia and Alabama with fear that
the cotton might find its way to a market down the Chattahoochee
or the Alabama, and thus transfer commercial leadership to another region. In 1827, South Carolina chartered a railroad to run
west from Charleston to Hamburg, at the falls of the Savannah,
in the hope of diverting cotton to Charleston from Savannah, and
to compete for the business of upland Georgia. The road was open
in 1830, and was 136 miles long, the first railroad of considerable
length to operate in the United States. It failed to accomplish its
purpose, for Charleston could not hold its own as the cotton empire shifted; but like the other improved highways between the
sections it helps to measure the interest the East developed in the
West during the period of the great migration.

The attempt of the East to hold the West, and to make its control permanent and effective, passed into its second phase during
the period of internal improvements. The earlier phase of the
problem was political; the later economic. In the earlier instance
it was uncertain whether the political bond would hold, and
Jefferson made haste to strain the Constitution to save the Union.
He thus bought Louisiana. In the later phase, Clay's effort to
induce the Union to promote internal improvements for the economic development of the United States was resisted by presidential opposition until private and State initiative undertook the
task. The Erie Canal was the only successful improvement for
many years, but it inspired imitation and opened a new period of
economic development. The East took part, attracted by western
profits. The West undertook public works on its own account in
order to open up the country and disseminate prosperity. But the
alignment of the West, with the East or with the South, remained
uncertain for another generation; and not until both North and
South called upon it in the Civil War was it ready with an answer.

CHAPTER XXX

THE WESTERN INTERNAL IMPROVEMENTS

THE years of the administration of John Quincy Adams, 1825–1829, mark the great inauguration of internal improvements. The Government of the United States was assisting in the work. Private capital and State resources were pledged to it. The Erie Canal was completed, and the eastern cities entered the race for western trade. The railroad period was opened with the Baltimore and Ohio, and the South Carolina Railroad. Inspired by the activity of the East and their own enthusiasms, the western States began improvements. In the summer in which he opened the Erie Canal, Governor Clinton made a special trip to Ohio to join in the inception of two local public works that were to make the Ohio River run uphill, and deliver commerce for Cincinnati and Cleveland, *en route* to New York.

The distribution of population in the Old Northwest in 1825 was still confined almost exclusively to the southern slope of the region on the Ohio River and its tributaries. Except in Ohio there was no large group of settlers north of the watershed; and even here the few communities that skirted the Lake Erie shore had an average density of under eighteen to the square mile. The Ohio tributaries were not useful to the innermost settlements as carriers of commerce. Zane's Trace had become a flourishing road for the eastern interior of the State. The United States began in 1825 to build the National Road, in extension of the Cumberland Road from Wheeling, in order to meet the need of the remote frontier. On July 4, 1825 it broke ground at St. Clairsville, a few miles west of Wheeling, where the new road was to branch off from Zane's Trace. But Governor Morrow of Ohio did not grace the occasion with his presence, for a more important ceremony was being held the same day at Licking Summit, near Newark, where the National Road was to be crossed by the new Ohio Canal. The turnpike period was no longer at its height, and the canals had captured the imagination of the promoter.[1]

The prospective opening of the Erie Canal had much to do with

[1] G. W. Dial, "Construction of the Ohio Canals," in Ohio Archæological and Historical Society *Publications*, vol. XIII.

the form taken by the Ohio public works. Not since the first settlements had there been a route for the exchange of goods between the East and the upper Ohio Valley. The development of such seemed to be the condition precedent to solvency throughout the West. The example of New York inspired the States to action on their own account and stimulated a thorough study of the topography of the country in the search for available routes.

The survey of canal sites revived the importance of the primitive conditions that determined the course of exploration and missionary activity during the French régime. Long before the first whites came, the Indians knew all of the interlocking streams that flow between the Lakes and the Mississippi Valley. They knew the currents, the distances, the length and convenience of the portages. The same elements that led to the frequent use of certain of the portage routes between the sections, and to the neglect of the others, affected their availability for canals. Where there was a river there was water for the canal; and where the grades were light the canal could be dug with fewest locks.

There were two good portage routes east of Ohio that invited the inspection of the canal engineer. Of these the easternmost left Lake Erie near Dunkirk, New York, reached Lake Chautauqua in a few miles, and thence used the Allegheny River all the way to the Ohio. A little further west, another started inland at Erie, and made a short cut to French Creek, that joins the Allegheny at Franklin, Pennsylvania. The Mahoning River, that cuts across northeast Ohio into Beaver Creek and the Ohio, afforded another route, for its headwaters interlock with those of the Cuyahoga.

The most direct of the Cuyahoga lines, and one that intrigued the attention of Ohio from the earliest surveys, led to the head of the Muskingum, and thence to the Ohio River at Marietta. Cleveland was at the northern terminus of this line, and the community around Marietta was the oldest, if not the largest in the State. Next west of the Cuyahoga lay the valley of the Sandusky River, with a spacious harbor at its mouth on Lake Erie. There was no village of importance as far west as Sandusky Bay in 1825, but there were scattered settlements along the river, whose residents had a large view of the importance of their future. The portage from the Sandusky led directly to the Scioto, in whose valley lived the Virginia and Kentucky settlers who had found their way to the Virginia Military Reserve. The new Ohio capital at Columbus was on the Scioto, where the National Road crossed the river. Below it were Circleville and Chillicothe.

Another of the Ohio canal routes was that of the Great Miami, from Cincinnati through Hamilton to Dayton, along the line of frontier forts built by St. Clair and Wayne to protect the country from the Wabash tribes. From the sources of the Great Miami, the Auglaize continues the line to the Maumee at Defiance, where Wayne erected his fort in 1794. Toledo Bay, at the mouth of the Maumee, provided the site for a terminus on Lake Erie. Here was the region claimed by both Ohio and Michigan Territory, the future center of the "Toledo War." Its canal values gave to that war its intensity.

The available portages did not cease at the western boundary of Ohio. Indiana possessed the Wabash, with a short carry between Fort Wayne and the Wabash River. When Wayne built this fort after the battle of Fallen Timbers he selected the one site from which the traffic of the Indians between Lake Erie and the Ohio could most easily be policed. There was no other Indian route as good as the Wabash, but engineers and scouts knew that it would be easy, if desired, to get from Lake Michigan to the upper waters of the Kankakee, and thence to the Illinois River and the Mississippi. The canal routes from Lake Michigan were secondary in importance to those from Lake Erie because of the devious course through Lake Michigan and Lake Huron. The insignificant Chicago River, emptying into the head of Lake Michigan by the side of Fort Dearborn could sometimes be followed in wet weather without a portage to the Illinois and the Mississippi. On the prairie marshes behind Fort Dearborn there was almost no obstruction to the canoe. Further north on Lake Michigan there was a possibility of striking west from Milwaukee to the Rock River, that runs parallel to the Lake, and not far inland. This would connect with the Mississippi at Rock Island. Still further north, Green Bay pointed to the old route most traveled from the Upper Lakes to the Mississippi, by way of Lake Winnebago and a chain of lesser lakes nearing the bend of the Wisconsin River where the town of Portage was eventually built.

The three States concerned, Ohio, Indiana, and Illinois, began their surveys of these routes in the twenties, under the spell cast by the action of New York. They found that the obstacles to be overcome were financial rather than mechanical, and that at all times they were involved in a mesh of politics. When the States avowed a determination to spend State money to improve prosperity, every settled section desired to share the advantage, and few regions were magnanimous enough to pay the bills while other regions profited.

The Ohio legislature was deadlocked for a time by the rival claims of the three excellent routes across the State. The commissioners began their study as early as 1822. The final decision, approved in 1825, was to undertake two canals. The Ohio Canal was to be a compromise between the easternmost routes, joining the Cuyahoga and the Scioto, to the disgust of Marietta and Sandusky, which were left off it. The "Fire Lands" people, for whom Sandusky was the port of entry, were too determined to accept defeat. They shortly undertook the Mad River Railroad on their own initiative. Meanwhile, however, the Ohio Canal was begun at Licking Summit in 1825. Around Cuyahoga Falls, near Akron, farmers began immediately to raise wheat for the eastern market. By 1831 the canal was in use between Newark and Cleveland, and a fleet of steam packets made frequent trips between Cleveland and Buffalo. In 1832 the canal was completed to its southern outlet at Portsmouth. The Ohio celebration that might have commemorated the termination of the task was abandoned because of an epidemic of cholera that swept the frontier in October, 1832. But the real monument to the canal was the rapid growth of a prosperous strip of farming country along the route, much as the Erie Canal had built up a similar strip across western New York. The grain from Ohio poured in to the warehouses of New York City, to the dismay of eastern farmers whose soil was outclassed by the fresh prairie soils now brought to use. Cleveland, which had only grown to a scant thousand inhabitants in the quarter century after Moses Cleaveland surveyed it, swelled to forty-five hundred by 1834, and kept on growing. The Democratic politicians, who had tuned their notes to the responses of the southern democrats who built up the Northwest, found it necessary to learn a different song for the counties north of the National Road. The northern invasion of the Old Northwest began to upset the solidarity of that section.

The second of the canals decided upon by Ohio was projected up into the country behind Cincinnati. Governor Clinton made the speech of dedication on July 21, 1825, at Middletown on the Great Miami, about halfway from Cincinnati to Dayton. The Miami Canal, as it was commonly called, made slower progress than the Ohio Canal because the resources of the State were in-sufficient to carry on two major operations at once. There was a good market for the Ohio canal stocks. Eastern men of means took some millions of them. The process of financing western im-provements with eastern money got slowly under way as the im-provement programs were launched, and never after 1825 was the West entirely without some eastern aid in its ventures. The period was over in which western development was limited by the resources that western funds could provide. The new financial ties provided at once a source of constant irritation between East and West, and a closer and more reliable union.

Dayton, at the northern end of the first section of the Miami Canal, was not reached until 1839; much of the delay being due to the panic of 1837. Congress, in 1827, came to the aid of the canals by voting not only a free right of way through the public lands, but a grant of free sections as well. Within the next few years one half of the lands lying within five miles of the canals on either side were used by the States concerned to advance the Miami, Wabash, Illinois, and Rock River canals. Alternate sec-tions were retained and granted, so that a map of the canal lands took the appearance of a strip cut from a checkerboard, with the red squares devoted to the improvement, and the white reserved by the United States for sale. The proponents of the grants urged them on the ground that Government lands would be more than doubled in price by an adjacent canal, and that it was only fair for the Government to share the unearned profit with the States whose sacrifices made the improvements possible. Even with Government aid the Miami Extension to Defiance was not open until 1845, two years after Indiana initiative had procured the building of a canal the whole length of the Maumee from Toledo to Fort Wayne.

The Wabash and Erie Canal had the advantage of following the best known route, and the disadvantage that its completion re-quired the concurrence of two States. It was surveyed under the act of 1824, and in the same year Congress provided it with a right of way; adding in 1827 the grant of five sections of public lands per mile. It was not begun until 1832, the year in which the Ohio Canal was finished; and it was sadly delayed by the financial stringency caused by the panic of 1837. In 1843 the canal was in operation from Toledo to Lafayette, on the Wabash. It was in later years projected further and further down that stream, to

Terre Haute, and then to Evansville. But before it could become as important as the Ohio Canal had been, it was out of style, and railroads were the rage.

The Illinois and Michigan Canal was started under desires similar to those of Indiana and Ohio and received the same kind of aid from the United States.[2] Surveys were made for it in the twenties and the commissioners in 1830 platted a town at Fort Dearborn to be its Michigan terminus, naming it Chicago; but the first steamboat did not anchor off the shoal mouth of the Chicago River until the summer of 1832. The prairie State still had no northern end, its population in 1830 being confined to the river bottoms of the Ohio and Mississippi, and the angle between them. The National Road would have crossed this southern angle had it not been abandoned, incomplete, at Vandalia. The panic caught Illinois so hard that little construction could be put through before the early forties. After 1843 the canal was rapidly built and in 1848 it was an accomplished fact.

Even the Wabash Canal was not as significant as its promoters hoped. It never quite justified the wailing note of *DeBow's Southern Review*, that it was "stretching its line down the banks of the Wabash, and as fast as it extends itself, it sweeps the whole products of the valley up the river, against its natural current, to the Eastern Markets, by way of the Lakes." This was the motive of the Northwest in the period of canal building but only the Ohio Canal approximated success. Even Illinois lost interest in the Illinois and Michigan Canal before it was finished in 1848. All the States received sharp lessons in the risks of public business, and this era of public ownership as well as of the canals reached its end.

The canal period could never have flourished in the earliest frontier phase of any State, from lack of population, wealth, and business. It came to life as the first positive effort of the States to utilize their wealth in the direction pointed out by Clay's American System; and was supported in the hope that such a use of capital would increase returns and spread prosperity. The building of canals through unsettled regions, where land was hardly worth the Government minimum of $1.25, was justified upon the plea that population would increase, and that taxable values would grow rapidly enough to warrant the outlay. The movement failed in

[2] J. W. Putman, "Economic History of the Illinois and Michigan Canal," in *Journal of Political Economy*, vol. XVII.

the Northwest from lack of skill and funds. In the Southwest it was never far advanced, for the southern man of means needed all his capital to hold his slaves and had little free for investment.

The positive results of the canal construction were most felt within the area indicated by Buffalo, Pittsburgh, Cincinnati, and Toledo. Here the canals distributed immigration, and collected the freights. Business relationships were established with the East, though they were not neglected with New Orleans. The fleets of steamboats increased on western rivers in spite of all canals, and New Orleans maintained a worthy rivalry with New York.

The western public works and the struggle of the East to reach the western markets, gave wide advertisement to the frontier regions in the years after 1825. There was a falling off in migration after the boom year of 1819, and the burden of debts was not forgotten until the twenties were well advanced. But every new enterprise taken up after 1825 called new attention to western opportunity and stimulated the movement of population. The canal lands, as they came upon the market, advertised specific regions. The opening of the Ohio Canal marks the beginning of another period comparable to the great migration, although there were fewer States to be created as a result. From 1832 until 1837 this wave of population flowed in swelling dimensions over the regions of the older settlements and out upon the public domain. For the first time since the beginning of the western movement the areas of available lands were limited. Behind the agricultural frontier there was a population of towns and farms growing more dense each year. Beyond it stood a barrier made up of the international boundaries of the United States, the desert across the Mississippi, and a solid Indian frontier that had come into existence since the inauguration of John Quincy Adams. This Indian frontier placed a limit upon expansion as well as upon the imagination of the American people.

CHAPTER XXXI
THE PERMANENT INDIAN FRONTIER, 1825-1841

WHEN the international boundaries of the United States were stabilized by the English treaty of 1818 and the Spanish treaty of 1819, it appeared to contemporaries that the country had reached the limit of its external growth. There was no serious thought that either Canada or Mexico would become parts of the United States, and even when the exhilaration of patriotic holidays was felt there were few whose flights of fancy reached a nation that stretched beyond the Rocky Mountains. Clay accepted the fact of national completeness, and devised his American System for the further-ance of its internal advantage. Monroe and Adams accepted it, and the former made his memorable gesture of defiance of the European world in his message to Congress in 1823. The War Department accepted it, and carried out its reorganization after the War of 1812, upon the supposition that the United States had little to fear from foreign enemies, and was chiefly concerned with in-ternal police along the border. The chain of frontier forts, from Fort Smith to Fort Howard, were testimony to this view; and in the course of erecting them, the War Department and the President learned much of the native races for whose control and pro-tection they were built.[1]

The new States that were the legacy of the great migration es-tablished a new frontier of organized government for the United States. After 1821 the further boundary of the States ran from Lake Erie, at Toledo, around Indiana, Illinois, Missouri, Tennes-see, Mississippi, and Louisiana, to the Gulf of Mexico. From the standpoint of the War Department the new States raised a cer-tainty that could not be ignored. The history of the States thus far showed that no white community lived contentedly with an Indian community in its vicinity. Even the organized territories protested when the tribes were not removed fast enough to please

---

[1] F. L. Paxson, *The Last American Frontier* (1910). Lewis Cass discussed these experi-ences in "The Removal of the Indians," in *North American Review*, vol. xxx; Annie H. Abel gives intense detail in *Indian Consolidation west of the Mississippi* (1906); Ruth A. Gallaher has reconsidered the matter in "The Military-Indian Frontier, 1830-1835," and "The Indian Agent in the United States before 1850," appearing in recent volumes of the *Iowa Journal of History and Politics*, 1917.

them; but the States expected to be freed of them. Georgia made this the price of its cession of western lands to Congress in 1802; and was repeatedly complaining because the Cherokee, which was the tribe chiefly concerned, showed a preference for staying where it was. Thus far it was a simple matter, when dealing with the tribes, to persuade them to surrender their old homes, and to drift further west. But the time had come, by 1821, when the available region of the West was narrowed down by the boundaries of the United States, and the western boundary of the several States. If, as was certain, Arkansas and Michigan Territories should rise to statehood; if a State should be formed north of Illinois, and perhaps another north of Missouri, it would become a difficult matter to tell the tribes where they might go when they were dispossessed by the pressure and demands of encroaching white populations. At no time in the past had a serious effort been made to formulate a policy for handling the Indians, except the short-lived effort of England, in which the Proclamation Line played a weak part. From pillar to post, the Indians had been driven in a piece-meal fashion. There was the ancient practice of shifting them towards the West, but no statesman or philanthropist had worked out a policy telling why and how this should be the case.

John C. Calhoun, as Secretary of War for James Monroe, was custodian of Indian rights and interests, as well as the agent for their chastisement when things went wrong. Under his direction the army was reorganized, the forts were arranged for, and the Indian problem was studied now that its solution was becoming pressing. He submitted the results of his study to the President and the latter transmitted them to Congress on January 27, 1825. The report of Calhoun contained long summaries of the numbers, location, and condition of the various tribes with which the United States had to deal. "One of the greatest evils to which they are subject is that incessant pressure of our population, which forces them from seat to seat," he wrote. "To guard against this evil . . . there ought to be the strongest and most solemn assurance that the country given them should be theirs, as a permanent home for themselves and their posterity."

As Calhoun and his countrymen looked upon the domain of the United States, there was no permanent home for the tribes within any State; and none in a region that white men were likely to desire. But beyond Missouri lay the great area of the Plains, with the Rockies, Canada, and Mexico as its thither boundaries. The best scientific opinion had reported with emphasis that white men could not live here. Yet the plains abounded with game, upon which the Indians were most accustomed to live. The Rockies were a barrier, the plains were a social waste. Here was a spot almost providentially designed to be the Indians' home; and Calhoun advised the President to "acquire a sufficient tract of country west of the State of Missouri and the Territory of Arkansas, in order to establish permanent settlements in that quarter."

Monroe accepted the conclusions of Calhoun and urged them upon Congress as almost his last official act as President. "The great object to be accomplished is, the removal of these tribes to the territory designated . . . . conveying to each tribe a good title to an adequate portion of land . . . . by providing . . . . a system of internal government . . . and, by the regular progress of improvement and civilization, prevent . . . degeneracy." Congress received the recommendation with favor; and for the next fifteen years it, as well as the various Presidents who followed James Monroe, remained firm in the belief that the future of the United States would permit a permanent policy of devoting to Indian occupation the whole of the territory remaining west of the organized States.

There were three steps in the fulfillment of the frontier policy advocated by Monroe and approved by his successors. First, Congress must by suitable legislation make it possible for the War Department to carry on the negotiations and give the necessary assurances to the tribes; and the Senate must approve the treaties negotiated. Second, room must be found for the eastern or emigrant tribes in a country already occupied by western or plains tribes. These must be induced to allow the emigrant Indians to settle and enjoy the new homes in peace. Third, the tribes east of the frontier must be persuaded to transfer their eastern lands to the United States and to accept western lands in exchange for them. The process was long and involved, but it was carried through.

The approval of Congress was given. A group of treaties made with the western Indians in 1825 gave a sort of pledge that was followed up by specific laws of 1828 and 1830, in which the policy of colonization was described as an accepted thing. In 1832 Congress recognized its responsibility to the emigrants and created a Bureau of Indian Affairs in the War Department, under a Commissioner whose duty was to care for the Indian wards. Two years later, the great charter of the frontier Indians was enacted in the Indian Intercourse Act, which forbade any white person, without license from the Indian Commissioner, to set foot in the Indian Country. The Indian Country became a legal entity, comprising the areas reserved to various tribes by the several treaties. A large part of it was further safeguarded by clauses in the treaties that the tribes should never be required to move away from the new homes granted to them. The guarantee of permanence, together with that of freedom from injurious contacts with members of the white race, was at the base of the Indian policy. Unless it could be upheld no one thought the policy could succeed. Under various clauses of the removal treaties, the United States assumed responsibilities towards the emigrant tribes that had not existed previously. Annuities were promised to some tribes, in part payment for the lands they gave up. Schools were promised, to teach the Indians letters and trades. In some cases blacksmiths and other artisans were to be maintained by the United States. There was a serious attempt to carry out the suggestion that once the tribes had been shifted to their final place of residence they must be lifted to a higher scale of civilization by the Government of the United States.

Preliminary negotiations with the resident western tribes were taken up in the summer of 1825, when important councils were held with the Osage, the Kaw, and the tribes of the Upper Mississippi. Governor William Clark, of Missouri, long experienced in such matters, framed the treaties with the Osage and Kaw in June. These tribes had long resided in the western part of Missouri and Arkansas and had already ceded so much of their claims as was included in Missouri. They now surrendered all the rest, except a limited reserve apiece, that opened in the west upon the buffalo country of the high plains. The Osage reserved a fifty-mile wide strip, running west from the Neosho, along the present southern boundary of Kansas; the Kaw retained a thirty-mile strip along the Kansas River, well west of the Missouri line. The country vacated immediately along the border of Missouri was to be used for colonization purposes.

Running northeast from Missouri to Lake Michigan lay the valley of the Upper Mississippi, still inhabited by the native tribes and not yet needed by prospective farmers. In this region the purpose of the United States was to consolidate the tribes and maintain the peace. The forts at Rock Island, Prairie du Chien, and

St. Paul existed for this purpose; and at Prairie du Chien, Governor Clark and Governor Lewis Cass of Michigan Territory assembled the Sioux, Chippewa, Iowa, and Sauk and Fox nations. It was a long and formal council, with over a thousand Indians drawing rations upon its last day, August 29, 1825. It was conducted as most councils were with food, drink, and presents, with kind words and powerful exhortations. At its close the tribes agreed to keep the peace, to recognize the sovereignty of the United States, and to accept suitable boundaries among themselves. The Sioux pledged themselves to respect a line drawn across the present State of Iowa, as boundary between themselves and the Sauk and Fox; and another line a little east of the Mississippi, as between themselves and the Chippewa.

The colonization of the eastern tribes was a tedious process. In many cases they did not wish to go; in others it was hard to induce the Indian mind to crystallize, or to settle the differences between the braves who were ready to sign agreements and those who wanted a higher price or better terms. The negotiators for the Government included many men who were old hands at this work, having taken part in the negotiations for removals before the frontier policy was conceived. The novel element in the frontier policy was not in the removal of tribes to western lands but in the deliberate acceptance of the policy, the determination that it should be final, and the selection of a permanent tribal home. There had been innumerable single transactions of the same general character since the days of the treaties of Fort Stanwix, Hard Labour, and Fort McIntosh.

Year by year, after 1825, as the details of the permanent Indian frontier were worked out, the eastern margin of the reserves developed into an irregular but solid line from the Red River to Green Bay. There were three sections to it, with differences in character, but alike in constituting a permanent line between the races. The southern extremity of the Indian frontier was west of Arkansas Territory and before its consolidation was completed Arkansas became a State in 1836. The middle region, abreast of Missouri and Iowa, touched the Mississippi near the lead mines and was shaped after the creation of Iowa Territory in 1838. The northern section represented the equilibrium reached between Indian occupation and white settlement in Minnesota and Wisconsin Territory after the latter was created in 1836. Parallel developments in the dozen years between the inauguration of Adams and the

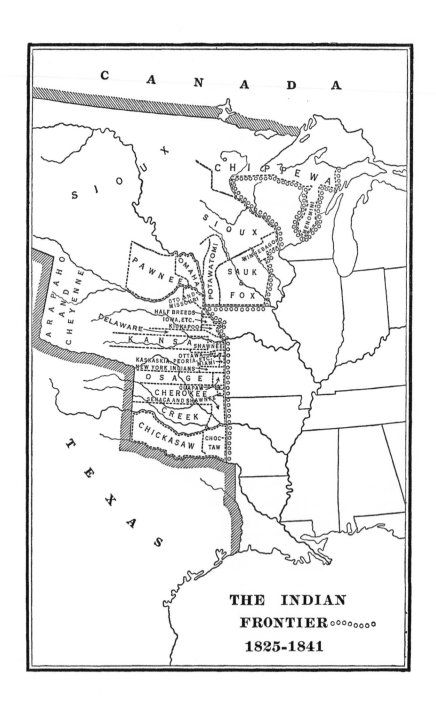

THE INDIAN
FRONTIER ·◦◦◦◦◦◦◦◦
1825-1841

panic of 1837 were the eastern competition for western trade, the western experiments with improvements in transportation, the ripening of the slavery feud between the North and the South, and the completion of this solid Indian front as a western barrier to further American extension.

The southern section of the Indian frontier was a border section with Mexico and Texas, the international line of 1819 crossing a region whose partition between two countries the natives hardly recognized. The Osage and the Comanche were the most important of the tribes whose compression was necessary to make room for the immigrant Indians. The tribes that moved in started to move before Monroe evolved his policy, and while Arkansas Territory extended to the western boundary of the United States at the one hundredth meridian. These were the five great nations of the southeast States, the Cherokee, Creek, Seminole, Chickasaw, and Choctaw. Until after the war of 1812 these tribes lived in Georgia and Mississippi Territory and ran over into the Spanish dominions of Florida without regard for national ownership. The Jackson campaigns began their transfer to the country beyond the Mississippi, and General Jackson concluded several treaties with them in furtherance of this removal. The tribal governments that they set up when at last colonized west of Fort Smith bore closer resemblance to real governments than did those of any other tribes adjacent to the American border. The northernmost of them, the Cherokee, settled on the Arkansas River and owned north to the Osage line at the thirty-seventh parallel.

The removal of the Cherokee and the Seminole nations attracted more attention than the removal of all the other tribes, because the latter struggled violently against going, and the former could not be moved fast enough to satisfy the State of Georgia. The administration of Adams was filled with angry complaints from Georgia and attempts by that State to force the Cherokee out and extend its own laws over the lands they occupied. The pledge of the United States to remove these Indians, given in 1802, was urged by Georgia as justification for insistence. In the end the Cherokee gave way after they had blocked the settlement of western Georgia and eastern Alabama for a decade. The Seminole war was the outgrowth of the refusal of the Seminole to abide by the treaty of 1832 in which they agreed to migrate with the Creeks. They subsequently confirmed the agreement in 1833, and in 1834 were called upon to move. Instead of moving they procrastinated;

quarrels arose over the possession of fugitive slaves who had taken refuge among them; they imbedded themselves in the swamps and forests of central Florida. And through the whole administration of Van Buren a large part of the army was engaged in searching for the recalcitrants. Most of them were removed during the forties, but the Seminole war was a baffling irritation for many years.

The middle section of the Indian frontier began at the northern limit of the Cherokee country and extended to the northwest corner of Missouri. In 1836 this corner was pushed further west by the addition to Missouri of a triangular area lying between its former western boundary and the Missouri River. From south to north the colonized tribes were given small reserves in exchange for the larger areas they had occupied further east. At the extreme southern end of the middle section the Quapaw and the united Seneca and Shawnee were in the angle between the Arkansas River and the State of Arkansas. North of these was a Cherokee strip allotted to the Cherokee because their main reserve was inadequate. Further to the north came the New York Indians, Miami, Ottawa and Chippewa, Piankeshaw and Wea, Kaskaskia and Peoria, Shawnee, Delawares, Kickapoo, Oto and Missouri, and Omaha. By 1841 they presented a solid front west of Arkansas and Missouri. The Omaha, the most northern tribe in the series, agreed by treaty in 1830 that their territory lay west of the Missouri River between the mouths of the Platte and the Big Sioux, and ceded to the United States their claims east of the Missouri. They were a native rather than an immigrant tribe, and shared with their neighbors to the east the condensation that was typical of the northern section of the Indian Country.

The peace treaty of 1825, at Prairie du Chien, was the first step in consolidating the northern part of the frontier. The tribes of this region, at this time, comprised the Chippewa who lived along the southern shore of Lake Superior, and the Sioux whose various groups dotted the valleys of the Upper Mississippi and the Missouri and extended west from the Great Lakes to the Rocky Mountains. South of the Chippewa along Lake Michigan as far as the Milwaukee River were the Menominee; south of these the Potawatami whose claims extended as far as Fort Dearborn and the Chicago River. The tribes along the Mississippi, south of the Sioux, were the Winnebago on the Wisconsin River and the Sauk and Fox whose range was on both sides of the Mississippi above the Illinois and Missouri. In 1825 there had as yet been little pressure upon these tribes, for the agricultural frontier was still far southeast of the site of Chicago. There were sparse settlements around the old fur-trade forts, and a handful of miners at the lead diggings on the Mississippi, but the Indians were still in undisputed possession of their lands.

Immediately after the treaty of Prairie du Chien, the shift of population to the Northwest began to unsettle it. From the Erie Canal came a swelling stream of colonists. In advance of them came prospectors to work the lead mines. Before 1830 the Winnebago and the Sauk and Fox were under foot, and had to be restrained for their own protection. During the next ten years, while the Jacksonian wave of migration reached its crest, all of the tribes between Lake Michigan and the Mississippi were either removed or condensed. By 1841 they had been pushed back, clearing most of Wisconsin and part of Iowa. The Menominee remained at Green Bay, but west and north of them the Wisconsin River valley had been given up, the Chippewa receding into northern Wisconsin and upper Michigan, and the Sioux retiring across the Mississippi. The Potawatami had been removed bodily from their residence around Chicago to a tract ceded by the Omaha, east of the Missouri. The Sauk and Fox had been forced across the Mississippi and had been compelled to cede a strip along the western side of that river, and the Winnebago had been colonized west of the Mississippi between the Sioux and the Sauk and Fox. The front of the Indian Country was unbroken from the Red River to Green Bay and Lake Michigan.

The Indian policy of James Monroe was worked out more fully and permanently than most American policies have been. The States were so glad to get rid of the tribes that they were willing participants, and gave it a longer life than it otherwise would have had. But the Presidents concerned, Monroe, Adams, Jackson, and Van Buren, did not waver in their support of it. Their consistent support forces the historian to conclude that they believed it a policy that could be maintained. Founded as it was upon the supposition that the States would never extend west of Missouri, and in the face of the evidence accumulating after 1830 that the Far West was to play a factor in American development, the living policy testifies to the firmness of the American conviction that the United States was ripe, mature, and complete in the decade of the twenties. "They are on the outside of us, and in a place which will ever remain on the outside," said a committee of

Congress at the end of Jackson's second term. "This strip of country, which extends from the province of Mexico to Lake Winnipeg on the North," said Catlin, who knew the Indians and the West, "is almost one entire plain of grass, which is, and ever must be, useless to cultivating man."

"The plan of removing the aboriginal people who yet remain within the settled portions of the United States to the country west of the Mississippi River approaches its consummation," wrote Jackson in his annual message for 1835. "It was adopted on the most mature consideration of the condition of this race, and ought to be persisted in till the object is accomplished, . . . The past we can not recall, but the future we can provide for. . . . The pledge of the United States has been given by Congress that the country destined for the residence of this people shall be forever 'secured and guaranteed to them.' . . . A barrier has thus been raised for their protection against the encroachment of our citizens. . . . After the further details of this arrangement are completed, with a very general supervision of them, they ought to be left to the progress of events." By the end of 1840 most of the tribes had been removed to the frontier, the Indian Country was solid, and the administrative details of the arrangement were complete. The American citizen, by his own enactment, no longer possessed a right to advance his settlements towards the West.

In the final stages of the Indian frontier policy, Congress and the War Department took up the problem of the permanent policing of the line of reserves that had been created. Every settled border region adjacent to the frontier was fearful of attacks from the Indian side, and was under the temptation to indulge in illicit and profitable trade in whiskey with the tribes.

The concentration of Indians along the new Indian front was real. In 1837 the Commissioner of Indian Affairs estimated that the Indians of the United States aggregated more than three hundred thousand, distributed as follows:

Resident among the States	12,415
Under agreement to emigrate	36,950
Emigrant Indians in West	51,327
Indigenous western tribes	231,806
	332,498

The Secretary of War, in 1837, recommended "a chain of permanent fortresses along that line, and a competent organization of the militia of the frontier states" as the best means of maintaining the peace; and the army was at work upon a survey of a western road authorized by Congress in 1836. This military road was to connect the Red River with the Mississippi at Fort Snelling, running West of Arkansas and Missouri. It was never built but its discussion kept the project of the frontier alive. The commander of the army in the West, General E. P. Gaines, recommended in 1838 that the cordon of military posts along the border be built of stone, to outlast the century at least; and that they be connected with military bases at Memphis and St. Louis by railroads that should be built by the army in time of peace. He pointed out that a parallel road along the frontier would be as helpful to marauding Indians as to their military police, but that railroads radiating from convenient centers would be abreast of the times and would make easy the quick shift of troops from one front to another. His proposal, like all the rest, failed of fulfillment, for the situation of the United States changed rapidly in the next few years. While the Indian frontier lasted, the defense of the frontier settlements was entrusted to moving bodies of United States troops, to a regiment of mounted dragoons that were enlisted early in the thirties, and to the militia. The governor of the new State of Arkansas declared in his inaugural, in 1836, "When the hardy yeomanry are disciplined and properly trained to arms, they are the 'bulwark of our country.' They are the 'chief defense of nations.'" They were at least the chief reliance of Democratic leaders for the next three quarters of a century.

CHAPTER XXXII

THE MISSISSIPPI VALLEY BOOM

SIMULTANEOUSLY with the adoption of the Indian frontier policy, the people of the United States again gathered themselves together for another wave of migration, and a new inundation of the West. The last wave, the great migration, reached its crest in the panic year 1819. For nearly a decade thereafter the migration was subnormal and the active East held its people home with the opportunities created by growing manufactures and internal improvements. The new wave formed even before Adams ceased to be President, and reached its largest about 1837. Permeated with the ideals for which Andrew Jackson stood and bringing his philosophy to its fulfillment in the constitutions of the Mississippi Valley, it may reasonably be described as the Jacksonian migration. The great migration completed the organization of six new States between 1816 and 1821. The Jacksonian migration had a smaller field in which to operate, for the frontier of the States now came close to the Indian frontier. Its political landmarks included only two new States, Arkansas and Michigan, which filled in interstices of the map; but it developed the region of the Upper Mississippi, where the territories of Wisconsin and Iowa appeared and projected American influence outside the United States into Texas, where a new republic claimed its independence in 1836. The whole Mississippi Valley was filled with the noise and upheaval that came with the new boom period, and western politics creaked under the new strains put upon it.

The whole population of the United States rose from 9,638,453 in 1820 to 17,069,453 in 1840. Of this increase of almost seven and a half millions, more than four millions were to be found in the States and territories west of the Appalachian Mountains. The total western population was about 6,300,000, not counting the elements in the population of New York, Pennsylvania, Virginia, and the Carolinas that might with propriety be counted as western; and this total was nearly two hundred per cent more than it had been in 1820. The whole United States increased about eighty per cent in twenty years. The eastern States, even with the help of their frontier elements, increased only some sixty per cent in the same period. The States of the old South, east of the mountains, increased but twenty-eight per cent. These variations in rapidity of growth caused much concern in a country that had grown to expect more than twenty-five per cent increase in a single decade. The jealousies among the sections, the southern fear of both East and West, and the eastern acidity on western problems may be explained in part by natural rivalries.

Furthest away from the settled region of the United States, the Upper Mississippi Valley was the meeting place of currents of settlers originating in the sections hitherto existing; and became the battle ground for the conflict of their ideals. When the governors signed the treaty at Prairie du Chien in 1825 there was still no pressure upon the Sioux and their immediate neighbors to give up their lands. The territory of Michigan extended across the two peninsulas from Lake Huron to the Misissippi, but there were no counties in this western half and no need for them until after the Winnebago war of 1827. Fort Winnebago was founded to keep the peace and protect the Indians in their rights, but it really served to make it safe for an invading column from the eastern States to enter the lead district and discover the attractions of the prairie openings and the hard wood forests of Wisconsin. In 1829, it was reported that twelve million pounds of lead were mined. Galena was booming at the northwest corner of Illinois, there were miners working the old diggings of Dubuque across the river in the Sauk and Fox country, and Mineral Point had been established by the prospectors in Michigan Territory. Iowa County was created in 1829 by the legislature of that territory so that the illegal occupants, for the settlers had no rights as yet, might have institutions of orderly government.

A second stream of miners and farmers ascended the Mississippi from the settlements of Missouri and southern Illinois. Most of these had southern grandparents and represented the continuation in the third generation of the migration that poured into the Appalachian valleys in the period of the Revolution, and over the western ridges at the end of the eighteenth century. Their habits in the early years in the lead country gave rise to nicknames that have stood the test of time. The "badgers" came up the river, dug in, and stayed as permanent members of a new community; the "suckers," like their finny namesakes, came up in the spring, and returned to Illinois before winter.

An early badger, and one of the most distinguished, was Henry

Dodge,[1] whose family tree portrays a typical course of frontier life. His ancestors made their first American appearance in early Massachusetts, and passed through years of residence in Rhode Island and then Connecticut. His father served in the Revolution, was wounded at the Brandywine, married the daughter of a Scotch-Irish settler at Carlisle, Pennsylvania, took up his residence at Kaskaskia where his brother was Indian agent, and moved with the infant Henry to Ste. Genevieve in the lead mining district of the Spanish province of Upper Louisiana. The purchase of Louisiana brought the Dodges back into the United States and Henry, now a strapping man, was of the sort that could thrash nine grand jurors for presuming to indict him for near-participation in Burr's conspiracy. The War of 1812 brought to Henry Dodge military duty and the rank of colonel. He sat in the convention that made a constitution for Missouri, and in 1827 was attracted by the reputation of the Illinois lead mines to ascend the Mississippi and to establish himself in what was soon to become Iowa County, Michigan Territory, near the present town of Dodgeville. The Indian agent wrote of him that he lived "in a small stockade fort near the principal mine. There are about twenty log houses in the immediate vicinity, besides several more remote. He has a double furnace in constant operation, and a large quantity of lead in bars and in the crude state." He resided there in calm defiance of the law, shipped his lead to New Orleans, and bought a generous estate when the Indian lands came finally upon the market. More than any other he personified the Upper Mississippi Valley from 1827 to 1850. He was a vigorous Unionist in 1832, decrying the right of any State to nullify a law of Congress; yet saw no inconsistency in his own refusal to obey the law.

The lesser immigrants, who followed Henry Dodge, came more numerously to the northern counties of Illinois, and were soon at outs with the Sauk and Fox Indians. The unfortunate treaty of St. Louis, signed in 1804, was at the root of the misfortunes that this tribe underwent. In this treaty, the east bank of the Mississippi, between the Wisconsin and the Illinois, was ceded to the United States subject to the right of the Sauk and Fox to continue to occupy it until the United States should sell it. No squatter had any right here against the Indians; but the large acreage of

[1] The archives of the upper Mississippi Valley have been combed for papers relating to this border hero, and the results are well displayed in Louis Pelzer, *Henry Dodge* (1911), and *Marches of the Dragoons in the Mississippi Valley* (1917).

cleared ground around the Sauk and Fox village at Rock Island was a constant temptation to the more adventurous of the prospectors. The double lure of lead and the Illinois prairies brought them in and during the summers of 1830 and 1831 they squatted upon the cornfields of the Indians.

The Indians resented this encroachment, as was their right, and Black Hawk, their principal brave, blustered at the settlers and threatened to put them out by force. The squatters made as strong an appeal to the governor of Illinois and the commander of the United States garrison at Rock Island as though they were the injured parties, instead of rank trespassers. In 1831 General Gaines forced Black Hawk to promise to stay west of the Mississippi, and leave the whites alone. But in April, 1832, Black Hawk was back again, crossing the river with a body of warriors estimated at between six and eight hundred.[2] There was panic in the lead country, and among the frontier farms of Illinois; but Henry Dodge held the Winnebago in check, preventing them from joining Black Hawk in a vain attempt to block the course of history. The Illinois militia was called out by Governor Reynolds, and General Atkinson brought his regulars from Fort Armstrong to a rendezvous at Dixon's early in May. Here the road from Chicago to the lead mines crossed the Rock River, and along this road were pouring the settlers from central Illinois and Indiana who were coming overland in wagons to the new country. In July General Winfield Scott arrived at Chicago with regulars from the East, including the cadet corps from West Point that was hurriedly sent to the defense of the frontier.

The frontier politicians who served with the Illinois militia in 1832 continued long to talk about their experiences, as though the campaign had been a war. Black Hawk lost his belligerent desires as soon as he saw a force raised against him, and retreated in haste. His direct line back to the Mississippi was cut off, so he ascended the Rock River, making a long detour through northern Illinois and southern Wisconsin, as he hurried to the rough land along the Wisconsin River near the Dells. The pursuers followed, not too closely. They conducted a running engagement through the Four Lakes district where Madison was later built, and drove him down

[2] F. E. Stevens, *The Black Hawk War* (1903), is a careful antiquarian study; the local historians of Michigan, Illinois, Iowa, and Wisconsin have conserved the last verifiable details of this inglorious campaign. J. Reynolds, *My Own Times* (1879). The famous autobiography of Black Hawk, first published in 1833, is now available in M. M. Quaife, *Life of Black Hawk, Ma-Ka-Tai-Me-She-Kia-Kiak* (1916).

to the Mississippi bank. On August 2, while Black Hawk and his discouraged warriors were crossing the river to the Iowa side, they were set upon, shot, drowned, and captured; and the chief himself was handed over to the army after he sought refuge with the Winnebago. In September what was left of the Sauk and Fox concluded a treaty of submission and cession, in which they agreed to stay west of the Mississippi and surrender a strip along the right bank of that river some fifty miles in width. The Black Hawk cession, as this was called, was the first title acquired by the United States in Iowa.

The peaceful Indian possession of the Upper Mississippi that was in force in 1825 was gone by 1832. The new equilibrium to be established was worked out in recognition of new territories to be formed north of Illinois and Missouri. The Sauk and Fox, who were construed to be the aggressors, were punished by the loss of their home. The Winnebago and the Potawatami were induced to follow them beyond the Mississippi.

The Winnebago met General Scott and Governor Reynolds in treaty council at Fort Armstrong in September, 1832. General Dodge was there, as friend of the tribe, for they had not resented his residence among them. They agreed to leave the country east of the Mississippi and to accept for temporary residence a tract between the Sioux and the Sauk and Fox, on the west bank, along the neutral strip that had been established between these ancient enemies after the Prairie du Chien negotiations of 1825. The Potawatami and their relatives from the Ottawa and Chippewa tribes were convened in a council at Chicago a year later. They had earlier than this reduced their claims to a strip extending along the western shore of Lake Michigan from Chicago to the vicinity of Milwaukee. They now accepted a substitute reserve west of the Sauk and Fox in the Iowa country and became emigrant Indians to the new frontier. Ten years later after they were in residence along the east side of the Missouri, in former Omaha country, their agent commented upon the rapidity of shift: "Although it is but ten years to-day since that treaty was concluded . . . the tide of emigration has rolled onwards to the far West, until the whites are now crowded closely on the southern side of these lands, and will soon swarm along the eastern side, to exhibit the very worst traits of the white man's character, and destroy, by fraud and illicit intercourse, the remnant of a powerful people, now exposed to their influence."

With the Indians removed from the space between Lake Michigan and the Mississippi, and with the General Land Office ready to run township lines and to open the new lands for sale, the time came for the development of the Upper Mississippi Valley. The spring of 1833 beheld a rapid flow of population along the three routes that led to northern Illinois, southern Wisconsin, and the Black Hawk Purchase. Squatters were at the Mississippi long before the country beyond it was ready for their use and the army had a vexatious task in ejecting those who could not wait for the appointed day. The difficulty of administering the land laws, which provided that there could not be any legal entry upon the lands until after they had been surveyed and offered formally for sale, was increased by a growing habit on the part of Congress of allowing preëmption rights. The theory of preëmption was that certain individuals already in occupation of parts of the public domain when the surveys were made had an equity in their improvements that entitled them to protection. Congress granted this, by special act, allowing such occupiers to buy their land at the minimum price in advance of the general sale. Hence the word "preëmption"; and hence the impossibility of holding back the general rush of settlers until the advertised date, when it was common knowledge that others, who had pushed in through the guards, would be allowed to profit by their law breaking. The Black Hawk Purchase was occupied in the summer of 1833, although it had as yet no government and the settlers' only guarantee of order was their own good sense.

Keokuk, Burlington, Davenport, and Dubuque, all of them river towns, were quickly born along the Black Hawk Purchase and developed hopes of future greatness that time could not fulfill. They were paralleled, on the western shore of Lake Michigan, by Chicago, Southport (Kenosha), Milwaukee, and Manitowoc, each of which saw itself as a connecting link between the fleet of lake steamers and the new towns and farms that were multiplying every spring. The Jacksonian migration was approaching its crest in the years after the Black Hawk War and these hopeful towns were the most remote of its disturbances.

Michigan Territory, enlarged after the admission of Illinois, extended from Lake Huron and the Detroit River to the Mississippi, without much population in either of its detached portions until after 1825. It established county government for the lead country in its extreme western end before 1830 and was itself enlarged after the Black Hawk cession. The new boundaries were designed to be temporary; but for the present they carried the jurisdiction of the territory as far west as the Missouri River and as far south as the northern boundary of the State of Missouri. Most of the new area was Indian Country, under the protection of the Indian Intercourse Act that was passed two days after the Michigan enlargement. It was as yet uncertain where the balance would be established between the Indians and the whites along the northern section of the frontier, and meanwhile some form of government for the settlers west of the Mississippi could not be avoided. Michigan promptly created two counties, Dubuque and Des Moines, separated by a line drawn west from Rock Island, and thus allowed the first Iowa residents to work out their own destinies.

The statehood movement in Michigan gave the terminal date at which the extension of its area must cease, and Congress took up at the same time the admission of Michigan and the organization of a new Mississippi Valley territory. There had been agitation for a division of Michigan for several years, led by Morgan L. Martin, a New York emigrant residing at Green Bay, and George W. Jones, of the lead region, who was Michigan territorial delegate in Congress in 1836. The territory of Wisconsin was the result of their activity, created in the spring of 1836, and including all of Michigan Territory outside the boundaries established for the State of Michigan, thus extending from Lake Michigan to the Missouri River. Henry Dodge, of Mineral Point, was appointed governor by President Jackson, and speedily convened his first legislative council at the village of Belmont in Iowa County. There were six counties in his original domain, two west of the Mississippi and four east. His territorial census found 10,531 inhabitants west of the river, and 11,683 on the eastern side. The local news was cared for by the *Belmont Gazette* and the *Dubuque Visitor*, while local finance was made more chaotic by the incorporation of the Miners' Bank to operate at Dubuque.

As soon as Wisconsin Territory was launched [3] it became apparent that its form was temporary, and that the flow of emigration would speedily procure its division into at least two commonwealths. The routes leading up the Mississippi were shorter and more direct than those around the lakes, and the southwest portion of the territory was growing more rapidly than the eastern.

---

[3] Moses M. Strong, *History of the Territory of Wisconsin, from 1836 to 1848* (1885), is almost an autobiography.

The first legislative council appreciated this and established a seat
of government near the geographical center of the eastern section
of the territory, finding a name for it in that of the venerable
Madison, who died in the summer of 1836. Two years later Congress recognized the trend of events and created the Territory of
Iowa, comprising the portion of Wisconsin west of the Mississippi.
There was southern opposition to the creation of additional northern territories that were likely to be free and to threaten the balance of power in the Senate; but George W. Jones, who had now
become sponsor for Iowa, and who was in Congress as the Wisconsin delegate, appears to have caught the southern leaders napping.
In the territorial census of 1838 there were shown to be 22,859
inhabitants in Iowa and 18,189 in Wisconsin; the former in a
compact body along the Mississippi, the latter in two flourishing
and rival sections, one on Lake Michigan and one on the Mississippi. There has been no moment since 1838 when the politics of
Wisconsin have not depended upon the balance of these two
sections.

The northern section of the Indian frontier was worked out during the early stages of the organization of the upper Mississippi
territories. Since the beginning of the century it had been the
scene of the great activities of the fur traders. First the British
and then the American companies had established their factories
and trafficked with the Indians between the lakes and the Missouri. Pike found traders at St. Paul, and Lewis and Clark found
them at the Mandan villages. After 1819, the United States post
at Fort Snelling was the center of trading, and for nearly twenty
years the traders had no rivals, until in 1837 Governor Dodge, and
the Indian agent at Fort Snelling, Taliaferro, convened the Chippewa and the Sioux for a new adjustment. Two treaties, concluded
that autumn, opened much of northern Wisconsin to white entry.
The Chippewa receded east and north, towards Lake Superior,
surrendering the timberlands of the Wisconsin Valley. The Sioux
ceded what claims they had left east of the Mississippi, most important of which was the rich pine country of the St. Croix Valley.
The farmer was slow in following the retiring Indians north of a
line drawn from Fort Winnebago to Fort Snelling, but the lumber-
men rushed in to establish a new frontier of their own and to lay
the foundations of the first large private fortunes that the far
Northwest produced. Down the St. Croix, the Chippewa, and the
Wisconsin to the Mississippi, down the Mississippi to the eager

buyers in the prairie States, the logs were floated every spring. After 1837 the northern section of the Indian frontier was stable for a decade, with two new territories nestling in between it and the frontier States.

CHAPTER XXXIII

THE BORDER STATES: MICHIGAN AND ARKANSAS

"The great rage even here in this part of Ohio is to sell & go West!" wrote an intelligent young teacher from Carthage, Ohio, early in 1837. Carthage was only a few miles north of Cincinnati, on the line of the canal to Dayton, and in a region that expected much from the internal improvements that were under way. But the Jacksonian migration was at its height, and the stories of successful development and speculation set in motion not only the social elements that were normally relied upon for the outfitting of new frontiers, but many of the staid and settled members of society. The migration picked up its people everywhere. There were Yankees from tidewater who moved with it to the extreme borders of the West; there were southerners from the coastal plain who found their way to Missouri or to Texas. No one has estimated how large a percentage of the whole American population was swept from its moorings by either the hope of improvement in a new location, or the positive discomforts of the old. The great migration was shaped by strong incentives to shift out of the East. In the Jacksonian migration the attractiveness of the West was the impelling force. In this, as in the earlier movement, the through migrant was the exception; the typical one was seized by the current where he happened to be, and was carried only a short distance towards the actual border. The heaviest contribution of the current was deposited in the parts of the West that already had the most population, while the most apparent was on the edge where every cabin stood out sharply against the background of loneliness.

The 6,300,000 inhabitants of the western States in 1840 included, as has been seen, over 4,100,000 who were new since 1820, and introduced new strains and stresses in the system of American politics because the newer elements were not spread over the country in the same proportions as the old. In 1820, Kentucky and Tennessee, the oldest West, boasted 980,000 inhabitants, and had a safe ascendency over the northwest and southwest neighboring groups. The northwest group, colonized largely through or out of Kentucky, included the three States, Ohio, Indiana, Illinois, and the territories of Michigan and Missouri, and comprised 840,000. The southwest group included the States of Alabama, Mississippi, and Louisiana, and the new territory of Arkansas, and had reached a total of 354,000.

The Kentucky-Tennessee ascendency was gone in 1830, for although the region had received a healthy increment in numbers, advancing to 1,370,000, the northwest neighbors had grown to 1,590,000. The southwest group, with the plantation now directing the course of its economic development, reached 670,000 at the same time. In ten years more, the ascendency was still further disturbed, for the plantation country grew to 1,400,000 whereas Kentucky and Tennessee had attained only 1,610,000. The old West was still growing with more than average rapidity, but it could not hold the pace with the abnormal increases of its younger rivals. The northwest group in 1840 was not only far ahead of the old West, but was as weighty as the old West and the plantation West combined, counting 3,330,000 inhabitants at the census. In all three areas the usual forces of development were intensified; the northwest group of States had additional contributions from the northern sources of immigration which had hitherto been less than fully developed. The Erie Canal made possible the New England and New York outpouring over the West.

The western sectional balance of 1840 shows that the West was less solid than it had been when Jackson was elected, and much less so than in 1800. The preponderance in numbers of the country north of the Ohio River over its more southern neighbors foreshadowed what the next two decades· were to bring about: — a preponderance within the Northwest of the northern strains among its population. For the purpose of this tabulation Missouri has been counted among the States northwest of Kentucky. If, however, its 383,000 inhabitants of 1840 should be subtracted from the Northwest and added to either of the other sections, the discrepancy in growth, though lessened, would still be overwhelming. ·

The creation of Iowa and Wisconsin Territories marks the extension of the Jacksonian wave of settlement into the most northwest corner of the United States. Michigan, which became a State in 1837, rose in population from 8000 in 1820, to 31,000 in 1830, and 212,000 in 1840. Indiana and Illinois each increased by more than the total Michigan population in the single decade closing in 1840, and Ohio increased nearly thrice as much. But these were already States, and the influx though disturbing did not yet upset society or politics. In the Territory of Michigan the invasion brought about a completely new alignment.

The roots of the white occupation of Michigan were thrust among the Indian inhabitants during the sixteenth century, when the fur trade began to attract the speculators of New France. By the eighteenth century the portages and the other strategic points were known, and Cadillac soon planted his station at the narrows between Lake Erie and Lake St. Clair. Detroit became a natural sentinel over the traffic between the lakes, although much of the business evaded it by following the canoe route further north, by way of Georgian Bay and Lake Nipissing. The French, and then the English, made their station at Detroit, not with an eye for settlement but to dominate the fur trade. When England surrendered the frontier posts after Jay's Treaty, the business of Detroit was too valuable to be sacrificed, and at Malden, across the river and a little below it, a new agency was developed. Hither came the Indians from the Wabash and further south; and here was the objective of Hull's forlorn campaign of 1812.

Not until 1805 were the dispersed inhabitants on the upper lakes numerous enough to warrant a separate territory; but in this year Michigan was set apart.[1] Detroit was its seat of government, but few of its people ever visited it, for they were spread as far north as the outlets of Lake Michigan and Lake Superior, and lived the mixed life of backwoodsmen. Few of them were without some admixture of French blood, and as a whole they constituted the residuum of generations of fur traders rather than the advance of farming pioneers. There was a belief that died hard that the land was unfit for farming. In the north were great forests that had as yet no market. The extensive areas of swamp were overwhelming in the discouragement they imposed upon the prospector. But more influential in retarding advance until after 1825 was the absence of any developed thoroughfare from a settled region of the United States to Michigan. When Hull was ordered to hold Detroit and to take Canada, his army broke its own road through the untrod wilderness, as Braddock and Forbes had done in reaching the Ohio forks.

There were only eight thousand inhabitants in Michigan in

[1] George N. Fuller, *Economic and Social Beginnings of Michigan* (1916), is useful. The Michigan Pioneer and Historical Society *Collections* began to accumulate volumes, somewhat indiscriminate for many years, in 1874. The great local collections of materials are those of Clarence M. Burton, in Detroit, and of William L. Clements, now a treasured possession of the University of Michigan.

1820, although some premonitions of change were visible. The area of the territory had been extended in 1818 by the addition of the remnant of the Old Northwest outside Illinois. Green Bay and Prairie du Chien were ancient communities, but they added little population to the backwoods eddy. More significant than their addition was the appearance, in 1817, of *Walk in the Water*, the first steamboat on the waters of Lake Erie. The Erie Canal was begun in this year and steadily thereafter the number of adventurous speculators increased to take advantage of events. Buffalo, Cleveland, Sandusky, and Toledo made a prompt appearance and development; and at Detroit there were new settlers who anticipated a boom period for Michigan. Congress allowed a territorial delegate to Michigan in 1819, and in the next decade the legislature organized the lower tier of counties to receive the incoming settlers.

Although there were only 31,639 settlers in Michigan in 1830, the number was growing so rapidly that in 1834 a territorial census enumerated 87,273, and the legislative council prepared to agitate for statehood. There was no enabling act by Congress, but the enterprising legislators read the Ordinance of 1787 for themselves and asserted that they had an unalterable right to form a constitution and State government when they possessed 60,000 free inhabitants. The territory accordingly enabled itself, without waiting for Congress to act, and in May, 1835, a convention assembled at Detroit. Of the eighty-nine members of the Michigan constitutional convention, fifty-two were originally from New England or the Middle States, and eighteen had passed the formative period of their manhood in New York. The constitution that they framed seems to have been written in the belief that the good times of the boom period were to last forever. The restrictive provisions of the western constitutions of the next fifteen years are lacking in the Michigan document. It provided that men should qualify for the franchise on a short term of residence, and that the legislature should insure prosperity by encouragement of internal improvement schemes. It claimed for Michigan the boundary stated in the Ordinance of 1787.

The adherence of Michigan to a southern boundary along a line drawn due east from the southern tip of Lake Michigan stirred up the only serious obstruction to its admittance.[2] So far as the South

[2] Annah M. Soule, "Southern and Western Boundaries of Michigan," and "The Michigan-Indiana Boundary," in Michigan Pioneer and Historical Society *Collections*, vol. xxvii.

was concerned there was no strong resistance, for Arkansas Territory was far enough along to be paired with the northern State. But Ohio was in guilty possession of a tract that Congress had assigned to Michigan in the Ordinance of 1787, and was able to prevent its entrance except on terms that were acceptable to itself. Indiana had been granted by Congress a strip ten miles wide north of the Ordinance line, and Ohio had claimed a wedge-shaped tract south of the north cape of the mouth of the Maumee River. Neither Ohio nor Indiana would yield anything to Michigan, in spite of the unalterability of the Ordinance, and in spite of the threat Michigan made by calling out the militia to protect the territory.

The influence of Ohio upon Congress and the national Administration was greater than usual in 1836, for a presidential election was impending, and Jackson was more than anxious to secure the choice of his friend and protégé, Martin Van Buren. The success of this scheme was threatened by an opposition plan to name local worthies whose combined strength might be enough to keep Van Buren's electoral vote down below a majority of the electoral college. Hugh L. White, of Jackson's own State was in the field, and William Henry Harrison of Ohio. It was no time for Jackson men to run an unnecessary risk of losing the vote of Ohio by despoiling that State of the piece of Michigan that it had seized. In June, 1836, Michigan was authorized to become a State, under the Detroit constitution, after accepting the unavoidable boundaries of Indiana and of Ohio, the latter now receiving its first legal sanction. Whatever politics was included in the vote was vain, for Harrison carried Ohio by a majority of over eight thousand. But Michigan lost its share of the eternal compact of 1787, and, what was more concrete, the harbor at Toledo and the terminus of the Wabash and Miami canals. A convention held at Ann Arbor, Michigan, in September, rejected the terms of this conditional admission; but in December another though illegal convention thought better of the refusal and accepted the inevitable. Michigan became the twenty-sixth State in the Union in January, 1837, having been delayed behind Arkansas by the wrangle over the Toledo strip.

Arkansas Territory, like Michigan, was in an eddy, and was reached by a current of population only when that current rose above its usual banks. The part of the Mississippi River that washes its eastern border was quite as remote from the standpoint of settlement as the Upper Mississippi around the lead mines. Either way population approached, Arkansas was a long way off. For the settler floating down the Ohio and Mississippi in his ark, there was no need to go as far as Arkansas. There was ever an abundance of fertile soil on the Ohio, or in Missouri. The stream of settlers was soaked up before it reached Arkansas Post at the mouth of the Arkansas River. Similarly, the migrant through New Orleans who sought unimproved territory, had to fight his way past the attractions of the black soil of Mississippi and Louisiana, and to work his way against a stubborn current before he could reach Arkansas. There was no territory of the name of Arkansas before 1819, and no need for one. The creation of Arkansas in that year was more for the relief of Missouri which was too straggling, than because the group of residents in the Arkansas Valley was of importance.[3]

In its original form Arkansas Territory extended from the Mississippi to the western boundary of the United States at the one hundredth meridian, between the State of Louisiana and the Territory of Missouri. There were Indian tribes in its western half, and Congress had intended to put more there. Not until 1828 was the western boundary of what was to be the new State worked out. After this time Arkansas was bounded on the west by the Choctaw from the Arkansas River at Fort Smith to the Red River, and by the Cherokee from Fort Smith north to the southwest corner of Missouri. It was the only State whose limit of extension was determined by Indian rights.

The social penetration of Arkansas followed, for most part, the course of the river up to the Indian Country, although Congress between 1821 and 1833 marked a military road from Memphis to Little Rock. The Arkansas River was full of obstructions in the form of timber washed downstream, and it was a long time before these were removed. American ingenuity, developed in this task of removing snags from navigable rivers, attracted much attention during the thirties, and the name of Henry M. Shreve became widely known because of his success in designing a snag boat. The removal of the great "raft" of the Red River that had ever impeded the development of northwest Louisiana, was his work, and under his direction the Arkansas was cleared.

The spontaneous ripening of Michigan into statehood was fol-

[3] J. H. Reynolds, "Western Boundary of Arkansas," in Arkansas Historical Society *Publications*, vol. II, summarizes the history of one of the most elusive boundary lines.

lowed by similar development in Arkansas, although the population was growing much less rapidly in the latter territory. A constitutional convention for the territory met in the Baptist meeting house at Little Rock in January, 1836, on the call of the legislature and without authorization by Congress. The Michigan congressmen-elect were already in Washington, urging the acceptance of the new constitution recently framed at Detroit and approved by the people. The Arkansas members used in their deliberation the recent southwest constitutions, notably those of Alabama, Mississippi, and Tennessee, as well as that framed in Virginia in 1829, from which they took most of the bill of rights. In both Mississippi and Tennessee the constitutions in force were recent revisions made necessary by the shifting population and rapid growth of the Jacksonian migration in these States. In spite of the fact that the other southern conventions had been following the precedent of Mississippi, which submitted its constitution to ratification in 1819, the Arkansas delegates signed their frame of government when they were satisfied with it, and declared it in force by promulgation.

The appearance of the Arkansas constitution in the spring of 1836, while Congress was deliberating over that of Michigan, made it possible to link these territories as Maine and Missouri had been joined, as Illinois and Alabama, and as Indiana and Mississippi. Indeed since the admission of Louisiana, in 1812, there had not been a single State admitted entirely upon its own merits. The rise of an affirmative slavery propaganda threw an emphasis upon the southern desirability of maintaining a balance of slave and free States in the United States Senate. Louisiana was the eighteenth State, and made the ninth in which slavery was to be a permanent institution. Thereafter the force of sectionalism was so great that no State either slave or free could be admitted unless it was accompanied by a companion State of the other type. The Michigan-Arkansas pair of 1836 was followed in the next decade by Iowa-Florida and Texas-Wisconsin. After Wisconsin there was no further territory available for the manufacture of slave States except in the Southwest that had been conquered from Mexico, and the South in the middle of the century set about to procure the repeal of the restrictive provisions of the Missouri Compromise. There is much reason to believe that slave labor, as the basis of an industrial system, had spent its force before 1860, but the momentum of the machine that had been erected upon it after 1812 was sufficient to propel the South into the disastrous attempt to secede in order to safeguard it. The sectional deviation that is revealed by the census of 1840, and the uneven development of the West, widened the split between the interests of slavery and free labor, and made it impossible for the former to win the Civil War.

In June, 1836, Congress authorized the admission of Arkansas and Michigan, under the constitutions of their choice, with the restriction upon the latter concerning its southern boundary. The law was ineffective upon Michigan until January 26, 1837. Arkansas, on the contrary, came in at once, and was able to cast its electoral vote for the presidential candidate of Jackson's choice. Van Buren was the choice of two thirds of its voters. The population of Arkansas in 1840 was 97,574; that of Michigan was 212,267.

CHAPTER XXXIV

THE INDEPENDENT STATE OF TEXAS

THE deliberate attempt of the leaders of the southern political machine to safeguard and conserve the institution of slavery, has been a subject for repeated attack and criticism from northern historians. It was indeed a disturbing element in the politics of the nineteenth century, but it was by no means the only force that tended to give shape to party controversy. The abolitionist historians, and the great learning of Hermann von Holst, gave wide currency to the idea that the settlement of Texas was an organic part of the pro-slavery attempt, and that both the creation and the annexation of Texas were to be regarded as parts of a gigantic conspiracy of slaveholders. Since the publication of the *Constitutional History* of von Holst, materials have come from the archives of the independent State of Texas that bear a different testimony. The studies of Garrison, Barker, Rives, and Justin H. Smith make it possible to reconstruct the Texas story, and to show it not as a conspiracy but as a normal fragment of the Jacksonian migration.[1] The fact that the land of Texas happened to be owned by a foreign nation no longer conceals the other fact that the social laws determining the extension of the frontier applied to the whole expanse of the western border, south as well as north. The remote consequences of this wave of population are to be found upon social "beaches" in the Upper Mississippi Valley, where Wisconsin and Iowa took shape, and on the coast of the Gulf of Mexico, along the line of the Spanish road from San Antonio to Nacogdoches, where Texas became important. Texas and Wisconsin were equally the consequence of the westward movement.

Until about the time of the Mexican revolution in 1821 there was no appreciable pressure of the American agricultural frontier upon the Texas boundary. The northern extension of New Spain had stopped, so far as its own driving force was concerned, before

[1] George P. Garrison, *Texas* (1903); Justin H. Smith, *Annexation of Texas* (1911); George L. Rives, *The United States and Mexico, 1821–48* (1913); Eugene C. Barker, the worthy successor of Garrison in the University of Texas, has traversed the whole early history of the State in the *Quarterly* of the Texas State Historical Society, now continued as the *Southwestern Historical Quarterly*. Garrison, and his pupils, Barker and Bolton, founded a distinctive school of investigators of southwestern history.

it reached the Sabine River. In the latter part of the seventeenth century, when Marquette, Joliet, and La Salle were establishing French claims to the Lower Mississippi, the Spanish rulers attempted to make a foothold in the same region. They appreciated that this was to be a frontier of empire. They occupied eastern Texas and established various missions among the Indians, but found it necessary to abandon most of them. At the northwest corner of the State of Louisiana, where the Red and Sabine rivers approach each other, their military frontier established itself *de facto*. The French built a post at Natchitoches in 1713. The Spanish were entrenched some years earlier than this on the Rio Grande, at San Juan Bautista, near Eagle Pass; and in 1718 they advanced to San Antonio and there constructed a town, a presidio, and a mission. The Spanish road from Eagle Pass, through San Antonio, to the Red River at Natchitoches, became a great highway for the priests and soldiers upon whom Spain relied to hold her empire. There were numerous missions and forts that were shifted from place to place as the exigencies of Indian and French warfare required, and at the upper end of the road, around Nacogdoches, on a branch of the Rio Neches, Spain kept a permanent guard.[2]

The transfer of Louisiana to Spain, in 1762, was accepted by that country with some reluctance. Spain gained little satisfaction and no profit from the new province except that Spanish control at New Orleans made it possible to relax the frontier garrisons of Texas. When the period of Spanish rule of Louisiana ended in 1803, Natchitoches was revived as an outpost, and the Spanish military authorities in Mexico proceeded to restore their control of the road to San Antonio. But there were few Americans *en route* to Texas who had to be turned back.

The few instances of border contacts between the United States and Spain before 1819 indicate the trifling importance of the boundary. Many of them had to do with the fixed or movable property of the Red River Valley. Burr gave it out, as one of his explanations, that he expected to take up land grants along the Red. Upon the plains bordering this river there were large herds of cattle and wild horses, the former valuable for their hides, the

---

[2] Herbert Eugene Bolton, after bringing out his *Guide to the Materials for United States History in the Archives of Mexico* (1913), produced in quick succession *Athanese de Mezières* (1914), and *Texas in the Middle Eighteenth Century* (1915), both books giving new meaning to the Texas-Louisiana border.

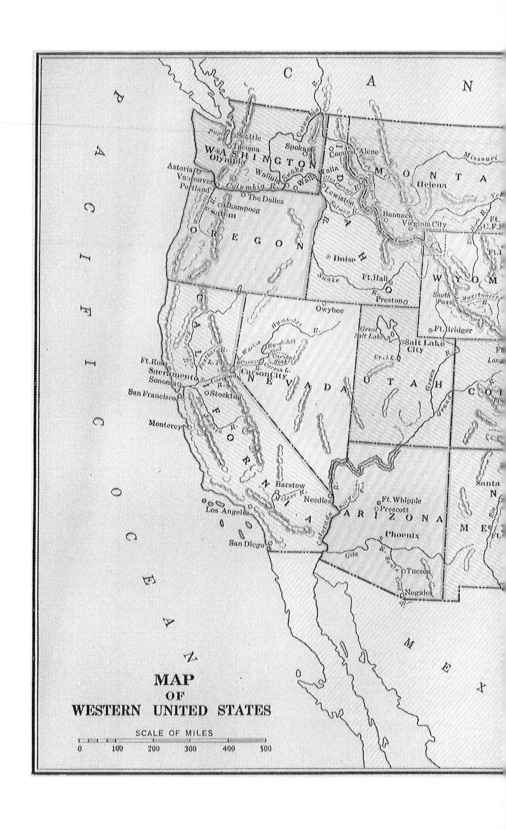

MAP
OF
WESTERN UNITED STATES

SCALE OF MILES

0   100   200   300   400   500

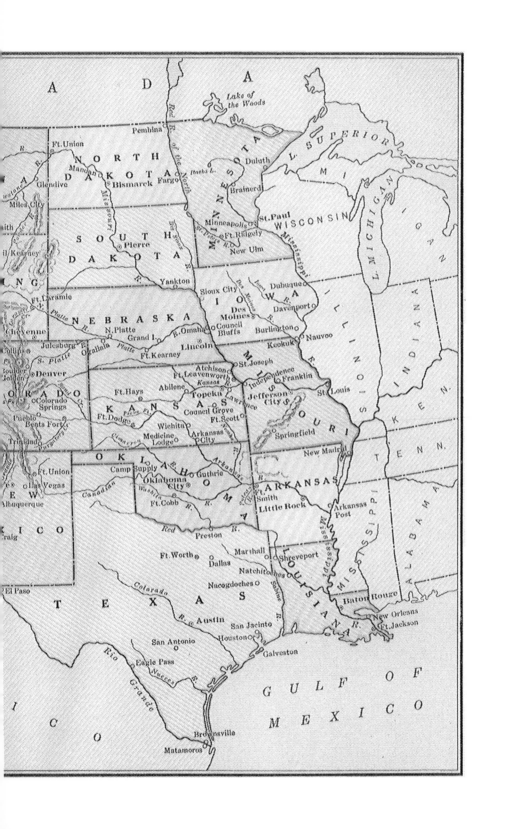

latter for purposes of trade. The vagrant hunter and the horse thief were unwelcome visitors on the Spanish side of the line, and occasional adventurers were killed in fights or executed after trial by the Spanish authorities. In 1811 a band of traders tried to take a train of pack mules to Santa Fé, but were inhospitably received and jailed. In 1819 an American named Long proceeded from Natchez to Nacogdoches to bring about the independence of Texas; but his provisional government had no success and he was driven out by the Spanish royalists. In 1821 Mexico became independent of Spain and the occupied American frontier reached the State of Missouri. From this date the American border was close enough to make trade interesting, and the Spanish or Mexican reluctance to allow contacts disappeared.

Towards the end of the great migration the first steps were taken to bring the cotton lands of Texas within range of the pioneers of the Southwest. Mississippi had become a State in 1817, Alabama in 1819, settlers were flooding Louisiana and working their clearings up the Red River, and one Moses Austin of Missouri Territory undertook a speculation in Spanish land titles.

The life of Moses Austin was as typical of the frontier as was that of Henry Dodge. He was born in Durham, Connecticut, married a wife in Philadelphia, learned to be a miner in Virginia, and migrated to the lead mines of Upper Louisiana while Spain was still in control of them. Here he became naturalized as a Spanish subject, only to have his nationality changed by the retrocession and sale of Louisiana. In 1803 he was once more an American citizen, with a special knowledge of the Spanish provinces. When the advance guard of the Ohio Valley migrants reached Missouri, he looked ahead into Texas as a field for profitable speculation.

In 1820 Moses Austin was at San Antonio persuading the Spanish authorities to allow him to import American settlers to a tract between the San Antonio road and Galveston Bay. He was successful, but died before the patent was issued; and his son, Stephen, took up the task he dropped.[3] The Mexican revolution intervened and the royalist grant prepared for Stephen Austin required confirmation by the native government of Iturbide before it acquired validity. When Iturbide's short-lived empire was overthrown, the congress of the republic issued a second confirmation. In 1825 the legislature of the Mexican state of Texas and Coahuila passed a

---

[3] The Austin papers, edited by Eugene C. Barker, are in process of publication by the American Historical Association.

general colonization law, and when the Jacksonian migration took shape there was an open highway leading to the Rio Grande.

The Mexican experiment in colonization was ill-advised, but it is not certain whether this was due to the corruptibility of the Mexican rulers or to some fantastic notion that American colonies could be made to live happily among the inhabitants of Texas. The bulk of the native population of Mexico was, as it still is, composed of Indians of unmixed blood. The simple, easy-going, illiterate lives of these had been little affected by centuries of Spanish occupation and control. They showed high powers of resistance to the forces of civilization and although they were in many regions controlled in worldly as well as spiritual affairs by the priests at the missions, they developed little independent spiritual or economic life. There were also many half breeds, mestizos or mulattoes according as the mixture was Indian or black; and there was a small minority of white persons of Castilian blood. By 1821 the currents of emigration had slowed down and most of the Spanish in Mexico were born there, and some of them took pride in the name of creole that was given them. The aristocracy was made up of these creoles and Spanish and included individuals of European education and large wealth. The young men of this class took readily to political intrigue and were widely ambitious of military glory. They lived by the management of the lower classes on their great ranches and plantations. The extensions of occupied territory had for centuries been made under government direction. There was no class in Mexico similar to the American frontiersmen or capable of doing their work in developing natural resources.

Blind to the consequences of letting in the American frontiersman, the local government continued the policy of making grants of land to promoters along the San Antonio road. The Government was resisting the overtures of the United States to buy a part of Texas, yet used Americans to colonize the land in question. The British diplomatic representative in Mexico observed the trend of events, and as early as 1825 warned both the Mexican foreign office and his own. "They are suffering," he said, ". . . by an absurd mixture of negligence, & weakness, the whole disputed territory . . . to be quietly taken possession of by the very men, whose claim to it, they are resisting here. . . . [The] whole of the lands between the rivers Sabine and Brazos, have been granted away to American settlers, and . . . the tide of emigration is settling very fast in the direction of the Rio Bravo. . . . On the most moderate computation, six hundred North American families are already established in Texas; their numbers are increasing daily, and though they nominally recognize the authority of the Mexican government, a very little time will enable them, to set at defiance

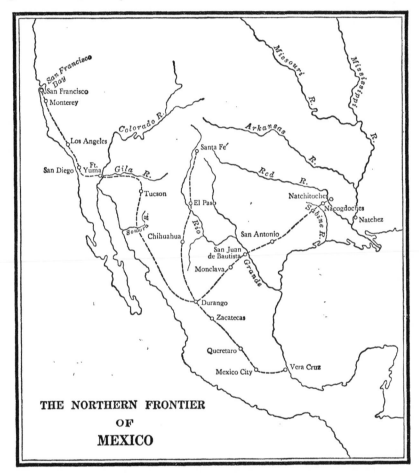

THE NORTHERN FRONTIER
OF
MEXICO

any attempt to enforce it. . . . [The settlers are] American — Backwoodsmen, a bold and hardy race, but likely to prove bad subjects, and most inconvenient neighbors."

By 1830 the American colonists in Texas were perhaps twenty thousand in number. True to the general conditions of the migration they came most numerously from the nearest settled regions, Louisiana, Mississippi, and Tennessee. Naturally they were southern by birth and education and among them were some few who had slaves in the United States and took them into Texas. A single good slave was often worth as much as a whole section of government land at the standard price of $1.25 an acre. But most of the Texas settlers expected their speculation to prosper and looked forward to the time when they might turn their small farms into large plantations, stock them with slaves, and join the aristocracy. Of necessity the Texas community was part and parcel of the American South.

The Mexican enthusiasm for American colonists in Texas weakened about 1830 when a law was passed prohibiting further immigration. But Mexico had no administrative machinery capable of enforcing the law and the current was now too powerful to be resisted. The parents and grandparents of the new Texans had been too long accustomed to browbeat the Indians, to intrigue with Spanish officials, and to defy their own Government. Their relatives had elected Andrew Jackson in 1828, and like them they worshiped the ideas of democracy and home rule. The Mexican effort to stem the tide, and to prohibit slavery among them, was treated as their kinsmen in South Carolina were at the moment treating the laws of the United States. South Carolina in 1832 made a gesture of nullification, led to it by the dogmatic teaching of Calhoun and his political school. Americans in Texas had even better grounds for declining to be swallowed up in a centralized government or to permit their institutions to be Latinized by Mexicans.

The mental attitude of Stephen F. Austin is a fair summary of the status of Texas with reference to Mexico. The studies that Professor Barker has made in the Austin papers, which have been preserved in great abundance, indicate that from the issuance of his grant in 1821 until 1832 Austin was unswerving in his loyalty to the terms of the contract. He sought in good faith to bring in families of sound character, of Roman Catholic faith, and willing to take and observe oaths of loyalty to the country of their adoption. The spirit of separation that showed itself before 1832 in some of the other settlements of Americans in Texas did not spread into the Austin grant.

Between 1832 and 1834 the spirit of Austin began to waver. Texas had been promised home rule, without receiving it. Instead, Texas was a part of a state of Coahuila and Texas, in which the Coahuila majority of natives might permanently overbalance the

Americans living east of San Antonio. There arose a necessity for a separation of Texas from Coahuila, and its admission as a separate state in the Republic of Mexico. But this was denied by the Mexican congress, whose internal ructions threatened the existence of the federal principle in Mexico in any form. The Mexican civil war between Bustamente and Santa Anna imperiled the peace of the republic and forced the Texans to take sides. Since Santa Anna professed to be a constitutionalist, anxious to overthrow the principle of centralization, he gained the support of Texas. But when he was victorious, he revealed the insincerity of his professions, and sought to make himself head of a centralized state. The autonomy of Texas was denied, its militia was cut down, and a military governor supplanted its legislature. Austin was in doubt until 1834. Then his mind cleared, as he saw that Texas could not live in the Mexico of Santa Anna. After 1834 he worked for independence.

The motives at work in favor of Texas independence were the frontier dislike of coercion, and an American fear of Mexicanization. In addition to these, there was a motive based on property rights. The earlier of the settlers had come in under legal Mexican grants, and received titles good under any Mexican law. Later arrivals speculated much in titles that were something less than perfect. There was ever a chance that a powerful Mexican Government would annul many of the grants, and there were great areas of ungranted lands that would be at the disposal of an independent government in Texas. The whole American border was aflame with land speculation after 1833, and this homely motive played a considerable part in steadying Texans in a conclusion to separate which they might well have reached on other grounds.

In October, 1835, Texas held a convention at Austin, and framed a constitution for itself. Michigan had just finished one; Arkansas was just about to begin one. All were unauthorized, and found their origin in the spontaneous desires of frontier groups for autonomous government. The Texas convention faced the question whether to make a constitution for use within Mexico, or to work for independence, and decided in favor of the former alternative. But the course of the Mexican Government in the next few months was such that in March, 1836, another Texas convention adopted a declaration of independence. The conservatives were losing their hope of an agreement with Mexico, and the immediate immigrants were almost to a man for separation. The new constitution accepted the common law as a basis for the criminal code, followed the structure of the United States Constitution where it was practicable, and permitted the Spanish law of property to remain in force.

The Mexican army and the Texas militia were already engaged in civil war when the declaration of independence was promulgated. Santa Anna was in the field to preserve his realm. There was heavy fighting at San Antonio, where the Texas defenders took refuge in the Alamo, and where those who survived the engagement were murdered by the victorious Mexicans. Davy Crockett and James Bowie were among the slain, but their souls, like John Brown's, went marching on. In April, 1836, General Sam Houston, who commanded the largest of the Texas forces, was attacked by Santa Anna on the San Jacinto River and completely dispersed the Mexicans. Santa Anna was captured as he fled, and under duress signed a treaty as president of Mexico recognizing the independence of Texas and the territorial claim of that republic as far south as the Rio Grande. The Mexican congress repudiated his authority to do this, and the facts of occupation had given no warrant for so extensive a region; but Texas never receded from its claim.

The Territory of Wisconsin was created the day before the battle of San Jacinto, and its people were no more certain of their Americanism than were those who won the freedom of Texas. Independence for Texas was conceived as a first step to incorporation in the United States. Texas agents were immediately sent to Washington to demand it, but found Jackson hesitant even to recognize the independence of the State. The election of 1836 was approaching, and there were already enough northern enemies of the Administration without arousing all the opponents of slavery who would see in Texas an attempt to build up the slave power. After the election of Van Buren it was still impossible to procure the admission of Texas. Formal recognition took place, and diplomatic agents were exchanged, but Texas was obliged to bear itself as an independent republic until 1845. The Jacksonian wave of migration came to an end in 1837. An anti-Jackson party, the Whigs, rose to life and victory. And the necessities of slavery politics determined the future of Texas. The financial collapse that visited the United States in 1837 temporarily diverted the thoughts of the country from speculation and growth to curtailment and recuperation.

CHAPTER XXXV

1837: THE PROSTRATE WEST

THE rage for emigration and speculation, and the high prices based upon an abundance of paper money, grew in intensity during the Jacksonian migration, producing an unbalanced economic life that could have no other end than financial collapse and general bankruptcy. But while the going was good, the tide of development flowed so fast that few could hope to stand against it. Over the whole West new villages appeared without forewarning, and former villages became cities at a single leap. What happened at Chicago was repeated elsewhere, on a similar scale. "Here," wrote a careful reporter, "the rise in real property and the influx of migration are unexampled in the Western World. Lots in Town with small improvements are selling at from 10 to 15000$, the right of preemption on qr. sec. of Land are worth from 8 to 10,000$. Several persons former citizens of . . . [Parke County, Indiana, near Terre Haute] have become immensely wealthy merely by settling on a tract of Land & improving it sufficiently to hold the preemption, and money is a sure drug. Altho this looks incredible it is nevertheless true. The emigration to the northern part of Illinois is unprecedented. Whether this state of things can last long or not I can't say, it seems hardly possible." The craze that John G. Davis saw when he wrote this letter in 1835 was wider than he knew; but he did not overstate it.[1]

Interlocked with the migration, stimulated by it, and itself an incentive to it, the internal improvements program of the western States reached full development at the same time. The source of the demand for internal improvements was the universal western conviction that there could not be solvency and prosperity without a market for the crops. The Erie Canal was a powerful stimulant, and the open rivalry of the seaboard communities for western trade kept the idea alive. The Ohio Canal, first among the western works to reach completion, gave wide advertisement to western ambitions, and the other canals, undertaken about the same time, did not have to be argued in the West. The Black Hawk War gave publicity to Illinois and its neighborhood. The removals of

[1] The late J. G. D. Mack, of Madison, Wisconsin, generously made available the papers of his ancestor, John G. Davis.

Indian tribes towards their new frontier homes held the attention of the country. About 1832 the abnormal forces drawing emigrants to the west became considerable, and in the following year they were reinforced by hard times in the Atlantic cities.

The American State took upon itself a new character during the booming years of this period. Heretofore the people had been content with a State that levied as few taxes as possible, and kept the courts open to litigants. Beyond its function as preserver of the peace, the State had few duties. The initiative in life was in the hands of the citizen, who disliked the suggestion of control. Public education had not yet built up a horde of salaried teachers. The militia was a go-as-you-please organization, without many military attributes. The revenues of government were not large enough to arouse cupidity or to make their control a matter of consequence. Politics were fought on personal issues and theories of government. The State was not in business.

Chief among the influences that drove the American State into business was the American System of Henry Clay. Under his teaching the West accepted the doctrine that there must be improved routes of communication in order to provide access to markets. These roads called for money; yet not only was private capital lacking, but private capitalists were not accustomed to investment in the stock of improvement companies. The legal side of such securities was yet inchoate. The powers of promoters, the control of corporations, the rights of the State with reference to corporations, the protection of the stockholders, were still to be worked out with pain, loss, and inconvenience to a multitude of innocent investors. Meanwhile, the works were needed. The United States, through its taxing system, might have become the source of the funds had not the strict constructionists interposed a barrier through Madison and Monroe. The States were the only other possible recourse, and when New York led off with the building of the Erie Canal there began a new period both in the use of capital and the activities of the State.

Every year after the inauguration of the Erie Canal witnessed an increase in State investment in improvements. To maintain their ascendency or to get new business, the tidewater States plunged into popular but ill-considered projects. The western States also responded to the enthusiasms of their people, and with each year of the Jacksonian period migration became more lavish in their commitments.

The greatest of the Ohio improvements were undertaken before 1830, and the State stocks, sold to raise the funds, found a ready market in eastern centers of capital. Indiana broke ground for the Wabash Canal at Fort Wayne in 1832, and gave charters to private railroad corporations to build a group of radiating roads from Indianapolis to the borders of the State. In January, 1836, its legislature responded to the idea that it was the right of every section of the State to have public money invested for its advantage, and enacted a general scheme of roads, railroads, and canals. It broke ground in 1836 for the Whitewater Canal. It had no advice as to where the money was to be found or whether the works would be self-supporting when done; but the enthusiasm was too strong a political force to be resisted.

Illinois followed its eastern neighbors and in the same year took over as a public work the canal from Lake Michigan to the Illinois River, which had been considered for a decade. It also agreed to nearly fifteen hundred miles of railroad, the most important lines of which were to be a central road, from Galena to the junction of the Ohio and Mississippi, a northern cross line to run somewhat south of Chicago, and a southern cross line at about the latitude of Terre Haute. It sold nearly five million dollars' worth of bonds in the following year to finance the schemes, and spread the burden without a quiver upon a new farming population that included only 157,445 inhabitants in 1830, and 476,183 in 1840. The rural legislators saw to it that a road, a bridge, a canal, or a railroad was provided for every corner of the State. The State that voted such enterprises was perhaps not more completely hypnotized than the investor who advanced the funds.

Missouri could not escape the "speculative intoxication" and in the legislative session of 1837 authorized seventeen railroads with an aggregated capital of seven millions.[2] In Michigan the entry upon a program was of course delayed until the territory became a State; but in 1837 the legislature caught up with the race and embarked upon the construction of three parallel railroads across the peninsula. It authorized as well the improvement of more than three hundred miles of rivers and the construction of over two hundred miles of canals. The governor was directed to borrow five million dollars on the credit of the State. The State had a population of 212,267 in 1840.

The southern States were caught by the contagion, but escaped

[2] There is a good book on this, John W. Million, *State Aid to Railways in Missouri* (1896).

some of the worst consequences because they happily lacked enough credit to become involved. The southern leaders bewailed the fact that the plantation country had no local capital for investment except in farm property and slaves. They found it harder to borrow on the credit of the State than did the northern communities. On July 4, 1836, a railroad convention was held at Knoxville that discussed the needs of the South without uncovering practicable ways and means. The Charleston politicians had a keen concern in a "great southern railroad" that might build up a southern rival to New York. Robert Y. Hayne was chairman of the Knoxville convention, and spoke to delegations from every State south of the Potomac, as well as from Indiana and Illinois. But a Cincinnati and Charleston railroad could not be built on oratory, and ten years later the South was still holding meeting after meeting in the hope of finding an "Open Sesame" to the treasures of internal improvements.

By the winter of 1836–1837, every western State, like nearly every western citizen, had pledged its future upon the success of speculative ventures, whose mere continuance was contingent upon free access to capital and the perpetuation of good times. The capital facilities had been increased by both the hypnotic influence of successful speculation and the financial policies of the Government of the United States. The number of private banks in the United States, operating each under its special charter from some State, rose in number from 506 in 1834 to 788 in 1837; and all of these issued their bank notes which circulated as money as far as the credit of the bank could float them. The merchant found it necessary to watch the notes with care, for there were counterfeits in large number, and the straggling, depreciated notes of insolvent banks were always a danger. But the banks increased in number under the natural pressure of customers for more facilities for credit.

The individual banks grew in size as well. The best estimates of the amount of bank notes in circulation in the United States show that from 1820 to 1830 the *per capita* issues of such paper actually declined from $6.96 to $6.69. But with the swell of the migration and the accompanying need for credit to move the population and to finance the State improvements, the issues of circulation rose more than proportionately with the number of banks. In 1835 there was in circulation $9.86 *per capita;* in 1837, $13.87. The approximate doubling of currency in seven years made money easy, and lightened the burden upon the debtor who could each year repay his debts in smaller buying values than he borrowed. As money became more plentiful and declined in value, prices rose. Valuations increased with the rise in prices; and properties that might have warranted loans of $1000 in 1830 appeared by 1837 to warrant loans of double that amount, without any necessary improvement in the inherent value of the property itself. As inflation became general the banks each year did their business in the adjusted values. Their assets were composed of long-time mortgages that were at best a dangerous foundation for issues of bank notes payable on demand; and that at worst might not be collectible at all because of the inflation of the values upon which they were issued. When the bubble should be pricked, and prices drop to reasonable levels, many pieces of property would not command a sale price equal to the debts against them, let alone an equity to the owner. The conditions in 1819, in over-investment and inflation, were repeating themselves in 1836 under the normal stimuli of a mass migration.

An abnormal stimulus to the tendency to inflation was provided by the financial policy of Andrew Jackson, expressed in his treatment of the second Bank of the United States. The trying experiences with inflation and deflation that the West passed through between 1811 and 1825 left permanent impressions upon the men who bore their brunt. By 1829, when Jackson became President, the actual hardships had receded into memory, and prosperity was widespread; but the older generation of the West could not escape the reactions from having passed through a period in which the typical farmer was hopelessly in debt and was terrified by the high probability of losing his equity in all he owned. It was human nature to forget easily the boom years, in which the debtor got off cheaply from the full repayment of his debt, and to recall only the other slope of the curve in which the debtor was paying back more than he had borrowed. The hardships worked upon society by the cycles through which prices revolve, with periods of inflation and deflation alternating to destroy property values, are only to-day beginning to receive the consideration they deserve. The whole United States had suffered acutely from the deflation of the early twenties but the West had suffered most uniformly. And although its pangs were lessened before 1829 there was a tendency, easy to revive, to believe that the steadying hand of a great bank in lessening inflation was really oppressing the people of the frontier.

Jackson had no special grievance against the Bank of the United States in the first year of his presidency and acquired one only when his trusted political lieutenants suggested that the branches of the bank were being used for party purposes by his political enemies. The charge appears to have been untrue, and to have been advanced because the branches stubbornly refused to be used for such purposes by Democratic politicians. Jackson's supporters included the great masses of western people, inspired by emotional concepts of democracy, and eastern political machines in which idealism was carefully subordinated to the getting of votes. In New York and Pennsylvania, in particular, the Democratic organization had discovered the truth that Governor Marcy later perpetuated in his aphorism, "To the victors belong the spoils." The party leaders, when victorious, rewarded their followers with public jobs. The incidental injury to public service was disregarded in the more immediate party advantage.

When Jackson became President, he held the usual Democratic belief that existing officeholders were dangerously aristocratic, and that the Government ought to be purged of them. His friends who wished the jobs encouraged the idea. There was a wholesale clearance of offices in Washington, and before the end of 1829 the Democratic leaders were reaching out to control the patronage within the Bank of the United States and its branches. Nicholas Biddle, president of the bank, supported the branch officials in their refusal to be converted into a political machine. The branch at Portsmouth, New Hampshire, was then attacked for alleged favoritism to anti-Jackson men; and the President was drawn into the fight by his loyalty to and confidence in his friends. His latent doubts about a national bank were revived and were expressed in his annual messages of 1829, 1830, and 1831. Few but the political leaders of his machine were with him in his attack, for the Bank of the United States was useful and widely popular. It had reduced the chaos of uncontrolled bank notes to reasonable order, and the money of the United States was upon a coin basis and the banks were solvent.

In 1831 and 1832 the managers of the Bank of the United States organized their friends in their defense and persuaded Henry Clay, as the leader among anti-Jackson men, to take up their cause. They reasoned that if Jackson injured the bank he could not be re-elected in 1832; and that by vigorous protest they might even stop his attack. In Congress, a bill for the recharter of the bank was brought up in 1832 in order to force the fighting in time to use it as an issue in the presidential election. Biddle overreached himself in his desire for aggressive fighting, for nothing confirmed Jackson in his impressions more than resistance to them, and his personal popularity was so overwhelming that the mere fact of his antagonism to the bank was enough to convert many who otherwise would have been entirely acquiescent in its policies. If ever a good cause was spoiled by lack of quiet tact, this was it.

The bank bill of 1832 passed Congress, where the large Jacksonian majorities nevertheless approved the bank; but Jackson vetoed the bill as unwise and unconstitutional. He went to the people on the issue, and was reëlected in spite of it.[3] He interpreted the result, however, as a vindication of his course, and in 1833 undertook to restrict and weaken the object of his enmity. The Bank of the United States was at this time the depository of public money, and collectors of customhouses or land offices deposited their daily receipts in the nearest branch. The western politicians upon whom Jackson was now chiefly relying, Francis P. Blair and Amos Kendall, had been through the Kentucky fight over the stay laws and the courts, and appreciated the political possibilities of an attack upon the institutions that controlled credit. As a first measure Jackson sounded his Secretary of the Treasury upon the transfer of the United States deposits from the Bank of the United States to other banks, which lay within his discretion; but McLane refused to humor the President and was shifted to the State Department. The new Secretary of the Treasury, Willam J. Duane, was a Philadelphia Democrat of such convictions and antecedents as a party man, that it did not occur to Jackson to ascertain his opinions in advance of his appointment. But Duane refused pointblank to shift the deposits, and when asked to resign, declined to do so. Duane was therefore removed from office and in his place came Roger B. Taney, who as Attorney-General in the cabinet had already volunteered to carry through the removal of the deposits.

Under Taney's direction, by order of the President, the public receipts after October 1, 1833, were not deposited in the Bank of the United States but were placed to the credit of the United States in other local banks. Amos Kendall, as fiscal agent, had made the contracts with the private banks designated to receive

[3] Presidential campaigns are now attracting their historians; Samuel R. Gammon, *The Presidential Campaign of 1832* (1922).

the funds. It was commonly charged that banks with Democratic directors were specially favored and that in places where there were no banks groups of local Democrats were encouraged to form them, tempted by the promise of the deposit of public money. The money on deposit in the Bank of the United States, at the moment of the cessation of new deposits, was drawn upon by United States disbursing officers until exhausted, but was not removed at once. The bank and its branches were forced to readjust their business in order to honor the Government drafts, and to prepare to wind up and pass out of existence at the expiration of the bank charter in 1836. This involved a curtailment of loans that brought into the business world the first premonition of an end to the period of open speculation. Wherever there was a branch bank, in 1833, there began a forced curtailment that brought disaster to business and employees, that threw unemployed men upon the market, and that increased the element in the population that was ripe for change of residence and the search for occupation. When the Bank of the United States closed its doors in 1836, said *Niles' Register*, "We are now rid of the 'monster,' and our citizens will no longer be compelled to borrow its money at *six per cent* interest, but be left free to pay from *seven to fourteen* per cent. as circumstances and their necessities may require."

In the winter of 1833–1834 the customers of the steadiest and most reliable of the American banks were turned adrift, unable to secure their loans; while the less solvent institutions, freed from the scrutiny of the Bank of the United States became recipient of large public deposits which they were at liberty to lend to new customers. The normal consequence of this was to lessen the safeguards of credit, and to make it easier to procure loans on inadequate collateral and at inflated valuations. The migration was rising towards the crest and individual borrowers were bidding for credit with which to carry out their ventures. Every successful venture stimulated a crop of imitators, and speculation fattened on itself. The United States, at the same moment, came into possession of larger revenues than anticipated, and these increased the size of public deposits until fears for their safety were aroused in even the Administration that had deliberately broken down the safeguards.

In 1832 the United States was forced to reconsider the policy of a protective tariff by the recalcitrance of South Carolina. Since the first tariff of 1816 the forces favoring protection as a policy had become compact and sectional. The South was guided by men like Calhoun to a belief that protection was an unfair tax for the benefit of the North. The law of 1816 was extended and enlarged in 1824 and again in 1828. In 1832 it was further revised, and Jackson by signing it showed that whatever he thought of Henry Clay, he had no unconquerable aversion to Clay's policy of an American System. Jacksonian Democracy did not fear central government as such, as Jefferson's did; it only feared central government directed by its political enemies.

Calhoun, who had been organizing southern opinion to meet this issue, led South Carolina into nullification in the fall of 1832. Jackson was disposed to fight the issue through, the more so because he had now broken with Calhoun and classed him among his enemies. But the compromisers in Congress, led by Clay himself, were willing to meet South Carolina halfway; and in 1833 there passed a compromise tariff to lower the rates gradually until after 1840. Under the new law the customs receipts, hitherto the chief financial reliance of the United States, had severe fluctuations after 1833, and in 1834 the total revenue of the Government fell away a third, from thirty-four millions, to twenty-two. But in 1835 and 1836 the customs increased rapidly, and the proceeds of sales of the public lands jumped to new heights that not only overcame all deficits from the tariff but established new levels for gross income. In the five years before 1834 the average annual revenue of the United States Government was $29,000,000; in 1835 it was $35,430,000; in 1836 it was $50,826,000.

The sales of public lands, which were always an accurate means of gauging the rapidity and spread of the development of the frontier, rose to new volume with the Jacksonian migration. The Public Land Office, first organized in 1812, was submerged in the inundation of patents; and in 1833 there were over twenty thousand such title deeds awaiting the personal signature of the President of the United States when Congress for the first time allowed him to employ a clerk to do this work. This was before the greatest period of purchase began, for not until 1835 did the total land sales pass the high mark of five million acres set in 1819. The prospective settler could buy outstanding revolutionary land scrip, or bounty warrants of 1812, or purchase from the States some part of their school lands, or buy canal grants, voted for the western canals. The direct sales of the General Land Office were not the whole, but they suggest the trend of the total. In 1834, something over four million acres were sold. The total for 1835 was fifteen million. In 1836 it was twenty million acres.

The money realized from land sales averaged close to the $1.25 fixed by the law of 1820 as the minimum price. At this rate it placed in the depository banks in 1834, $4,857,000; in 1835, $14,757,000; in 1836, $24,877,000. The daily receipts of the local registers of the land offices were deposited by them in the nearest depository banks, and became banking capital immediately, available for loans. Against this capital, the United States was by 1835 drawing for running expenses, but the receipts were heavily in excess of any need that the Government had for money. There was a surplus of receipts over expenditures of more than ten millions in 1831, 1832, and 1833. It dropped to three millions in 1834. In 1835 it rose to eighteen millions; in 1836 to twenty. For many years the excess receipts had found a proper use in the retirement of the public debt. But at the end of 1834 the last of the debt was paid off, and the United States was without a creditor at home or abroad. The accumulating surplus now became a menace, a temptation upon Congress to extravagance, a license for the banks to make reckless loans, and a risk to the Government because of growing fears for the solvency of the depository banks.

There was no credit in the land sales, yet the surplus represented a huge credit transaction in which the United States might become the loser. The buyer of public land paid for his purchase with money, much of which was borrowed at the bank upon a valuation agreed on by him and it. The receipts went into the treasury, and then into the bank on deposit. It was at once reloaned and became the means of further purchases, which in cycle increased the money on deposit and again enlarged the fund to be lent. The United States had no land buyers on its books as debtors, but for every cent of the cash on hand a bank was debtor, and the ease with which the United States could get its money was limited by the ability of the banks to realize upon their assets. Jackson worried about the reality of the public funds in 1836; and Congress was beset with schemes for dissipating the surplus revenue.

By auto-intoxication the boom of 1835 and 1836 approached the bursting point. The more speculation, the greater the fund for speculation. A halt was called when Congress passed, in the summer of 1836, a bill to regulate the deposit of public money and to distribute it among the States. There were various means proposed for getting rid of embarrassing surplus. As the election of

1836 came on, criticisms of the Administration included some
based upon the fact that the Government was collecting so much
more than it needed to spend. The Distribution Bill provided that
on January 1, 1837, the treasurer of the United States should balance his books, set aside a working capital for himself of five millions, and prepare to deposit the rest among the States in four
quarterly installments. This money was not to be given to the
States, for strict constructionists believed this to be unconstitutional. It was to be placed with them on deposit only, subject to
a right of recall, which, however, was not expected to be exercised.
The basis of deposit was the ratio of representation in Congress.
The first quarterly payment was to be made at once.

As January 1, 1837, approached, the depository banks were
driven to the kind of curtailment that had embarrassed the Bank
of the United States in 1833. They knew of the drafts against the
Government deposits that would remove part of their banking
funds, and were forced to accumulate money to meet the drafts.
The wave of unrestrained speculation was halted; and as the
second and third installments came due in April and July, 1837, it
was apparent that the machine could not be checked without a
smash. On May 10, 1837, the banks suspended by prearrange-
ment, and the panic of 1837 was a fact. The fourth installment of
the distribution was never made because Van Buren called Congress to meet in special session to repeal the law.

In addition to the Distribution Bill which retarded the whirl of
speculation, there was a Specie Circular that made it more severe.
The Administration fears for the safety of the surplus were increased by the wide variety and uncertain character of the paper
money with which business was transacted. Jackson tried to get
from Congress in 1836 a law limiting public receipts to coin. He
failed in this, but as soon as Congress had gone upon recess, he
issued on July 11, 1836, an executive circular "to repress alleged
frauds, and to withhold any countenance or facilities in the power
of the government from the monopoly of the public lands in the
hands of speculators and capitalists, to the injury of actual settlers
. . . and of emigrants." He directed receivers of public money to
accept no money but gold and silver, except in case of *bona fide*
resident settlers buying not over 320 acres of public land. By thus
discrediting the paper of the banks, he discouraged land sales and
called a halt to speculation.

With the banks in suspension, there was wild depreciation among the bank notes, and numerous failures of banks and customers. Business stopped. Land sales fell off at once. Tariff revenue declined, because the country stopped buying. There was a deficit in receipts of twelve millions in 1837, and eight and a half millions in 1838. The farmer lost both his high prices and his market; and was fortunate if he did not lose his farm. For the next five years the United States was engaged in the painful work of settling the accounts created by its long financial debauch; and the western States acquired an enduring distrust of banks of issue. The new constitutions between 1837 and 1850 almost without exception show how a feeling against all banks was become an essential part of the belief of Democrats of the school of Andrew Jackson. As late as 1843 when the West could jest about some of its experiences with substitutes for money, a newspaper humorist wrote of the admission prices of the National Theater at Cincinnati: ". . . box tickets, two pair of chickens and a dozen eggs — pit ditto, three pounds of butter, and a cabbage head — gallery, any quantity of peas and potatoes. *N.B.* Fresh meats, poultry, and all the vegetables of the season can be obtained at the box office on the most reasonable terms for cash."

By the time the United States recovered from the depression that followed the panic of 1837, it had passed into a different era of American history. The foundations of public opinion of the twenties had disappeared. National expansion had carried the domain to the Pacific. Railroad communication had become the dominant form of internal improvement. Corporation business was well established. An industrial society was rising in the East to offer a new form of contrast to the agrarianism of the frontier. And the plantation system was entrenching itself in Democratic politics for its struggle for existence.

CHAPTER XXXVI

THE TRAIL TO SANTA FÉ

IN the five years of depression that followed the panic of 1837 the United States abandoned the policy of the Indian frontier, without quite knowing why or how. Until the actual crash the various agencies of government, supported by public opinion, continued to administer the established system. After the recovery from the depression, it was taken for granted that the system was obsolete, although there was no formal act that abandoned it. By 1843, when there were at one moment over one thousand actual home-seekers starting across the Indian Country for residence in Oregon, it was obvious that there was something wrong with the idea that the Indian frontier could be perpetual. Earliest among the specific forces that were destined to break it down was a growing interest in traffic with New Mexico that took on the form and name of the Santa Fé trade.[1]

The northern provinces of Spain in America were developed at the terminals of radiating roads that joined on the Mexican plateau in the State of Durango. They were not established as the result of a persistent occupation of the country, but represented a conscious adaptation for the purpose of national defense. Texas, New Mexico, and Upper California, each at the end of its long overland trail, took on modern shape about the time of the American Revolution. They were the attempt of Spain to defend herself to the north against the border competition of France, England, and Russia.

The civilization of these provinces was old but lacked the element of progress. The few Spaniards who lived in them had no ideal of making permanent homes but were disappointed if they failed to find wealth that could be appropriated and carried off. There was no general emigration from Spain to the colonies. What trade there was, was limited to monopolistic trading companies, and the dangerous conditions of the Spanish Main in the seventeenth and eighteenth centuries gave much justification to the Spanish policy of limiting the traders to a few ports of entry which

---

[1] Katherine Coman, *Economic Beginnings of the Far West. How we won the Land beyond the Mississippi* (1912).

they might reach only under official convoy. The oceans swarmed with pirates, privateers, and the public war vessels of enemies of Spain. Vera Cruz was maintained as the port for Mexico and the northern provinces, and the economic development of New Spain was limited to the traffic that could be carried on through that port.

The Spanish exploiters took naturally to the high country of Mexico, avoiding the plains along the coast. They were in search of precious metals and thought to find these only in the mountains. They soon learned of the endemic diseases that made the tropic flats perilous places for them to dwell. From Vera Cruz they pushed inland directly to the City of Mexico, and then spread south and north along the backbone of the continent. Their great road from Mexico ran north through Querétaro, Zacatecas, and Durango. Here it developed the eastern branch to Eagle Pass, San Antonio, and Nacogdoches, at whose northern extremity Texas appeared. It developed a western branch through Sonora to the Santa Cruz Valley and the Gila. The main line continued a little west of north to the Chihuahua Desert, across this to El Paso del Norte and thence up the valley of the Rio Grande del Norte. The northern terminus of the central road became New Mexico, with a capital at Santa Fé, about the time the English were making their first foothold upon the Atlantic seaboard.

At the beginning of the nineteenth century, New Mexico was separated from the American border by a thousand miles of plains and mountains. Even if it had not been the policy of Spain to prevent foreign intercourse with its colonies, the distance and difficulty of access would have protected Santa Fé and its related towns from American approach. There was no American understanding of the nature of the Spanish colonial civilization until in 1807 the Spanish outposts arrested Zebulon M. Pike and his escort and conducted them as prisoners through the forbidden regions. Pike's book gave the first picture of the slow-moving society, with its antiquity, its adobe houses, and its great herds, that called itself New Mexico.

Pike saw a market in New Mexico, if only it could be reached. The colonists, Spanish and Indian, had means, but nothing to buy. They dwelt more than fifteen hundred miles away from Vera Cruz with the connecting highway often impassable except for mule trains. There were few commodities that could stand the freight charge of delivery in Santa Fé. There were few local manufactures and few artisans of any sort. The Spanish had no idea of working out their own economic future with local resources. The ordinary Yankee "notions," that every storekeeper in the States

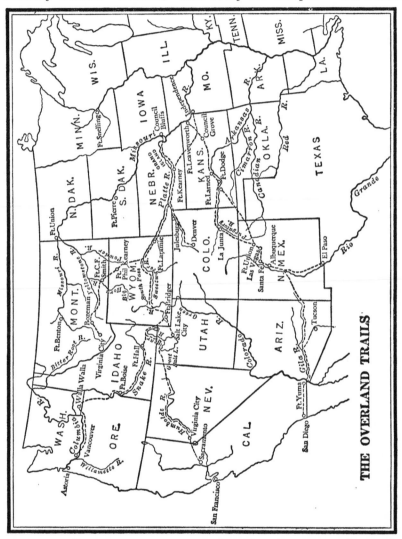

THE OVERLAND TRAILS

carried at all times, were scarce and costly. Spoons, cutlery, mirrors, needles, and thread were needed and lacking. There were silks and silver plate and other costly goods of little bulk, but the market was unsatisfied without even knowing what it lacked.

Pike described the New Mexico market in his book. Just as he printed it, the so-called Hidalgo revolt took place in Mexico, and there was a pretense of erecting a republic independent of Spain. A group of American traders, led by one McKnight, equipped a pack train in 1811 and set out across the plains from St. Louis, intent upon testing the truth of the stories of a free market at Santa Fé. They found the market, but it was not free. The Hidalgo revolt was suppressed, the Spanish authorities at Santa Fé were vigilant, and the adventurers paid for their temerity by jail sentences. It was still too soon to build up a traffic across the plains. And in 1819, when Spain and the United States established the Louisiana boundary, it appeared as though there might never be an occasion for it. The trade with Santa Fé had aroused a mild amount of cupidity, but not more than the fur trade with the Indians was sustaining all the time.

The Spanish barriers broke down in 1821. Even before Spain was displaced by independent Mexico in that year, the Spanish had dallied with the idea of encouraging American immigration into Texas, although without appreciating its possible consequences. When the news of the Mexican revolution reached the Missouri border in 1821, William Becknell hurriedly gathered a stock of goods and took the packs across the plains. He left Missouri in the late autumn, so late that his friends believed he could not get through. But in the early spring of 1822 he returned, heavy with profits, keen to repeat the trip, giving the word that the trade was open. That spring he took three wagons through to Santa Fé, revealing thereby the fact that the so-called American Desert could be easily traversed.[2]

The Santa Fé traders were an annual occurrence after 1822. In the early spring of each year they assembled their goods on the border, at St. Louis, or Franklin, or Independence. As the Missouri settlements ascended the river, the "jumping-off" place moved with them, reaching the mouth of the Kansas River at the western boundary of the State in 1831. At Independence, or its predecessors, the horse traders assembled with horses and mules for sale; the blacksmiths and wheelwrights opened their shops to repair and build the wagons. The harness-makers freshened up

[2] The *Missouri Historical Review* has naturally specialized somewhat in Santa Fé matters; it printed in 1910, "The Journal of Captain William Becknell, 1821." Elliott Coues assembled much bibliographical and topographical learning in his notes to *The Journal of Jacob Fowler, 1821–22* (1898).

CHAPTER XXXVII

THE SETTLEMENT OF OREGON

In the spring of 1832 the North American border was alive from Assiniboia, where the Hudson's Bay Company was aware of a need for institutions of government, to the plains of Texas where the impossibility of assimilating American blood with Mexican was being revealed. Around Fort Garry, where the Red River of the North joins the Assiniboin, the British traders had a group of residents, some of whom had come thither from Pembina a few years before. Their number was approaching five thousand, and since the foundation of the settlement in 1811, they had been ruled by one-man power, the resident factor of the company. They now received from the paternal hand of the great company a local council of government that controlled the affairs of the half-breed families and made the adjustments necessary along their long cart route to Fort Snelling and their canoe route to the ports on Hudson's Bay.

The Canadian extension projected around the northern flank of the Indian frontier as those of Mexico did around its southern end. In neither Canada nor Mexico did the problem resemble that of the United States for in neither was there a continuous pressure of farming population upon the Indian occupants of the soil. The artificial line that the United States was still engaged in drawing between the two civilizations was not necessary farther north or farther south. The activity of 1832 was at each end and at the middle of the American frontier.

Independence, Missouri, was the focal point of this unusual ferment. In addition to the Santa Fé traders, whose outfitting needs had brought the village into existence, there were in 1832 at least three other bodies of men engaged in similar work and eager to hurry across the frontier as soon as the grass was ready for their stock. There was a fifth body that was preparing a steamboat to ascend the Missouri River to a new high mark of navigation.

The American Fur Company whose *Yellowstone* was the first steamboat on the Upper Missouri, relied originally upon the keel boat for the fur trade. For many years the traders had laboriously ascended the Missouri to the Mandan villages, or above, and had brought down at the close of the winter hunt great bales of fur. There was a large element of risk in spite of the friendly current that worked with the trader on the homeward trip, for when the boats capsized the cargo was frequently lost and even lives were sometimes endangered. The early narratives tell of the shifts to which the shipwrecked trappers resorted to improvise new craft. The bull-boat, framed of saplings, and covered with hides of buffalo, with the seams sewed by hand and waterproofed with clay and tallow, was a possible though not in any sense a convenient vehicle. It spun with the current like a top; it was as unseaworthy as a tub and only dire necessity could excuse its use. The value of the goods to be taken up to the Indians each year and the much greater value of the pelts brought down, led to the construction of the *Yellowstone* and the discovery that many hundreds of miles of river were navigable in flood time. The steamboat was taken up beyond Council Bluffs in the season of 1831 and to the mouth of the Yellowstone River in 1832 where there was a trading post named Fort Union. For nearly thirty years to come, the annual steamers of the company kept pushing the head of navigation further towards the continental divide, and ended only in 1859 when they were within a few miles of the falls near the one hundred and eleventh meridian, where Fort Benton was maintained. The expedition of 1832 gave to this trade new dimensions and permanency; and every trapper who came back after a season's hunt in the Montana valleys had new observations to refute the common idea that here was an uninhabitable desert. If these hunters had been more literate, they would have weakened the idea more promptly. They knew the whole interior of the continent decades before it was surveyed or portrayed on any chart, but their hard-won observations were rarely reduced to maps and writing, and lesser men who later made the maps took most of the credit.[1]

Captain Benjamin L. E. Bonneville, a French-born officer of the regular army, was at the head of another of the trans-frontier parties of 1832 and started for the Columbia Valley early in May. He had been granted leave of absence from the army, to take a private party of trappers to the Rocky Mountains and commanded a well-equipped force of more than one hundred men. Jim Bridger, who was with him, long remained a picturesque figure among the scouts, and later erected Fort Bridger, an important

[1] James C. Bell, *Opening a Highway to the Pacific, 1838–1846* (1921), has a good bibliography.

trading post west of the famous South Pass of the Rockies They were after furs and took wagons along to bring them back. Their trip was destined to outstay Bonneville's leave, but the tales they brought home carried the lore of the mountains from the level of camp-fire legend to that of recorded fact. Washington Irving immortalized the trip in *The Rocky Mountains: or Scenes, Incidents, and Adventures in the Far West; digested from the Journal of Captain L. E. Bonneville* (1837). The literary exploitation of the Far West began at this time, carrying the frontier of letters far beyond the field that James Fenimore Cooper developed in the *Leather Stocking Tales.*

Another "captain," whose party was outfitting at the bend of the Missouri in 1832, was William Sublette, whose title was not based on any commission but was freely conferred by the tongues of his admiring contemporaries. He and his brother Milton were professional hunters whose range of travel made them familiar with the country of the trails long before the trails were worn. They and their associates had operated out of St. Louis for more than a decade. One of the parties, under General William Ashley, had in 1823 discovered South Pass, the rolling plain between the Sweetwater head of the North Platte and the westward streams that make up the Colorado and Columbia. A similar adventurer, Jedediah Smith, had traversed the whole of the Nevada desert and had entered Spanish California more than once.[2] Sublette, like Bonneville, was after furs: and unlike him, he knew his business.

Nathaniel J. Wyeth took yet another party upon the plains in 1832. His ambition was to develop a permanent seat of trade in the Oregon Country and to get there overland. He recruited his company in Boston and was the object of a somewhat embarrassing interest as he crossed the States to the Missouri border, for his knowledge of the plains was less than his pretense. His party, after a few weeks of camp and drill on an island in Boston Harbor, went by sea to Baltimore, there took the cars to Frederick, whence they walked to Brownsburg. Here they took steamboat to Pittsburgh, thence to St. Louis and from there bought passage to Independence. But they grounded at Lexington and were forced ashore, to walk the rest of the way to the western boundary of the State. A quaint boat that they brought with them, a cross between a dory and a prairie schooner, attracted more attention than the

[2] H. C. Dale, *The Ashley-Smith Explorations, and the Discovery of a Central Route to the Pacific, 1822–1829* (1918).

fact that this was a real commercial venture and testimony to a new interest in the Far West.[3]

So numerous were the enterprises of 1832, and so much in excess of those that had been undertaken in the years before, that it is safe to ascribe the beginning of a strong trans-frontier influence to this year. The whole United States, internal as well as external, was in commotion. The bank attack was on, and South Carolina was defiant. Black Hawk was leading his braves up the Rock River Valley; the frontiersmen of Maine were on the verge of private war with the Canadians of New Brunswick over their boundary troubles; the Seminole of Florida were uneasy over the forced migration west. The Oregon Country made its appearance beyond the western horizon, to induce first a traffic and then a migration of home seekers.

Under the treaty of 1827 with England, the Oregon Country was held in joint occupation by the two claimants, subject to the right of either to terminate the agreement on one year's notice. It had taken a generation for the Pacific front of the continent to assume even this degree of definition in the affairs of England and the United States, for at the close of the Revolutionary War neither country had advanced a claim to possessions here. The ancient occupation of North America by Spain and Russia had extended spheres of influence that met somewhere in the vicinity of the Columbia River, but no boundary agreement had been settled upon before the British and American wedge of influence was thrust in between these countries from the eastern side of the continent. The western ripples of the War of 1812 washed upon the Pacific, and Astoria was among the spoils of war. The United States became, piecemeal, the assignee of whatever claims Spain possessed, in addition to new rights based upon visitation and development. Through Louisiana was acquired the full right of approach to the eastern side of Oregon. By the treaty of 1819 Spain formally relinquished her claims to territory north of the forty-second parallel. But the matter was academic to both British and American statesmen, and the English treaty of 1818 ran the international boundary between Louisiana and Canada as far as the continental watershed, and left Oregon beyond that ridge in joint control. For a ten-year period the joint occupation was to last, according to the first agreement; then it was altered

[3] Thwaites reprinted the journal of the Wyeth party with other Oregon narratives in *Early Western Travels.*

to permanent joint occupation, subject to the right to terminate and force a division if either claimant should so desire. During the life of the ten-year bond, England came to an agreement with Russia whereby that empire withdrew its claims to anything south of fifty-four degrees, forty minutes, north latitude, leaving a clearly defined rectangle with the name of Oregon. By 1832 Oregon was a definite place, between the Rockies and the Pacific, north of forty-two and south of fifty-four-forty; but there was still no special reason why it belonged to one of its claimants more than to the other.

In 1832, although the amount of travel across the border was considerable, there was no destination beyond it that possessed such a lure as Texas or the lead country; and for another ten years more the Oregon business was little more significant than that of Santa Fé. But as the decade advanced there was added to the motive of the fur trade a second motive that brought a different type of adventurer upon the plains and left a different type of life in the Columbia Valley. The period was one of eager missionary activity among the churches, Catholic and Protestant, and the establishment of new missionary fields carried the workers into remote corners of the world. The Indians of the Oregon Country were never reached by the Spanish missions, yet were described by explorers from the time of Lewis and Clark as possessing fine qualities of manhood and character. The Methodists sent a group of missionaries to serve these tribes in 1834, and the next year a band of Presbyterians followed them. In 1836 Dr. Marcus Whitman, who had gone halfway with the party of 1835, and had returned to the States for reinforcements, took a wagon across the Rockies and with his bride set up near the junction of the Columbia and Snake rivers the Waiilatpu Mission.[4] In 1840 the Jesuits sent out Father de Smet and founded a mission on the Bitter Root.[5]

The little groups of practical Christians at the missionary establishments laid the foundations of agricultural occupation of Oregon. The fur traders before them had indeed maintained permanent stations, such as that of the Hudson's Bay Company at Fort Vancouver, where the Willamette enters the Columbia. But their

[4] The real services of Dr. Whitman have been discredited by the unreasonable claims made by some of his surviving associates and their partisans; Myron Eels, *Marcus Whitman* (1909); W. I. Marshall, *Acquisition of Oregon; and the long-suppressed Evidence about Marcus Whitman* (1911); Edward G. Bourne, "The Legend of Marcus Whitman," in his *Essays in Historical Criticism* (1901).

[5] H. M. Chittenden and A. T. Richardson, *Life, Letters, and Travels of Father Pierre-Jean de Smet, 1801–1873* (1905).

people were transients, and their trade depended upon preventing the development of farming settlements. The mission homesteads, however, were built up as models for the Indian converts; and their workers had the ideal of reclaiming the Indians not only from paganism but from savagery. They sought to establish industry and a productive life in place of the vagrancy of the nomad hunters. They built permanent houses and cleared the surrounding fields. Within a year or two they discovered the charm of soil and climate characteristic of the Columbia country; and their letters home revealed these attractions in addition to those of saving souls. In the latter task they were not more successful than other workers among the tribes, for the Indians in tribal state possessed vast powers of resistance to civilizing influence. But as farmers they were triumphant. Their descriptions were so attractive that relatives and friends sought occasion to join the annual caravans from Independence, and each year saw a slight increase in the number of Americans in the vicinity of Fort Walla Walla and Fort Vancouver. All of them found in Dr. John McLoughlin, the factor of the great company at Fort Vancouver, a friend, counselor, and banker.[6] These settlers raised the question as to how long the country could get along without either a formal government or a national sovereign. Joint occupation became precarious as soon as either English or Americans wanted to occupy Oregon.

By appointing Dr. Elijah White to be Indian Agent for the United States in Oregon in 1842, the question of control was definitely raised and emigration thither was encouraged. White's party included 130 persons, with 18 wagons. The same year, the War Department sent the son-in-law of Senator Benton, John C. Frémont, a young officer of the regular army, to explore the road to South Pass. The trail was well known and a formal exploration was hardly needed, but Frémont managed to identify himself so completely with this and the other routes to the Pacific that the nickname "pathfinder" clung to him throughout his life, and he appeared to have discovered the various trails instead of merely first recording them on an accurate map.

The Oregon Trail followed the valley of the Platte River to its source in the Rocky Mountains.[7] The emigrant started at Inde-

[6] F. V. Holman, *Dr. John McLoughlin* (1907).

[7] Henry Inman and William F. Cody, *The Great Salt Lake Trail* (1898); Francis Parkman, *Oregon Trail* (1846); Harrison C. Dale, "The Organization of the Oregon emigrating Companies," in Oregon Historical Society *Quarterly*, vol. XVI, — a magazine indispensable to the historian of the Northwest. All of these matters are well summarized in Joseph Schafer, *History of the Pacific Northwest* (1905).

pendence or some point above it on the Missouri. In the forties, with the beginning of settlement in Iowa, there were several roads developed across northern Missouri and southern Iowa, that led to the Missouri River south of the mouth of the Platte, which is among the Council Bluffs. Anywhere between the mouth of the Platte and that of the Kansas the traveler might cross the river and make his entry to the plains. There was one well-traveled road that went with the Santa Fé Trail for some distance to a point on the divide between the Osage and Wakarusa rivers, and then branched northwestwardly to the Platte River at the head of Grand Island. Between this road and the line of the Platte River were many trails radiating from the head of Grand Island to points on the Missouri River. Any of these might be taken by the Oregonian; and all of them were bad since at the time of their use in May the river and creek bottoms were afloat, and the wagons had to fight alternate mud and ridges. The streams of the region ran generally across the line of march.

From Grand Island until the forks of the Platte were reached (near Julesburg, Colorado) the road was good and the grades were easy. On either side of the river, or up its dry channel, the wagons could advance so regularly that the life of their occupants fell into a standard routine. From the mouth of the north fork, which the trail followed, the country became more hilly; and above the mouth of Laramie Creek it speedily became mountainous. The Sweetwater branch of the North Platte rises near South Pass, through which the Oregonians made their way. Frémont got this far in 1842 and explored the mountains on either side of the pass before returning to the United States. The travelers pushed on across the various tributaries of the Green River and began their downward course at the headwaters of the Snake. The journey from the Missouri to the Willamette was all of two thousand miles long, and about half the distance was rough going that tested the perseverance of the migrant and the endurance of his stock. Around Green River the road was extremely rough, and the water was almost undrinkable. Alkali was everywhere, offensive to men and animals. Disease and hardship left their marks upon both, and the trail was by 1842 marked with graves, bones of oxen, and the discarded household goods of those whose wagons broke down or whose stock gave out. In the following spring the flood of migration struck the trail, and more than a thousand emigrants gathered at the Missouri crossings in May.

Between 1837 and 1842 there was less than the normal shifting of population in the United States. The grandiose schemes for advancing prosperity had fallen flat in the former year. Some of the debts were actually repudiated by the States that incurred them; others were compromised with the creditors; the individual farmer had speculative obligations to meet, and yet lacked a market for the only goods he could produce. There was no region that by its prosperity attracted the floating population. The aspirations of the discouraged frontier produced a new political party and elected William Henry Harrison President in 1840, much as they had elevated Jackson to the same office twelve years before. The growing repute of Oregon was the first thing to break the spell. The westward movement revived in 1843.

Every year after 1842 a larger party met at the Missouri and crossed to Oregon. Congregating at the edge of the Indian frontier and pushing across it, the emigrants had many contacts with the Indians colonized there, and the plains tribes beyond them. Fort Leavenworth became more important as the strategic center of the region, and along the trail various posts were opened where travelers might replenish their outfits. Except for such supplies as these stations carried in stock and the game that could be shot along the march, the emigrant train was dependent upon itself for a period of from four to eight months. In 1846 Congress allowed the War Department to garrison selected spots for military posts. The first of these, near the head of Grand Island in the Platte, was 310 miles from Fort Leavenworth and was called Fort Kearny, after Stephen Watts Kearny, first lieutenant-colonel of the dragoon regiment. Farther out the trail, 337 miles west of Fort Kearny, an old adobe trading post at the mouth of Laramie Creek was bought and became Fort Laramie. For thirty years nearly everything that affected the Sioux of the plains was in some way associated with this post. Beyond South Pass were private posts at Fort Bridger, Fort Hall, and Fort Boisé. In the numerous journals that have survived the migrations, these spots stand out as the landmarks of the trail. After 1845, the emigrant commonly carried in his kit a copy of Frémont's journal with a useful map of the country as far as the Pacific.[8]

When the Oregon Country was spoken of by emigrants, they

[8] J. C. Frémont, *Report of the exploring Expeditions to the Rocky Mountains in the Year 1842, and to Oregon and North California in the Years 1843-'44* (28th Congress, 2d Session, Senate Document 174).

generally meant the long fertile valley of the Willamette River, running north from California to a junction with the Columbia at Fort Vancouver. Here the Americans took root, from Portland up to Salem. There were smaller groups around Whitman's mission on the Walla Walla; in the valley of the Grande Ronde which the settlers had to cross between Snake River and the Walla Walla there were a few. The mission workers and the employees of the Hudson's Bay Company were of much aid to them as they arrived in Oregon ragged, footsore, and often hungry at the approach of winter. Even before White arrived with the emigration of 1842 there was a need for government. He made it his business to guide the community in this direction in the following spring.

The benevolent despotism of Dr. McLoughlin was overturned by the American Oregonians in May, 1843, when they formed at a convention held in a place called Champoeg, a local government based upon the laws of Iowa Territory. They had no laws, no land titles, and no rights, but they erected one of the spontaneous governments of the frontier that met their minimum needs until Congress was ready to make them into a territory. They sent a messenger to Washington to ask such treatment, but Congress had not yet given notice under the treaty of 1827 and was not ready for action.

Oregon became a national political issue before any steps were taken to solve it as a social problem. Between 1841, when Harrison's death in office turned the Presidency over to John Tyler, and the inauguration of Tyler's successor in 1845, a Democratic administration made ready to incorporate Texas in the Union. The unwillingness of the Senate to ratify a treaty of annexation forced the issue into politics on the eve of a new election. The Democrats embraced it, came out with James K. Polk for the "reannexation" of Texas; and added "the whole of Oregon or none" as a slogan to sweeten northern public opinion. The policy was not advanced as one of expansion but was defended upon the ground that both tracts belonged to the United States of right. Polk accepted both with sincerity and determination but found it convenient to agree to a compromise upon Oregon in 1846. On June 15, James Buchanan, Secretary of State, negotiated a treaty with England whereby the forty-ninth parallel, the old line of 1818, was extended to the Pacific Ocean. It was a reasonable compromise of a matter in which neither side had a good case against the other. The campaign cry, sometimes phrased as "fifty-four forty or fight," lacked a sound justification in fact. The treaty left the Columbia River in the United States.

With the rising interest in Oregon and the migration across the frontier, the Indian policy of 1825 was quietly dropped, and the region of the plains, from being a providential boundary to check American dispersion, became an annoying impediment to communication between the coasts. There was yet no white use found for the plains, and no tendency of the agricultural frontier to advance by the old process into the country directly west of Arkansas, Missouri, and Iowa. But the travel through and across the Indian Country dispelled the notion of its universal barrenness. The War Department did not even try to enforce the provisions of the Indian Intercourse Act as to white entry into Indian Country. The military posts authorized in 1846 were in contemplation of a permanent use of the trails, and between the forty-second parallel and the forty-ninth the United States was now for the first time in ownership of a tract facing the Pacific Ocean. Congress was dilatory in meeting its responsibility for the new possession and did not create the Territory of Oregon until 1848.

CHAPTER XXXVIII

THE "STATE" OF DESERET

THE belief that the Indian frontier was to last forever was almost universal in 1832 and was accepted with as little question on the frontier as in the East. No testimony to this is stronger than that which was given unconsciously by the prophet of the most militant of the border sects, Joseph Smith of Palmyra, New York, founder of the Church of Jesus Christ of the Latter Day Saints. This leader announced in 1830 that it had been revealed to him that his church was to conduct missions among the Gentiles who were to be won back to the fold and among the Indians whose savagery was to be reclaimed. In this year he printed his bible, *The Book of Mormon*, completed the formal organization of the church and dispatched missionaries to the Indian Country. In the following summer, led by the reports of the first missionaries, he declared that revelation had indicated the spot where the church was to be established for all time. He named Independence, Missouri, as "the land of promise and the place of the city of Zion," and visited it in person to dedicate the tabernacle. Here with the Gentiles on one hand and the Indians on the other, he expected the Mormon Church to fulfill its mission.

The Mormon Church, first under Smith and then under his more stable successor, Brigham Young, played an active part in frontier thought for thirty years. Its rise and structure indicate the intellectual and spiritual uneasiness of the border settlements. Its spectacular trek in search of Zion brings it in line with the other forces that carried American interests toward the Pacific in the decade after the Jacksonian migration.

The ferment of the twenties included many revolts besides the beginnings of Mormonism.[1] Jacksonianism was one manifestation of it, and the most pervasive. Anti-masonry was one, giving the first view of the aspirations of the new community around the eastern end of Lake Erie. Scientific thought was in upheaval because of the speculations of the young scientists just back from their studies at the new German universities. Occasional historical students, drilled in the new critical scholarship of Niebuhr, were challenging

[1] W. A. Linn, *The Story of the Mormons* (1902).

tradition with evidence. Individuals were breaking from the creeds of every Christian church and were demanding the right to give their own interpretation of the documents containing the revelations of Jesus Christ. Even so broad a body as the Society of Friends, that had no creed, was split into followers of the orthodox faith and those of Elias Hicks. Ralph Waldo Emerson laid down his preaching as a minister of the Unitarian Church and took up the teachings of a philosopher at large. On the frontier, where religion had ever been more emotional than elsewhere in the United States and where the waves started by the great revival of 1801 had not entirely spent their force, strong preachers took their congregations with them and founded personal churches. Humanitarianism was afoot, and movements for temperance and abolition of slavery were taken up with religious passion. It was a poor prophet who could not gain a few converts, whatever he taught; and an unstatesmanlike one who could not build them into a new church. The nation was ripe for spiritual leadership and yearned for voices speaking with authority. Scores of new movements came to light. Those that outlasted the voice and personality of the founder became important indexes of the religious capacity of the United States. Of these none was more significant than the church that Joseph Smith established.

Palmyra, New York, lies in that region south of Lake Ontario to which the Erie Canal brought tumultuous development in the twenties. Before 1817 the country was almost untouched by white men; a decade later it gave birth to the Anti-Masons who upset the political balance of Jackson and developed into the new Whig Party. Among the pioneer families who came early to Palmyra was one from Vermont, bringing with it a lad named Joseph Smith. Smith was so inconspicuous in boyhood that the later recollections of his contemporaries seem artificial and forced. He was never identified with either steady farm work or any trade. He began to dream visions in the early twenties, and in 1827 had revealed to him the golden plates on which was inscribed the Book of Lehi. No one else saw the plates, for it was revealed to Smith that if any unhallowed eye gazed on them, the individual would be consumed by holy fire. He translated them from behind a curtain, his writer taking down the words as he dictated the history of the lost tribes of Israel, who were no other than the American Indians. The narrative of the Book of Lehi was lost, but a later, fuller narrative, the Book of Nephi, was published in 1830 as the *Book of Mormon*. It has been said that there was a revelation printed on the title page threatening with "pain of death" any person who should sell it for less than one dollar and a quarter.

The informal organization of the Mormon Church took place before the publication of its book of scriptures; it became formal in 1830 after the receipt of a revelation on church organization that specified Smith as the divine intermediary. Other apostles who believed that they were receiving revelations were informed that they were mistaken. The new teacher picked up his first converts as dozens of others were doing in the same period. He differed from the rest in that he kept a firm grip upon the faithful, made tithes a real thing for them, and accumulated from their contributions a fund for advancing the interests of the church. It was difficult for critics and dissenters to stand up against his personality, reinforced by a claim of direct revelation.[2]

In 1831 the church took up a temporary residence at Kirtland, Ohio, a little east of Cleveland, where the Ohio Canal was about to aid in the agricultural development of the community. Its scouts at the same time sought for a permanent site for Zion and selected Independence. There are said to have been one thousand converts in 1831, and a steady stream of these was started by the missionaries who carried the gospel. There was little in the gospel that might not have been found in the sermons of border preachers, some of whom were among the earliest converts. The historical content of the Book of Mormon bore a resemblance to that of parts of the Old Testament. It was believed that the chosen missionary received at once a gift of tongues enabling him to visit his field and discourse in the appropriate vernacular. The proselytes, as they came in, were allowed to contribute to the welfare of the church and were put to work under the centralized direction of Smith and his assistants. A store, a sawmill, a hotel, a tannery, and a bank were run as part of the establishment; and there was none of the dissipation of initiative on individual jobs that was characteristic of the other settlements of the neighborhood. The reputation of the Mormon community that was spread abroad was that even the thoughts of the faithful were under control, and the votes, too; and that they were a close-knit unit out of sympathy with the individualistic opinion of the frontier. They were immediately unpopular, adding provocation by their complete ac-

[2] T. B. H. Stenhouse, *The Rocky Mountain Saints: A full and complete History of the Mormons, from the first Vision of Joseph Smith to the last Courtship of Brigham Young* (1874).

ceptance of the teaching that in good time they would dominate the world. The panic of 1837, on top of the tense relations with neighbors already existing, made it necessary to abandon the temporary Kirtland post; and Zion itself had already been abandoned for similar reasons.

Independence was revealed as Zion and dedicated in 1831. Construction was begun and colonization progressed, making the place ready for the headquarters of the church to move thither. But Independence was not a good situation for the peace of mind of a new community. It was frequented by individuals, traders and farmers, who had no use for members of a group and who derided the teachings of Smith. The native Missourians resented the influx of converts and the prospect of permanent notoriety and found means of annoying the Mormons. There was retaliation on both sides, hard feeling and violence, and in 1833 Zion was abandoned in favor of Far West, a new station north of the Missouri River in an unsettled part of what was then Clay County.

Until the non-Mormon farmers encroached upon the settlement at Far West, about 1836, there was peace and development there. Then the normal extension of Missouri brought pressure upon it. The peculiar cohesion of the Mormons became again a cause of affront. By the time the Kirtland colony came west, it was necessary once more to move in order to procure freedom from pressure. In 1839 Smith discovered a deserted village in Illinois named Commerce, built and abandoned by one of the experimental communities. It lay in an angle of the Mississippi River, a little above the mouth of the Des Moines, and was bought at a bargain price, and renamed Nauvoo. The legislature of Illinois was willing to grant a special charter to the new town and a special amendment of the militia act, giving the town officers complete control of the local military force. Smith had means of getting himself and his associates elected to these offices. As an *imperium in imperio* Nauvoo became populous and independent, having perhaps ten thousand inhabitants in 1842. And up the river came the constant stream of new converts, more than replacing the exodus of disappointed members who dropped away.

The expulsion of the Mormons from Illinois, like the three other expulsions that they suffered, reveals the frontier brand of intolerance. The church claimed that it was punished for conscience' sake; the neighbors maintained that corrupt political influences and intolerable manners brought it about. It began to be whispered that personal immorality was prevalent, and that the leaders of the church, at least, had taken numerous wives. The political leaders of both Whig and Democratic parties began to distrust Smith, who seems to have promised political support to both factions; only to announce that he expected himself to be elected President of the United States. In the tense party feeling of 1844, the Mormons found themselves disliked and distrusted by both parties, and there was schism even at Nauvoo. There were charges and countercharges, mob violence and arrests, and at last Joseph Smith and his brother Hyrum were taken from the jail at Carthage, Illinois, and shot. Their lynching was the final stroke. Migration again became the order of the day, and the new leader, Brigham Young, looked about for a refuge where they might live their life in peace. He saw no spot in the United States, and cast his eyes across the border to the northern part of Mexico, beyond the Rocky Mountains.

Of the fifteen thousand Mormons at Nauvoo in 1846, approximately twelve thousand stayed by the church in its troubles and crossed into Iowa Territory early in the winter. They abandoned their homes and their improvements. There was no market for a whole town site. They marched with what movables they could pack into their wagons, and made their way through southern Iowa to the Council Bluffs during the next summer. They wintered in camp in the Pottawattamie country near the Council Bluffs, while Brigham Young conversed with guides who knew the plains and made his plans for 1847.

In the spring of 1847 the valley from their camp site down to Independence was crowded with the wagons of the overland migration. This was the fifth summer of heavy emigration, and the numbers ran into hundreds of wagons and thousands of persons and live stock. Oregon was the chief objective, but there was unusually heavy freight to Santa Fé because of the needs of the army that had marched there in 1846. And there was a minority that intended to turn south at Great Salt Lake and go to California. Part of the Oregonians had been diverted to California by the stories of climate and soil, as early as the migration of 1845.

The Mormons broke camp in June, 1847, to march as a body over the Oregon Trail, but Young, with a selected band of prospectors and seventy-three wagons, hurried ahead in April to choose a stopping place. He did not take any one into his confidence, but he had evidently determined that the Mormons could gain isolation by establishing a kind of life that the separate farmers could not live. He had learned of irrigation and thought to apply it in a part of the desert, believing that the close organization of the Mormon Church could carry it through, whereas the individualistic and poor typical farmers of the frontier could not imitate it. He traveled rapidly up the Platte, not along the south bank, which was the usual course of the Oregonians, but on the north side which became thereafter the Mormon Trail.[3] From South Pass he pushed southwestward to the rim of the basin that surrounds the Great Salt Lake. The company arrived there July 22, with Young sick and a day behind the leaders; but here he immediately recognized the chosen land, and set his party to work on the first irrigation ditch and the potato patches. He staked his vision against the judgment of the plainsmen. Jim Bridger promised him that he could not raise a crop in the Great Salt Lake Valley.

The main column of the Mormons was on the trail in the summer, in several bodies. Before leaving winter quarters, Young provided them with an order of march, regulating the number and equipment of the bodies, and organizing them for safety and protection. The practical wisdom of the order shows that he had learned much about the dangers of plains travel from the people he interviewed in 1846. A station was left behind in Iowa at Kanesville, later to become the town of Council Bluffs, that served as a forwarding post for the main settlement. Young wanted independence, but he had no idea of absolute isolation. He traveled back on the trail himself as soon as he had selected the site for the City of the Great Salt Lake, to encourage the main body and to manage the affairs. A regular post and express service between the Missouri River and the new settlement was maintained.

Only despotism could have accomplished the results that the Mormons brought about in the remaining thirty years of Brigham Young's life;[4] and only a wise and benevolent autocrat could have maintained the grip upon the members of the church that made them willing to put up with the despotism. After the first season,

[3] F. L. Paxson, "T. Turnbull's Travels from the United States across the Plains to California," in State Historical Society of Wisconsin *Proceedings*, 1913, is the journal of an emigrant over the Mormon Trail in 1852, and has full notes and maps.

[4] See the judicious and careful narrative of this in Hubert Howe Bancroft, *History of Utah* (1889). Richard Francis Burton, *The City of the Saints, and across the Rocky Mountains to California* (1862), is a picture by a traveler of wide experience, and is still readable.

in which there was some scarcity, there was an abundance of food and rough comfort for every one. The farms and ditches were extended up and down the valley that runs east of Great Salt Lake, and south to Utah Lake. Temporal, spiritual, and civil affairs were so closely blended that it is almost impossible to disentangle them. The church itself undertook the large supply services in transportation and merchandise and showed itself a capable judge of personal capacity, in taking into the hierarchy all of its members who showed power of leadership. Bishops were numerous, making it possible to reward with rank and title every one of importance. As the colony grew through the arrival of converts, new sub-colonies were marked out, but they were not planted in the go-as-you-please manner of most frontier developments. Instead of this, the officers of the church made the reconnoissance, selected the site, and then told off enough members of each craft or line of business to make the venture a success. Young did not tolerate any rival to himself in the management of Mormon affairs, but the graded hierarchy under him gave ample chance for recognition to the abler members of the church. And when individuals dissented or deserted, means were found to silence or evict them.

The new gospel that the Mormon missionaries preached did not repudiate the teachings of Christianity, but was like that of Mohammed in accepting all that had gone before and adding to it a new revelation. It laid great stress upon the material benefits that the Saints were to enjoy and upon the earth that they were ultimately to inherit. It taxed its followers heavily and gained the persistent support that comes from sacrifice. It rewarded the unusual members, and dominated the ordinary. It became an experiment in state socialism like nothing else that the United States had seen or was to see until the war organization of 1918.

The mutterings against Mormons and Mormonism did not cease with the departure of the church from American territory into Mexican. The American suspicion of secret organization could not be silenced, and to the average frontier community there was something dangerous in the discipline under which the Mormons moved. The indiscreet promises of some of the missionaries were an additional affront, for they suggested that when the church was ready, it would precipitate a war of destruction against the Gentile world. More influential perhaps than either of these causes of unpopularity were the rumors of immorality that appeared in Nauvoo and have never been dissociated from the church.

It is stated by an apologist for the Mormons that Joseph Smith knew the "rightfulness" of "plural marriage" as early as 1831, the same having been shown to him by revelation. But in the early days of the church, with converts drawn chiefly from the ordinary families of the frontier where the sanctity of the marriage vows ranked high, it was no time to practice it. He did not take his first plural wife until 1841, and the scant evidence that exists raises a doubt as to whether this act was that of an inspired prophet or merely of a lustful man. On July 12, 1843, he announced in secret the text of a revelation concerning plurality of wives and celestial marriage, making it incumbent upon single women to be bound to some man during life in order to enjoy the full pleasures of salvation after death. The revelation included a special message directed to his first wife, Emma, bidding her not to interfere with the additional wives that the prophet brought into her household; and unbelievers have thought that perhaps the jealousy of Emma may have been the real occasion of the revelation. The church membership was by this date growing rapidly and among the converts there was a preponderance of women; unusual on the frontier where single women were extremely scarce and where the demands of husbands-elect shortened to a minimum the widows' period of mourning. After the secret revelation, Smith and Young, and their intimate counselors, availed themselves of it to build up plural families in private. But they sternly denied both the families and the revelation in public. In at least one case an indiscreet missionary who preached the doctrine was driven out of the church by excommunication.

The rumor that the leaders were living immoral lives persisted in spite of all denials, and asserted that the bishops and other dignitaries were practically compelled to take plural wives in order to fasten them more firmly to the church. In August, 1852, the dogma was publicly announced at a special conference of the church, and Brigham Young took the offensive in defending its morality and spiritual soundness. From this date there was no concealment. When Young died in 1877 he left seventeen wives housed in a row of dwellings in his capital city. It does not appear that polygamy was ever universal among the Mormons, and there is much evidence that many women detested it, but most of the study and interpretation of the meaning of the church has halted around this fact, and has thus missed seeing the success of the order as a colonizing agent.

With the planting of the Mormon settlement in the midst of the desert in 1847, another objective was created to direct and stimulate migration over the trails. Every year since 1843, this had flowed by thousands. In Oregon, spontaneous local government was started in 1843; in the Salt Lake basin it assumed the name of the State of Deseret and took shape in 1849.

There is no evidence that shows whether Brigham had received a grant of land from Mexico authorizing his settlement of 1847. When he framed his plans, he sought to get outside the United States and away from chronic persecution on the border. But the conditions that had pursued the Mormons from their foundation continued to follow them. While they were on the march through Iowa, Polk led the United States into the Mexican War, and sent an army across the plains to Santa Fé. Before they left winter quarters in 1847 the actual conquest of California was over; and before they had finished their new home the United States had taken title to the land they occupied. There was nothing to do but make the best of the facts and to seek from the United States the same sort of autonomy they had received from Illinois. In March, 1849, a convention met in the City of the Great Salt Lake to frame a government.

The Mormon Church itself performed what functions of government were indispensable prior to 1849. The population included none but willing members of the faith who were ready to accept church leadership, and who had lost the American passion for separation of church and state. The convention of 1849 followed a call directed to "all the citizens of that portion of upper California lying east of the Sierra Nevada Mountains." It agreed to send a memorial to Congress to create a territorial government and framed a constitution for the region under the name of Deseret. The boundaries of the projected State were generous enough to include Utah, Nevada, Arizona, and southern California as far as the harbor of San Diego. The form of government was substantially that of the States of the Mississippi Valley. The provisional officers were elected in March, 1849, and left the control exactly where it had been before the framing of the constitution, for Young was chosen as governor, and church officials were placed in every elective office. It was an efficient government; more so than the spontaneous governments of Oregon or Franklin had been. And non-Mormons passing through its jurisdiction often had reason to be glad of its existence. The legislature of

Deseret sent a delegate to Congress that summer. But anti-Mormon influences were already at work, and members of the other branch of the Mormon Church (the non-polygamous group who were expelled while the church resided at Nauvoo) were pointing out the evil influence of Brigham Young. No action was taken by Congress for another year; but in Deseret the people lived safely and happily under a government of their own creation.

Oregon and Deseret were two spontaneous colonies beyond the Rocky Mountains that owed nothing to Congress for their foundation. They were joined in the autumn of 1849 by a third, California, which framed a constitution for itself at the old Spanish village of Monterey, and demanded immediate admission as a State.

CHAPTER XXXIX

THE WAR WITH MEXICO

THE Republic of Texas remained independent for nine years after 1836 because of the unwillingness of President Martin Van Buren to risk its annexation to the United States, and the inability of President John Tyler to bring it about. Its secession from Mexico at the moment when slavery became the controlling issue in American politics was an unfortunate accident, from the standpoint of speedy admission to the Union. There was no northern territory ready to be admitted with it, after the admission of the Arkansas-Michigan pair; and there was a growing disinclination on the part of northern leaders to admit more slaveholding States upon any basis. The leading nations of Europe recognized the independence of the Texas Republic, but the mother country, Mexico, remained resentful and refused to admit that the insurrection of 1836 had been successful. The Mexican relations with the United States, strained on their own account, were made more difficult because of the Mexican belief that the loss of Texas was the result of a deliberate American conspiracy.

The first serious attempt to accomplish the admission of Texas was made by President Tyler after the reorganization of his cabinet.[1] The presidential election of 1840, at which William Henry Harrison and John Tyler were elected by the Whig voters, was a successful revolt of dissatisfactions that had accumulated during the twelve years of Jackson and Van Buren. The Whigs carried all the northern States except New Hampshire, Illinois, and Missouri, and overturned the Jackson forces even in Kentucky and Tennessee. The revolt was inspired by much the same spirit as that with which Jackson himself had been victorious, and the personnel of the winning ticket indicated the price that the Whig leaders were willing to pay for insurance of success. Tyler, the

---

[1] Justin H. Smith, *The War with Mexico* (1919), will be a landmark in the historiography of this period for a long time. He, and all other writers on the Southwest, owe a debt to the great collector and preserver of local records, Hubert Howe Bancroft of San Francisco, who wrote, edited, or signed nearly forty great volumes of Pacific Coast history between 1874 and 1890. From his collections, now owned by the University of California, there come frequent volumes in the *Publications* of the Academy of Pacific Coast History, directed by Herbert E. Bolton.

Vice President, was a southern Democrat in every sense except in his personal hostility to Andrew Jackson. He had nothing but this in common with such of the Whigs as were inspired by real ideas. When the Hero of Tippecanoe, his chief, died after a month in the White House, the Whig victory was substantially nullified, for Tyler thought in terms of southern ascendency. Most of the cabinet of Harrison left Tyler at the first opportunity. Webster, Secretary of State, remained longest, for he was engaged upon an intricate negotiation with England that was completed only in the Webster-Ashburton Treaty of 1842. When he resigned at last, and Calhoun finally became Secretary of State, the way was open to advance the Texas question.

Calhoun's desire to annex Texas was based upon his determination to insure the safety of slave labor in the South. Not only was an additional slave State to be desired, but there was a danger in allowing an independent nation to be slipped in between Mexico and the United States. He feared that England and France might carry on projects of their own in Texas, and that their influence might lead to an abolition of slavery there. The Texan leaders encouraged this fear by talk of their inability to live without connection with some larger nation, and spoke freely of the possibility that they might be compelled to seek either an alliance with Europe or incorporation as a colony. Texas had no desire to enter upon such a course, but found that American interest in annexation was stimulated by the thought of rivalry.

In April, 1844, Calhoun concluded a treaty of annexation with Texas. Before the Texas minister would sign it, he had to be assured that if Mexico made the treaty a cause for further war the United States would do everything in its power to protect Texas against punishment. England was trying to compel Texas to abolish slavery, but Calhoun was not quite frank when he asserted that this attempt was the cause of American action. The treaty failed of ratification by the Senate in June, but the Democratic Party had by this time nominated James K. Polk and made Texas and Oregon a party issue.

All through the autumn of 1844 the United States resounded with cries for the "reannexation of Texas," and "fifty-four forty or fight." The Texans, said Tyler, in his message on the treaty, "are deeply indoctrinated in all the principles of civil liberty and will bring along with them in the act of reassociation devotion to our Union and a firm and inflexible resolution to assist in maintaining the public liberty unimpaired. . . . " The South, in general, was for both slavery and expansion; the West was for expansion and not greatly concerned over slavery; the East had a strong minority opposed to both. Polk was elected in November, not because of a national mandate to carry out the Democratic promise, but because Clay's trimming between the forces for slavery and against it alienated northern Whig votes. Clay carried his own section of the West, Kentucky and Tennessee, but lost New York. The abolitionist candidate, James G. Birney, attracted three times enough votes to have elected Clay. Could Clay have held one third of Birney's little vote, he would have gained New York and would have become President in 1845. As it was, however, Polk, though a minority candidate, won the election and interpreted the victory as approval of expansion.

Tyler, too, interpreted the election as meaning Texas, and the Congress whose Senate rejected the annexation treaty in June, was ready for incorporation in the short session after election day. A joint resolution for annexation by either act of Congress or by a new treaty was passed in March, 1845, and before Polk took the oath of office a messenger dispatched by Tyler was on his way to Austin. The republic assented to annexation in June, and on July 4 a convention assembled to draft a new constitution suitable to an American State.

One of the members of the Texas convention spoke of the fact that the people of the new State came largely from "the highly respectable and democratic States of Arkansas and Missouri," illustrating again the general rule that frontier populations drifted but a short average distance. But Arkansas and Missouri were both too young for many of their citizens to have been born there. Of the sixty-one delegates in the convention the *Arkansas Banner* reported eighteen as having been born in Tennessee, from six to eight each in Virginia, Georgia, and Kentucky, and the rest scattered in smaller numbers over the whole East. "The delegates to the Convention, for intelligence, integrity and worth, would rank high in any country," wrote an Austin correspondent of the Charleston *Courier*. "There is not, perhaps, much of brilliancy, but a great deal of matter-of-fact sense and sound knowledge; and I predict that we shall form and send to you a sound and sensible Constitution. . . ." The delegates were as good Jacksonians as though they were already in the United States; they wore crêpe a week in honor of the memory of Jackson, who died in June, 1845, and granted to one of their number, General Sam Houston, a leave of absence that he might make a pilgrimage of affection to Jackson's home at the Hermitage. The constitution bore the imprint of the newest word in popular rights: married women were allowed to retain control of their own property, and the homestead of the farmer was exempted from judgment in the collection of his debts. For many years to come, married women's property rights and homestead exemption were the rallying cries of border democracy.

Before Texas was declared a member of the United States by act of December 29, 1845, the administration of President Polk was aware that annexation would probably occasion war with Mexico. The Mexican press and Government were enraged at the United States and a noisy war party was welcoming a certain cause of war. Martial ideals were violent among the Mexicans, whose young men rejoiced in flaming uniforms and military rank. Their army was overgeneraled and short of privates; its spirit was overbearing and hypnotized the Mexican leaders into the belief that a war would be brief and glorious and would forever end the American menace. Contempt for the commercial disposition of the United States was as pronounced as the belief in Mexican prowess.

The detailed diary that Polk began to keep in the spring of 1845 makes it possible for the historian to see the inside of the presidential mind.[2] He came to office not only convinced of the justice of both Oregon and Texas, but determined to find a means of adding to the United States, California, New Mexico, and parts of other provinces of northern Mexico. He was willing to acquire these peacefully, bartering for them the numerous financial claims that the United States and its citizens held against the government of Mexico. But if Mexico should determine to go to war about Texas, he would welcome it. He told his cabinet that "in making peace we would if practicable obtain California and such other portion of the Mexican territory as would be sufficient to indemnify our claimants on Mexico and to defray the expenses of the war . . ." Eventually when Mexico seemed to be slower in going to war than he expected, he drafted a message to Congress asking for a declaration against that republic on the ground that the United States had enough grievances to justify a war for their satisfaction.

In the summer of 1845, while the details of annexation were

[2] The Chicago Historical Society rendered a real service when it permitted the publication of its manuscript of this diary under the careful editorship of Milo M. Quaife, in 1910.

being worked out with Texas, and Texas was nervous from its fear of Mexican attack, the United States made preparations for the eventuality of war. These involved orders to the part of the army that was stationed near Texas, to the fleet commanders in the Gulf of Mexico and the Pacific, and to the single consul, Thomas O. Larkin, whom the United States maintained at Monterey in Upper California.[3] Almonte, the Mexican minister at Washington, broke off relations with the State Department upon the passage of the Texas resolution, and his government in July recommended that war be declared against the United States as soon as annexation was consummated. General Zachary Taylor, who was in command in the Mississippi Valley, was ordered in June, 1845, to proceed towards the western boundary of Texas, to prevent a Mexican invasion; and was later informed that the Rio Grande was the western boundary. He did not take his station on that river until the following winter, but in April, 1846, was near the mouth of the Rio Grande, opposite the Mexican village of Matamoras.

The fleet commanders also were instructed what to do in the event of a war with Mexico. The forces in the Gulf were ordered to occupy Vera Cruz, which under Mexico as under Spain was the main port of entry, and the chief contact point with the outside world. The vital parts of Mexico were protected by the wide expanse of roadless deserts to the north and by tropic lowlands, impregnated with disease, between Mexico City and the sea. Only through Vera Cruz could the heart be reached, and military opinion was uncertain whether even here it could be accomplished. Commodore John D. Sloat, who had seven small war ships in Pacific waters, was ordered in June, 1845, to seize Upper California at once upon learning of a state of war. This meant, to him, the port of Monterey, which was the most important spot upon the western coast.

Larkin, at Monterey, was informed of the status of affairs in a dispatch sent by Secretary of State, Buchanan, in October, 1845, and delivered in April, 1846. He was told that the United States would make no attempt to detach California from Mexico, but would welcome its freedom, self-obtained. It hoped, otherwise, to acquire California through purchase. The guarded language of his instruction was sufficient to indicate to Larkin that the Adminis-

[3] Larkin's papers are available in "The United States Consulate in California," edited by R. W. Kelsey in Academy of Pacific Coast History *Publications*, vol. I.

tration expected him to stir up the "spontaneous" revolt; and he proceeded to get in touch with the Americans near Monterey.

In addition to the orders to Taylor, Sloat, and Larkin, which were natural preparations for a state of war that seemed to be imminent, there was another American measure of 1845, whose meaning is still involved in mystery. Captain John C. Frémont, with a small detachment of troops, appeared in the vicinity of Monterey in the spring of 1846. The results of his exploring parties of 1842 and 1843 were now in print, but no documents have been found to justify or explain his invasion of northern Mexico with an armed party in 1845. On this, his third trip, he reached the Sacramento Valley in the autumn of 1845, and wintered near San Francisco Bay, in spite of orders from the Mexican officers to take himself and his men out of California. He does not appear to have been ordered here as a part of the impending war, for in the spring he moved north toward Oregon. Yet his presence at all is hard to reconcile with the conditions proper to a time of peace. His connection with Senator Benton, who may have known more than has been printed, and who may not have been averse to having a member of his family on the spot, seems to have a significance. At any event, in May, 1846, Frémont claimed to have received verbal orders from a marine lieutenant named Gillespie and marched his men back to the Sacramento where they were on hand when the news of war arrived.

The war that Polk anticipated and that the Mexican Government threatened, lingered in its beginning; and as the spring of 1846 advanced the President took measures to hasten it. He turned to the long docket of unsatisfied demands in the files of the State Department and convinced himself that these would justify a war. They consisted of grievances arising from the chronic disturbances of Mexican politics. From the moment of Mexican independence in 1821 there was a course of revolt, counter-revolt, and confiscation that had dire results upon the property of foreigners resident in Mexico. What one ambitious dictator seized, the next one repudiated; and foreign claims kept the Mexican minister of foreign affairs always explaining and never satisfying, for the government did not become either steady or solvent. During Jackson's administration events reached such a state that the President asked Congress for power to institute reprisals in case Mexico continued to avoid acknowledgment or settlement. In 1839 Van Buren succeeded in extracting from Mexico an agreement to arbitrate the claims; but his successors could not make Mexico pay the awards. A new treaty of 1843 provided for the satisfaction of these, and Mexico made three quarterly payments before it defaulted again; and additional new claims were accruing all the time. In December, 1845, the United States had more than six million dollars' worth of unadjusted claims, and in May, 1846, the cabinet approved Polk's determination to use armed measures to collect the debt. But before the war message was finished and sent to Congress, the news arrived in Washington on May 9, 1846, that a detachment of General Taylor's army had been attacked on the Texas side of the Rio Grande and defeated in an engagement on April 24.

The news reached Washington on a Saturday. On Monday Polk shifted his reason for the war, and sent in a message declaring that it already existed. "The grievous wrongs perpetrated by Mexico upon our citizens throughout a long period of years remain unredressed . . ." he declared. "The cup of forbearance had been exhausted even before the recent information from the frontier of the Del Norte. But now, after reiterated menaces, Mexico has passed the boundary of the United States, has invaded our territory and shed American blood upon the American soil." Congress supported the President in his declaration, although the country was lukewarm, and the Whig Party was openly critical. An Illinois congressman of that faith, Abraham Lincoln, later made caustic inquiry whether the spot on which the blood was shed was actually a part of American soil; and in New England James Russell Lowell turned his poetic gift to a satire of the war party in the *Biglow Papers*.

Whether Mexico was the aggressor or not, it was impossible to have the war without going for it, and the army of the United States was in no condition for prompt attack or defense. It was necessary to raise and train the militia of the States, and to find commanders who could be trusted to carry out the Administration purpose. The ranking generals of the regular army were Zachary Taylor and Winfield Scott, both veterans of the War of 1812 and both Whigs. They presented a cruel dilemma. As Whigs they might be indifferent in prosecution and wreck the war; or, worse, they might succeed and wreck the Administration. The first Whig President, Harrison, had been a military hero; if there should be a second Whig hero in 1848, no Democrat was likely to be able to withstand him. There was talk of asking Congress to revive the office of Lieutenant-General and of appointing Colonel Thomas Hart Benton to the supreme command; and Benton would have been willing. His Democracy was excellent, but Congress was unsure of his military talent, and the thing fell through. Taylor and Scott were relied upon to win the war and Colonel Stephen W. Kearny was selected to coöperate with them.

The military strategy of the war comprised three border attacks upon Mexico and one blow at the center. Scott was chosen for the last and sent to New Orleans to build up an expeditionary force. In March, 1847, he landed his force near Vera Cruz; and six months later, on September 13, assaulted the fortress of Chapultepec, that guarded the City of Mexico. The next day he raised the American flag over the capital of the enemy. Taylor, in the same months, earned his nickname of "Old Rough and Ready" in the triangle of northeast Mexico that is indicated on the map by Matamoras, Monterey, and Tampico. Colonel Kearny led his Army of the West against New Mexico and into Upper California.

Texas, New Mexico, and California, the three outposts of northern Spain in America, were not vital in the life of Mexico, but were accessible to the United States. Taylor held Texas, and by occupying the Mexican states west of the Rio Grande established the American purpose at this point. The duty of Kearny, assigned him in the early summer of 1846, was to raise an army on the Missouri border and march overland to New Mexico and California. The war was started too late for his expedition to have the advantage of the best pasturage on the plains; but Colonel Benton, who knew all the conditions of plains travel, assured the War Department that the army could get through if it left the Missouri before the end of July.

In addition to this detachment of regular troops, increased by enlistments, Missouri was called upon for militia, and one of Kearny's captains was sent to Council Bluffs, where the Mormon leaders let him have a battalion of about five hundred of their young men. Kearny, with his main body, moved along the trail to Santa Fé in July. Until he reached Bent's Fort on the Arkansas River, where the route to Santa Fé turned southward, there was no danger and no need for military organization. Between this point and Las Vegas, he maintained a military watchfulness. In the mountains between Las Vegas and Santa Fé, he learned from Mexican captives of armies raised against him and ambushes planted in the cañons; but none of these materialized and he marched into the

capital of New Mexico unharmed, on August 18. He declared
New Mexico annexed to the United States, gave it a territorial
form of government and proceeded down the Del Norte upon the
way to California. In a few days his plans in this direction were
changed, because he met a small party of dispatch bearers commanded by Colonel Christopher Carson, who carried the glad
news that California was already taken. It was no longer necessary for Kearny to lead an army through the arid valley of the
Gila River and across the desert of southern California, and he
sent it back, save for an escort with which he hurried on to fulfill
his mission; for his orders directed him to assume the military
governorship of California once it was conquered. In December
he entered San Diego. The notes and sketches made by W. H.
Emory, one of his party, became the basis for a report and guide
book to the country between Fort Leavenworth and San Diego
that ranks in importance with Frémont's volume on the road to
Oregon.[4] The army that Kearny left behind him on the Rio
Grande, proceeded under Colonel Doniphan to invade Mexico by
way of El Paso, and there established connection with the right
wing of Taylor's force.

The establishment of peace with Mexico was begun even earlier
than the opening engagement of the war. After the rupture of
diplomatic relations in 1845 Polk sent to Mexico a special commissioner, John Slidell, to undertake the purchase of New Mexico
and Upper California. He hoped to pay for this by having the
United States assume the financial claims against Mexico. Slidell
spent the winter of 1845–1846 in Mexico in a vain attempt to
carry out his instructions. The Mexican Government would not
even receive him as a minister.

A second attempt to reach an agreement was made at the time
of Scott's invasion, when the chief clerk of the State Department,
N. P. Trist, was sent to Mexico in April, 1847. Like Slidell, Trist
was to try for a peace ceding California and New Mexico; in addition he was instructed to try to get Lower California. Trist traveled with Scott's headquarters and was a cause of great dissatisfaction to the commander, who resented his presence there, although
eventually the two found a basis for common action. In July and
August there were numerous proposals and counter-proposals
with the Mexicans, but until after the occupation of Mexico City

---

[4] William H. Emory, *Notes of a Military Reconnoissance from Fort Leavenworth to San Diego* (30th Congress, 1st Session, Senate Executive Document 7).

in September, it was not possible to start serious negotiations. The treaty was at last signed at Guadalupe-Hidalgo on February 2, 1848. In this agreement Mexico accepted the line of the Rio Grande, which the Texans had extorted from General Santa Anna after the battle of San Jacinto; and an extension from it westward from El Paso, along the Gila to the Gulf of California, and thence to the Pacific, south of San Diego Bay. The United States, on its part, assumed the claims against Mexico and paid $15,000,000 to Mexico in cash. The Senate ratified the treaty; with regret not because it added territory to the United States, but because the desires that had grown with war were not completely satisfied. There was a minority that wanted Chihuahua and Sonora and there were some who thought that now was the time to take all Mexico and annex it. The conquered republic had little to say in the settlement, for the victor had taken what he pleased and retained what he wanted, on his own terms.

CHAPTER XL

THE CONQUEST OF CALIFORNIA

THE transfer of title to Upper California and New Mexico and the adjustment of the Texas line came at the close of the Mexican War; but the real conquest of California was so nearly concluded before the war began that the Treaty of Guadalupe-Hidalgo was only a recognition of the accomplished fact. Upper California was the newest of the provinces of Spain, created because of the dangers impending upon the northern frontier; and lost because those dangers were greater than the power of the nation that foresaw them. It was the terminal of the westernmost of the three great highways originating in Durango and extending as arteries to the furthest outposts of the old empire.

Alta California, and indeed Baja California, the long peninsula south of it, lay outside the scheme of Spain in America until after the settlement of Philadelphia, and the overthrow of James II by William of Orange.[1] The priests and soldiers who carried Spanish civilization into the interior reached Santa Fé nearly a century earlier and were familiar with the plains of Texas and the trail to Nacogdoches long before 1687, when the Jesuit, Father Eusebio Kino, built his convent near the head of the Santa Cruz River, south of the future site of Tucson.[2] From this station he operated for the rest of his life, baptizing thousands of Indians with his own hand, and traversing every part of the country between the Gila and the Sonora rivers. He believed that California was an island, and the maritime exploits of Spain were so modest that the real topography of the Pacific Coast remained long a mystery. It was indeed a closed sea, calmly appropriated by Spain, without contest except by an occasional freebooting privateer like Sir Francis Drake, who skirted the American coasts about 1579.

The occupation of Lower California began shortly after Kino settled in Sonora, and for the eighty years that elapsed before Spain expelled them from America (1767) the Jesuits were active in planting missions among the Indians. The Spanish crown, in

---

[1] Irving B. Richman, *California under Spain and Mexico* (1911); T. H. Hittell, *History of California* (1885), shares with Bancroft the distinction of voluminous detail.

[2] Herbert E. Bolton, *Father Kino's Memoirs* (1919).

1697, authorized the creation of a Pious Fund to be raised by contributions from the charitable and to be expended in this work. Loreto, on the Gulf side of the peninsula, was the first fruit of this enterprise, and eighteen missions in all were built under Jesuit control. Kino lived long enough to learn that Baja California was a part of the continent, and published in 1705 a map that showed it as a peninsula. The Jesuit establishments extended north to near the head of the Gulf of California, and when they were expelled, their country was given over to the Dominican order, while the Franciscans received a free hand north of them, above the latitude of San Diego Bay, in Alta California. At the same moment the occupation of Alta California became a matter of grave concern to a far-seeing statesman of New Spain, José de Gálvez.

The European treaties of 1762 and 1763 brought problems to Spain as to England, when the former possessions of France were divided between these two. Spain was not anxious to receive Louisiana or to extend the frontier to New Orleans; and took few steps to amalgamate Louisiana and Texas. It was regarded as a buffer province, and its possession brought a clearer vision of the dangers that threatened the kind of empire that Spain maintained. On the north were the fur traders of England and Russia, whose annual hunts brought them each year nearer to the Spanish outposts and put in danger the policy of monopoly and isolation that Spain encouraged. The English settlers were to the east, and it took few months to reveal the weakness of the Proclamation of 1763 in restricting their occupation to the Atlantic seaboard. The cessions of 1763 brought them nearer to New Orleans. Their more adventurous traders were already pushing up the valley of the Arkansas River. The time would come when English or Russians, or both, would press in upon New Spain. Hence Gálvez memorialized the crown to reorganize the provinces and to occupy Upper California. The creation of the Provincias Internas in 1776 met a part of his desire. The military expedition she proposed were under way in 1769.

San Diego Bay was the first objective in the occupation of Upper California. A small naval expedition sent from the new port of San Blas, on the west coast of Mexico, visited the bay at about the same time that an overland expedition reached San Diego from Lower California. The soldiers and priests in the latter were led by Father Junípero Serra and Governor Gaspar de Portolá and established a mission and a presidio at their destination in the summer of 1769. In the next few years their followers overran California, as far north as the valley of the Sacramento. Portolá, himself, advanced far enough in the autumn of 1769 to discover what no Spaniard had hitherto expected; that there was a great land-locked harbor behind the Golden Gates, and that San Francisco Bay was more important as a strategic point than either San Diego or Monterey which was occupied in 1770. There was no Spanish establishment on San Francisco Bay until 1776, and no town bearing its name until after the American conquest.[3] In the course of time a village called Yerba Buena grew up outside the presidio and was occupied by the civilian hangers-on of the Spanish occupation. But it remained true here, as elsewhere in Spanish America, that there was no steady stream of Castilian emigrants coming to make new homes and carry on the fight against nature. Only those Spaniards who failed to attain their desire of an independent fortune were willing to remain exiles from home. The successful exploiters of America went back. Those who remained hovered under the walls of presidio or mission, or procured grants of land in the valleys and developed an easy-going ranch life, in a hospitable country.

The Spanish defensive thrust, inspired by Gálvez as *visitador general*, and executed by him as Minister of the Indies, stopped at the northern border of the bay of San Francisco. Alta California was never extended much above the mouth of the Sacramento River. Every extension lengthened the line of communication to Mexico City and increased the cost of holding it. The Spanish crown had no money to sink in the venture and the Spanish people had no desire to occupy the land. By the close of the eighteenth century the frontier of Spanish occupation was rubbing against that of Russia; and from the East, the advance guard of English and American influence was pushing across the Rocky Mountains.

For about fifty years after the occupation of Upper California, Spain maintained here a life of Arcadian deprivation. Land was cheap and plenty, and live stock found its own food and flourished without care. Wealth in the form of herds was easily obtained, and the genial climate lessened the importance of clothing and shelter. The land barons, with holdings running up into the thousands of square leagues, lived much like those of New Mexico in their adobe ranch houses. Their wives and daughters were able to wear jewels and silks, and to tread the clay floors of their homes in

[3] Z. S. Eldredge, *The Beginnings of San Francisco, 1754–1850* (1912).

satin slippers that had made the journey from Seville by way of Vera Cruz. Their half-breed dependents were the offspring of Indian women who had married soldiers discharged from the army at the presidios. The field laborers, so far as they had them, were the Indians themselves; for whom the acceptance of Christianity meant baptism and labor. There was the same sort of isolation from the currents of the world as prevailed at Santa Fé, but it was tempered somewhat by the fact that the Pacific Ocean was coming to be dotted with flags other than those of Spain. The whalers from the northern Pacific and the vessels on the China trade persisted in touching at San Diego and Monterey in spite of the refusal of Spain to welcome them there. They wanted water, potatoes, and fresh vegetables or meat. They had fish to sell and often Yankee notions. Few of the governors whose duty was to rebuff them were stern enough to resist the influence of presents or bribes, and the Spanish system throve on graft. There were, therefore, occasional contacts with foreigners and a small amount of trade in goods that Santa Fé could not get. There were even a few deserting seamen from the ships, who stayed in California and were tolerated by the Spanish residents. In 1846 there were not many more than six thousand Mexicans or Spaniards in all of Upper California.

The golden age had begun to change before 1830, when in Texas the attempt was made to exclude further American immigration by law. The Spanish boundary treaty of 1819 defined the northern and eastern limits of California just in time to give point to the trespasses that were being made by American fur traders and explorers. In 1823 General William H. Ashley, of the Rocky Mountain Fur Company, found the South Pass, through which his successors trod the way to Oregon. In the same year Jedediah S. Smith hunted in the country around the Great Salt Lake. Before Smith lost his way on the Santa Fé Trail in 1831 and was murdered by the Indians, he had crossed and recrossed the Nevada Desert, and spent winters both in Oregon and in California. After the fuller development of the Oregon Trail in 1832, the stragglers who wandered south into California became more numerous, and before the 1843 migration to Oregon the charm of California was receiving advertisement from the professional occupants of the Far West.

Johann August Sutter, a German who having acquired Swiss citizenship gave it up for Mexican naturalization, became the most active center of American influence in California in the year 1839. He settled on the south bank of the American River, which is one of the largest eastern tributaries of the Sacramento, somewhat above the junction of the streams. The modern city of Sacramento lies in the angle south and east of their junction. Here Sutter founded his New Helvetia, in Mexican territory, but as far removed from the activities of the Mexicans and their officials as could be accomplished without arousing adverse attention; and here he bought from the Russian-American Company their trading station, Fort Ross, which was the farthest south of Russian penetration. After 1840, Sutter with his fort, his farms, his herds, and his henchmen, was a continuous source of apprehension to the Mexican authorities at Monterey, although they gave him official standing as an alcalde, or petty magistrate. He became, as well, the friend and outfitter of the stragglers who crossed the Sierra Nevada. Most of the passes from the Nevada Desert to the coast, whether above or below Lake Tahoe, descend on the western side to some of the tributaries of the American River. The first sign of civilization that the trader or explorer saw was Sutter's ranch. In its owner they found a man of cultivated interests, ready to help them and to supply their needs. In California, Sutter played much the same part that Dr. McLoughlin played in Oregon.

The Oregon migration of traders and missionaries, as has been seen, was an annual affair after 1832, and made a small beginning with homeseekers led by Dr. White in 1842. Thereafter the emigrants were numbered by thousands, and the trail from Independence to The Dalles, where the Columbia River breaks through the Cascade Mountains, was crowded with wagons and marked with the wreckage and graves of the emigrant trains. As early as 1841 occasional members of the procession avowed their destination to be not Oregon, but Upper California. The fact that this belonged to Mexico was no more of an obstacle than was Mexican ownership of Texas; or than the Sauk and Fox hunting rights in Illinois had been to the prairie farmers.

The historian of *The Trans-Mississippi West* (1922), Professor Cardinal Goodwin, tells of the excitement caused along the Missouri border by one of the earliest of the California "boosters," a French trapper, Robidoux by name. Robidoux had been West, and described California as "a perfect paradise, a perpetual spring." He made it appear like the Garden of Eden, when he declared that there was freedom from chills and fever. "There never was but one man in California who had the ague," he asserted. "He was from Missouri, and carried the disease in his system. It was such a curiosity to see a man shake with the chills that the people of Monterey went eighteen miles into the country to watch him." In 1841 a caravan of forty-eight, whose secretary, John Bidwell, has left among the Bancroft manuscripts *An Immigrant's Recollections of a Trip across the Plains*, went from Missouri over the familiar Platte trail to the vicinity of Fort Hall on the Snake River. Here they made their own trail across the alkaline plains to the Humboldt River, which they followed down its course until it empties into its "sink." They found their way across the Sierra Nevada and into the southern side of San Francisco Bay where the party was broken up.

Every year after 1841 there were parties on the trail for California. In the winter of 1843 Frémont visited the country. His first expedition to South Pass in 1842 was followed the next season by a trip to the mouth of the Columbia. From The Dalles of the Columbia he turned south. The maps of 1843 were still inaccurate in their details of Pacific topography, and it was in particular uncertain whether there was any great natural highway to the coast south of the Columbia. It was known that the Colorado was not a highway. Its deep, rough gorge constituted an almost impossible barrier from its head, at the junction of the Grand and the Green, to its mouth at the Gulf of California. Except at two or three places abreast of the southern part of California, it has not been possible to take a railroad across the cañon; and even at these crossings the steep sides of the ravine through which the river bottom runs have offered refractory problems in engineering. At Yuma, near the mouth of the river, was the easiest way across, where the Spanish priests and explorers had found their way through from Sonora to the Pacific. There was a party of emigrants who used this route, going from Missouri to Santa Fé, and through Yuma, in 1841. But the Colorado River itself constituted a barrier for all time.

The maps of the early nineteenth century, based on rumor and the reports of missionary parties, showed a River Buenaventura, rising near Great Salt Lake and flowing into the Pacific through a pass not far from Lake Tahoe. Undoubtedly the maps were founded upon a visit to the upper course of the Humboldt River, and the assumption that it must find its way to the sea. The fact that the stream empties into a lake and marsh, known as the Humboldt Sink, could be ascertained only by observation. Frémont set the issue at rest in the winter of 1843–1844, when he moved south along the Sierra Nevada, from the Columbia to southern California, and proved that the Buenaventura was a myth. His journal and map, published the next spring, helped to disseminate true knowledge of the coast district. Several hundred emigrants crossed the trail to California in 1844 and 1845. In the latter year, an organized effort was made to meet the Oregon caravan at Fort Hall, and to divert a large fraction of it to California. In 1846, in spite of the state of war, the emigrants crowded the trails and California ranked with Oregon in the public mind.

The Donner party of 1846 has commonly been mentioned to illustrate the hardships and dangers of the California trail. It shows, quite as pointedly, the fact that California, of itself, had become an objective of the westward drift. The Donners, George and Jacob, and their party, were among the hundreds of Mississippi Valley farmers who made up their minds to experiment with the Far West in the winter of 1845. They made their preparations carefully. They had considerable property and some ready money. There were eighty-seven in their immediate group, which acquired a special identity west of South Pass. Up to this point, they marched with the caravan. Here they refused to be guided by the common judgment and insisted on trying a cut-off running south of Great Salt Lake, instead of keeping the main road across its northern end. They were slowed down by inexperience and poor guides and reached the Sierra after winter had closed in. The heavy drifts of mountain snow held them prisoners and buried their live stock. The rescuing party in the spring found that they had cut firewood from the topmost branches of trees of considerable size, because the snow had hidden everything else. Thirty-nine of the party died. The fact that their sufferings were due to stubbornness and ignorance did not lessen the catastrophe or intimidate others from venturing upon the plains.[4]

The Mexican War hastened the annexation of California but did not cause its conquest. This was under way before the war began. The peaceful penetration that carried the frontier of the United States into Texas and Oregon was at work and must have produced the same results in California. When the rumor of war

---

[4] A child of the party wrote in her old age Eliza P. Donner Houghton, *Expedition of the Donner Party and its Tragic Fate* (1911). The women and children were all brought through.

reached the Americans on the bay of San Francisco they possessed the initiative to act for themselves.

The Bear Flag Republic sprang to life before the declaration of war was known to the Americans in California. The preliminary instructions, prepared in 1845 for Sloat and Larkin, were forwarded in duplicate to these agents, and one set of them came through in the hands of A. H. Gillespie, whom the President sent as a dispatch bearer. Gillespie delivered the instructions to Sloat in writing; to Larkin he repeated them verbally, having committed the original to memory and then destroyed it. He visited Monterey, and Yerba Buena and New Helvetia, and then pushed on northward in search of Frémont's camp. He brought Frémont back to the Sacramento, although it is still a mystery what he said to him, or what he had a right to say. In June Frémont made a camp on the Feather River, which is the next great eastern tributary of the Sacramento, north of the American Fork. The Americans of the region at this time convinced themselves that the Mexican authorities were raising a force to expel the foreigners. They organized a raiding party, seized a herd of Mexican horses, and on June 14 raised the flag of revolt at Sonoma. They made a flag carrying a red star and a bear, and called themselves an independent republic. They invited Frémont to put himself at the head of their movement; and he, after a modest hesitation, accepted the responsibility. Their career was cut short by the arrival of Sloat, with news of the declaration of war, and orders to seize Monterey and possess himself of California.

The resistance of the Californians to the American conquest was brief and slight. The Mexican troops were too few in number to offer serious obstruction, and the Mexican population was dispersed over too wide an area to be mobilized for defense. The bond of union with Mexico was fragile at best and was weakened by the glimpses of the outside world that Californians had gained because of their position on the Pacific. The forces of Sloat, Frémont, and the revolutionists were joined in July, and Commodore Stockton who soon arrived to relieve Sloat continued active coöperation to make the conquest permanent. San Diego and Los Angeles were occupied, as well as all the places around the bay. There was a revolt of the Spanish in southern California in the autumn, and Stockton was temporarily forced to abandon both San Diego and Los Angeles. But in December Kearny arrived by the Yuma route, and early in January, 1847, all resistance ceased. Thereafter the only trouble of the American commanders in California was whether Stockton or Kearny was in command, with authority to govern the province until the President should otherwise direct. Each had sweeping orders, from the Secretaries of War and the Navy respectively; and each was disposed to insist upon his own supremacy. They took it out upon Frémont, who had no orders at all, and was their junior. By giving him inconsistent commands, they forced him to disobedience; and eventually they arrested him and sent him east for court-martial.[5]

In December, 1847, Polk discussed with Congress the fact that New Mexico and California "are now in our undisputed possession, and have been so for many months, all resistance on the part of Mexico having ceased within their limits." He did not propose to relinquish either of the provinces, since only by holding them would the United States be able to procure an indemnity for the war and its precedent grievances. "Mexico commenced the war," he said, "and we were compelled in self-defence to repel the invader and to vindicate the national honor and interests . . ." He recommended that Congress extend the "civil jurisdiction and laws of the United States" over them at once, without waiting for formal treaty of relinquishment from Mexico. He urged again, as he had urged in 1846 and 1845, that a territorial government be provided for the settlers in Oregon. The only government they possessed was a temporary and extra-legal agreement of their own, which was "wholly inadequate to protect them in their rights of person and property, or to secure to them the enjoyment of the privileges of other citizens." In less than two years the thrust of migration to the Pacific had changed the balance of the United States, pushing its borders northwest to Puget Sound and southwest to San Diego Bay, and forcing upon the attention of Congress the political disposition of a domain half as large as the whole United States had been before 1845. Once more the frontier had called the tune; but this time the politicians of the East and South were locked in a struggle of their own which must be settled before they could adjust western problems on their merits.

[5] John Charles Frémont, *Memoirs of my Life Including in the Narrative Five Journeys of Western Exploration* (vol. I, 1887). The publication and profit of Grant's memoirs greatly stimulated autobiography writing.

CHAPTER XLI
FAR WEST AND POLITICS

THE hope of President Polk that Congress might in 1847–1848 take up and adjust the government of the region beyond the Rockies was doomed to disappointment. At the opening of the session Scott was in Mexico City and the other generals were in undisputed possession of their conquests; but the treaty was not signed, and storms of politics were rising in intensity. During the following spring the treaty of Guadalupe-Hidalgo was completed, and the American factions set to on the issue of slavery in the territories. The northern forces that had tried to limit the war with David Wilmot's proviso that there should never be slavery in the territory to be acquired, hoped to beat the party of Polk in the presidential election that was impending. They chose a southern Whig and a military hero, Zachary Taylor, as their party chief, and elected him over Lewis Cass, Democrat, of Michigan. It was not a clear contest, and Taylor was again a minority President, as Polk had been; and as in 1844 the victory was due less to the power of the candidate than to the fact that a split in New York factions kept its preferred party from carrying the State. With New York reversed, Cass would have won, as Clay would have won in 1844.

The measures for organizing the Far West were pushed during 1848 without much result. The free soil demand was that the status of slavery must be settled first and that it must be forbidden in the whole area. Polk believed that it would be a fair compromise to extend the line of 36° 30′ to the Pacific and prohibit slavery north of that line. Calhoun advanced the doctrine later summarized in the words "the Constitution follows the flag," and declared that the Constitution was already in force in the Far West, and by implication legalized slavery everywhere. Webster denied that the Constitution could affect anything but States in the Union and said that the Far West was already free because there had not been slavery in either Oregon or California. The southern politicians became devotees of the Missouri Compromise because by declaring its effectiveness to make Oregon free, they could claim that it made the other territories slave.

A bill to organize Oregon, New Mexico, and California was debated in 1848, but when it passed in August only the first territory survived the debate. Polk signed the Oregon bill August 14, 1848, and explained at length that he did so only because Oregon was so far north of 36° 30′ that it was certain to be free in any event. The remaining problems of the conquered territory could not be solved this year, or even the next.

After the creation of Oregon Territory there remained four concrete questions respecting the new country. Nearest home was a question on the Texas boundary. The United States had espoused against Mexico the Texas claim to the Rio Grande as a western boundary, but was not disposed to admit the validity of the claim as against itself. The province of New Mexico, which the United States and not Texas had taken, always included both sides of the Del Norte, or upper Rio Grande. To concede the whole of the Texas claim would throw into Texas half of New Mexico. On the other hand, if the Texas claim were denied, it would discredit the American contention that by the annexation of Texas "American soil" was extended up to the Rio Grande. There was need here for a careful compromise, and Texas, aware of its opportunity, was hopeful of passing its revolutionary debt to the United States in return for territorial concessions on the Del Norte.

Beyond Texas were three territorial problems. The Mormon State of Deseret was organized in 1849. Some form of government had to be allowed to these settlers, however unpopular they were. If population and solvency alone were to count, they were as ripe for admission as a State as many of their Mississippi Valley predecessors had been. There must also be a territory for New Mexico, and since Spain had never drawn any boundary between the Rio Grande and the Salt Lake basin, this line must be drawn with reasonable regard for the facts of settlement and convenience. Finally there was a population in California, with a Spanish civilization, and an American admixture, and a boundary fairly well defined by fact.

In addition to the various bases of settling their relationships that prevented action during the final months of Polk's tenure of presidency, there was still one more that Taylor confided to the retiring President as they drove to the Capitol for inauguration. This was to let them organize themselves and go; to relieve the United States from the responsibilities of States so remote from the seat of government, and to let the Rockies continue to be the western boundary of the American people. For a President who had based his policy upon the expansion of the national domain nothing could have been more heart-breaking from his successor.

While Congress debated and parties fulminated upon the Far West, the course of development continued without hindrance, so altering the problem as to reduce to unimportant dimensions that part of it which Congress could by legislation affect. Migration into Oregon and California was stimulated by the new notoriety of the region. The caravans of 1846 were surpassed by those of 1847; these in turn were small compared with those of 1848. And in 1849 the dimensions broke all records because a new factor had come in. Gold was discovered on Sutter's ranch, and the whole world turned its attention toward El Dorado.

The active life that found its center on the Sacramento, where Sutter's establishment gave a focus to the various currents of American penetration, was stimulated by the events of the Mexican War. Sutter found a ready market for his live stock, and as a community of Americans grew up on San Francisco Bay, the need for supplies of food opened the doors of a new prosperity to him. The little village of Yerba Buena throve under American occupation. Early in 1847 it had an American alcalde, for most of the victors accepted the Mexican law as still in force and operated through it. There were legal discussions whether the conquest had destroyed all law, and left California in a state of nature, or whether Mexican law remained intact, or whether by the fact of conquest the Constitution of the United States became immediately operative. But Congress worried over these matters more than the settlers, who took over the government, renamed Yerba Buena, calling it San Francisco, in January, 1847; and who plotted a town site along the water front. The frontier passion for speculation in real estate followed the flag, whether the Constitution did or not.

In the following winter Sutter undertook to manufacture lumber for the San Francisco market. He chose a site about forty-five miles above his fort, on the south branch of the American, where there was a good water power, and employed a handy man, one J. W. Marshall, to build the mill. Marshall was able to hire as laborers some of the discharged members of the Mormon battalion who had been brought to California with Kearny's force. He found loose flakes of gold in the bottom of the mill race on January 24, 1848, and hurried down to the fort to break the news to Sutter. They tried to keep the matter secret, for Sutter knew his mill would pay and had his doubts about the gold. But by the middle of March the California paper printed it, and the floating population of the coast started towards the diggings.

The gold was not hard to find. Auriferous rocks underlie the continental divide from Central America to the Yukon, and since the beginning of the present geological era the mountain streams have been washing free particles away from their lodes and depositing them in the sand banks at the bottom of their precipitous courses. In the thirty years after Marshall's discovery, the mineral empire was extended in every direction, and thousands of camps sprang up around one discovery or another.[1] The first prospectors could start without either experience or equipment. The shovel, pick, and pan were the only indispensable tools. Water was necessary, and deposits where there was no natural supply of water waited for their development until engineering methods became more sophisticated. Meanwhile, along the bottoms of a multitude of streams, prospectors washed the sand and gravel, and watched the sediment for shining particles, and found them. When the first placer miner discovered gold on a new stream, he and his associates organized a mining district and adopted laws determining the number of running feet of river bottom each claimant was entitled to, and the distance up the hills on either side that the claim might go. They decided how much work the finder must do to establish a claim and how much to hold it. They recorded on their informal books the claims and their transfers and did the work so well that when the laws caught up with the prospectors, it was generally enough to give legal effect to the agreements already in force.[2] Mining law upon the American frontier was a spontaneous growth, embodying some of the experience of Welsh and Spanish miners, but mostly representing the practical adjustments reached on the ground by men used to self-government. It differed from the land law in that it was not the work of non-resident legislators or social theorists.

In the summer of 1848 the tributaries of the American became the center of interest on the Pacific. San Francisco was almost entirely desolated, as its able-bodied population boarded up their

[1] William J. Trimble, *The Mining Advance into the Inland Empire* (1914), University of Wisconsin *Bulletin*, No. 638.

[2] T. M. Marshall, *Early Records of Gilpin County, Colorado, 1859–1861* (1920), vol. II of University of Colorado *Historical Collections*, contains many documents illustrating the habits of a typical mining community; C. H. Shinn, "Land Laws of Mining Districts," in Johns Hopkins University *Studies*, vol. II.

houses and shops and hurried to the diggings. The local paper, the *Californian*, that might have become an invaluable historical source, suspended publication May 29, 1848, for it, too, had joined the rush. The news spread up the coast, and from Oregon there came a stream of men down the Sacramento Valley. It spread down the coast and speculators hurried up from Mexico and the Latin states. They came from Hawaii and China and Japan as fast as the news could carry out, and chance sailing ships could bring them back. San Francisco sprang to life again, after a temporary unconsciousness, because of the profits of the supply trade. By the summer of 1848, immigrants were passing through the town by thousands, and enough gold dust was coming back from the diggings to prove that the discovery was a fact.

Consul Larkin reported to the State Department, on June 1, that twenty thousand dollars' worth of gold had come into San Francisco in the preceding two weeks. He visited the camps on the American in person in June, and Governor Mason followed him later in the summer. Their official reports described the intensity of the rush. Every one seems to have gone to the diggings except Sutter, who stuck to his ranch and was harvesting a wheat crop, to sell it at thirty-six dollars a bushel. Troops deserted the army detachments in California or on the western plains. Seamen abandoned their ships in port and left the vessels stranded without men to move them.

The news of the discovery reached the States in time to be given to the public when Congress met in 1848, but Polk's *Diary*, which generally pictures the President's thoughts, shows that he was slow in realizing that the course of western development had been changed. California was lifted by a single stroke from the status of a remote frontier to be settled gradually as farmers were willing to risk the trip, to that of a speculative adventure that would attract in a single year more than enough people to warrant an immediate State. The President was slow to see it; but shipmasters at every Atlantic port felt its significance, and announced sailings at once to San Francisco or to the Isthmus of Panama. When the vessels sailed they were crowded with passengers, young men predominating, inspired with the gambler's hope.

In the ordinary routine of business, Congress had made provision for regular communication with California in 1848. It had authorized a mail route thither, to be carried by water and the Isthmus. The contractor, William H. Aspinwall, had sent steamers in ballast around the Horn to carry on the western leg of the route. They left the East before the news arrived, but learned it as they touched at South American ports. When they reached Panama, they found waiting there a clamorous crowd, brought by steamer from New Orleans or New York, demanding instant passage to San Francisco. The immigration of 1849 began with the landing at San Francisco of the first installment of the ocean-borne gold seekers, February 28, 1849.

The water route was the rich man's method of getting to California. The cost was heavy but the trip was quicker and less laborious than on the overland route. This way went the merchants and public officials: as well as the gamblers and parasites, for the idea of easy money brought into the migration a social element notably lacking in the ordinary movements to a new frontier. The great mass of the gold seekers, however, were forced to be content with the same methods that the Oregonians and the Mormons had been using for many years. They prepared their wagons, stock, and outfit in the late winter; and in the early spring took to the roads across Iowa or Missouri that came to a focus upon the great bend of the river, between Independence and the Mormon town of Kanesville, at Council Bluffs.

The Platte route was by no means the only land way to California. There are numerous records of companies of emigrants who followed the Santa Fé Trail and Kearny's road beyond it to southern California. Other southern routes converged at the Yuma crossing of the Colorado River. There were trails across Texas to El Paso; and thence to Kearny's road. Some parties crossed Mexico and followed the padres' trail through Sonora to the Gila River and the Colorado. But the first reported diggings were upon the northern side of San Francisco Bay, to which the Platte and the Humboldt gave the most direct access. Even the "southern mines" were well north, being upon the feeders of the San Joaquin River, with Stockton as their supply center. The San Joaquin and the Sacramento empty into the same arm of San Francisco Bay.

The emigration of the "forty-niners" was the largest and most heterogeneous that the plains had seen. It was not made up of persons selected as closely as most other migrations were. There were more bachelors, for the gold fields were not regarded as a place for women. There were more who were so poor that they could not provide even the simple outfit of the farmer emigrant.

There were many who were not farmers at all, for the lure of gold caught the townsmen. There were many who had failed at everything, as well as young men with their future still before them. There were numerous companies that maintained close order upon the march and drew their wagons at night into the corral for safety. But there were others who traveled alone, and some in light wagons who hurried along much faster than the procession. Many were so inexperienced that they began to discard equipment that they could not carry before they reached Fort Kearny on the Platte.

The Mormons on Great Salt Lake received the forty-niners as a direct interposition of providence for their benefit. The first year in the desert, 1847–1848, tested the Mormon organization and courage, for in the flight from Nauvoo they had left behind or lost much of their movable property. Not until they harvested their crop of 1848 were they free from danger of starvation. When they brought in the early crops of 1849, they knew that the procession of gold seekers would want supplies and that they could provide them. Many a Mormon farmer did a profitable business in live stock, picking up the emaciated animals of emigrants for a song, fattening them for a few months, and selling them again at a fancy price. Few of the forty-niners had much money, but they had goods — furniture, tools, farm implements that they could not carry further with their animals dropping exhausted, but which the Mormons needed. The exchange was unavoidable for the miners, and profitable for the Mormons, who by the end of 1849 were well-organized, well-fed, and well-supplied.

The tide of gold seekers continued to flow for many years. In 1850 there were 92,597 persons whom the enumerators could find in California; in 1860, 379,994. The local historians have tried to estimate the annual accessions, the most reliable guess being that of Hubert Howe Bancroft, himself an immigrant of 1852. Bancroft set up in business in San Francisco and began at once to collect printed and manuscript materials for the history of the Pacific Slope. To-day, in the library of the Academy of Pacific Coast History, his collection holds for its region the place held by the Draper Collections of the State Historical Society of Wisconsin in the history of the Old Northwest. It was Bancroft's estimate that some forty-two thousand persons completed the trip by the Platte route to California in 1849. But the volume of emigration cannot be measured by the survivors, for after the first few weeks the Californians were met every day by the returning procession of those whose courage or supplies had given out and who were returning home. And near every camping ground the fresh graves and wooden crosses gave a clue to the multitude that died. A cholera epidemic accompanied the march as far as Fort Laramie, with a mortality of perhaps five thousand; and in the dry valley of the Humboldt there were starvation and thirst for many more.

In the first months after the overturn of Mexican power in California the executive duties of government fell upon the shoulders of the army. Stockton exercised the powers, and then Kearny, and later a series of deputies whose right to rule was founded upon the power of the President as commander-in-chief of the armies of the United States. The ratification of the treaty of cession made no change in this, for until Congress saw fit to act, there were no American laws that could extend to California of their own force. Americans elected themselves to local offices, and the native Californians, who had had little use for Mexico, accepted the new rule and coöperated with it. The recommendations of Polk to Congress in 1847 brought no result. He repeated them in 1848 with still no result. He left office with forebodings as to Taylor's western policy disturbing his mind.

When Congress adjourned without action, in March, 1849, and the size of the migration indicated that the whole scale of California affairs was to be magnified, there was concern about the civil status of the colony in San Francisco and in Washington. Taylor was less dangerous than his threat, and responsibility and knowledge made him give up the idea that the Pacific communities must be allowed to go. Instead of this he sent a confidential agent to California a few weeks after his inauguration, with word that the mining camps had better draw up a constitution for themselves and make immediate application for admission to the Union. General Bennett Riley, who now commanded the troops in California, was instructed to coöperate with such a movement, and the immigrants themselves were more than ready. Beyond the limited amount that could be done by voluntary association in the mining districts, by self-help, and by an occasional vigilance committee formed by outraged citizens, the community had no accepted basis of law and order.[3] Men went armed, and the nature of both their business and their play made altercation and combats

---

[3] Porter Garnett, *Papers of the San Francisco Vigilance Committee of 1851*, in Academy of Pacific Coast History *Publications*, vol. i; Mary Floyd Williams, *History of the San Francisco Vigilance Committee of 1851*, in University of California *Publications in History*, vol. xii.

frequent. There was gold dust, quickly got and as quickly spent. There were grog shops, gamblers, and dance halls without number, to prey upon the miners. The men themselves were mostly young and care-free. There were few family ties to make for decency and self-restraint. Yet the community did not disintegrate into anarchy. From the first arrivals, the average immigrant believed in law; and there was a steady development of orderly habits that culminated in a constitutional convention, held at Monterey in September, 1849.[4]

A native Tennesseean, William M. Gwin, who had come to California from Louisiana, carrying with him a copy of the new constitution of Iowa, was the most influential member of the Monterey convention. His associates were chosen by free male citizens of the United States or the conquered area, aged twenty-one, and actually resident in California. They came from thirty States and from a wider range of economic and social conditions than was usual in a new frontier. Their work, says Professor Thorpe, illustrates "the potency of those political ideas which, in the opinion of so varied a body of delegates, were best fitted to survive." There was a slight majority of members from free States, and a much stronger opinion that slavery was not fitted to California conditions. The miners objected to having claims worked by slaves, as a few of them tried to do; and obstructed the attempt of some slave owners to take out claims in the names of their slaves as well as their own. Gwin printed the constitution of Iowa in an edition with wide margins, on which changes were noted by the delegates. The new State forbade the institution of slavery in its basic law, after a thorough debate of all the aspects of the subject that took up nearly half the whole time the convention was in session. It limited the suffrage to free white citizens. The constitution was submitted to the people in November and was ratified by the huge majority of 12,061 to 811 votes. A State government was elected in December, and a congressional delegation led by Gwin and Frémont, senators-elect. When Taylor met his first Congress in December, 1849, a new State had been formed and was asking admission on terms not fixed by the slavery politicians, but by its own free citizens.

[4] R. D. Hunt, "Genesis of California's First Constitution," in Johns Hopkins University *Studies*, vol. XIII, is one of the institutional monographs inspired by Herbert B. Adams; more elaborate is Cardinal Goodwin, *Establishment of State Government in California* (1914). The first governor of California, who was also an Oregon emigrant, has left Peter H. Burnett, *Recollections and Opinions of an old Pioneer* (1880).

The adjustment of the territorial problem of the Far West, now three years overdue, was no longer subject to theoretical legislation. The only region likely to have a large population had settled its own status. There were still details to be worked out respecting the Texas-New Mexico boundary, and the government of New Mexico and Utah; but the southern leaders, dismayed and exasperated by the California development, sought compensation in other directions and uttered again the threat to break the Union. A convention, attended mostly by southern Democrats, met at Nashville in June, 1850, to consider plans of action in the light of the existing federal situation, as the New England Federalists had done at Hartford, in December, 1814. It failed to recommend the extreme step of disunion, for in the meantime the national leaders had brought forward a scheme of compromise that was based upon a frank and admitted fear of secession. The Compromise of 1850 was carried into effect in a series of laws that were signed by the President in September, 1850. It was not Zachary Taylor who signed them, however, for he had died in July, 1850, and had left the office for Vice President Millard Fillmore, a New York Whig.

Henry Clay introduced his resolutions for "the peace, concord, and harmony of the Union," in January, 1850; and they were the subject of continuous and solemn debate for eight months. They could never have been passed as a body, for each of the measures aroused bitter antagonism in some quarter of Congress. Only by breaking them up into several laws, each of which might pass by its own separate majority, could they be enacted. The moderates prevailed, led by Clay, and by Webster until he left the Senate to become Fillmore's Secretary of State. California was admitted. Texas was given ten million dollars in return for a suitable boundary indicated by the Missouri Compromise line (36° 30'), the meridian of 103°, and the parallel of 32° thence to the Rio Grande.[5] New Mexico and Utah were organized as territories and separated

---

[5] Marcus Baker, *The Northwest Boundary of Texas* (U.S. Geological Survey *Bulletin*, 1902); W. J. Spillman, "Adjustment of the Texas Boundary in 1850," in Texas State Historical Association *Quarterly*, vol. VII; I. J. Cox, "The Southwest Boundary of Texas," in Texas State Historical Association *Quarterly*, vol. VI. The meridian of 103° (Greenwich) is slightly east of that of 26° (Washington), although the Spanish treaty of 1819 uses the two systems as the same. Congress has used both, New Mexico being bounded west by a Washington meridian and east by a Greenwich meridian. Many good map makers are led into slight errors because of this lack of identity in the two systems; and the confusions are made worse because in some instances an erroneous survey, made in good faith, has finally been accepted as though it were really the legally designated line. The western boundary of the Texas panhandle, which the law fixes at 103°, is a good test of map-making accuracy.

by the parallel of 37°, except for an extension of New Mexico northward to 38° at the northeast corner. The South received its compensation in that no word was said about extending the Missouri Compromise line across the territories to California, the omission leaving slavery to be settled by local option in Utah and New Mexico. It received also a rigorous amendment of the fugitive slave law of 1793. It was forced to tolerate a concession to northern radicals in the prohibition of the slave trade in the District of Columbia.

The ambition of the leaders of the State of Deseret to become a State in the Union was postponed gratification, because of objections to Mormon polity. The constitution that the handful of Americans in New Mexico offered for approval was ignored. The three territories and one State now organized for the people beyond the Rockies were a sufficient recognition of their importance, and even this strained the bonds of the Union almost to the snapping point. The anti-slavery leaders did not claim a right to interfere with slavery in the States and were thus forced to use the creation of territories as the occasion for presenting their reform. Their aggression drove the planter leaders of the South to panic and extremity.

CHAPTER XLII

PREËMPTION

THE resonant phrases with which Daniel Webster answered Hayne of South Carolina, in the debate of 1830, were destined to become before his death an integral part of the consciousness of the North and West. They translated into language that the man in the street could read and understand, the legal concepts that John Marshall had embodied in his great decisions. The Union was above the States, he said. Within its proper sphere, the Union was supreme. "Liberty and Union" were in his mind; but they were "one and inseparable"; and the southern view of a Constitution violable and voidable at pleasure was incompatible with the pregnant phrase with which the Constitution describes itself as the "supreme law of the land." In the battle of the sections that was to ensue, Marshall provided the constitutional ideas and Webster popularized them, until every schoolboy of the North could recite the peroration of the *Reply to Hayne.* But it has sometimes been forgotten that the occasion of this memorable debate was the conflict of ideas in the sections, respecting the treatment of the public lands; and that Webster, quite as much as Hayne, or Calhoun his master, was animated by the hope of retaining for his region the alliance of the West.

Always there has been a sectionalism in the United States — the ancient rivalry of the tide-water against the frontier West, or the newer struggle, shaped by slave labor and the plantation, pitting East against South, with the West as the coveted ally. The American System of Henry Clay was a product of the latter and sought to bind East to West in an alliance of mutual interest. The protective tariff was for the East, and the internal improvement system was for the West. If it had been possible to devise a treatment of the public lands mutually advantageous, the alliance might have become permanent, and Clay might have reached the height of his ambitions. But the essential interests of the western States ran counter to those of the industrial communities that flourished under the system of the tariff. The West wanted free access to the lands, active migration, and speedy development. The eastern leader saw with regret the draining off of population, for in excess population he found his factory workers at a declining labor cost. He opposed free land as naturally as the West desired it.[1]

The philosophy of the Ordinance of 1787 was generous in its vision of the procession of new States to be formed out of the public domain, but was ever modified by the tide-water ascendency over the disposal of the lands. The general laws of 1800 and 1820 differed chiefly in their details of method for accomplishing the same end, the production of a net revenue from the domain. The former tried high price and long credit, and was a demoralizing failure. The latter established the long-lasting rate of $1.25 per acre and produced the tidal wave of revenue that preceded and induced the panic of 1837. But down to the moment when that wave began to swell in 1832, the gross revenue from the lands was only thirty-eight million dollars, whereas the United States had paid out on their account the larger sum of forty-nine million dollars.

The public domain was not a financial success, whatever it was as a social agency. Yet the terms of its administration were so important to the people of the frontier States as to dominate their thoughts. Under the law of 1820, the Ohio and Mississippi Valleys passed from the first phase of frontier existence into the second, the tier of commonwealths beyond the Mississippi took shape, and Oregon and California received their earliest increments of population. Every year it became more clear that no one theory on the domain could satisfy all, and that clash of interest here might well break down the alliance that Henry Clay had labored to build up.

The East and North would have been best satisfied with the working of the system if it had been possible to charge and collect a high price for the western farms, to slow down the movement of population thither, and to turn a net revenue into the Treasury of the United States. With revenue in hand and labor supply built up at home, the interests of industry would have been protected.

The States of the South shared in large measure the frontier belief that a price for land was a burdensome tax upon the settler, but had even stronger reasons for combating the program offered by the East. A large revenue, administered by the Government at Washington, tended to exalt the Union as against the States; and they were becoming so sensitive upon the matter of slavery control

[1] William E. Dodd, *Expansion and Conflict* (1915), is a brilliant discussion of this scheme by a southerner who knows the West.

that they felt bound to impede every extension of national power. Therefore, the South was willing to support a lowered price, or none at all. The supposition that a high land price would build up an industrial population in the North was an additional reason for southern opposition. In the southern mind the tariff was evidence of sectional favoritism, unfair, if not unconstitutional. Every northern movement to check the extension of the frontier added to this conviction and helped prove to the South the selfishness of northern policy. In the arguments, overtures, and contests among the sections it was not possible to reduce the public lands to one acceptable formula. Cession, donation, graduation, distribution, and preëmption became technical words, everywhere understood, and capable of rousing lofty emotions, or frenzy of denunciation according to the orator and the audience.[2]

An outright cession of the unsold lands to the States in which they lay, would have pleased most of the newer States. They resented the continuation of Federal control within their limits, and begrudged the acreage of public land which the Government did not sell and they could not tax. If the land was as yet unsurveyed, and not upon the market, they criticized the slow movements of the General Land Office. If it was on sale, without a buyer, there was a painful prospect of its remaining thus indefinitely. The price appeared to be too high. The settler was impoverished by the debt due for his land, in the midst of millions of acres that the Government could neither sell nor use. Before Benton of Missouri had sat out his first six years in the Senate, he was demanding a cession of unsold lands to the States, as well as a donation to actual settlers of land that did not immediately find a buyer at the regular price.

Donation to the settler was as popular in the West as cession to the States, and in one form or another would doubtless have followed such cession. As Benton and his followers pressed the idea through the decades, they discovered additional reasons why the farm-maker was a public benefactor and entitled to remuneration. Some of the newer constitutions made by the frontier States in the forties embodied the principle that the homestead of the settler ought to be free from legal attachment for the payment of debts, and that every debtor, however insolvent, ought to be allowed to

[2] The most useful studies of this are Raynor G. Wellington, *The Political and Sectional Influence of the Public Lands, 1812–1842* (1914); and George M. Stephenson, *The Political History of the Public Lands from 1840 to 1862. From Preëmption to Homestead* (1917).

retain a minimum property. It was only a slight elaboration of this idea when the leaders came to demand that the homestead itself should be given freely by the Government to every man who would reclaim it from the unoccupied domain. This became the homestead policy that reached success in 1862 after an increasing agitation for a generation.

Graduation was urged by the Western States as a partial concession to their interests, and one more likely to be attained. In every region, when a new tract of sections went on sale, the buyers at the public auction took the choicest pieces of land, often at fancy prices. Later, in accordance with the law, the remainder went on private sale at the standard price, and many settlers took their farms at this rate. But there came a time in the affairs of every land office when sales declined although there was much land unsold. The bad lands had no buyers, and the section-seekers balanced carefully the desirability of the less attractive acres. But there was no reduction in price for the sections that remained unsold; and in theory they would remain forever Government land until some buyer should come along willing to pay the price. It was reasonable to urge that after lands had long remained without a buyer they should be reduced in price. Unless there were some scheme of graduation there was no way of getting rid of the Government as a land-holder; and there was no equity in forcing the buyer to pay as much for the remnants as had been charged for the original fresh lands. Benton was the great advocate of graduation, and every few sessions brought up a bill for it in Congress, to show by the roll-call who were the genuine friends of western development. Yet he systematically failed to get it passed.

Cession, donation, and graduation were generally unpalatable to the East and acceptable to West and South; but distribution was the reverse. The national solution of any problem had a natural appeal to Henry Clay, and he could not appreciate the fairness of giving away national property to a few States or a few thousand citizens. Moreover, the East so deeply opposed the western solutions that the adoption of one of them would threaten Clay's balance of power. He evolved, accordingly, the plan of distribution. This meant, *not* the distribution of the public lands to the States in which they lay, but the distribution of the proceeds of land sales among all the States, according to the ratio of representation in Congress. In 1833, the year after that in which he had been the National Republican candidate for the Presidency, he worked through Congress a bill embodying his ideas of compromise, only to run afoul of the equally insistent ideas of Andrew Jackson.

Clay's Distribution Bill of 1833 gained votes from sections that had little in common, because of its inconsistencies and compromises. Easterners voted for it because seven eighths of the net receipts were to be distributed among all the States. Some westerners approved because one eighth of the net receipts was to be given directly to the State in which the land lay, thus complying in part with the demand for cession. The southerners who voted for it were attracted by a different law passed at the same time, the Compromise Tariff of 1833, in which Clay granted them a gradual but effective abolition of the system of protection. But Jackson withheld his approval from the bill, and in December, 1833, explained to Congress that the measure was a violation of the fundamental agreement that the lands were to be used equally for the common purpose. He saw a breach of faith in the favoritism that gave one eighth to the frontier States. He had already urged Congress to fix a price "barely sufficient to reimburse to the United States the expense of the . . . system," and he wanted to withdraw the system from the States. "It cannot be doubted," he said, "that the speedy settlement of these lands constitutes the true interest of the Republic. The wealth and strength of a country are its population, and the best part of that population are the cultivators of the soil. Independent farmers are everywhere the basis of society and true friends of liberty."

After the veto of Distribution in 1833 the discussion of the public lands became almost inextricably involved with matters of national finance and sectional politics; and the theme thereafter falls within that discouraging limbo of things that never happened. Prosperity came and went; and was followed by panic and repudiation. The surplus revenue arose to embarrass the Treasury, and part of it was "deposited" with the States under the act of 1836. It was not "distributed" because of the growing constitutional qualms of southern politicians; and what objections these had to distribution of surplus applied equally to distribution of the public lands. Clay kept steadily at his project, however, in spite of the lukewarm attitude of the West towards it; but his opponents gained momentum in their demand for cession or donation. In 1836 a distribution bill seemed so probable that Jackson was driven to draft a veto message, but the bill failed of passage. In 1840, following the Whig victory and the success of William Henry

Harrison, Clay took steps to utilize the victory for the passage of distribution, and in 1841 gained the dubious triumph of an ineffective law.

This Whig victory of 1840 was an incongruous event.[3] The same border passions that advanced Jackson to the Presidency in 1828, ejected his successor from that office twelve years later. The Whigs as a party were so nearly inarticulate that they did not dare to reduce their beliefs to writing, lest it should cost votes. Instead they nominated Harrison, as a border hero, and Tyler as an anti-Jackson martyr, and asked every dissentient section to vote the ticket for whatever reason seemed best to it. Harrison was a "log-cabin" candidate, and drew enough scattered support to gain his office. His western compatriots, as soon as election was over, and even before inauguration, demanded fulfillment of the kindly pledges that both candidates had made them.

Clay, though a westerner, was a Kentuckian; and in Kentucky there were no public lands. His support of distribution would hardly have been possible had he come from one of the States of the Old Northwest. Benton, much better than he, represented the true western attitude upon this subject. And Benton, in the short session of Congress between the election of Harrison and the inauguration, put through the Senate a "log-cabin" law, to adjust the land system according to the frontier demand. Neither cession nor donation was practically possible, though either would have received western approval. He accordingly based his bill upon the principle of preëmption.

There was nothing new in the idea of preëmption itself. In nearly every Congress since 1800 the matter had been discussed, and repeatedly Congress had permitted preëmption of lands as a means of offsetting some of the inconveniences of the system of sales. It happened constantly, as the area of agricultural occupation advanced westward, that settlers found themselves living on farms that they had improved, but to which they had neither title nor prospect of getting one. They often entered this precarious status with eyes open, trusting to luck or politics to relieve them; at times they found themselves in it because of the defects of the land laws. In either case the frontier farmers did not surrender without a fight the lands upon which they were trespassers before the law.

[3] Arthur C. Cole, *The Whig Party in the South* (1913), contains colored maps showing the distribution of the southern vote, 1836–1852.

There was no legal way for a farmer to get upon a farm in the public domain until after the Indian title had been quieted by the United States and the land surveyed, and the area opened to sale following the regular period of advertisement and proclamation. But Indian titles were often not quieted before settlers were crowding around the edges of the reservations and casting their covetous eyes upon the tracts from which they were legally barred. And Congress made appropriations for the survey of ranges of townships less freely than would sometimes have been convenient; while in spending the appropriations along the border it was equally impossible for Congress or the Commissioner of the General Land Office to anticipate the amount of sections that ought to be surveyed in each region of development in order to have an adequate area of land available for sale. When new tracts were thrown upon the market, there was always the problem of keeping settlers off the unoffered land until the appointed day. And when available lands were exhausted before the buyers were satisfied, there was no satisfactory way of keeping the surplus of settlers off the land, sale or no sale.

The first right of preëmption was voted by Congress in 1801, to relieve certain settlers who had bought their farms from John Cleves Symmes, only to find that their locations were outside the tract to which that speculator received title from the United States. In consideration of their bad luck and the fact that they had gone ahead to improve their tracts, they were allowed to buy the farms in question as soon as these were offered for sale, in advance of the auction, at the minimum price of $1.25. Buying ahead of the auction, at the minimum price, was the essence of this and every other preëmption act that Congress passed. This is what the very word "preëmption" meant.

As the years went on, other groups of settlers asked for the passage of special laws granting them the privilege. Sixteen similar special acts were passed before 1841, sometimes occasioned by genuine distress, sometimes to relieve persons who had deliberately trespassed relying upon the chance of a plea to Congress. In these years the western opinion was forming that no one but the occupier had a moral right to the public lands; that the speculator in particular was an enemy of the public; that any price was an affront. "When settlers are compelled to travel more than one hundred miles to enter lands, they will appeal to Congress for preëmption rights, rather than incur the fatigue and expense of a journey to that extent through a trackless wilderness," wrote one observer of the process. The willingness of Congress to pass such exemptions, of course, added to the difficulty of administering the land sales, for as a harassed district attorney wrote, the Government tolerated in these cases, "a trespass in the citizen which subsequently perfects a *title* in himself," and a premium was placed upon violations of the law. The commissioner protested in 1836, "the preëmption privilege that may be considered as little else than a mere benevolence, enabling the adventurer to appropriate to himself the choicest lands, most valuable mill-sites, and the localities for towns, at a vast cost to the public."

The preëmption laws were nevertheless passed. Until 1830 they were special in character; then they were made general, conferring the privilege upon whatsoever citizens might anywhere have so trespassed within a stated period of months. In the thirties, while the land system was the football of politics, its administration was breaking down because of the soft-heartedness of Congress.

It was breaking down as well because of the tough-mindedness of the settlers. The law-abiding frontiersman who went to the land office prepared to bid for his farm as the law directed, was challenged by a vision of two situations that seemed equally unfair. In one, there was a possibility that a moneyed speculator, with no intention to develop the land himself, would bid on it, and thus either get it or raise the price for the farmer-buyer. If the prospective farmer-buyer was already residing on the tract as a squatter, the whole value of whatever improvements or clearings he might have made, was at stake, for he had no rights before the law. Confronted by the danger of high price or loss of improvements, or both, he was ready for any means of saving his position.

The other situation was that of the preëmptioner — the specially favored trespasser, whom Congress had relieved from the necessity of bidding against speculators at the auction, and who was sure to get his acres at minimum price. Why, asked the farmer-buyer, should one farmer buy at auction, when another, no better, is allowed the minimum? The man who obeyed the law was at a disadvantage in comparison with either the speculator or the preëmptioner. The spirit of the frontier corrected this disadvantage as well as it could, even though this entailed a systematic violation of the land laws.

In Iowa Territory this systematic violation was best organized and most successful, although the "claims club," which was the tool employed, appeared on many other new and developing frontiers. The technique was simple and required as raw materials only a group of squatters who had settled on part of the domain before the land was legally open to them. In the eastern countries of Iowa just behind the Black Hawk cession, there were plenty of these, for the volume of migration in 1833 and 1834 had been underestimated by the Land Office.[4]

The first formal step of such a group to save the equities in the farms that they were illegally improving, and to avoid an auction price, was to form a claims club or association. This club would elect officers and provide its secretary with a book for the records. Each one of the members would then describe to the club the farm he had appropriated, in the language of the Government survey if possible, otherwise by metes and bounds; and if no other member objected, the secretary would then record the claim. If two or more members disputed a single tract, the club adjudicated the contest.

For the remainder of the life of the claims club its secretary acted as an informal recorder of deeds. He made notes of changes and transfers, and sometimes had the backing of the club in passing-on a squatter's claim to heirs. He continued this service until the day approached when the receiver of the local land office, having completed the surveys of townships and sections, proclaimed that upon a given day the land would be offered for sale at auction to the highest bidder, and warned citizens of the legal penalties attached to any collusive action that might lessen the free bidding or reduce the proceeds to the United States.

It was towards this day that the whole life of the claims club was directed. The members of the club, already in occupation of part of the area that was to be auctioned off, attended the sale in a body, with such weapons as their spirit might dictate. The secretary attended, too, armed with his book of records and transfers. As the clerk of the sale called off the description of the sections, one by one, the secretary of the club looked into his book to see who was living on it, and bid for the land at the minimum price of $1.25 per acre. Then he, and the occupier, and the other members

[4] Benjamin F. Shambaugh, "Frontier Land Clubs or Claims Associations," in American Historical Association, *Report*, 1900. There are many references to this type of law-defeating organization in the *Annals of Iowa*, the *Iowa Historical Record*, and Professor Shambaugh's own *Iowa Journal of History and Politics*. An Alabama conspiracy of the same type is described in *American State Papers, Public Lands*, vol. VI, 187.

of the club surveyed the gathering to see whether any other bidder thought it wise to make a bid.

It generally happened that prudence kept other bidders quiet, and the "free auction" resulted in a sale of the farm at the price that would have been paid if a preëmption law had already been passed covering these settlers and this region. There were cases, however, when strangers in ignorance, or speculators with courage, sought to buy; only to run the risk of bodily violence or social ostracism. The spirit of the community resented any interference with the squatter's right as the frontier saw it. Grand juries could rarely be induced to indict for these flagrant violations of the law; and after indictment, petty juries of the vicinity could not be expected to convict.

Between 1820 and the panic of 1837 the frontier crystallized its opinion that any price for the land was an imposition and that the auction was an affront. Special preëmption acts became more sweeping, and claims clubs were resorted to in many more cases than there are surviving records to substantiate. It was not practical politics, as yet, to persuade the tide-water element in Congress to accept the homestead principle in its entirety, so the demand took the form of universal preëmption rights. These, if granted, would allow the settler to squat more nearly where he pleased, and to perfect a title when the lands should come on sale by merely proving his occupation and improvement of the land and paying a minimum fee.

The "log-cabin" bill of Senator Benton that passed the Senate in February, 1841, was such a bill providing for general, prospective preëmption. But the Whigs were able to prevent its passage in the House. The session ended, Harrison was inaugurated and died, and John Tyler who had disapproved of both preëmption and graduation, became President. But Tyler was impressed with the financial needs of the States, which since the panic of 1837 had been unable to meet their budgets, and he advised Congress that he would favor a distribution scheme, for the proceeds of the land sales, providing this did not compel Congress to raise moneys in excess of the amount contemplated by the Compromise Tariff of 1833. Under this act the rates were to be reduced to a flat twenty per cent ad valorem after June, 1842.

A new distribution bill thus took shape in the session of 1841, with Henry Clay leading to its support the representatives of the eastern States. In neither Senate nor House had he a working

majority favoring his proposal, and hence he had to pay a price in
each. The western Representatives demanded and secured a pre-
emption amendment, couched in much the same terms as Benton's
bill that failed earlier in the year. The southern Senators procured
a guarantee that distribution would cease if a war should ensue, or
if Congress should raise the rate on imports above the level of
twenty per cent. It thus became the Distribution-Preëmption
Bill, to which Tyler gave his assent, September 4, 1841. By its
provisions, the proceeds of the land sales were to contribute ten
per cent to the States in which the lands were sold, while the balance, after paying the cost of administration of the system, should
be distributed pro rata among all the States. But this distribution
was to cease whenever the duties on imports should exceed twenty
per cent. So preëmption became a universal right under liberal
conditions that lasted with little change for half a century.

It was a typical Clay compromise; but the only part of it that
lasted was the principle of preëmption that he opposed. Before
the law had any effective influence, Congress was driven to raise
the rates and abandon the Compromise Tariff of 1833 because of
the Treasury deficits that still lingered after the panic of 1837. A
new high tariff was passed in 1842, and the distribution clauses
therefore lapsed. Preëmption became a settled policy and the year
1841 assumed a significance in the development of the public
domain equaled only by the years of the other basic laws, 1787,
1800, and 1820. Under the preëmption law, the frontiersmen who
were thronging into the upper Mississippi valley and across the
plains to the Pacific, and who were raising the density of settlement in all the public land States, found it less onerous to solve
that basic problem of their life, the acquisition of a clear title to
their land.

CHAPTER XLIII

THE FRONTIER OF THE FORTIES

THE State of California was the fruit of the manifest destiny that drove American settlers to the Pacific, and it took on its personal identity because of the accident that gold was found at the end of the rainbow that the migrants were pursuing. The fight that its admission to the Union entailed and that shaped the terms of reconstruction of the rest of the territory conquered from Mexico, nearly wrecked the Union, and only Clay with his fertile compromise of principles, saved the day. In the Mississippi Valley, meanwhile, the panic of 1837 was receding into the past. The great crest of land sales, reached in 1836, was a matter to be remembered, but not to be repeated. The high prices, induced in part by the flood of paper money, had subsided; and while deflation was, as always, painful to the debtor, the West was healthier when the deflation was accomplished. Two pairs of frontier States were added to the Union in the decade preceding the admission of California — Texas and Wisconsin, Iowa and Florida. The difficulties that the pioneers of Iowa and Wisconsin surmounted on their way to statehood illustrate the aftermath of panic in the Mississippi Valley.

The Territory of Wisconsin was divided by Congress in the spring of 1838, and on the western side of the Mississippi River the "Iowa District" was given legal recognition as Iowa Territory. There were more than forty-one thousand settlers in the two territories north and west of Illinois by this time. They had nearly doubled in numbers within two years and were increasing more rapidly every day. The northern element among them was still small; but up the Mississippi and across the prairies from Indiana and Illinois larger numbers came from the southern bases of frontier growth. They were insistent upon home rule, and they had an additional reason for welcoming it, founded in the panic of 1837.

The insane confidence that led the States into their internal improvement schemes of 1836, and that made their voters believe the politicians who told them that every county could have its railroads at once, was gone before 1840. Instead they possessed now a burden of debts, for whose satisfaction they could not find a means. The future, no longer rosy, was darkened by a promise of heavy taxes to pay back the squandered loans. Individual farmers, who had mortgaged their lands in the enthusiasm of the moment, discovered that the debt was frequently larger than the whole value of the property. There was an exodus from Indiana and Illinois, made larger because of the desire to escape taxation. New immigrants from the East looked at the tax-rate and pushed on to further fields. The territories, Wisconsin and Iowa, profited by the dubious reputation of Illinois, and after 1837 found themselves in hectic growth, doubling their numbers every few months.

A movement for the dismemberment of Illinois is one of the evidences of the financial state of mind of the early forties. Anywhere in the State, citizens were ready to give anything reasonable for relief from taxes. Neighbor States were dropping the burden and indulging in frank repudiation.[1] The northern counties of Illinois, above the latitude of Chicago, reminded themselves that this portion of the State had been intended by Congress, in the Ordinance of 1787, to be a part of the fifth Northwest Territory, Wisconsin. For several years their leaders talked of secession and annexation to a territory with a lower tax-rate. The movement came to naught, for no State may be divided without its consent, and no one fancied that Illinois would submit to partition. But the desire illustrates a frame of mind that helped along the speedy colonization of Iowa.

"Burlington is the largest, wealthiest, most business doing and most fashionable city, on or in the neighborhood of the Upper Mississippi . . ." wrote a contributor to the *Iowa Territorial Gazette*, under the stimulus of the Fourth of July enthusiasm of 1840. "We have three or four churches, a theatre, and a dancing school in full blast." Well placed on the Mississippi, midway between the Des Moines and Iowa rivers, Burlington was a natural port of entry for the Black Hawk purchase. And when the great Sauk and Fox cession, made in 1842, opened the interior of the territory, the procession of settlers through the river gateways became an orderly mob. The children of the South predominated for some years, but in Iowa there was a larger admixture of long-distance migrants than was usual on the border, because by 1840 travel was entering upon its modern conditions.

The river steamboats had begun to ascend the Upper Mississippi many years before Iowa attracted attention. One reached

[1] William A. Scott, *The Repudiation of State Debts* (1893).

the post at Fort Snelling as early as 1823. But not until the later thirties were these craft either numerous, safe, or cheap. By 1840, however, packets were plying regularly from Pittsburgh to all the Ohio ports and St. Louis; and from St. Louis upstream to the head of navigation. Emigration ceased to be a matter of downstream drifting on a flatboat, or painful overland travel with the farm wagons and live stock across the prairies. The steamboat was quicker and not much more costly for those who were content to take deck passage. Among those who disembarked at the Iowa river towns were many for whom the frontier was a complete novelty, and whose homes were far away.[2]

Ephraim Adams and his "Iowa Band" composed one of the bodies that lessened the frontier uniformity of Iowa. His party was made up of Congregational ministers and their families, from Yale and Andover, who came on missionary duty. The foreign missionary associations were sending their representatives to Oregon, Hawaii, and the Far East; this was a home mission project and resulted in the opening at Grinnell of a little college that has continuously stood for devotion and sound education. Its people, and their friends, made the frontier democracy of Iowa less completely Jacksonian than most of the Mississippi Valley was at this moment.

There were, nevertheless, fifty-one Democrats among the seventy-two delegates who gathered to frame a constitution for Iowa in October, 1844. At any time after 1840 there would have been abundant precedent for the formation of a State government, and more than once other territories had proceeded with the constituent work without waiting for Congress to enable them. In 1840, and again in 1842, proposals for holding conventions, at the initiative of the governors who were ambitious for statehood, were rejected at the polls by the settlers; but in 1844 the project passed. The discussions in the convention that ensued give, as usual, a picture of the grievances that called for immediate remedy, and the modifications in basic law suggested by the experiences of the frontiers of the forties.[3]

The debate over banks is the most instructive that the scanty

[2] Seymour Dunbar, *A History of Travel in America* (1915), has been less widely known than it deserves. In no other place is so varied a collection of cuts and descriptions of steamboats and other agencies of American transportation.

[3] Benjamin F. Shambaugh, *History of the Constitutions of Iowa* (1902); he edited in 1907 *Proceedings of the Fiftieth Anniversary of the Constitution of Iowa,* in which there is a keen discussion of frontier ideas by Andrew C. McLaughlin.

records preserve, for the passion for bank notes had been succeeded by an aversion to banks of issue. The high prices and inflation of the boom period were justly attributed to overeasy banking, and the farmers, as a body, were imbued with a Jacksonian antipathy toward any bank. The merchants among the people, and the easterners, were less sweeping in their condemnation, but there were few as yet to take positive ground that banks were necessary tools of commerce. The constitution forbade the chartering of any bank without a referendum, and made the liability of stockholders extend beyond the amount of stock held, to the whole property of the stockholder. The application to corporations of this legal principle of partnership was of course destructive of the corporation and was meant to be.

The second of the great Iowa debates was over boundaries. As a territory, Iowa possessed the broad sweep of domain between the Mississippi and the Missouri, north of the State of Missouri. The convention did not expect to retain all this, but there were doubts as to what ought to be asked of Congress, and what might be obtained. The local opinion was in favor of a Mississippi frontage as far north as the St. Peter's or Minnesota River and a western extension to the Missouri. With these ambitions, the boundary clause of the constitution was constructed.

Congress, meanwhile, had other ideas. There was among the southern representatives a disposition to keep an Indian tract on the east bank of the Missouri, to limit the extension of Iowa as Arkansas had been limited by the reserves of the Five Civilized Tribes. It was necessary to admit Iowa, in order to make a balance for Florida, which was now declaring itself ready; but it was not necessary to make a huge free State in the Northwest. In March, 1845, before the Iowa constitution had been submitted to the people, a bill passed Congress admitting Florida and Iowa, under the constitutions they had framed, but cutting down the boundaries of the latter to a strip along the Mississippi only, as far north as the mouth of the Mankato River. Curtailed both north and west in its territorial dimensions, Iowa rejected the constitution, and put off admission.

In the spring of 1846 a second constitutional convention met to revise the constitution of 1844, and to propose to Congress a compromise boundary. The extension of the State to the Missouri River, south of the present northern boundary, was the new proposal, which Congress ratified in time for Iowa to become a State in December, 1846. The second constitution was changed only in details from that of 1844, and banks of issue were still forbidden. What opposition there was among the Iowa Whigs was inspired chiefly by this prohibition.

Florida, which became a State under the original act of 1845, was like Maine, a detached eastern frontier at the date of its admission. It had remained, protesting, in territorial status since 1822. "The whole policy of this Government, and all the principles upon which its institutions rest," declared the Florida petition, "are adverse to the long continuance of a Territorial Government over any portion of the citizens of the country." But population had come in slowly. Much of the land was a tangle of swamp and forest and over what was arable there lay a cloud of Spanish titles and land claims. The reluctant Seminole, who agreed to emigrate and then recanted, made Florida a scene of prolonged warfare. The people framed a constitution upon their own initiative in 1838, which Congress put off accepting until its act of 1845. The New York *Herald* rejoiced in "Florida and Iowa as stars to the Union, which will secure a Democratic Senate for the support of the measures of the new administration." The *Arkansas Banner* echoed the thought: "It must be pleasing to every true-hearted democrat to contemplate the permanent triumph and establishment of his principles. Florida, and Iowa, which is large enough to be ultimately divided into two States, are both decidedly democratic. Texas will come into the Union almost unanimously democratic. It, in not many years hence, will constitute four or five States — all of which will most certainly be democratic. . . . It is certain, therefore, that whiggery is doomed — it has gone down with its great champion — while the star of democracy has ascended the political horizon never to go down again, but to brighten with the waste of years!" At the next census, in 1850, Florida had 87,445 inhabitants; Iowa 192,214.

The "star of democracy" that illumined the firmament in Iowa and Texas shone as well over the region between Lake Michigan and the Mississippi, which constituted Wisconsin Territory after the division of 1838. Before 1845 there were three settled areas within the territory, each with a distinct set of characteristics. In the southwest counties, it took a keen eye to see any difference between Wisconsin and the Iowa people across the Mississippi. They had nearly all ascended that stream in their homeseeking quest. They had much the same admixture of southern and middle

State forbears. They were Democrats and "ultra" in their democracy.

But the eastern limit of southwestern Wisconsin was in the vicinity of the Four Lakes, where Madison had become the territorial capital. Here Henry Dodge, himself one of the most typical of the southern entrants, presided as governor during the better part of Wisconsin's territorial existence. East of Madison there was still in 1846 what a Milwaukee editor described as a "vacuum" extending thirty miles or more to Lake Mills; and by this vacuum of unoccupied frontier, eastern Wisconsin was separated from the West.

Along the lake shore, Wisconsin was before 1846 an unbroken succession of towns from Green Bay to the Illinois line. Milwaukee, the most important, was in caustic debate over the relative prospects of Chicago and itself. And around or behind these towns were social influences far different from those of the remote frontier. The lake steamers brought their cargoes and their passengers directly from Buffalo; whither they had come from the seaboard States or the New York frontier. The South was at a discount; and here were to be found what were rare in the Mississippi Valley — increasing colonies of foreign born. The German and Irish immigration that began in the forties provided thousands of settlers for the eastern Wisconsin towns and farms; and the Germans, indeed, talked of the possibility of founding a German State.

In southeast Wisconsin was an overflow from Illinois and Indiana, of typical frontier character, but of slighter southern aspect than the Mississippi Valley stream. Its people were often the second generation of Erie Canal migrants, who had stopped for one generation on the northern slope of the Old Northwest. Or if they came of Kentucky stock, they were insulated by another generation from the southern influence. In the southern counties along Lake Michigan, and up the valley of the Rock River and on the fertile plains between, they made a prosperous, conservative farmer population.

The cleavage that was to wrack the political structure of the Northwest in the next two decades was already visible in Wisconsin. In 1844 a territorial abolition society was formed in Milwaukee, and a southwestern politician hoped to fasten on the eastern leader of the Wisconsin Whigs "beyond all doubt, the charge of abolitionism." It was in 1842, when a citizen of Richmond, Indiana, ventured to ask him what he thought of abolition‹ ism, that Henry Clay made his fatal response, "Go home, Mr. Mendenhall, and mind your own business." The settlers whom the North contributed to the Old Northwest were refusing to mix with those who derived their ideals from the South.

In the summer of 1846, after various attempts at spontaneous statehood had been defeated in Wisconsin, Congress passed an enabling act, and for a third time reduced the area that the eternal compact in the Ordinance of 1787 had assigned to the last State to be constructed in the Old Northwest. The first reduction occurred when Illinois in 1818 was allowed its strip north of Chicago; the second when Michigan was compensated for the Toledo strip of which Ohio despoiled her, by the grant of the upper peninsula, between Lakes Superior and Michigan. Wisconsin was now cut short of the Mississippi River, which had been designed as her western limit, and was instead offered statehood only in case she would accept the St. Croix River as her boundary. This curtailing of Iowa and Wisconsin made room for an additional Mississippi Valley State (Minnesota), but caused real and reasonable disappointments.

Like Iowa, Wisconsin made two constitutions before her inhabitants were satisfied, but the reasons for the rejection of the first basic law were different in the two cases.[4] Iowa choked over the boundary. In Wisconsin the different conceptions of the meaning of democracy, that have kept the State in continuous uproar since its creation, occasioned a struggle that was only partly settled when the second constitution was accepted in 1848. "There is a striking dissimilarity between the habits and customs of the people of the Mississippi Valley and the old Eastern States," wrote a well-informed writer in the *Wisconsin Democrat* in 1846: "the eastern and western portions of our Territory are made up principally of these divisions, hence there must of necessity exist strong prejudices between them which time and intercourse alone can eradicate."

There were noticeable among the delegates of the first convention representatives of the "progressive Democracy," who were Simon-pure Jacksonian extremists; of the "retrograding Demo-

---

[4] F. L. Paxson, "A Constitution of Democracy — Wisconsin, 1847," in *Mississippi Valley Historical Review*, vol. II. The State Historical Society of Wisconsin, fortunate in the services of Draper, Thwaites, Kellogg, Quaife, and Schafer, has published voluminous materials on the official and popular debates over the constitutions.

cracy," who were disposed to question the eternal soundness of the Jacksonian financial program; and of the Whigs, who showed an eastern conservatism by being interested in property rights and believing in banks. The progressive Democrats were in control and offered to the territory a constitution forbidding the chartering of banks and the issuance of paper money, providing for elective judges, allowing the farmer to save his homestead from judgment for debts, and securing to married women the possession and control of their property. These were principles by which to test the "ultraism of the age," and they were all embodied in the constitution. There was an additional principle, of more political significance, in the requirement for the franchise of one year's residence and an oath of allegiance to the United States. The eastern sections of Wisconsin were filling so rapidly with immigrants that the western democrats foresaw themselves swallowed by a population of foreign antecedents and strove by this restriction to put off the evil day.

The issues were drawn over the constitution before the convention adjourned and submitted the document to the people at the polls. Marshall M. Strong, of Racine, one of the Lake Michigan communities, was unable to restrain his indignation as the convention inserted one radical article after another. He resigned his seat in the convention in disgust and went home to organize a coalition of "Retrograding Democrats" and Whigs, to fight the ratification of the constitution. He was successful. The alliance opposed with vigor the prohibition of banks and gave moral support to the aliens who wished to vote at once. The progressive Democrats, or "tadpoles" as their opponents called them, converted their sentiments to verse of a sort:

> "The Federal party can't endure,
> So much indulgence to the poor;
> The Bank Democracy begrudges
> The People's power to choose their judges;
> The Married woman's clause they say,
> With grief will turn each husband grey;
> But still the worst of all disasters,
> Is banishing their dear 'shin-plasters.'"

But singing did not help them, and the constitution went down, with only three counties in the territory giving it a majority.

The year 1847 was devoted to reflection and party reorganization. Upon post-mortem analysis, it was seen that the definitive item in the rejection was the prohibition of banks. Every month the streams of immigrants emptied more thousands of eastern and foreign residents into the territory. The population of 30,945, of 1840 swelled to one of 305,391 in 1850. The bank party wanted to make a new constitution, and the radical Democrats gave up their hope of defeating it. A Whig territorial delegate to Congress was chosen in September. Governor Dodge assembled the legislature in special session in October to call a convention once more, and in December this convention met in Madison.

The second constitution, accepted in the spring of 1848, and still in force in 1923, was a sweeping revision of the first. Hardly a phrase came through unchanged. The alterations in intent were fewer, however; and the one of these that carried the new basic law to victory forbade the legislature to charter any bank until after a referendum on the subject; when, should the referendum be affirmative, they might construct a "general banking law," which should be ineffective until ratified by the people at a general election. When, in 1852, this law was enacted and approved, it may be said that the Mississippi Valley had passed through the wave of Jacksonian thought, and had begun to confront the issues of a new generation. Wisconsin became the thirtieth State in May, 1848, and there was an appropriateness in the fact that one of the first senators was Henry Dodge, who found as a colleague at Washington his own son, Augustus Cæsar Dodge, Senator from Iowa.

The fight over the Wisconsin constitutions was a significant struggle that might have taught the politicians of the forties many useful things, had they possessed the insight to understand it. Thus far the settlements north of the Ohio River had been similar to and an outgrowth of those of the old West. The Jackson Democracy, and its imitation, the Harrison Whigs, grounded themselves in the typical frontier experiences and prejudices. The further the frontier penetrated, the greater weight it acquired without changing its fundamental character. The diversion of its tendencies, due to the plantation and slave labor conditions of the cotton country, had attracted notice in the early twenties, and the Gulf States became a group apart. The diversion due to the flooding of the northern slope of the Old Northwest with northern and foreign immigrants was less promptly appreciated, for it was taking place within the older States of Ohio, Indiana, and Illinois. There were few who realized that in a few years the control of these

States would be in contest, and that they would be forever lost to southern political manipulations. In Wisconsin, in 1848, there was eastern influence enough to defeat the banking prohibition, which had come to be regarded as typical among the Jacksonian constitutions. Every western State north of Kentucky under these Jacksonian influences made a constitutional revision after 1837. Wisconsin gave the first decisive check. It was still possible in both Iowa and Wisconsin to send two Democrats to the Senate upon the first election, but the votes that wanted banks were growing and could not be permanently satisfied with Democrats. In the presidential election of 1848, Taylor, the Whig, was elected without getting the electoral vote of any of the five Northwest States, or of Iowa. Yet Lincoln, in 1860, carried every one of them. The struggle in Wisconsin was merely an opening skirmish in the political battle that was to increase in deadly intensity for a dozen years.

Although the Mississippi Valley was largely unconscious of the changes in political balance that were impending, it felt that it was growing away from the primitive conditions of the first migrations. The rivers were crowded with steamboats, and the politicians had given up preaching that turnpikes would be the economic salvation of the country. The canal period had come and gone. The high hopes that surrounded the completion of the Erie Canal (1825), and the Ohio Canal (1832), had evaporated before the Illinois-Michigan Canal became an accomplished fact, in the year of the Wisconsin admission. A new era was opening dazzling promises of wealth and growth. In the same year, 1848, what may be regarded as the first through railroad of the West made a complete line of communication between Lake Erie and the Ohio, from Sandusky to Cincinnati. The railroad age became a reality in the same decade in which the party of Andrew Jackson lost its grip.

CHAPTER XLIV

THE RAILROAD AGE

"*The Valley of the Mississippi:* The greatest in the world, take it all in all. Situated as it is, between the two oceans, it will yet command the commerce of the world, and that commerce may be centred in New Orleans." This was the toast that John C. Calhoun gave at a banquet in the St. Charles Hotel at New Orleans, in the fall of 1845, before he took passage on the *S.S. Marie* to ascend the Mississippi to Memphis. At Memphis he was due to attend the great railroad convention where politicians and business men of the Middle West and South dazzled themselves with glimpses of the future and sought to find ways and means to bring the West in line with the railroad movement that was at the moment sweeping the world.

It was an anachronism of some interest that the statesman of reaction should have thought to attach himself to the forefront of progress. A constructive politician in his youth, Calhoun in middle life devoted his logical intellect to building a defensive philosophy around States' rights and slavery; and felt bound, therefore, to oppose whatever development of society seemed likely to interfere with State sovereignty. Yet in 1845 he thought it worth while to make the laborious journey from his South Carolina home to Mississippi, to New Orleans, and to Memphis, to engage in railroad propaganda. He was for the moment at leisure. With the termination of the Tyler Administration in March, he had vacated the office of Secretary of State, and he was not yet returned by his loyal State to his seat in the United States Senate. Some thought that he was looking forward to the presidential nomination of 1848, and a cynic wrote from Washington a little later: "Suppose you get up a great North Western convention [at Chicago], and invite him [Calhoun] to attend it," he will find a constitutional way to improve not only the Mississippi, but the northern lakes and harbors. Certainly he was not blind to the hold that the railroad movement had acquired over the western mind, or to the fact that no southern statesman was likely to be elected President unless he could capture the imagination or interest of the West.

It was no new thing for transportation to be close to western interest. In the fundamental analysis of border life, after the procuring of the land itself, and the capital with which to develop it, the marketing of the crop contained the key to prosperity. The bulky agricultural staples of the West constituted nearly the sole produce that could be converted into money with which to pay debts or buy land. They could not be sold or consumed at home. Their bulk and weight made them costly to move to distant markets. Whatever device promised to lessen freight rates, whether by roads, or vehicles, or by the legal control of the carriers, was certain of a western hearing, and almost certain to inspire a western movement in politics. The National Road and the canals between tidewater and the western rivers had had their day, yet the attainment of wealth and happiness were still the mirages that lured the West from election to election.

The broadening use of steam was the promise that inspired the new movement and brought the frontier, almost for the first time, into contact with the industrial revolution. This revolution — the change from hand work to the use of power machinery — began after the invention of the stationary engine in the eighteenth century and made Western Europe a new world. It cut it off sharply from all preceding history, altering the habits of workers, the distribution of population, and the application of capital. It increased the amount of manufactured goods, at a cheapening cost and thereby added to the physical comfort of every life.

It not only cut Europe off from its past, by the sharp change in conditions, but it cut it off from contemporary America. The open frontier and the abundance of land made it hard to drive Americans into factories; and the scarcity of American capital made the rise of manufactures doubly slow. By 1850, America was at least fifty years behind Europe, with reference to the industrial revolution, and many of the differences between American and European civilization, noticeable to all, were consequences of this.

But when the industrial revolution passed from power machinery to locomotion, when the stationary engine was adapted into the traveling engine, America took hold more rapidly; for there were more premiums to be gained by quick transport in America than by manufacture. The experiments of George Stephenson with steam locomotives, from his *Blucher* (1815) to his *Rocket* (1830), were watched in America as eagerly as at home; and before his *Rocket* was put in regular use on the Liverpool and Manchester Railway, the American railroad movement had begun. It was on a different scale indeed from that of England or France, for capital was scarce and distances were huge. In a sparsely settled country, the effort to build any railroad was of necessity extreme; and to build it well was out of the question.

The Baltimore and Ohio and the South Carolina railroads were the first of consequence in the United States and were built under conditions that were experimental as to roadbed, track, motive power, rolling stock, and financial organization. Their builders acquired more valuable experience than they did profit. But between the year in which the Baltimore and Ohio broke ground (1828), and that in which the Preëmption Act was passed (1841), every center of population along the seaboard began to build its roads.

The early railroads, almost without exception, were as local as the turnpikes had been. Where there was already a profitable traffic, it was profitable to project a railroad. Because of engineering difficulties, few of the early lines crossed large rivers. Their builders preferred, instead, to radiate from the cities up into the country which they supplied, and from which they drew their provisions. The growing coal industry north of Philadelphia provided an incentive for various roads tributary to that city and New York. Only by accident did the railroads, in the early period, connect two cities of similar importance. When such connections were made and through circuits were provided, it may be said with reason that the preliminary period of railroading had ended.

During 1841, Boston became connected with Albany as nearly as this could be done by rail. There was a local line from Boston to Worcester, another running west from Worcester to the Berkshires at West Stockbridge, and a third thence to Greenbush, on the Hudson, opposite Albany. A ferry trip was unavoidable, as well as two changes of cars, for the traveler who desired to make the journey. But such travelers could not be squeamish, and for another generation journeys by rail were attended by many of the inconveniences of stage coach travel.

It became possible in the next year to push through from Albany to Buffalo, although the corporate grouping known as the New York Central Lines was still a projection of the future. But it required perseverance to make this trip, for the lines involved were the Mohawk and Hudson, Utica and Schenectady, Syracuse and Utica, Auburn and Syracuse, Auburn and Rochester, Tonawanda, and Attica and Buffalo. At every terminal point there was a change of cars, a delay in making connections, and generally a change of gauge. Inn-keepers felt that it was their perquisite to entertain the traveler overnight between trains, and it was common for the roads to arrange schedules with this in view. As late as 1854 the citizens of Erie, Pennsylvania, rioted and destroyed trackage when the two roads meeting there made a standard gauge connection and proposed to run their cars through without delay.

But after 1841 the number of through routes in the eastern States became so numerous that both travel and freight shipment acquired increased speed. The next dozen years are those of the trunk line competitions, in which the period of canal rivalries among the eastern cities is duplicated by a period of railroad rivalry for access to the interior markets.

The Baltimore and Ohio was projected as a trunk line at its inception, but it was hindered by inexperience, lack of means, and panic, and only in 1852 was pushed to the Ohio River. It was five years more before there was a continuation west of the Ohio to Cincinnati and St. Louis. The northern trunk lines, started later, reached their destinations with less vexatious delay. These were the Grand Trunk, the New York Central, the Erie, and the Pennsylvania, all lying north of the Baltimore and Ohio; and the Memphis and Charleston and the line from Richmond to Chattanooga lying south, with the Vicksburg road still incomplete at the outbreak of the Civil War.

The Grand Trunk, a Canadian road, with open water outlet at Portlánd, Maine, and western terminus at Port Huron in Ontario, was, after its completion in 1853, as important in the development of the American Northwest as though it were the possessor of a roadbed entirely within the United States. The New York Central, next south, was built up by consolidation of the local lines along the Mohawk route, and operated until 1853 against the harsh competition of the State-owned Erie Canal. Its superior grades, and the uniformly fertile valleys that it traversed, gave it such advantages, however, that if traffic with the interior of the United States were determined by competition alone, the New York Central would outstrip all competitors, and the metropolis of New York City would be even more overwhelming than it is.

The Erie was a single project, between the Hudson River opposite New York City, and Dunkirk on Lake Erie. It served a tier of southern New York counties that had not derived benefit from the

Erie Canal, and struggled for many years against the handicap imposed by the State, that did not propose willingly to allow any railroad to compete with the canal. It was begun in 1835, and finished sixteen years later at a moment when, by accident, a citizen of Western New York, Millard Fillmore, was President of the United States. The ceremonial train that was run to commemorate the opening was a worthy follower of the *Seneca Chief* that bore DeWitt Clinton and his associates east from Buffalo in 1825. It was the first railroad, under a single management, to bridge the gap between the Atlantic and the interior waters, and is thus the earliest trunk line.

The Pennsylvania Railroad was chartered in 1846, and bought from the discouraged State the entire plant of the system of internal improvements that had been completed twelve years earlier. It built a railroad from Philadelphia to Pittsburgh, and by 1852 was running trains, broken only by a short stage link at the summit of the Appalachians, where the tunnel was still under construction. The tracks ran through unbroken in 1854. The Baltimore and Ohio was the southernmost of the northern trunk lines, with a course almost entirely north of the Ohio and the Potomac.

The southern trunk lines were of necessity longer and more expensive than those of the North. There was for them no water route comparable to that of the Great Lakes or the Ohio River, to shorten the railroad distance between tidewater and interior navigation. They must be built all the way from the coast to the Mississippi in order to function with success. From the thirties the project of a Cincinnati and Charleston Railroad excited the southwestern imagination, but it came to naught. Piecemeal, a series of lines came to life from the Chesapeake to Richmond, and thence west, and up the Great Valleys to Knoxville and Chattanooga. Hence the western end of the Memphis and Charleston made connection with the Mississippi River; while the main line of the Memphis and Charleston gave to Charleston an interior connection in substitution for the one she had sought at Cincinnati.[1] The Vicksburg road, through Jackson and Montgomery to Atlanta and Savannah, was not a factor in the railroad era before the Civil War.

In the building of the trunk lines there is shown the keenness of the eastern cities for improved intercourse with the West; simul-

[1] St. George L. Sioussat, "Memphis as a Gateway to the West," in *Tennessee Historical Magazine*, 1917.

taneously the local western lines were born, to serve local needs or to connect with the trunk lines, or both.

Where the first railroad of the West was built is an antiquarian matter of some uncertainty. At the moment of the panic of 1837 there were several small projects under construction, and at least one possessed both track and a steam locomotive. This was the Erie and Kalamazoo, which was open from Toledo to Adrian. Its locomotive, the *Adrian No. I*, arrived by boat at Toledo in June, 1837. But there was no railroading of any significance in the West before the panic, and none after it for a decade. Not until 1847 was there a western line connecting two points of importance; or a thoroughfare between the Lakes and the Ohio before 1848.

The Indianapolis and Madison, eighty-six miles long, was put in operation during 1847, at the close of which year the United States possessed 3205 miles of track, with 660 nominally operating in the Northwest. The map of the year shows the mileage radiating mostly from the towns at the head of Lake Erie. The road that first reached a through connection was the Mad River and Lake Erie, which joined, at Springfield, Ohio, a road to Cincinnati. Sandusky, the Lake terminus of this first through road, was driven to railroad building by the political decision in Ohio which left its citizens without the advantage of a canal port. In the rest of Ohio there were no other important railroads even begun, for the Ohio Canal, and the Miami and Wabash canals traversed the regions of largest population and wealth and retarded railroad enthusiasm. Sandusky, piqued at this neglect, built the railroad for itself, and there were some weeks after the summer of 1848 in which the shortest way from the East to St. Louis was by New York, the Hudson, the Erie Canal, the Lake Erie steamboat, the Mad River Railroad, and the Ohio River steamer. After this date, the canals fell rapidly into desuetude, with declining use, and with revivals more for political effect than to serve an economic end. It has never yet been possible for an inland water highway in the United States to recover its ascendency once a railroad has paralleled it. The Erie Canal, the Ohio River, the Great Lakes, and even the Mississippi have all had their periods of dominance and of eclipse.

In addition to the desire to provide railroad service for a given locality, the western railroads engaged in a race for the prizes in terminal advantage which were Chicago and Indianapolis. In this they were able to secure eastern backing, since the trunk lines were not content to touch the Ohio or the Lakes and desired to push through to Chicago or to the Mississippi. In the next four years after the opening of the Mad River Railroad nearly nineteen hundred more miles of track were put in use beyond the Ohio River. The lines ran southwest from Cleveland and Sandusky, through Cincinnati and Indianapolis, and as far as Terre Haute on the Wabash. From Toledo and Detroit they ran almost due west around the tip of Lake Michigan to Chicago.

The race for Chicago is a dramatic story of the years 1848–1852.[2] The beginning is laid in the hopes of the fresh young commonwealth of Michigan, expressed through its earliest legislature in 1837, for three parallel railroads across the lower peninsula, from Monroe, Detroit, and Port Huron. Work was started on the southern and central of these lines, and in the early forties the State faced bankruptcy because of its enthusiasms. The unfinished public works were sold to private companies that assumed the names of Michigan Southern and Michigan Central and resumed construction, with Chicago as a goal.

The State of Indiana lay as an obstruction in the way of success for either of these lines. They could not get to Chicago except across that part of Indiana that touches Lake Michigan; and without a legislative franchise they could not even enter the State. Indiana was reluctant to grant the right. Its chief interest lay in the development of the central part of the State, around Indianapolis, and the southern end. It saw no advantage in being party to the elevation of Chicago as a potential rival for western ascendency. The legislature accordingly refused charters for the Michigan roads, and these felt driven to devious means of accomplishing their purpose. The New Albany and Salem, a line which Indiana had already chartered, was induced by the Michigan Central to build and lease a small piece of track from the Michigan State line to that of Illinois. The Northern Indiana did the same for the Michigan Southern, and in the spring of 1852 both Michigan lines entered Illinois. They did not go into Chicago over their own tracks, but prevailed upon the Illinois Central Railroad and the Chicago and Rock Island to allow them as non-competitors, to use their respective stations and terminals. West of Chicago local

[2] F. L. Paxson, "The Railroads of the 'Old Northwest' before the Civil War," in Wisconsin Academy of Sciences, Arts, and Letters, *Transactions*, vol. xvii, has annual sketch maps. A group of Wisconsin students, R. E. Riegel, R. S. Cotterill, and F. W. Prescott, are now in collaboration upon a graphic and statistical history of all the ante-bellum railroads of the United States.

lines had already built as far as Rockford, on the Rock River, near the Wisconsin line.

By the end of 1852 the lines tributary to Lake Erie had swept west and southwest across the Old Northwest. By the end of 1853 Chicago had a connection with St. Louis and a fairly direct one with Indianapolis. In 1857 the Ohio and Mississippi was completed from St. Louis to Cincinnati, there to meet the Cincinnati and Marietta; and across the Ohio from Marietta was a through line east over the Baltimore and Ohio. By the end of 1860, the last building season before the Civil War, there were 9514 miles of railroad in the Old Northwest, out of some 30,000 miles of railroad in all the United States. The Northwest was covered with a close-meshed railroad net that brought good transportation within hauling distance of nearly every occupied farm. Grand Haven on Lake Michigan, La Crosse on the Mississippi, and St. Joseph on the Missouri constituted the railroad frontier, and a line connecting them falls not far from what was the agricultural frontier as well. Prior to 1860 the advance of the agricultural frontier was determined by the natural roads, aided as far as might be by the navigable rivers. But now that the railroad had caught up, the future was to be a different story, with population spread and dispersion accelerated because of ease of movement, and with the general shift and advance of the frontier determined, not by the horde of individual homeseekers, but by the conditions under which new railroad lines could acquire the financial means of existence. Finance and transport did not cease to be vital in western economy; but they changed their technique.

CHAPTER XLV

LAND GRANTS AND THE WESTERN ROADS

THE peculiar features of the camp meeting — its concentration of interest, its emotionalism, and its reliance upon mob psychology — were more fruitfully applied in matters of religion and politics than in those of business. In the great western revival at the opening of the nineteenth century it was discovered that the accumulated emotions of the frontier could be released in camp, under the exhortations of powerful preachers, and that the frontier families, wearied with the loneliness of their habitual existence, welcomed the chance to lay aside for a time their worldly affairs and devote themselves to intense doses of religious experience. The religion of the West was shaped by this discovery, and thereafter those churches flourished best whose methods permitted them to take advantage of it.

The politics of the West grew up under somewhat similar conditions. The political leader on the stump bore close resemblance in method of life and type of persuasion to the itinerant preacher. The audiences that were collected to listen to party speeches were lusty under punishment, and absorbed long hours of eloquence. It was not worth while to leave home and travel half a day or more for a short speech. The parson preached morning and afternoon, to congregations that made a day of it. The politician did the same; and at moments of keen political excitement, meetings were organized that lasted not a few hours but several days, until the countryside was impregnated with political emotion. The Whig campaign of 1840 was conducted like a religious revival, taking its cue from the Jackson movement of a dozen years before. Both movements were alive with grand intangibles and heroic virtues, whose effect upon the mind was semi-religious, and whose propagation went best under the conditions that the recurrent camp meetings had made universal in the West. The rise of the convention method in the United States, whether used for politics, religion, or business, appears to have a close connection with this frontier trait.

When the camp meeting was applied to the promotion of railroads, its efficacy broke down. It was productive of conviction but not of cash; and without cash, and the capital for which it stood, the best of convictions made no railroads. As early as 1836, Robert Y. Hayne of South Carolina was in the chair of a convention at Knoxville, to discuss the "great southern railroad" from Cincinnati to Charleston, and to find ways and means for its immediate construction. The belief was still prevalent that the United States had reached its growth. On the western border the Indian reservations made a nearly solid barrier beyond Missouri. General Gaines was using his ingenious mind in the elaboration of a system of radiating railroads to police the Indian Frontier, and Congress was accepting the idea of the great western road from Red River to Lake Superior. The southern politicians were aware that their hold on the West would be improved if they could create economic bonds that would operate for them as the Erie Canal was doing for New York; and that without these bonds they might be left stranded with the lapse of time.

But although it was easy to establish the conviction that there ought to be a Cincinnati and Charleston Railroad, no railroad was forthcoming, for the southern system produced little free capital for investment, and northern capital was finding abundant profitable use at home. The great southwestern convention of 1845 was a renewed attempt to give vitality to southern and western transportation, with Calhoun in the chair this time, instead of Hayne. There were said to have been at Memphis nearly six hundred delegates, from sixteen States, with local auditors who filled every corner of the Methodist Church, where the convention sat. The resolutions that they passed make clear their need for improvement of the rivers and the building of connecting railroads, but show no conviction on either of the vital matters of capital or constitutionality. The South could not control the former, and could not turn to the National Treasury with confidence as the West could do, because of its denial of the right of the Government at Washington to make internal improvements.

There were eighteen States, instead of sixteen as at Memphis, whose delegates met in Chicago on July 5, 1847, to discuss western improvements from a different angle.[1] The local press prided itself upon the fact that this was really a general movement and not so

[1] Robert S. Cotterill has made the most intimate study of the railroad conventions, publishing his conclusions in "Southwestern Railroads and Western Trade," in *Mississippi Valley Historical Review*, 1917, and "Memphis Railroad Convention, 1849," in *Tennessee Historical Magazine*, 1918.

sectional as that of the Memphis gathering. Horace Greeley himself was there, as correspondent of his New York *Tribune*, now six years old, and as propagandist for a closer dependence of the Ohio Valley upon the Middle Seaboard States. The gathering had a strong Whig flavor too, whereas Memphis was generally Democratic. It also had a specific animus, contributed to it by the President of the United States.

In the preceding summer James K. Polk approved the free trade tariff of 1846, and spread despair among the northern Whigs. He followed this by a veto, in August, of a river and harbor bill, upon which the hopes of the West were founded. "By one dash of James K. Polk's pen our prosperity has been checked — our hopes crushed, in defiance too, of the votes of both Houses of Congress and the known will of the people," was the wail of the Milwaukee *Sentinel*. The bill thus blocked carried appropriations for deepening river channels, and protecting harbors everywhere in the West. In deliberating upon it, Polk had an appreciation of the difficulties of a President elected by a coalition of western and southern votes, for the internal improvements that were the West's meat were the South's poison. He was as determined, however, as any of the Scotch Irish on the frontier in which he had been bred, and stuck to the course he mapped out for himself.

The Chicago Convention, twenty-three hundred strong, it is said, exhorted the country to the improvement of rivers and harbors, and the completion of the intersectional railroad lines; and in the following year the first piece of railroad iron was spiked down within the limits of Chicago. It headed towards Galena, while at the same time the roads in Michigan were gathering up their strength for the race for Chicago and the traffic of the prairies.

The local conventions were innumerable after this time. They preached the same doctrine, and revealed the same universal facts that the West had little capital for investment, and the South almost none at all. The typical procedure, when a line was incorporated and a company organized, was for the president of the railroad to print his stock certificates and carry them east, or to Europe, to peddle them around the haunts of concentrated wealth, in the hope that some magnate might be induced to buy them at a discount, and thus enter upon a speculation that might work to the development of some part of the interior of the United States.

At St. Louis, in October, 1849, was a third of the conventions of propaganda. Thomas Hart Benton was the presiding genius of this demonstration, and he had by this date convinced himself that he was the political patron of far-western railroads. Always interested in the development of the remote frontier, Benton, from his first entrance into the Senate in 1821, was its spokesman. He had seen the trade to Santa Fé rise and Oregon become a fact. Slower than some to visualize the possibility of a railroad to the Pacific, he had now been impressed by its probability. With grand oratorical gesture, he pointed to the Far East and India, and showed how it could be made tributary to the United States if only there were a railroad to the Columbia River; and how St. Louis was the natural junction point for such a road with the Mississippi River system. Missouri laid down its first track in 1851 and had a transverse railroad to St. Joseph by 1859, but still the excitement and the resolves failed to uncover the ways and means of wholesale railroad building. With all the noise and propaganda, there was but one railroad of any consequence in the West before 1849.

It was a difficult matter throughout the United States to get the railroad movement started, but every obstacle, except the intellectual adherence to older methods because they were older, was stronger in the West than elsewhere throughout the Union. The more specific problems, to be attacked before the railroad net could become a fact, were how to raise the capital, the form of the debt, the control of expenditure, and the relation of the railroad to politics and the State.

There had been few large capitalistic adventures in the United States or in the world, before the advent of the railroad movement, and most of the wealth of society was in the hands of its owners, to be invested in driblets upon the simpler projects of trade and manufacture. The State was nowhere in business. Except for purposes of war, where every nation borrowed what it could and took by taxation what it was able to collect, there were few occasions when society needed to get together large sums of fluid capital. Before the rise of the factory system, the world got along through small business, with the individual or the partnership quite able to finance the ventures. Such a concern as the East India Company, or the other huge trading corporations of the period of colonial expansion, were more like states within states than they were like private business, and in general they provided no precedent for the growth of private commerce. In America they actually evolved into self-governing commonwealths, and in India into an independent government. No line of continuity that they founded runs unbroken into the big business of the twentieth century.

There was no need for the financial machinery of large enterprises so long as the enterprises were small. When, however, the construction of roads, canals, and railroads began to arouse an interest, and it became apparent that no single capitalist, or even partnership, could provide the total, or would incur the whole risk, the promoters of the new era set about to find a means of assembling enough capital for the task, and to devise methods of making the speculations safe and profitable.

The number of conceivable methods of raising the needful millions was small: the State might take from the people by taxation, it might borrow from the wealthy and repay out of either taxes or anticipated earnings, it might persuade Congress to do either of these, or it might allow many individuals to contribute small sums through the medium of some kind of joint stock enterprise. In fact, each of these methods was used, but as time went on, society passed into a period of corporation finance, in which in addition to all the uncertainties about the primary ventures there were added the uncertainties about the organization and working of corporations as tools of enterprise.

The Cumberland and National Roads were built by the United States, out of proceeds of taxation and the sale of public lands, but Congress declined to follow up the precedent thus set, and turned deaf ears to appeals on behalf of the Erie Canal, and most of the later flood of special improvements. Jackson's veto of the Maysville Turnpike Bill became a classic upon the dangers involved in public participation in local improvements. Certain sorts of improvements of rivers and harbors Congress was willing to carry out at public cost, and the bill for these grew into a public scandal, but it stayed shy of ventures that were projected as remunerative investments. The States were less self-restrained in these ways than Congress and learned an abiding lesson during the panic of 1837. Thereafter it became almost impossible to interest a State in an improvement at its direct cost, until the day of the automobile arrived to bring back the period of wide-open roadmaking.

Occasionally Congress was prevailed upon, in the earlier phases of the railroad movement, to buy a block of stock in an enterprise, as a public contribution. Thus the Portland Canal at Louisville, and the Baltimore and Ohio Railroad received a modicum of aid. But this in principle was even more dangerous than direct construction, for it incurred the risk while leaving the management in private and often irresponsible hands. The States were more generous in this direction and less conservative; and in the excitement of the new movement they passed laws authorizing the minor governmental districts, like towns or counties, to bond themselves and invest the proceeds in railroad stocks. The promoters of the roads stressed always the quasi-public character of the work, as they sought aid, and pointed out the scarcity of private wealth; but as the enterprises took shape, the public bodies who financed them found that the profits, if any, were likely to take a private direction. After the panic of 1837 it became less easy to induce any governmental division to place its credit in the hands of private promoters.

There was left the joint stock corporation. Year after year the legislative bodies that had passed through an era of bank charters were approached by agents solicitous for railroad charters. It was often true that these had no funds in hand and no promise of any, but they asked and the legislatures granted permission to build roads, with terminals often vaguely stated, or not at all, and corporate privileges loosely drawn and filled with "jokers" behind which the promoters could take refuge when their sins came home. The legislatures, in this traffic, suffered the same injuries to their morale and prestige that they suffered when lands were formerly sold by private law or banks were so incorporated. The progress of American legislation from special to general laws on banking and incorporation, runs through the first half of the nineteenth century and is accompanied by a noticeable improvement in conduct and ethical standards. The harsh experience that taught legislatures to abandon the practice of private legislation was much of it acquired during the railroad boom between 1841 and 1857.

Once the charter was voted, the promoters were at liberty to sell stocks and bonds with almost no restraint. There was no general public scrutiny upon issues. The law of corporate liability was so inadequately worked out that creditors could not know how far it was safe to advance funds. In some of the States, the earliest corporation laws made every stockholder personally responsible for all the debts of the corporation, thus passing on the principle of the partnership to the stock company. The effect of this was to make a person of wealth unwilling to subscribe to the stock of any company, lest he be required to "hold the basket" when the affair fell through. The principle of limited liability of shareholders to an amount pro rata with the number of shares held, was gradually established. In some States there was double or triple liability, but the general rule eventually made the stockholder responsible only for what his stock actually called for.

But with liability fixed, there was no way of controlling the price at which stock was sold or to insure to any buyer fair treatment with his associates. The bonded debt was equally uncertain. As soon as a new company acquired any property there was a temptation to mortgage it, nominally to advance the business but often to rob the treasury. Bonds were marketed at the discretion of officials. The shareholder in an early railroad corporation ran a small chance of receiving dividends on his investment, but was almost certain to receive a valuable and costly education in the methods of experimental corporation finance. The engineering methods involved in making a roadbed were still experimental; the mechanical principles of steam locomotion were in large measure conjectural; the corporate mechanism was still on its trial trip. It is no wonder that the thirty thousand miles of railroad before the Civil War were generally built at a loss, often became a matter of disgrace, and occasionally grew into a gross public scandal.

Throughout the United States the railroad movement was attended with these uncertainties and difficulties. In the West they took on an aggravated form because of the general scarcity of capital. It was an added disadvantage of the West that much of the ownership of its railroads was absentee in character, due to the sale of stocks and bonds in the markets far away from home. This bred misunderstanding, for the investor cared little for anything beyond his dividends, and had slight personal knowledge of the conditions of the country upon whose prosperity he held his mortgage.

Extreme cases that help to explain the later attitude of the West toward corporations, may be found in the Yankton bonds and the Watertown mortgages. In the former instance, a county in Dakota Territory bonded itself to aid a promised railroad. The officers of the road took the bonds, disposed of them in the East and built no road. When the time came to pay the principal and interest on the bonds, the farmer issuers, oppressed by a sense of the grave injustice done them, could not see why they should be held to meet the obligation. In the East, in consequence, the idea spread that the West was willing to repudiate its debts; the West was confirmed in its notion of the dishonesty of corporations and the rapacity of creditors.

The Watertown mortgages were a Wisconsin issue.[2] They were first mortgages on farms along the line of a proposed railroad. The promoters had sold the farmers stock, taking the mortgages in return, for the farmers had no cash to subscribe. The mortgages found eastern buyers, yet the road remained a dream. The aggrieved farmers sought by every means to evade the payment of the mortgages on the ground that they had been defrauded, as indeed they were. And before the matter was settled by a final compromise, the misunderstandings between the sections had been intensified and made more permanent.

The devices to which western communities were driven to finance their railroads were so extreme that a political premium was placed upon whatsoever ingenuity should discover a means of shifting the burden. In the end they turned to Congress, following a well-traveled line of thought that the West has used whenever it has felt a need. They persuaded themselves, and then their rulers, that the public lands afforded a proper source for an endowment of railroad construction, and after 1850 there began a period of wholesale land grants inspired by this idea.

There was no novelty in looking to Congress and the land for help. The appropriation of a part of the proceeds of the land sales to the construction of roads, was as old as the century. Not only did the West look automatically to the lands as an available endowment for schools, universities, and State institutions, but Congress as an owner of land was held to have an even interest with the States in whatever should increase the value of real property, and there was no doubt that railroads would accomplish this.

The full history of the appropriation of public lands for internal improvements would include innumerable grants of the actual land needed for the construction through the public domain of roads and canals.[3] No such enterprise could be executed in the West without crossing Government property, and Congress always granted the necessary right of way. When railroads made

[2] Fred Merk, *Economic History of Wisconsin during the Civil War* (1916). The above paragraphs were written considerably before the appearance of Thorstein Veblen, *Absentee Ownership* (1924), which contains an elaboration of their idea, with much embroidery.

[3] John B. Sanborn, "Congressional Grants of Land in Aid of Railways," in University of Wisconsin, *Bulletin*, vol. v.

similar demands, the response was the same. The right of eminent domain which alone made it possible to build a railroad along a suitable right of way, could not run against the United States, and hence the Federal grant was an indispensable prerequisite. These grants of roadbed were generously conceived and went beyond the narrowest needs of the routes. The Illinois and Michigan Canal, in 1822, was allowed ninety feet clear on either side of the canal. The Tallahassee Railway, in Florida, which never got beyond the projector's drawings, was allowed thirty feet clearance on either side in 1834. The West expected such treatment, and it would have been churlish or impolitic to refuse, and before the railroad demands became numerous the policy was well established. In 1852 Congress reduced the matter to the form of a general statute: whenever a railroad should be chartered within the next ten years, and completed within the next fifteen from the date of the act, it was granted in advance a right of way of one hundred feet through the public domain, with the privilege as well of taking extra space as needed for its stations, and cutting timber whenever this could be found.

The act of 1852 settled the question of the right of way, but made it no easier for the company to finance the grades or find the rolling stock. The West wanted more than mere toleration and asked confidently for an endowment, and could point to the precedent of certain of the canals which had been so treated. In connection with the Ohio, Indiana, and Illinois canals, Congress had aided the States to build by allowing them a number of sections along the line, so many on either side, alternately located like the red squares of a checker board. Well before the panic of 1837 the agents of western railroad projects were begging Congress for alternate-section land grants, on the double grounds that the roads could not be built without them and that the roads would so greatly raise the value of the remaining lands that Congress might endow freely and yet remain the gainer by the gift. In the next ten years the Senate frequently approved the idea, for in the Senate the equal representation of the States gave to the newer States a distended influence. But the House of Representatives long stood firmly against such an appropriation. In 1850 this opposition yielded, and the period of the land grants for railroads really opens.

A central railroad for Illinois was the project over which the winning battle was fought. The idea intrigued the prairie statesmen from an early date. Illinois was a long and slender chain of river settlements, from the lead mines in the Galena region to the marshes at the junction of the Ohio with the Mississippi. It had at the beginning no town of importance, and much of its shore line was so low as to be flooded with the freshets that came as regularly as the spring of the year. Inland a little, the vast prairies took shape, where "the soil, for the most part was of a rich, black, deep mould, of unsurpassed fertility, capable of producing in the greatest abundance wheat, rye, corn, oats, and fruits and vegetables of all kinds. But, with all their productiveness, the quarries and mineral wealth had remained comparatively unsettled and uncultivated. . . . These lands had been in the market subject to private entry for a third of a century at a mere nominal value, and yet in very few instances were purchasers found for them. Remote from markets, without facilities for transportation and with roads almost impassable, the cost of handling the products of the lands to a market, and the time employed therein, amounted to almost as much as the value of the land." [4] For fifteen years before Senator Douglas was successful in unloosing Federal aid to reclaim this Illinois Garden of Eden, his predecessors were working at the task.

As early as 1836 the central road idea was recorded among the Illinois statutes in a special charter to a corporation that was to connect the southern end of the State with the Illinois River at the terminus of the Michigan canal. The canal itself was not yet built (nor was it completed for a dozen years), and the Sauk and Fox lands north of it were hardly freed of their native inhabitants, but the imagination of the youthful State was hard at work. The next year, the project was included in the long list of improvements that the State was proposing to construct itself; and money was voted, which, had it existed, would still have been far from adequate to the most limited conception of the road. It did not, however, exist, it could not be improvised, and with the panic, the idea was indefinitely postponed. As a part of the State projection, however, steps were taken to create a southern terminus.

The junction of the Ohio and Mississippi was an inviting strategic point for commerce upon the map, but a reconnoissance of the country showed that for miles in every direction it lay below high water and that only through extensive drainage and levee construction could the tip of Illinois be made habitable. There

---

[4] W. K. Akerman, *Historical Sketch of the Illinois Central Railroad* (1890); Howard G. Brownson, *History of the Illinois Central Railroad to 1870* (1916).

was no village there until in 1837 the State created Cairo by legislative fiat; and Cairo lived a precarious and moist existence for half a century.

A third attempt at a railroad was made in 1843, but it, too, failed. Its promoters invited Congress to allow them to preëmpt a share of the lands through which the road should run, but the time was not yet ripe. Settlement was indeed expanding, and Galena had become a bustling place at the northwest corner of the State. Chicago, too, was on the map; and from Chicago settlers were marching into the interior towards the Rock River. The strategic year that turned the central project toward success was 1847, when the improvement convention at Chicago gave wide advertisement to the northern prairies, and when Stephen A. Douglas moved his home to that young city.

Douglas was a Yankee immigrant, who had edged into Illinois politics in the preceding decade and who sat as a Representative in Congress from 1843 to 1847.[5] He became a Senator in 1847 and was already entrenched as an agile and persuasive Democratic leader. The elderly giants with whom he sat were rounding out their generation without having succeeded in solving their critical problems of sectionalism. Webster, Clay, Calhoun, and Benton, whose voices had advised the Nation since the War of 1812, were still moving their combinations against each other without bringing order from chaos. Douglas brought a new note into the discussions and saw that to men of his generation belonged the future and untold success if only they could reconcile the conflicting currents of interest. He approached the solution as a product of the frontier, unhampered by doubts as to constitutional powers, and captivated by the ideas of the railroad age. He became a leader in the railroad movement from the moment of his settling in Chicago and organized in Congress the votes needed to make the Nation a partner in the work.

There were two main lines of thought that led to a land grant for the endowment of a railroad. One was the old idea of internal improvements which was popular enough on the frontier, but was the particular dogma of the Whig party rather than the party to which Douglas belonged. Few southern Democratic votes could be procured through stressing this. The southern statesmen, however, valued the territorial property of the United States, and John C. Calhoun saw no harm in using a part of the public domain

---

[5] Allen Johnson, *Stephen A. Douglas* (1908), understands both Douglas and the West.

to improve the value of the rest. He rejected the idea as a step in internal improvements but was willing to support it as an investment. And his vote was just as good on one theory as another. In the session of 1848 Douglas put through the Senate a land grant bill but failed to get it through the House. The next Congress saw the bill emerge triumphant in a different shape.

Even such southern Democrats as were willing to invest public lands in railroads were lukewarm respecting a road more than three hundred and fifty miles long in the State of Illinois. And eastern Whigs, interested in the better development of communication with the West, could see only a local project in an improvement that would merely parallel the Mississippi River and increase the commerce to the Gulf. In its old form the scheme called for a railroad between Galena and Cairo; Douglas added to it in 1848 a branch from a central point to Chicago, which gave it an interest to the East. The South found that the local project had blossomed into a national one in 1850, for a road from the Ohio River to Mobile was provided also. As an early "Lakes to Gulf" enterprise, it now conciliated all the votes that were to be influenced.

In addition to a generous right of way the law provided that there should be granted to the States through which the road should run six sections of public land, alternately placed, for every mile of track. This would mean that the finished road would run through a twelve-mile strip, checkered with retained and granted sections. It provided also that the price of the reserved sections should be raised to a double minimum, of $2.50, so that the cash worth of what was retained should equal what the whole was worth before the grant. If any of the railroad sections should prove to be occupied by a preëmptioner, or under other grant, the railroad was at liberty to select another section in exchange or indemnity for it, if it could find one, on the alternate principle, not more than fifteen miles from the track. The grant area thus extended six miles on either side; the indemnity area nine miles farther in each direction. The grant was made not to the Illinois Central Railroad itself, or to the Mobile and Ohio, but to the States through which the line was to run, to be by them devoted to the railroad purpose.

The bill of Senator Douglas became a law September 20, 1850, without attracting much attention outside the deliberative bodies that passed it. It constituted a large step towards the solution of the financial question which blocked the frontier railroads. It made the Nation a partner, and provided legislatures with an excuse for scandal, and promoters with a fund to waste; yet without it the West would have waited long for its railroads and its development. For the next twenty-one years there was never a moment when requests were not before Congress for additional gifts for roads that seemed as useful as the Illinois Central; and in nearly every session the requests were granted. The Middle West was covered soon with its mesh of railroads, the Illinois Central itself being completed by 1856. And the vision of Federal aid that had been realized for local purposes was harnessed to more grandiose schemes as Douglas and his friends developed the idea of substituting for the overland trails a railroad to the Pacific Ocean.

CHAPTER XLVI

KANSAS-NEBRASKA AND THE INDIAN COUNTRY

On the frontier of the forties the transition began that was to change the United States from its agrarian simplicity to urban and industrial complexity, that was to transform the method by which the settlement of the unoccupied wastes proceeded, and that was in another half century to drive the frontier off the map. The people of that frontier were Jacksonian, whether they thought of themselves as Democrat or Whig, and they were engaged in writing into their State constitutions the truths of Jacksonian experience, which they expected to last forever. Their farms were filling in the chinks over all the settled area and were pushing the new lines against the wilderness of the Upper Mississippi, the plains of Texas, and the valleys of the Pacific Coast. Behind the outlying farms, modern methods in the guise of railroads were catching up; and before the period was ended the railroad frontier, aided by national gifts, reached the Missouri River at its bend. Here it found that the main agricultural frontier, which spread over the State of Missouri in the twenties, had paused on the edge of the higher plains and the scantily watered region that early travelers had designated as the American Desert. The period of the forties, so far as economic development is concerned, begins with the revival of activity after the panic of 1837 and continues unabated until checked and terminated by the panic of 1857.

The agricultural frontier, reaching the bend of the Missouri about the time that Monroe laid down his Indian policy, did not cross the Missouri or seriously encroach upon that policy for thirty years. In spite of the hundreds of thousands of emigrants who sought better conditions in Oregon or California, the western edge of farms remained substantially permanent, a little east of Independence. It could not have remained permanent if these migrants had seen anything that they coveted, for the United States never developed either law or opinion strong enough to balk a frontier that once set itself in motion. The country of the Indian Frontier was not a desert but it was less attractive than the well-watered farm lands of Indiana, Illinois, or Wisconsin. Its staple crop of grain was not marketable in the absence of roads or navigable rivers. Until the railroads reached it, it was possible to leave the Indians in undisputed possession. The trails ran through it, and the emigrants traveled along the trails, without desiring as yet to stop and acquire land. As late as 1853, the Commissioner of Indian Affairs, George W. Manypenny, reported that there was no serious encroachment of squatters upon the lands of his wards west of Iowa and Missouri.

Before the acquisition of the Southwest, and the Compromise of 1850, the Indian Frontier policy had been abandoned although not formally repudiated. With the development of heavy traffic along the trails the Government had stopped the further definite colonization of Indians. This was indeed substantially complete by 1841 and needed no further legislation or administration. The treaty arrangements with the Indians for the next decade were again fragmentary negotiations, as they had been before 1825. At the head of the Mississippi the Sioux, Sauk and Fox, and Winnebago were under continuous pressure as the Iowa and Wisconsin pioneers worked out their destiny. In 1851 there were notable new Indian conferences, but they can scarcely be connected with any organized Indian policy.

The great Sioux cession in Minnesota Territory is the outstanding negotiation with the Indians of the border in 1851.[1] As early as 1837 the Sioux of this region ceded to the United States all their lands east of the Mississippi, and Fort Snelling at the junction of the St. Peter's and Mississippi was the only haunt of white men among them. When Iowa and Wisconsin in turn became States, there was turned adrift the northwest part of their territorial area. By this time some five thousand settlers had moved in, to resent being deprived of all the institutions of government. They were Wisconsin Territory until that became a State; then they were nothing. They, however, sent H. H. Sibley as a delegate to Congress, just as though they were still possessed of territorial status, and Congress allowed him to sit and paid his salary. In March, 1849, his bill to create a Territory of Minnesota became a law. But Minnesota being almost entirely within unceded Sioux lands had no room for a swelling population, save in the angle between the St. Croix and Mississippi rivers, that had once belonged to the Northwest Territory.[2]

[1] The *Minnesota Historical Collections* have gathered many reminiscent articles on the Indian problem. W. W. Folwell, *Minnesota* (1908).
[2] N. West, *Henry Hastings Sibley* (1889); Wilson P. Shortridge, *The Transition of a Typical*

In 1851 Governor Alexander Ramsey conducted treaty councils with the Sioux, in which they agreed to cede all their claims to territory east of the Red River of the North and the Big Sioux River (constituting now the western boundary of Minnesota) excepting a strip twenty miles wide along the Upper Minnesota River. The compensation promised to the tribes was considerable, but its payment was diverted because at the moment of signing the cessions the tribes were persuaded to sign an agreement that claims of the traders against individual Indians should be satisfied out of the fund before the proceeds should be divided. The traders saw to it that their claims were greater than the whole purchase price; with the result that the tribes had the mortification of seeing their lands disappear without an equivalent in any form that they could understand. To make matters worse, the encroaching settlers moved upon the lands as soon as the treaty was signed and before the Senate had ratified or Congress appropriated the purchase price. "I used all my efforts to prevent this state of things and to induce the white population not to occupy the land until it could be done lawfully," declared the local Indian agent. "I called on the military at Fort Snelling to assist in removing improper persons; but they refused to act. The current of emigration became irresistible, and the country is virtually in the possession of the white population." By 1860 there were 172,023 residents in this new territory.

The treatment of the Minnesota Indians was tragically unfair, as the agricultural frontier swept over them and left a train of grievances to drench the Minnesota farms with blood before they were forgotten. Further west on the open plains the other tribes of Sioux, and their relatives, were brought into negotiations in the same summer, and only less unfairly dealt with.

The Upper Platte Agency at Fort Laramie was an important strategic point as soon as the columns of emigrants began to march up the Platte Valley, *en route* to the Sweetwater and South Pass. There was rarely any serious disturbance, but the emigrants were continually complaining of the thieving and beggary of the plains Indians, while they themselves were violating the Intercourse Act and selling whiskey to the natives. In 1849 the Secretary of the Interior, as one of his earliest official acts, for his office was new that year, recommended that funds be provided

Frontier with Illustrations from the Life of Henry Hastings Sibley (1922); Marcus L. Hansen, *Old Fort Snelling, 1819–1858* (1918).

for a great council with these tribes along the trails. In the follow-ing year the funds were available, and the agent at Fort Laramie began the difficult task of rounding up his wards.[3]

As the Indians were scattered on the plains from Canada to the Arkansas River and could never be easily diverted from their hunts or hurried to a meeting place, there were months of prepara-tion necessary before the tribes began to drift in during the summer of 1851. They came from all directions, Sioux mostly, but also bands of Assiniboin, Arikara, Grosventres, Crows, Cheyenne, and Arapahoe. The councils were held under the direction of Thomas Fitzpatrick, the local agent, and at their close the as-sembled braves recognized the right of the United States Govern-ment to build roads and posts at pleasure, agreed not to commit depredations upon emigrants, and accepted the council presents as well as the promise of an annuity of $50,000, for fifty years. The Sioux agreed that their proper range lay north of the Platte Trail; the Arapahoe and Cheyenne similarly accepted as theirs the country between the Platte and the Arkansas. The United States Senate, in its wisdom, amended this treaty to read fifteen instead of fifty years, but otherwise treated it as though it were in force. It was not possible to send it back to the tribes for resubmission, and it never really had the force of law. Yet in spite of the cancel-lation by the Senate of seventy per cent of the compensation promised in the agreement, the tribes, in general, kept the peace.

The lack of deliberate evil intent, which pervaded the Indian affairs of the forties, disappeared shortly after the negotiation of the Fort Laramie Treaty and in the next few years they appear to have been directed by persons who knew only too well what they wanted. In the summer of 1854 the first land office in the Indian Country was opened across the border from Missouri, to retail to settlers the tribal lands that had been dedicated to perpetual Indian use. The double forces of slavery propaganda and railroad extension had met, to bring about the repeal of the Missouri Com-promise, and to force the unwilling frontier of the farmers to en-croach upon the old Indian frontier. The Civil War period had begun and was for the moment marching hand in hand with the forces that were to make secession an impossibility.

[3] James C. Maline, "Indian Policy and Western Expansion," is an excellent study in University of Kansas *Bulletins*, 1921; Lucy E. Textor, "Official Relations between the United States and the Sioux Indians," in Leland Stanford Jr., University *Publications*, 1896.

The suggestion that a railroad might some day be constructed to the Pacific was made as soon as the American imagination began to play upon the idea of any railroad. And as soon as the earliest pioneers had crossed South Pass, this route began to impress itself as the desirable one. By a process of elimination, no other route could be of practical importance until after 1846, for until then Spain controlled the Pacific Coast north to 42°, and the British half of Oregon silenced discussion of any line north of Puget Sound. The only way to get to the Pacific was through Oregon and down the valley of the Columbia. The early missionaries called attention to the moderate grades that prevailed along the whole Oregon Trail, and editors gave space from time to time to letters whose writers figured out the costs of such a road and descanted upon the advantages. So long as these believed that it could be built for ten thousand dollars a mile, the practical value of their suggestions was less than the sentimental.

But every year after the panic of 1837 railroads became more of a reality, the Pacific settlements were of greater consequence, and the obstructions in the way of a road became a matter of keener regret. These obstructions were of two sorts. The physical obstruction was some two thousand miles of unoccupied plains and mountains; the political was the policy of Government which consecrated forever to Indian use a compact barrier of land bounded on the east by the Indian frontier line, and on the west by the territories that faced the Pacific. By 1850, the engineers were aware that it was entirely possible to build a road, if it could be financed. In the same year the Indian Country received a definite western boundary along the lines of the new territories of Oregon, Utah, New Mexico, and Texas. Within this Indian Country the treaty obligations of the United States were such that the Indians could not be dispossessed without national stultification; and until dispossessed, the country could never be settled by whites, and support a railroad.

By 1850 reasonable men supposed that a Pacific railroad would some day be constructed. They owed much of their enlightenment to the general influences of the railroad era and much to the specific propaganda of the first great devotee of Pacific railroads, Asa Whitney, of New York.

Asa Whitney was a merchant in the Chinese trade. For over half a century American ships had been circling the Horn, with furs for China, to bring back silks, tea, and the objects of art that still fill the cupboards and cabinets of seafaring families. Whitney visited China and beheld with his own eyes the inexhaustible market for American goods. He returned to devote his life to the promotion that should make this traffic a possession of the United States. A railroad to the mouth of the Columbia River would cut many months from the dreary ocean voyage and would pass the wealth of the Orient through the port of New York. "There is the East; there is India!" exclaimed Benton when he had been educated to the point of believing in the continental railroad. Whitney, long before him in the field, presented to Congress a specific petition for a railroad charter in 1845.

The Whitney memorial, bearing the date of January 28, 1845, is embedded in the public documents of the second session of the Twenty-eighth Congress. It describes the trade in rhetorical fashion and suggests that the obvious line for the railroad is one beginning at a suitable point on the Great Lakes. It asks of Congress a charter and a land grant. Five years before Senator Douglas and his allies put the Illinois Central bill through Congress, Whitney was begging for a strip of the public domain sixty miles wide, along the route of his projection. He explained in detail that he would build the road with the cheap European laborers who were thronging in through New York from Ireland and Germany; that he would pay these as little as possible in cash and as much as possible in land; that each construction gang, when paid off, would settle along the route as a nucleus for the future population; and that in their trade there would be found a profitable traffic for the railroad from the opening of its first section.

Whitney was immediately recognized by *Niles' Weekly Register* as "prince of all projectors," but he was born too soon. Although he easily convinced his hearers that his scheme was practicable, he could not live down the suspicion of being a visionary himself. He made a survey west from Milwaukee in the summer of 1845 and ran a publicity service whose results can be seen in papers all over the United States. He went, in succeeding years, on speaking trips, visited State legislatures, addressed them in their assembly chambers and invariably passed out a sheaf of blank petitions which his interested auditors used to bombard the members of Congress. "This enterprising gentleman . . . has perhaps more than any man in the country illustrated the importance of a connection with the Pacific," said *DeBow's Review* in 1849.

At the moment when the acceptance of Whitney's idea became

so general that his scheme was regarded as reasonable, other events removed the simplicity that attended it until 1846. In that year the United States acquired the undisputed ownership of a part of Oregon and entered upon the war which made California a possession of the country. There had been but one road to Oregon; but now that California was American, the Santa Fé Trail and the various routes through Texas to San Diego and San Francisco became practical. There developed among the Mississippi valley localities a rivalry to possess the profits of a continental railroad, and in the nation at large a jealousy of sections, lest the other section should reap the profit.

The frontier of the forties, excited by the future profits to be earned by the local railroads that grew apace, and absorbed in the local selfishness that was the touchstone of success, presented a western front in which several localities might contest with reason for the terminal of the Pacific railroad. The city of New Orleans, which already thought of itself as the metropolis of the interior, believed that the best route would run due west through Texas and New Mexico to the Colorado River at Yuma, and thence to Southern California. Vicksburg had its devotees, and there, as well as at Memphis, was insistence upon a line that should thread the cotton plains of Texas, to El Paso and Yuma. Cairo, to which the new Central Railroad was expected to bring the business of Illinois, had a vision of western trade, as had St. Louis which already monopolized the fur trade and the western outfitting business. The youthful city of Chicago, which in imagination saw the bonds that were to connect it with the Atlantic, saw the Platte trail inviting a railroad to the Pacific; a future which Milwaukee was disposed to contest, for Milwaukee had similar ambitions of its own. And before Whitney's voice was silenced by his retirement, the tip of Lake Superior, where Duluth now is, had its supporters as the farthest west of the Great Lakes.

The log-rolling of the localities, after 1846, forbade the authorization of a railroad, and even if there had been no other difficulties than the mere selection of a route there must have been a long deadlock. The larger sectionalism was the reflection of the slavery controversy that placed the slaveholding States in a compact group, ambitious for itself and even more jealous of anything that might enhance the opportunities of the rival section. The agitation of Whitney and his followers proceeded after 1845, and the more it convinced, the more it aroused emotions to block its fulfillment. In 1853, after the voice of California had entered the debate, the most that Congress could do was to authorize a series of surveys of possible routes to the Pacific.

WASHINGTON TERRITORY 1853

OREGON TERRITORY 1848

ROCKY MOUNTAIN DIVIDE

UNORGANIZED INDIAN COUNTRY PROTECTED BY TREATIES AND ACT OF 1834

MINNESOTA TERRITORY 1849

CALIFORNIA 1850

UTAH TERRITORY 1850

NEW MEXICO TERRITORY 1850

IOWA 1846

MO. 1821

ARK. 1836

L.A. 1812

TEXAS
ANNEXED 1845

ORGANIZATION OF THE WEST
1850-1854
Frontier Line of 1850 ooooºººººoo

"If any route is reported to this body as the best," said Gwin, the new Senator from California, "those that may be rejected will always go against the one selected." His pessimism was warranted for southern Senators were openly admitting the existence of a Pacific railroad majority and hoping that enemies of the road might accomplish its defeat by stirring up dissensions among its friends. It was possible, however, to place in the Army Appropriation Bill of 1853 a sum of $150,000 to be spent by the Secretary of War for the maintenance of survey parties in the field.[4] The Secretary to spend the money was Jefferson Davis, of Mississippi,

[4] The results of these surveys are conveniently digested with excellent bibliographies, in George L. Albright, *Official Explorations for Pacific Railroads* (1922).

whose political connections were already crystallized and whose mind was not likely to be convinced in favor of any route that would serve the North.

But the friends of a railroad knew that there were other things than prejudice and politics to impede the construction of a line along the Platte trail. The Indian Country was a continuous menace to their interests. It could be said with truth that a southern line would cross the mountains more easily and be less blocked by snow in winter than a northern route. It could also be said, and this carried much real weight, that Congress had already brought into existence a continuous zone of organized States and territories, Louisiana, Texas, New Mexico, and California, through which the railroad would run. Every mile of the route would be available for colonization, with no limitations except the fertility of the soil and the nature of the terrain. In December, 1853, this was reinforced by the Gadsden Purchase from Mexico of the Gila Valley, through which was known to run a specially appropriate right of way for such a road.

But any northern route was barricaded by the Indian Country which now stood as a monument to the short sight of those who in 1825–1841 built it up as a perpetual western boundary to the States. There were none now who thanked God for the American Desert and the Indian tribes that prevented straggling of the people across the continent. Instead a demand arose that the Indian Frontier be abolished, that the tribes of the border be made to cede their lands again and that a right of way for the agricultural frontier be acquired west of the Bend of the Missouri. The Commissioner of Indian Affairs was directed in 1853 to undertake the negotiations and remove the tribes.

With such treaties in mind, Manypenny, the Commissioner, visited the Indian frontier in the summer of 1853 and found the tribes in residence there, just as they had been colonized twenty years or more before.[5] He had no stomach for the job, for the wording of the colonization treaties and their even more solemn implication forbade the creation of any organized territory within treaty limits; and the tribes had shown no desire to abandon their guarantees. They were not even under pressure of population,

---

[5] The *Annual Reports* of the United States Commissioner of Indian Affairs afford a running picture and comment on Indian matters. They include not only the operations of the Commissioner for the period, but have detailed reports from the several agencies. Manypenny subsequently wrote *Our Indian Wards* (1880).

which had in the past given a justification to many of the removals, and Manypenny found almost no squatters or prospectors
among the tribes. It was a political demand that he was serving,
to remove the obstacle to railroad building and to create territories to placate the southern Democrats. The front of the tribes
that were now to be disturbed began at the north with the Omaha,
in the angle between the Missouri and the Platte. South of these,
the more important Indian nations were the Oto and Missouri,
the Sauk and Fox, the Kickapoo, and the Delawares who were in
the angle north of the Kansas River, with an outlet to the game
range of the western plains. The Shawnee were south of the
Kansas; and below them the Kaskaskia and Peoria, the Piankeshaw and Wea, and the Miami. Yet further south there was a
reserve that was ascribed to the New York Indians, which these
had never been willing to occupy.

Without enthusiasm, most of the tribes of the border signed the
treaties that were offered them in 1853 and accepted compensation
and territory elsewhere. But about half the nations refused to
yield completely to the pressure and adhered to reduced reserves
within the limits of their possessions. Of these the Delawares were
the most important, since the Delawares reserve touched the
Missouri border at Independence and was a direct impediment to
settlement of the Kansas River Valley, or the region around Fort
Leavenworth. Where tribes were stubborn, Manypenny accepted
partial cessions and made an agreement that the ceded lands
should be administered by the United States in trust for the ceding
nations; that the acres should be sold at public sale to the highest
bidder and that they should not be offered at the usual minimum
price of $1.25 until after the lapse of three years. In July, 1854,
Congress opened a land office in what was to be Kansas, for the
sale of the Indian lands thus acquired. But it made no serious
effort to keep preëmptors off the trust lands, which the contracts
required to be sold at auction. Grave scandals grew out of this
neglect, but the tribes were too weak to make an effective resistance. "By alternate persuasion and force," wrote Manypenny in
his annual report after the negotiation was completed, "some of
these tribes have been removed, step by step, from mountain to
valley, and from river to plain, until they have been pushed halfway across the continent. They can go no further: on the ground
they now occupy the crisis must be met, and their future determined."

The statesmen who framed the Compromise of 1850 believed that it was necessary to save the Union and that without it the plantation States would try the remedy of secession. If this should occur, it was believed by many that the States of the Mississippi Valley would of necessity follow the South because of the dominating influence of the Father of Waters as a trade route. Canals had been given up as an economic panacea, and the significance of the through railroads was not appreciated by even the most enthusiastic promoters of the railroad movement.

The Compromise saved the day, and secession was averted until it was too late for it to succeed. But the elder statesmen agreed that another such struggle would wreck the Union, and pledged themselves, after the passage of the measures in the autumn of 1850, not to revive the question of slavery, but to treat it as a settled issue. In his inaugural address the next President, Franklin Pierce, in 1853, gave his unhesitating support to the measures of 1850 and expressed the fervent "hope that the question is at rest." He spoke, however, to a new political audience, for Webster, Clay, and Calhoun were dead, and Benton had been repudiated by his State. Pierce had behind him a victorious Democratic party, entrenched in both houses of Congress, but it was marshaled by new generals, Jefferson Davis, William H. Marcy, and Stephen A. Douglas. Two of these were in the cabinet; the third was party leader in the Senate.

The only unorganized part of the United States after the Compromise of 1850 was the Indian Country, running from Texas to Canada, and from the Missouri border to the Rockies. So long as it endured, it constituted a barrier which the most hopeful railroad projector could hardly expect to pass, and its significance was fully appreciated by southern leaders who pointed to their own open strip as the obvious route. In the Congress that expired in 1853 the signs indicated that the barrier would not be allowed to stand, in spite of treaties and southern support. The railroad surveys were ordered, the Indian cessions were demanded, and a bill to create a Territory of Nebraska covering most of the Indian Country passed the Senate. In the debates over this, opposition was based upon the good faith which was pledged against it, and the bill failed of enactment. It reappeared in the first session of the new Democratic Administration, accompanied by a report from Douglas of Illinois, the chairman of the Senate Committee on Territories.

The motive of Senator Douglas in pushing through Congress in 1854 a bill for the territorial organization of the Indian Country has been one of the great moot points in the interpretation of American history. To his surprise and dismay, his measure broke the charmed silence, and let loose all the attack upon slavery that the old leaders had hoped to stifle. Mr. James Ford Rhodes, whose monumental volumes are still, with right, the guide of the student through this period, felt able to assert with confidence, "that the action of the Illinois Senator was a bid for Southern support in the next Democratic convention." And most historians have agreed with Mr. Rhodes. But of recent years Professor Frank H. Hodder, whose diligent research in the history of the West has been done from the angle of a professor in Kansas, has collected much testimony to indicate that Douglas was primarily a railroad statesman. He shows with great plausibility and what approaches proof, that Douglas's leadership was wrapped up in the economic advantage of his adopted State and of his home town, Chicago. The South was averse to further northern territories from which slavery could be excluded and averse also to aiding any northern railroad to the Far West. To get support for a railroad measure out of a Congress in which the Democrats were so strongly entrenched it was necessary to pay a price. And this Douglas unquestionably paid.[6]

As he first brought in his bill in January, 1854, it still provided for a single territory of Nebraska, but he had discovered that in spite of the Missouri Compromise it was not necessary to exclude slavery from it. The principle of the Compromise of 1850, he said in substance, was the right of each territorial community to determine for itself the character of its local institutions. California had come in free because it so desired; Utah and New Mexico had been organized without requirement upon slavery. There were many, moreover, he advised, who doubted whether Congress ever had the right to exclude slavery from any of the territory of the United States. Accordingly, in the spirit of 1850, he urged the creation of Nebraska Territory without a word on slavery.

Within the next few days his ideas grew. Kansas was cut apart from Nebraska, and embraced that part of the former huge territory that fell between the thirty-seventh and fortieth parallels. This was obviously to give a chance for each of the sections

[6] Frank H. Hodder, "Genesis of the Kansas-Nebraska Act," in Wisconsin State Historical Society *Proceedings*, 1912; but compare P. O. Ray, *The Repeal of the Missouri Compromise* (1909).

to gain a State. An amendment was also added to the bill that said in explicit words what Douglas's original measure had said by inference. It declared that the Missouri Compromise was repealed, that there might be no misunderstanding on the subject.

From January until the end of May the battle raged, with the South finding its price and supporting with growing enthusiasm the repeal of the Missouri Compromise. But in the North, instead of gratification that now a means was being found to build a central railroad, a new political party was born to fight the extension of slavery; and even northern Democrats joined in the denunciation of Douglas and his bill. The disturbance was out of all proportion to the expectation; what seems to have been conceived as a piece of log-rolling in order to let the railroads cross the plains became a fight of vital consequence. Its leader did not weaken from the storm he had provoked. Instead he found and developed further reasons to justify his attitude on the Missouri Compromise and convinced his friends that popular sovereignty was a new and great interpretation of the frontier ideal of democracy. He was doubtless not blind to the fact that if he could succeed in getting slavery transferred to the realm of popular sovereignty and out of national politics, there would be an excellent chance for him to lead a united Democratic Party where he would.[7]

The new Territories of Kansas and Nebraska were created May 30, 1854, and together embraced the whole Indian Country except the part between Texas and the thirty-seventh parallel, which is to-day the State of Oklahoma. A land office was opened, and the sections acquired from the Indians by Manypenny's treaties were thrown open to the preëmptioner. But the passions of the debate prevented the territories from being settled in the normal fashion that had recently been witnessed in Iowa and Texas. There was no drift to Kansas or Nebraska until politicians started one by propaganda. North and South the cry was heard against permitting either section to colonize and thus determine the future of the territories. Northern philanthropists gave of their wealth to aid societies to assist able-bodied men to go to Kansas, to make it free. Southern politicians urged the sons of the South to keep it slave. The response to these heated calls came mostly from the north, for persons wealthy enough to have slaves generally took

[7] From "consent of the governed," through "popular sovereignty," to "self-determination," there has been a marked similarity of teaching among Democratic statesmen. Andrew C. McLaughlin, *Lewis Cass* (1891).

little part in frontier advance. The southerners contented themselves with riding across the border, *en masse* from Missouri, to vote a southern ticket on election days. Kansas became "bleeding Kansas" in a few months as partisans of the sections clashed, but the bloodshed was lessened because of the scant number of settlers who came in.[8]

Pierce, and after him Buchanan, did what Presidents could do to make a slave State out of Kansas. They favored the slave minorities that called themselves the people and disapproved the action of the free settlers, who were the majority. Four governors of the territory were appointed in as many years, in the vain search for a man who could manage Kansas. The factions on the ground made four constitutions in the same period, but were properly balked in their aspirations for immediate statehood, for when the decade came to an end there were only 107,206 people in Kansas; and in Nebraska but 28,841. As a means of settling the slavery question the Kansas-Nebraska Bill was even less than a total failure. It was hardly more important as a means of promoting emigration. But it was a success in removing the barricade of the Indian Country and preparing the way for a railroad to the Pacific.

[8] W. E. Miller, *Peopling of Kansas* (1906).

CHAPTER XLVII

"PIKE'S PEAK OR BUST!"

THE panic of 1857, like its predecessor twenty years before, separated two waves of migration. Two sharply contrasting types of effort met at this point; and two geographic areas whose common boundary is the line of the Bend of the Missouri, assumed modern form in the successive periods. There was to be in the new era, and in the western region of the plains, little of the gradual growth that was distinctive of the advance of the agricultural frontier from the line of the Proclamation of 1763 to that of the Missouri Bend. This had been a continuous process, without haste and without cessation, until it brought Missouri into the Union in 1821. Then its pressure to the west had stopped for a period of thirty years. Rounding out its conquests north and south, it remained a Mississippi Valley movement. The advance after the panic of 1857 was thus not from a new frontier into a newer, but from and through a community in Missouri and Iowa whose institutions had lost much of the rawness of frontier beginnings and were taking on an aspect of settled prosperity. The country from Lake Michigan to the Missouri was indeed yet chiefly agricultural, but it was becoming mixed with the complex contacts of the railroad age and the first stages of industrial society. Cincinnati and New Orleans, the centers of wealth in the West at the beginning of the century, were now great cities; but their dominance over the Mississippi Valley was being contested by St. Louis and Chicago, the newer growths of the steamboat and railroad ages.

The town of St. Louis was rounding its first century of settlement in the fifties.[1] In this hundred years it had seen the rise and decline of the Missouri fur trade, the advent of the flatboat migration and the arrival of the river steamers. It had found the reason for its existence in the supply trade of the farming country around it, and in wholesale business which it could command from its strategic position near the head of river commerce. Benton, in his oratorical moments, spoke of fifty thousand miles of navigable

---

[1] L. U. Reavis, *St. Louis: The Future Great City of the West* (1875), possessed an ironical title even at the date of its publication.

inland waters in the Mississippi system and tributary to St. Louis, and he had been reluctant to envisage any other type of commerce. Half of Benton's mileage was imaginary, so far as it was available for anything bigger than a flatboat in flood time, yet there was enough to insure the rise of an important city at the mouth of the Missouri River.

At the time of the admission of Missouri, St. Louis was a town of some 5000 inhabitants, and twenty years later it boasted 16,469. The Jacksonian migration was abroad by this later date, and in the next two decades the city grew tenfold, to 160,773 in 1860. This was, in 1860, a considerable body of citizens, more numerous than the whole population of Delaware, nearly as large as that of the whole State of Minnesota, and half as large again as the Territory of Kansas possessed in the same year. These two decades were those of the fullest development of the steamboat traffic, and the sloping levees at St. Louis were ever crowded with the bustle that accompanied it.[2] Separated by the river from contact with the eastern railroad net (a contact not made until the opening of the Eads bridge in 1874), St. Louis looked to the West for its railroad conquests. On July 4, 1851, it broke ground for the first of its State-aided group of radiating lines.[3] The State was sponsor, exchanging bonds for mortgages on the railroad properties. But it was fifteen years before the main line west from St. Louis, which it grandiloquently called the Pacific Railroad of Missouri, completed its track parallel to the Missouri River, through Jefferson City to Kansas City. Six years earlier than this the Hannibal and St. Joseph Railroad had made the crossing of the State to the Missouri River above the bend; but this had been accomplished not under the stimulus of Missouri, but at the prompting of the northern rival of St. Louis, the city of Chicago on the lakes.

The upstart town, as Chicago appeared to St. Louis eyes, showed signs of rapid growth at about the time of the memorable river and harbor convention of 1847. It may have had sixteen thousand inhabitants then, living on the marshy tract south of the mouth of the Chicago River and struggling against the continuous attacks of wind, dust, and mud. The antiquarians could recall a few families and a Government fort dating from the first years of

[2] Mark Twain, *Life of the Mississippi* (1883), is the classic description of this environment, in which Tom Sawyer and Huckleberry Finn were born to live forever.

[3] Robert E. Riegel, "Trans-Mississippi Railroads during the Fifties," in *Mississippi Valley Historical Review*, vol. x; "The Missouri Pacific Railroad," in *Missouri Historical Review*, vol. xviii.

the century; and at the evacuation of this fort in the War of 1812 there had occurred one of the worst disasters of that conflict. For twenty years more Fort Dearborn and its environs remained far in advance of agricultural settlement, and no steamboat is known to have made a landing there until in 1832 one of them acted as army transport, bringing General Winfield Scott and his eastern troops to the relief of the border threatened by Black Hawk. Hastened by the emergency they had made the trip from the Chesapeake, by way of the Erie Canal, in eighteen days to Chicago. On Scott's recommendation, cordially reinforced by the local interests, Congress undertook the construction of a harbor there, and the Illinois and Michigan canal commissioners had already platted a town site at the northern end of the canal.

In the next fifteen years the beginnings of Chicago occurred, and there developed a rivalry with the other lake towns, St. Joseph, Michigan City, Southport, Racine, and Milwaukee, out of which Chicago emerged, triumphant. Its great special advantages were its access to the prairies of northern Illinois, and the congestion of trails, as overland settlers from the East rounded the tip of Lake Michigan, before spreading out west and northwest. The convention of 1847 developed local self-confidence, the first local railroad started towards Galena in 1848, and four years later the two railroads from Michigan made their entry. Chicago became the center of an intricate railroad net in the fifties, while St. Louis was still projecting ways and means. The opening in 1857 of the long line from St. Louis to Cincinnati, thence to Marietta and Baltimore, parallel to the Ohio River, did not alter the fact that Chicago was the railroad center and that the dominance of St. Louis was grounded upon the river traffic. There were 29,963 Chicagoans in 1850, and 109,260 in 1860. Ten years more, and the last census in which St. Louis led, showed St. Louis 310,864; Chicago 298,977. In 1880 Chicago was more than 150,000 ahead of its rival.

The prosperity of the fifties was great everywhere in the United States. In the South it was King Cotton that made the fortunes, in the North the rise of manufactures, in the West the transformation of agricultural frontier into complex commonwealths. Everywhere railroad mileage was one of the best indices of excitement and prosperity; and of the thirty thousand miles of 1860, nearly nine tenths were laid down between the Mexican War and the financial crisis of 1857. If one looks at the productive industries from which the wealth for this investment was acquired, one sees chiefly the agricultural, for mineral exploitation was in its infancy, and the rising manufactures were still generally too small to supply American consumption. At the beginning of the period little of the capital was found abroad, for the European investor was wary of Americans after his experience with the default and repudiation that followed the panic of 1837. But as years advanced and the era of prosperity became better founded, foreign capital was available to supplement the savings of the older States.

The agencies for spending were further developed than those for accumulating. The banking system of the United States went from bad to worse after the expiration of the Second Bank of the United States. The balance of trade drained coin out of the country to pay foreign creditors, and there was no important American source of precious metals until after 1848. The Whig Party, where it could, supported banks; but there was no official machinery for their oversight. The fifteen hundred institutions that carried on the business of the country at the end of the fifties, were uncontrolled and speculative and possessed of most of the dangerous elements that marked the banks of the period after the War of 1812. The better bankers, with a half century's experience, knew more about banking, but they were in constant fight with the wild cats and the inflationists who flourished under the banking rule of *laissez faire*. Currency was still unreliable and inadequate, and credit machinery was unevenly distributed, while the amount of credit at hand was progressively affected by the sequence of years of extra heavy investment.

The time came, as come it must, when the capital available was less than the aggregate demands of the country, and some one must perforce do without. The railroads, the farm developments, the roads and bridges, and the plants of the growing cities, as well as the factories where the artisans worked and the new houses in which they lived, progressively tied up the accumulated capital, much of which yielded no income, or none as yet. The period of prosperity lasted longer than it otherwise would have done, because in the middle of the fifties the American grain found a strong market abroad created through the closing of the Russian wheat fields in the Crimea. While the Crimean War lasted, the prosperity of the United States was secure. The prosperity of the South was sure even after the peace, because cotton was just finding its unlimited market, and the sewing machine was increasing

the consumption of cotton faster than the planters could harvest
and gin it. In the winter of 1856–1857, with the war over, the
business of Europe began to return to its normal channels, and the
market for the American surplus broke. The railroads that were
still in search of lenders, found that they could not place their
stocks and bonds to any advantage, and a general stringency
served notice that the moment was approaching for a cessation of
activities and a liquidation of debt.

There need not necessarily have been a destructive panic, although it is hard to see how much suffering could have been
avoided, with the construction enterprises stopping because they
had no money for pay-roll use or for purchase of material. But the
failure of a great financial institution, the Ohio Life Insurance and
Trust Company on August 24, 1857, was the spark that set free the
explosive forces of financial apprehension. A writer in *Hunt's
Merchants' Magazine* pointed out that the new electric telegraph
acted as an intensifier for the crisis, for it flashed the bad news
instantaneously to every section of the country, and the depression instead of working out in waves from the center of disturbance
to the circumference of the frontier, struck everywhere at once.
Banks failed, one hundred and fifty, perhaps. Notes that had
been used as currency lost their value. Persons with assets tried
to realize upon them all at once, and the markets for securities
broke. This was the first panic in the experience of the new stock
exchanges, and they were caught unready and at a loss. In the
autumn of 1857 the Middle States, the East, and the Northwest
were financially prostrate, and unemployed persons congregated
in the towns, while broken farmers thought of abandoning their
places and seeking better fortune elsewhere. In the Mississippi
Valley, whose whole social aspect had been changed in twenty
years since the last great panic, men were torn loose from their
moorings during 1857 and 1858, and set to looking for a new means
of easy wealth.

Just about Christmas, 1858, the news reached Omaha that gold
had been found among the foothills of the eastern slope of the
Rockies, in what rumor described as the Pike's Peak Country.
This was enough to set the drifting population on the march, and
the mineral empire budded with mining camps in the next few
months. It would have attracted a large migration, even in time
of general prosperity as California did in 1849, but it now was
visited by a body of seekers inflated by the depression of the East.

The antecedents of the Pike's Peak discovery run back to the excitement of 1849. The forty-niners by tens of thousands were summoned across the continent by the lure of gold which few of them were to find. Some lost their courage and turned back *en route;* and some came home disillusioned by the reality of El Dorado. Others remained in California to live and farm, and found a reason for existence which had not been before them when they started. A few found gold, and fewer still retained it. And an indefinite, but large number, remained forever seekers. These last acquired the habit of the roving life; with a pick and pan, a burro and a few camp tools they spent their lives prospecting the mountain valleys. They pushed far down into Mexico and South America and far up to Alaska and the Yukon; they appeared in the gold fields of Australasia and Africa; and the casual camp fire in any mining region thereafter was likely to stir up a flood of reminiscence that covered the mineral regions of the world. Many of them are known to have continued their search on the American Continental Divide throughout the fifties, and there were frequent unfounded rumors of discoveries that stirred the pulse of the ambitious everywhere.

In the summer of 1858 two or three hundred such prospectors were at work along the mountain wall directly west of Kansas Territory, in a region that had escaped development.[4] From the Bend of the Missouri, the Oregon Trail pushed off northwestward, and the Santa Fé Trail southwestward; and between the trails, with their backs against the foothills lived the Arapahoe and Cheyenne Indians. The emigrant trains had passed them for a quarter of a century, without much molesting them, so complete was the immunity of the so-called American Desert from the activities of settlers. Even Kansas and Nebraska Territories, now four years old, and each located at the mouth of a great river draining the Indian Country, had not brought much change to the range Indians in their western ends. Kansas-Nebraska was politics rather than settlement in its inception, and politics it still remained. A prosperous agricultural border would not have had numbers of men free to be prospecting during the farming months of 1858; yet there were men from Lawrence and Lecompton who

---

[4] F. L. Paxson, "The Territory of Colorado," in *American Historical Review,* vol. XII; Jerome C. Smiley, *History of Denver. With Outlines of the earlier History of the Rocky Mountain Country* (1901), is unusually accurate and well illustrated. Clyde L. King, *History of the Government of Denver* (1911).

were out in force. The precise date of their discovery of gold near Pike's Peak is not recorded. Sometime that autumn they found it in the sand banks at the mouth of Cherry Creek, one of the affluents of the South Fork of the Platte River, twenty-odd miles south of the fortieth parallel, and hence in Kansas Territory. Pike's Peak was ninety miles away, but it was the one spot in the vicinity that the border knew by name.

Before winter set in, Denver City was in existence, drawing its name from the then governor of Kansas. Quills of gold dust had been sent down the Platte trail to Omaha, and the handful of prospectors had decided that among themselves they contained the raw materials for a new territory or even State. Following a conference in one of their cabins, men were found willing to go to Washington to ask a territorial government and to Lecompton to ask the creation of counties by the legislature of Kansas. Congress, deadlocked by the slavery fight, was incompetent to do anything, but Kansas responded by authorizing the organization of five new counties, west of the 104th meridian.[5] This was less than the autonomy that the Denver settlement desired, and in practice there was no government except what the miners made for themselves.

The news of gold rioted along the border settlements as that from Sutter's Fort had done a decade earlier. The western papers took up the story, and soon were printing itineraries to the Bend of the Missouri, and thence to Denver. It was no grueling trip like that to Oregon or San Francisco, but an easy seven hundred miles from the Missouri River. Few prospectors went out in the winter of 1858–1859, but in the spring of 1859 their camps lined the Missouri from Independence to Council Bluffs; and early in April their march across the plains began. They used the heavy wagons of the prairie schooner type, and also the light carriages of the border. They went on horseback with pack animals, and some who lacked worldly means took their cue from the Mormon emigration and pushed their baggage before them in light two-wheeled hand carts. This had been a much-used means by the Mormons for bringing in their poorer converts, and it was successful in the hands of Pike's Peak gold seekers. "Pike's Peak or Bust!" was a common slogan, printed in the papers, and painted on the canvas

---

[5] There are complete sets of county maps in Helen G. Gill, "The Establishment of Counties in Kansas," in Kansas Historical Society *Collections*, vol. VIII; and F. L. Paxson, "The County Boundaries of Colorado," in University of Colorado *Studies*, vol. III.

of their wagons. Before the season was over, more than one wagon was stranded along the trails, with the frank confession painted on the wagon flap, "Busted, By Gosh!" Passing, meeting, overtaking the emigrant trains, were to be found also the coaches of a regular passenger service, the Leavenworth and Pike's Peak Stage and Express Company that made better time than the prospectors and that carried into Denver City in June no less a personage than Horace Greeley, on a journalistic trip of observation. One of his colleagues had been printing there *The Rocky Mountain News* since April 23.

William Tecumseh Sherman was at Fort Leavenworth in April, 1859, and wrote for the information of his brother, John: "At this moment we are in the midst of a rush to Pike's Peak. Steamboats arrive in twos and threes each day, loaded with people for the new gold region. The streets are full of people buying flour, bacon, and groceries, with wagons and outfits, and all around the town are little camps preparing to go west. . . . Strange to say, even yet, although probably twenty-five thousand people have actually gone, we are without authentic advices of gold. Accounts are generally favorable as to words and descriptions, but no positive physical evidence comes in the shape of gold, and I will be incredulous until I know some considerable quantity comes in in the way of trade."

The earlier residents of Denver, and the mining camps along the foothills, north and south, anticipated the throng of gold seekers; and those who owned mining claims that promised well were fearful of a rush that might wash them away and dislocate their mining titles. As in California, they had formed mining districts immediately on the discovery. They took further steps during the winter to prepare a government. There were named camps at Golden, Boulder, Black Hawk, Central City, Idaho Springs, and Georgetown, and delegates from these met in Denver in April to consider statehood. This gathering issued a call for a more regular convention, which met in June, after the advance guard of the fifty-niners had begun to countermarch. The first Pike's Peak gold was placer dust, easily washed from the creek bottoms in many places, but not abundant enough to make many miners rich. The quartz lodes, when found upstream, were so refractory that they could not be mined or smelted without great outlays of labor and capital, which the average miners could not command. Gold production was mining company business, and as soon as the eager crowds saw this, most of them started back to the States. By June so many were homeward bound that it took a stout heart to believe that there would be any one left by fall. The June convention adjourned until August to see. In August it was somewhat encouraged, and framed for the consideration of the voters a State constitution and a memorial to Congress asking territorial status. The latter prevailed at the polls, and a delegate was sent to Washington at once. "Here we go," wrote Byers in his *Rocky Mountain News*, "a regular tripple-headed government machine; south of 40 deg. we hang on to the skirts of Kansas; north of 40 deg. to those of Nebraska; straddling the line, we have just elected a Delegate to the United States Congress from the 'Territory of Jefferson,' and ere long, we will have in full blast a provisional government of Rocky Mountain growth and manufacture."

The Territory of Jefferson became a reality when a new convention, in October, framed a territorial government to last until Congress should respond to the request for legislation. The area claimed covered eight degrees of longitude, from 102 to 110; and six degrees of latitude, beginning at the 37th parallel. R. W. Steele, who was elected governor, met his first legislature on November 7, 1859.

There was no action by Congress upon the application for a new territory in either the session of 1858 or that of 1859. The slavery deadlock was complete, and the same forces of sectionalism that prevented Pacific railroad legislation prevented the creation of new territories whose political complexion might be in doubt. The existing territories that were ready for statehood were not excluded from the Union, but Congress would go no further.

Minnesota and Oregon were the new States that finished their probationary period just after the panic of 1857. The former made its constitution in the panic year, in a fashion that was novel then and has remained unique. Its convention was bicameral, and the basic law was framed in agreement by two houses.[6] But the double organization was not intended by the legislature that called it. It grew instead out of the fierce slavery fight in the election, and a split among the delegates into two bodies each claiming to be the constitutional convention. The rival bodies sat side by side, and drafted two constitutions, which were so much alike that it was possible to procure an agreement on the document upon

[6] William Anderson, "A History of the Constitution of Minnesota, with the first Verified Text," in University of Minnesota *Research Publications*, 1921.

which the people were invited to vote. The State government that was elected was Democratic, with H. H. Sibley as first governor. Congress, perhaps because of this, admitted Minnesota May 11, 1858.

The Oregon convention met at Salem in 1857, without an enabling act, after the people had demanded admission since 1850. The generous boundaries of 1848 had been reduced by Congress in 1853, when Washington Territory was formed north of the Columbia River. The territory was still further reduced for statehood purposes, its eastern part being added temporarily to Washington. It too was Democratic, and so received the votes in Congress that were needful for admission, February 14, 1859.

The population of the Territory of Jefferson was drawn from States and territories where the Republican movement was strong, and where the Democratic Party did not expect to find a voting majority. The appeals of Jefferson fell therefore upon deaf ears, but although legislation could be postponed, the fact could not be concealed that a new principle had entered into the problem of territorial creation with the discovery of Pike's Peak gold. This was the utilization of the mineral empire.

The territorial maps for the period of the fifties show that the Rocky Mountains were regarded only as a barrier, inconvenient for purposes of emigration and railroad building but convenient for purposes of boundary making. Oregon, Utah, and later Washington, were given the Rocky Mountains as eastern limits while for Kansas and Nebraska they formed a western line. The thought that in the mountain area there might be any resource that would compel the creation of mountain States was unborn until the prospectors found gold on Cherry Creek. Discoveries came thick and fast after this, and before Governor Steele had been two years in office no one could believe that one territory would meet the need. Even that one was deferred until secession occurred in the winter of 1860–1861 and the southern Democratic votes went home.

The census enumerators found 34,277 persons in Colorado in 1860; too few for a State, but sufficient to continue the demand for local and autonomous government. On February 28, 1861, President Buchanan signed a law cutting away from Kansas and Nebraska, on the east, and Utah and New Mexico on the west, the new Territory of Colorado. The name Jefferson was discarded, and the boundaries to which the miners aspired were reduced.

Colorado extended between the thirty-seventh and forty-first parallels, and between the twenty-fifth and thirty-second meridians west of Washington. Denver became the capital city. At the same time, the, Arapahoe and Cheyenne Indians, upon whose domain, under the agreement of 1851, the miners were an intrusion, were persuaded to recognize the inevitable and make a cession of the land along the foothills. This was done at Fort Wise, on the Upper Arkansas, where a trader named Bent had long maintained a post in the early days of the Santa Fé traffic. Here the tribes, among whose leaders Black Kettle was the best known, accepted a new reserve on the north bank of the Arkansas River, in the angle west of Sand Creek, and ceded to the United States the hunting range lying between the Platte and Arkansas rivers. The Arapahoe and Cheyenne retained the right to live and hunt in the ceded country as long as it continued unsold, but they ceased to have the rights of wild Indians of the open plains.

It remained for President Lincoln to organize the territory whose organic act Buchanan signed. Lincoln appointed as governor a former army officer named William Gilpin, a visionary and near-poet of Pennsylvania Quaker stock, who wrote prophetic books on the future of the Rocky Mountain country.[7] Gilpin arrived in Denver at the outbreak of Civil War hostilities, and found himself adrift on a disturbed frontier, with the Government too much preoccupied at the moment to listen to his cries. Colorado for the next few years lived a precarious life, amid Confederate plots and Indian uprisings. Its mineral development never again induced a population as large as that of the boom year of the fifty-niners. Its inhabitants took slowly to agriculture and were two decades in finding a permanent basis for existence. With their advance the frontier march beyond the Missouri begins and a new period of national development opens.

[7] William Gilpin, *The Central Gold Region* (1860); *The Mission of the North American People* (1873).

CHAPTER XLVIII
THE FRONTIER OF THE MINERAL EMPIRE

For ten years after the discovery of gold in the Pike's Peak country, the map of the Rocky Mountain area was in a condition of continual revision, as Congress, on half knowledge or worse, tried to keep the institutions of government abreast with the activities of the gold seekers. The task was great and involved because gold was everywhere; it was elusive because the gold was generally in small amounts; and great communities, gathered hurriedly by a new find, dispersed as quickly when the limits of the deposit were ascertained.

The new Colorado Territory was the first step in the procedure of breaking up the mountain wastes into orderly governments to meet the needs of the shifting population. It was accompanied by other steps, however, which had been deferred like Colorado because of the deadlock over the slavery question, and which were released in the closing days of Buchanan's administration, after the southern obstructionists had gone home. These were the admission of Kansas, the organization of a new territory, Dakota, for the farmers of the upper Missouri country, and the creation of an overflow mining territory east of the California line, for the Washoe gold and silver seekers.

Kansas, in spite of the war that had raged over its plains, was not much of a State even in 1861. Most of its settlers lived in its extreme eastern counties, near the rivers that were its sole connection with the Union. Two hundred miles west of Missouri was still the open range, and the village at the old Council Grove, where the caravans had been in the habit of completing their protective organization, was on the actual frontier even yet. The Jayhawkers and the Blue Lodges, and Old John Brown at Osawatomie, had kept up the turmoil; but there had not been a rush of incomers on any terms.[1] The fourth State constitution, made at Wyandotte in 1859, and ratified by what people there were that autumn, waited for acceptance by Congress for more than a year.

[1] Oswald G. Villard, *John Brown: A Biography Fifty Years After* (1910), is one of the most exhaustive books of its kind. But historians are not in complete agreement on John Brown; a local interpreter is Hill P. Wilson, *John Brown, Soldier of Fortune: A Critique* (1913).

The southern vote would not play true to itself, and admit that Kansas was entitled to be a free State if it so desired, yet it had, in 1854, welcomed Douglas's discovery that the people had a right to determine their institutions for themselves and that popular sovereignty was superior to the Missouri Compromise. When Kansas was at last admitted in 1861, Congress cut off its western portion, at the 25th meridian, in order to make room for Colorado Territory whose creation was only a matter of a few weeks.

Dakota Territory was formed under an act of March 2, 1861, and included all of Nebraska Territory lying north of the 43d parallel. In addition, it embraced a fragment of domain that had been without government since 1858, and whose people provided the motive force for the whole transaction. The admission of States and the creation of territories was never an exact process, and more than once Congress, without intending it, did destruction as well as construction by its laws. Thus in 1848 the admission of Wisconsin, with a western boundary at the St. Croix River, turned adrift a settled part of the territory between that stream and the Mississippi. This became a part of Minnesota in 1849. Similarly the admission of Minnesota in 1858, with a western boundary near Sioux Falls on the Big Sioux River threw away the angle between the Big Sioux and the Missouri, into which settlers had entered by way of the Missouri Valley. This large triangular tract, west of Minnesota as it now is, and extending to the Missouri River, was added to the northern slice taken from Nebraska, to form Dakota. At the lower end of this triangular area, was a village of Yankton, near the mouth of the James River, and for a hundred miles or so along the Missouri near Yankton there was an occasional farmer. Not until 1868, however, did Joseph Ward bring here his bride and undertake to found a parish and a college for the Congregational Church.[2] Several hundred miles north of Yankton, at Pembina on the Red River of the North, were a few more residents who had come there with the Canadian settlement, and who maintained a precarious connection with the world by means of an annual ox-cart caravan to Fort Snelling. The creation of Dakota was only incidentally concerned with the content of the Rocky Mountain empire, and belonged to the western margin of the agricultural frontier. Like Kansas and Nebraska, Dakota was not under heavy pressure of settlement.

Nevada Territory, born the same day as Dakota, was rather a

[2] George H. Durand, *Joseph Ward of Dakota* (1913).

supplement to California than a following of the new principle of subdivision of the mountain area, although in fact it accomplished such a division. In the same summer of 1858 in which prospectors found gold on Cherry Creek, there were other wanderers at work on the eastern slopes of the Sierra Nevada, near Lake Tahoe and the arbitrary eastern boundary of California. On the eastern slopes of Mount Davidson they found silver rather than gold, although there was much gold with it, and the new camp was "on the public highway to California," where tens of thousands of emigrants had passed, without seeing the wealth beneath their feet. The mining district took its name at first from Lake Washoe, at the foot of Mount Davidson, and it drew its people mostly from the California towns, although some came "from Kansas and Nebraska, from Pike's Peak and Salt Lake." [3]

This was in the extreme western end of Utah Territory and had had thus far no interest except as the route of the California trail, along the Humboldt Valley. The Mormon colony on Great Salt Lake kept its hand on the highway, principally through the maintenance of service stations for emigrants. Carson County, Utah, was founded on the trail in 1854; Carson City, near Washoe Lake, sprang into life in 1858. Not until the spring of 1859, when the famous deposits known as the Comstock Lode were found, did the Washoe mines arouse much interest, and then they were outshone in the public eye by those of Pike's Peak. But that autumn, as at Denver, the Carson City miners made themselves a constitution and organized a spontaneous State, which they pretended was superior to the government of Utah Territory.

The eastern boundary of Nevada Territory was placed in 1861 at the 39th meridian west of Washington, and California was invited to assent to a western boundary along the watershed of the Sierra Nevada. When California failed to do this, which meant a reduction of territory for her, Nevada was given an additional degree along the eastern side, making the 38th meridian the boundary. In 1864 there was a further extension to the 37th meridian, and an addition to the south which carried Nevada beyond the 37th parallel to the Colorado River. At Carson City a territorial government was set up, whose most important member, Samuel Langhorne Clemens, was the private secretary of the ter-

[3] H. H. Bancroft, *History of Nevada, Colorado and Wyoming* (1890); Albert Bigelow Paine, *Mark Twain: A Biography* (1912), has rare interest and gives a vivid picture of this place and period.

ritorial secretary. The overland journey of "Mark Twain," with his brother Orion Clemens, to this new post in the summer of 1861, has become a classic jaunt, immortalized in *Roughing It* (1872). The mining camp which occasioned their trip would have justified itself, if it had done no more than bring to this new type of frontier its greatest artist.

A few thousands of the fifty-niners stayed in Colorado to help set up a State; some fewer thousands remained in Nevada for the same purpose. But many times their number ranged over the mountains between, and north and south, under the unsettlement that the Civil War brought into many minds and subject to the hypnotic influence of the search for gold. There were drifters, who kept on drifting, war or no war. There were deserters from Union armies and from the Confederacy. There were sympathizers with both causes who left home because of unpopularity, and there was an admixture of that class that "left their country for their country's good." Once in a while, spurts of loyalty, or the reverse, set a mining camp aflame. There were personal conflicts that revealed how many men were sensitive enough to fight, if not loyal enough to stay at home to do it. Before the war was over the succession of camps that followed the discoveries into every corner of the mountains provided reason for as thorough a subdivision of the mountain West as Congress need ever undertake.

In the summer of 1860 gold was found in the Clearwater Valley, one of the eastern tributaries of the Snake River. The new field was somewhat northeast of the main Oregon Trail, which cut across the great bend of the Snake, towards Walla Walla; but it was not so far that miners from Oregon and Washington Territory could not flock there in the spring of 1861. Five thousand, or more, were on hand by mid-summer and brought Lewiston to life, in the angle between the Clearwater and the Snake, and in the heart of the reserve of the Nez Percé Indians. As the news spread, they kept on coming. "The Idaho miners," said H. H. Bancroft, "were like quicksilver. A mass of them dropped in any locality, broke up into individual globules, and ran off after any atom of gold in their vicinity. They stayed nowhere longer than the gold attracted them." In quick succession they spread to the Salmon River, another eastern tributary of the Snake, and to the Boise. They pushed south of the Snake to the Owyhee, and at every station they found more gold and planted temporary camps. By 1862 Congress was under pressure to create a territory for them, for the seat of Washington was too far west and that of Dakota too far east.

Before Congress acted on the problem of the Snake River miners, there was a like problem of Missouri River miners. The Columbia and Snake, and their eastern tributaries, interlock upon the northern continental watershed with the headwaters of the Missouri, and the Bitter Root Valley, although it drains into the Pacific, is as easily accessible from the east as from the west. It was through this country that Lewis and Clark went in 1806; and in 1853 Isaac I. Stevens at the head of the northern survey for the Pacific railroad.[4] Stevens was deeply impressed with the fertility of the valleys and the ease of crossing the divide, and his reports to the War Department are full of the confident rhetoric of the convert. No great trail had crossed the continent here, however, because of the lack of a population around Lake Superior to feed it, and because of the ease of access to the main Platte trail.

For a generation before gold was found in the Bitter Root and the Beaverhead, the Missouri had been put to occasional use. In 1832 the fur traders' steamer reached Fort Union at the mouth of the Yellowstone.[5] Later, as spring freshets encouraged greater penetration, the boats worked their way farther up the shallow stream, until in 1859 they made a new head of navigation near the great falls of the Missouri, at Fort Benton. Nearly every year thereafter, until the railroad came, the boats reached Fort Benton, with annuity goods for the northwest Indians, supplies for the trappers and fur traders, and with emigrants who became more numerous after the suspicion of easy gold got abroad. West of Fort Benton, to Walla Walla, was the obvious route for a cut-off, to shorten the overland journey. Congress authorized in 1855 a road from the Falls of the Missouri to Fort Walla Walla, and John Mullan was placed in charge of its construction. It was passable by 1860, but few emigrants used it because of the rarity and uncertainty of the river connection at Fort Benton. It none the less attracted attention when the miners sought the upper affluents of the Missouri and Columbia.

Missoula County, Washington Territory, was organized in 1862 for the benefit of miners in the Bitter Root, and Boise County a few months later for the prospectors on the Boise branch of the

---

[4] Hazard Stevens, *The Life of Isaac Ingalls Stevens by his Son* (1900).

[5] Hiram M. Chittenden, *History of Early Steamboat Navigation on the Missouri River Life and Adventures of Joseph La Barge* (1903).

Snake River. The rush to Bannack City and Virginia City, east of the Continental Divide, drew miners away from Boise City. Virginia City claimed fifteen thousand inhabitants at its maximum; but in its turn it contributed to the headlong rush to Last Chance Gulch, one hundred and thirty-eight miles north, on the road to Fort Benton, where Helena appeared in 1864.

The waters of Bill Williams Fork of the Colorado River yielded up their gold and attracted miners to the southwest fields. The exploitation of this region, which lay off the traveled roads, was a by-product of the Civil War, and the march of California volunteers. Colonel James H. Carleton's California column, some eighteen hundred strong, marched across the California desert, and up the Gila River Valley, to the relief of the Union forces in New Mexico in 1862. There was little fighting for them, but they were compensated by the opening of the placer deposits of the Colorado Valley — "one of the richest gold countries in the world," Carleton declared the next spring in a letter to Halleck. But the conditions that made for easy prospecting made it hard to keep an army in the ranks, and Carleton complained constantly of the frequent desertions of his men who could not withstand the lure of the gold fields. He even suggested that a mining regiment might be the solution, meaning one whose soldiers should be practical prospectors and compensated in part by leave to spend a share of their time among the hills. The new field created an interest in a part of New Mexico Territory where none had been before and diverted attention from the Rio Grande, as well as from the ancient villages of the Santa Cruz Valley, near Tucson.

It was no new thing to find precious metals in New Mexico. The Spanish missionaries had discovered silver deposits which had already been worked by the Indians, along the old Sonora Trail to the head of the Gulf of California. Nogales, Arizona, is where the Santa Cruz crosses the Mexican boundary to-day. At Tucson, a little north of this, the stream reaches the valley through which the Southern Pacific Railroad has found its way. Still further north, the Santa Cruz would make a junction with the Gila River if it were not swallowed up in the arid sands of Arizona on the way. Tucson was the village of the Spanish miners; and after the Mexican War and the Gadsden purchase, American prospectors visited the country seeking to reopen the silver mines. A former officer of the regular army, named Mowry,[6] with southern associates,

6 Silvester Mowry, *Arizona and Sonora* (3d ed., 1864).

revived the diggings, and started a movement as early as 1856 for the division of the Territory of New Mexico. They even had a constitutional convention at Tucson in 1860, without arousing Congress to action in their behalf. They disappeared before the advancing column of Carleton, for their sympathies were with the Confederacy.

The placer gold of the Colorado River and the Bill Williams Fork drew miners to the western end of New Mexico. Carleton reported in 1863 that "*it will be absolutely necessary* to post troops in that section of the country; indeed the capital of Arizona will be sure to be established *there*. All of the people of Tucson, our teamsters and employés generally, who could possibly get away, have already left for that region." There were about twenty-five thousand Indians in the western end of New Mexico, and under seven thousand whites, at the time of the gold discoveries. It was a fair inference from the experience of the other mining camps that these numbers would speedily be increased.

The miners were more diligent than Congress in developing the mineral empire, but every success of theirs reacted upon Washington. After the passage of the Colorado, Nevada, and Dakota acts, Congress became involved in the maze of war legislation and was never able to give systematic consideration to the demands for additional subdivisions of the Rocky Mountain country. It was sympathetic enough, but not well informed as to the prospects of permanence for any community, and its legislation was founded chiefly upon temporary expediency. With this there was mingled a willingness on the part of the war party to encourage the creation of new States or territories that might be expected to be loyal to the United States.

No new territory was created in 1862, but in 1863 Arizona and Idaho were added to the list. The former was detached from New Mexico, February 24, 1863, and included that portion of the older territory lying west of the 32d degree of longitude west of Washington. In its original form, its northern line on the 37th parallel continued west to the California boundary, thus including in Arizona a triangle northwest of the chasm of the Colorado and entirely detached. Part of this tract was separated and added to Nevada in 1866. The first territorial capital was where Carleton had advised, at Fort Whipple, which became the town of Prescott. In a later period the capital was often shifted, coming to rest presently at Phoenix on the Gila River.

Idaho was created a week after Arizona, at the expense of the adjacent territories of Washington, Utah, Dakota, and Nebraska. It included a huge rectangle north of Colorado and Utah, between the 27th meridian from Washington and the eastern boundary of Oregon, thus reducing the Dakotas and Washington to their present dimensions. There was, however, no effective economic or political unity created in Idaho. The ridge separating the miners of the Missouri from those of the Snake was a barrier to unity, in spite of the geographic nearness of the two systems of camps. Before the territory could be organized with the seat of government at Lewiston (which the territorial governor, W. H. Wallace, selected because it was close to his home in Washington), there was a demand for partition, and the separation of Montana. "To attempt to restrain miners would be, to my mind, like attempting to restrain the whirlwind," wrote the Indian agent at Lewiston, who knew. Congress speedily responded to the facts of the shifting prospectors.

In May, 1864, autonomy was provided for the camps at Bannack, Virginia City, Deer Lodge, Pioneer, and Missoula, with the Bitter Root Range as their western limit, and an extension down the valleys to the Dakota line.[7] Montana thus acquired its present boundary at the start and held its first legislative assembly at Bannack the following winter. Idaho territory was cut down to greatly reduced dimensions, and the southwest rectangle of its domain, corresponding roughly to Wyoming, was attached to Dakota for governmental purposes.

After 1864, the political map of the United States was on the verge of completion, with only the division of the Dakotas and the establishment of Wyoming Territory left undone. The former was postponed until the time was ripe for their admission as States. The latter came in 1868. It would doubtless have come earlier had important mining camps arisen within the limits of the present State. The few mines caused no boom, and the transit through the area along the familiar Oregon Trail was the only important fact that lessened the Indians' possession of this hunting range of the eastern slopes. When Wyoming Territory was freed from Dakota and set up for itself in July, 1868, the causes were the completion of the Union Pacific Railroad across its breadth and the establishment of the town of Cheyenne at the junction where a southern line branched off to Denver.

[7] The Montana Historical Society *Contributions* are full of pioneer reminiscences.

Between the discoveries of 1858, and the Wyoming Act ten years later, the subdivision of the mineral empire was completed. The map told a new story, and the new conditions brought into American politics by the influence of the dispersed settlements of the miners, were affecting the courses both of economic development and political balance.

The war Government at Washington made what use it could of the changing Far West. Lincoln was a practical statesman, and foresaw the situation that might result when after victory the votes of the South might be added to those of the northern Democrats who had hampered the prosecution of the war. Its consequence might well be the delivery of the United States into the hands of those who had risked their lives to wreck it, and those who had countenanced, or, at most, mildly opposed the experiment. To offset this, he searched the plains for new communities that might be susceptible of development into States with Union sentiments. Before the decade of mining excitement was over, Nevada, Nebraska, and Colorado, not to mention the western portion of Virginia, were brought within the range of statehood politics.

The admission of West Virginia was a war measure, defensible, if at all, only on the ground that a state of civil war justifies the acceptance of frauds that are useful in their consequences. It was well known before Virginia seceded that her western counties were opposed to the course, and the Virginia ordinance of secession was carried by tide-water votes. The counties in the piedmont and mountains were divided in their desires; those of the West were antagonistic. It was accordingly possible for Union sympathizers in the Wheeling district to start a movement for the division of the State and the creation of a loyal West Virginia. The domineering politics of eastern Virginia had nearly provoked such revolt many times before the war; secession brought it to a head.

But under the Constitution of the United States, no State boundary may be changed without the consent of the State concerned; and Virginia was in active revolt against the United States. A revolutionary Virginia government was therefore organized in the western counties, within Union lines; and this under the protection and at the wish of the war Government, gave the consent required. Congress accepted it as though it were real, and in 1863 permitted the Senators and Representatives of West Virginia to take their seats.

With the Government in such need and Congress in such a

mood, it was not surprising that in the session following the creation of West Virginia, bills should pass to enable the three ripest territories to frame constitutions and enter the Union. Nevada and Colorado were enabled on the same day, March 21, 1864; Nebraska a month later, April 19, 1864.

The proceedings in Colorado came to naught. A convention in Denver made a constitution in July, which the voters promptly rejected. The reason for rejection appears to have been the heavy taxation that might be expected to follow admission, incident to the setting up of a State establishment. A second convention, irregularly assembled the following summer, made a constitution which the people accepted; but by this time Lincoln was dead and Andrew Johnson was in no mood to be a party to the increase of the radical Republican vote. Johnson found reasons to decline to issue the proclamation of admission for Colorado, and Senator Sumner in the ensuing debates opposed action because, whereas it required a population of one hundred and twenty-seven thousand to be entitled to one Representative under the apportionment act, Colorado had a total not exceeding twenty-five thousand. Congress nevertheless passed a bill to admit the territory, which Johnson vetoed May 15, 1866. The bill was passed again the next session and again vetoed. In spite of the fact that by 1867 the radical Republicans were repeatedly passing reconstruction measures over the veto of the President, it was impossible to procure the votes for Colorado. It remained outside for ten years more.

Nevada made better headway than Colorado. There was on hand at the date of the enabling act a constitution made in 1863, which was touched up for presentation in 1864. The arid wastes of the territory, and the scanty population were overlooked by a Government that needed votes. Since time was pressing, with the presidential campaign of 1864 approaching, the enabling act provided that upon the completion of a suitable constitution the President should admit the new State by executive proclamation. Strict constitutionalists raised a mild question whether this was not an evasion by Congress of its own duty to perform the act of admission, but the scheme prevailed, and on October 31, a few days before the critical election, Lincoln proclaimed Nevada as a State. To William M. Stewart, its first Senator, he is reported to have said, "I am glad to see you here. We need as many loyal States as we can get." [8]

[8] William M. Stewart, *Reminiscences* (1910), is so inaccurate that too much credence ought not to be placed on any of its statements.

In Nebraska the procedure for admission limped, but was finally effective. There had been little settlement in the ten years since the creation of the territory, and this was confined to a string of villages along the Missouri, below the Platte. Omaha was but a name. Fort Kearney (the settlers refused to spell correctly the name of the soldier, Kearny) was beyond the region of settlement.[9] The convention chosen under the enabling act of 1864 never met, for at the same election the people had been asked whether they desired to form a State, and like Colorado they voted no. In the legislature of 1866, however, a constitution framed by a group of Omaha lawyers was brought in as a bill, passed and submitted to referendum by the people. It passed by a scant majority of one hundred, in a total vote of under eight thousand; and was accepted by Congress as sufficient. Johnson vetoed the bill for the admission of Nebraska the day after he vetoed Colorado for the second time, but the measure was just enough better than the Colorado bill to receive the votes needful for passage over the veto. Nebraska became a State March 1, 1867.

The exploration of the mineral empire and the creation of the mountain territories were natural consequences of the extension of the frontier of the miners beyond that of the farmers. The farming frontier was still content to remain at the Bend of the Missouri while the miners were organizing the thousand miles beyond. The admission of the plains States was politics rather than frontier development. But the new processes started after the panic of 1857 could have only one outcome in the end — the disappearance of all the open frontier and the creation of a final group of States.

[9] Albert Watkins, "History of Fort Kearny," in Nebraska State Historical Society *Collections*, vol. XVI; J. Sterling Morton and Albert Watkins, *Illustrated History of Nebraska* (1905–1913).

CHAPTER XLIX

THE OVERLAND ROUTE

THE gossip of the miners as they gathered around the camp-fires or sought shelter in their flimsy shacks, is not usually to be rated as sound historical source, nor did it often become the starting point for great movements either in politics or business. But one of their persistent rumors, told in his cups by many a prospector, connected their vital need with the Government of which they saw so little. The legend begins with a wakeful miner, on a moonlight night, in camp anywhere south of the California Trail. The hero rolls over in his blanket, looks across the desert, and there in the distance sees what causes him to rub his sleepy eyes and look again. It is usually a huge white camel, less often black, and sometimes followed by a herd of lesser camels who clearly recognize him as their lord. The story is generally told by one who has no confidence of being believed, and who is entirely unaware that on June 18, 1856, a train of camels did march into San Antonio.

Edward Fitzgerald Beale [1] was in command of this camel corps, the first and last in American experience, and had himself urged the action which had resulted in an appropriation by Congress, an expedition to the Levant to procure them, a voyage home to Indianola, Texas, under Lieutenant David D. Porter, and the launching of the experiment of acclimating the ship of the Arabian desert upon the arid wastes of the American Southwest. For the next two years the camel corps was tried out under all the conditions of travel over the desert. "They are the most docile, patient, and easily managed creatures in the world and infinitely more easily worked than mules," their enthusiastic commander wrote the Secretary of War. He rode them, used them as pack animals, and as draft animals; he ascertained the advantage of their padded feet over the fragile hoofs of mules and horses; he noticed their ability to go without a drink, and reported that on one crossing of the Southwest he never once went out of his way to give them water. A writer from Los Angeles in 1858 wrote that "Gen. Beale and about fourteen camels stalked into town last Friday

---

[1] Stephen Bonsal, *Edward Fitzgerald Beale. A Pioneer in the Path of Empire, 1822–1903* (1912), has rescued this story from its grave among the Government documents.

week and gave our streets quite an Oriental aspect." The experiment convinced Beale that the camel was the solution of the traffic problems on the trails, but it convinced few else, and in the end the herd was scattered. It is quite probable that the romance of the startled miners may have had some foundation in wandering strays from the camel corps. It is certain that the attempt to solve the problem was real, and that this was only one among many efforts to lessen the isolation of the scattered camps and to draw together the dispersed colonies of Americans throughout the West.

A few months before Porter was sent to the Levant to get his camels, Jefferson Davis, the Secretary of War who sent him, was engaged in serious study of the preliminary reports of the detachments of engineers who had been sent upon the plains under legislation of 1853. Five lines of survey had been run to the Pacific, in the search for "the most practicable and economical Route for a Railroad," and most of the surveyors had ended by becoming violent partisans of the particular routes that they explored. "The time for a great national railroad has not yet come," wrote William Tecumseh Sherman, who was acquainted with the work. But Davis reported to Congress, February 27, 1855, that "A comparison of the results . . . conclusively shows that the route of the 32d parallel is . . . 'the most practical and economical route for a railroad from the Mississippi river to the Pacific ocean.' This is the shortest route . . . its estimated cost [is] less by a third than that of any other of the lines . . . it could be executed in a vastly shorter period."

It was perhaps natural for Secretary Davis to believe in the southernmost, or thirty-second parallel, route, for it would connect New Orleans with San Diego, but it was impossible to induce Congress to authorize construction either here or elsewhere. The decade of the surveys passed without action to bridge the gap by a railroad, or to bring the settlements on the Pacific, or along the roads thither, closer to the States than the ordinary means of wagons and horses would accomplish. But pressure for quicker service was mounting higher, and Congress was in a mood to authorize the marking of wagon roads and the quicker carriage of the mails.

One unforeseen consequence of the great distance to Oregon, Utah, and California was unusual isolation. The ordinary frontier communities were only a few miles ahead of their immediate predecessors and roads were always in process of construction in their immediate rear. Down the Ohio, and up and down the Mississippi, and their various tributaries, the communities pushed without ever getting bitterly detached. Short cuts, like Zane's Trace, or that to Natchez, could always be relied on to lessen distances, and post routes were established to serve the outposts as rapidly as these had any need for mails. But it was a different matter to follow up the emigrants to Oregon and California. The Mormons established their own stage and express from the Missouri Border, and Congress provided a water route to San Francisco in the spring of 1849. The next ten years were years of experiment in the methods of overland communication, culminating in the overland mail, the pony express, and at last, the chartering of the Pacific railroad. Throughout the decade, no camp was so remote that it abandoned the idea of an improved route. From every quarter of the Union there came in upon Congress the bewildering demand for roads and mails. And since the isolated regions were mostly in the territories upon the public domain, it was Congress rather than any State that must work out the solution.

The first long distance mail routes were conducted like the caravans that used the same trails over which they ran. The carrier, whether for the Great Salt Lake Valley Carrying Company or for the Independence–Santa Fé service of 1849, drove by day and camped by night. He made somewhat better time than the emigrant wagon, for he used a lighter vehicle, with a smaller load, but the conditions that he had to meet were those of every emigrant.

A demand for something better arose soon after the admission of California, and thereafter the Senators and Representatives of this State were ever pressing their needs upon Congress. The railroad surveys of 1853 were in part a response to their urge. The Post Office Appropriation Act of 1857 carried authorization for a service of a different type. This was to be an expedited mail, with wagons running day and night and speeded up by relays of fresh stock.[2]

The Postmaster-General was directed by this act to advertise for bids for a mail to California in not over twenty-five days from

[2] The best-known account is F. A. Root and W. E. Connelley, *Overland Stage to California* (1901), although Glenn D. Bradley, *The Story of the Pony Express* (1913), and W. L. Visscher, *The Pony Express* (1908), are of use. Alexander Majors, *Seventy Years on the Frontier* (1893), is the memoir of a freighter. Curtis P. Nettels has searched the local sources for his "The Overland Mail in the Fifties," in *Missouri Historical Review*, vol. XVIII.

the Mississippi River. The route was to be selected at his discretion, but the contractor was to be allowed to hold his contract for a period of six years, so that the cost of his investment might be spread. The many bidders for the route, in the summer of 1857, included most of the freight carriers of the plains. This business had already reached a high development, and hundreds of wagons were always at work, not for emigrants, but with goods for the army posts, or Indians' annuity goods, or traders' supplies for Santa Fé, or for the mining camps as these appeared. The romance associated with the early caravans on the Santa Fé Trail had nearly gone. In its place the slow-moving cloud of dust and the rumble of the wheels, the cracking of the whips and the profane admonitions of the drivers to their mules indicated a growing and laborious traffic. A writer in 1860 thought there were eighteen thousand freight wagons in constant operation.

The contract for the overland mail was awarded in the autumn of 1857 to John Butterfield, who was given a year to get ready to haul the coaches. In his *Annual Report* of that year the Post-master-General explained the award, and the route that had been selected. Aaron V. Brown, the Postmaster-General, was a southern man, and an appointee in the cabinet of a Democratic President, James Buchanan. His preferences may have been like those of Jefferson Davis, for the Kansas war was now on, and the line between the factions was sharply drawn. But there was much to justify his decision that the route should start with two eastern termini at St. Louis and Memphis, making a junction near Fort Smith on the western boundary of Arkansas, crossing Red River near Preston, Texas, thence west across Texas to El Paso, and into California by the Fort Yuma entrance. Nothing could convince the northern critics that this selection was not wholly due to politics. Yet there was reason in a route that would not be snowed up and impassable for several months each winter and that would cross the mountains at as low and practicable elevations as possible.

A special reason for avoiding the central trail in 1857 was the fact that in this year the Mormon Church was at war with the United States, resisting the authority of Federal officers. An army was on the plains, under command of Colonel Albert Sidney Johnston, with orders to bring the rebellious church to terms; but at the moment when the contract was let, it was still uncertain whether they would be his terms, or those of Brigham Young. In September, 1857, an emigrant party from Arkansas to California was brutally massacred at Mountain Meadows in Utah by John D. Lee, and it was commonly believed that the Mormon Church was officially responsible for the outrage.[3] The inability of the United States to police the central trail was good reason for running the mails another way.

On September 15, 1858, Butterfield started his stages on a semi-weekly service from San Francisco to Tipton, Missouri (then the western terminus of the railroad from St. Louis to Kansas City). The distance as the route ran was 2795 miles, and the first east-bound coach, carrying an inspector of the Post Office, made the trip in twenty-four days, eighteen hours, thirty-five minutes actual time. "I cordially congratulate you upon the result," President Buchanan telegraphed to the successful contractor. "It is a glorious triumph for civilization and the Union. Settlements will soon follow the course of the road, and the East and West will be bound together by a chain of living Americans which can never be broken."

It was indeed a triumph of a sort, for Butterfield had been busily at work during his year of preparation, constructing a plant across the plains. In order to keep the stages running at the required average of nearly five miles per hour, day and night, it was necessary to have fresh teams ready for the stage at intervals of not much more than ten miles. There were no roads, and the wagons were hauled over the uneven plains where the going was least rough. It was heavy pulling at best. At worst, there were streams to ford, mud holes to get mired in, rocky sections where progress could not be made faster than a walk, and occasional smooth stretches where the animals could be urged to a gallop. The romantic artists have generally pictured the overland stages swaying and tossing as the horses were driven at a run; it would be more truthful to show their slow plod through shifting sands.

As close together as fresh relays were needed, Butterfield built him a cabin and a corral, and stationed a stock tender. His freight wagons hauled hay and grain for the animals to these stations, and were ever at work replenishing their stores. When the stage drove in, the tired horses were unharnessed, and waiting teams were brought up to replace them; while the tired passengers in the coach climbed down to stretch their legs. Less often than the horses, the passengers and drivers needed attention, and every

[3] J. P. Dunn, *Massacres of the Mountains. A History of the Indian Wars of the Far West* (1886).

few stations came a "home station" where in addition to the corral and haystack, there was a house, an eating place and perhaps
a blacksmith or wheelwright. In the arid waste, tires fell from
shrunken fellies and the wheel was in danger of shaking apart unless promptly repaired. There is a frequent picture of the overland
traveler in forced camp by some stream, while the wheels were
soaking to swell out and hold the tires in place. The rough roads
were hard on hoofs as well as wheels. The blacksmith was always
in demand, and sore-footed animals, resting in the corrals, were a
constant expense of the establishment.

At the home stations food could be procured, but not beds, for
the traveler kept going without a rest. "Twenty-four mortal days
and nights — twenty-five being schedule time — must be spent in
that ambulance; passengers becoming crazy with whisky, mixed
with want of sleep, are often obliged to be strapped to their seats;
their meals, dispatched during their ten-minute halts, are simply
abominable, the heats are excessive, the climate malarious; lamps
may not be used at night for fear of non-existent Indians; briefly
there is no end to this Via Mala's miseries," wrote one traveler
who knew how to live in many lands.

The Abbott-Downing coach, which in the course of time became the standard wagon on the trail, was built at Concord, New
Hampshire, for a generation before it was tested on the plains. At
a pinch it could carry fourteen passengers, nine of them inside, and
five, including the driver, on the box or on the roof seat. Its wide-
tired, heavy wheels were nearly as capable as those of the prairie
schooner. Its body was slung on stout leather braces, and was
sheltered from the weather by leather curtains. At the rear of the
body was a projecting "boot" with leather cover, in which the
scanty luggage of the passengers was carried. Twenty-five pounds
of personal baggage was the usual allowance for the three weeks'
journey; and the unavoidable hardships of the trip made it not
surprising that many of the passengers carried almost their whole
allowance in a jug. It was on the boot that the mail sacks were
packed, and if there was more mail than could be accommodated
here, the sacks rode inside, to the exclusion of passengers. Mails
had the right of way under the contract, and passengers must
yield to them if necessary. In the trip that Clemens made to
Nevada, he and his brother were the only passengers. He described in unfading language their struggle with the sacks that
shared the interior of the coach, and the experiences in learning to

sleep while riding the box with the driver. It was a triumph of organization to run the overland stage to California, and a feat of endurance to survive the trip.

Under the contract of 1857, Butterfield was to receive $600,000 a year for three years, but during the first year of operation the Government receipts from his route were only $27,229.94. The Postmaster-General described it, in a flush of enthusiasm over its inception, as a "conclusive and triumphant success"; but the next year, 1859, he was sobered by the slight revenue from it, and reported that, "Until a railroad shall have been constructed across the continent, the conveyance of the Pacific mails overland must be regarded as wholly impracticable." The service was to be justified upon national grounds, if at all, but the Postmaster-General thought the cost was excessive. There were in addition to the overland stage two not-expedited services, one from St. Joseph by way of Albuquerque to Stockton, California, and one from Independence to Salt Lake and Placerville. Each of these brought in a revenue negligible in relation to its cost.

The arrival of the railroad at St. Joseph, in 1859, established a new convenient point of departure from the Missouri River, but the Butterfield mail coaches continued to run over the line opened in 1858, until the Civil War compelled a rearrangement of the system. The heaviest freight was hauled over the Platte trail, in spite of the Post Office decision that the Texas route was superior. The tide of emigration to the Pacific that poured over the Platte trail after 1842 never slackened in its use of this as the most practicable for summer travel. When it became necessary in March, 1861, to take the overland mail away from danger of Confederate interference, there was enough equipment already along the Platte and the California Trail beyond it, to make the shift an easy one.

No single influence did more to give prominence to the Platte trail than the decision to use it for the pony express, which was started in 1860. The execution of this project was largely the work of Alexander Majors, of the freighting firm of Russell, Majors, and Waddell; its promotion was due to Senator Gwin of California. Gwin, who wanted a railroad, accepted the survey of 1853 as better than nothing. He induced Congress to allow the expedited mail service of 1858, but was not contented with it. The development of Colorado and Nevada, with their mining camps not far from the direct road to California, reinforced his demands for a relay pony service, unencumbered by stages or passengers, that might carry important mail through to the coast in much less than the twenty-five days of the Butterfield contract. Through his insistence the private firm organized the pony express, with blooded horses stationed at relays from nine to fifteen miles apart. Light men, or boys, were hired as riders, and drilled to rush through the Indian Country unarmed, relying on speed for their protection. On April 3, 1860, the express was begun, with riders starting simultaneously at each end; at Sacramento, and at Atchison, Kansas, across the river from St. Joseph. Their first run beat the best record of the overland mail coach by two weeks, and they promised a ten-day schedule. Their best run carried Lincoln's inaugural address to Sacramento in seven days and seventeen hours. Although they charged a fee of five dollars for the smallest tissue letter that was bundled into the saddlebags, the express was never a financial success. The Post Office objected to it because of the law against private mail services. In October, 1861, it ceased, partly because the money of the firm was gone and Russell, Majors, and Waddell were bankrupt; but more because on October 26, 1861, the Pacific telegraph was open, with a line 3595 miles in length, from New York to San Francisco.

In the summer of 1861, the Platte trail was a national highway, with as much significance and as great a length as any continuous road has had. The pony express riders were upon it, and the overland stages. The freighters were innumerable, the wagons of prospectors and farmers moving west were much in evidence. There was little tendency to permanent settlement anywhere along the line, but the mining population was developing junction points at short intervals where branch roads led off into the new diggings, and brought back not only the gold as dug but the imperative demand for more wagons, more mails, more roads, and a railroad to the Pacific. Butterfield and Russell, Majors, and Waddell drop out of the story soon after 1861. Their place is taken by the picturesque Ben Holladay, a man ignorant of letters but full of the enterprise and gambler's instinct that made him for the next four years a magnate among the traffic organizers of the plains. He sold out in 1866 to the rival firm of Wells, Fargo, and Company, an organization that lived so long as to forget its freighting origin, and to become one of the greatest of the railroad express companies.

The organization of the overland mail could not have occurred before the war with Mexico, for the United States had no real interest on the Pacific; it could not have lasted beyond 1869, for in that year the railroad was finished. It rose and fell within two decades, and never was it looked upon as more than a temporary institution, since even before it was conceived there was a general conviction that a railroad would be built as soon as Congress could surmount the sectional and local partisanship that blocked the selection of any route.

As the fifties advanced, the number of competing routes was reduced and standardized. Secretary Davis surveyed five in all under the law of 1853, but there were not five that survived the test of criticism. The northernmost was discarded for practical purposes, in spite of the enthusiastic commendation which Stevens, its surveyor, gave it. It was too academic to talk of a line from Minnesota to Washington, with no population on either Lake Michigan or Puget Sound at the ends, and neither population nor important resources along it. The middlemost was discarded as well. It was a hobby with Senator Benton to urge that best of all the routes was one along the thirty-seventh parallel, through the Sangre de Cristo Range of southern Colorado. No suitable direct grade was discovered here, or has been since; and the gorge of the Colorado River was as real a barrier to it as the mountains, but Benton persisted in advocating it, and Frémont made an independent survey for it. With these two possibilities eliminated, there remained the line of the Platte trail, where every one had known since 1835 that a railroad could be built, and the two southern lines known as the thirty-fifth parallel route, through Albuquerque, and the thirty-second parallel route, Davis's choice, from New Orleans, through El Paso and Fort Yuma.

In the decade of deadlock, there was nearly always a railroad bill before Congress, though there was no possibility of its passage. Senator Douglas, in 1855, the session after his triumph with Kansas-Nebraska, had a politicians' bill for three complete railroads — northern, central, and southern. There was no need for more than one, and no belief that even one could earn dividends, but he was ambitious on any terms to build a line through the Indian Country that he had subdivided. His bill passed the Senate, but met in the House the opposition of Benton, who had now lost his Senate seat and was obliged to content himself with the status of a Representative from the St. Louis district. Benton amended the Douglas bill to provide for one central trunk line and three eastern feeders over the plains to Lake Superior, Missouri, or Iowa, and Memphis. The bill failed to become a law, and at no time before the Civil War was there a better chance to pass one.

While Congress was deadlocked over the matter of route, the machinery for building such a road, when authorized, was being developed. There was a long debate whether it should be by the Government, as Benton wished, or by a private promoter with Government aid, as Whitney wished. Before 1857 it is likely that if a road had been authorized it could have been Government-built. After the financial experiences of that year the Government could not be driven into business.

But there was a well-developed procedure for Government aid which Douglas had launched in his Illinois Central Bill of 1850. The public lands were there, miles of them unbroken by any plough. If it was reasonable to give millions of acres of the most fertile land of Iowa, Illinois, or Wisconsin to aid in railroad building, it was more reasonable to extend even greater aid to railroads on the plains, where not many as yet expected ever to see a crop. The Illinois Central grant was followed by demands from every western State for similar generosity, and some of the eastern States asked why if the West was to receive lands for railroads, the East should not receive lands for something else. It was answered to this that the railroad land grants were not a gift but an investment by the Government, and that through their use the value of what remained was more than doubled. The Government sections within the limits of the railroad grants were held at double minimum price, or $2.50 per acre. President Fillmore approved railroad grants amounting to 8,198,593 acres; Pierce approved grants of 19,687,179 acres more. The prevailing type of grant was like that to Illinois for the use of the Illinois Central; six sections per mile of track, to be selected alternately with indemnity limits of fifteen miles on either side. The policy of extending aid of this sort was continued through the Civil War and down to 1871. When Donaldson summed the matter up in 1880, for record in his *Public Domain*, the land grant railroads actually built amounted to 15,430 miles, and it was estimated that their lands would exceed 155,000,000 acres.

A group of business men in California launched the enterprise that eventually was finished as the Union Pacific Railroad. Leland Stanford, governor of the State, Collis P. Huntington, Charles C.

Crocker, and Theodore D. Judah were interested in the charter issued to the Central Pacific Railroad Company of California early in 1861. Judah was the engineer, and ran a survey along the main trail to the Carson Valley that summer. He found nothing but engineering difficulties, for the California end of a railroad was obliged to climb the continental divide and to indulge in heavy mountain construction. Judah was an enthusiast, however, and hurried to Washington that autumn with plans and profiles. He had the support of the California delegation in Congress, as well as the advantage brought to his project by the Civil War.

Before the Civil War there was a reasonable choice among the three best routes, but after secession the two southern lines were out of the question for the same reason that shifted the overland mail to the Platte trail in 1861. There could be no national railroad in Confederate country, and even Missouri was ruled out, as somewhat dangerous. In the summer of 1861, it was not yet certain whether this State would cast its lot with the South or remain in the Union. Judah died that winter before his lobby was successful, but on July 1, 1862, a bill was signed by Lincoln to carry out his enterprise.

It was provided in this bill that a railroad should be constructed from the western border of the State of Iowa to San Francisco Bay, by various corporations already in existence, and one that was to be chartered directly for the purpose. The Central Pacific of California was to construct the western end, within the limits of that State. From the eastern boundary of California, to a point on the one hundredth meridian, the Union Pacific Railroad Company was to do the work. East of this meridian were to be four branches to Missouri River points at Kansas City, Atchison, Council Bluffs, and Sioux City. The main line to Council Bluffs was left to the Union Pacific, the others were ascribed to various corporations.

Private corporations were to build the railroad along the route now crowded with the wagons of the overland service. But the Government was to aid in various ways, by right of way, by land endowment, and by a loan of credit. The right of way was stated as four hundred feet, with extra ground as needed for yards or sidings, and with the privilege of cutting wood and stone from adjacent portions of the public domain. The land grant was to consist of ten sections per mile of track. The loan of credit was to be secured by a first mortgage on the finished railroad and was to be in form of United States bonds, advanced at the rate of sixteen thousand dollars per mile of track.

The passage of the Union Pacific Act did not build the road, and although its promoters were urging it as a war measure, the Civil War was ended before serious construction began. But the act opened a new period in railroad legislation, and in the disposal of lands. The old fiction of granting the lands to the States instead of directly to the roads was abandoned now. This road was to operate in the territories rather than in the States, and the sensitive southern consciences were gone. The northern members of Congress had no aversion to the idea of direct Federal aid. The overland route was thus the occasion for establishing a new wide-open policy of treatment of the public domain. The policy became even wider before the railroad spanned the route.

CHAPTER L
THE PUBLIC LANDS: WIDE OPEN

THERE were no railroad land grants made by Congress in the Administration of James Buchanan, 1857–1861. There occurred instead the last stand of the sectional influences against the newer view of National power and responsibility that was gaining ground through the logic of events and the advocacy of the western States. Discussion there was in abundance, and had Congress been left free to act there would have been legislative results, for the Republican Party was gaining in strength every month. Many of the Democrats from the North and West were willing to vote with them. But Buchanan stood true to the political alliance that he represented and had no comprehension that the United States might become a government of action. Whatever bills escaped destruction in committee or in either House, he vetoed. In his veto messages of the Homestead Bill and the Morrill Act may be found classic and final statements of the Philosophy that Calhoun had elaborated to protect the South. During these four years of deadlock various western forces were dammed up, any one of which might have gained in time enough head to break the dam. One was the demand for a railroad to the Pacific, and land grants for other lines; this was partly successful before Buchanan was elected and waited for final fulfillment until after he retired. A second was the evolution of agricultural outlook that beheld the passing of the simple farmer, at work with only his own hands and ancient tools, and that saw rising to change his task the various aids of science and machinery. A third was the swelling demand of the free-soil West, repeating the old formula that it was an outrage to charge the pioneer for the farm that he created and insisting that the United States grant him a homestead. All of these found their best expression through the leaders of the Republican Party, and all were successful in the first Republican Administration.

The Union Pacific Act, assuaging one of these demands, was partly founded on the notion that it was good business to give away half the region affected by a railroad, in order to double the value of the other half. But the American farmer was now thinking of more than mere acreage and original cost, as he considered the factors of success. Thus far his agriculture had been laborious in its execution, and primitive in theory and in practice. He was now conscious that science and mechanics might affect his profits.

The conservatism and ignorance of the rustic has been a familiar theme since the dawn of history. The more sophisticated classes in society have looked upon the farmers with a mixture of contempt and scorn, while literature has invariably depended on them to furnish the material for humor and burlesque. The isolation of the farmer in a roadless world accounts for much of this; the routine character of his work and the conditions under which it must be performed, account for the rest. Farming early became a conventional task, in which formal education had no part, and in which from father to son, by precept and example, the routine methods were handed down. The simple tools, plough, flail, and sickle appear in the earliest of our pictorial records. They were in use when America was discovered, little changed from their forms of antiquity. The frontier farmer, and indeed the farmer everywhere, was using them almost unmodified when the American States gained their independence. The settlers of the Appalachian valleys knew only this sort of agriculture, helped out by some rotation of crops and rule-of-thumb selective breeding of domestic animals. The children of the valleys picked it up and carried it down the Ohio to the West. Through inheritance and isolation it was hard to prove that anything they knew was wrong, or that a better method was good enough to overcome the curse of novelty.

The American farmers suffered for their conservatism and the backwardness of agriculture, and out of their suffering emerged the remedy. It was not long after the settlements pushed into the Great Valley before the farmers of the seaboard found that they could not meet the competition of the frontier. The wheat and corn of the virgin farms came cheaper to the market than the farmers on the older fields could raise them. Each new improvement of a road intensified this competition somewhere. It was true that sometimes the spread of settlement brought better soil into use. More often the old farm had been used up. The soil was exhausted by repeated cropping, which the partial rotation did not cure. The use of manures was rare, for domestic animals were mostly out at pasture. Commercial fertilizers were not known, except that perhaps lime was sometimes used to sweeten soil.

The movement to improve the method of agriculture began with eastern farmers who felt it necessary to fight off competition, or who responded to the idea that the country gentleman needed to set a good example. Some of them imported at great expense blooded rams and bulls as sires. Diomed, the great race horse that won the first Derby at Epsom in 1780, was brought to America in his old age to head the stud of a Virginia gentleman. Agricultural societies, with exhibitions and prizes for country produce, became common early in the nineteenth century. And as region after region passed out of its era of primitive fecundity, its people turned eagerly to whatever might sustain its prosperity.

The German universities took the lead in substituting science for tradition as a guide for agriculture. The chemical experiments of Liebig at Giessen were paralleled and followed with such intensity, that by 1850 something was known of the theories of fertility. The publication of the *Origin of Species* (1858) brought down upon Charles Darwin's head the reproaches of theology, but gave a new reasonableness to the ideas of selective breeding of animals and plants. Before 1860 there was much that could be learned respecting the connection between science and agriculture, and a demand arose for a technical education that might train young men to be better farmers than their fathers. In 1857 Michigan broke ground in this direction by creating the first American State College of Agriculture. Iowa followed in 1858, Minnesota in 1859, and the drive was on whose natural direction in the West must be a demand for Federal aid in the propagation of agricultural theory.

Justin S. Morrill, of Vermont, chairman of the Committee on Agriculture in the House of Representatives, took the lead in Congress and became the father of the agricultural colleges. He brought in his first bill in the winter after the panic of 1857, when the frontier was deep in depression, and ready for any remedy. In his speeches defending the measure, Morrill dwelt upon the larger social consequences of agricultural education. He described the injury wrought by the drift of young people from the farm to the city, and the usefulness to the Republic of a solvent, intelligent, agricultural class. The cities of 1857 were filling, also, with new immigrants; and in politics an active nativist movement was reinforcing any arguments that would lead in strengthening the American element in the American population. The Morrill Act passed the House at once, and the Senate at the next session. Buchanan vetoed it in February, 1859.

"The Constitution," declared Buchanan, as he gave expression to the reasons animating the last stand of the old school, "is a grant to Congress of a few enumerated but most important powers . . . which can be best or alone exercised beneficially by the common Government. All other powers are reserved to the States and to the people. For the efficient and harmonious working of both, it is necessary that their several spheres of action should be kept distinct from each other. This alone can prevent conflict and mutual injury. Should the time ever arrive when the State governments shall look to the Federal Treasury for the means of supporting themselves and maintaining their systems of education and internal policy, the character of both Governments will be greatly deteriorated." He regarded the grant of lands as extravagant and unwise in a time of depression. The basis of the proposed distribution was twenty thousand acres for each Senator and Representative; the lands to go to the State concerned for the "endowment, support, and maintenance of at least one college where the leading subject shall be, without excluding other scientific or classical studies, to teach such branches of learning as are related to agriculture and the mechanic arts . . . in order to promote the liberal and practical education of the industrial classes in the several pursuits and professions in life." The provision for industrial education was a graft upon the parent idea, as the Mobile and Ohio provision had been upon Douglas's Illinois Central Bill. The real motive of the act was agricultural education; but it was necessary to win over city votes.

The veto checked the movement for the present, but the Morrill Act was revived in 1862, passed without any serious debate, and signed by Lincoln the day after he approved the Union Pacific Bill. The delay resulted only in increasing the amount of the grant from twenty thousand acres per representative to thirty thousand. It was provided that each State, where possible, should take the lands from the unassigned public domain within its limits. As Buchanan had pointed out, however, some four fifths of the amount went to States in which there were no lands. These received land scrip for the appropriate number of acres. They were not permitted to locate the lands themselves, and become owners of real estate within the limits of another State, but they were at liberty to sell or assign the scrip and use the proceeds for the purpose of the act. In all, 9,600,000 acres were thus allotted in the next few years, in addition to 1,165,520 acres already given to the State universities, and 67,893,919 acres accruing to the States in the shape of sections sixteen and thirty-six, for the common schools.

Science, invited to the aid of the farmer, was slow in coming. Every State, in time, accepted the gift under the Morrill Act and opened one or more agricultural schools. Morrill had not debated the educational side of his proposal as fully as the social, and Congress had not even tried to examine the educational leaders of the day as to the practicability of the scheme. Higher education was almost entirely classical in 1862. Eliot had not yet begun his revolutionary attack upon the Harvard curriculum, and the college or university presidents, clerical for the most part, would have had little to suggest to help the new establishments. It was long before the agricultural colleges taught enough agriculture to justify themselves. The experiment stations that were to mean much for agriculture in the next half-century, were slow in starting and had technique to develop as well as personnel to train. But the movement was begun to educate the most conservative of classes and abolish the rustic.

Mechanics came sooner to the farmer's aid than science, and here the United States led the world. In Europe the supply of land was relatively limited and was all appropriated; while labor was plentiful and cheap. Hand labor survived long under these conditions, and the incentive to devise labor-saving machines was less than in America, where the supply of land was unlimited, and every farmer's profits were measured by the acreage he could cultivate. The ingenuity of Eli Whitney brought about a revolution in cotton culture, and innumerable other minds were induced to work on other inventions. The contractors on the Erie Canal and the National Road experimented with contrivances to pull stumps and move dirt by wholesale. Nearly every village blacksmith shop concealed some device on which the craftsman worked when business was slack, and over whose future development his mind strayed to dreams of wealth.

Typical of these was Robert McCormick, a Scotch-Irish resident of the Shenandoah Valley. Farmer and blacksmith by turn, he watched the procession of emigrants to the western lands and himself worked on one of the most alluring of the problems, that of harvesting the wheat crop. His neighbors cut their wheat with the heavy cradle, and brought in the crop only after the most wearisome labor of the farmer's cycle. The cradle was an improvement upon the scythe, for it left the grain neatly piled on the ground, ready to be bunched and bound; and the scythe was in its turn an improvement over the sickle with which grain had been harvested since the dawn of history. But sickle, scythe, and cradle all involved heavy and slow manual labor, whereas the crop, when ready to be harvested, needed to be cut at once. The limit on wheat production was not the acreage that could be planted, but the amount that could be cut, bound, and stacked in the few days after it was ripe and before it spilled. Mechanics, everywhere, were searching for the solution, as McCormick was. About 1831 he gave it up. It was not hard to devise a machine to cut dry, erect, wheat straw, on even ground; but to get one that would operate over rough terrain, with the straw wet, soft, and tangled by summer storms, was more than he could do.

In the year that Robert McCormick gave it up, his son Cyrus H. McCormick built a model that would work.[1] It can probably never be determined how much Cyrus learned from his father's efforts, and what he devised himself, although his father and his brothers joined in declaring him to be the inventor of the reaper that he patented in 1834. The basic elements that McCormick included in his machine remain in the structure of the most advanced harvesters to-day. There was a reciprocating knife, with triangular, saw-tooth blades, each protected by a conical sheath. The conical sheaths were thrust among the stalks as the reaper advanced, while a great reel overhead swept the grain against the sheaths and the knives that worked in and out among them. The grain fell as cut upon a horizontal platform built in the rear of the knives, and the operator, with his rake, gathered the stalks into convenient sheaves from off this platform. The binder was added a generation later, and the thresher was improved and refined, but the McCormick invention was the turning point for agriculture from a hand industry to one of science and machinery.

There were three reasons why the reaper was slow in being adopted by the farmers of the West. One was their conservatism, that made them reluctant to believe that it would work. It was several years before the inventor could find a buyer for his first machine. A second was the semi-mountainous country in which

---

[1] Herbert N. Casson, *The Romance of the Reaper* (1908), and *Cyrus Hall McCormick: His Life and Work* (1909), are too superficial to do their theme justice. Reuben G. Thwaites, "Cyrus H. McCormick and the Reaper," was prepared from the papers of the McCormick family and printed in State Historical Society of Wisconsin *Proceedings*, 1908; but the treasures of the important agricultural library of the McCormicks are yet to be worked.

it was invented. The harvesting capacity of the reaper was so great that a farmer needed for it larger fields than the valley of Virginia afforded. At best it was an expensive machine that could be used only a few days in the year. The modern thresherman has surmounted this by beginning to harvest the wheat on the southern plains, and then following the crop as it ripens to the northernmost limits. But the early farmer needed more acreage before he could use the reaper to advantage. The third obstacle was the fact that it involved an additional need for capital. The farmer was used to buying his land, but did not control much more capital than was needed for this. His tools were all cheap, and many of them he could make himself. In order to prepare his mind for the new outlay, and to procure the means to finance it, much education and preparation was in order. As these were done, the farmer became a business man, and broke with the old traditions of agriculture.

McCormick sold his first reapers in the early forties, as farmers recovered from the depression of 1837. He sold them himself, being both manufacturer and salesman, and in the course of his travels, he discovered the endless prairies of northern Illinois, where a wheat field might run for miles without a hill to throw the reaper off its course. In 1847, when he was disposing of some two hundred machines a year, he moved his factory from the rolling country of the Shenandoah to Chicago. If his fellow townsmen had known it, his arrival was more significant for them than the Rivers and Harbors Convention over which they were much excited that summer. There was no railroad in Chicago as yet, and the Illinois Canal was incomplete, but McCormick picked out Chicago to become the center of a new kind of agriculture, and pioneer of a new era. In 1851 the inventor, now possessing an improved machine that had grown with the tests of use, took the reaper to the World's Fair at London and demonstrated before a hostile audience that in agricultural machinery the United States could lead the world. The use of the reaper spread with the frontier of the fifties. At the end of the decade the McCormick plant was turning out four thousand a year, and had built up extensive side lines of other agricultural machines, while rival manufacturers were contesting his patent rights and offering the farmer a range of choice.

The availability of the new agricultural machinery came at the moment when the obstructions to the freest use of the public domain were breaking down, and when railroads had so far supplemented the older water routes that the crop could get to a market wherever it was raised. The changes that came with the machines, caused by them in part, and in part by the opening of the rural mind to science, were far-reaching in their consequences. Of course they saved labor, making many thousands of men free to fill the Union armies in the Civil War. They educated the farmer, making him at once business man, mechanic, and a large employer of labor, and thus helping to break up the isolation of the rural class. And they increased the rate at which it was possible for the West to absorb the farm lands of the public domain. The profits to be got out of wholesale agriculture had once before stimulated the South to push the area of cotton culture. It now inspired the West to push to fulfillment the homestead policy.

There was an inconsistency in the western demands that broke down the last of the restrictions on the lands. Every community wanted railroads so badly that it was willing to vote alternate sections for every line. It was clear that these grants could not produce revenue for the roads unless they were sold, and the sections which the Government retained were held at double-minimum, and yet the West advocated them.

The grants of lands to the States for education in general, or agricultural education, or public works, had again little value unless the lands were sold at a profit. Yet it was possible for a western spokesman to advocate all these and still believe that the Government ought to give a free farm to each citizen who would reclaim it.

The inconsistency between using the lands to raise money, and giving them away, was clear to the Free Soil Democrats, who, in 1852, included in their platform a specific demand for a homestead policy, declaring, "That the public lands of the United States belong to the people, and should not be sold to individuals nor granted to corporations, but should be held as a sacred trust for the benefit of the people, and should be granted in limited quantities, free of cost, to landless settlers." The inconsistency became clear enough to the settlers, too, in the decade that followed the Civil War. But during the fifties the West wanted both railroads and free farms and failed to realize that one might block the other.

There would have been a homestead law before the Civil War, if it had not been for James Buchanan. The movement for free lands was approaching a head, and within the new Republican

Party there were few who did not believe in the policy.[2] A law permitting any head of a family or alien who had declared his intention to become a citizen, to occupy a quarter section for five years, and then buy it for twenty-five cents an acre, passed both houses of Congress in the summer of 1860. It did not make the land free, but the reduction in price was so sweeping that the homestead opinion accepted the law as a fair compromise and called it, "A Bill to secure Homesteads to actual Settlers on the Public Domain." Buchanan vetoed it for the same reasons that induced him to veto the Morrill Act of the year before: it was in his opinion unfair and unconstitutional. It was not expedient, he thought, "to proclaim to all the nations of the earth that whoever shall arrive in this country from a foreign shore, and declare his intention to become a citizen, shall receive a farm of 160 acres, at a cost of 25 or 20 cents an acre, if he will only reside on it and cultivate it." This was, however, the stand not only of the adherents of the revenue theory of the public lands and of the strict constructionists who denied the powers of the Government, but also of the sections that feared the growth of a free farming West that might overbalance the South.

Lincoln signed the Homestead Bill, May 20, 1862. The only result of Buchanan's veto was to delay the policy two years, and abolish the price of twenty-five cents an acre. Its privileges were now extended to "any person who is the head of a family, or who has arrived at the age of twenty-one years, and is a citizen of the United States, or who shall have filed his declaration of intention to become such," with the exception made necessary by the war then raging, "and who has never borne arms against the United States Government or given aid and comfort to its enemies."

The homesteader was allowed a quarter-section of minimum lands, or half a quarter of double-minimum, on five years of residence and cultivation. The Pre-Emption Act was not repealed, but remained in force for those who did not desire to acquire title by residence or cultivation; and any homesteader was specifically allowed, at any time after his original entry upon the lands, to commute his homestead entry to a preëmption, and buy the land at the regular price.

On January 1, 1863, the first homesteaders made their entry on the public domain, the agricultural college lands were made ready

---

[2] James T. Dubois and Gertrude S. Mathews, *Galusha A. Grow, Father of the Homestead Law* (1917), naturally gives Grow more credit than he earned.

for the States, and the railroad lands were held before the eyes of railroad builders to speed their efforts. The public lands were entered upon the last great period of their existence; to remain wide open for the next twenty-five years, until they were closed not by a change of policy but by the fact that the resources of the Nation were exhausted. In the census of 1880, and in the *Report* of the Commissioner of the General Land Office for that year, it was noted that practically all of the farm land had been taken up. The open frontier disappeared, and with it vanished the most American of all the American forces that have operated on society. After 1862 the history of the American Frontier is in its final chapters.

CHAPTER LI

THE PLAINS IN THE CIVIL WAR

THE influence of the Civil War in making the United States a nation has long been a theme of patriotic writers and orators. They have pointed out how Lincoln's decision to maintain the Union, and the consolidating forces let loose by the military operations of the United States, changed the character of the Federal Government. A fair implication from many of their interpretations is that if there had been no Civil War the United States would have remained a loose Government, without power and without program.

From the standpoint of the plainsman, or the prairie farmer who appeared a generation before him, the error of this theory of American history is much like that of the statesman of the Old South, whose information as to American development ceased to grow after the Mexican War. The course of industry and transport, after the panic of 1837, had but one end, and that was an interstate organization of the business of the United States and a growing pressure upon Congress to provide the machinery for its direction and control.

The historian who finds the key to nationality in the Civil War has given too little attention to the necessary implications of the building of the railroads, the multiplication of territories, the land grant policies, and the complications these created. The Middle West and the Far West were the political creatures of the United States and looked to the Nation for coördination and support. They looked thus before the Civil War and kept on looking during that momentous struggle. New reasons for their dependence sprang up during the war itself, and were disconnected with it. The only effect the Civil War had on the Pacific railroads and the Homestead Act was to delay their accomplishment. The mining camps demanded roads, railroads, and post offices, without reference to the war, and the mere fact of their existence implied a necessary enlargement of the activities of the National Government in the ensuing years.

But the error of the historical interpreter is one of the study and the library, subject to correction and repair. The error of the statesmen of the Old South was more costly, for it deprived their calculations of a vital factor, whose presence and proper appraisal might have altered the course of history. They believed that the whole Mississippi Valley, including the tributary basin of the Ohio, was still bound up with the current of the Father of Waters and that true western interest must forever lie with that power which should be able to control the outlet of the Mississippi at New Orleans. This was good doctrine for James Wilkinson and inspired a wise policy in the Spanish rulers who bought off the leaders of the Old West. It was good doctrine for Thomas Jefferson, too, who was driven by it to buy Louisiana and preserve the Union. It was not bad doctrine in the forties and early fifties, when the steamboat traffic of the Mississippi was at its height and the gaudy cabins of the floating palaces carried up and down the leaders of western and southern politics, business, and society.

But it was bad doctrine after the railroad era gained its stride, and it became worse every day after the trunk line railroads reached Chicago. The South formed an opinion and then closed its mind. Its orators continued to talk of the dependence of the Ohio Valley on New Orleans, at a moment when the banks of New York were filled with the paper and securities of the Northwest. The panic of 1857 made the error worse, for the North and West were prostrate, while the South still had in cotton a source of untouched prosperity. The grave analyses of southern writers, showing the panic to be due to a faulty economic organization of the rest of the Union, and the South to be impregnable in its economic situation, helped to confirm a general hope that the South could get along well alone and that the Northwest would ultimately follow it out of the Union. Wherefore, in part, secession; and a war that saved the Union, if it did not shape its future growth.

It is easy after the event to show how southern mistake and faulty analysis failed to see the unifying of the North and West by the normal process of industrial growth. Every northwest State gave its vote to Lincoln in 1860. And after the election, instead of following the South into the Confederacy, the Ohio Valley sent its young men, by hundreds of thousands, into the Union armies. No State that had been in actual contact with free territory went with the Confederacy. In all the Border States, Delaware, Maryland, West Virginia, Kentucky, and Missouri, the forces of Union were strong enough to offset the overtures of the South. It was not always easy to do this. West Virginia, as has been shown, was wrenched away from Virginia by sheer force. Kentucky muttered and sent many men into the Confederate armies, although the State refrained from secession. In Missouri there was civil war, followed by guerrilla warfare in which both Union and Confederate forces were involved. The old lines of communication, that had run from north to south since the first settlement of the Mississippi Valley, gave way to new bonds between East and West. When the South closed the Mississippi to commerce, the traffic of the upper valley hesitated for a few months and then found outlet eastward over the trunk line railroads; and the recovery of the Mississippi by Union forces in 1863 failed to send it back. No inducement has since been found to divert the interior commerce from the railroads to which the South drove it, or to restore to the Mississippi its ancient prestige.[1]

Each of the sections inherited a part of the far frontier, when the split occurred, and on the border of the plains the farthest flung of the engagements of the Civil War took place. Nothing that occurred in the way of fighting west of the Mississippi had any bearing upon the outcome of the test of strength that was under way between Washington and Richmond, and that was working its way up the Cumberland and Tennessee towards the Chattanooga gateway to the Old South. But the frontier, with its sparse population, was disturbed by what small portion of the war it had and revealed something of its capacity for action and its incapacity for sustained defense.

The southwest extremity of the frontier battle line touched the Rio Grande at El Paso and then ran north with that river to the northern portion of New Mexico. Here Texas tried to establish a military frontier in 1861, and west of it the Confederacy hoped to acquire the wealth of the Mowry mines in the Santa Cruz Valley. Confederate forces under General Henry Hunter Sibley swept up the Rio Grande in the autumn of 1861, unimpeded by Federal defenders of the region. Some of the United States commanders had turned their posts and property over to the Confederacy. Colonel E. S. Canby alone stuck to his post at Fort Craig, without yielding to, or retarding, the advance of Sibley. The Confederate army passed around him and went on up the river to Albuquerque and Santa Fé.

A logical objective for Sibley was the new Colorado Territory

[1] Carl Russell Fish, "Economic Conditions in the Northwest, 1860–1870," in State Historical Society of Wisconsin *Proceedings*, 1907.

to the north, which he might have reached through Las Vegas and over the Raton Pass. But in Colorado Governor William Gilpin was fearful of attack from the south and suspicious of alleged disunion conspiracies among the southern members of his community. Without authority from Washington, or funds to pay them, Gilpin raised two volunteer regiments, which he marched south to the Santa Fé Trail and over it to relieve Canby. The Confederate offensive was checked south of Fort Union on the Santa Fé Trail, there was unimportant fighting between Fort Union and Albuquerque, and by April, 1862, the retreat of Sibley left the Rio Grande in Union hands. A few weeks later, reinforcements arrived from California, in the form of Colonel Carleton's column that had advanced from Yuma through Tucson. Carleton was left in possession at Santa Fé, with men more interested in the new mines of Arizona than in their military problem.

The Rio Grande episode took place in a country sparsely inhabited, where the few residents were indifferent to the struggle going on before them. The Mexicans of New Mexico were easy going and illiterate, and neither helped nor hindered either of the hostile forces. The Santa Fé Trail along which it occurred was itself some hundreds of miles in advance of the settled portion of either Union or Confederacy.

But near the eastern end of the Santa Fé Trail, where it left the Bend of the Missouri, there was fighting of a different sort, with a militant local population ready to take part at any moment. Here was Kansas, still sore from its own civil war of the preceding decade. Here, too, was Missouri, with its policy as a State in bitter dispute, and with an antipathy to the "Jayhawkers" of Kansas, which it took no pains to disguise. Close by was Arkansas, sparsely settled, more primitive than either Missouri or Kansas, and full of partisans of the Confederacy. In these three States the sympathizers of both sides were already yearning to get at each others throats and needed only the call to arms in 1861 to set them loose.

The result was guerrilla warfare and private violence. It is not possible to separate the events that may have had some military meaning from those that were only acts of revenge or private grudge. There were raids on both sides, and murder, theft, and arson. Bands of ruffians held together for considerable periods with no other purpose than that of plunder. The military commanders of the Union forces, with their headquarters at Fort Leavenworth, had generally no definite enemy to confront, but were at their wits' end to keep the civilian population from destroying itself. The term "border ruffians" had been used in the days of the Kansas war to describe the gangs of southern sympathizers who ravaged the Kansas settlements; it continued to be used throughout the Civil War.

In August, 1862, one of the guerrilla leaders, Quantrill by name, led his band to Lawrence, Kansas, in the most famous of the border raids.[2] The town was surprised, and sacked without resistance. When the enraged population in return sought to harry the Missouri border, General J. M. Schofield, who had been unable to protect them, restrained them from doing damage. In the following year a Missouri expedition was organized in Arkansas and fought its way through southwest Missouri to Kansas City and Westport before it was broken up. The border warfare was at all times a vexatious and useless waste, revealing more of the passions of the border people than of the military problems of the Union.

In addition to the border raids, the Confederacy has been charged with the promotion of Indian uprisings. The Indians of the plains became generally uneasy in the sixties, after a decade of relative tranquillity in the fifties, and this change has been ascribed to Confederate policy. No important evidence has been brought forward to confirm this. Only in the Indian Country immediately west of Arkansas did events clearly conform to such a policy; and here with reason, for the Confederacy included this portion of the Indian Country within its limits. There was a Confederate Indian Office that extended control over these tribes, substituting itself for the United States Bureau of Indian Affairs. It drove out the Union Indian agents, compelling the tribes to enter into new agreements with their new sovereign. In the long run its activities were useless to the Confederacy and disastrous to the tribes, for the United States regarded this defection, though under compulsion, as treason. After the Civil War was over, the Five Civilized Tribes were punished by a confiscation of the western half of their ranges; and the lands so acquired were used for the recolonization of various tribes that were taken off the plains. But it was easy to assert that whenever unusual disorder appeared among the Indians, the Confederacy was responsible for it.

The earliest of the serious Indian disorders of the Civil War occurred on August 18, 1862, when the Sioux of Minnesota, led by Little Crow, ravaged the valley of the Minnesota River, and

___

[2] William E. Connelley, *Quantrill and the Border Wars* (1910).

slaughtered some hundreds of its unsuspecting inhabitants.[3] The blow came at a moment when the Union was in despair, and Lee was contemplating his first invasion of the North. Pope had succeeded McClellan, only to be outgeneraled by Lee at the second battle of Bull Run. The outlook in Europe was black. It was hard to avoid the suspicion that the desolate frontier above New Ulm, and the exiled survivors who rushed in panic to that village and Fort Ridgely, were consequences of the military measures of the Confederacy. The Secretary of the Interior thought so; and whether they were or not, the whole Minnesota frontier west of St. Paul, and extending to the Yellow Medicine River, was aflame with murder.

But the records of the Indian Office show other and sufficient causes and make it unnecessary to turn to the theory of Confederate intrigue. The Indian agents in Minnesota knew what was wrong, and had for a decade, since the Ramsey treaties of 1851, been protesting against the abuse of the Sioux bands by Congress and the Senate. The latter body had, in its full power over treaties, amended part of the promised reserve out of existence. The former had been overdeliberate in appropriating the treaty funds. And when the money came at last, long after the preëmptioners had swarmed over the ceded lands, the accumulated traders' claims against individual Indians ate up the payment and left little for distribution.

The result of the slow and partial compliance of the United States with the agreement signed by the tribal leaders in 1851, was to split the Sioux into two factions: the "farmers" and the "blankets." The former, in what was typical Indian fashion, accepted the inevitable and made the best of it. They settled down to farm life on the limited reserve, took care of their crops and live stock, and the men generally symbolized their transition from the wild to the tamer state, by putting on trousers like the white man. The blanket Indians, on the other hand, remained irreconcilable. The young braves who had not come to realize the power of the superior civilization, and the untamed, and the malevolent, and the indolent, accepted the annuity goods as they came around; but accepted them with surly demeanor, and despised the more com-

---

[3] Isaac V. D. Heard, *History of the Sioux War and Massacres of 1862 and 1863* (1863); the local historians have difficulty in agreeing upon the total loss. Heard placed it at 737, but more recently it falls to 490 in the well-checked lists of M. P. Satterlee, *A Detailed Account of the Massacre by the Dakota Indians of Minnesota in 1862* (1923).

pliant tribesmen who put aside the blanket and went to work. The agents saw trouble coming many years before it arrived. The sense of grievance soaked in, and it called for no more than a chance accident to provoke an outbreak.

Such an accident occurred in Meeker County, in the broad angle between the Mississippi and the Minnesota rivers, on August 17, 1862, when five white settlers were murdered. No one has suggested that the affair was premeditated, but once it was done, the guilty Indians and their innocent friends realized that punishment was almost certain to follow and to hit them without discrimination. They therefore struck first, blanket and farmer Indians alike, ravaging the frontier for two hundred miles and seizing women and children as captives and hostages. For a few days the braves remained in the vicinity of the settlements around and above New Ulm; then they took to flight up the Minnesota River towards the unsettled country beyond the Yellow Medicine.

By the end of August the pursuit was under way, with the Minnesota militia led by the officers of the young State. Appeal was made to the United States Government, and General Pope, no longer useful in the East after the second battle of Bull Run, was sent out to take command. They followed the tribes and the prisoners up the river, afraid always that the Indians would add to their outrage by further mutilation and murder of the women and children. In September they caught up with them and defeated them in battle. Little Crow and the more guilty leaders fled from the field and took refuge among relatives in Dakota Territory. The so-called "friendly" Sioux remained to surrender, and to return the prisoners to Henry Hastings Sibley who commanded the militia. "The Sioux war is at an end," Pope declared in October, but as the women and girls came home and told the story of their captivity the whole Northwest was swept with a demand for the extermination of the Sioux.

The Government was in a dilemma. Viewed as a war, the Sioux prisoners had done only what Indians nearly always did when the tribes went to war, and the United States had insisted upon handling them with treaties and calling them nations. The prisoners were entitled to protection, and an occasional voice from the frontier, like that of Bishop Henry B. Whipple, called attention to the repeated provocations the savages had received. But the opinion of the border called the prisoners murderers and demanded revenge. Several hundreds of the Sioux were tried by military commission at Fort Snelling, and found guilty of murder, rape, and arson. Mobs of citizens from St. Paul tried to take the matter of punishment into their own hands, and for some days maintained a state of siege around the fort. In the end President Lincoln pardoned all but thirty-eight of the savages, but these were hanged on a single scaffold at Mankato on December 26, 1862. The rest of the Sioux prisoners were soon transported to a Dakota reservation; the fugitives were pursued and scattered by troops under Pope's orders. The Minnesota outbreak was a natural consequence of a faulty system of Indian administration, made worse by the pressure of an active frontier. This pressure kept up and was injuriously felt wherever the use of the trails and the extension of the mining camps brought groups of white men into contact with the Indian tribes.

The Colorado problem arose when the fifty-niners rushed to the camps of the Pike's Peak Country and intruded upon the range assigned in the treaty of 1851 to the Arapahoe and Cheyenne. This tribe, at Fort Laramie, agreed that its country lay between the Platte and the Arkansas, and east of the divide. Living was easy here, for across the range the buffalo herd drifted north every spring, and south in the autumn. With even the primitive bow and arrow, the Indians could extract a livelihood from the herd; and as they acquired more horses and firearms, the buffalo became their basis of existence. The natural tendency of the travel along the trails to Oregon and Santa Fé was to break up their herd and waste the game, but the huge numbers of buffalo seemed to defy extinction as long as no regular settlements were made within the Arapahoe and Cheyenne country. The growth of Denver and the formation of the new territory forced a revision of the plans under which the Arapahoe and Cheyenne had lived in peace since the Treaty of Fort Laramie. While Congress was engaged in the final debates over Colorado Territory in 1861, the Indian agent at Fort Wise negotiated a treaty with the tribes concerned. He summoned the Indians to his Upper Arkansas Agency, on the river near the point where the trail to Santa Fé turned southwest along the line of the Purgatory or Las Animas River. Here was one of the several sites of Bent's Fort; and here there had been traders' stations of some sort, with little break since the country was visited by Zebulon Montgomery Pike, in 1806.

The first concentration of the wild tribes of the plains was accomplished in the Treaty of Fort Wise. North of the Platte, the

Sioux still remained at large on the open range; south of the Arkansas, the Kiowa and Comanche retained their freedom, although the agents were asking for a means of restraining them. But between the two rivers, the Arapahoe and Cheyenne now accepted as their definite home a triangular tract in southwestern Colorado in the angle of Big Sandy Creek and the Arkansas, and about ninety miles in breadth. Fort Lyon, near the junction of the streams, became their new agency, and the tribes ceded to the United States the rest of the range, outside the reserve, although retaining the right to hunt over it until it should be further disposed of.

The Sand Creek Reserve was never a success. It comprised perhaps the most dry and desolate region of the whole Arapahoe and Cheyenne country, and had no special virtue except that none of the more important routes of travel actually traversed it. The Indians never lived here, but remained in wandering camps, becoming more sullen and despondent as they watched the heavy traffic over the main stage line to the north and the spread of isolated farms where there was enough water to maintain a little stock. There was slight trouble, however, until the summer of 1864, when, by premeditation, the stage line was attacked along most of its length from Fort Kearney to Denver.

Governor Evans, of Colorado, saw the uprising coming in the early summer, when immigrants reported on the sullenness of the tribes, and the necessity for strict military organization west of Fort Kearney. There was further testimony to it in sporadic attacks upon isolated farming families, so many indeed that towards the end of June he sent a proclamation to the friendly Indians, warning them to collect around the agencies to avoid "being killed by mistake." Four concentration posts were named in the message: Fort Larned, in central Kansas, for the Kiowa and Comanche; Fort Lyon, on the Sand Creek Reserve, for the southern bands of Arapahoe and Cheyenne; Camp Collins, in northeast Colorado, for the northern bands; and Fort Laramie for the Sioux. He promised rations and protection for the friendly bands that might assemble here; and destruction for the wild bands that remained on the warpath. It was after this warning, and in spite of it, that Ben Holladay's stage line was broken up. There were Indian attacks at nearly every station, haystacks and buildings were burned, and stock was driven away. Few lives were lost, but damage to property and nerve was considerable; and as late as September one of the Indian agents wrote that, "Communication with the Missouri river is now almost entirely cut off. All coaches are provided with a large escort, and the trains crossing the plains collect and travel together for protection."

There was no response to Governor Evans's invitation to the bands to gather round the agencies until the summer came to an end, and autumn frosts lessened the comfort of life on the open plains. Then the Arapahoe and Cheyenne began to drift in to Fort Lyon, declaring that they were friendly and had always been so. The agent here took a party of them to Denver, late in September, for conference with Governor Evans and Colonel Chivington who was in command of the Colorado militia. This was an embarrassment to the authorities who were now ready for a campaign against them. Chivington received, on the day of the conference, a telegram from General S. R. Curtis who commanded the military department, saying, "I want no peace till the Indians suffer more." The Governor accordingly promised them nothing, lectured them severely, and sent them back to make what peace they could with the military authorities in the field. None the less, the bands continued to gather around Fort Lyon and were directed by the agents there to go into camp on Sandy Creek, a few miles above the station. Among them was Black Kettle, leading chief of the Arapahoe and Cheyenne, who declared his friendship, sought relief, and joined the camp.

Colonel Chivington completed his preparations for a campaign, organizing some nine hundred men in two militia regiments. He marched them in November, not out on the plains where there were still some warlike bands at work, but down the Arkansas to Fort Lyon, where the tribes had been invited to assemble, and where they were now peaceably in camp. From Fort Lyon he marched up Sandy Creek to the camp, which he attacked without warning, killing indiscriminately braves, squaws, and children. He justified the attack by declaring that in the wigwams his men found numbers of fresh white scalps and fragments of mutilated bodies. His men retaliated in kind, with mutilation and slaughter. He and his authorities called it a punitive campaign. The Commissioner of Indian Affairs described it as a massacre, in which Black Kettle's people were "butchered in cold blood by troops in the service of the United States." It has never been possible to fix the responsibility with satisfying accuracy, for many of the braves professing peace were actually fresh from the warpath; but the episode, as clearly as that in Minnesota two years earlier, pointed to the impossibility of leaving Indian relationships upon their old basis much longer.

After the Chivington massacre, the Arapahoe and Cheyenne bands took to the plains again, until in October, 1865, a new treaty was made with them on the Little Arkansas, near Wichita. They surrendered the Sand Creek Reserve, accepting the promise of a new one on the Cimarron River, partly in Kansas and partly in lands confiscated from the Cherokee. But the Senate never confirmed this, and until 1867 the Arapahoe and Cheyenne remained a tribe without a home.

The Sioux of the plains, who had restricted themselves at the Fort Laramie conference to the range north of the Platte, remained at peace through the fifties in spite of the fact that the Senate had cut down the promised annuities by seventy per cent. They were not encroached upon by settlers during the decade, nor by miners except at the end of the period. The camps established in the Bitter Root Valley, and along the heads of the Missouri River in 1862 and immediately thereafter, raised new problems of transportation, but did not crowd actual settlers up against the Indian hunting grounds. Like the Arapahoe and Cheyenne, the Sioux of the plains lived the wild life, dependent chiefly upon game for food and clothing.

Among the stipulations of the Fort Laramie Treaty (which never had the force of law, because never fully ratified), was one that bound the Sioux to permit the free opening of wagon roads, and the unmolested passage of emigrants along them. Any damage done to emigrants was to be paid for out of annuity funds. In 1854 a minor episode occurred that revealed something of the problem. It centered around a stray cow, abandoned by a Mormon train on the Platte. This animal, sick and emaciated, was killed and eaten by a Sioux band; whereupon other Sioux, perhaps through virtue, or because they had not been numbered at the feast, carried the news to the agent at Fort Laramie that a cow had been stolen. The agent, instead of charging the animal against the next annuity, or dismissing the case because the owner had not complained, reported to the military commander at the post, and he dispatched a punitive party commanded by a young lieutenant, Grattan by name, to arrest the thieves. Through some mishap the party was taken as a war party, and the Sioux attacked and wiped out the detachment. The next summer a regiment was marched upon the plains to discipline the offenders, and Fort

Pierre was later taken over as an army post on the Missouri River. There was no organized resistance, and the punishment was promiscuous, with every probability that whatever Indians had incurred real guilt were out of reach.[4]

It was not until 1865 that the Sioux of the plains became unmanageable. Orders were sent from Washington that year to survey a new wagon road cut-off to the mines of western Montana Territory. It was to leave the main trail near Fort Laramie, proceed northerly down the Powder River, east of the Big Horn Range, and then bend west to the Yellowstone River and the Bozeman mines. This was the Bozeman Trail, and might have become an important emigrant road had not the Sioux, and their determined chief, Red Cloud, sternly prohibited it. The survey party of 1865, under General P. E. Connor, marched down the route, to the Rosebud River, returning in the autumn in what can only be regarded as a careful retreat. They found Indians hostile, and ready to pick off stragglers or stampede stock. This was the heart of the buffalo range, and Red Cloud declined to consider its surrender.

In 1866 Colonel H. B. Carrington was sent out from Fort Kearney to mark the road, protect emigrants and build a chain of posts from Fort Laramie to Bozeman.[5] He built Fort Phil Kearny at the point where his road left the Powder River, and Fort C. F. Smith at the crossing of the Big Horn. But his force was so small that after separating the construction parties and the garrisons, he was compelled to hold the defensive in a hostile country, where the defensive was interpreted by the Sioux as a confession of weakness. His men were inadequately armed, with left-over rifles from the Civil War; whereas the Indian Office was yearly issuing to the Indians, rifles of recent manufacture and superior accuracy.

As Carrington settled into winter quarters, his orders to the posts and men under him were peremptory; to remain on the defensive, to fight only when attacked, and then to do no more than was necessary to insure safety. He repeated his directions more than once, for his men were restive under inaction, and many of the younger officers hungered for engagements and promotion. On December 21, 1866, his wood-cutting train signaled back to

---

[4] The industrious and romantic Cyrus Townsend Brady has *Indian Fights and Fighters: The Soldier and the Sioux* (1904), and *Northwestern Fights and Fighters* (1910).

[5] Grace Raymond Hebard and E. A. Brininstool, *The Bozeman Trail* (1922), relates the story of the episode, and contains admirable maps.

headquarters at Fort Phil Kearny, that they were surrounded by attacking Sioux. There had been more than one fight of this character before; and Carrington sent an expedition to relieve and bring in the train. Before these started, under Fetterman, a new officer of his command, he repeated his admonitions against taking an aggressive. The troops dashed out of the fort, passed over a low range of hills and disappeared forever. When they failed to come back, further relief was sent, which found the dead and mutilated bodies of every man in Fetterman's command. The evidence showed that upon leaving the post they had seen Indians and had pursued them instead of continuing upon their mission; and the Indians had led them into a successful ambush.

The Civil War was over before the Fetterman massacre occurred, and the conditions that were so often ascribed to Confederate intrigue continued although the Confederacy had become a thing of the past. The army of the United States was commanded by men who had seen long service in real war, and in the War Department there were resources that overshadowed the scanty numbers of Indians and their limited equipment. Yet there was no peace on the plains. There was instead, as the confusion of the war passed away, and the United States could see it better, a crisis in Indian affairs caused by pressure from all sides, and increasing penetration of their ranges. There was as well the question whether the Bureau of Indian Affairs was adequate for its task, and whether the ideals of an army were the proper ones to dominate the men who were charged with the policing of the plains. It was a crisis that could end only in the extinction of the tribes, should events continue as they were. And the administrative system could not be altered for the better unless the United States should rise to new levels of organization and better standards of government.

CHAPTER LII

THE UNION PACIFIC RAILROAD

If there had been no other reason why the Indian policy must proceed upon a new course after the Civil War there would still have been cause enough for the change in the fact that the Pacific railroad was becoming a reality, and that from either side of the Continental Divide a railroad track was piercing the plains and mountains. It had been long in starting. As late as 1848, the New York *Herald*, that knew enough to know better, avowed in seriousness that "This whole project is ridiculous and absurd. Centuries hence it will be time enough to talk of such a railroad." During the delay, the plains had become an open book, traversed in every direction and mapped and described from every angle. The emigrants had continued to march across the continent in unbroken procession and with them the stage lines and the freighters had served to establish the routes and emphasize their length. The delay was long enough for the builders to learn how to construct so great a work, and for Congress to devise the means of aid. The "centuries hence" were reduced to decades, when the passage of the Union Pacific Act of 1862 opened the period of actual construction.

The national assistance offered the road in the original act seemed to be generous. The ten sections of public lands and the loan of sixteen thousand dollars of United States bonds per mile, would begin to accrue as soon as the first brief division of forty miles was completed and accepted by the federal inspectors. These could then be marketed, in order to provide funds for constructing additional divisions. The promoters of the company were required to raise only a small initial capital, to build the opening divisions and cover the necessary overhead. But even this small amount proved to be beyond their capacity, for the Civil War was calling for great loans to the Government, and was providing abundant outlets for the investment of free capital. Persons with money to invest found better opportunities at home in every section of the Union than were afforded by the stocks of a railroad on the plains. Even the warmest advocates of the Pacific railroad had not convinced themselves that the road would pay. It was to be a national enterprise justified by the intangibles of national pride and protection. There might be a profit for the actual builders, but little was expected from operation. Hence the stock found no market, and there could be no more bonds except as a second mortgage. The United States loan was to be a first mortgage upon the property. Only an over-hopeful speculator could believe that the railroad would earn enough to satisfy the interest charges of this mortgage, to meet the charges on a second mortgage, and leave a surplus for dividends upon its stock.

The Central Pacific of California accepted the terms of the act of 1862 and proceeded with its surveys, while the new Union Pacific corporation was organized as provided in the act. But neither company showed vitality for five years, and the road that was urged so strongly as a war measure was hardly begun until the war was over. Ground was broken at Sacramento for the Central Pacific, in February, 1863, and a few miles were running before the end of the year. By the end of 1865 there seem to have been about sixty miles in operation, thirty more in 1866, and forty-six more the following year, making a total of 136 miles at the beginning of the building season of 1868. The construction was hindered by lack of capital, and the extreme difficulty of the engineering problem in the Sierra; but the Union Pacific that had only the gentle rolling plains to cross built even fewer miles, forty in fact, by the end of 1865.

Congress revised the enabling act in 1864, taking into account the lack of confidence in the future of the road, and the way in which its first mortgage obstructed further loans. The most important changes in the law were the doubling of the land grant, which now became twenty sections per mile of track, and the shifting of the Government loan to the status of a second mortgage. The railroads were permitted to borrow on first mortgage bonds to the amount of the Government loan. Investors who had no interest in second mortgage bonds or stock felt differently about a first mortgage, substantially guaranteed by the Government's holding of a second mortgage of the same amount. It was already required that the roads should have a standard gauge of four feet, eight and one half inches, so as to permit the exchange of rolling stock with the larger railroad systems of the East.

Under the law of 1864 both companies found financial support and gained momentum. Their speed was further increased by a law of 1866 concerning the junction point at which they should meet. The original act provided that the Central Pacific should build within the State of California and meet the Union Pacific on the eastern border of that State. In the law of 1864, the Central Pacific was given permission to build 150 miles into the State of Nevada; and about this time President Lincoln made an executive ruling that gave a new aspect to construction in Nevada and Utah. The original law provided that the loan of bonds by the United States should be at the rate of sixteen thousand dollars per mile; with the proviso that this should be doubled in the rough foothills, and trebled to forty-eight thousand dollars in the heavy mountains. It was left to the President to determine the points at which the double and treble subsidies should begin to accumulate. His ruling threw the relatively flat country of the high Nevada plateau into the mountainous class, and both of the companies made a rush for the privilege of constructing here. The Central Pacific watched every move of Congress, with a careful lobby, and saw that no law was passed unless it received some favor. In 1866, it induced Congress to repeal the junction point and permit each road to build what it could, and to make a junction where the tracks should happen to meet.

Then began the race of construction, with the bond loan as the prize for performance. At the moment when the Arapahoe and Cheyenne and the Sioux were beginning their forlorn struggle against compression and extinction, the railroads increased the size of their gangs upon the plains, and in 1867, 1868, and 1869 built as never before. For a period of sixteen months in 1868 and 1869 every working day saw an average of two and a half miles of new track laid down. And in the spring of 1869 the work was done, 638 miles by the Central Pacific, and 1038 by the Union Pacific to the junction point.

The incidents of construction were so picturesque as to receive more general attention than was usually accorded railroad building now that the novelty of it had worn off. The material difficulties of the builders were great. From both ends they were building into an unoccupied waste, where they must carry with them their gangs, their habitations, and everything their men might need except fresh meat. With every mile laid down, the work became more complex, for over the increasing length of track must move from the first day not only the building materials but the equipment for daily life of large communities, and the communities themselves.

The terminal towns early caught the attention of the visitors upon the roads. During the busy seasons the railroad camp might easily run to ten thousand men, for all of whom shelter must be provided. The mining camps had taught them how to do this. The men slept in tents or wood frames covered with canvas or rough wood shacks. Along the disreputable street deep with dust or mud in the center and flanked by the hitching rails for horses, were the stores and houses. Their wooden fronts ascending to a parapet above the roof made an ambitious showing that was often belied by their canvas backs. Saloons, dance halls, and gambling dens were innumerable. After work there was nothing to do but wait for to-morrow, and while away the time with the parasites who swarmed along the line. "Hell on Wheels" was the appropriate name that Samuel Bowles of the Springfield *Republican* bestowed upon the town he visited in 1868. "Hell would appear to have been raked to furnish them," he said, "and to it they must have naturally returned after graduating here."

The towns were temporary, yet none was so forlorn that some speculators did not appear to hope that it would be permanent. As soon as the site was selected, a town would be platted, streets named for the heroes of the Civil War, and lots put on sale. Among the forms of gambling that flourished was the speculation in real estate; and after each town moved on, leaving its empty shell behind it, it left also a harvest of blasted hopes.

Out of these railroad towns the construction trains proceeded every morning, carrying the whole working population to the job. It was not always a safe task. On the Union Pacific there was continuous friction with the Indians whose range was invaded. The meat hunters had constant trouble and sometimes gangs of workmen were attacked, so they were sent to their tasks armed to resist. From the chief engineer, General Grenville M. Dodge, down to the section hands, many of the builders were men of military experience. Soldiers discharged from the army in 1865 and 1866 sought work with the railroad. They "stacked their arms on the dump and were ready at a moment's warning to fall in and fight," said Dodge. They could arm a thousand men from the track train, experienced soldiers commanded by seasoned officers. And after the day's construction work, thus guarded, the trains carried them back to the shacks at night.

Every so often, when the track head was forty or fifty miles in advance of the terminal town, they knocked off work for a day and moved the town. Tents were taken down, bags and boxes were packed, frames of houses were disjointed, and piled in rough mass upon the cars. The whole moved forward to a new place at the head of the track. An observer at the site that was to be Cheyenne, has reported the arrival of the train at that bare station: "The guard jumped off his van, and seeing some friends on the platform, called out with a flourish, 'Gentlemen, here's Julesburg.'" And what had been Julesburg that morning was taken off the cars and set up to be Cheyenne that night. The terminal town of the Central Pacific was a Chinese camp, for Governor Stanford and his associates had repaired their local labor shortage by importing cheap coolie gangs. It was less expensive and more orderly than the Union Pacific camp, for the Chinese workers saved their pay, lived on rice, and wasted less than the Irish laborers who dominated on the eastern end.

The engineering problems varied on the different ends of the line. At neither base was there access to a stock of supplies. San Francisco Bay was remote from places of manufacture, with the result that all the heavy tools, the rails, and the rolling stock came by ocean route, with heavy freights and long delays. At the eastern end of the line, there was no railroad connection when construction began. St. Joseph was a railroad terminus, but no line crossed Iowa as yet to Council Bluffs, which was selected as the starting-point. The supplies were freighted up the Missouri from St. Joseph or St. Louis, or from places more remote. The Union Pacific was burdened with the unnecessary condition that it should begin not at the Missouri River but at the western boundary of the State of Iowa. This was a provision offered to their constituents by the Iowa delegation and meant that a long and costly bridge must be built across the Missouri River before the railroad itself could get far under way. Most of the American railroads were still crossing important rivers on car ferries, for the manufacture of steel was not yet far enough advanced to make the steel truss bridge practicable; and there was no satisfactory substitute for it. The western road had an abundance of wood and stone in its vicinity with which to do the heavy work of construction, but the eastern road ran through a treeless plain, with long stretches where neither of these essential building materials was at hand. Neither of the tracks was held down by the engineers to a standard maximum gradient, but both were built along the natural configuration of the country unless the ascents were prohibitive.

In spite of the generous aid offered by the United States in the act of 1864, both roads found it hard to raise money as needed to pay the costs of construction. In both cases the same men who controlled the stock of the company organized and controlled as well contracting companies to which were let contracts for construction of the line. In this way they expected to get their profits out of the speculation. On the western end it was the firm of Charles C. Crocker and Company that had the lion's share of business; on the eastern, it was the Crédit Mobilier of America.

The Crédit Mobilier of America was a Pennsylvania corporation, created by special legislative act. It was organized with general powers, but without special purpose, except that its promoters proposed to sell their charter to some group of speculators who needed corporate privilege without running the gauntlet of legislation to get it. The Union Pacific men soon gained control of it, and through it the road was built. A Congressional committee later reported that the Union Pacific had cost about fifty million dollars to build, and that the railroad paid the builders this price and an additional profit of about twenty-three million dollars.

The procedure was to let the contract for a given section at a stated price, and to pay the builders partly in cash, of which the railroad had little, and more in the securities it could control. It possessed under the law common stock, first mortgage bonds, and the United States bonds which constituted the second mortgage. All of these fluctuated on the market, so that it is almost impossible to say with precision what the cost of any transaction came to. Mr. James Ford Rhodes, who is familiar with business practices of the period after the Civil War, and who has made a careful study of the Crédit Mobilier, has reached the conclusion that in the year 1868, the largest year of the Crédit Mobilier, the holder of a share of stock in the company received as dividends:

230 per cent first mortgage bonds
515 per cent Union Pacific stock
60 per cent cash

All of the securities were far below par, the Union Pacific stock running as low as nineteen cents on the dollar, but Mr. Rhodes's computation is that the holder of a $100 share of Crédit Mobilier stock received in 1868 dividends worth $341.85; and it is his judgment that the profit was not excessive considering the short life of the investment and its risk.

The profits would probably not have attracted attention had not one of the promoters, Oakes Ames, a Massachusetts congressman, sold blocks of this stock to his colleagues, lending them the money with which to pay for it until the dividends should earn the cost. The New York *Sun* brought out the facts of this scandal during the presidential campaign of 1872, showing that a long list of Congressmen and other public officers had accepted these doubtful profits from a company that existed only because of acts of Congress. The Crédit Mobilier case became the text for innumerable sermons on political reform, while Oakes Ames, exposed and censured, died broken by the blow. It was only by such heroic finance that the Union Pacific was able to meet its bills during the years of actual construction.

The race for mileage was begun after the legislation of 1866, and during the next two years the two great lines were brought within sight of completion. But as the year 1868 progressed there arose a doubt as to whether the advancing ends would ever meet. The law did not say where that point should be, or require the roads to build along a common survey. Each chose its own route, and a prospect arose of two overlapping lines, each continuing indefinitely. Congress intervened at this stage, and fixed upon the north shore of the Great Salt Lake where the junction should be made.

At Promontory Point in Utah, or rather at a point directly north of its base, the last spike was driven May 10, 1869. Sidney Dillon, president of the Union Pacific, drove it in the presence of officers and guests from both coasts, while throughout the United States bells were rung, meetings were held, and orators called attention to the meaning of the event. Among the many poets of the day, Bret Harte stood out with his much quoted verse:

> "What was it the Engines said,
> Pilots touching, head to head
> Facing on a single track,
> Half a world behind each back?"

He let the eastern engine get the worst of the argument, and permitted the West, which he, beyond most writers of the day could understand, to carry off the honors:

> "'You brag of the East! *You* do?
> Why, *I* bring the East to *you!*
> All the Orient, all Cathay,
> Find through me the shortest way;
> And the sun you follow here
> Rises in my hemisphere.'"

Never again could the wild Indians range the plains from the Rio Grande to the Assiniboin. The Pacific railroad split the northern and southern plains forever. It destroyed the possibility of the wild life as a permanent condition. The year after the celebration at Promontory Point, the section of the Union Pacific that crossed the plains was paralleled from Denver to the Missouri River by the Kansas Pacific Railroad, which was connected with the main line at Cheyenne. The Kansas and Nebraska towns threaded upon these railroad lines, pushed out into the Indian Country, and their people gave words and definiteness to the demand that there must be a new chapter, and a final one, in the history of the American Indian.[1]

[1] J. P. Davis, *History of the Union Pacific Railway* (1894), was long the standard secondary work. There now are admirable accounts in Nelson Trottman, *History of the Union Pacific. A Financial and Economic Survey* (1923).

CHAPTER LIII
THE DISRUPTION OF THE TRIBES

By 1869, almost an even century after the Treaty of Fort Stanwix, it had become impossible to treat the Indians as separate independent tribes without doing violence to the facts of their life or to the reasonable demands of civilization for the use of the land over which they hunted. The theory of the Fort Stanwix Treaty was obsolete, as was that upon which Monroe and his successors acted after 1825.. There could not be an Indian civilization maintained in its original form by the legislative enactment of the white race. If the Indian could not put his land to use, another would. In the process of experience by which this fact was learned the Indian tribes declined in civilization and took on the worst attributes of the stronger race. The benevolent theorists, who desired to protect the tribes from actual destruction, were in the older communities of the East. On the frontier, in actual contact with them, lived aggressive men who were realists in life, and saw in the Indians an incumbrance upon the earth. Only an absolute despotism, with high ideals and a powerful machinery of government could have saved the tribes, and this did not exist in the United States. It is not necessary or fair to call the process *A Century of Dishonor* (1881), as Helen Hunt Jackson did in her literary indictment of our Indian policy, for the only conscious policy of the Government was honorable and generous. But the American machine was far from being exact or competent; and through the different agencies at play, the defects of legislation and administration, and the incompetence of the Indians themselves, a result was attained after a century of American independence that was not far different from what a policy of conscious dishonor might have brought about.

In advance of the completion of the Union Pacific, Congress was stirred by the manifest uneasiness of the Indians and the loud recriminations of the frontier States and Territories, to undertake an investigation of the status of the border. The Minnesota outbreak attracted attention after a long period in which the relations were relatively peaceful. The Chivington massacre kept interest alive and raised more doubts as to whether all the right was on one side.   The Fetterman affair at Fort Phil Kearney was quite as glaring.   The points of view from which the long chain of events was to be examined were displayed and argued in the reports of the Government bureaus concerned and in the press.

The Bureau of Indian Affairs, which had been a part of the Interior Department since 1849, was under grave suspicion of incompetence and corruption.   There was not always a pretense of making appointments of agents or other officials on the basis of fitness. Like the rest of the civilian establishment of the United States, it was riddled with the spoils system.   On the accession of a new President, the Commissioner of Indian Affairs expected to be removed to make room for a friend of some friend of the President. The new incumbent proceeded to assign his patronage where it would do the most good in a political way; with the frequent result that the Indian wards of the United States were placed in the charge of incompetents, perhaps even drunkards or crooks.   At best they could become useful only after years of service at the expense of their charges; but by the time they had learned enough to cease to be a liability on the system, their terms of office came to an end with a new election.   It is to the credit of human nature that as many of them were honest and conscientious as were, but the natural result of the system was to defeat whatever good intention Congress had in its legislation.   One case taken at random illustrates what often happened.   The agent of the Yankton Sioux in 1863 was like his associates charged with agency supplies which he was supposed to issue for consumption as needed.   He appears from the testimony taken by the committee that investigated his conduct to have required his Indians, who could not read or write, to make their mark early in the fiscal year upon vouchers covering his whole stock.   He then issued what he must and sold the rest to his own profit.   It was common to find cases in which flour, bacon, and other supplies for Indian consumption were delivered spoiled, yet paid for in full.   There was often collusion between agents and contractors.

The defects of the Indian administration were damaging, but the virtues were almost as embarrassing.   The good agent became at once the friend of his tribe and took their point of view.   He trusted them beyond warrant and saw clearly their necessity to have weapons of the most improved character in order to fight evenly the lessening game.   He kept on issuing rifles and ammunition to them up to the verge of outbreaks, and more than once the army was sent to repress tribal troubles hot upon the issue of Indians' rifles more modern than the troops themselves carried. Naturally the army that was always sent for to restore peace was indignant at the agents who were so often immoral, corrupt, and injudicious.

But the army was itself under suspicion nearly as grave. Its members had no responsibility except when there was trouble afoot. The officers were generally good men, for the spoils system did not permeate the military establishment, and there was a pride of service that kept most officers free from the abuses to which agents yielded. But the army was a fighting machine, whereas the Indians needed an effective police. Congress failed to provide a system of law to cover Indian affairs, and crimes in the Indian Country had no adequate means of detection or punishment. There was only the martial law, which treated the Indians as enemies rather than as petty criminals or drunken murderers. When, as in Minnesota in 1862, a local affair took place, the tribes knew that the punishment would be sweeping and fall alike upon the innocent and the guilty. There was an incentive for the good Indians to join the bad and for both to take captives with whose bodies they might barter for better terms. The tribes so often were willing to give up members guilty of murder or robbery as to justify a belief that a system of police, manned perhaps by the Indians themselves under white officers, would have been able to maintain order at less cost of life and money. The Fetterman massacre appears to have been caused less by Indian hostility, than by martial spirit in officers who ought to have approached their task as policemen. At Sand Creek in 1864 the congregated Indians bore testimony to the fact that peace might have been established by negotiation, and that the martial ardor of Colonel Chivington was itself one of the obstructions to peace and good understanding.

Mutual recrimination between the army and the Indian service could not, however, solve the problem, and Congress was inspired by the Chivington affair to create a Committee on the Condition of the Indian Tribes which began its work in March, 1865. Its members, in various groups, visited the scenes of trouble, taking testimony as they went, which they published in an illuminating *Report* in January, 1867. They reached without difficulty the conclusion that the principle of permitting the Indians to exist as roving tribes was no longer tenable. They could not agree upon the measure of guilt to be ascribed to the various parties to the special outrages they investigated, but they saw the poverty and homelessness of the once wild tribes, and the impossibility of maintaining peace without giving them better security and support. While they investigated, the engineers put through the Union Pacific, and it became more imperative to quiet the plains, so that the trains might run without interruption. The way in which Black Kettle's warriors had extinguished the Holladay stage line in 1864 was a valuable object lesson.

As a result of the *Report on the Condition of the Indian Tribes* (1867), Congress created a peace commission in the summer of 1867, with instructions to restore peace on the plains, to secure an unimpeded right of way for the railroad, and to recommend a permanent policy for dealing with the Indians. Two years later a volunteer and non-political Board of Indian Commissioners was organized as a permanent adjunct to the Bureau, to advise the Commissioner and oversee his contracts and finances. Peace was brought about, although not without difficulties that further illustrate the conflict between the civilian and military methods of approach.

The northern Indians were invited to meet the peace commission at Fort Laramie in September, 1867, and runners were sent upon the plains to carry the summons to the dispersed bands. But when the commission arrived at the scene of the council the Indians were not there. Instead of coming to confer, Red Cloud of the Sioux sent in word that peace would recur when the United States formally abandoned its attempt to build the Powder River road and withdrew the garrisons. Only after six months' delay was the council held in April, 1868; and in the resulting treaty the road was given up, while the Sioux accepted as a permanent reserve the southwest corner of Dakota, west of the Missouri River, and guaranteed in return peaceful transit on the plains. Other treaties were made with the Ute, Shoshoni, and Bannock tribes across the divide, whereby these Indians withdrew to condensed areas. Congress, that summer, created Wyoming Territory, and completed the political organization of the West.

The tribes of the southern plains were induced to meet the peace commission, in October, 1867, on Medicine Creek, eighty miles south of the Arkansas. The braves of the Kiowa, Comanche, and Apache were there, as well as the Arapahoe and Cheyenne who were still vagrant and homeless after the Fort Wise Treaty of 1866.

These last had had one more intimidating lesson as to the difficulty of doing business with the army.

In the spring of 1867 General Winfield S. Hancock, who had been assigned to command the army on the plains, made a demonstration of American power along the Arkansas. He took the local agents with him, and had a fully equipped army, with infantry, cavalry, artillery, and a pontoon train, and proposed to warn the tribes to keep away from the trails to the Southwest. In March he was at Fort Larned, where the Pawnee Fork comes in from the west to join the Arkansas. Here he decided to visit in force the Arapahoe and Cheyenne village, then encamped on the Pawnee Fork, about thirty-five miles away from the Santa Fé road. The Indians objected to this, and the agents protested, but Hancock persisted. As he approached, the population of the camp took to flight, leaving their tents and belongings behind them, and the tribe gave their visitor the cold welcome of a deserted village. He destroyed their property, treating flight as a hostile action and proceeded in imposing state to Fort Dodge, on the Arkansas, near the crossing of the one hundredth meridian. The peace commission had this to overcome before they could persuade the Indians to gather on Medicine Lodge Creek for the October conference. Here, the Kiowa and Comanche surrendered their claims in the panhandle of Texas and accepted part of the confiscated lands in Indian Territory between the Red River and the Washita; while the Arapahoe and Cheyenne were placed in the Cherokee outlet, between the Arkansas and the Cimarron.

With the conclusion of the treaties that guaranteed free passage for the railroad the trouble was not yet over. There was peace for the moment, and the Indian agents, with incorrigible confidence, issued to the tribes the special gifts that Congress made available in 1868. During the periods of declared war the ration issue had of course been stopped, and the Indians were reduced to destitution. Arms and supplies were issued to the Arapahoe and Cheyenne in July and August, 1868. Almost immediately sporadic murders of settlers took place in Kansas along the western margin of the settlements on the Solomon and Saline forks of the Kansas River. The young braves, at least, were on the warpath again, and General Sheridan, who had replaced Hancock, undertook to restore order by an attack upon the base from which they operated. Most of the Indians were in the west end of the Indian Territory, south of the outbreaks. Camp Supply was newly built on the North Fork of the Canadian, and toward this post in the autumn several columns of troops advanced from New Mexico, from Fort Lyon in Colorado, and south from Fort Hays in central Kansas. Major-General George A. Custer, with the Fifth Cavalry, U.S.A., led this last detachment. The peaceful Indians had been ordered to congregate at Fort Cobb, under General Hazen, for protection and rations; and the hostiles had been advised to keep away.

Black Kettle none the less came in to Fort Cobb toward the end of November, claiming to be at peace. Hazen refused to receive him, ordering him away from the fort. The Indians pitched their tents on the Washita, toward which place Custer headed his advance. The punitive column had crossed from Fort Hays to Camp Supply in November; it left the latter place November 23, marching heavily through the snow. On November 27 it surprised and completely destroyed Black Kettle's village, killing without discrimination braves, women, and children. Custer's battle on the Washita was not a war, but a punishment, for the period of possible Indian wars was over. The tribes were now so widely scattered, and so poor, and the railroads made mobilization of military forces so easy, that the rest of the Indian story is one of localized disturbance and overwhelming retribution. In 1876 Custer himself was the victim of his gallantry and the system.

The northern Sioux, whose affairs occasioned this catastrophe, settled down after 1868 upon their reserve in Dakota, with the Missouri River on their east, the open Powder River range upon their west, and the Black Hills in the center of their territory. The encroachment that they sought to avoid in this reserve, came none the less. By 1872 the Northern Pacific Railroad reached the Missouri River at the Mandan village. Worse than that, gold was found in their Black Hills, and increasing rumors of the wealth of the find came out. In 1874 Custer was sent into the Black Hills to ascertain the extent of the discoveries and the degree of penetration by white prospectors. Disturbed by the threats of dislodgment involved in this, the Sioux were further irritated by the dishonesty of the agents at Red Cloud's agency. A group of geologists, on an exploring trip from Yale University, turned their attention from rocks and fossils to flour and bacon, in 1874, and charged over signatures of honor and distinction that the agency affairs were a disgrace.[1] Nothing happened to the agent, however,

[1] Professor O. C. Marsh, *A Statement of Affairs at the Red Cloud Agency, made to the President of the United States* (1875).

and by the autumn of 1875 the various Sioux bands were dispersed over the plains, all disgruntled, and the young braves menacing.

In the winter of 1875 the Sioux were ordered in to the agency on pain of being treated as hostile, and when they failed to obey, three columns of troops were sent out to round them up in 1876. Custer commanded one of these, and pursued his charges into a destructive ambush. He and his men were slain June 25, 1876, under conditions that make it clear that he behaved more courageously than wisely, but that make it clearer that the army was at a disadvantage in policing Indians.

In the summer of 1877 there was an outbreak among the Nez Percés, equally illustrative of the hard lot of the Indians and the inadequacy of the machinery for handling them. The Nez Percés, whose habitat was the Snake Valley, were notably upstanding, honest, and friendly Indians. The first blow to their friendship was in 1862 when the town of Lewiston was planted in the heart of a reserve that had been guaranteed them in 1855. The next year a treaty was negotiated, by which the Clearwater country was made available for white entry, but many of the Nez Percé braves refused to be bound by it because they had not personally given it their assent. The Indians never reached a point at which they recognized a tribal government competent to bind by its action all the members of the tribe. Chief Joseph, the leader of the non-signatory Nez Percés, kept his followers under control, but they lived where they pleased in the country that the treaty had pretended to transfer. Attempts were made by President Grant to bring Chief Joseph to terms, the Secretary of the Interior, Zachariah Chandler, being sent on mission to him in 1876; but Joseph remained moderate and firm in his refusal. The next year a casual brawl gave occasion for punishment, and the Nez Percés fled from the Snake Valley. General O. O. Howard led in the pursuit, gaining every day a higher respect for the character and capacity of his opponent.[2] The fugitive Indians did no damage as they went, and even paid the frightened farmers for the supplies they took. Howard failed to catch them, though he followed them across Idaho and Wyoming into Montana for seventy-five days. On the Missouri River they were at last maneuvered into the grasp of

---

[2] Brig.-Gen. O. O. Howard, *Nez Percé Joseph. An Account of his Ancestors, his Lands, his Confederates, his Enemies, his Murders, his War, his Pursuit and Capture* (1881); Nelson A. Miles, *Serving the Republic. Memoirs of the Civil and Military Life of Nelson A. Miles, Lieutenant-General, United States Army* (1911).

another military force, commanded by Nelson A. Miles. After every outbreak, whatever the cause, there were further cessions, and increased consolidation of the tribes, as well as increased inability to break out again.

The changing Indian problem, after the completion of the Union Pacific, gradually induced changing methods. In 1871 Congress put an end to one of the vicious details of the system by abolishing the treaty. From the first treaty made by Congress at Fort Stanwix in 1784, down to 1871, 370 treaties were concluded and ratified. In all of these the form of negotiation with an independent nation had been observed, and the Senate had confirmed by the constitutional approval of two thirds. The fact that the Indians could not comprehend the full meaning of a treaty and lacked the institutions for enforcing one, was not the primary reason for abolishing this method of negotiation. The moving condition now was the jealousy of the House for the Senate. The treaty method gave to the Senate legislative power over a domestic problem; and the House that was expected to pay the bills demanded that it be consulted in the agreement. In the Indian Appropriation Bill of 1871 it was provided that no future agreements should be made without the approval of Congress.

With the exception of occasional local outbreaks, the tribal relations were generally peaceful after 1871. For this, the Indian Commissioner claimed the credit. The Board of Indian Commissioners claimed credit, too, and in their annual reports pointed out how their wisdom and disinterested moderation gradually diverted the tribes from the road to war to the paths toward peace. The real reason is to be found in the closing of the open frontier; but the change was not the less genuine, whatever the cause.

"The Indian Service is primarily educational," declared the Commissioner of Indian Affairs in his *Annual Report* for 1909, after a generation of the changed conditions.[3] His conclusion is borne out by the testimony of the intervening reports, since the last of the tribes were placed upon reduced reserves. While the Indians were wild and roved the plains, the educational work possible among them was limited. The religious denominations conducted missions, but the influences toward civilization were

[3] W. J. Harsha, "Law for the Indian," in *North American Review*, 1882. Indian Commissioners have had a habit of writing of their duties; George W. Manypenny, *Our Indian Wards* (1880); Francis E. Leupp, *The Indian and his Problem* (1910); Charles L. Slattery, *Felix Reville Brunot, 1820-1898* (1901).

offset by the lure of the tepee and the irresponsibility of wild life. The mission schools, however, showed that the Indian children were capable of education, and reservation day schools were multiplied as the tribes became more constant in their residence.[4]

The educational task of moulding the child who returned at night to the home of savage parents was too great not to arouse complaint. The agency boarding school was the response, and parents were persuaded to entrust their children to white teachers, among whom they lived during the impressionable years of their lives. But institutional schools, at best, were dehumanized; and at worst their personnel was that of the rest of the Indian service, political and incompetent. The Commissioner under President Hayes did much to remedy this, and pointed out that there ought to be a merit system for appointments. Not until the Civil Service Act was passed in 1883 was there statutory authority for removing these places from the reach of the spoilsmen, but before this time a third type of school had been devised, in the non-resident boarding school.

In 1879 a young officer named Pratt received permission to assemble a group of boys and girls from various border tribes in the old Carlisle Barracks, in Pennsylvania, there to educate them. He opened the school that fall, installing a trade-school education and sending the students in the summer vacations to live and work with selected families of the neighborhood. Here they learned the white man's standard of life, acquired his tastes, and formed relations of mutual respect with the people whom they met. For nearly forty years the Carlisle school was a model that was imitated by some thirty other non-resident boarding schools. Carlisle was closed down in 1918, when the army needed the plant for invalid rehabilitation, and when the progress of citizenship among the tribes had again changed the nature of the Indian problem.

Long before the tribes were condensed upon reserves, it was foreseen that the Indian could not be civilized and enabled to cope with individualistic neighbors until the communal influences of the tribe could be broken down. As early as 1817 one of the treaties with the Cherokee provided that an individual Indian might at his request be separated from the tribe and acquire citizenship. But the courts ruled that citizenship was not their

[4] Martha L. Edwards, "A Problem of Church and State in the Eighteen-Seventies," in *Mississippi Valley Historical Review*, vol. XI.

inherent right, and that even the Fourteenth Amendment to the Constitution did not confer citizenship upon them when it asserted that "all persons born or naturalized in the United States and subject to the jurisdiction thereof" should be citizens of both the nation and the State of their residence. The Commissioners of Indian Affairs therefore urged continually upon Congress a policy that would break up the tribal autonomy and throw the Indians upon their own exertions.

A great advance in the theory of dealing with Indian wards was made under President Hayes, whose Commissioner E. A. Hayt installed a modified merit system. It was time for this, for in the previous administration it was shown that the trader at Fort Sill was paying annually for his appointment, and Grant's Secretary of War was receiving the money. Hayt recommended sweeping changes in his first *Annual Report:* the concentration of the tribes should continue until complete, education should be pushed, rations should be reduced as rapidly as possible to encourage individual responsibility, a special code of reservation law should be passed, a system of Indian police should be set up, and, chiefly, tribal holding of land should give way to ownership of land in severalty.

Congress moved slowly along the path indicated by Hayt and his successors. In 1887, in the Dawes Act, it laid down a general principle for dividing up the lands. The tribes were to be allowed to grant fixed areas to all their members, and to sell to the United States whatever there remained above the amount required for this. The proceeds of the sale of the surplus were to constitute a tribal trust fund, administered for their interests by the United States, which was also to act as guardian for the Indians to whom land in severalty was granted. These wards were not to be allowed to sell their lands or to dispose freely of them until such time as they appeared to have sufficient sense of responsibility to warrant it. There was a real danger that the Indians would not appreciate the significance of private lands, and would barter them away at once and become dependents upon the Government without either tribe or land. As rapidly as the individual owners received their certificates of competency, they were to become full citizens of the United States. The treatment of the Five Civilized Tribes was different in detail from that of the other wilder Indians, but the principle of steering all of them toward full citizenship with its privileges and responsibilities was now established. In 1906, in the

Burke Act, further safeguards were provided for Indians who were still incompetent to protect themselves, and further discretionary authority for the Commissioner in granting them citizenship. The lands bought by the United States in the execution of the policy of severalty were turned into the public domain and opened to entry under the general laws. This brought about in most instances only a moderate addition to the area of agricultural development; in the Indian Territory it provided a tract for which no government existed until in 1890 Congress established there the Territory of Oklahoma.

Long before the Burke Act was passed, or Oklahoma was ready for statehood in 1907, the Indian problem had lost its larger meaning, and the Indians had come to be one of the lesser difficulties in the road to Americanization. The undigested alien groups of the large cities, and the status of the negro in an industrial world, had far greater bearing upon national welfare. The Indians were no longer a military risk, and the scores of army posts that dotted the West with reason and propriety in the decades of Indian wars lost their significance. In place of Indians and wild game, the vast distances of the old range had come to breed great railroad systems and to be the propagating ground of social panaceas. This was the last American frontier, yet it was true to precedent in regarding its immediate needs as universal in character, and in demanding that the whole attention of the United States be devoted to their solution.

CHAPTER LIV

THE PANIC OF 1873

THE last phase of the history of the American frontier runs from the building of the Union Pacific until the frontier disappeared. This covers less than twenty-five years in time; in place its setting is the high plains, which the explorers first described at the opening of the century. The process was different from that with which any earlier frontier was opened up, for now the railroads were not only bringing settlers to every entrance around the margin, but were penetrating every remote oasis that blossomed in the heart of the Far West. Events moved more rapidly than had been possible in earlier migrations; yet the process would have been completed a decade sooner, had it not been impeded by the great depression that followed the Civil War. The panic of 1873 produced a despondent state of mind that induced eastern intellectuals like Godkin, Lowell, and the clientele of the *Atlantic Monthly* to despair of the future of America. It angered the West, slowed its development, and gave rise to great movements of reform.

It would be possible to write an economic history of the North and West that would show a rapid growth unhindered by the Civil War. The panic of 1857 had run its course by 1861, and the United States was ready to enter upon an era of industrial development. The losses had been written off and new capital had been accumulated. In spite of the war the new era opened. From 1861 to 1865 there was a stimulated prosperity due to the war demand for manufactured commodities. The cities grew in size and number, improving their plants each year. Profitable farming was pushed north and west, and new railroads were worked in to complete the existing system. In spite of the capital drawn off for war purposes, there was money for investment in every sort of business. Immigration in the ten years of the sixties brought into the country nearly as many persons (2,500,000) as were enrolled in all the Union armies.

The western aspect of this period of investment and boom had for its chief feature the building of railroads, with the Union and Central Pacific system as the most spectacular single item. When this was chartered in 1862, after long agitation, and as a war measure, there was no call for more than one main line, and no excuse for another. South of Iowa the Confederacy was so strong as to preclude the development of a Missouri or a southern railroad. North of Council Bluffs the settled frontier was still so far east of the Missouri River that no one could have justified an additional road at that moment. But with the advance of years the regional ambitions that impeded the Pacific railroad in the fifties came again to life; and after 1865 the southern aspirations, with northern backing, could again be presented to Congress. Regardless of their probable profits, more roads had to be chartered, and more lands dedicated to their use.

On July 1, 1864, Congress chartered a second land-grant continental railroad, the Northern Pacific.[1] The route was Whitney's and then Stevens's. The gentle slopes on either side the divide, and the narrow space of useless mountains along this route attracted the attention of all of its surveyors. Stevens believed it was the best of all despite the adverse ruling of his chief, Jefferson Davis. The one most difficult stretch, from the mouth of the Yellowstone to that of the Snake, was colonized by the Montana and Idaho miners at the moment when the Union Pacific received its grant. From these camps arose demand for a second line, with one Josiah Perham at its head, advocating a "People's Pacific Railroad Company."

The organic act of the Northern Pacific called for a railroad from the head of Lake Superior to Puget Sound, and provided for it the usual right of way through the public domain. The land grant was the most generous yet allowed, comprising twenty sections per mile in the States traversed (which would be Minnesota and perhaps Oregon), and forty in the territories. There was no loan of bonds such as had accompanied the Union Pacific, for Congress had already repented of this form of railroad encouragement.

The Atlantic and Pacific Railroad was chartered two years later, July 27, 1866, to build along the line of the thirty-fifth parallel survey. There was already one of the Missouri railroads built southwest from St. Louis to Springfield, and its terminus was accepted as the starting-point for the Atlantic and Pacific. West of Springfield the project showed the line running across Indian

---

[1] Louis H. Haney, *Congressional History of Railways* (1908–1910), is highly factual, but contains an accurate digest of materials on the governmental side of the land grants. It originated in two *Bulletins*, Nos. 211 and 342, of the University of Wisconsin.

Territory and northern Texas, through Albuquerque on the Rio Grande, and across the Colorado River at the Needles into California. The land grant was like that of the Northern Pacific, and there were no bonds. There was a significant proviso, secured by the watchful efforts of the California railroad men, which authorized a California road, the Southern Pacific, to build a line of its own to join the Atlantic and Pacific on the eastern border of the State, and to receive the same land-grant as the invading road.

The Texas Pacific Railroad was authorized March 3, 1871. Its eastern end was fixed near the head of navigation of the Red River, at Marshall, Texas. From Marshall there were promising eastern connections through Shreveport to New Orleans, and through Texarkana to St. Louis. West of Marshall the project passed through Fort Worth, crossing Texas on its longest diameter, to El Paso, whence it followed the thirty-second parallel survey to Fort Yuma and San Diego. It received what was now the usual grant of twenty and forty sections, and no bonds. But its grant was less important than it would have been had the United States possessed any land within the State of Texas to be granted. The Texas lands were retained by Texas when that republic abandoned its independence to enter the United States. Its legislature was willing to help the through railroads, and eventually the people of Texas had to face a railroad question not unlike that which the United States finally confronted. But neither the Atlantic and Pacific nor the Texas Pacific could receive anything in Texas from the United States.

The Texas Pacific was the fourth and last of the land-grant continental railroads. Before 1871 the slow construction of the roads across the plains suggested questions of policy, and raised doubts as to the wisdom of such lavish subsidies. The period inaugurated with Douglas's Illinois Central grant in 1850 came now to an end. Until 1862 all of the grants were made through the State Governments to the railroads in question; after that year some of them accrued directly to the railroads. The continental lines, conceived as such, were only four, although other lines that eventually crossed the plains were put together out of smaller roads. The local roads of the Mississippi Valley continued to receive land-grants up to the very end of the period, which at least one statesman of national importance had reason to regret. It was almost impossible for members of Congress to keep clear of the speculative interests that desired the lands. In the Crédit Mobilier exposure it was revealed how many of them were willing to take an unearned profit.[2] In 1869 the Speaker himself, James G. Blaine, helped one of the lesser lines, the Little Rock and Fort Smith, to save its privilege, and then begged for financial advantages because of his services. Whatever usefulness was in the land-grant policy at its inception was outlived in the twenty-one years before it was abandoned in 1871.

The Union and Central Pacific interests were lukewarm at the thought of additional Pacific railroads in a country where there was hardly business for a single line. The financial difficulties that the first of the continental roads had to confront, and that delayed completion for seven years after chartering, were monumental for the new roads. None of these had United States bonds to use, and none found private capital eager to take the risk. The Northern Pacific and the Atlantic and Pacific were chartered well ahead of 1869, but the Union Pacific was opened that summer, and there was yet no prospect that a rival road would be begun. Railroad development was being pushed within the States, and across the central plains, by men who were mostly deaf to the grandiose schemes of additional continental lines.

The Denver and Rio Grande, and the Atchison, Topeka, and Santa Fé were perhaps the most notable of the more regional lines that developed during the later sixties, the latter having the advantage of a grant made to the State of Kansas in 1863. The former was the work of a group of Philadelphia promoters, headed by General William J. Palmer who took up his residence south of Denver at a place soon known as Colorado Springs. The town of Denver made a connection with the Union Pacific at Cheyenne in June, 1870, and the following summer General Palmer broke ground for his ambitious scheme to capture the Santa Fé trade for Colorado merchants. By the summer of 1872 they were running the road one hundred and twenty miles, to the Arkansas at Pueblo, and were faced by a temptation to change their program. A little above Pueblo the Arkansas emerges from a deep gash in the Rocky Mountains, known as the Royal Gorge. Through this ravine it was possible to get a railroad, and only one, to western Colorado and eventually to Salt Lake City. The Denver and Rio Grande would have appropriated the route without a question had its ambitions not been challenged by the Atchison, Topeka, and Santa Fé.

[2] J. B. Crawford, *Crédit Mobilier of America. Its Origin and History* (1880).

The Atchison, as this road was often called in its early years, was designed to follow the Santa Fé Trail from the Missouri River. Atchison, on the west bank opposite St. Joseph, was a natural starting-point, and before the end of 1872 the railroad built the whole length of Kansas and earned its land-grant. Outside Kansas, it was on its own resources, and was divided in interest between Santa Fé and Salt Lake City. As it ascended the Arkansas, and the Denver road approached that river from the north, there was a competition between the two roads that extended from their financial offices to the construction gangs that finally fought with picks and crowbars over the possession of the narrow gorge above Pueblo. The quarrel was smoothed out in the next decade, but the two lines gained much advertising from it.

The railroad mileage of the United States increased from 30,635 as reported in the Census of 1860, to 52,914 in 1870, and 92,296 in 1880. In spite of generous land-grants the financial problems remained severe, and the least promising roads paid the highest interest charges and developed the most slowly. The Northern Pacific completed a paper organization immediately after its incorporation, but was five years in finding a financial backer. In 1869, under the inspiring leadership of Jay Cooke, it came to life.

The name of Jay Cooke of Philadelphia was one to conjure with in 1865.[3] Coming to Philadelphia as a banker on the eve of the Civil War, he was then unknown and unimportant. He acquired standing through selling on profitable terms a block of Pennsylvania war securities that was rated unsaleable by older and more seasoned bankers. He completed the transaction through enthusiasm and patriotism, and sold the securities to doubting investors on the argument that whether they paid or not, the sale of the securities was indispensable to the preservation of the Union. There was as yet no general public market for investment securities, most of the new issues having to find their takers among the banks and brokers and men of large means. Cooke added to his enthusiasm and patriotic determination to help win the war, a belief that in nearly every American family there was a small nest egg of real money. Often this was held out of circulation; and the notion that it was hidden in an old stocking under the feather bed was not far from the fact. Much of it was

[3] Ellis P. Oberholtzer, *Jay Cooke, Financier of the Civil War* (1907), is not only invaluable at this point, but is one of the frankest of our biographies of commercial magnates.

available on notes signed by borrowers of the neighborhood, for every region had its local men of means who lent at usurious rates, bought tax titles, and acquired property below its worth at foreclosure sales. Cooke's contribution to American finance was in the discovery that there was a potential investing public, of great numbers and considerable means; and that the problem was how to acquire the confidence of the common people who owned the money.

From his success with Pennsylvania bonds, Cooke progressed at once to the sale of United States bonds, gaining immediate fame. Repeatedly, as Secretary of the Treasury Chase called for bids for issues of the bonds that he was required to place in overwhelming issues, Cooke was the banker who bid highest for them, and secured the contract. His defeated rivals attacked him for alleged collusion with the Treasury; but when the tests of their charges came at the next offering, it was Cooke who bid the highest, on the lowest allowance for handling. More than once he took issues for which the trade would not bid at all, until at last he became the unofficial agent of the Treasury for floating loans.

He found the ultimate buyers among the common people. His methods of advertising the loans included propaganda through the press, dodgers given out at the post offices, and advertisements in the local and religious weeklies that found their way into the careful families who had gold and needed to be assured that it was safe to let it go. He was never too busy in his Philadelphia office to receive in person the country buyer of a single bond, to accept the payment, and to give his word that the United States would pay. He also combed Europe for buyers, and when the English and French bankers preferred to put their faith in securities of the Confederate States, he took his samples to the Germans, Dutch, and Swiss, who bought heavily at the market price. How much he did to win the war can only be a matter of guesswork; but when it was over, his name stood out at the head of the list of American financiers.

His credit was impregnable. He had promised that the country would pay, and it did. Every buyer who bought bonds below par through him, paying in greenbacks that were even further below par, thought well of the investment. The United States paid interest charges in gold. After the war the market price of the bonds rose rapidly, at a time when the buying power of the dollar was increasing. The investments made through Cooke were so profitable that he found himself with enhanced repute, and with a large class of devoted customers who looked to him to keep them provided with sound investments. There were no more bonds of the Government to sell, and he turned necessarily to railroad and manufacturing bonds, disposing of them readily in the booming years of bus'ness that followed the surrender of Lee in 1865.

In 1869 Jay Cooke became convinced that the statements of Josiah Perham and Isaac Stevens were true, and that the northern strip of territory across the United States needed only a railroad to enable it to develop into a prosperous farming country. Michigan and Wisconsin were already booming, and the timber millionaires who appeared out of their northern woods gave a foundation for encouragement. The Wisconsin railroads were pushing towards St. Paul, which was to be brought into communication with Chicago in 1872. Beyond St. Paul was the long wagon trail of the Red River ox-carts, over which the annual supplies of the Canadian Northwest had been hauled for many years. It was suspected that wheat could be grown to advantage in the valley of the Red River of the North once an outlet to a market was provided for it. It was the belief of many that the Canadian Northwest itself was attached to the British Empire by the slightest thread, and that its real destiny was with the United States.

Jay Cooke accordingly became the financial underwriter of the Northern Pacific Railroad in 1869, and acquired the determining influence upon its destiny. He selected as its point of departure the head of Lake Superior, which he had himself visited in 1868. He bought heavily in lands around Duluth, to take advantage of the increment in values when the railroad should become a fact, and he gained control over the Lake Superior and Mississippi River Railroad, already building between St. Paul and Duluth. From a point on this line, near Duluth, he commenced actual construction for the Northern Pacific early in 1870. He was already singing the praises of the investment to prospective buyers of the stock and land.

For the next two seasons the Northern Pacific built steadily through the untouched Indian country, winding its way among the lakes of northern Minnesota. It crossed the Mississippi River at Brainerd, and reached the Red River at Fargo; thence it pushed on, almost due west to the Missouri River which it reached in 1873 at a point opposite the Mandan Village where Lewis and Clark wintered in 1804–1805. It was appropriate in 1873 to call this new station Bismarck. The ultimate destination was the Columbia River. For the present Cooke gave up the idea of building across Washington Territory to Puget Sound, contenting himself with procuring a control of the Oregon Steam Navigation Company which maintained an adequate system of river steamers on the Columbia below the junction of the Snake, and with which it did not seem profitable to offer railroad competition.

There is no room to doubt the sincerity of Cooke in promoting the Northern Pacific, despite the fact that there was no traffic to justify the regular running of trains over the 471 miles of track between Bismarck and St. Paul. He believed in it with the same enthusiasm that had marked his confidence in the United States; and sold the securities at home and abroad to investors who accepted his word. But he hypnotized himself. His prospectus was as much too hopeful as the early estimates of Lewis and Clark were too pessimistic of the future of the plains. It was not, after all, a part of the Garden of Eden that he was tapping; nor could the drifting snows of winter be made to yield to any persuasive language of the prospectus writer. Yet he not only sold the stock, but bought it, to the exasperation of his partners who did not believe as wholly in it as he did. During 1872 he found it necessary to buy increasing amounts himself in order to provide funds in accordance with the terms of his underwriting.

The boom of the later sixties reached its crest not far from the date when Cooke underwrote the Northern Pacific. Since 1861 the United States had been spending, investing, and destroying property without check. The agricultural extension of the decade, as usual, was on credit, and covered the farms with a blanket of debts. The purchases of farm implements were a new source of demand for farming capital. The railroads represented a drain upon the accumulated savings of some one; and those lines that were not immediately revenue-producing effected an absolute withdrawal from use of the capital involved. The Civil War was fought. No one dares say how much it cost, for no accounting system can cover all its charges. But for a period of four years nearly two and one half million men were withdrawn from productive work — and were devoted to the labors of destruction. The South was left flat and bankrupt, with its whole pre-war movable wealth to be replaced. In spite of the heavy increase in productivity, and the accumulations of new capital, the American people developed new demands for wealth more rapidly than they saved it. In the early seventies they reached a stage in which the process of railroad building and other investment could continue only if money could be obtained abroad on reasonable terms. The further west one went in the United States, the completer the blanket of debt and the more universal the debtor status. What was typical of the West was universal in the South.

In the winter of 1872–1873 the European market ceased to absorb enough American securities to enable American development to proceed without a check. Local crop failures in Europe produced a cessation of investment, and American scandals gave the United States a bad name. The Tweed ring exposure in New York City was disheartening. General John C. Frémont was jailed in France under charge of promoting the European sale of bonds in a "land-grant" railroad that had not received its land-grant. The Crédit Mobilier scandal exploded in September, 1872. Cooke nevertheless was willing to do himself what he invited his customers to do. He bought Northern Pacific until his solvency depended upon a market that he could not revive. On September 18, 1873, his partners closed the doors, and admitted bankruptcy, with the Northern Pacific as the chief contributing factor.

It was, of course, more than the Northern Pacific, for the depression was everywhere, and for ten days panic was so wild upon the New York Stock Exchange that the governors of that clearing house closed it down and refused to allow sales to go to record. When they reopened at the end of the month, the crisis was a thing of the past; but so was the period of prosperity that had been ushered in with the outbreak of the Civil War. For the next five years the development of the plains was postponed. The construction gangs were disbanded, for there was no money to meet the pay roll or to buy the iron. The hard times induced a period of reflection and gave rise to frontier demands for legislative relief, such as had followed the earlier panics of 1819, 1837, and 1857. The complete absorption of the frontier was postponed another decade.

CHAPTER LV
FRONTIER PANACEAS

There were two general conditions that prevailed over the West when the panic of 1873 occurred. One was the debtor status; the other was the intensified dependence upon markets for prosperity, and upon railroad transportation to reach the market. Each of these was so general as to bring the frontier population, or the near frontier population, into close accord. And when the depression became acute this accord was translated into political manifestations, much as the banking theory had become political in the Jackson period, and the Mississippi Valley aspirations in the early years of the Republic. Elsewhere throughout the Union were large numbers of citizens who felt as westerners did. This was always the case. But nowhere, except near the frontier, where life was standardized by the oppressive hand of economic barriers, could the opinion become homogeneous and the reaction universal. The debtor status produced the greenback movement; the transportation problem gave rise to the Patrons of Husbandry or the granger movement.[1]

The greenback movement made its first appearance in the Ohio Valley States, and spread thence because of its appropriateness to the actual frontier and to the South where the Civil War had turned back the hand of time. Its first clear proponents were from Ohio, whence the name, "the Ohio Idea," that was associated with it for a time. Its advocates were to be found in both great parties, but only the Democrats in their national platform of 1868 were willing to put in words the demand that "where the obligations of the government do not expressly state upon their face, or the law under which they were issued does not provide, that they shall be paid in coin, they ought in right and in justice, to be paid in lawful money of the United States." The "lawful money" referred to was the legal tender greenback currency of the Civil War; the purpose was to prevent deflation, to aid the debtor, and to lay a tax on wealth.

The United States was forced upon a paper basis early in 1862

---

[1] The editor of the Springfield, Massachusetts, *Republican*, Samuel Bowles, describes the West of his period in *Our New West* (1869).

because the currency system had broken down and because a weak Treasury made a forced loan inevitable. At the outbreak of the war the country was upon a gold basis, with the actual currency consisting largely of bank notes, redeemable in gold coin. It was theoretically as legal to redeem them in silver dollars, but the theory was unimportant since, from the date of the currency law of 1834 fixing the relative weight of the dollars at 16:1, almost no silver dollars had been coined. Silver, undervalued at that ratio, found more profitable use in other forms than money. Gold alone was minted and used, and by 1861 the assumption of business was that when a dollar was called for, a gold dollar, or one redeemable in a gold dollar, was meant. There had been general suspension of specie redemption during the panic of 1857, but the banks had resumed payment before the war broke out.

The resort of the Government to paper drove the banks to cease redemption in specie for the period of the war. The dollar thereafter became the paper dollar, whose value was whatever the hope or fear of the Nation might ascribe to it. The public creditor was compelled to accept it; but he protected himself by raising the price of what he had to sell. The private creditor suffered confiscation when he was paid off in the depreciated paper, the loss being the difference between the gold value of the paper, and gold at par. From 1862 until 1864, when the greenbacks reached their lowest price (about thirty-five cents on the dollar), the loss was borne without means of evasion by every owner of property, every recipient of wages, and every person who lived upon a fixed income. The man who had a debt to pay absolved his debt on a basis more profitable each month as the buying value of the legal tender dollar declined.[2]

During this period of depreciated currency the United States incurred its debt which amounted to $2,846,000,000 in the autumn of 1865, and the farmers, merchants, manufacturers, and railroads incurred theirs. Most of the loans were made in dollars, and payable in dollars. The United States had been unable to borrow only gold, and had been compelled to allow the buyer of its bonds to pay in greenbacks, which the Government again reissued. The contract for repayment sometimes called for coin, but more often did not specify what sort of money should be used. The passage of the legal tender acts, creating a paper money which the Government itself accepted, gave the basis for a demand that it was

[2] Wesley C. Mitchell, *A History of the Greenbacks* (1903).

reasonable for the Government to pay out the kind of money it had itself received. There is much indirect evidence to show that the general expectation at the time of creation of the loans was that they should be paid in gold; and that without this confidence the public credit would have sunk even lower than it did.

When the war was over the first desire of the Treasury was to resume specie payments, an act which the world has ever accepted as marking the return of national solvency. This involved getting rid of the greenbacks in some way, by funding in bonds with the rest of the war debt, or cancellation, or redemption and destruction. The Treasury urged it, and Congress in 1866 authorized the retirement by destruction of $4,000,000 worth of greenbacks by the Treasury each month.

The act was no sooner passed than mutterings arose. The grievance was that the contraction of the currency to this extent (for there was no other money to replace the greenbacks thus destroyed) would lessen the amount of available money, that this would be followed by appreciation of the value of the dollar, and that as the result of this the payment of debts would be made more difficult, commerce would be impeded, and the holder of United States bonds or other investments would receive a more valuable dollar than he had lent. Men who had never felt a sense of outrage when the depreciating greenbacks wiped out the accumulated savings of the people, became indignant when their appreciation threatened to add to the burdens of the debtor. There were many debtors, and their political representatives voiced an appeal that the West and South accepted as valid almost without argument. This was "the Ohio Idea." It went to the extent of protesting against any withdrawal of the greenbacks; and beyond that it advocated that the greenbacks ought to be used as "lawful money" to pay the interest and principal of all bonds whose face did not call for coin. In 1868 Congress repealed the law for the withdrawal of the greenbacks, after $44,000,000 had been cancelled, and the outstanding total had been reduced to $356,000,000. The only other available money in 1868 was the national bank notes, amounting to $295,800,000.

The Democratic Party yielded to the greenback demand although its candidate in 1868 declared himself opposed to that portion of the platform. The Republicans, on the other hand, denounced "all forms of repudiation as a national crime," and demanded the payment of the debt in "the spirit of the laws under which it was contracted." A resolution pledging the faith of the United States to coin payments and early resumption was passed early in Grant's first term. In 1870 a funding bill was passed authorizing the funding of the Civil War bonds in long term bonds payable principal and interest in coin. Under this, most of the outstanding debt was refunded in the next nine years. In 1875 a Resumption Act was passed, directing the Secretary of the Treasury to accumulate a gold reserve in order to resume the issuance of coin in exchange for greenbacks in January, 1879.

Between 1865 and 1879 the value of the greenback dollar rose to par. Increasing confidence in the solvency of the United States had much to do with this. Increasing business that called each year for more money for its needs was in part responsible. The credit of the Government became impregnable as it became clear that Congress would not avail itself of any technical right in order to lessen the burden of its obligations. It would have been discreditable repudiation for the United States to issue an inferior currency for the purpose of lightening its national debt.

But as the dollar rose to par the debtors' grievance became more intense. It was quite true that the creditor was in a position of advantage because of the way in which deflation was working out, and that the debtor was each year paying back a dollar that had a higher buying value than the year before. The same debt took more bushels of wheat or pounds of cotton. The loss inflicted upon the owners of property during the war by inflation and a depreciating medium now fell quite as unfairly, upon the larger section of the people who were in debt. "The Ohio Idea" came to represent a determined grievance, bad enough in the prosperous years immediately after the war and unbearable during the panic after 1873.

In 1876 a National Greenback party ticket was in the field headed by the venerable Peter Cooper of New York. In this party the "rag baby," as the eastern papers called the greenbacks, found a friend. The greenback orators asked why the money that was good enough for the soldiers during the war was not good enough for the money lender after peace, and spoke of the greenback issue as "the child of war and the savior of the country." Cooper received the sympathy of much of the West, but not the votes. In 1880 General James B. Weaver of Iowa was candidate of the same cause; and in 1884 General Benjamin Butler of Massachusetts. The program of cheap money was not strong enough to detach

Republicans from the party ticket when it came to election day, but the large vote that greenback and other inflation measures could command in Congress, in both parties and at almost any time, indicates the non partisan uniformity of western economic opinion.[3] By 1879, when resumption took place, western conditions like those of the rest of the country, were improving. The greenback had come so close to par that it lost its capacity to arouse either hope or fear; and the responsible citizens of the West, having paid their debts and acquired credits in the bank, lost their desire or interest to depreciate the currency. Always when in debt, the frontier has been susceptible to inflationist theories of finance, but this time it recovered before it gained its point.

An abiding distrust of banks, corporations, and creditors was left in the western mind as the greenback movement subsided. And if this was not enough to provide a permanent basis for political cohesion, an additional influence was brought to bear by another of the factors of the frontier situation. The vital force of land economics has been stressed on many occasions; the greenback movement was only one aspect of the western sensitiveness to matters affecting its access to credit for its development. Its route to a market, upon which permanent solvency depended, was now over the railroads. Transportation had become a tax. Whether too heavy or not, whether fair or discriminatory, the tax was so universal that its control came as a new element into the political consciousness of the country, and there arose a frontier protest against leaving this general tax to be levied for private interest by private corporations.[4]

The protest against the railroads came earliest, of necessity, in the section where the issue was clearest and least mixed with other issues. During the early period of railroad construction, the new methods of communication were thought of as local, and supplementary to preëxisting methods of transportation. Few were so visionary as to suppose that railroads would ever be able to outcompete the water routes. The rivers that were well established before the railroads came were expected to continue to bear their share. So were the canals. Until after the outbreak of the Civil

---

[3] Two valuable collections of personal manuscripts of greenbackers are the Ignatius Donnelly papers (Minnesota State Historical Society), and the Luman H. Weller papers (State Historical Society of Wisconsin).

[4] John D. Hicks, "The Political Career of Ignatius Donnelly," and "The Origin and Early History of the Farmers' Alliance in Minnesota," in *Mississippi Valley Historical Review*, vols. VIII and IX.

War there were few railroads that were not forced to take into account the rival attractions of some natural highway or water route. The lines that made up the New York Central system, or the Pennsylvania, had for competitors the lake steamers and the Erie Canal. The Illinois Central had ever beside it the Mississippi. The Ohio River was regarded as a permanent highway for the freights between Pittsburgh and the Gulf of Mexico. Only the experience of the Civil War, in which the trunk lines gathered up the business and clung to it even after the Mississippi had been made a Union stream, suggested that there was in the railroads a power to dominate the situation, and to offer a service so impelling as to eliminate its rivals. Could this be done, there was nothing to prevent the monopoly of transportation from falling to the railroads or to prevent them from loading the business with "all the traffic would bear." In proportion as the exchange of commodities between the sections became more common, or necessary, the routes and costs became unavoidable, and it fell into the power of the men and corporations who controlled these carriers to wield destructive powers — perhaps for the common good, but perhaps also for lust of power, personal advantage, or corporate profit.

The first clear glimpse of this prospect was caught on the prairie farms north and west of Chicago, where the condition of the natural routes prevented the development of any highways similar in importance to the Lakes or the Ohio River. North of the latitude of St. Louis the Mississippi is so shallow and treacherous as to lose its carrying capacity. The smaller local streams were none of them safely navigable. But the only crops the country could as yet produce were cheap and bulky. The corn and wheat of the Illinois and Iowa farms could not be raised with profit during the earlier stages of the development of these States; similarly Wisconsin and Minnesota lagged. The country northwest of Chicago began to develop only after the opening of the Erie Canal, and grew to economic importance only as railroads threaded their counties to bring out the crop. There was here a degree of dependence upon the railroad not equaled in any other large section of the Union. Even here it could not be seen so long as the major emphasis was upon the construction of the lines, and the times were good. With the lines done, and the times hard, the one firm thing that the suffering farmer could see was the irreducible freight rate, set high because the railroad was a private business operated for profit, and because ill-advised individual speculation had often built two roads where one would have done, or one where none could be supported. Most of them were wastefully, ignorantly, and, often, dishonestly constructed. The heavy fixed costs of the bonded debt, and the pressure of stockholders for dividends, held the railroads to the task of squeezing their revenue out of the country, regardless of its economic condition. There was here no alternative route to moderate rates by competition, and no complex business entanglement to obscure the relation of the railroads to prosperity.

The railroads that were added to the mileage of the United States between 1860 and the panic of 1873, brought most of Iowa, Minnesota, and Wisconsin within their net, and enabled their spectacular growth. In these three States the population rose from 1,623,000 in 1860 to 2,684,000 in 1870. Illinois alone increased more than 800,000 in this decade. These and the million newcomers in the three neighbor States were drawn in by high prices for farm products, easy money, and fertile farms. By 1870 their leaders were wondering how it was to be possible to pay the debts incurred in the process.

The new constitution framed by the State of Illinois in 1869 and 1870 indicates that the old apprehension that had been directed toward the banks in the Jacksonian constitutions was now directed toward the railroads and the grain elevators. The latter were declared to be "public warehouses," whoever might own them; and provisions for the regulation of both types of utilities were written into the constitution. Acting under these new powers, the legislature in 1873 created a Railway and Warehouse Commission with a revolutionary power, to fix the rates. The idea that such utilities were subject to public control swept rapidly across the Northwest States, as the public came to appreciate the quasi-taxing power of railroad and elevator rates. In 1874 Minnesota created a commission with power to fix rates; and in the same year Iowa and Wisconsin both enacted complete tariffs of maximum rates as statutes. The movement for regulation was already well started before the panic of 1873 occurred. The resulting hard times, with a slack market and falling prices, accentuated still further the rigidity of the freight rates, and made it easy to diabolize the influence of the railroads in the economic life of the country.

The tendency to seek for a cause of agricultural depression turned politics against the railroads, and brought to life a spontaneous organization among the farmers to further their own interests. The farmer of the Middle West was a different type of man in 1870 from what he had been after the panic of 1819. He had then allowed the political leaders to shape his remedies, and had followed Henry Clay or Andrew Jackson according to his frame of mind. But he had been incapable of organization upon an agrarian basis, and had possessed the undiluted individualism of the remote frontier. The Middle West farmer was no longer on the actual frontier, although some frontier traits still lasted. The plains farmer, developing railroad lands, or double-minimum lands that the Government had reserved, was less of a frontiersman than the Democrat of 1820, even though his tasks were much the same. He had access through railroad, telegraph, and newspapers to the centers and ideas of the world. He had more formal education, and had become something of a technician through his use of machinery. He had more banking knowledge, for he had more obligations. He had more normal contacts with his fellows, and was susceptible of organization.

The Patrons of Husbandry was one of the numerous societies formed after the Civil War when a craving for formal association was showing itself throughout American life.[5] Its avowed purpose was to extend the advantages of education and relaxation to farmers, and to improve their position by association and self-help. Its organizers, some of them Government workers at Washington, saw the South as the natural field for the ventures of the Patrons of Husbandry, for in the South farming was on the verge of a complete reorganization because of the abolition of slavery. But the society did not take hold. There was no demand for it, and the local granges that it formed had few members. Its mechanism comprised local chapters, or granges, to whose meetings farmers and their families came for picnics and discussion. Women were admitted, and the children came along as they must to any gathering attended by their parents. The granges were by profession non political, existing for social and economic advantage.

The local granges were gathered into State granges, and these in turn into the National grange, at whose congresses large matters of agricultural policy were discussed. The imposing title of the

[5] Solon J. Buck, *The Granger Movement. A Study of Agricultural Organization and its Political, Economic, and Social Manifestations* (1913), is a model study; Fred E. Haynes, *Third Party Movements since the Civil War with Special Reference to Iowa* (1916) is more general than its title promises, because Iowa has never entirely missed a reform movement.

society soon dropped from use, leaving the grange as the real name. The granges began to grow in number and membership after 1870. As the farmers' grievances crystallized the granger movement spread. In the South it never became dominant, but in the country northwest of Chicago it swept the States. In 1872 and 1873 its membership leaped by thousands, reaching perhaps 1,600,000 at its height. Its contemporary historian[6] gave its temper in his preface: "For several years past the country has been suffering from evils of which all have been conscious, but which none had the courage to remedy, until the Grange took up the cause of the oppressed. Prominent among these are the burdens that have been fastened upon the people by the reckless and unscrupulous course of the great Railroad Monopolies that have sprung up in our midst. These vast and powerful corporations have inaugurated a series of abuses which have gradually and effectually undermined the solid basis upon which our finances were supposed to rest. They have debauched and demoralized our Courts and Legislatures; have bribed and taken into their pay the high public officials charged with the making and execution of our laws; have robbed the nation of a domain sufficient to constitute an empire; have flooded the land with worthless stocks and other so-called securities; have established a system of gambling at our financial centers that has resulted in a monetary crisis which must cover the whole land with ruin and suffering; have set at defiance the laws of the land, and have trampled upon individual rights and liberties, openly boasting that they are too powerful to be made answerable to the law."

It was but natural, when the Northwest was thoroughly aware of its grievances against the railroads that elections should turn upon this issue. The grange itself played a small part in politics, but the grangers were also citizens, whose whole history was a succession of episodes in which the Government of the United States, or of the States had been turned to for economic relief. The granger laws, passed by the legislatures at the bidding of their constituents, were designed to bring the railroads under the control of law, and to assert the right of the public to share in their control.

[6] J. D. McCabe [Edward Martin, pseudonym], *History of the Granger Movement; or, The Farmer's War against Monopolies* (1874), was a popular subscription work when the movement was at its height. It economized in illustrations, lifting some of them with only a tendencial change in captions, from John H. Beadle, *Our Undeveloped West; or Five Years in the Territories* (1873).

The first reaction of the eastern owners of railroads to the granger laws of Wisconsin, Iowa, and Illinois was one of open contempt and antipathy. The antagonism was everywhere worse because the money invested in western railroad property was commonly drawn from centers remote from the railroads themselves. Absenteeism served to accentuate the normal differences due to the relation of debtor and creditor. Many provisions of the rate laws were unworkable because the angry farmer legislators had not known enough to make a rate, and were inspired only by the determination that the rates should come down. The railroads took advantage of this and paid little attention to the legal rates. They claimed that any such fixation was an interference with their constitutional rights.

The railroad defense against rate fixing by public authority was based upon two lines of argument; one, that it was against the clause of the Constitution of the United States giving Congress power "to regulate commerce among the several States," the other, that it involved a taking of property without "due process of law"; and both came eventually before the highest courts for determination. The greatest of the State decisions was by the Chief Justice of Wisconsin, Edward George Ryan, who in September, 1874, completely upheld the right of the State to legislate on rates. The Supreme Court of the United States heard arguments upon several cases rising under the laws of the various States, and handed down its basic decision in the spring of 1877, in the case of Munn vs. Illinois. Chief Justice Waite, who delivered the opinion, followed the Wisconsin argument, and showed how since time immemorial the English common law had given to the people the right to establish rules "requiring each citizen to so conduct himself, and so use his own property, as not unnecessarily to injure another." This had applied to ferries, common carriers, hackmen, bakers, and millers; and maximum charges had long been fixed for services rendered. "When private property is devoted to a public use," he said, "it is subject to public regulation." The Supreme Court upheld the granger laws as fair in principle, and not interfering with the constitutional powers of the United States Government. It was a blow to the ideas that had hitherto prevailed in the conduct of private business in the United States, to have the public admitted as a partner in the venture, and it marked a great turning point in the development of American Government. It is significant that the point was first pressed by the West, and found its earliest victories in the region where frontier simplicity first revealed it. It was another case in which the frontier grievance was translated into a national policy.

CHAPTER LVI

THE COW COUNTRY

THE Indian Country, as Monroe and Calhoun conceived it, and as it was executed between 1825 and 1841, was the product of one frontier situation. It came inevitably, with the need to provide for the native races; its setting was contributed to by the misconception of western resources and the Rocky Mountain barrier of the United States; it was destroyed as the natural consequence of the development of the Pacific Slope.

The overland mail service was similar in its development. It could not have been imagined before the Mexican War; it could not have been avoided after it; and its term of life was ended not by forces operating within itself but by the external influence of the railroad movement.

The railroads themselves induced and destroyed a third episode whose habitat was on the high plains. Between the close of the Civil War and the completion of the continental railroad system, 1865–1885, they both brought the cow country into being and destroyed it forever. The initial fact that began the short life of the cow country was the discovery, about 1865, that beef cattle could be bred and fattened on the plains, and delivered by the railroads to the markets in the Middle West, more cheaply than beef could be produced locally upon the farm.

Food was the least of American problems, whether in the older settlements or along the frontier margins. There was rough plenty everywhere after the first years of new development. The native Indian corn in its various forms of meal, hominy, whiskey, and pork, was a sure preventive of starvation. Travelers among the seaboard towns, in the eighteenth century, reveal the fact that in the more favored regions there was even a cuisine based upon the fundamentals, supplemented by wild game and the various forms of sea food. But the cuisine was in most places satisfying rather than attractive; plentiful rather than varied. Pork, chicken, and less often veal, were the reliance for the meats. Beef was generally poor. The domestic cattle on the farms were poor milkers and yielded inferior beef, while the lack of facilities for preserving fresh meat drove the country dweller to dry his beef or corn it. But such as it was, food was plentiful, and was everywhere locally obtainable.

In the earliest chapters of frontier expansion one reads of swine raised for the market, and marching to it. The settlers of the Valley turned their hogs loose, allowing them to multiply and adapt themselves to life in the open. The animals became wild and self-supporting; and from time to time they were gathered into droves and driven eastward over the common trails. Furnishing their own transportation, western swine became a competitor of eastern farm-grown hogs early in the nineteenth century. A little later there are records of cattle driven to Louisville or Cincinnati; or to St. Louis or Chicago. The furnishing of meat, fresh or packed, was generally a local task, and the growing towns had little difficulty in finding enough animals in their immediate vicinity. Cincinnati became an early packing center, developing a large trade down the river. The South provided the only considerable market aside from local needs, for only in the South did a rural population fail to raise its own food. The economics of the plantation made it seem profitable to keep the negroes in the cotton field and buy their pork, rather than to diversify their work by requiring them to produce it at home. In every considerable town the stock yards and the slaughter houses were unavoidable nuisances, which local government tried to abate somewhat by regulation, but which were offensive all the year and foul in summer. As the cities grew, and dwellings encroached upon the margins of the stock yards, the problem was raised of the degree of power possessed by the municipalities to suppress useful business for the common good. With every chapter of city growth, there was another arrangement of the slaughter pens, and a revived protest against permitting herds of swine, sheep, and cattle to be driven through the city streets. In Chicago, where a packing industry second only to that of Cincinnati was growing up, a group of speculators bought a half section of prairie lands on Halsted Street, consolidated all the various dealers' interests, and opened at Christmas, 1865, the Union Stock Yards. It was large consolidation, but Chicago was a growing city, with an export trade. The consolidation was a natural process following a generation of s'aughtering activity. Nothing was further from the minds of the men who put it through than that, at the moment of the opening of the Union Yards, the business of preparing food was on the eve of a complete and permanent revolution.[1]

[1] Rudolf A. Clemen, *The American Livestock and Meat Industry* (1923), has a sound historical basis, is minutely analytical, and contains a full bibliography.

At about the moment when Chicago consolidated its yards, and other cities thought it necessary so to do, it was discovered that the high plains possessed a new resource.[2] In the autumn of 1866, the rumor runs, some teams of bullock trains were stalled by snow upon the plains of western Nebraska. The freighting business was at its height. Every western camp required a minimum of supplies which could be obtained only from the East and delivered only in prairie schooners, hauled by oxen. Since the beginning of the overland migrations in the early forties the freight traffic had grown in volume. The army on the plains was a heavy consumer of supplies. The stage companies had stations to be provided. The Indian agencies received annual caravans of goods for the use of their wards. And the patient ox pulled the load.

The oxen that figure in the story were abandoned when a snowfall made it impossible to continue the journey that season. The drivers cached the wagons as well as they could, pegged down tarpaulins over them, and rode their horses back to the Missouri, charging the oxen up to unavoidable loss. In the following spring they returned to the caches, with new animals, to take the abandoned wagons to their destination. They expected to find the whitened bones of their abandoned stock, but found instead the animals themselves, sleek, fat, and ready for the block.

It ought not to have occasioned much surprise, but the idea was new. It was common knowledge that the buffalo herd lived on the open plains, drifting north each spring with the fresh pasturage, and south each fall before the winter frosts. The Indian had found the bison a general purpose animal, that provided food, clothing, shelter, and fuel. The rough pelt of the beast was not valuable enough to bear the cost of carriage for long distances, but as soon as settlements reached the margin of the buffalo range the hides were valued locally for coats and robes. Among the earliest freight shipments from the rail heads of the continental railroads were bales of buffalo skins that could now for the first time seek a remote market. The swain of the seventies did his winter courting in the moderate space afforded by his cutter, and warmed by the generous thickness of the buffalo robe.

The southwest roads, as soon as they impinged upon the plains of Texas, found similar freights in bales of hides of beef cattle.

[2] F. L. Paxson, "The Cow Country," in *American Historical Review*, vol. XXII; and Clara M. Love, "History of the Cattle Industry in the Southwest," in *Southwestern Historical Quarterly*, vol. XIX, give many details and references.

There were wild herds of these, the offspring of strays from the old Spanish settlements, that were acclimated to the Texas plains, and that had bred themselves to a resilient and vivacious long-horned stock. Too tough for their flesh to have a market, they first acquired value when their hides could be collected and shipped to the tanneries, leaving their carcasses to bleach upon the plains.

The advent of the railroad coincided with the discovery that beeves could winter in the open on the plains, and brought significance to what had always been known about the plentiful crop of spring grass. There arose at once a cattle industry through which the cow country became a reality. The approaching railroads of the later sixties found waiting for them the herds of stock at Marshall, Dodge City, Abilene, or Ogallala. The promised profits of the business were large, entry upon it was easy, the ice machine and the refrigerator car made it possible to conserve the product, and the growing city population in the East provided a hungry market.

The great plains, from central Kansas to the Rockies, and from the Rio Grande to Canada, became the cow country, and remained the cow country until the open range was closed. The incidents of the business were simple, but were new to frontier agriculture. They grouped around the problems of breeding, the round-up, the long drive, and the marketing process, each of which became standardized almost instantaneously with the appearance of the traffic.

The breeding was concentrated on the Texas plains, which had proved their fitness by the presence of the wild herds. The cows of these herds became the mothers of calves that were destined from birth for the butcher's block. In the mild climate of this region there was a low mortality of mothers and offspring, and the herds roamed at pleasure over vast stretches of pasturage that no one owned but the State of Texas. The resulting meat was naturally tough, but as soon as a market appeared steps were taken to improve the breed. The mothers were preserved, prolific and resourceful, breeding sturdy calves. For sires, imported bulls were selected and brought in — Short-horn, Hereford, Polled Angus, and Galloway. The scrub bulls were rapidly weeded out of the herds, and each spring saw a better crop of calves. Regardless of their owners, the herds ranged together over the plains. Once a year at least the owners coöperated to identify and select the stock that was ready for the market.

The round-up was the earliest of many picturesque events that attracted public attention to the new industry; yet the institution was by no means new. The cattle were marked by brand upon the flank, and branding as a means of identification was of ancient origin. There were brand books early in colonial history, for they could not be avoided as long as cattle ranged at large. When the time came for the round-up, generally in May, at which time the spring calves were large enough to eat the fresh grass, yet not too large to heel behind their respective mothers, the neighborhood came suddenly to life. The various breeders, with their men, made a great circle around the margins of the grazing ground of their herd, and drove slowly to the center. There was wisdom in the slow drive, for anything that excited the animals injured their condition, and might even incite them to destructive and suicidal stampedes. Their destination was some convenient central camp or station, where a branding gang was organized, with pens and with as many different irons as owners.

As the herds came in, the yearling steers, branded the season before, were cut out of the herd, and penned in a corral, where each owner could identify and select his own. The cows, with calves at heel, were driven to the branding pens, where each calf was given the brand of the mother that it followed. The stray calves, that could not be identified by filial affection, were herded by themselves, to be divided and branded, pro rata, at the close of the round-up. There was no sure way of determining parentage for these. Mavericks they were called, taking their name from a too enterprising rancher who had acquired notoriety by cutting out the unbranded calves before the round-up, and marking them with his own brand. After the round-up was completed, the cows and calves were turned loose again to pasture upon the public ground, while the yearlings were made ready for the "long drive," or sale, or both.

At this point in the story the cowboy made his principal entrance. During the period of breeding, the cattle ranged over a wide area with little attention, and much of the help used at the round-up was of a temporary character. But from the moment that the yearlings were separated from the herd it became necessary to employ men to live with them, keep them from danger, guard them from cattle thieves, and deliver them finally to an ultimate buyer. This was a relatively new occupation for the border, and recruited its men from the ranks of drifters. The cow-

HISTORY OF THE AMERICAN FRONTIER

boys became as definite a type as the border ever produced. They worked in small gangs, living in the saddle, and operating from a headquarters on wheels — the chuck wagon, where was the cook, as well as the materials for their sketchy camps. Emerson Hough has told *The Story of the Cowboy* (1897), Philip A. Rollins has more deliberately collected the facts of his life in *The Cowboy* (1922), Frederick Remington has immortalized him with pencil and brush, and John A. Lomax, in *Cowboy Songs* (1910, with many reprints), has collected the folk-songs which whiled away his loneliness. Hermann Hagedorn has revealed him through the eyes of one of his most eminent appreciators in *Roosevelt in the Bad Lands* (1921). The cowboy remains, a generation after he disappeared, one of the most thrilling characters of fiction and American romance. The great showman, Col. William F. Cody (Buffalo Bill), made him an international figure in the most distinctive of American entertainments.

From the round-up the steers were started towards the slaughter house, in the custody of bands of cowboys. Many of the animals were driven to the nearest rail head, so that Hutchinson and Dodge City, in Kansas, on the Santa Fé, became the earliest of the cow towns. After the round-ups the various herds moved slowly across the public domain to these points, where the buyers from the East came to meet them. The cowboys had nothing to do with the sales; the owners of the cattle made the negotiation and the steers changed hands. From these towns long trains of cattle cars carried their freight to the cattle pens. In the towns the cowboys, relieved of the unbearable tedium of stock guarding on the plains, found recreation and dissipation. The cow town in the later seventies took the place held a little earlier by the railroad terminal camp, and by the mining camps of the early sixties. It was the most lawless place known, where armed men gambled away their substance, and shot away their lives, unconcerned with the orderly progress of society.

But only a fraction of the steers started so promptly for the market. Most of them, in the vicinity of the Kansas cow towns changed owners, but not habits. Their southern breeders sold them to northern feeders, who left them on the plains, in charge of new gangs of cowboys. Here began the long drive, as it was in fact, and as the border soon denominated it. From Texas up to the Canadian Northwest stretched an unbroken expanse of native grass, plentiful enough for grazing purposes. Animals could be fattened here at government expense, with the owners paying only moderate amounts for stock tending. The cowboys started their charges northward, letting them set their own pace, grazing and ripening as they went. From central Texas, across the Indian Country soon to be Oklahoma, through Kansas west of Dodge City, ran the route of the long drive, which ended for some years at Ogallala, a station on the Union Pacific in western Kansas. This became another cow town, with all the local accompaniments of cattle barons, bad men, romping cowboys, and gambling halls. When the Northern Pacific began to build, it created a station still further north, lengthening the long drive to the Yellowstone, above the Bad Lands of Dakota. Here in Montana Territory, near Fort Keogh, Miles City arose, and Glendive, somewhat below Miles City, where the Northern Pacific first touches the Yellowstone. In later years the long drive occasionally pushed across Montana to Saskatchewan, and the Canadian Pacific near Moose Jaw and Regina.

Eventually the cattle were destined for an eastern market, and their owners, during the long drive, were carefully watching the market and hoping to get a top price. At the northern destinations the steers were packed into the cattle cars and freighted to Chicago or Kansas City. It was never practicable to slaughter them on the plains, although some ventures of this sort were made. As the cars of steers pulled into the packing cities, the buyers sought the stock yards, and paid what they chose; for the owners could not do anything with the animals but sell them. From this fact, and because the owner was at the mercy of the packer, arose an additional phase of the cow country, the ranch. If the owner could hold his cattle cheaply, and ship only when the market was right, he could improve his price. It was too expensive, however, to employ the gangs of cowboys forever, even if a tract of land suitable for holding the herd could be obtained. At just the strategic moment, invention caught up with the necessities of the treeless plains, and Yankee ingenuity devised the wire fence.

Early in the eighties, cowmen developed northern ranches, near the Union Pacific or Northern Pacific. Their equipment included a dwelling and a grazing area of the public domain; either fenced or protected by their " squatter right." Upon these ranches they turned the steers at the end of the long drive, and here they held them, sometimes for another year. Such a ranch as this Theodore Roosevelt became interested in shortly after leaving college.[3] At

[3] Theodore Roosevelt, *Hunting Trips of a Ranchman* (1891).

Chimney Butte, where the Northern Pacific crosses the Little Missouri in Dakota Territory, he buried an investment, acquired robust health and much experience, and learned to know his West.

The range cattle business, with the cow country as its habitat, sprang into life almost full fledged from the beginning. While it was still young it made its imprint upon American life at many points. First the flood of cattle upset the equilibrium at the stock yards, and the farmer raisers of cattle found themselves hit by the competition of range cattle, quite the equal of their own, and growing finer every year. Next the packers found an endless supply of cattle, and enlarged their industry. Around the yards grew packing towns, with not only the slaughter houses, and the usual packing impedimenta, but new products and new processes. It was some years before the legend arose that the only part of the animal that could not be turned to profit was the squeal; but soon the hides, the hair, the bones, the hooves, the blood, and the entrails became the raw materials for new manufactures and the source of enduring profits. Refrigeration and the happy invention of a tin canning machine changed the form in which the meat sought the consumer. Fresh beef, tinned, was soon ready for export; and meat in sides, in chilled cars, emigrated from the West to introduce new panic among the growers and butchers of the East.

The fact seems to be that the United States could well afford to eat more meat, and liked the new beef better than its former supply. The flood of beef from the range lowered the price and induced increased consumption. It started an export trade that in the seventies spread the new competition one stage further, to Europe. Beef shipments on the hoof, in the form of frozen sides, in tubs, and in tins flooded western Europe, and stimulated the growth of protective policies in England, France, Germany, and Italy. In some countries frank protective duties sought to keep out the cheap American rival of the native beef. In others the same end was attained indirectly through the imposition of quarantines. It was conveniently discovered that American cattle were subject to diseases that made them a menace to European herds, and unfitted their flesh for consumption. Out of these competitions arose still new complexities for the traffic.[4]

The transportation of the animals and the meat gave business to the railroads, which sought to follow the prevailing practice and

[4] Joseph Nimmo, *Report in Regard to the Range and Ranch Cattle Business* (48th Congress, 2d Session, House Executive Document 267, Serial 2304).

charge all the traffic would bear. The struggle over rates and the fierce competitions and secret rebates, brought the industry into the clutches of the railroad problem. The magnitude of the great packing firms allied it with the terrifying problems of monopoly. The suspicion that the meat might be tainted or diseased created a demand for government control. Only when the United States could certify that it had watched every stage of the process, and could guarantee the product, could it break down the European wall of quarantine. In 1884 the Bureau of Animal Industry in the Department of Agriculture opened a new chapter of government inspection and control.

The natural effect of the panic of 1873 was to set a limit to the growth of the beef industry so long as the period of depression lasted. With the return of prosperity about 1879, the cow men felt the boom, and the cow country hurried on to the most active period of its prosperity. The government as a silent partner, owning the grazing grounds and contributing free grass, was at the basis of the bonanza; but the cattle barons acted as though their activity was of right, and from 1879 to 1885 each year saw the trails more crowded with herds, and the long drive more densely populated with steers and cowboys. The very conditions that created the prosperity, compelled the dissolution.

As suddenly as it arose, the cow country disappeared in the last half of the eighties, for reasons as obvious as those that caused it. Overstocking of the plains was among the primary causes. It was cheap and easy to build up a herd. There was no natural limit to the number of cattle that could be bred in Texas, and the widely advertised profits of cattle raising overplayed the hand. Since nearly all were trespassers on public land, there was no basis for concerted action to reduce the size of the herds to something approximating the demand. Cattle growers associations were formed, but could rarely reach agreements or enforce them. The range became crowded, the pasturage scarce, and the flood of steers at the stock yards placed both breeders and feeders at the mercy of the railroads and the packers.

The railroads that made the cow country possible destroyed it as they normally progressed. Along the eastern margin of the plains was the line of agricultural settlements. During the sixties this line was retarded in its westward progress by continuous Indian friction. But with the cessation of Indian wars and renewed railroad building, the migration of the farmers was resumed. Every homestead taken up in Kansas, Nebraska, or Dakota, restricted the region of free grass; for the farmer did not welcome the drifting cowboys, and enforced their proprietary rights with shotguns and wire fences. The nesters, as they were called, were as incompatible with the open long drive as farmers had ever been with the wild Indians of the frontier. Two kinds of civilization could not well endure together and at once. Before 1885 the rapid settlement of the plains had thrust the open range into western Kansas, and narrowed its extent.

At the northern end of the range, the economies of the cattle men themselves served to restrict their opportunity. Every enclosure built at a northern ranch forced all other cow men to drive around, or blocked them off from running water and the finest pastures. The files at Washington are filled with complaints of this. Shotgun law was effective. Often the carriers of the mails found their well-known routes barricaded by new fences and determined cowboys who cared nothing for the law. Between the homesteads of the nesters along the eastern margin of the range, and the larger enclosures of the ranches near the northern railroads, an end of the open range was brought in sight. Every western railroad broke it up, and every town enlarged the area where the cow men were unwelcome.

The fear of disease added to the restrictions by 1884 and 1885. Much of the European prejudice against American cattle was founded upon business rather than upon hygienic considerations. But there was some disease. There was Texas fever, and hoof and mouth disease, both readily contagious, and spreading infection widely among the herds. The long drive was admirably adapted to spread disease. By actual contact, an infected herd carried disaster all along the trail. The ground that it grazed over became infected, and subsequent cattle picked up the disease. The business contained the seeds of its own destruction.

The plains States recognized the threats against the prosperity of the industry and sought to protect themselves by creating boards of health, and enforcing quarantines. The United States owned the domain, but Kansas, Nebraska, and Colorado controlled the local government. When these, by 1885, had enacted rigorous laws against the driving of foreign cattle across their borders, the long drive necessarily came to an end, and with it ended the cattle business on the free-grass basis. As a final phenomenon there appeared in 1884 and 1885 a demand from the cattle owners associations that the Government of the United States itself intervene again, and set aside a national quarantined cattle trail from Texas to Canada, and continue at its expense in the partnership so profitable to the cow men. The national cattle trail was impracticable, but its very suggestion identifies the cow country as a normal frontier episode.

The cow country thus became a phenomenon of the last American frontier. It could not have appeared before the railroads reached the eastern margin of the great plains; it could not have taken shape had the plains been available for immediate agriculture, as were States like Iowa and Illinois. It could not survive the completion of the railroads and the inevitable penetration of the plains by farmers. Without the coincidence of wire fences, refrigeration and packing technique, its development must have been curtailed. But with all these, it rose to a spectacular and ephemeral prominence, calling attention once more to the American Far West at the very moment when the Far West and the frontier were to disappear forever.

CHAPTER LVII
THE CLOSED FRONTIER

THROUGH the completion of the continental railroads the cow country found its Nemesis and the open frontier was destroyed. The period of destruction falls into two episodes, separated by the depression after 1873. In the earlier of these, the railroad charters were enacted by Congress, the land-grants were provided, and the first promoters began the search for funds with which to do the work. The projects stopped literally in their tracks when the panic struck them. They remained abandoned for several building seasons, during which the companies passed through the pangs of failure, foreclosure, and reorganization. They were not revived until the dawn of prosperity was again visible, in the administration of Rutherford B. Hayes. By 1879 they were all again at work, with a nervous activity that brought them to completion in five years more.

The name of Henry Villard is intimately connected with the events that led to the completion of the Northern Pacific. Villard was a German immigrant, a newspaper man who thought his work as correspondent in the Civil War worth the bulk of the space in his *Memoirs* (1904). He acquired an interest in the railroad situation when, after the panic of 1873, he was employed as special representative by German investors who had taken stock in this company at the instigation of Jay Cooke. As head of various stock or bond holders committees he was drawn into the mesh of reorganization; and he had a head for strategy that let him see vital factors that the Northern Pacific was itself overlooking. He observed that the line ran only to Wallula near the mouth of the Snake River, and that by voluntary decision the Northern Pacific was to entrust its coast business to a river steamboat system. He watched his chance to acquire control not only of the navigation company, but of the Oregon Railroad, already existing in the Columbia Valley. These he merged into the Oregon Railway and Navigation Company, with which he declared war upon the Northern Pacific while the latter was resuming construction and finishing its main line after 1879. The president of the Northern Pacific, Frederick Billings, still saw no menace in the fact that no freight could reach the coast without paying tribute to Villard's consolidation, and refused to come to a traffic agreement.

In June, 1881, Villard organized his "blind pool," for whose unrevealed purposes he borrowed from his New York friends. With the resulting funds he quietly acquired control of the Northern Pacific, as well as of the Oregon Railway and Navigation Company, transferring the joint holdings to a new holding company, the Oregon and Transcontinental. At the next meeting, he voted Billings out of the Northern Pacific, himself into the presidency of the three related corporations, and proceeded to complete the lines. In September, 1883, he celebrated the driving of the last spike of the Northern Pacific, by running his "Golden Spike Special" across the continent, laden with a company of distinguished guests, to whom he revealed the resources of the new empire. There was still no State between Minnesota and Oregon, and no immediate prospect of any, but he could show the rising tide of migration towards the newly opened country. There was no titter of realization stirred up by his advertising device. Continental railroads were ceasing to be a novelty. Even the New York *Nation*, which he had acquired in 1881, refused to show excitement, for Godkin wrote ". . . the country can never feel again the thrill which the joining of the Central and Union Pacific lines gave it." [1]

At the moment of its completion, there was promise and threat of competing railroads paralleling the Northern Pacific on either side. To the north, the Canadian Pacific was hurrying west under the driving force of Donald A. Smith, later to become Lord Strathcona. To the south, James J. Hill was maturing his plans for extensions of the St. Paul, Minneapolis, and Manitoba into Montana, and across the divide. In 1885 the Canadian Pacific was finished. Hill completed the Great Northern in 1893. A northwest empire, dependent upon these roads, and spreading the granger States, was beginning to take shape.

The southern plains[2] were teeming with railroad gangs between

[1] Eugene V. Smalley, *History of the Northern Pacific Railroad* (1883), was prepared under Villard's direction, and provides for his line a better history than most railroads possess. There is much relevant material in Joseph G. Pyle, *Life of James J. Hill* (1917); George Kennan, *E. H. Harriman, a Biography* (1922); and Beckles Willson, *Life of Lord Strathcona and Mount Royal* [Donald A. Smith] (1915).

[2] There is no adequate biography of any of the promoters of the southwestern continental railroads, and the scattered chapters in the writings of Hubert Howe Bancroft remain the most trustworthy guide.

1878 and 1884. Before the panic, the Atchison, Topeka, and Santa Fé built its track across Kansas, parallel to and south of the Kansas Pacific, and the Union Pacific. It now revived and expanded its activity toward the southwest, while Texas and California became breeding ground for railroad projects.

The group of Californians who first became interested in railroads through their association with the Central Pacific, held together as the only resident group that the Far West produced. Most of the lines were absentee owned, and were directed by men whose only knowledge of the West was of its capacity to be exploited. The Californians, however, clung to their local interests with tenacity and success. They procured clauses in the acts of the Atlantic and Pacific (1866) and the Texas Pacific (1871) authorizing the Southern Pacific of California, which they owned, to build east to a junction with each of these continental lines on the eastern boundary of the State of California. Both of these branches were finished and ready for business before the main lines reached the junction point. Through this, the situation which confronted the Northern Pacific at Wallula was repeated when the successor of the Atlantic and Pacific reached the Colorado River at the Needles, and when the Texas Pacific, having crossed Texas, approached El Paso. The Southern Pacific, indeed, though having no continental franchise of its own, was able by its vigor, and its branch-line privilege, to dominate both southern lines, and to direct them towards a consolidation of railroads.

The Texas Pacific, halted near Fort Worth by the panic, was reorganized and revived about 1878 by Southern Pacific influence. The California connecting branch, from San Francisco to Fort Yuma on the Colorado, was built between 1865 and 1877, but had no hope of continuation eastward except as the Southern Pacific interested itself. The legislatures of Arizona and New Mexico, and the State of Texas, were accordingly besought for charters, under which the Southern Pacific between 1879 and 1882 crossed Arizona along the Gila River route, and crossed New Mexico to El Paso on the Rio Grande. It even built into Texas some ninety-two miles, to Sierra Blanca, at which point it made a connection with the Texas Pacific, bound west. In January, 1882, through cars were first run from California to St. Louis over this line; in October they were run to New Orleans as well. But the completion of this only partly satisfied the aspirations of the Southern Pacific for connections with the East.

A second Southern Pacific line across Texas and Louisiana from Sierra Blanca to New Orleans was made available by February, 1883, through the purchase and merger of various local lines of southern Texas. The population of Texas was not yet strung along the route of the Texas Pacific, although cotton farming was causing a boom in the country around Fort Worth. The original Texas was settled on the San Antonio road, and between it and the Gulf of Mexico. The Galveston, Harrisburg, and San Antonio road was a local Texas line, started to serve the needs of the country near the coast. This and others were merged, new links were built, and when the through trains ran into New Orleans in February, 1883, they skirted the bend of the Rio Grande, passed through San Antonio and Houston, and crossed Louisiana as near the coast as the engineers could build the tracks. This was to become the main line of the Southern Pacific.

A third Southern Pacific connection was the product of the combined efforts of the western group and the old Atlantic and Pacific, reinforced by the Atchison, Topeka, and Santa Fé. When the Atlantic and Pacific collapsed in 1873, with trackage to Vinita, Indian Territory, its land-grant seemed likely to be forfeited through nonfulfillment. The length of Indian Territory, where whites could not lawfully reside, and northern Texas and the panhandle, where the cattle were becoming numerous, did not promise a profitable basis for railroad construction. Though it was reorganized in 1876 as the St. Louis and San Francisco, reorganization did not instill in it a breath of life until its associates lent their aid. The Atchison, Topeka, and Santa Fé had by this time followed the old Santa Fé Trail to the Rio Grande, and had descended that stream toward El Paso. At Deming, New Mexico, its track crossed that of the Southern Pacific. It was now heading deliberately for Mexico City, through an affiliated line, the Mexican Central, which reached its destination in March, 1884. The unused land-grant of the Atlantic and Pacific attracted the attention of the Santa Fé managers, in spite of the fact that the time limit had expired. Congress was often kind to railroads that needed time extensions. It was therefore arranged to enable the construction of the section of line from Albuquerque to the Needles, nominally under the charter of 1866. The Southern Pacific meanwhile built its Mojave branch from Barstow, California, across the desert to the Needles. Over this new through line Pullman cars were running into St. Louis before the end of 1883.

The complex western net of railroads was carried to substantial completion in the first half of the decade of the eighties.[3] Railroad mileage was climbing up in relation to population throughout the country. In 1860 there were 985 miles per million inhabitants. This increased to 1380 miles in 1870; to 1858 miles in 1880; and to 2625 miles in 1890. Thirty years later the mileage had not yet reached 3000 miles per million. The relative changes brought about by the abnormal construction of the eighties were largest in the Far West, where the Pacific roads were the most extensive single accomplishments. The completion of the system was widely advertised, for new transportation circuits were of general interest, and corporations as large as the Northern or Southern Pacific were novelties. The latter system of lines attained additional prominence for itself when its owners brought the various corporate components into orderly relation with each other.

There was an intricate network of contracts, through which the California magnates controlled and built the Central Pacific, and the various Southern Pacific roads. There were other feeder lines that were controlled by one or another of the group. In 1884 the State of Kentucky was prevailed upon to incorporate the Southern Pacific Railroad Company, for whose stock the various members of the California group exchanged their holdings in the several roads. New unity in management was thus gained, permanence was secured, and the fact that the holding company was a creation of a State in which none of its lines were operated gave promise of lack of legislative interference. State governments were becoming more interested in railroad affairs, since the granger cases had upheld their right to regulate, and even Congress was rapidly approaching a time when it must exert an influence in the name of the United States. In November, 1883, most of the railroads, by common agreement, took one significant step toward their adjustment as a national system; they agreed to adopt a system of time zones within which one standard should be used by every road. This abolished at a stroke much of the confusion that had hitherto attended long-distance travel, and pointed to the fact that the railroads were becoming one problem for the Nation, rather than thirty-eight problems for as many States.

As the continental railroads opened their lines they brought within easy reach every considerable section of the Far West, and

[3] F. L. Paxson, "The Pacific Railroads and the Disappearance of the Frontier in America," in American Historical Association *Report* (1907).

abolished the isolation that had thus far been a characteristic of the American frontier. They bore heavily upon the open frontier in another way through their stimulation of sales of the public lands, and their wide advertisement of the resources of the West. It was still the basic task of the frontier farmer to secure his farm. Hitherto he had in practice been limited in his selection to the zone of public domain adjacent to the established agricultural frontier. He could now penetrate to every part of the West, and thus with better access, and wider publicity, the process of divesting the United States of title was pushed ahead.

There were many ways in which the migrant of the eighties could procure his farm.[4] He could still buy it outright under the Preëmption Act of 1841. In spite of repeated urging from the General Land Office, Congress failed to repeal this law when it was made needless by the Homestead Act of 1862. This latter act was best known of all the land laws, and the attractive invitation to go west and receive a free farm from the United States was heard around the world. During 1883, original homestead entries were made by 56,565 persons, making a total of such entries since the law enacted of 608,677. The picture of more than half a million free families cultivating the domain was inspiring — but untrue. Only a third as many, 213,486 had completed the terms of residence and cultivation required by law and received their final entry from the Land Office. The Homestead Act was a telling advertisement, but many prospective homesteaders decided that it was better to buy the farm outright, commuting it under the Preemption Act, as was permissible. Many others, who reached the frontier under the lure of the Homestead Act, decided to buy railroad lands, out of the generous land-grants, or school lands from one of the States. But the various ways of obtaining lands met the needs of the different types of farmer headed west, and no one need cavil at the statement of Donaldson in *The Public Domain* (1884), that the Homestead Act "stands as the concentrated wisdom of legislation for the settlement of the public lands. It protects the Government, it fills the States with homes, it builds up communities, and lessens the chances of social and civil disorder by giving ownership of the soil, in small tracts, to the occupants

[4] The earliest systematic sketch of our land system was left to be done by a Japanese student, Shosuke Sato, "History of the Land Question in the United States," in Johns Hopkins University *Studies*, vol. IV; Albert Bushnell Hart wrote one of his earliest monographs on "The Disposition of our Public Lands," for vol. I of *Quarterly Journal of Economics*. They have not had adequate successors.

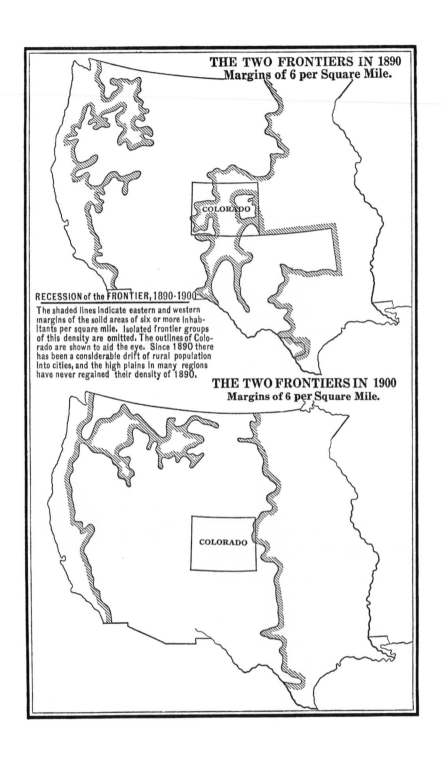

THE TWO FRONTIERS IN 1890
Margins of 6 per Square Mile.

COLORADO

RECESSION of the FRONTIER, 1890-1900

The shaded lines indicate eastern and western
margins of the solid areas of six or more inhabitants per square mile. Isolated frontier groups
of this density are omitted. The outlines of Colorado are shown to aid the eye. Since 1890 there
has been a considerable drift of rural population
into cities, and the high plains in many regions
have never regained their density of 1890.

THE TWO FRONTIERS IN 1900
Margins of 6 per Square Mile.

COLORADO

thereof. It was copied from no other nation's system. It was originally and distinctively America, and remains a monument to its originators."

If the land laws had met the other needs for soil as well as they met those of the small frontier farmer, the history of the tenth decade under the Constitution would have been more orderly and satisfying than it was. They failed, however, to protect the public interest in mineral rights, or water powers, or irrigation projects, and they provided no legal method whereby the legitimate wholesale user of land could obtain his need. Much of the country brought within reach by the railroads was mountainous, and without appreciable value; much was useful only for its timber; much had only a grazing value; yet the law treated it all as though it were destined to cultivation by the small farmer.

The cattle companies were the most conspicuous sinners against the spirit and letter of the law. Timber was not yet scarce enough in the United States for there to be much concern at the mounting forest holdings that certain groups of speculators were bringing together; and low-grade coal lands, which abounded in the domain, or oil fields whose value was not yet appreciated, failed to stimulate public interest. But the cattle barons trod on their neighbors' toes, destroyed the lesser cow men, and forced their law-breaking to the attention of the country.

There was no objection to the use of Government grass upon the open range, so long as the country was not needed; but the cattle industry required large enclosures, to safeguard the stock as well as to lower the cost of cattle tending. The need was for acres by the thousand, or ten thousand; whereas the law issued it in sections and fractions thereof. The real requirement of the rancher for a large tract that he could control, the cheapness with which he could fence it with barbed wire, the public opinion of the locality which did not discourage such seizure of the public domain, and the laxity of Congress which would not appropriate enough money to permit of a real police and inspection of the public property, all contributed to the multiplication of illegal inclosures. These were to be found by 1885 everywhere when the cattle appeared in numbers; they were most numerous on the northern plains, in Nebraska and Montana, near to the shipping points on the continental railroads. The technique of the fencer began usually with the lawful acquisition of title to a small tract of land. By homesteading, preëmption, or purchase otherwise, he secured a tract fol'owing the meanderings of some stream suitable for watering the stock. Without such water right, secure'y possessed, it was unsafe to venture upon the business. When, however, he had gained title to both banks of a stream for several miles, his possession made it impossible for any other rancher to get to the water, or to use the dry grazing grounds on either side of the stream. The rancher often enlarged his owned holdings by requiring his employees to enter homesteads or preëmptions, and transfer them to him. This was strictly illegal, for the law fulminated against collusive entries, and insisted that personal use alone warranted either homestead or preëmption; but there was no machinery to enforce the law, and no local opinion to warrant enforcement.

There never had been a time when the frontier concerned itself with the maintenance of the common rights over the domain. The Government had more generally been regarded as a somewhat impertinent outsider who thrust barriers between the citizen and the land he wanted. On this last frontier, the prospective homesteader complained when he found that the cattle man had illegally enclosed trails, water rights, and pasturage that the homesteader might have used; but events were moving too rapidly for this feeling to acquire political weight. It was easier to direct public attention to railroad encroachments, for the land-grant railroads owned a large acreage which they held for occupation. In many cases the roads had failed to be completed on time, and the grants had become void, or at least voidable. The Commissioners of the Land Office early brought this status to the notice of Congress. The question arose whether public land withdrawn from entry on the filing of a railroad plat should return automatically to entry when the time limit expired without fulfillment; or whether, as the roads insisted, it required a special act of Congress to bring this about. If forfeit for noncompliance, the questions appeared as to what should be forfeit — the whole grant to the railroad, or the lands opposite the sections not finished on time, or only those not finished at all. It was a matter of complex business, whose equities worried successive Secretaries of the Interior, and had political implications that made it impossible more than to approximate justice. It was at least a triumph of national policy that the whole grants to the Texas Pacific were canceled for cause, and remained canceled in spite of the active and efficient lobby of the Southern Pacific, which wanted to receive them as assignee.

The difficulties of administering the General Land Office in the face of such a migration as was now under way were great. They were alleviated by the fact that the task was nearing its end. The population map of 1880, as shown by the census report, revealed the fact that the best farm lands of the public domain were all disposed of, and that recent entries were carrying the farmers dangerously close to the sub-humid plains and the high mountains. There was room for some further advance before 1890, but not much. At every census since the first in 1790 the line of six inhabitants per square mile had shifted west, forming a positive measure for the advance of the frontier. The line of 1890 was so broken and irregular, and approached so near, at various places, to the western line that was swinging east, that obviously the frontier task was done. In 1900, indeed, the line shows an absolute recession. The migrations of the eighties were over-large; and the enthusiasm of the settlers, recruited by alien immigrants, and stimulated by lenders with money to advance on farms, and railroads with lands to sell, planted more farmer families on the western plains than the plains could hold. Between 1880 and 1890 the typical American frontier process reached its end.

CHAPTER LVIII
THE ADMISSION OF THE "OMNIBUS" STATES

In the period of depression after the panic of 1873, Colorado, the thirty-eighth State, was admitted to the Union in 1876. It brought no change in the boundaries upon the political map of the United States, for these lines had become substantially complete after the organization of Wyoming Territory in 1868. It established, however, a western status that remained unchanged for thirteen years, until new States had ripened under the boom of the eighties.

During these thirteen years approximately two thirds of the total area of the United States lay under autonomous State governments, and one third was dependent upon the will of Congress. Of the total area, 3,026,789 square miles, the eight territories of Dakota, Montana, Idaho, Wyoming, Washington, Utah, Arizona, and New Mexico, and Indian Territory which last was not a territory at all, comprised 938,015 square miles. They occupied an unbroken tract from Canada to Mexico, and varied in breadth from nearly twenty-seven degrees of longitude along the Canadian line to five degrees at the narrowest part, Utah. Their region had much of it been included in the legendary American desert, or the Indian Country. Their first institutions of government had mostly originated in the demand of mining camps for home rule. The oldest of them, New Mexico and Utah, had rounded over a quarter century since their creation; the newest, Wyoming, was still in its first decade. All of them bore testimony to the fact that while mineral resources were capable of inspiring territorial talk they rarely provided a sound basis for civil organization unless supplemented by extensive agriculture. The white population, 150,220 in 1860, had grown to 271,166 in 1870, and to 606,810 in 1880. Ten years later, with the inclusion of most of the 325,464 Indians which were now enumerated, the gross population of the area was 1,908,803.

The three States of Kansas,[1] Nebraska, and Colorado shared

---

[1] William E. Connelley, *The Life of Preston B. Plumb, 1837–1891* (1913) and *Ingalls of Kansas* (1909), pictures through the lives of two senators "the founding of a great State," and the "passing of an old order." Plumb was so typical that William H. Crane copied him

with the territorial area in many of its characteristics. They were set up in the undulating plains that rise gradually from the Missouri River to the watershed of the Rockies. In 1860 their population of 170,324 had been close to that of the territorial area; but with the earlier influence of the continental railroads bearing upon them, and their closer proximity to eastern sources of emigration, they grew to 527,256 by 1870. In 1880 they had far outstripped the territorial area, having 1,642,825 inhabitants; and in 1890 this was increased to 2,904,013. They possessed home rule, which gave them greater political influence than their territorial neighbors, but their social age was about the same and their difference was that of greater size rather than of inherent quality. There was no new State admitted after Nebraska (1867) until Colorado (1876); and political considerations as well as immaturity had much to do with the long interval after Colorado until the next admissions in 1889.

Colorado limped and lingered in its advance toward statehood. Under its first enabling act it rejected admission in 1864. When it thought better of it, and approved admission the following year, the President of the United States had changed from Lincoln to Johnson, and presidential policy had also changed. Johnson did not want additional Republican States and found excellent reasons for refusing to admit Colorado with its scanty population, its vagrant habits, and its low taxable wealth. After the completion of the Union Pacific and its Kansas Pacific branch, agriculture awoke on the eastern slopes of the mountains, and the tributaries of the South Platte and the Arkansas yielded water for irrigation ditches that induced a more permanent prosperity than Colorado Territory had yet witnessed. Thereafter another enabling act came easily in 1875, and a constitution was framed at Denver in 1876.

The second Colorado enabling act was passed on the last day upon which the Republican party had a majority in Congress for a period of six years. Beginning with March 4, 1875, Grant was confronted with a Democratic House of Representatives, including a Democratic delegate from Colorado Territory. The opposition developed hopes that from Colorado might come three Democratic electoral votes in 1876, and Patterson, the delegate, encouraged this belief. But the new State was admitted by proclamation on

in every detail in his make-up and manner in *The Senator*, and Plumb himself trimmed the actor's beard to make the resemblance more complete.

August 1, 1876, and cast its vote for Rutherford B. Hayes the following November; without these three, or with them reversed, Samuel J. Tilden would have become President of the United States. It was small wonder that in ensuing Congresses, members of both parties looked upon new States with reference to their influence upon presidential aspirations, and that Democrats resolved not to increase the burden of votes that might be cast against them. Throughout the administration of Hayes, 1877–1881, there was continuously a Democratic House of Representatives to block the admission of Republican territories as States, and after an intermission of a single Congress, the blockade lasted until the end of the Fiftieth Congress in 1889. During the four years of Cleveland's administration, 1885–1889, the blockade was from the other side, with a Republican Senate suspicious of every statehood proposition that might turn out Democratic.

After Colorado, the likeliest territories were Dakota and Washington, each of which had the beginnings of a solvent population. The massacre of Custer and his men in 1876 drew attention to Dakota and its resources. In the southwest corner of the territory, the region of the Black Hills was filling in with mineral prospectors, and the stage coach running north from Cheyenne on the Union Pacific to Deadwood kept alive a tradition that had largely died after the overland stage was withdrawn. When Colonel William F. Cody organized his first Wild West show in 1883 he capitalized the general interest in the cow country and the mining camps, and made the attack upon the Deadwood coach a spectacular feature of his performance. When he took his show to England in 1887, royalty was more intrigued by this than by any other episode, and his autobiography tells many stories of the experiences of "Buffalo Bill" when he held the reins, and the then Prince of Wales insisted upon riding around the arena on the box.

The Black Hills brought advertising to a remote part of Dakota, and suggested an ultimate division of the territory. There were already two clearly defined tracts, one in the northeast, where the wheat lands of the Red River of the North were tapped by the Northern Pacific Railroad, the other in the southeast, where farmers from Iowa and Minnesota had naturally overflowed from these States and occupied the angle between the Missouri and the Big Sioux rivers. When James Bryce traversed this territory with Villard's ceremonial train in 1883, he witnessed the laying of a corner stone for a new capitol building at Bismarck, where there were hopes rather than inhabitants. "The confidence of these Westerns is superb," he wrote. "Men seem to live in the future rather than in the present: not that they fail to work while it is called to-day, but that they see the country not merely as it is, but as it will be, twenty, fifty, a hundred years hence, when the seedlings shall have grown to be forest trees." The starting of a capitol at Bismarck was evidence that in Dakota the intention was to enter the Union as two States. Universities were established at both Grand Forks, on Red River, and Vermilion, on the Missouri, so that institutions might be ready for each half when the division came.

Bills for the admission of Dakota were before Congress during the session of 1882–1883, but failed to pass. The defeat was due to Democratic opposition, reinforced by a vigorous protest from a group of Republicans. The Republican protest was founded upon the fact that Yankton County had made no provision for the payment of its issue of railroad bonds, whose holders sought to compel payment by exclusion. "I believe that all the objections which have been hitherto urged against the passage of that bill are purely partisan and malignant," declared John J. Ingalls, Republican Senator from Kansas; and he knew much of both partisanship and malignancy. With the defeat of this measure, the moment of possible admission was passed, and there was no chance for success until after the election of 1888.

In Dakota spontaneous attempts at statehood kept aspirations alive through the years of partisan blockade. A constitution was drawn up at Sioux Falls in 1883, and another at the same place in 1885. The United States Senate, which was Republican, repeatedly passed enabling acts for the division of the territory and the admission of its parts. The House as consistently rejected the proposals, searching for arguments in the size of the population and the allegation that division was a measure being forced upon an unwilling northern half of the territory. In 1888 the Senate again had under consideration a division-admission bill, with no hope of passing it through the House, when the result of the presidential election disclosed the fact that after March 4, 1889, the Government of the United States would be Republican in all its branches. This removed the blockade. The question now immediately became not whether Dakota could be admitted, but how many other territories would be admitted with it.

Washington Territory had a local statehood movement in 1878, at the moment when the renewal of active building on the Northern Pacific gave promise of a brightened future. The convention sat at Walla Walla, for most of the people were yet in the southeast corner of the territory, near the Columbia River. The Puget Sound country and the Spokane country were somewhat later in their development. To the Walla Walla convention it seemed reasonable that upon admission Washington should be enlarged. It had become evident that so much of Idaho as lay north of the Salmon River was attached to Washington by much closer ties than those that bound it to the southern portion of itself. Lewiston desired to be in Washington. In 1887 a bill annexing this Idaho panhandle to Washington got so far as to pass Congress, to be defeated by the pocket veto of President Cleveland. But the Territory of Washington was still a territory in 1887, nine years after framing its constitution. The blockade kept it out.

Between Dakota at the east, and Washington at the west, the line of the Northern Pacific brought the northern half of the territorial area into easy access. Montana and Idaho were both crossed by its track. Wyoming lay south, but was close enough to be affected. The cattle that traveled up the long trail, across eastern Wyoming where Red Cloud made his successful stand in 1868, passed naturally down the Powder River and the Big Horn to the Yellowstone Valley, and thence found shipment east from Miles City and Glendive. The searching pen of Owen Wister has preserved the picture of the Wyoming of this period. His *Virginian* (1902) is among the most real of American heroes, and is one of the most accurate of our historical portraitures. But Wyoming was a thoroughfare rather than a destination, and its scanty population (62,555 in 1890) left it without real right to immediate statehood. Idaho, a little more populous than Wyoming (88,548 in 1890) had a similar situation.

Montana was somewhat further advanced than Idaho or Wyoming, and profited by the publicity given it by the Cœur d'Alene mining rush of 1883–1884, and by the growing enclosures of the stockmen. Its people held a convention at Helena, in 1884, under the presidency of William A. Clark, and memorialized Congress for immediate statehood, without result. They received an unusual favor from President Cleveland, however, when he appointed as territorial governor in 1885 one of their own citizens, Samuel T. Hauser.

Carpet-bagging was a usual feature of the territorial governments. At a time when most of the appointive offices were used to reward party services, it was too much to expect that officials in the Indian service, or territorial, should be selected upon any better basis. Within the States most of the Federal appointees had at least the virtue of residence in the communities in which they served, for every President had political bills to pay, or hopes to advance, in every constituency. But the territories had no presidential votes to cast, and no influence to fear or favor. They were like the reconstruction governments of the post-bellum South. The political carpet-baggers of the territories could do less damage than those of the southern States, for they had smaller communities to operate upon, and much less money to spend, but in principle they were generally as un-representative. The "consent of the governed," which meant much to most Americans on the Fourth of July, meant little to them when it came to the territorial Americans subject to their discretion. The political appointees of the territories were liable to become a statehood ring, lobbying for admission, and intriguing for the elective jobs. In most of the territories it is difficult to separate their ambitions from the genuine aspiration of the population for statehood.

Quite as characteristic of the far western territories as their carpet-bagging governments was their somewhat lawless reign of law.[2] The institutions of settled society came irregularly into the open territories where population was sparse and included a heavy percentage of drifters. In the older territories the farmer population spread definitely and permanently across the fields. There was at once a settled group, tied up with the future of the region, possessing homes and property, and forming the basis of orderly government. But with the rise of the mining camps it was apparent that this frontier must develop in a new way, and that order was to be an acquired characteristic, difficult of attainment.

The lawlessness of the mining camp and the cow town received wide notoriety, and was turned to literary uses by Bret Harte and Mark Twain.[3] Self-help lasted in these regions longer than on the agricultural frontiers, for the good reason that unless self-help was immediately available at need, it might be too late for any help. The men, good and bad, went armed, and the bad man had every

[2] Thomas J. Dimsdale, *The Vigilantes of Montana, or, Popular Justice in the Rocky Mountains* (2d ed., 1882).

[3] Charles H. Shinn, *Mining Camps. A Study in American Frontier Government* (1885).

advantage in the earlier phases of far western life. In every community, however, there came a time when local opinion asserted itself, often with catastrophic outcome. The vigilance committee made a formal appearance upon the mining frontier as early as the first decade in California, with good citizens organizing as volunteers to suppress the bad. The justice thus rendered was of necessity summary and abrupt, and sometimes indiscriminate. But the stabler portion of a community was confronted with a real dilemma when it had to choose between longer tolerating murder or worse and taking the law into its own hands. A few sessions of the vigilance committee were likely to pave the way for the inauguration of a reign of law.

When the election of 1888 was followed by the last session of the Fiftieth Congress, in which for the last time the Democrats possessed a majority in the House of Representatives, there was great activity among the statehood advocates. The Dakota bill, which had passed the Senate at the previous session, was before the House; the majority of the latter now determined to yield, and by yielding to acquire something for itself. "If these territories be not admitted this session," declared one of the Democratic leaders, "they will surely be admitted under Republican auspices in the next Congress." The Dakota bill was therefore reported out, but amended to "omnibus" proportions by the addition of Washington and Montana, and by New Mexico, which was expected to be Democratic. It was taken for granted that the northern territories, first settled during the Civil War, and long officered by Republican appointees, would enter as Republicans.

The lifted blockade, which was apparent to the Democrats of the House, was as apparent to the Republicans of the Senate. Although they had long scolded the Democratic wickedness that excluded Republican States, they had no mind to admit any Democratic States themselves. The Senate received back its amended bill, and amended it again, striking out New Mexico, and dividing Dakota, leaving the bill with still four territories in the "omnibus." Twice the bills were sent into the committee on conference before an agreement could be reached on terms satisfactory to the victorious Republicans. The House gave up the now unequal fight, and Cleveland, on February 22, 1889, signed the Omnibus Bill for the admission of four new States.

In the summer of 1889 the Far West was noisy with its constitutional eloquence. The Omnibus Bill provided that conventions should meet, to frame constitutions, or to revise those that had been made spontaneously.[4] In South Dakota the Sioux Falls constitution of 1885 was revamped. In North Dakota, Montana, and Washington new ones were put together. In Idaho and Wyoming, where there was no authority at all, conventions met at Boise and Cheyenne and framed documents similar to those of the four enabled States. At Santa Fé, New Mexicans gathered and did likewise. At Salt Lake City there was no special constitutional movement, for Utah had been continuously aspirant for forty years. But within the Mormon Church a change was taking place, and the following spring it was revealed to the members of the church that a belief in the doctrine of plural marriage was not necessary to salvation. This, for Utah, had become a condition precedent.

The terms of the Omnibus Bill required that the several conventions should frame constitutions along certain lines. There was still, and ever had been, doubt as to the constitutional right of Congress to set terms for the admission of a State. In the United States Constitution it is simply stated that "New States may be admitted by the Congress into this Union," and the law is clear that, once in the Union, there is no difference among the States, they being equally free and equally dependent. Advocates of complete States rights maintained that Congress had no concern except to see that a republican form of government was erected by a State constitution. Advocates of restriction held that since no power could compel Congress to admit any State, and since none could enter the Union without Congressional permission, Congress thus acquired a discretionary power that it could exercise according to its pleasure. Whatever the law, Congress was beyond control, and whatever injustice might be complained of, there was no means of enforcing redress.

Missouri learned this fact when the constitution of 1820 forbade the entrance of free negroes into the State, and Congress refused to permit the State to function until this prohibition was interpreted away. There was no means of controlling the action of a State once in the Union; until admission it had a master in Congress that it must respect. The precedents of the Civil War period enhanced the importance of the strategic position of Congress. It was discovered that the sort of power claimed by Con-

[4] John D. Hicks, "The Constitutions of the Northwest States," in University of Nebraska, *University Studies*, vol. XXIII.

gress as a whole could be used by either House, since each, under the Federal Constitution, is sole judge of the elections, returns, and qualifications of its own members, and has actual power to exclude or expel. The Confederate States were not permitted to resume their functions in the Union until they submitted to a long series of exactions set for them by the victorious Congress. Some of these were internal, which they might have amended away after readmission; others were permanent in consequence, such as the requirement to ratify the Thirteenth and Fourteenth Amendments. When Nebraska was admitted, shortly after the Civil War, Congress followed the same procedure, stated terms of entrance, and directed the President to examine the constitution of the new State, and to admit it by proclamation upon satisfying himself that the requirements of Congress were fully complied with.

Colorado was similarly admitted in 1876, under a law passed in 1875. On this occasion an attempt was made to test the validity of admission by proclamation, on the ground that Congress had no right to delegate to another agent the power to admit a State. The protest had a real meaning, when the Democrats in the House contested the seat of the first Republican congressman-elect from Colorado in 1877. If the contest could be made effective, it would tend to establish the fact that Colorado was still not a State, that its electoral vote of 1876 ought therefore not to be counted, that Rutherford B. Hayes ought to be deprived of the three Colorado votes, and that without these he would lack a majority and be forced to vacate his office. It was an ambitious program, which collapsed when the House seated the Republican member.

The Omnibus Bill, in section four, required certain "irrevocable" pledges of the new States: (1) that there should be perfect toleration of religious sentiment, (2) that claim to public lands and tribal lands should be expressly renounced, and that taxes should not fall heavier upon lands owned by citizens of other States than upon those owned by resident citizens, (3) that territorial debts and liabilities should be assumed and paid, that (4) systems of public schools should be provided "free from sectarian control," (5) that the constitutions should be republican in form, that (6) they should make no distinction "in civil or political rights on account of race or color, except as to Indians not taxed," and that (7) the constitutions should not be repugnant to the Declaration of Independence and the Constitution of the United States. There was no difficulty in obtaining compliance under all these heads. In addition, the new constitutions were made a catalogue of the new ideas of government and control that had survived the Civil War and blossomed amid the economic changes of the eighties.

The great length of the new documents was one of the most visible facts. Increasingly the constitutions were recording the distrust which Americans were coming to feel towards their own governments. Every constitution was clearer upon the things that the legislatures could *not* do than upon the ends to be attained by legislation. There were long clauses to prevent the granting of favors to corporations, banks, or railroads; there were sections reflecting the experiences of the granger movement, and asserting the public right over common carriers. There was the usual manhood suffrage, and in one of the new constitutions of 1889, that of Wyoming, there was woman suffrage as well. The constitutions approximated codes rather than organic laws, and there was a costly paradox in that they showed an intent to develop programs of State action, yet drew iron-clad restrictions to make such programs ineffective.

Early in November, 1889, President Harrison issued a series of proclamations admitting the four States of the Omnibus Bill; their Senators and Congressmen, all Republican, took their seats when the Fifty-first Congress met the following month.[5] The exigencies of the party contributed to the success which was accorded by this Congress to two of the territories that had been left outside the Omnibus Bill, yet desired statehood. It was in this session that Thomas B. Reed, of Maine, earned the title of "Czar" by his courageous career as Speaker of the House; and it was only by a stern party administration that a majority was held together to support his rules. In the Senate there was a fairly easy situation, but every member was needed every day in the House. The five new Republicans of the Omnibus States were useful to their party. Two more from Wyoming and Idaho were added in the summer of 1890. On the merits of the case, both States might easily have been excluded, but the party needed votes, and Congress was fatigued by the long wrangle over admission of territories, that had been heard for more than ten years. New Mexico, with Democratic tendencies, was indeed rejected; Arizona was impossible; Utah had seen the light, but had not yet been permitted to make a constitution.

[5] F. L. Paxson, "The Admission of the Omnibus States," in State Historical Society of Wisconsin, *Proceedings*, 1911.

CHAPTER LIX

THE DISAPPEARANCE OF THE FRONTIER

WITH the admission of the Omnibus States, and the two others that trailed into the Union after them, the work begun by the old Congress of the Confederacy was substantially completed. The thirteen original States were supplemented by thirty-one that had been admitted to the Union. The forty-four that now constituted the United States embraced in their territory not only all that the founders had ever dreamed of, but much that had been willingly conceded to the desert. The huge territorial area of 1876 was forever broken up. Never in so short a time had so large an area been at one stroke lifted to statehood, nor so many States been added, as these six that entered the Union in less than nine months. The process that is fundamental in the American empire, and that marks it as different from any of its predecessors, was nearly worked out.

The American process, outlined in the legislation of the Continental Congress in the Ordinances of 1784 and 1787, contemplated a motherland and dependent colonies, like any other empire; but differed from others in the promise that dependency was a temporary status, to be terminated by the transition from social adolescence to adult stature, and to be marked then by full admission to all the privileges of the nation. The spirit of freedom and progress, encouraged by frontier conditions, gave rise to this new theory of imperialism. The United States never seriously wavered in its adherence to it. The Ordinance of 1787, in all its fundamentals, was as effective in the admission of Wyoming or Idaho as in that of Vermont or Ohio. It was never necessary to revise its principles. Congress had modified details as the years rolled on, but had left the substance intact.

Perhaps one of the reasons why the pledge of 1787 continued to bind was the fact that the American Federal Government did not develop a governing caste, or a colonial office. The plague of the spoils system was the horde of inefficient placemen who abused the territories; its salvation was their inefficiency and impermanence. If American conditions had bred at Washington a colonial office like that of England, the normal tendency of an effective bureau-cracy might well have been to block the development of States and to induce a reinforced conviction that territories were not yet ready for admission. But there is no evidence that a policy was ever developed for the government of the territories. Their officers were given their commissions, generally to reward political services. They were then turned loose, subject only to the restrictions that the courts and the appropriation bills might place upon their conduct. The President was too busy to interest himself in their affairs. The State Department had no agencies of control. The Indian Bureau, the Land Office, and the War Department all exercised some concurrent jurisdiction with the territorial officers, and there was some interlocking of functions, but no American ever made a reputation founded upon his knowledge of territorial affairs, and his success in administering them. When the Spanish War resulted in transferring detached colonies to the control of the United States there was no going establishment ready to receive them, despite the fact that in a century the country had raised forty-two governments from dependent status to full participation. It became necessary to attach the island colonies to a bureau in the War Department, unhappily so efficient as to preclude any early granting of full autonomy.

In the course of admitting the new States Congress devised mechanisms for giving effect to the policy of the legislation of 1787. Statehood was never forced upon any community although it was sometimes, as in the case of Nevada, offered in so tempting a fashion as to accelerate the movement. Colorado declined the offer of 1864, as did Nebraska, and upon several occasions territories refused to accept the first terms offered them by Congress. Iowa rejected admission upon the first terms because of the boundary involved. Arizona and New Mexico declined joint admission in 1906.

The pressure was more commonly the other way, with territories demanding admission earlier than Congress was ready to accord it. The first three new States, Vermont, Kentucky, and Tennessee were hardly to be regarded as creations of the United States, for all had been formed prior to the Constitution. They were unfinished business of the Revolution. But Ohio, the first State to be guided through all the preliminaries by Congress, was the occasion for the passage of the earliest of the enabling acts, whereby Congress kept its control over the details of the statehood process. The enabling acts gave formal authority to proceed, fixed the qualifications of voters and shaped the conventions, and dictated the further terms to be complied with before admission. Of the thirty-one States added to the Union since Ohio, more than half, eighteen, have operated under enabling acts; and of the thirteen not enabled, two already possessed statehood before their independent admission and one was a free republic. These were Maine (a part of Massachusetts), West Virginia (a part of Virginia), and Texas. The virtue of the enabling policy, from the standpoint of Congress, was the vantage it gave for determining in advance of admission the full compliance of the State with policies of the Government of the United States. The political theorists of some of the States have engaged at times in the profitless discussion as to whether it is the act of Congress that creates the State, or the act of the people in framing and ratifying the constitution. The impossibility of an American State existing outside the Constitution and continuing to be American, makes the date set by Congress for admission the one of practical significance, however much the people may believe that they have become a State at any earlier time.

The growth and spread of democracy have been revealed not only in the content of the State constitutions, but in the method in which they have come into effect. The first revolutionary constitutions were often framed by the legislatures which had seized full authority, and which declared the basic laws to be operative without further sanction. By the date of the Philadelphia Convention, in 1787, it had come to be believed that a legislative body chosen under an old basic law was incompetent to form a new constitution, and that a special convention chosen by the people for this purpose was indispensable. But it was accepted in theory that when such a convention met it embodied the full sovereignty of the people, could perform legislative as well as constituent functions, and could not only construct a new constitution, but promulgate it and give it force. The earlier new States were admitted under constitutions thus promulgated, and the radical democrats of the age of Jefferson saw nothing inconsistent with their democracy in this assumption of power by a constitutional convention. The Mississippi convention of 1817, for reasons which have not been clearly established, broke from this practice, and submitted its constitution to a referendum by the people, which referendum gave it validity. The new method was in close accord with the democratic ideas of the Jacksonian period, and soon became general. Five subsequent States adhered to the old process, Illinois, Alabama, Missouri, Arkansas, and Florida, but all the rest preferred to submit the constitution to popular ratification. Illinois was the only northern State after Mississippi to promulgate an original constitution. The same procedure was extended to the ratification of amendments and to most of the new constitutions that the States made as they outgrew their original constitutional garments.

The earlier habit of Congress was to await the action of the territory under the enabling act and to pass a law admitting the State after the presentation of a constitution. Missouri was an exception to this, for the ultimate admission of that State depended upon an examination of the degree of its compliance with terms that Congress set. The President admitted it by proclamation. There was a similar provision in the case of Nevada, and thereafter admission by proclamation became a general rule, broken only by Wyoming and Idaho whose completed constitutions Congress accepted without further action. In the case of Arizona this method of admission was complicated because the President of the United States objected to a provision of its constitution, and declined to exercise his power to admit the State. The natural result of the frequent repetition of the steps in making and admitting new States was to keep alive a familiarity with constitutional matters, and to engender among the people the habit of self-government.

After 1890 there were four additional States to be anticipated, and only four. None of these was to be the orderly result of frontier advance, and each was to be admitted in its own time and in its own way. Utah, New Mexico, and Arizona were territories, unripe or unfit for immediate action; Oklahoma was a new creation of the year in which the Omnibus States were formed.

Oklahoma was given the usual territorial form of organization in 1890 after a dozen years of active contest over the future of the Indian Country. Thrust in between Texas and Arkansas, this was the southern tip of the tract which, by Monroe's Indian policy had been forever devoted to Indian occupancy. The Indian Intercourse Act of 1834 provided for the exclusion of white residents, and safeguarded the native inhabitants. The Five Civilized Tribes were already colonizing the eastern end of the tract beyond Arkansas when the policy was undertaken. In succeeding years, as the course of events undid the work of Monroe's policy, the Indian

Country was reduced; and with the Kansas-Nebraska legislation of 1854 it was stabilized between the Red River and the thirty-seventh parallel. The Indian Country had at this time the limits of the present State of Oklahoma, except for the narrow strip north of the Texas panhandle, which was not Texas or anything else, and acquired the name of No Man's Land.

The Civil War resulted in the confiscation of parts of the Indian lands as a penalty for adherence to the Confederacy,[1] and various plains tribes were colonized west of the Five Civilized Tribes in the succeeding years. The tract was commonly miscalled Indian Territory, although it possessed no government of territorial form; none at all in fact, since the federal laws did not operate within the territory to control vagrant whites who intruded, and the resident tribes had no lawful jurisdiction over such intruders. It became a refuge for fugitives from adjacent States and for adventurers who intermarried with Indian women. When the cattle industry developed, the Indians who owned the land were allowed to lease the grazing rights to cattle companies, whose stock tenders thus acquired a sort of right to reside within the forbidden area.[2] Through these the fertility of the plains between the Arkansas and Red rivers became widely known; and it was learned as well that in the heart of Indian Territory were tracts of land to which the United States had acquired title from their former tribal owners. During Hayes's presidency attempts began to occupy these ceded lands in the central part of Indian Territory upon the pretext that the preëmption and homestead laws extended automatically over them. Oklahoma was the name spontaneously given to the area.

The western end of the Indian Territory was continuously upset during the decade of the eighties. Around it and through it new railroads were bringing in their thousands of colonists, some of whom did not try to keep their covetous eyes off the plains of Oklahoma. In the southwest angle, Texas maintained a claim to a large piece of the country, alleging that the north fork of the Red River was the correct boundary fixed in 1819, rather than the South Fork, which the United States claimed. Texas organized Greer County here and refused to admit United States ownership

[1] Annie H. Abel, *The American Indian as a Slaveholder and Secessionist* (1915), a learned and exhaustive work.

[2] President Cleveland canceled these leases, seeing no reasons why the cattle corporations should confer on their employees privileges denied to ordinary citizens by the intercourse laws. R. M. McElroy, *Grover Cleveland* (1923).

until the Supreme Court in 1892 (in the case of United States *vs.* Texas) rejected the Texas claim. At the northwest angle was No Man's Land, for which Congress had no provision at all. Here the cowboys put together a short-lived local government under the name of Cimarron, in 1887, with Beaver as their principal settlement. But at the very center, between the Canadian and Cimarron forks of the Arkansas, and west of the Creek Nation, the chief disturbances of Indian Territory were on the plains of Oklahoma.[3]

As early as 1879 Hayes was obliged to warn by proclamation groups of prospective squatters that the Oklahoma lands were not open to settlement. The "boomers" were congregating openly at convenient points on the border, principally at Arkansas City in Kansas, just north of the point where the Arkansas River crosses the Indian Territory line. The proclamation was ineffective, and the emigrants were arrested by federal troops, and escorted outside the Indian Country. Nearly every year after this the same attempt was made; speculators advertised freely that these lands were open, and Presidents proclaimed as often that they were not. When surplus lands became available under the Dawes Act of 1887, and more of the acreage became United States property through agreement with the Creek and Seminole, the inducements to try to acquire the lands were increased. Among these ceded lands were some that Congress required to be added to the public domain. One of the earliest official acts of President Harrison was the issuance of a proclamation opening Oklahoma to entry at noon, April 22, 1889.

There was as yet no territorial government, and the Oklahoma boomers were not of the type of the ordinary frontier farming families. They were speculators, and many of them had real money. By sunset of the entry day there were noisy boom towns at Guthrie and Oklahoma City, the plains were crowded with riders hurrying towards regions where they hoped to locate, and the land offices had long queues of prospective entrymen. For a year they lived in relative peace, under a few United States marshals, governed largely by their own good sense. In 1890 Congress gave them a territory whose irregular limits were extended from time to time as more land became available. When the Omnibus States were admitted to the Union it was certain that eventually Oklahoma must be admitted too, but whether it should be

[3] Roy Gittinger, *The Formation of the State of Oklahoma* (1917).

in conjunction with Indian Territory and the Five Civilized Tribes, or alone, was less clear.

Before the status of Oklahoma could be settled, Utah finished its long probationary period and became a State. It had behind it the novelty of the Mormon settlement in the desert, the odium of revolt against the United States in the Utah War of 1857, and above all the curse of polygamy. From the moment when the revelation concerning this was made public in 1852, American opinion forbade serious talk of statehood for a polygamous community. The peculiarities that had made Mormons unpopular at Kirtland, Independence, Far West and Nauvoo were now enlarged so as to be overwhelming and unforgivable. The Mormon settlement throve under the joint influence of its own industry and the careful statesmanship of Brigham Young, but it was never possible to dissect its institutions and determine where church stopped and state began. In 1862 Congress passed a law making bigamy in the territories a federal offense, but since Mormon juries could not be expected either to indict or convict on this charge, and there were few Gentiles there, the law was a dead letter. Not until after railroad connection was established shortly after the completion of the Union Pacific Railroad did the Gentile population of Utah become a minority strong enough to be respected; even then it was sometimes soured by the fact that among its leaders were many Mormon renegades.

The Edmunds Acts of 1882 created a commission government for Utah, and indicated the earliest determination of the United States to break up polygamy. It required the commissioners to make up a new list of voters, denying franchise, office, and even jury service to polygamists, and excluding believers in polygamy from jury service in cases of trials of offenders under the cohabitation sections of the law. The property of the church was for a time seized and held in trust, while the non-Mormon inhabitants were given control of the territorial machinery. Vigorous prosecutions of Mormon leaders who adhered to their polygamous families resulted in numerous convictions and sentences, which Federal authority now showed no disposition to relax.

Under this régime, the Mormon church abandoned polygamy. This was formally announced at the church convocation in 1890, the act being generally accepted as a public surrender. In the clash of controversy it has not been possible to determine how large a part polygamy actually played in Mormon affairs. No

Mormon historian has been allowed to tell the whole statistical truth, and no Gentile has been able to. The question of its survival has often been a matter of religious or political controversy since 1890, but the discussions have uniformly contained more heat than light. In 1893 President Harrison, on the recommendation of the Utah Commission and the appeal of the leaders of Mormon opinion, issued a general amnesty to Mormons who had respected the law since 1890, and in 1894 Congress enabled the territory to become a State. In January, 1896, Utah was admitted under a constitution that repudiated polygamy.

After 1896 there remained New Mexico, Arizona, and Oklahoma Territories, of which the last and youngest was much the farthest advanced, with 398,331 inhabitants in 1900. Its neighbor, still known as Indian Territory, with a preponderant Indian population, had 392,060 inhabitants. In both, the increase was accelerated by the convenience of railroad approach, and the scarcity of other homestead lands in the public domain. In various places talk was heard of irrigation as a means of bringing arid lands under cultivation, and Congress had gone so far as to provide a general survey of irrigation sites on the public domain. But the total area of the valleys that might some day be put under ditch was a slight percentage of the mountainous, arid, and otherwise useless remainder of the public lands. Oklahoma contained as good land as the best had been, and grew instantly into a populous and prosperous territory once the barriers were lifted. It was vocal, too. It demanded statehood, keeping its desires before Congress at every session. By 1902 there was serious consideration of another omnibus bill that might take care of all the remaining territories, and in 1906 such a bill was passed for the admission of Indian Territory and Oklahoma as one State, and New Mexico and Arizona as another. The latter combination was declined by the people concerned.

By 1906 the Dawes Act had been in operation so long that the time was approaching when many of the former tribal members would become citizens of the United States, owning their estates in fee simple, and managing them themselves. The Burke Act of that year provided further guidance for the Secretary of the Interior in administering this citizenship, while in the autumn a joint convention sat to frame a constitution under the name of Oklahoma. The resulting constitution, under which President Roosevelt admitted Oklahoma in 1907, was long and intricate.

Its seventy pages carried to the extreme the same tendencies to make a code rather than an organic law, that were visible in the constitutions of 1889. The population of Oklahoma was mixed and exuberant, but lacked most of the typical characteristics of the older frontier States.

Arizona rejected union with New Mexico in 1906, and was thus compelled to remain in territorial status for a few more years. There was a clash of populations here, the New Mexicans containing a strong element of Mexican stock, and being in many places only partly Americanized after half a century of annexation. In Arizona most of the inhabitants were American, with a prejudice against the Mexican. Here there was also a strong corporate interest, since the development of mines had brought into the territory much outside capital and many men to work it. This development was not entirely by pioneers of the ordinary type, but by company towns which were as concentrated in their management as the Mormon colonies in the desert valleys north of them.

The enabling act for Arizona and New Mexico was passed in 1910, and both territories framed their constitutions in the following year. Their admission came in 1912, with New Mexico a few weeks ahead of Arizona because the latter had met with a form of obstacle unique in the history of statehood. It had embodied in its constitution all the most modern suggestions for reform including a group of measures then on the firing line of insurgency — initiative, referendum, direct primary, and recall. The last of these aroused the opposition of the President of the United States, William H. Taft, whose training as a judge, and whose conservative temper made him recoil at the idea of a recall of judges. He declined to issue the proclamation for the admission of Arizona so long as this principle was a part of the constitution. Appeal was made to Congress, but Congress, even wi h an opposition in control of the lower House, upheld the President. It was first suggested that there should be a special referendum on the article on recall, but the President would have none of this, and vetoed the bill. He signed a bill a few days later, permitting the entry of Arizona only after the offending article should be excised. Arizona complied, and was admitted. The following election it flaunted its freedom in the face of the nation by amending its constitution and putting back into it the principle of the recall.

This ended the story. With forty-eight States participating in the Union, the task was complete, and all of the main body of American territory had fulfilled that part of its destiny which had to do with the reclaiming of successive frontiers, and the erection thereon of self-governing States, autonomous yet integrally a part of their imperial system. The frontier had disappeared, and with it had been removed by the time the work was done, that special influence that has made American history unique.

There was still no cessation in the steady pressure of the newer West upon the Nation. With the admission of the Omnibus States the open frontier came substantially to an end, but the newest members of the Union were alive with complaints, and their younger associates were in fullest sympathy with them. The United States had yet to meet the attack of the Populists, the Progressives, and the various Farmer-Labor combinations. But the distinctive frontier influence was undergoing transmutation into agrarian influence, and the struggle was henceforth to be less a contest between the older sections and the young, and more a struggle of the agricultural elements of society against the industrial. The first century of American independence was dominated by the influence of the frontier; its second seems likely to be shaped by industry and the pressure of the outside world.

THE END

INDEX

Abbott-Downing coach, 464.

Abilene, Kan., cow town, 536.

Abolitionism, in Northwest, 397.

Absentee ownership, attitude of frontier, 97, 416, 417.

Adams, C. F., on battle of New Orleans, 177.

Adams, Ephraim, Iowa Band, 394.

Adams, Henry, as historian, viewpoint, 107n., 111n., 133n., 172n.

Adams, J. Q., Spanish negotiations, 181–85; presidential candidacy, 249, 257; and internal improvements, 249, 258; begins canal, 266.

Adams, John, peace negotiations, 41; as minister in England, 79; presidency, 108.

Admission of States, early evidence of probability, 50, 54; and Ordinance of 1784, 62; promise in Ordinance of 1787, 68; and free self-government, 88; Vermont, 88, 89; Kentucky, 90; Tennessee without enablement, 94; Ohio, 125–29; policy of enabling acts, 126, 565; Louisiana, 148; Indiana, 195–97; Illinois, 197; Mississippi and Alabama, 210; domain considered available (1819), 211, 212; Missouri and Maine, 217–19; Arkansas, 286, 301, 302; Michigan, 298, 299, 302; Texas, 353, 354; California, 378, 379; Iowa, 394–96; Florida, 396; Wisconsin, 398–400; Minnesota, 445; Oregon, 446; Civil War and political need, 456; West Virginia, 456; attempt for Colorado, 457, 555; Nevada, 457; Nebraska, 458; Colorado, 554–56; later political scrutiny, 555–58, 560, 563; Dakotas, Washington, Montana, 557, 560–63; Congress and requirements in constitutions, 561–63; American theory of imperialism, 564; not forced on territories, 565; essential act, 566; conventions and ratifications, 566; by presidential proclamation, 567; Utah, 571; Oklahoma, 571; New Mexico and Arizona, 572.

Agriculture, colonial, 2, 3; as chief industry, 113, 439; railroads and frontier, 409, 426, 544, 549; Missouri River and frontier, 423; and Crimean War, 440; conservative conditions, 472; rise of efforts for improvement, 473; first colleges, 473; Morrill Act, 473–78; improvement and public-land policy, 477; new type of western farmers, 529; plains, and cattle industry, 541; agrarian influence and unrest, 573.

Alabama, population (1820–50), 209; terri-

tory, 210; statehood, 210, 567. *See also* Southwest.

Albany, N.Y., early railway connection, 404.

Albany Congress, and Americanization, 8.

Alien and Sedition Acts, 108.

Almonte, J. N., leaves, 355.

Alton, Ill., distributing center, 194.

Alvord, C. W., as historian of frontier, 7n., 8n., 36n.

Amelia Island, occupation, 182.

American Fur Company, development, 214; Missouri River traffic, steamboats, 331, 452.

American Revolution, and autonomous spirit, 32; frontier phase, 33, 40; and Canada, 34; Burgoyne's campaign, 34; in Northwest, Clark, 36–39; in South, 39, 40; peace negotiations, boundaries, 41, 42, 57, 84; land warrants, 53, 60.

American System, frontier attitude, 157; elements, 244–49, 381; as administrative policy, 249, 258, 268; attitude of South, 254, 255; political weakness, 255.

Americanization, during colonial times, 1, 2, 5, 7, 8, 11, 17, 32, 40; of frontier as process, 43.

Ames, Oakes, Crédit-Mobilier scandal, 500.

Amherstburg. *See* Fort Malden.

Anti-masonry, rise, 341.

Apache Indians, Medicine Creek Council, 505.

Appalachian system, piedmont frontier, 6; settlement of valleys, 6, 7, 23; frontier crosses, 16–18, 20, 24.

Arapahoe Indians, Fort Laramie Council, range, 426; unmolested, 442, 488; cession (1861), new reserve, 447, 488, 489; war, 489–91; homeless, 491; Medicine Creek Council, 505, 506; Hancock's raid, 506; renewal of trouble, Custer's raid, 506, 507.

Arikara Indians, Fort Laramie Council, 426.

Arizona, precious metal discoveries, 453, 454; territory, boundaries, 454; and Southern Pacific, 546; declines joint statehood, 571, 572; admission, recall question, 572. *See also* Rocky Mountain.

Arkansas, boundaries, 213, 300; territory, 211, 213; population (1820–40), 217, 302; statehood, constitution, 286, 301, 302, 567; slow development, 299; riparian settlement, 300.

Arkansas Banner, on new Democratic States, 396.

Grosventre Indians, Fort Laramie Council, 426.
Guadalupe-Hidalgo Treaty, 360.
Guilford Courthouse, battle, 40.
Guthrie, Ok., founding, 569.
Gwin, W. M., California constitutional convention, 378; senator, 378; on Pacific railroad routes, 430; and pony express, 465.

Hagedorn, Hermann, on cowboy, 538.
Hamilton, Alexander, and strong government, 104–06; land report, 120; and Burr, duel, 144, 145.
Hamilton, Sir Henry, in American Revolution, 36, 38, 39.
Hancock, W. S., Indian raid, 506.
Hanna, C. A., study of frontier, 17n.
Hannibal and St. Joseph Railroad, construction, 438.
Hard Labour Treaty (1768), 14.
Harmar, Joseph, Indian expedition, 76.
Harper, Robert, ferry, race, 17.
Harper's Ferry, 17.
Harris's Ferry, 17.
Harrison, Benjamin, proclaims States, 563; opening of Oklahoma, 569; amnesty for Mormons, 571.
Harrison, W. H., delegate, career, 121, 124; land bill, 121; governor, 125, 191; and Burr, 146; Indian councils, 161, 162, 192; and Tecumseh, Tippecanoe, 163–65; and squatters, 164; military ambition, 165; Thames River, 173; and advertisement of West, 189; and slavery, 198; presidential candidacy, support, 338, 386.
Harrod, James, station, 29, 89.
Harrodsburg, station, 29, 89.
Harte, Bret, on Pacific railroad, 500; on lawlessness, 559.
Hartford Convention, 253.
Hauser, S. T., governor, 558.
Hawkins, Benjamin, as Indian agent, 174.
Hayes, R. B., Indian policy, 511; Colorado vote and election, 556, 562; and Indian Territory squatters, 569.
Hayne, R. Y., railroad convention, 314, 411; occasion of Webster debate, 381.
Hayt, E. A., Indian policy, 511.
Hazard, Samuel, colonial scheme, 22.
Hazen, W. B., and Indians, 507.
Helena, mining camp, 453.
Henderson, Archibald, study of frontier, 24n., 83n., 90n.
Henderson, Richard, Transylvania, 27, 29, 30, 88; Nashville, 30.
Henry, Patrick, and Clark's expedition, 37.
Herkimer, Nicholas, Oriskany, 35.
Hickory Ground, Jackson's fort, treaty, 175.
Hicksites, 342.
Hill, J. J., Great Northern, 545.

Hinsdale, B. A., study of Northwest, 71n.; on frontier posts, 82.
Hodder, F. H., on Douglas's motive, 434.
Holladay, Ben, overland mail, 466.
Homesteads, exemption, 354, 383, 399; demand for public-land policy, 384, 478; bill (1860), veto, 478; act, 479; and preëmption, 479, 549; effect of act, 549.
Hoosiers, 194.
Horseshoe Bend, battle, 175.
Hough, Emerson, on cowboy, 538.
Houses, frontier, 114.
Howard, O. O., and Nez Percés, 508.
Howe, Sir William, and Burgoyne's campaign, 35.
Hudson's Bay Company, Fort Garry, 214, 331; Oregon Country, 335.
Hulbert, A. B., on Braddock's expedition, 20; study of frontier, 18n., 20n., 65n.
Hull, William, governor, 141; in War of 1812, 171–73.
Humanitarianism, movements, 342.
Humboldt River, trail, 366. See also California Trail.
Huntington, C. P., Central Pacific, 468.
Hunt's Merchants' Magazine, on telegraph and panic, 441.
Huntsville, Ala., settlement center, 174, 209.
Hutchins, Thomas, public-land survey, 63.
Hutchinson, Kan., cow town, 538.

Idaho, mining camps, 451; territory, boundaries, 455; divided, 455; Nez Percé war, 508; Washington and panhandle, 557; admission, 563. See also Rocky Mountain.
Illinois colonial scheme, 22; Clark's expedition, 33, 36–39, 42; territory, boundaries, 148, 162; population (1810), 191; (1820), 192; (1830–40), 313; river towns, 194; statehood, boundaries, constitution, 197, 567; slavery question, 198; Egypt, 199; and Bank of United States, 236; canal routes and system, 270, 273; squatters and Black Hawk War, 288–90; boom in northern, 311; internal-improvement schemes, debt, 313; debt and emigration, 393; debt and attempted dismemberment, 393; Illinois Central, 418–21; regulation of railways and elevators, 528. See also Northwest.
Illinois and Michigan Canal, land grant, 272; construction, 273; right of way, 418.
Illinois Central Railroad, project, 418–20; land grant, 421.
Illinois River, canal route, 270.
Immigration, colonial races and Americanization, 1–5, 7, 8, 11, 17, 32; Wisconsin settlers, 397.
Imperialism, or Americanization, 8; after French and Indian War, 8; and procla-